Aid for Trade and Development

Following in the wake of the World Trade Organization's engagement with Aid for Trade, this book brings together a range of perspectives around this emerging issue. The collection of articles in this volume presents many of the ideas elaborated through research conducted by International Lawyers and Economists Against Poverty (ILEAP) since 2005 and is intended to provide a basis for further study. Since many of the contributions on Aid for Trade to date have come from the North, the book looks to deepen the debate by forwarding voices and experiences from the South. The book traces the evolution of Aid for Trade from its beginnings and examines the global architecture, modalities, and costs associated with its implementation. Drawing on lessons from national and regional experiences, this book further explores ways in which Aid for Trade can both move forward and become a real tool for poverty reduction in beneficiary countries.

ILEAP is an independent, not-for-profit organization whose overriding goal is to promote pro-development outcomes in international negotiations. Established in 2002, ILEAP provides professional backstopping capacity and support in trade negotiations to a variety of beneficiaries in Africa and the Caribbean.

ILEAP provides practical, timely, and independent interdisciplinary trade advice and assistance in trade negotiations to developing countries. For more information, please visit our website: www.ileap-jeicp.org.

AID FOR TRADE AND DEVELOPMENT

Edited by

Dominique Njinkeu and Hugo Cameron

ILEAP | INTERNATIONAL LAWYERS AND ECONOMISTS AGAINST POVERTY

JEICP | JURISTES ET ÉCONOMISTES INTERNATIONAUX CONTRE LA PAUVRETÉ

CAMBRIDGE UNIVERSITY PRESS

CAMBRIDGE
UNIVERSITY PRESS

Shaftesbury Road, Cambridge CB2 8EA, United Kingdom

One Liberty Plaza, 20th Floor, New York, NY 10006, USA

477 Williamstown Road, Port Melbourne, VIC 3207, Australia

314–321, 3rd Floor, Plot 3, Splendor Forum, Jasola District Centre, New Delhi – 110025, India

103 Penang Road, #05–06/07, Visioncrest Commercial, Singapore 238467

Cambridge University Press is part of Cambridge University Press & Assessment, a department of the University of Cambridge.

We share the University's mission to contribute to society through the pursuit of education, learning and research at the highest international levels of excellence.

www.cambridge.org
Information on this title: www.cambridge.org/9780521757256

First published 2008
First paperback edition 2009

A catalogue record for this publication is available from the British Library

Library of Congress Cataloging-in-Publication data
Aid for trade and development / edited by International Lawyers and Economists Against Poverty.
p. cm.
Includes bibliographical references and index.
ISBN 978-0-521-88951-3 (hardback)
1. Economic assistance – Developing countries. 2. Developing countries – Commerce. I. International Lawyers and Economists Against Poverty.
HC60.A45296 2008
338.9109172'4–dc22 2007043674

ISBN 978-0-521-88951-3 Hardback
ISBN 978-0-521-75725-6 Paperback

CONTENTS

CONTRIBUTORS

PROFESSOR DAVID OLUSANYA AJAKAIYE joined the African Economic Research Consortium (AERC) as Director of Research in October 2004. Prior to that, he had worked at the Nigerian Institute of Social and Economic Research (NISER), Ibadan, for 29 years. While at NISER he rose to the rank of Professor of Economics in 1992. Over the years he served as Head, Research and Consultancy Unit (1988–1992); Director, Economic Development Department (1993–1998); and Head, Macroeconomic Modelling Unit (1998–1999). In 1999, he was appointed Director-General, a position he held until he joined AERC in 2004. Prof. Ajakaiye was a member of various planning bodies in Nigeria, including the Joint Planning Board and the National Council on Development Planning. As a consultant, he has worked with several international organizations, including the African Capacity Building Foundation (ACBF), the International Development Research Centre (IDRC), the Carnegie Corporation, the UK's Department for International Development (DFID), the European Union, and the World Bank. He has been editor of the *Journal of Economic Management* (1995–2002) and Business Manager of *African Journal of Economic Policy* (1994–2004). Prof. Ajakaiye was a John Holt Scholar at the University of Ibadan (1971–1974), where he obtained his BSc degree in economics in 1974, and a NISER Fellow at Boston University, USA (1978–1984), where he took his MA (1982) and PhD (1984). He specializes in economic development policy analysis and development planning using a variety of quantitative techniques including econometrics, input-output analysis, and computable general equilibrium (CGE) models. He has published several books, monographs, and journal articles and chapters in books, all in the area of economic development.

AMBASSADOR HAVELOCK R. BREWSTER. Most of Ambassador Brewster's career has been in the service of international institutions and government. Among the positions he has held were Ambassador of Guyana to the European Union, Austria, Belgium, and Germany. He was also Executive Director for the Caribbean at the Inter-American Development Bank and previously Special Research Advisor and Director for Trade in Primary Commodities at the United Nations Conference on Trade and Development. He has served as a consultant and advisor to a number of international organizations, governments, and universities. He began his career in academia at the University of the West Indies and was the first Professor of Economics at the Cave Hill campus. He graduated in economics from the University of Durham, England, and Dalhousie University, Canada. Mr. Brewster's numerous publications are in the fields of trade and development, economic integration, and development finance. He is currently Alternate Executive Director for the Caribbean at the Inter-American Development Bank.

DERYCK R. BROWN is a development practitioner with over fifteen years' experience in research, consulting, project and policy work mainly in the Caribbean Community (CARICOM). He has worked closely with donor agencies and CARICOM member states in the delivery of trade-related technical assistance and capacity-building projects. He served as Lead Negotiator for CARICOM at the Consultative Group on Smaller Economies in the Free Trade Area of the Americas (FTAA), leading the region's efforts in relation to the Hemispheric Cooperation Program and the Regional Integration Fund. Mr. Brown has undertaken consulting assignments for the United Nations Development Programme (UNDP), the Inter-American Development Bank (IADB), the International Labour Organization (ILO), the CARICOM Secretariat, the Caribbean Export Development Agency (CEDA), and the United States Agency for International Development (USAID), among others. He is from Trinidad and Tobago.

MASSIMILIANO CALÌ is Research Officer at the Overseas Development Institute (ODI) in London. His current research interests include analysis of constraints to trade in services in African countries, the effects of natural resources booms in developing countries, the impact of trade openness on the geographic distribution of economic activity, and the economic determinants of large urban agglomerations in developing countries. Prior to ODI, he has worked in Latin America (Italian Embassy to Bolivia and the Economic Commission for Latin America) and South Asia (Asian Development Bank and the private sector in India). Mr. Calì studied at the University of Pavia, Italy, and at the University of East Anglia, UK, and is currently completing a PhD in economic geography at the London School of Economics.

ALDO CALIARI is Coordinator of the Washington-based Center of Concern's Rethinking Bretton Woods Project. He carries out research on the use of international law to advance the Center of Concern's economic and social justice advocacy agenda. Immediately prior to joining the Center in 2000, he completed a master's degree at American University on international legal studies, specializing in international human rights law, where he was honored with the Outstanding Graduate Award. In 1997 he received a law degree from the Universidad Nacional de Tucuman Law School. After getting his law degree, and before starting his master's at American University, he worked as an attorney in Argentina.

HUGO CAMERON is International Trade Negotiations Expert at ILEAP, where he has focused on issues around Aid for Trade since 2005. He was previously Director of Trade and Environment at the Geneva-based International Centre for Trade and Sustainable Development (ICTSD). From 1998 to 2004 he edited ICTSD's trade publication *BRIDGES Weekly Trade News Digest*. He has assisted the government of Tanzania on trade negotiation issues, including fisheries and health and safety standards. Mr. Cameron holds degrees from Simon Fraser University and McGill University.

RAMESH CHAITOO is the head of the Services Trade Unit at the Caribbean Regional Negotiating Machinery (CRNM) based in Barbados. He is responsible for monitoring, analyzing, and participating in services trade negotiations and advising Caribbean governments on negotiating strategies and options. As a researcher, trainer, and consultant, Mr. Chaitoo has many years' experience in trade policy matters. Prior to joining the CRNM, he was a Senior Associate at Carleton University's Centre for Trade Policy and Law in Ottawa, Canada. He has provided training to officials in Canada, the Caribbean, Central America, Bangladesh, and other countries. He has also conducted trade-related consultancies for several governments and international agencies. Mr. Chaitoo is a graduate of Carleton University, the University of Cambridge, and the University of the West Indies.

ANTONI ESTEVADEORDAL is Manager of the Integration and Trade Sector at the Inter-American Development Bank (IDB) since July 2007. He has expertise in trade policy, economic integration, and regional cooperation policies in Latin America and the Caribbean, Asia, and Europe. He is responsible for the IDB operational support, technical assistance, and the policy research program on trade development issues and regional integration initiatives. He coordinates several joint initiatives with the WTO, ADB, EU, OECD, OAS, and UN agencies. Before joining the IDB he taught at the University of Barcelona and Harvard University. He has published widely in major journals, including *American Economic Review*, *Quarterly Journal of Economics*, *Review of International Economics*, *Journal of Economic Integration*, *Journal of World Trade*, and *Economia*. He has also contributed to several books and edited most recently *Integrating the Americas: FTAA and Beyond* (with Dani Rodrik, Alan Taylor, and Andrés Velasco; Harvard University Press, 2004); *Regional Public Goods: From Theory to Practice* (with B. Frantz and T. R. Nguyen; IDB-ADB, 2004); *The Origin of Goods: Rules of Origin in Preferential Trade Agreements* (with O. Cadot, A. Suwa, and T. Verdier; Oxford University Press-CEPR, 2006). He has coordinated several IDB reports such as "Beyond Borders: The New Regionalism in the Americas" (IDB, 2002); "The Emergence of China: Opportunities and Challenges for Latin America and the Caribbean" (IDB-Harvard University Press, 2006), and "Regional Rules and the Global Trading System" (IDB-WTO, forthcoming, 2007). He holds a PhD in economics from Harvard University and a BA in economics from the University of Barcelona.

J. MICHAEL FINGER is known for his seminal work in several areas of international economics: how the GATT/WTO system relates to development; trade restrictions, for example, safeguards and antidumping in Latin American trade liberalization; and the commercial value of intellectual property in poorer communities. Dr. Finger retired from the World Bank in 2001. While there he served as Lead Economist and Chief, Trade Policy Research Group and was the Bank's initial Coordinator for the Integrated Framework for Trade-Related Technical Assistance to Least Developed Countries. He has since served as Resident Scholar at the American Enterprise Institute and consultant to a number of developing country governments, to the United Nations Food and Agricultural Organization, and to the UN Millennium Project Task Force on Trade. He held the chair of Vernon F. Taylor Distinguished Professor of Economics, Trinity University, San Antonio, Texas, in 2004 and 2005, and has taught at the China Foreign Affairs University, the University of

Berne, the Stockholm School of Economics, and Duke University. Before working at the World Bank, Dr. Finger held key positions at the U.S. Treasury Department and the United Nations Conference on Trade and Development. He holds a PhD in economics from the University of North Carolina. Dr. Finger is author or editor of six books and author or co-author of a long list of articles. Having done high-level applied analysis as well as having taught at several universities, his work combines the assiduity of a scholar and the outlook of a practitioner.

PAOLO GIORDANO holds a PhD from the Institut d'Etudes Politiques de Paris (Sciences Po) and an MA from the Bocconi University of Milan. He currently serves as a Trade Economist at the Integration and Regional Programs Department of the Inter-American Development Bank, where he coordinates country strategies, regional programs for the Mercosur region, and the Trade and Poverty Trust Fund. He conducts policy-oriented research programs in areas related with the quantitative evaluation of trade policies and is involved in country and regional policy programming, as well as in financial operations related to trade and regional integration. Before joining the Bank he was an Appointed Professor at the Mercosur Chair of the Institut d'Etudes Politiques de Paris (Sciences Po), lecturing in international economics, trade policy, and Latin American development. In his career, he lectured in several European universities, organized and participated in international meetings, published in international refereed journals, supervised graduate students, and worked as a consultant for international organizations. Mr. Giordano speaks five languages and has extensively resided and traveled in developed and developing countries for academic and professional purposes. His latest edited books are *An Integrated Approach to the EU-Mercosur Association* (2002), *Asymmetries in Regional Integration and Local Development* (2005), and *Desarrollo rural y Comercio Agropecuario en América Latina y el Caribe* (2005).

GERRY HELLEINER is Chairman Emeritus of the Board of International Lawyers and Economists Against Poverty (ILEAP) and Professor Emeritus (economics) and Distinguished Research Fellow at the University of Toronto's Munk Centre. He has held posts at Yale University, the University of Ibadan, the University of Dar es Salaam, the Institute of Development Studies, the World Institute for Development Economics Research, and the University of Oxford. He served as the research director of the Group of 24 and chaired the boards of the North-South Institute. He currently serves on the executive committee of the International Development Research Centre, the executive board of the African Capacity-Building Foundation, the Program Advisory Committee of the African Economic Research Consortium in Nairobi, and the UN Committee on Development Planning.

BERNARD HOEKMAN is Research Manager of the International Trade Group in the Development Research Group of the World Bank. Before taking up his present position, he managed the international trade and global integration activities of the World Bank Institute's Economic Policy Division. He has worked extensively in countries in the Middle East and North Africa. Between 1988 and 1993 he was on the staff of the GATT Secretariat in Geneva. He is a graduate of the Erasmus University Rotterdam, holds a PhD in economics from the University of Michigan, and is a research Fellow of the London-based Centre for Economic Policy

Research. His current research focuses on the functioning of the multilateral trading system (WTO), international transactions in services, the relationship between competition and trade policy, the economics of regional economic integration, and channels of international technology diffusion.

FAIZEL ISMAIL is the head of the South African Delegation to the World Trade Organization, Permanent Mission of South Africa to Geneva. Prior to this he served as South Africa's chief director for export and investment promotion and also as director of foreign trade relations in the Department of Trade and Industry, where he had also worked as consultant for multilateral trade relations. Mr. Ismail holds an MA in development studies from the University of Sussex and an LLB from the University of Natal.

ANNEKE JESSEN is Senior Operations Specialist at the Inter-American Development Bank's Integration and Trade Sector. She is the Departments' Regional Coordinator for the Caribbean and responsible for the Bank's integration and trade-related technical cooperation programs with the CARICOM Secretariat, the Caribbean Regional Negotiating Machinery, and other regional institutions in CARICOM. She has led the design and implementation of numerous Bank operations in the Caribbean and has written extensively on CARICOM trade and integration issues. Her most recent publications include "The Caribbean Community: Integration among Small States," in McKinney, Joseph A. and H. Stephen Gardner (editors), *Economic Integration in the Americas, Routledge Studies in the Modern World Economy* (forthcoming); "Deepening and Diversifying International Trade," in Rojas-Suarez, Liliana and Carlos Elias (editors), *From Growth to Prosperity: Policy Perspectives for Trinidad and Tobago*, IDB: Washington, DC, 2006; and "Trade and Integration as a Strategy for Growth," in Rojas-Suarez, Liliana and Desmond Thomas (editors), *Barbados: Meeting the Challenge of Competitiveness in the 21st Century*, IDB: Washington, DC, 2006. Before joining the Bank in 1996, she worked for five years as Research and Project Coordinator at the Institute for European-Latin American Relations (IRELA) in Madrid. Ms. Jessen, a Danish citizen, holds degrees from the Universities of Aarhus and Copenhagen and from the Johns Hopkins University's School of Advanced International Studies in Washington, DC.

JESSICA LUNA is an economist, working as consultant at the Integration and Trade Sector at the Inter-American Development Bank (IDB). She prepares technical research papers and policy-oriented documents on issues related to trade policy, regional integration, and economic development. Ms. Luna participates in the design and implementation of trade-related Bank's operations for Latin American countries, particularly for the Andean countries. Before joining the Bank, she was an economic advisor at the Ministry of Foreign Trade and Tourism of Peru for the World Trade Organization (WTO) and Free Trade Area of the Americas (FTAA) negotiations. She led Peru's delegation at the Negotiating Group on Subsidies, Antidumping and Countervailing Duties (NGADCV)–FTAA and coordinated Peru's position for WTO Agriculture Negotiations. Ms. Luna conducted economic analysis on agriculture, market access, trade remedies, and safeguards and provided advice for dispute settlement cases in which Peru was involved. Ms. Luna, a Peruvian citizen, holds a master's degree in public administration in international development from the John F. Kennedy School of Government at Harvard University and BA in economics from Universidad Catolica del Peru.

PROFESSOR WILLIAM LYAKURWA is Executive Director of the African Economic Research Consortium. He joined African Economic Research Consortium (AERC) from the International Trade Centre based in Geneva, Switzerland, in 1993, where he held the post of Senior Trade Promotion Advisor. Mr. Lyakurwa has, since 1994, held the positions of Director of Training and Deputy Executive Director until his appointment to the position of Executive Director in March 2003. Mr. Lyakurwa received his PhD from Cornell University, USA, in 1978 as the culmination of notable academic performance in economics at undergraduate and postgraduate levels, from the University of Dar es Salaam, Tanzania, to Cornell University, USA. He has consequently been enlisted as an advisor and consultant to governments, regional bodies, multilateral institutions, and international and nongovernmental organizations. Mr. Lyakurwa has served as Chair and member of several policymaking boards in Tanzania and internationally. He was the Chair of the PTA/IDRC Project Management Committee (1993–1997) and of the NORDIC/SADCC Trade Advisory Group (1989–1994) and is currently the Chair of the COMESA Project Management Committee (2000 to the present). He was also a member of the steering committees of the OAU Policy Analysis Support Unit based in Addis Ababa, Ethiopia; the Secretariat for Institutional Support for Economic Research in Africa (SISERA) based in Dakar, Senegal; and the Centre for Environmental Economics and Policy in Africa (CEEPA) based in Pretoria, South Africa. He has also served as Chair and Head of several national committees on trade and capacity building. Mr. Lyakurwa has published extensively in local and international journals as well as contributed chapters in books, research, and discussion papers. He has a wealth of experience in research, graduate training, and "hands-on" human resource management, and has a keen sense of appreciation of the challenges of implementing the Consortium's programs in an evolving continent.

BEDE LYIMO is an economist in the Tanzanian civil service, currently on sabbatical leave. He has worked with the Ministry of Industry, Trade and Marketing for more than twenty years in various capacities, including two years as Assistant Director, Multilateral Trade Programmes, following which he was responsible for multilateral trade negotiations. He has participated extensively in negotiations under the Doha Development Round, including consultations on the Enhanced Integrated Framework and Aid for Trade. At the moment he is Chief Executive Officer of the Better Regulation Unit (BRU), Ministry of Planning, Economy and Empowerment. The BRU is a unit coordinating the implementation of major legal and regulatory reforms focusing on formalization of property rights in Tanzania, harmonization of business registration procedures, and regulatory licensing and labor law reforms, with the support of four bilateral development partners, that is, DFID, DANIDA, SIDA, and The Royal Netherlands Government, as well as the World Bank. Mr. Lyimo is a Tanzanian and received his degrees at the University of Dar es Salaam, Tanzania, and the Catholic University of Leuven, Belgium.

DOMINIQUE NJINKEU, a national of Cameroon, is Executive Director of ILEAP. Mr. Njinkeu has researched and published on African development issues, trade and regional integration, and international negotiations. He has worked previously for the African Economic Research Consortium (AERC) in Nairobi, Kenya, as the Deputy Director of Research. He also held research positions at the Council for the Development of Social Science Research in Africa (CODESRIA) in Dakar, Senegal, and the Government of Cameroon. He has taught at the University of Yaoundé in Cameroon; at the Université Laval, Quebec; and at Southern Illinois University.

DR. E. OLAWALE OGUNKOLA is a reader in the Department of Economics at the University of Ibadan, Ibadan, Nigeria, and a senior research Fellow both at the Centre for Econometrics and Allied Research (CEAR) and Trade Policy Research and Training Programme (TPRTP). He has consulted widely for various bodies in Nigeria, Africa, and internationally, including the World Bank, the United Nations Development Programme (UNDP), the UK Department for International Development (DFID), Food and Agriculture Organisation (FAO), the African Union Commission (AUC), and the Economic Community of West African States (ECOWAS). He was a visiting scholar to the International Monetary Fund (IMF) in 2001. He was a visiting lecturer at the National University of Lesotho (2000–2002). He has been a resource person to the Regional Trade Policy Course (RTPC) of World Trade Organization (WTO) since 2002. He has published extensively in the area of trade and regional integration, with particular focus on Africa. He holds a PhD degree from the University of Ibadan, Ibadan.

SHEILA PAGE is a senior research associate of the Overseas Development Institute, London. From 1982 to 2005 she was a research fellow there. Previously she was at Queen Elizabeth House, Oxford, 1972, and the National Institute of Economic and Social Research, 1972–1982. Her current research interests include how and why developing countries participate in international negotiations and trade relations between developed and developing countries, including Special and Differential treatment and EU-ACP arrangements. She has also advised developing countries in multilateral and regional negotiations. Her publications include *Special and Differential Treatment for Developing Countries in the WTO*, with Peter Kleen (2005), *Developing Countries in GATT/WTO Negotiations* (2002), *Regionalism among Developing Countries* (2000), *World Commodity Prices: Still a Problem for Developing Countries? How Developing Countries Trade* (1994), *World Trade Reform: Do Developing Countries Gain or Lose?* (1994), and *Trade, Finance and Developing Countries* (1989).

PIERRE SAUVÉ is a visiting fellow of the International Relations Department at the London School of Economics (LSE), in London, UK, where he also serves as a research associate of the School's International Trade Policy Unit. He was a visiting professor at the Institut d'Etudes Politiques (Sciences Po) in Paris, France, in 2003–2004, where his teaching activities focused on a range of "newer generation" trade issues at the interface of trade, investment, competition, and regulatory reform. Since January 2003, he has served as a Paris-based consultant with the World Bank Institute. During 1993–2002, he served as a senior economist and division head within the Trade Directorate of the Organization for Economic Cooperation and Development (OECD), where he oversaw the Directorate's work on the post-Uruguay Round trade agenda. He has advised the governments of a number of OECD and developing countries and has served as a consultant to a number of regional and multilateral organizations, including the Agence Intergouvernementale de la Francophonie, the Asian Development Bank, the Asia-Pacific Economic Cooperation Forum (APEC), the European Commission, the European Institute for Public Administration, the Inter-American Development Bank, the Swedish International Development Agency, UNCTAD, and the WTO. He is the author of numerous articles and monographs on policy issues relating to international trade, investment, and the regulation of industry.

SOK SIPHANA, a Cambodian national, is Director of the Division of Technical Cooperation Coordination at the International Trade Centre (ITC) since October 2003. After working in the private sector in the United States, he was a consultant for small businesses and international organizations such as the World Bank and the Asian Development Bank. He also worked as a legal expert for the UN Development Programme. In May 1999, he became Vice Minister in Cambodia's Ministry of Commerce. In this capacity, he worked extensively on issues related to trade promotion, trade policies, trade and development, the commercial legal framework and economic integration. He was also a key player in Cambodia's accession to the World Trade Organization. He has written abundantly on trade and development, legal and investment issues and has worked closely with the donor community. Mr. Sok is holder of a master of business administration from the Century University of New Mexico, USA, a juris doctor in law from the Widener University School of Law in Delaware, USA, and is currently completing a PhD in law and economics with the Bond University School of Law in Queensland, Australia.

AMANDA SUNASSEE LAM has been working in the areas of trade and private sector development for the last fourteen years. She started off her career in the private sector in Mauritius and very quickly moved into development work. She worked for some of the main development agencies such as UNIDO, UNDP, AusAid, and EU and has over that time acquired a deep understanding of the donor systems and of regional integration issues in the Indian Ocean region, COMESA, SADC, and Southeast Asia. She has been actively involved in the SADC EPA negotiations and has been an observer on the East African Community Custom Union Negotiations. She has worked as a technical assistant to the governments of Curacao, Tanzania, and Lao PRD for the last five years and has been posted in Europe, Africa, and Southeast Asia, focusing on trade and regional integration and the ongoing WTO and EPA negotiations. She is currently working on the Multilateral Initiative for Trade the Integrated Framework in Lao PRD. Ms. Sunassee Lam is originally from Mauritius and was educated in the United Kingdom, at the Universities of Kent in Canterbury and School of African and Asian Studies (SOAS), University of London.

EDWARD MATHEW SUNGULA is the head of the Multilateral Trade Programme in the Ministry of Industry, Trade and Marketing, Tanzania. He has previously worked in the shipping industry for about twenty years within the confines of trade facilitation. He is the Integrated Framework (IF) coordinator in the IF focal point, which is the Ministry of Industry, Trade and Marketing, and has made several presentations on trade-related issues. He has worked and is still working closely with donors and multilateral agencies in the coordination of Tanzania's Diagnostic Trade

Integration Study (DTIS) preparatory phase. Mr. Sungula, who is the contact point for all World Trade Organization issues in the Ministry, received his first degree from the University of Dar es Salaam, Tanzania, and a Master of Science degree from Norwegian School of Management, Norway.

KATI SUOMINEN serves as International Trade Specialist at the Inter-American Development Bank in Washington, where she manages team research projects on global trade and economic integration issues and coordinates trade-related operations for Mexico. Her articles have appeared in such journals as *Economia of the Brookings Institution*, *American Journal of Political Science*, *World Economy*, and *World Trade Review*. She holds a PhD from the University of California, San Diego (2004), MA from the Boston University (1996), and BA from the University of Arkansas at Little Rock (1995).

DIRK WILLEM TE VELDE is a research Fellow in the International Economic Development Group at the Overseas Development Institute in London. He holds a PhD from Birkbeck College, University of London. His work includes publications on trade and investment policy and on the impact of foreign direct investment on development and labor markets in particular.

ANN WESTON is Vice President and Coordinator of Research at the North-South Institute in Ottawa, Canada. She joined the North-South Institute in 1987. Her current research focuses on the World Trade Organization and its implications for Canada and developing countries. She has conducted extensive research on the consequences of the North American Free Trade Agreement (NAFTA), resulting in a number of publications, notably the *NAFTA Papers: Implications for Canada, Mexico and Developing Countries* and *Jamaica after NAFTA: Trade Options and Sectoral Strategies*. She co-authored Women and the New Trade Agenda, published by UNIFEM. Before joining the Institute, Ms. Weston worked as Senior Economics Officer in the Economic Affairs Division of the Commonwealth Secretariat and as Research Officer at the Overseas Development Institute (ODI) in London. She received her degrees at the Universities of Sussex and London.

ACRONYMS AND ABBREVIATIONS

ACBF	African Capacity Building Foundation
ACP	African, Caribbean, and Pacific group of countries
ADB	Asian Development Bank
AERC	African Economic Research Consortium
AfDB	African Development Bank
AGOA	African Growth and Opportunity Act
ASEAN	Association of Southeast Asian Nations
BCI	IDB Business Climate Initiative
BCSI	Barbados Coalition of Service Industries
BEST	Programme for the Strengthening of the Business Environment of Tanzania
BOP	Balance of Payments
CAD	Canadian dollar (currency)
CAF	Andean Development Corporation
CAFTA-DR	U.S.-Central America-Dominican Republic Free Trade Agreement
CAP	EU Common Agriculture Policy
CARICOM	Caribbean Community
CARIFORUM	Forum of the Caribbean ACP States
CAS	Country Assistance Strategy
CB	capacity building
CDB	Caribbean Development Bank
CDE	EC Centre for Development of Enterprises (formerly CDI – Centre for Development of Industry)
CEMAC	Communauté Economique et Monétaire de l'Afrique Centrale
CFD	Caribbean Forum for Development
CG	Consultative Group
CGCED	Caribbean Group for Cooperation in Economic Development
CGE	Computable General Equilibrium
CGIAR	Consultative Group on International Agricultural Research
CGSE	Consultative Group for Smaller Economies
CIDA	Canadian International Development Agency
CMT	Cut, Manufacture, and Tailor
COMESA	Common Market for Eastern and Southern Africa
CPIA	World Bank Country Policy and Institutional Assessment
CRNM	Caribbean Regional Negotiating Machinery
CRS	OECD Creditor Reporting System

CSO	Civil Society Organization
CSR	corporate social responsibility
CTD	WTO Committee on Trade and Development
CTDSS	WTO Committee on Trade and Development – Special Session
CTF	Common Trust Fund
CTPL	Centre for Trade Policy and Law
CUTS	Consumer Unity and Trust Society (India)
DAC	OECD Development Assistance Committee
DANIDA	Danish International Development Agency
DDA	Doha Development Agenda
DFID	UK Department for International Development
DMCs	ADB developing member countries
DTIS	Diagnostic Trade Integration Study
EAC	East African Community
EADB	East African Development Bank
EBA	Everything But Arms initiative
EBOPS	Extended Balance of Payments Classification of Services
EBRD	European Bank for Reconstruction and Development
EC	European Commission
ECDPM	European Centre for Development Policy Management
ECLAC	UN Economic Commission for Latin America and the Caribbean
ECOWAS	Economic Community of West African States
EDF	European Development Fund
EDS	Export Development Strategy
EEC	European Economic Community
EIB	European Investment Bank
EIF	Enhanced Integrated Framework
EPA	Economic Partnership Agreement
ESA	Eastern and Southern Africa
EU	European Union
EUR	euro (currency)
FAO	UN Food and Agriculture Organization
FIAS	Foreign Investment Advisory Service
FONPLATA	IDB Financial Fund for the Development of the River Plate Basin
FSO	IDB Fund for Special Operations
FTAA	Free Trade Area of the Americas
G7/G8	Group of Seven/Eight developed countries
GAERC	EU General Affairs and External Relations Council
GATS	General Agreement on Trade in Services
GATT	General Agreement on Tariffs and Trade
GAVI	Global Alliance for Vaccines and Immunisation
GDP	Gross Domestic Product
GEF	Global Environment Facility
GNI	Gross National Income
GPGs	global public goods
GTFA	Global Trade and Financial Architecture Project
HCP	Hemispheric Cooperation Program
HIPC	Heavily Indebted Poor Countries
ICT	information and communications technology
ICTSD	International Centre for Trade and Sustainable Development

IDA	International Development Association
IDB	Inter-American Development Bank
IDRC	International Development Research Centre
IDS	Institute for Development Studies
IEG	World Bank Independent Evaluation Group
IF	Integrated Framework for Trade-Related Technical Assistance for Least Developed Countries
IFC	World Bank International Finance Corporation
IFF	International Finance Facility
IFIs	International Financial Institutions
IFTF	Integrated Framework Trust Fund
IGTN	International Gender and Trade Network
IIC	Inter-American Investment Corporation
IIRSA	IDB Initiative for the Integration of Regional Infrastructure in South America
IISD	International Institute for Sustainable Development
IITC	(JITAP) Inter-Institutional Committees
ILEAP	International Lawyers and Economists Against Poverty
ILO	International Labour Organization
IMF	International Monetary Fund
INT	IDB Integration and Regional Programs Department
INTAL	IDB Institute for the Integration of Latin America and the Caribbean
IPGs	international public goods
IRCC	Inter Regional Coordination Committee
ITC	International Trade Centre
ITD	IDB's Integration, Trade and Hemispheric Issues Division
JAS	Joint Assistance Strategy
JITAP	Joint Integrated Technical Assistance Programme
LAC	Latin America and the Caribbean
LATN	Latin American Trade Network
LDC	Least Developed Country
LOC	Letter of Credit
MCA	Millennium Challenge Account
MCC	Millennium Challenge Corporation
MDGs	Millennium Development Goals
MFA	Multi-Fibre Arrangement
MFN	Most-Favored Nation
MIF	IDB Multilateral Investment Fund
MIGA	Multilateral Investment Guarantee Agency
MoC	Ministry of Commerce
MPI	Ministry of Planning and Investment
MSME	Micro, Small and Medium Enterprises
MSN	Maquila Solidarity Network
MTS	multilateral trading system
NAFTA	North American Free Trade Agreement
NAMA	Non-Agricultural Market Access
NAO	National Authorising Officer
NEPAD	New Partnership for Africa's Development
NES	National Export Strategy

NFIDCs	Net Food Importing Developing Countries
NGO	Non-Governmental Organization
NGPRS	National Growth and Poverty Reduction Strategy
NIP	National Indicative Programme
NLF	IDB New Lending Framework
NPGs	national public goods
NSDP	National Strategic Development Plan
NSI	North-South Institute
NTBs	non-tariff barriers
NTF	AfDB Nigeria Trust Fund
OAS	Organization of American States
OCT	Overseas Countries and Territories
ODA	Overseas Development Assistance
ODI	Overseas Development Institute
OECD	Organization for Economic Cooperation and Development
OECS	Organization of Eastern Caribbean States
OIE	World Organization for Animal Health
OMVS	Organisation pour la Mise en Valeur du Fleuve Sénégal
PAIRAC	Appui à l'intégration régionale en Afrique centrale
PBLs	policy-based loans
PDLs	performance-driven loans
PER	Programme Economique Régional
PMGs/MBPI	Priority Management Groups/Merit-Base Pay Initiatives
PMU	(ACP) Project Management Unit
PPP	IDB Puebla-Panama Plan
PRI	IDB Private Sector Department
PRS/P	Poverty Reduction Strategy/Paper
PSD	Private Sector Development
PSE	Producer Support Estimates
PSIP	Public Sector Investment Program
R&D	research and development
RIBS	Regional Integration Budget Support
RIF	Regional Integration Fund
RIP	Regional Indicative Programme
RPTF	Regional Preparatory Task Force
RTA	Regional Trade Agreement
RTC	IDB Regional Technical Cooperation Program
RTIBS	Regional Trade Integration Budget Support
SACU	Southern African Customs Union
SADC	Southern African Development Community
SAP	Structural Adjustment Program
SARPN	Southern African Regional Poverty Network
SATRN	Southern African Trade Research Network
SDT/S&DT	Special and Differential Treatment
SEATINI	Southern and Eastern African Trade Information and Negotiations Institute
SIDA	Swedish International Development Agency
SME	small/medium enterprises
SPS	Sanitary and Phyto-Sanitary Standards
SPSP	Sector Policy Support Program

SQAM	Standards, Quality Assurance, Accreditation & Metrology
SSA	sub-Saharan Africa
STDF	WTO Standards and Trade Development Facility
SWAp	Sector-Wide Approach
SWOT	strengths, weaknesses, opportunities and threats analysis
TA	technical assistance
TBT	Technical Barriers to Trade
TCB	trade capacity building
TCBDB	(WTO/OECD) Trade Capacity Building Database
TD	Trade Development
TDI	Trade Development Index (UNCTAD)
TFRP	IDB International Trade Finance Reactivation Program
TIM	IMF Trade Integration Mechanism
TIPS	Trade and Industrial Policy Strategies
TPR	Trade Policy Review
TPRTP	Trade Policy Research and Training Programme
TRA	trade-related assistance
TRALAC	Trade Law Centre for Southern Africa
TRCB	trade-related capacity building
TRIMS	(Agreement on) Trade-Related Investment Measures
TRIPS	(Agreement on) Trade-Related Intellectual Property Rights
TRTA	trade-related technical assistance
TSIs	trade support institutions
TWN	Third World Network
UNCTAD	United Nations Conference on Trade and Development
UNDAF	United Nations Development Assistance Framework
UNDP	United Nations Development Programme
UNIDO	United Nations Industrial Development Organization
U.S.	United States
USAID	United States Agency for International Development
USTDA	United States Trade and Development Agency
USTR	United States Trade Representative
WAEMU/UEMOA	West African Economic and Monetary Union
WBG	World Bank Group
WHO	World Health Organization
WIDER	World Institute for Development Economics Research
WIRSPA	West Indies Rum and Spirits Producers Association
WTO	World Trade Organization

ACKNOWLEDGMENTS

From the very beginning stages of conceiving this volume and onward, we are grateful for the intellectual guidance received from a number of people and processes. The initial ideas began with discussions among a group of trade specialists at the steering committee of the DFID-funded project "Global Trade and Financial Architecture"[1] in 2005. These discussions took place in the context of both the September 2005 United Nations conference in New York to review progress toward the Millennium Development Goals, and of the autumn 2005 meetings of the World Bank/International Monetary Fund (IMF) Development Committee. Among other areas, the World Bank/IMF Committee considered a statement on trade capacity building that would later form the main building blocks of the Aid for Trade initiative. As the process developed, we became concerned that Aid for Trade could become another major effort fully designed by well-intentioned development specialists, with limited representation from the nonindustrialized world. We are particularly grateful to Susan Prowse, Bernard Hoekman, Ricardo Meléndez-Ortiz, Sheila Page, and Gerry Helleiner for their suggestions on the design and implementation of the emerging Aid for Trade architecture.

We are truly thankful to the many authors who gave their time, support, and feedback to the process of compiling this volume. In particular, we are indebted to them for their patience in what was an overly lengthy editing period for an issue requiring a timely response. Viewpoints put forward in this book by the authors remain their personal perspectives and do not necessarily reflect those of their own institutions or of ILEAP. At various stages, the papers in this book have been presented at in-country and regional stakeholder workshops, African ambassadorial retreats, senior official sessions, and African trade ministerial meetings. A special thank-you should go to the Commission of the African Union and to the African Group of Ambassadors in Geneva, in particular for their efforts during the tenure of the Aid for Trade Task Force in the first half of 2006. We would also like to thank John Sewell of the German Marshall Fund for his review of the initial book proposal, as well as Former Mexican President Ernesto Zedillo, Sweden's ambassador to the WTO Mia Horn af Rantzien, WTO Deputy Director-General Valentine

[1] GTFA Project (2005), *Strengthening the Global Trade Architecture for Economic Development: An Agenda for Action*. London: UK Department for International Development (DFID). See http://www.dfid.gov.uk/aboutdfid/organisation/itd-global-trade-fin-architecture-intro.asp.

Rugwabiza, and the AU's Commissioner for Trade and Industry Elisabeth Tankeu for their kind endorsements of the book.

In addition to the chapter authors, the book would not have been possible without essential contributions from a number of individuals. In particular, we would like to thank Max Brem and Jeffrey Phillips for their diligent work in copyediting texts and references; John Berger at Cambridge University Press for his patience and support throughout; Phyllis Berk for an initial chapter edit; David Primack for assistance in finalizing the edition; and a number of ILEAP staff (Elaine Wong, Francine Chanel, Roberto Estrada, and Daniel Briollais), who competently managed the contractual and administrative arrangements necessary for such an undertaking.

Importantly, this book, and the wider ILEAP Aid for Trade program of which it forms a part, would not have been possible without the support of Susan Prowse and Bernard Hoekman in mobilizing resources from DFID and the World Bank. Additional financial assistance was provided by the Netherlands Ministry of Foreign Affairs, Swedish International Development Agency (SIDA), United States Agency for International Development (USAID, via African Economic Research Consortium), the World Bank, the World Bank Institute, International Development Research Centre (IDRC, Canada), Canadian International Development Agency (CIDA), and the Ford Foundation. We thank them for supporting our work on Aid for Trade and in many other areas. The views expressed in this book remain entirely those of the authors and do not imply official endorsement by any of the sponsor organizations or agencies. Above all, we are grateful to the ILEAP Board of Directors for their overall guidance in keeping a tight balance between the search for development-promoting trade rules and comprehensive trade capacity building with a long-term perspective.

D. N. and H. C.

FOREWORD

GERRY HELLEINER

The World Trade Organization (WTO) is an imperfect institution. Certainly no less imperfect are the world's aid agencies and multilateral institutions that purportedly seek to stimulate development and reduce poverty in the world's lowest-income countries. Yet over the past few years, within and around the multilateral Doha Round of WTO negotiations, these imperfect trade and aid institutions have been newly intertwined in accelerated and intense discussion over the complexities of a relatively new buzz-phrase: "Aid for Trade." The phrase "Aid for Trade" still means different things to different people. For those long concerned with the desirability of overall "policy coherence" in the struggle against global poverty, trade and aid issues have always been closely connected. For others, immersed in their individual policy "silos" of trade or aid policy, the Aid for Trade concept presents a completely fresh challenge to earlier approaches. Within the WTO, the World Bank, bilateral aid agencies, and elsewhere, Aid for Trade debates abound.

Whatever the particular short-term outcome of current official discussion of Aid for Trade surrounding the Doha Round, the issues surrounding it are not going to disappear. Global poverty will continue to challenge the global community. Many countries will be unable to reach the Millennium Development Goals. The trade problems of the developing countries, particularly the lowest-income ones, show no sign of going away. Most analysts agree that the lowest-income countries will continue to require official development assistance, considerably more than they currently receive, for decades to come. Some of the latter external finance and technical cooperation will continue to be directly related to these countries' trading problems and possibilities. The Aid for Trade issues are therefore now undoubtedly here to stay. And so they should. But the Aid for Trade discussions have so far typically been quite lopsided in terms of the inputs from potential "stakeholders." The knowledge, experience, and views of the potential beneficiaries of new Aid for Trade financing and arrangements have been seriously underrepresented.

Trade and aid issues are highly complex. The roles that trade and aid can play in development and poverty reduction depend upon multiple factors, not least the influence and interplay of political actors with other objectives to pursue. In order to develop sensible objectives and formulate policies to attain them, policymakers in potential beneficiary countries, no less (and arguably more) than in donor capitals, must understand the issues. So should their political constituencies. Most of the Aid for Trade discussion to date has taken place at the international level, far removed from the specifics of daily policy practice in developing countries. In many of the lowest-income developing countries, key policymakers have been only dimly aware of the Aid for Trade debates that could have important impacts upon their people's trading and development prospects. If Aid for Trade is ever to assist in development and poverty reduction, it is critically important both that these national (and local) policymakers and their constituencies are aware of the issues to be addressed and that their inputs are fully registered and constructively utilized.

This volume seeks to gather in one place much of the key information and analysis that could inform those who have heretofore been relatively far from the international Aid for Trade discussion. What is this new Aid for Trade discussion all about? Why has it arisen at this time? What is its potential importance? Do earlier experiences offer lessons that might engender hope for fruitful outcomes from it? What should potential beneficiaries be looking for or worrying about? Its varied authors include many of those who have been directly involved in recent Aid for Trade debates. They also include those with direct hands-on experience in Aid for Trade beneficiary countries. Like other ILEAP/JEICP* products, this volume aspires to create greater transparency and better balance in important policy discussions in the sphere of trade and development over many years to come.

* International Lawyers and Economists Against Poverty/Juristes et Économistes Internationaux Contre la Pauvreté

Introduction: Aid for Trade and Development

HUGO CAMERON AND DOMINIQUE NJINKEU

1 Introduction

Under the right circumstances, trade liberalization can be an engine of growth. But if the benefits from reductions in tariffs and trade barriers are to be gained, at least two conditions must be met. First, favorable market access regimes need to be in place. Second, for low-income countries that face severe challenges such as lack of human, institutional, and production capacity, their integration into the global economy must be supported by development assistance targeted to enhance growth and trade. Such assistance must improve their competitiveness, their ability to meet standards in high-value export markets, and their institutional capacity to engage in trade negotiations and implement the outcomes. It must also take into account the potential negative effects stemming from trade liberalization.

Negotiations in the World Trade Organization's (WTO) Doha Round and in other fora[1] hold out the prospect of further market access for goods, services, and investment. But these negotiations also hold significant pitfalls. Many developing countries – particularly those reliant on only a few imports and exports – are vulnerable to trade-related policy shocks, price changes, and other adjustment costs. Reductions in their tariffs can have a significant adverse effect on scarce government revenues, further hampering their already weak ability to re-deploy labor from sectors negatively affected by liberalization. Across-the-board tariff cuts could hurt many countries reliant on preferential access to Europe and other developed economies. In addition, net food-importing developing countries could face higher food costs as reductions in agricultural tariffs and subsidies in developed countries lead to higher prices for previously subsidized goods.[2] At the same time, the policy options available to developing countries for shielding industries from strong global competition have shrunk under structural adjustment programs and successive rounds under the General Agreement on Tariffs and Trade (GATT) and WTO.

While support has been given previously to assist low-income countries to integrate into the multilateral trading system, it has been offered in a piecemeal fashion, and has tended to focus on improving trade policy capabilities rather than on

[1] Other important trade negotiating initiatives include the Economic Partnership Agreements (EPAs) between the European Union and regions in Africa, the Caribbean, and the Pacific (ACP); the U.S.-African Growth and Opportunity Act (AGOA), and regional trade integration processes.

[2] For further discussion of these adjustment costs, see Stiglitz and Charlton (2006), pp. 12–17.

building productive supply-side capacities. Because the underlying capacity problems have not been adequately addressed, the challenges faced by low-income countries in integrating into global production and trade persist.

Bringing low-income countries on board the global economy in a way that supports their long-term development requires a mix of policy reforms and investments across a broad range of areas – including infrastructure, training, the private sector, and institutional development. Programs targeting these types of interventions have become known as "Aid for Trade" – a concept that has recently received increasing global attention.

While various interpretations exist, Aid for Trade can be defined broadly as "any assistance intended to help countries to trade and, in particular, to help them take advantage of trade agreements" (Phillips et al., 2005). This involves strengthening trade capacity and reducing supply-side constraints such that low-income countries are able to contest markets. The chapters in this volume tell the story of how Aid for Trade has emerged as a key element of the development and trade negotiating agenda, and how it could best be structured and implemented to meet the needs of its beneficiaries. This introduction presents the main themes touched upon in the book. After reviewing some preliminary background, it traces the evolution of Aid for Trade and describes how the various chapters, taken together, present a clear picture of what Aid for Trade is and where it could be headed.

1.1 Hong Kong mandate and the Aid for Trade Task Force

Elements of Aid for Trade have existed for many years in bilateral and multilateral development assistance programs. The issue came to be recognized with the launch of the WTO's Doha Round – or Doha Development Agenda (DDA) – in 2001, which saw renewed focus on developing country concerns in the international trading system, including on trade-related technical assistance. At the WTO's Sixth Ministerial Conference in Hong Kong in December 2005, trade ministers acknowledged the wider supply-side role that Aid for Trade could play beyond technical assistance (see Box 0.1). Amid announcements of increased funding for trade capacity building from a number of developed countries (see Box 0.2), ministers invited the WTO Director-General to create a task force to provide recommendations on how to operationalize Aid for Trade.

The WTO Aid for Trade Task Force was created in early 2006, and delivered its report a few months later in July following extensive consultations (WTO, 2006). Taking as a guide the Paris Declaration on Aid Effectiveness[3] and the Hong Kong mandate from ministers concerning mechanisms to secure additional financial resources, the report emphasized that Aid for Trade financing be "additional, predictable, sustainable and effective." In all, the report outlined thirty-two recommendations for implementation by the WTO, donors, and beneficiaries to fulfill trade-related needs and monitor the progress of Aid for Trade activities. These included proposals for strengthening needs identification at the country level, strengthening

[3] The Paris Declaration, agreed by both donor and beneficiary countries in 2005, includes principles to guide aid delivery, including country ownership, mutual accountability, aligning aid to national development strategies, effective donor coordination, harmonization of donor procedures, transparency, and predictable and multi-year commitments.

Box 0.1. WTO Hong Kong ministerial mandate on Aid for Trade

"We welcome the discussions of Finance and Development Ministers in various fora, including the Development Committee of the World Bank and IMF, that have taken place this year on expanding Aid for Trade. Aid for Trade should aim to help developing countries, particularly LDCs, to build the supply-side capacity and trade-related infrastructure that they need to assist them to implement and benefit from WTO Agreements and more broadly to expand their trade. Aid for Trade cannot be a substitute for the development benefits that will result from a successful conclusion to the Doha Development Agenda (DDA), particularly on market access. However, it can be a valuable complement to the DDA. We invite the Director-General to create a task force that shall provide recommendations on how to operationalize Aid for Trade. The Task Force will provide recommendations to the General Council by July 2006 on how Aid for Trade might contribute most effectively to the development dimension of the DDA. We also invite the Director-General to consult with Members as well as with the IMF and World Bank, relevant international organisations and the regional development banks with a view to reporting to the General Council on appropriate mechanisms to secure additional financial resources for Aid for Trade, where appropriate through grants and concessional loans."

Source: WTO (2005), para. 57.

Box 0.2. Increased support for Aid for Trade

At the United Nations Millennium Summit in New York in September 2000, world leaders pledged to increase development aid for the realization of the Millennium Development Goals (MDGs), which have as their main target the reduction of poverty by half by 2015. Goal 8 of the MDGs has as one of its targets the development of an "open, rules based, predictable, non-discriminatory trading and financial system." At the International Conference on Financing for Development in 2002 in Monterrey, Mexico, world leaders agreed to increase development assistance in line with objectives set by the MDGs. More recently, the World Bank announced plans to increase infrastructure lending by US$1 billion per year to around US$10 billion by 2008. In February 2005, G7 finance ministers called on the World Bank and the IMF to develop proposals for additional assistance to countries to ease adjustment to trade liberalization and to increase their capacity to take advantage of more open markets. Subsequently, at the G8 summit of developed countries in Gleneagles in 2005, leaders agreed "to boost growth, attract new investment and contribute to Africa's capacity to trade."

Prior to and at Hong Kong, Japan, the EU and the U.S. all announced increases in resources for Aid for Trade. Japan announced US$10 billion over three years (though it later transpired that this is to be primarily in the form of loans). The European Union said it would increase its annual spending on Aid for Trade to EUR2 billion by 2010 – half from the Commission and half from member states, up from EUR400 million in 2005. The U.S. announced a doubling of annual Aid for Trade to US$2.7 billion by 2010, up from $US1.3 billion in 2005.

donor responses, and enhancing the beneficiary-donor link. The report also advocated improving monitoring and evaluation, and specifically proposed establishing a body in the WTO that would undertake periodic reviews of Aid for Trade, based on reports from relevant stakeholders, with a view to ensuring additionality and predictability of funding. To follow up its work, the Task Force proposed that the WTO Director-General set up a group to examine how to implement, monitor, and review Aid for Trade efforts and act on the report's recommendations.

The recommendations stopped short of specifying how Aid for Trade should be put into practice at the operational level, leaving this for later elaboration. As such, the report's recommendations should be seen not as an end-point, but as a launchpad for further reflection on how Aid for Trade can be structured such that it enables low-income countries to extract net benefits from their participation in the international trading system.

The Hong Kong mandate on Aid for Trade and the creation of the Task Force did not take place in an analytical vacuum. Responding to repeatedly-expressed concerns by developing countries on trade-related supply capacity issues, significant research had previously drawn out the key issues around Aid for Trade. In particular, the Global Trade and Financial Architecture Project (GTFA, 2005) coordinated by the UK's Department for International Development (DFID) and the UN Millennium Project Task Force on Trade (2005), were instrumental in clarifying previous political commitments in Aid for Trade.[4] Among other issues, these initiatives advocated the need for additionality of funds and for coherence at the national and international levels. They also served to bring Aid for Trade to the attention of trade and aid decision makers in North and South.

1.2 Origin of the book

Coming in the wake of the WTO's engagement with Aid for Trade, this book compiles the results of a work program developed at the International Lawyers and Economists Against Poverty (ILEAP). ILEAP has provided ongoing support to countries in Africa and the Caribbean from the inception of Aid for Trade concepts through the Hong Kong Ministerial and beyond. The work program focuses on elaborating the overall architecture of Aid for Trade; bringing forward African and Caribbean perspectives; and exploring specific Aid for Trade projects, including in services and trade facilitation. The collection of articles in this volume presents many of the ideas elaborated through ILEAP's research, and is intended to provide a basis for further study of the issue-area. Since many of the contributions on Aid for Trade to date have come from the North, the book looks to deepen the debate by presenting here a number of perspectives and experiences from the South.

Following this introduction, the book is divided into three parts. The chapters in Part I – **Aid for Trade Genesis and Architecture** – take a close look at the origins of Aid for Trade and examine the global architecture, modalities, and costs associated with its implementation. In so doing we attempt to frame the discussion with respect to how Aid for Trade can be classified, funded, and delivered, with an emphasis on the perspectives of beneficiary countries. In moving towards

[4] At the Gleneagles Summit in July 2005, leaders of the G8 developed countries agreed to increase aid to developing countries to build physical, human, and institutional capacity to trade, and to grant additional support for trade capacity building. See G8 (2005): para. 22 (a).

a way forward in Aid for Trade, it is important to take note of prior experience in delivery, and to draw lessons from these. Part II – **Aid for Trade in Action** – aims to do precisely this. The chapters in this part recount the implementation of past trade capacity building programs and explore what went wrong, what went right, and how these lessons can be applied to the future Aid for Trade agenda. Part III – **Way Forward** – points to three areas that have been under-represented in the Aid for Trade discourse: private sector development; infrastructure; and a regional approach. The chapters in this part offer concrete proposals for how these areas could be incorporated into the Aid for Trade agenda to ensure it maintains a focus on its core supply-side elements. Taken together, the three parts attempt to move toward the long-term objective of making trade an effective engine of growth and poverty eradication.

2 Part I: Aid for Trade genesis and architecture

Development support for trade-related areas has been around for many years. As Hoekman explains in Chapter 1, the legacy of Aid for Trade can be traced back at least to the 1980s, when support for the integration of developing countries into the global economy through liberalization of trade-related policies was a major aspect of the lending programs and activities of the International Monetary Fund (IMF) and the World Bank. With the advent of poverty reduction strategies in the 1990s, a larger share of development assistance was directed towards health, education, and public expenditure management, with less aid going to infrastructure, agriculture, and trade. In the late 1990s, many developing countries perceived a need to focus more on stimulating higher economic growth rates. This view was supported by several reports: for instance, the UN Millennium Task Force on Trade stressed that trade could do much to help achieve the Millennium Development Goal of halving poverty by generating higher growth rates. A similar message was expressed in the 2005 report of the Commission for Africa (2005).

The renewed recognition of the importance of trade for development led to an increased focus by the development community on the importance of removing barriers in export markets for firms and farmers in developing countries, and thus strong support for an ambitious Doha Round outcome. However, the support for global liberalization was accompanied by a strong emphasis on the need for complementary policies and investments in low-income developing countries.

The Aid for Trade agenda emerged at a time of lackluster advancement of development in the Doha Round. Key developing country concerns such as implementation of the Uruguay Round agreements[5] and special and differential treatment (SDT)[6] were marginalized as increasing focus turned to developed country issues in agricultural and industrial market access. In Chapters 1, 2, and 3, Hoekman, Ismail, and Finger argue that Aid for Trade must be conceived of as a fundamental component of what constitutes "development" in the multilateral trading system

[5] The Doha Round 'implementation' agenda includes addressing a list of imbalances from previous rounds, which developing countries felt had hindered the realization of meaningful gains from the new system of rules. Such imbalances include the lack of implementation of certain commitments and obligations on the part of developed countries (including special and differential treatment provisions), as well as difficulties encountered by developing countries in implementing their new obligations. See ICTSD/IISD (2003).

[6] SDT holds that global trade rules cannot apply equally to countries at different levels of development.

(MTS). As such, it goes hand-in-hand with the concept of SDT. Different and more favorable treatment for those countries less able to compete has become essential to ensuring proportionality in the commitments undertaken by developed and developing countries, reflecting their differing abilities to obtain benefits from the trading system. SDT has traditionally been put into practice by granting exemptions or longer implementation timelines for developing countries – essentially derogations from the WTO norm of nondiscrimination. One could argue that Aid for Trade is essentially another way of expressing SDT, one that can improve policy coherence by marrying greater overall nondiscriminatory access to markets to an enhanced ability on the part of low-income countries to exploit such access.[7] Indeed, one of the key Doha Round SDT proposals links to Aid for Trade by urging donors, multilateral agencies and international financial institutions to coordinate their work to "ensure that LDCs are not subjected to conditionalities on loans, grants and official development assistance that are inconsistent with their rights and obligations under the WTO Agreements."

Previous efforts at technical assistance and capacity building in trade, however, have tended to be relegated to the sidelines of the WTO, and have not addressed the lack of competitiveness of the trading system's poorest members. Initiatives such as the Integrated Framework for Trade-Related Technical Assistance for LDCs (IF) and the Joint Integrated Technical Assistance Programme (JITAP) (see Box 0.3), in which the WTO is a key player, aim to coordinate and enable technical assistance activities. But their effect has been limited by a lack of funding and inadequate focus on supply-side issues such as infrastructure or private sector development. By reorienting the discussion not only to comprehensive and coherent support to technical assistance for trade professionals but also to addressing the root supply-side causes of developing country disenfranchisement from the multilateral trading system, Aid for Trade has the potential to reverse this trend.

To a certain extent, prior to Hong Kong the WTO had already begun to recognize the importance of linking trade commitments with the domestic ability of poor countries to meet them, as discussed in Chapter 3 by Finger. In an agreement reached in 2004 (WTO, 2004),[8] language on the issue of trade facilitation mandated that "support and assistance should also be provided to help developing and least-developed countries implement the commitments resulting from the negotiations... It is understood, however, that in cases where required support and assistance for such infrastructure is not forthcoming, and where a developing or least-developed Member continues to lack the necessary capacity, implementation will not be required." While the "support and assistance" referred to show that WTO members were already taking note of the need for adequate supply-side assistance to be made available to meet obligations, they did so by relaxing the obligation to implement rather than by committing to address the core problems to enable smooth and progressive insertion of these countries in the international trading system. Thus while the trade facilitation commitment was an important milestone for linking technical assistance to trade obligations, WTO members at that stage were not ready to fully commit to helping developing countries exploit the benefits of the agreement.

7 See also Hoekman and Prowse (2005).
8 For language on trade facilitation see July 2004 Package, Annex D.

Box 0.3. The Integrated Framework and JITAP

Integrated Framework for Trade-Related Technical Assistance for Least-Developed Countries (IF)

The IF was launched in 1997 to facilitate coordination of trade-related technical assistance and promote an integrated approach to assist Least Developed Countries (LDCs) enhance their trade opportunities. It is a joint initiative supported by six agencies – the International Trade Centre (ITC), the International Monetary Fund (IMF), the UN Conference on Trade and Development (UNCTAD), the UN Development Programme (UNDP), the World Bank, and the WTO – and aims to coordinate the trade-related technical assistance provided by them. Although the IF initially made little progress, it was revamped in 2000 as a mechanism to mainstream trade into national economic plans and poverty reduction strategies. An IF trust fund was established to finance Diagnostic Trade Integration Studies (DTIS), which involve a comprehensive assessment of countries' barriers to trade. These are followed up by action plans for the delivery of trade-related technical assistance, with a view to mainstreaming trade into countries' Poverty Reduction Strategy Papers (PRSPs). The IF has two main funding windows – Window I, which is used to fund the DTIS (US$300,000 per country), and Window II, which is used to fund projects (up to US$1 million per country). As a result of various implementation gaps – including lack of donor uptake on DTIS – at the September 2005 IMF and World Bank Development Committee meeting it was decided that the IF should be enhanced and provided with additional resources. The Task Force charged with developing proposals for an 'Enhanced Integrated Framework' delivered its report in June 2006. Its main conclusions were: (i) raise the current level of funding (US$35 million) to a funding target of US$400 million over an initial five-year period; (ii) strengthen capacity in recipient countries to manage the IF process; (iii) create a new Executive Secretariat in Geneva, housed at the WTO Secretariat; and (iv) establish a monitoring and evaluation framework. The Task Force further determined that the IF should not be expanded to include non-LDC low-income countries, and that alternative or parallel structures will be needed for non-LDCs.

Joint Integrated Technical Assistance Programme (JITAP)

JITAP, established in 1998, is a trade capacity building program for selected least-developed and other African countries. Like the IF, it emerged following the conclusion of the Uruguay Round to respond to developing countries' technical assistance and capacity building concerns within the multilateral trading system. It is a joint initiative from the WTO, UNCTAD, and ITC. JITAP channels support from various donors into one program to help African country partners benefit from the multilateral trading system. In a first phase, eight countries participated in JITAP: Benin, Burkina Faso, Côte d'Ivoire, Ghana, Kenya, Tunisia, Uganda, and the United Republic of Tanzania. A group of eight new countries has been added for the second phase as of 2002: Botswana, Cameroon, Malawi, Mali, Mauritania, Mozambique, Senegal and Zambia. JITAP focuses on five sets of activities: (i) setting up Inter-Institutional Technical Committees; (ii) workshops to build national capacity on WTO negotiations; (iii) studies and export promotion strategies; (iv) setting up reference centers; and (v) participation of national experts in negotiation processes in Geneva. The fact that JITAP is an instrument that is available to all African (developing and least-developed) countries makes it a tool that could be adapted to channel part of an Aid for Trade package to countries in the region. This also makes it suitable for regional programs, which are likely to address problems of both LDCs and other countries within regional groupings together with LDCs.

In the context of the various global commitments on Aid for Trade (see Box 0.2), WTO members have acknowledged that support for improving trade-related capacity should be pursued for reasons that are inside as well as outside the current Doha Development Agenda. This is clarified further in Chapter 4 by te Velde, which examines Aid for Trade through a public goods lens. On the one hand, when viewed widely, Aid for Trade can support the conclusion of WTO negotiations and therefore contribute to the provision of "governance" public goods. On the other hand, several components of current and past Aid for Trade activities contribute to the provision of public goods or goods with externalities themselves, particularly in the areas of governance and knowledge production and dissemination. It is well known that the provision of public goods is undersupplied when left to the market, so aid could usefully support the public provision of public goods. With regards to governance, Aid for Trade can be seen as a key element of a global system of trade rules, and can help ensure this system is supportive of development. It also can help to raise knowledge levels both nationally in the form of impact assessments and trade development studies, and internationally in the form of awareness-raising. These are aspects that provide benefits to all users of the multilateral trading system.

However, gaps exist in the provision of public goods related to Aid for Trade, particularly with respect to determining the optimum level of delivery (country programs vis-à-vis global programs), impact assessments of changes to trade rules, and awareness raising at a global, regional and national level. In particular, serious constraints persist in conceiving and delivering Aid for Trade at the regional level.[9] This problem is exacerbated by the fact that many countries are operating along regional lines in the trade field, and effective Aid for Trade delivery may well require a regional approach. The WTO Aid for Trade Task Force recognized this, and recommended exploring the merits of establishing Regional Aid for Trade Committees, comprising sub-regional and regional organizations and financial institutions, to oversee the implementation of the regional dimension of Aid for Trade.

The explicit recognition of a WTO interest in and responsibility for aid at Hong Kong has offered the possibility that the supply-side concerns of the multilateral trading system's less-advantaged members will start to be taken seriously. Whether expectations are met for effective delivery and additional and predictable increases in trade-related aid will depend on a range of factors. These include a sustained commitment from donors, engagement from beneficiaries, and devising a workable Aid for Trade architecture. Together with te Velde, Chapters 5, 6, and 7 by Page, Calì, and Njinkeu et al. respectively explore in greater detail the modalities and architecture of Aid for Trade – namely how it can be defined, measured, and delivered.

2.1 What does Aid for Trade include, and how much will it cost?

For many, there is a great deal of confusion and some skepticism concerning what Aid for Trade is, who it is for, how it might work, and where the money will come

[9] Though they can bring significant benefits, particularly for landlocked countries, regional programs are associated with high transaction costs and coordination problems. They are further constrained by the fact that donor-beneficiary arrangements tend to be based at the national level and run counter to regional approaches. See IMF/World Bank (2006).

from. Aid for Trade implies costs for areas as diverse as trade-related technical assistance, regional integration, and infrastructure. In order to determine the magnitude of these costs, it is useful first to determine what exactly is included in Aid for Trade and how various aspects of it could be classified. This can provide useful indications for how it could be structured to best meet the needs of its beneficiaries.

2.1.1 *Narrow and Broad*

One way to categorize Aid for Trade, outlined in Chapter 5 by Sheila Page, is by differentiating aid for WTO-related costs from aid needed more broadly to help countries use trade as part of their development strategies. The "Narrow" category includes costs for implementation of multilateral commitments, as well as those related to preference erosion. The "Broad" category covers support for conventionally recognized trade policy capacity building; for infrastructure and other measures to build countries' ability to trade; for institutions that improve capacity to trade at both the country and regional levels; and for building up private sector enterprise in new export (or import replacing) areas. In determining what any Aid for Trade package should include, it is important to take into account the different types of needs identified, the different timing of needs, and the different principles that tend to guide the aid and trade discourses.

2.1.2 *Three pillars*

Another way to classify Aid for Trade, related to the above, is to group its different aspects into three broad pillars: supply-side capacity; trade system costs; and trade policy development. Chapter 7 by Njinkeu et al. takes a closer look at this categorization and reviews its implications for African countries. At its heart, the first pillar is about building productive capacities by enhancing the regulatory, human resource, and physical infrastructures that businesses need to produce goods competitively and to move and export these goods efficiently. It comprises both private sector development and infrastructure more broadly defined. The second pillar refers to the alleviation of costs incurred as a result of trade reforms, including those undertaken as a means of implementation of international trade agreements. Grouped under this category are costs incurred from implementation of trade rules; food price increases to net food importers; preference erosion; reductions in tariff revenues; and other economic and social costs related to adjustment in specific sectors. The third pillar outlines assistance needed to address the human resource capacity gap in trade policy making and implementation. If African governments are to formulate trade policy and negotiating positions that promote development and poverty reduction, they require a range of expertise at many different levels. This involves training as well as facilitating inputs from relevant ministries, the private sector, research institutions, and civil society.

2.1.3 *Aid for Trade Task Force*

The two classifications outlined in the preceding paragraphs are reflected broadly in the WTO's Aid for Trade Task Force Report, which defines six categories based on existing Aid for Trade programs:[10] (i) trade policy and regulations; (ii) trade development (for example, investment promotion and business support services); (iii) trade-related infrastructure; (iv) building productive capacity; (v) trade-related adjustment; and (vi) other trade-related needs. The report suggests that activities should be reported as Aid for Trade when they have been identified as trade-related priorities in recipient countries' development strategies such as the Poverty Reduction Strategy Paper (PRSP).

A better understanding of the scope of Aid for Trade helps to make informed estimates of the expected costs. Towards this end, Chapter 6 by Calì builds on the Narrow / Broad classification developed by Page in Chapter 5. Quantifying Narrow WTO-related costs tends to be more straightforward than calculating open-ended costs associated with infrastructure or private sector enterprise. Narrow costs are seen to amount to between US$2 billion and US$4.2 billion, depending on assumptions used. Based on past expenditures, broad costs have increased from US$11 billion in 2001 to US$17 billion in 2004, mainly driven by outlays in infrastructure. These costs would need to be maintained or increased to meet ongoing needs, and refocused towards countries and regions where needs are greatest. Notably, as Calì points out, a brief analysis of the largest recipients of Aid for Trade indicates that strategic geopolitical concerns – rather than need – tend to be the major drivers of aid allocation or increases. This tendency has serious implications for a long-term disbursement agenda that focuses on meeting actual needs rather than serving the short-term strategic or security goals of donors.

2.2 Who is involved?

A wide range of stakeholders are by necessity involved in Aid for Trade delivery. These include government officials in donor and recipient countries, international agencies such as the World Bank and the WTO, regional organizations, the private sector, the research community, and civil society. Effective implementation of Aid for Trade will require the involvement of all these groups at the appropriate levels.

Many of the elements associated with Aid for Trade are already covered in one form or another by various trade-related technical assistance and capacity building initiatives. Chapter 4 by te Velde reviews a number of these initiatives and assesses their role in delivery of trade-related assistance. At the multilateral level, beyond the Integrated Framework and JITAP, other programs include the IMF's loan-based Trade Integration Mechanism (TIM) that addresses aspects of compensation and adjustment finance, and the WTO's Standards and Trade Development Facility (STDF), designed to assist developing countries meet global food and safety standards. There are a multitude of other programs delivered by international agencies, including the World Bank, the UN Conference on Trade and Development (UNCTAD), the International Trade Centre (ITC), and the UN Development

[10] This classification is derived from that used by the WTO/Organization for Economic Cooperation and Development (OECD) Trade Capacity Building Database (2007), a compendium of all trade-related assistance programs. The database uses three categories to classify Aid for Trade: (i) trade-related technical assistance and capacity building; (ii) trade-related infrastructure; and (iii) building productive capacity. Chapter 2 by Ismail looks more closely at this classification.

Programme (UNDP). Regional institutions such as the Inter-American Investment Bank also play a role, particularly in loan-related support for infrastructure.

Bilateral assistance plays a crucial role in Aid for Trade. The European Development Fund (EDF) and its involvement with the ACP group through the Cotonou Agreement is an important channeling mechanism for trade-related assistance. In Chapter 12 in Part II, Sunassee takes a close look at the lessons learned from past experience with the EDF and its usefulness as an Aid for Trade provider. Other bilateral donors – including the UK, the Netherlands, Norway, Denmark, Sweden, Canada, and the United States – are heavily involved in Aid for Trade program support and delivery.

Non-governmental groups are also key players in articulating how Aid for Trade could be constructed and delivered, particularly with respect to enhancing its potential to reduce poverty. Chapters 15, 16, and 17 – also in Part II – by Lyakurwa et al., Weston, and Caliari respectively address the important role played by research networks and civil society in bringing fresh perspectives and providing intellectual backstopping to beneficiaries, international agencies, and donors.

2.3 Operational Modalities

All of the chapters in Part I touch on or propose aspects of operational modalities, or ways in which Aid for Trade might be structured and delivered. While the recommendations of the Aid for Trade Task Force served to reframe the discussion, they did not include concrete recommendations for implementation, so the issues raised in the chapters continue to be relevant to the wider reflection on architecture. We touch briefly on two of these below.

2.3.1 *Existing or new delivery mechanisms*

A central concern around delivery is to understand why current trade capacity building programs are not addressing needs (infrastructure, supply capacity, and the need to compensate for preference erosion), and whether new mechanisms should therefore be put in place. The idea of a stand-alone fund for Aid for Trade has also been raised by a number of commentators. For instance, both the Global Trade and Financial Architecture report (GTFA, 2005) and the Millennium Project Task Force on Trade (2005) recommended the establishment of an Aid for Trade fund. Page (2005) has proposed a fund to compensate losses suffered from preference erosion, while Stiglitz and Charlton (2006) have presented the idea of a "Global Trade Facility" to be housed at the World Bank. Despite these contributions, the WTO Aid for Trade Task Force declined to recommend the formation of a stand-alone fund. According to the Task Force report, existing mechanisms and programs should be used as much as possible. Specifically, donors and governments should establish in-country processes that build on what already exists, where appropriate. The Task Force further recommended exploring the merits of establishing Regional Aid for Trade Committees to oversee the implementation of the sub-regional and regional dimensions of Aid for Trade. In the case of the EU-ACP EPAs, for instance, this could be done though the joint programming and management of Aid for Trade via the existing aid delivery infrastructure in the EDF. What is clear is that Aid for

Trade cannot be managed by a single donor or institution, and no single approach is suitable for all countries.

2.3.2 *Country-led and sector-led funding*

Another recurring challenge in aid delivery, outlined by Page in Chapter 5, relates to country-led, as opposed to sector-led, approaches, and the question of what level should be used in delivering Aid for Trade. Country-led funding sees aid as a means of providing general support for all of a country's needs. In the case of trade, this would be expressed, for instance, by mainstreaming trade in PRSPs and country development strategies, with prioritization of trade-related projects at the discretion of each country. As a result, there is no guarantee under country-defined processes that trade-related areas will necessarily be prioritized. Sector-led, on the other hand, relies on so-called vertical funds that channel money to specific sectors, such as health, environment, or trade. Vertical funds can be best used for coordinating global solutions for specific global problems and ensuring that money is effectively distributed to a particular sector. While both PRSPs and vertical funds can suffer from a lack of ownership by recipient countries (depending on the process used), with vertical funds there is also the problem that other sectors in turn may demand their own vertical funds in order to avoid being "crowded out." The Task Force did not pass judgment on this issue, but rather emphasized the need for both a "country-driven" approach while also making targeted Aid for Trade funds available. The need to avoid donors making tradeoffs such as diverting funds from other sectors towards Aid for Trade reinforces previously-stated arguments around additionality. Chapter 9 by Siphana in Part II provides an example of a country's experience integrating sector-wide approaches as part of its national development strategy.

2.4 Aid for Trade and the EU-ACP Economic Partnership Agreements

While much attention has focused on the WTO and the multilateral Aid for Trade architecture, similar elements of the debate emerge in the trade and aid relationship between the EU and the African, Caribbean, and Pacific (ACP) group of countries, particularly with respect to the Economic Partnership Agreement (EPA) negotiations between them. EPAs are intended to shift the trading relationship between the EU and the ACP from so-called Lomé-based preferences[11] to six regional free trade agreements that comply with WTO rules. The process is guided by the Cotonou Partnership Agreement, which covers both aid and trade elements of EU-ACP relations. Article 34.3 of the Cotonou Agreement mandates EU economic and trade cooperation to "aim at enhancing the production, supply and trading capacity of the ACP countries as well as their capacity to attract investment. It shall further aim at creating a new trading dynamic between the Parties, at strengthening the ACP countries trade and investment policies and at improving the ACP countries'

[11] Signed in 1975 between the EU (formerly European Economic Community) and the ACP, the Lomé Conventions instigated non-reciprocal preferences for most exports from ACP countries to the EEC, together with financial benefits. There were four iterations, with the last one, Lomé IV, expiring in 2000. See http://www.acpsec.org/en/conventions/cotonou/cotonou_historical_note_e.htm.

capacity to handle all issues related to trade." In addition, Article 41.5 stipulates that the EU will support the ACP states' efforts to strengthen their capacity in the supply of services. This clause promises to pay particular attention to the enhancement of the competitiveness of ACP services related to labor, business, distribution, finance, tourism, culture, and construction and related engineering services.

As part of adjusting to and implementing the new EPAs, ACP countries will have to undertake a number of critical reforms. But if these countries are to benefit from the EPA negotiations, substantial investments in infrastructure and productive capacity will be needed. This is because ACP tariff reductions, together with loss of ACP market share from preference erosion, will need to be balanced out if the ACP is to mitigate painful economic restructuring. Although a number of these costs may be attributable to other ongoing trade liberalization processes such as the WTO and other regional and bilateral agreements, there will be certain costs directly attributable to the EPA negotiations. This is most apparent in the case of LDCs, which are required to make few commitments in the WTO Doha Round, yet are asked to comply with reciprocity requirements under EPAs. As a result, the Aid for Trade agenda is of particular significance for these countries. The Aid for Trade implications of EPAs are explored in Chapters 7 and 12 by Njinkeu et al. and Sunassee respectively, including how European funding could be used for programs that support much-needed regional integration within ACP regions.

3 Part II: Aid for Trade in Action

Following the outline in Part I of the various elements around the origin and implementation of Aid for Trade, the second part of the book draws on selected practical experiences with previous or existing trade capacity building programs. The chapters illustrate the multi-dimensional nature of the issues, and show how Aid for Trade has been delivered through different mechanisms and by a diversity of stakeholders at national, regional, and multilateral levels. Taken together, these experiences communicate lessons as to what Aid for Trade should and should not be, and how different stakeholders can be harnessed to move the process towards development and productive integration of low-income countries into the multilateral trading system.

3.1 Capacity building programs

Chapters 8 and 9 by Lyimo/Sungula and Siphana respectively provide examples of nationally-based delivery of trade capacity building programs – namely, the IF, JITAP, and Sector-Wide Approaches (SWAp) for investments in trade – and draw conclusions from these.

3.1.1 *The Integrated Framework (IF)*

The IF is a six-agency program launched in 1997 to facilitate coordination of trade-related technical assistance and promote an integrated approach that assists LDCs to enhance their trade opportunities. It has achieved mixed success. The experiences of Tanzania and Cambodia show that, while the program can help LDCs enhance their capacity to identify advantages and constraints in trade, it has failed to provide adequate financial and human resources to deliver the intended outcomes. The donor community has generally not responded adequately to the needs identified in the IF's Diagnostic Trade Integration Studies (DTIS), particularly in the areas of social and economic infrastructure. Unless the level of funding increases along the lines recommended by the Enhanced IF Task Force (see Box 0.3 above), it will continue to be unable to make a significant difference in implementing the Task Force's recommendations. As a result, the IF may not be well-suited for supporting macroeconomic adjustment, which has to date been mainly undertaken in African countries via the IMF and the EDF.

Another limitation of the IF is its scope, in the sense that it continues to apply only to LDCs; other low-income countries do not qualify. This issue was raised by the Aid for Trade Task Force, which recommended exploring the possibility of an in-country process modeled on the IF, but separately funded, for non-LDC low-income countries.[12]

If trade is to be fully mainstreamed into the PRSP process, country ownership is paramount, as is demonstrated by Cambodia's experience. Close coordination between affected areas of government, the private sector, and civil society organizations allowed Cambodia to develop a well-informed trade strategy based on in-country economic realities. This needs to be reinforced by close and ongoing coordination between government and donors.

3.1.2 *JITAP*

Established in 1998, JITAP is a trade capacity building program for selected least-developed and other African countries, administered by the WTO, UNCTAD, and ITC. It emerged following the conclusion of the Uruguay Round to respond to African countries' technical assistance and capacity building concerns within the multilateral trading system. JITAP can be a useful model for addressing government-level aspects of trade policy development and participation in rules making. However, JITAP would not be the most appropriate tool to handle an Aid for Trade package in its entirety, particularly in areas involving infrastructure or more complex adjustment-funding mechanisms. It is important to bear in mind that the volumes of funds that have been handled by JITAP in the past have been quite modest. On average, beneficiary countries have received approximately US$1.5 million over five to eight years. The flows of aid required under the Aid for Trade initiative, however, are much larger, given the focus on addressing supply-side constraints and infrastructure. Like the IF, the program is also limited in scope, specifically to African countries. However, this could mean there might be a role for JITAP in supporting regional capacity building efforts on trade within the continent's economic regional groupings.

The evidence from Tanzania shows that the training approach used by JITAP, based largely on workshops and seminars, provides very limited capacity for handling the practical aspects involved in implementation of trade policy. Experience emerging from the bilateral programs that paralleled JITAP activities highlights the benefits of longer-duration training schemes, as well as highly specialized

[12] Specifically, the sixty-six IDA (International Development Association) countries, as identified by World Bank lending criteria. See http://web.worldbank.org/.

postgraduate programs that cover the full range of trade development issues in building effective technical capacity for economic and trade analysis. In the long run, trade-related technical assistance should aim to build long-term human and institutional capacity, ensure local ownership, and create a framework for laws and legal regulations. This must be reinforced by building capacity in the public service such that ministers have competent staff that understand the technical details of trade policy. To build this capacity, short-term courses, conferences, and seminars should be seen a supplement to – not a replacement for – long-term training programs in areas such as economics and law.

3.1.3 *Trade SWAp*

The objective of a Sector-Wide Approach (SWAp) in trade is to ensure that ongoing and future trade and trade-related interventions match needs, that duplication is avoided, and that new commitments or possible future funding from bilateral and multilateral donors are reflected. Cambodia's SWAps in education, health, and public finance management show that they can be effective tools for aid delivery. While general experiences with SWAps for productive sectors tends to be weaker, Siphana argues that a well-designed trade SWAp can help coordinate responses to the needs identified as part of the IF process, but for which the IF has not been able to fund itself. Chapter 12 by Sunassee touches on SWAps as one of the preferred delivery mechanisms currently employed by the EU with its ACP partners.

3.2 Formulating Aid for Trade

The previous experience of the Inter-American Development Bank (IDB) in delivering Aid for Trade, together with that of Caribbean countries in the Free Trade Area of the Americas (FTAA) process, and between the EU and the ACP, are instructive for helping to properly structure Aid for Trade in future. This applies particularly to the areas of programming, coherence, availability of funds, and political considerations.

3.2.1 *Programming*

As described by Estevadeordal et al. in Chapter 10, the extensive experience of program delivery of trade-related assistance by the IDB in Latin America and the Caribbean (LAC) holds important lessons for other regions in the discussion around Aid for Trade. Since its creation more than forty years ago, the Bank has actively supported the development of trade-related infrastructure and supply-side capacities in its LAC member countries. Further, over the last decade, the Bank has built a solid track record in trade-related capacity building in LAC, developing both country-focused and region-wide approaches to the provision of such assistance. Through regular interaction with government authorities, the private sector and other non-state actors, it has developed a sound reputation in the LAC trade community, based on technical expertise, working experience and mutual trust. The chapter identifies no less than seventeen key lessons gleaned from this experience that are critical for those involved in future design and administration of Aid for Trade programs to take note of. These include building up local expertise, the usefulness of multi-sectoral approaches, monitoring and evaluation, and various elements around donor coordination – a priority also touched upon in Chapters 11 and 12.

3.2.2 *Coherence*

Strong coordination between donor and beneficiary countries and within countries is one of several aspects of effective Aid for Trade formulation and implementation. Expressed in the principle of alignment in the Paris Declaration, the discussion in Chapters 11 and 12 by Brown and Sunassee respectively emphasize its importance. Efforts by donors to base their overall support on partner countries' national development strategies will need to be reinforced by reducing bottlenecks such as overly-complex procedures and low absorptive capacity in beneficiary countries. This will require development partners to establish a fine balance between control and flexibility, while recipient countries need to become more proactive players. Coherence at the national level among trade and finance ministries is also paramount. In beneficiary countries, while trade officials may propose all manner of projects in the context of Aid for Trade, it is finance and development planning ministries that are the repositories of project planning expertise and the formal conduits to international financial institutions (IFIs). Many donors will only act on the authority of designated officials in finance and/or development planning ministries. For the requests of trade officials to gain traction in finance ministries, it is incumbent on them to bring these forward at an early stage in the funding process. Meanwhile, in donor countries, close coordination between development and trade ministries is also essential to help align funding with any commitments made in the trade sphere.

3.2.3 *Accessing funds*

A recurring problem, particularly for countries interacting with the EU, is that of gaining access to promised financial assistance. Experience has taught many beneficiary countries to be circumspect about assurances of receiving funds that may never materialize due to lengthy and unnecessarily onerous procedures for accessing them. The 8th EDF (1995–2000) replenishment, for instance, experienced low commitment and disbursement rates, resulting in a staggering EUR9.5 billion in uncommitted funds. Sunassee points to some improvements in this area since 2000 in EU funding administration. Recipient countries expect progressive improvements on this front as donors take on board and implement the Paris Declaration, including its provisions on reforming and simplifying donor policies and procedures.

3.2.4 *Political considerations*

At the outset of the WTO's Aid for Trade initiative, some concern was raised regarding the use of Aid for Trade as a negotiating tool to gain developing country buy-in into a wider Doha Round agreement. Developing countries have emphasized at every opportunity that any Aid for Trade must be viewed as a complement to, rather than being conditional upon, a fair market access package. A step was taken in this direction by de-linking Aid for Trade from the Doha Round single undertaking, but the experience of Caribbean countries in the FTAA nevertheless advises caution, as discussed by Brown in Chapter 11. In the FTAA negotiations, the offer of technical and financial assistance was used by the larger, wealthier countries – principally the United States – to provide an incentive to encourage countries skeptical about the advantages of the FTAA to continue with the negotiations and eventually sign on to the agreement.[13] However, while concessions and commitments made during trade negotiations are reflected in the final agreement and become legally binding and enforceable through the dispute settlement mechanism, technical assistance provisions tend to be non-binding "best endeavor" clauses. The other side of this coin is the dual role of negotiator and funder played by donor countries. In the context of the FTAA, most countries looked to the United States to provide the resources for trade capacity building. But the United States as a party to the FTAA negotiations was also in a position to manipulate the process by providing its aid selectively. Similar dynamics are also possible in the EPA context, where the trade negotiations are between countries at radically different levels of development and where the EU plays both a negotiating and a funding role.

3.3 Sectoral analysis: Aid for Trade in services

Services are of growing importance for low-income countries: over 50 percent of the GDP of many of these countries is made up by the services sector. The particular nature of services and of trade liberalization in services is such that there are a number of special features to the Aid for Trade debate in the sector that distinguish it from goods trade. In order to take account of the non-tariff nature of impediments to services trade, therefore, a tailored response is required for Aid for Trade in services. Chapters 13 and 14 by Sauvé and Chaitoo respectively outline the elements that could make up an effective agenda for Aid for Trade in services. Looking at the sector from an Aid for Trade perspective provides a useful illustration of an area where some of the main issues can be tested.

Chapter 13 by Sauvé identifies three broad areas in particular as requiring support: (i) the ability to negotiate from a more informed position; (ii) the capacity to better manage the process of market opening; and (iii) the ability to supply newly-opened foreign markets. Capacity building for supply-side constraints under (iii), however, should involve a different set of institutional actors than those concerned with the strengthening of trade negotiating or regulatory capacity due to the private sector focus. Taken together, such an approach could help address the clear deficit in negotiating, enforcement, and supply-side capacities that the majority of developing countries face under the WTO's General Agreement on Trade in Services (GATS).

[13] The U.S. Agency for International Development (USAID) assisted several Caribbean countries with the preparation of their trade capacity building strategies and action plans, and fed information directly back to the U.S. Trade Representative (USTR) on a regular basis. This constituted a conflict of interest in which the major negotiating power had also devised and funded a process that gave them ready access to detailed assessments of negotiating strengths – and, more importantly, weaknesses – of other countries at the table. See Chapter 11 by Brown.

3.3.1 *Lessons learned*

Many capacity building efforts in services have so far focused on helping negotiators and sectoral officials master the legal provisions of the GATS. But there are more pressing needs that are arguably more conducive to harnessing the pro-development potential of services liberalization. These include acquiring the analytical tools to determine a country's readiness to liberalize; developing government-wide negotiating strategies; and helping domestic service providers take full advantage of the market access opportunities arising from regional and multilateral liberalization efforts. In the experience of the CARICOM countries, as discussed by Chaitoo, technical assistance in services has largely taken the form of seminars or workshops for government officials. Unfortunately, these have limited impact on boosting trade in services from the Caribbean or any region, particularly when most domestic suppliers are at the level of small or micro-enterprise. To remedy this, more tangible investment in the development of regulatory regimes to allow market opening, as well as business-supporting or facilitation measures, are needed for services industries to overcome constraints and gain market intelligence as well as make themselves known. In an earlier publication, te Velde (2005) suggests that donors could focus on three areas in particular for building countries' capacity to participate in services negotiations:

1. Support national working groups on trade in services, and equip these with the tools and funds to solicit assessments of trade in services, or do the assessment themselves;
2. Foster regional networks at the sector level, so that interested parties (for example, the private sector, regulatory agencies, and central banks) learn from experiences within the region; and
3. Support the development of trade in services windows in multilateral organizations, such as UNCTAD and the World Bank, to explain GATS and its general implications, as well as to combine their strengths in providing sectoral expertise and assessments, at the level of capitals, and link with national working groups at the sector level.

3.4 Inputs from research networks and civil society

While beneficiary governments and donors remain the focal actors in Aid for Trade, a diversity of other institutions play key roles in delivery and support, and in formulating how trade-related assistance can be implemented to enable development and poverty reduction. Chapters 15, 16, and 17 by Lyakurwa et al., Weston, and Caliari respectively examine the functions of international research institutions and civil society organizations and how they help to articulate the Aid for Trade agenda.

3.4.1 *Research-policy linkage*

If a development perspective is to be reflected in trade rules and trade negotiations, it is imperative that low-income countries are able to determine their own offensive and defensive agendas, and move them forward them in relevant fora. To do this, they must be equipped with sufficient long-term and short-term domestic capacity to research, analyze, and engage effectively in a wide range of trade-related issues. Currently, many countries suffer a systemic lack of capacity in trade-related research and policy-making. This is characterized by grossly inadequate staffing of relevant government ministries and institutions, lack of qualified government personnel and scholars, insufficient academic institutions and opportunities, and inadequate coordination mechanisms both in capitals and during negotiation processes.

To fill this gap, global research networks can play a role in helping low-income countries develop national trade policies and participate in trade negotiations. This research requires further support to translate its findings into action, for instance by using funds for organizing national multi-stakeholder meetings to develop national policy positions. Research can also help to inform various ways in which Aid for Trade might evolve. For instance, studies on behind-the-border issues and others such as trade facilitation can help to identify how additional funding might support efforts to expand developing country trade and poverty reduction.

Chapter 16 by Weston evaluates the relevance of contributions from research institutions and networks by addressing whether they respond to developing countries' needs (*effectiveness*); whether they have had an impact on trade policies and practices (*management and efficiency*); and whether they have contributed to building longer-term capacity nationally and regionally (*sustainability*). The chapter concludes that Aid for Trade should be used to support Southern trade research networks, which remain scarce, including in governments, universities, parliaments, civil society, and the private sector.

3.4.2 *Keeping a holistic development focus*

By widening the debate around Aid for Trade to include elements of poverty reduction, development, human rights, environmental protection, and social justice, international civil society has helped to maintain a broader vision on the issue. In addition, like international research networks, civil society groups can provide essential backstopping research for low-income countries that lack this capacity. Caliari shows that international NGOs providing policy advice on Aid for Trade should seek to ensure that it reflects a holistic perspective that links trade and finance. Recipient governments need to be cautious about issues such as aid coordination, conditionality, and skewed governance, and must acknowledge the political impact of international financial institutions and donor policies in trade negotiations. Civil society organizations have brought to light research questioning the effectiveness of compensation mechanisms and foreign direct investment. Most civil society groups working on the issue agree that an effective Aid for Trade package must include aid to overcome supply-side constraints and aid to improve in-country policy analysis.

4 Part III: Way forward

From the start, Aid for Trade emerged as a renewed focus on the supply-side needs of low-income countries. It also emerged as a response to concerns raised by many of these countries that lessons need to be drawn from experiences in existing trade-related capacity building, particularly with respect to addressing their core competitiveness. Recall the WTO Hong Kong mandate on Aid for Trade, which stated that "Aid for Trade should aim to help developing countries, particularly LDCs, to build the supply-side capacity and trade-related infrastructure that they need to assist them to implement and benefit from WTO Agreements and more broadly to expand their trade." Moving forward, Aid for Trade must maintain its focus on supply-side elements. In particular, we identify three priorities that require increased attention in future:

- Enhancing private sector capacity to produce and trade;
- Improving trade-related infrastructure; and
- Focusing actions at the regional level.

These areas have suffered from under-representation in the Aid for Trade agenda. They are also closely linked. For instance, regional development banks can play a major role in financing infrastructure that benefits private sector development at the regional level. Chapters 18 and 19 by Brewster/Njinkeu and te Velde respectively address how programs in these areas might be elaborated such that they are prioritized in Aid for Trade delivery.

Under the aegis of Aid for Trade, it is often easier to identify immediate needs and compliance or implementation issues, but far more difficult to envisage longer-term needs relating to economic adjustment and diversification. As the primary driver of such processes, the private sector is a critical – yet often overlooked – stakeholder. Programs with appropriate funding schemes for business development projects applied at a suitable level must be included as an element of the Aid for Trade agenda. In this context, as outlined in Chapter 18 by Brewster and Njinkeu, the experience of the regional development banks can be instructive.

4.1 Scope of private sector Aid for Trade

There are two general means of support for private sector development: general support such as for rules and regulations, and specific support for sectors or firms. These can be complemented by actions in: (i) infrastructure preparation and infrastructure software (that is, technical cooperation); (ii) programs directly addressing the competitiveness of production processes and the quality of exports/exportables produced; and (iii) measures that directly promote the marketing of specific export/exportable goods and services. Prioritization of private sector support in these areas would have to be determined in the framework of negotiations directly between the specific private sectors concerned and donor agencies. Priorities should be expected to have a demonstrable connection to their effectiveness in enhancing export performance, and to the latter's attainability over the lifespan of the support project. Importantly, care should be taken to ensure that support is directed not at the international private sector but at building the ability of *domestic* companies within low-income countries to produce and export.

If Aid for Trade to the private sector is to be efficiently used, like other related Aid for Trade activities it must adhere to the principles of effective aid delivery.[14] As such, it would need to be integrated into more comprehensive national development

[14] See note 3 above on the Paris Declaration on Aid Effectiveness, as well as Cambodia's experience with the Integrated Framework outlined in Chapter 9 of this volume.

strategies or regional programs. Furthermore, as the primary actor in production and exporting, the private sector must be directly engaged in the design, management, and monitoring of any Aid for Trade intended to be of benefit to it. A necessary complement to these goals is human and institutional capacity building for the private sector.

4.1.1 *Development banks and infrastructure*

The role of multilateral and regional development finance institutions should not be overlooked in financing the infrastructure aspects of Aid for Trade, much of which is expected to come from loans rather than grants. Most development banks are highly liquid and under-spending in this area. At the IDB, for instance, infrastructure accounts for merely 23 percent of total lending, compared with the 65 percent devoted to the social sectors and governance. In the African Development Bank (AfDB), there has been stagnation in project lending at around the US$1 billion mark. The trends with respect to private sector investment in infrastructure are even worse: investment in this area has collapsed since 1998 and shows no sign of recovery. Total AfDB investment in infrastructure projects with private sector participation dropped from US$71 billion in 1998 to US$16 billion in 2003. Since there is now a relative abundance of loan capital, several of these institutions are actively promoting infrastructure projects using such innovative devices as flexible mixed private-public combinations and non-sovereign guarantees. In the trade-related infrastructure field, a specific Aid for Trade agenda might best be used in preparation and software projects, where there is no serious overlapping with other institutions. This could be a good means of accelerating investment in infrastructure construction by the multilateral development finance institutions.

The experience of the IDB provides an example of what is achievable in Aid for Trade from regional finance mechanisms. Chapter 19 by te Velde looks at the IDB and other examples of delivery instruments, including World Bank and bilateral donor projects. As the most active of all regional banks on Aid for Trade, the IDB has a strong track record of supporting infrastructure and supply-side capacity in the region, and more recently has also provided trade capacity building. According to an IDB report, "Aid for Trade is not new for the IDB: many of the Bank's traditional lending instruments were designed to support the very elements of what is today perceived as the broader aid-for-trade agenda, including infrastructure development (transport, energy and communications) and strengthening countries' productive capacities. The Bank also has a long track record of providing adjustment related lending, some of which has been directly related to trade" (Rey de Marulanda et al., 2006).

4.1.2 *Regional aspects*

Discussion of cross-border issues on aid at the regional level came to prominence at the WTO prior to Hong Kong at the September 2005 session of the Committee on Trade and Development (CTD). At that meeting, an assessment of the Integrated Framework sparked a discussion around what Aid for Trade measures might be made available to non-LDC developing countries (recall that the IF is only available to LDCs). The WTO Aid for Trade Task Force recognized this concern, and recommended exploring the establishment of "a separately-funded in-country process for non-LDCs." This is an important element of the discussion, particularly in Africa, as most sub-regions on the continent group LDCs with non-LDCs, creating potential barriers to regional coherence in Aid for Trade delivery. Since trade policy for many regions in low-income countries is being coordinated on a regional basis together with a strong push towards regional integration, this implies a regional approach for many aspects of Aid for Trade. However, most attention thus far has focused on delivery at the national level.

Chapter 19 describes three types of regional activities that could add value to national Aid for Trade programs: (i) support to help regional bodies take a coordinating role on regional trade issues, particularly for integration efforts appropriate at the regional level; (ii) support for knowledge sharing and learning within a region; and (iii) support for activities with cross-border externalities such as regional infrastructure projects. As mentioned by the WTO Aid for Trade Task Force, Regional Aid for Trade Committees could be set up to monitor how Aid for Trade is disbursed. Taking into account both WTO and EPA negotiations, such committees could facilitate a variety actions, including the monitoring of regional trade policy integration, implementation of needs assessments of cross-border Aid for Trade projects (for example, regional DTISs), and reviews of the adequacy of existing mechanisms for financing regional Aid for Trade.

REFERENCES

Commission for Africa. 2005. "Our Common Interest – Report of the Commission," UK: Commission for Africa.

G8. 2005. *Declaration*, Gleneagles: 8 July. http://www.g8.gov.uk/.

GTFA Project. 2005. "Strengthening the Global Trade Architecture for Economic Development: An Agenda for Action," London: DFID, http://www.dfid.gov.uk/aboutdfid/organisation/itd-global-trade-fin-architecture-intro.asp.

Hoekman, Bernard and Susan Prowse. 2005. "Policy Responses to Preference Erosion: From Trade as Aid to Aid for Trade," Policy Research Working Paper 3721, Washington, D.C.: World Bank.

ICTSD/IISD. 2003. "Implementation-related Issues and Concerns," *Doha Round Briefings*, Geneva: ICTSD and IISD.

IMF/World Bank. 2006. "Doha Development Agenda and Aid for Trade," prepared by the staffs of the IMF and World Bank, Washington, D.C.

Page, S. 2005. "A Preference Erosion Compensation Fund," *ODI Opinions* 35, London: Overseas Development Institute.

Phillips, Lauren, S. Page, and Dirk Willem te Velde. 2005. "Aid for Trade: What does it mean? Why should aid be part of WTO negotiations? And how much might it cost?," *ODI Opinions*, London: Overseas Development Institute.

Rey de Marulanda, N. et al. 2006. "Aid for Trade: The Inter-American Development Bank's Experience in Latin America and the Caribbean," *Integration and Regional Programmes Department*, Washington D.C.: IADB.

Stiglitz, Joseph E. and Andrew Charlton. 2006. "Aid for Trade: A Report for the Commonwealth Secretariat," London: Commonwealth Secretariat.

te Velde, Dirk Willem. 2005. "Revitalising services negotiations at the WTO: Can technical assistance help?," London: Overseas Development Institute.

UN Millennium Project. 2005. "Trade for Development – Achieving the Millennium Development Goals," *Task Force on Trade*, New York: UNDP.

WTO. 2004. *Decision Adopted by the General Council on 1 August 2004*, Doha Work Programme, WT/L/579, 2 August.

WTO. 2005. *Ministerial Declaration*, Ministerial Conference, Sixth Session, Hong Kong, 13–18 December 2005, Doha Work Programme, WT/MIN(05)/DEC, 22 December.

WTO. 2006. *Recommendations of the Task Force on Aid for Trade*, Aid for Trade Task Force, WT/AFT/1, 27 July.

WTO/OECD. 2007. "Doha Development Agenda Trade Capacity Building Database," http://tcbdb.wto.org/.

PART ONE

Aid for Trade Genesis and Architecture

1 **Aid for Trade:** Helping Developing Countries Benefit from Trade Opportunities

BERNARD HOEKMAN

1 Introduction

While differences persist regarding the appropriate role of government intervention to support or restrain trade, there is general agreement regarding the strong positive association between economic development and trade expansion. The World Trade Organization (WTO) promotes trade, and in that sense can be regarded as an institution that promotes development. However, despite the boom in world trade during the last thirty-plus years – in part under the stewardship of the WTO and before it the General Agreement on Tariffs and Trade (GATT) – and the increasing participation of many developing countries in the trading system, many observers are concerned about the impact of the WTO on the economic development prospects of poor countries (see, for example, Oxfam, 2002; Rodrik, 2005; Stiglitz, 2000).

These concerns often boil down to two specific problems. First, the WTO is driven by mercantilism: trade negotiations reflect a desire by countries to improve their access to export markets. The focus is on mutual reductions in the negative spillovers that national trade-restricting policies impose on other countries through the reciprocal exchange of market access "concessions." In the case of small developing countries that are of only limited interest from an export perspective, the system of reciprocity does not "work." Such countries cannot offer enough to induce larger traders – the most interesting markets – to improve access.

Second, common policy disciplines may not be appropriate for all countries. For example, taxing trade may be the most effective method for a government of a developing country to raise revenue, implying that reducing tariffs, even if in principle seen as desirable by a government, may be conditional on having put in place the capacity to reliably tap domestic tax bases. Increasingly, the ambit of the WTO extends beyond trade policy. While harmonization of domestic regulatory policies may reduce negative spillovers on foreign firms, there may well be strong economic efficiency rationales for regulatory diversity. Intellectual property protection is an example – relatively weak enforcement may well be first best for poor countries at early stages of development (Maskus, 2000). Even where it is agreed

The author is grateful to Kym Anderson, John Panzer, Susan Prowse and John Wilson for helpful comments, discussions and inputs. The views expressed in this paper are personal and should not be attributed to the World Bank.

that harmonization of substantive regulatory disciplines is appropriate, this may give rise to asymmetrically high implementation costs, in that the burden may fall disproportionately on poorer countries (Finger and Schuler, 2000).

The traditional approach to address such "development" concerns in the GATT/WTO has been through a mix of opt-outs from specific rules, a call for high-income countries to grant preferential access for developing country exports, and promises of development assistance. The focus of this paper is on the last two responses. Preferential access can be – and generally is – regarded as a form of aid that complements official development assistance transfers. Insofar as countries have preferred access to a protected market, this will generate rents (financed by consumers) for the preferred exporters. These are equivalent to a financial transfer.[1] Official development assistance – direct financial transfers – is delivered independently of the WTO: through development cooperation agencies working with recipient governments. Trade expansion may be a focus of specific projects and assistance programs, but insofar as this is the case, there has historically been very little if any connection or interaction with the GATT/WTO. Thus, development assistance was delivered in parallel to preferential access programs and special and differential treatment. This was by design: the WTO, and before it the GATT, focuses on the international spillovers created by national trade policies; development agencies focus on supporting efforts by governments to raise per capita incomes.

Since the launch of the Doha Round in 2001 there is an increasing recognition that this parallelism or independence may not be desirable. Efforts to mobilize more "Aid for Trade" – to allocate more (or a greater share of) development assistance to trade – reflect a view in parts of the development community (aid agencies, counterparts in developing country governments, development-focused NGOs) that there had been some neglect on their side of the potential power of trade as an instrument to reduce poverty. It also reflects a concern that more attention be given to ensuring that trade agreements "make sense" from a development perspective. This has resulted in both greater engagement in national trade policymaking in several traditional donor countries such as Sweden and the UK, and an increased emphasis on building capacity in developing countries to define and defend trade positions. Conversely, the trade community (trade ministries, WTO representatives) is more cognizant of the need to mobilize resources to support implementation of negotiated trade policy-related disciplines, and, more generally, to help governments deal with the adjustment costs associated with trade reforms and harness the opportunities created by trade liberalization.

This paper starts with a brief review of the status quo ante – the approaches that have been pursued in the past to address development concerns in the trading system (Section 2). It then discusses the genesis of efforts to complement the focus on (preferential) market access – using trade as a form of aid – with financial assistance to help countries realize the benefits of trade – "Aid for Trade" (Section 3). This is followed by a discussion of challenges and options for moving forward (Section 4) and concluding remarks (Section 5).

[1] In practice, these rents will be split between preferred exporters and importers (such as distributors and retailers). Olarreaga and Ozden (2005) and Ozden and Sharma (2006) show that the share accruing to exporters is well below 100 percent, and that smaller countries get smaller shares of the rents.

2 The status quo ante

Given that the only instrument GATT/WTO members have at their disposal is trade policy, it is not surprising that efforts to address development concerns by the trade community have focused on the instruments they control. That is, the approach taken by the GATT/WTO can be characterized as an effort to use "trade as aid." There are two dimensions to this approach. On the one hand, there is the focus of the institution on nondiscriminatory trade liberalization – which benefits all members, including developing countries, through better access to export markets and helping to lower their own barriers to trade. On the other hand, this effort to lower trade barriers on a most-favored nation (MFN) basis available to all other WTO members is complemented with positive discrimination in favor of developing countries through granting of *preferential* access to markets, as well as greater flexibility/opt outs for developing countries for specific GATT/WTO rules. This special and differential treatment emerged as part of the trading system in the 1960s. A rationale for the use of trade instruments was to complement aid with what was regarded as a more powerful development instrument. The case for discrimination in favor of developing countries was summarized by the phrase "trade, not aid."

A large literature has emerged since then analyzing the effectiveness and desirability of using such positive discrimination. Views differ.[2] Some argue that in principle the approach makes sense and has been successful for some developing countries, but in practice has delivered limited benefits because of the way it has been implemented. A good case can be made that the value of preferential access offered by developed countries was greatly reduced as a result of product exclusions and restrictive administrative conditions (rules of origin, quota limitations, and so forth).

Others are of the view that the use of trade discrimination as a form of aid has had significant downsides for recipients, in part because it has slowed down general liberalization on a nondiscriminatory basis and helped result in a more distorted global trade system. A large body of research has shown that discriminatory trade policies have been of limited use to many developing countries. While a number of countries benefited from such programs as a result of being granted quota rents on traditional commodities such as sugar and bananas, this arguably has worked against their export diversification. Moreover, the plethora of preferential access programs has encouraged the proliferation of reciprocal trade agreements, further distorting world trade flows and moving the trading system away from nondiscrimination.[3] The fact is that, despite preferences and special and differential treatment of developing countries, many of the poorest WTO members have seen their share of world trade stagnate or decline since the 1970s.

Both sides agree that a major factor impeding the use of preferential access programs is a lack of competitiveness and supply capacity in many of the beneficiary countries. Critics of the effort to use preferential trade as a form of aid regard this in part as a result of preferences, arguing that preferences create incentives for countries not to diversify, given that this would entail a loss of rents created by

[2] See, for example, Johnson (1967) for an excellent contemporaneous analysis and discussion. Pack and Saggi (2006) and Rodrik (2005) review the more recent literature.

[3] See, for example, the survey of the literature and the readings in Hoekman and Ozden (2007).

the ability to export to highly protected markets for products such as sugar and bananas in the EU.

The current approach used in the WTO to promote development is significantly *in*coherent (Hoekman, 2002). Shifting to other instruments that provide more direct assistance to improve the competitiveness of firms and farmers would improve policy coherence by marrying greater overall *nondiscriminatory* access to markets to an enhanced ability on the part of low-income countries to exploit such access (Hoekman and Prowse, 2005). Such considerations helped to put Aid for Trade on the agenda of international policymaking and the WTO.

3 The rise of Aid for Trade on the policy agenda

At the end of the Uruguay Round and the entry into force of the WTO agreement, there was a rather clear separation between the trade and development communities. One dealt with market access and trade policy rules, while the other dealt with a plethora of subject areas. This included trade policy and trade capacity in developing countries, but proceeded on a separate track – there was little, if any, connection to the WTO. One result of this separation, as noted in the preceding section, was that GATT/WTO members sought to deal with development concerns through the instrument of trade policy. A good case can be made that this was inefficient, often ineffective, and costly to the trading system by undermining the principle of nondiscrimination. At the same time, the development community, while not ignoring the trade agenda in developing countries, devoted far greater attention and priority to other matters.

What follows discusses some of the major forces that led to the emergence of Aid for Trade on the agenda. The discussion distinguishes between considerations that were particularly prominent in the trade community and those that influenced the development community.

3.1 Trade community perspectives

From a trade community and WTO perspective, two types of concerns proved important. The first revolved around what can be called the "Uruguay Round hangover," the gradual recognition on the part of many developing countries that the results of the Round and the entry into force of the WTO entailed numerous implementation obligations, some of which were "resource-intensive." A particularly influential paper by Finger and Schuler (2000) drew attention to the fact that the costs of implementation, if defined not just narrowly in terms of required legal and regulatory changes, but in terms of what is necessary to benefit from a specific WTO set of rules, could be high.[4] However, the primary instrument used in the WTO to address implementation problems was to grant transition periods to developing countries. Assistance to meet the costs of implementation was a matter for governments to request from national and international development agencies.

[4] Implementation concerns and a widespread perception that the Uruguay Round had been (and the trading system was) unbalanced (Stiglitz, 2000) were factors that led the Doha negotiations to focus on development; the negotiations coming to be called the Doha Development Agenda (DDA).

Relatively rapidly after the WTO entered into force, it was recognized that coordination was needed between such agencies and the WTO, and that it would be beneficial to create a mechanism to assist WTO members in obtaining assistance to address implementation challenges. This was the genesis of the Integrated Framework (IF) for Trade-Related Technical Assistance to Least Developed Countries, a result of the 1996 WTO Ministerial in Singapore. The IF was basically a coordinating device involving the WTO and five international agencies active in trade and development,[5] and was aimed at helping LDCs undertake needs assessments for trade-related technical assistance. It was intended that these needs would be addressed as part of the regular delivery of assistance by the agencies and/or bilateral donors. Essentially an unfunded mandate established by trade ministers, the IF achieved little in its early years. Over time its functioning was improved as the development community began to devote greater attention to the trade agenda. One important change was the creation in 2001 of a dedicated trust fund to finance diagnostic activities – which extended far beyond WTO implementation issues – and small technical assistance projects. While this helped to cover the costs of identifying trade-related priorities in LDCs, financing of these priorities was left to existing mechanisms for the allocation of development assistance. A perception on the part of LDCs that the IF was primarily a mechanism for studies and analysis, as opposed to an instrument to deliver more aid resources to deal with identified priorities, led to calls on their part for strengthening the mechanism and giving it substantially greater resources. The WTO Aid for Trade Task Force, which reported in July 2006, recommended bolstering the IF by creating a dedicated secretariat and a funding mechanism for its work program (to be undertaken by the agencies and contractors). This fund was recommended to be on the order of US$200–400 million. At the time of writing, the process of establishing this Enhanced IF was ongoing.

The IF is discussed at greater length later in this chapter and in other chapters in this volume. What matters in the genesis of Aid for Trade is that the IF was the first formal effort to bring development agencies into the trade/WTO picture. Moreover, it was an initiative that came from the trade community, not the development community. The same was true of another initiative launched around the same time: the Joint Integrated Technical Assistance Programme (JITAP). JITAP, a joint venture between the ITC, UNCTAD and the WTO, was more narrowly focused on the delivery of trade-related technical assistance to African countries. JITAP was more limited in terms of its country coverage (16 beneficiary countries), but in contrast to the IF was not restricted to LDCs. JITAP interventions aimed primarily at trade ministries and their immediate constituencies.

A second factor that increased the attention given by the trade community to aid (fiscal transfers) was the increasing difficulty in overcoming resistance to more liberalization – that is, achieving the "global public good." Progress on removing distortionary trade policies has been especially slow in the key area of agriculture. One reason for this could be that there is not enough "on the table" to be of interest to exporters in countries with high agricultural protection. The standard GATT/WTO

[5] The International Monetary Fund (IMF), the International Trade Centre (ITC), the UN Conference on Trade and Development (UNCTAD), the UN Development Programme (UNDP), and the World Bank.

approach to overcoming resistance to liberalization by groups who benefit from protection is to define a negotiating agenda that spans many areas. This helps to mobilize more support for reforms in "sensitive" areas such as agriculture by creating new opportunities for workers and firms that are active in other areas, such as manufactures and services. Through the reciprocity mechanism negotiators then seek to achieve enough concessions from trading partners to induce those who would gain from this strategy (exporters) to balance the domestic political opposition by groups who would lose protection.

While large emerging market countries maintain higher average tariffs and other barriers to trade than OECD countries, and thus can make "concessions" that will benefit OECD exporters, this prospect does not appear to be enough to mobilize the political support needed for significant reforms of agricultural policies. This suggests additional instruments may be needed to promote reforms in the North – one possibility being internal compensation mechanisms (income transfers). This can be seen as part of the Aid for Trade agenda, although many in the development community would argue this is a perverted expansion of the term given that it involves allocating scarce fiscal resources to groups who are often relatively well-off, and may reduce the amount available for development assistance. However, from a trade perspective, greater use of fiscal transfers, if it results in greater liberalization, may well be money well spent.

Moving from production and export subsidies to income support can be part of the solution to overcoming resistance to liberalizing access to highly protected markets. Income support policies are less distorting than production subsidies and much less trade distorting than border protection. A start has been made down this path by some countries. Australia, for example, is maintaining high consumer prices during the transition period of phasing out support for sugar, dairy, and tobacco farmers to finance a structural adjustment program for affected producers. The EU has put similar policies in place in the CAP reform context. Such policies imply a shift away from indirect transfers from consumers to producers through trade policies and towards greater use of fiscal instruments (including consumer levies/excises) to provide income support or adjustment assistance to (former) producers. This need not imply a net increase in the fiscal burden in either the short or medium term. On the contrary, the direct payments to farmers in OECD countries in 2004 amounted to US$113 billion, according to the OECD's Producer Support Estimate (PSE) calculations. The present value of a future stream of such payments is US$2.3 trillion. If the contribution by consumers in the form of higher food prices is added (based on the OECD's Consumer Support Estimate (CSE) for 2004), that present value would rise to US$5.3 trillion – providing ample scope to compensate producers for any loss in land asset value and net income resulting from phase-outs of protection programs. Such adjustment assistance programs should not be open-ended. The objective should be to partially compensate losers while ensuring there are incentives for the least efficient producers to exit from the formerly protected sectors.

For many smaller or poorer developing countries, the potential adjustment costs of liberalization are also of concern. However, given that these countries were not expected to make major liberalization commitments in the Doha Round, loss of preferences was a higher profile issue. Developing countries that benefit from extensive preferential access to OECD markets stand to lose from nondiscriminatory trade liberalization. Global liberalization may also increase the import prices they pay for some staples. For poor countries that have not diversified their economies and that depend on preferential access to major markets, there may be little immediate gain from multilateral trade reforms, especially if they do not undertake reforms of their own in trade and domestic economic policy to improve their competitiveness, reforms that may require investments and thus a need for financial resources (Hoekman, 2002).[6]

Adjustment costs are an inevitable outcome of ambitious trade reform, whether global or national. Addressing such costs, and putting in place a policy environment that assures households that the reforms will result in new job opportunities, is therefore an important political imperative (Bhagwati, 2004; Sutherland et al., 2004; Zedillo et al., 2005). Trade policy changes have important distributive consequences within and across countries. Some countries and many individuals in all countries may experience losses as a result of trade liberalization. In principle, aggregate gains will exceed aggregate losses,[7] so that it is possible to redistribute incomes to compensate the losers while still generating net overall benefits from the reform. In practice, however, political and technical constraints preclude full compensation. Political constraints include equity considerations: should those who introduced past trade-distorting policies at the cost of society as a whole be compensated? Technical constraints include limitations on the ability to tax and redistribute, and, more important, on the ability to identify losers and design compensation programs in a way that does not distort the incentives to adjust (Verdier, 2005).

Dealing with both the narrow WTO implementation agenda and the broader issue of adjustment costs and resistance to reform – the limits of reciprocity – could be facilitated by adding financial transfers/aid to the mix of instruments. The implication is a need for trade policymakers to bring those who control such financial instruments into the picture more directly than has been the case in the past. As mentioned, the IF was a first effort to move down this track, but in a very limited way – initially revolving around an effort to get the development community to assist in implementing already negotiated agreements, and then expanded to diagnose the broader set of trade priorities in developing countries. In the event, much of the push for more Aid for Trade came from the development side of the house, not the trade community.

3.2 Development community perspectives

Support for integration into the world economy through liberalization of trade-related policies was a major aspect of the lending programs and activities of the

[6] Recent research on this topic suggests that for most poor countries the aggregate impact of preference erosion would be limited. Administrative requirements (rules of origin), the exercise of market power by importers (retailers, distributors), product exclusions, and low MFN tariffs for most manufactures and natural resource-based products all imply that the effective value of preferential access is limited. Preference erosion is an important issue for some countries, but they are mostly middle-income economies. See Candau and Jean (2006); Dean and Waino (2006); Francois et al. (2006); and Low et al. (2005, 2006).

[7] Losses being the sum of adjustment costs and the present discounted value of the difference between the pre-reform and post-reform incomes of those individuals unable to ever find employment that pays wages at or above their pre-reform levels.

IMF and World Bank in the 1980s. In the 1990s there was a significant shift in the focus of these institutions towards reducing poverty directly and working more closely with governments to implement national poverty reduction strategies. A result of this shift in focus and modus operandi was that a larger share of development assistance was directed toward health, education, and public expenditure management, with less resources going to infrastructure, agriculture and trade. In the late 1990s, many developing country governments perceived a need to focus more on stimulating higher economic growth rates. This view was supported by several task force reports. Thus, the UN Millennium Project Task Force on Trade stressed that trade could do much to help achieve the Millennium Development Goal of halving poverty by generating higher growth rates (UN Millennium Project, 2005). The same message came from the Commission for Africa (2005).

The renewed recognition of the importance of trade for development led to an increased focus by the development community on the importance of removing barriers in export markets for firms and farmers in developing countries, and thus strong support for an ambitious Doha Round outcome. However, the support for global liberalization was accompanied by a strong emphasis on the need for complementary policies and investments in low-income developing countries. Background papers for the Millennium Project Task Force that assessed the likely impacts of the Doha Round on the poor in low-income countries, using household survey data, confirmed that there was great potential to reduce poverty through more trade but that other instruments are needed to realize this potential.[8]

The magnitude of the gains to poor countries from global trade reforms depends on actions to create new jobs, raise wages, and move producers out of subsistence agriculture. Global trade reform by itself will not ensure these outcomes. Domestic supply constraints are the main reason for the lack of trade growth and diversification in many of the poorest developing countries. Without action to improve supply capacity, reduce transport costs from remote areas, increase farm productivity through extension services, and improve the investment climate, trade opportunities cannot be fully exploited and the potential gains from trade will not be maximized. The needed reforms span numerous areas, many of them "behind the border." The specific interventions that will generate the largest payoffs must be determined case-by-case. The associated analysis and subsequent actions to address identified priorities will generally require resources that are likely to be in short supply in most poor countries, giving rise to a strong case for additional Aid for Trade as a complement to global trade reform (Prowse, 2006).

The agenda is huge. Among possible complementary reforms, research in this area identifies in particular actions to move households out of subsistence production and to improve productivity. Given that poverty is concentrated in rural areas that depend heavily on agriculture, trade opportunities can raise incomes but only if products are produced for the market. This may require active intervention to help households make the switch – through extension services, access to credit, and investments in infrastructure. Poor roads and ports, poorly performing customs, weaknesses in regulatory capacity, and limited access to finance and business

[8] See, for example, Balat et al. (2007); Gomez-Sosa and Soloaga (2007); Isik-Dikmelik (2007); Lara and Soloaga (2007); Nicita (2007a, b); and Soloaga (2007) as well as the contributions in Hertel and Winters (2006).

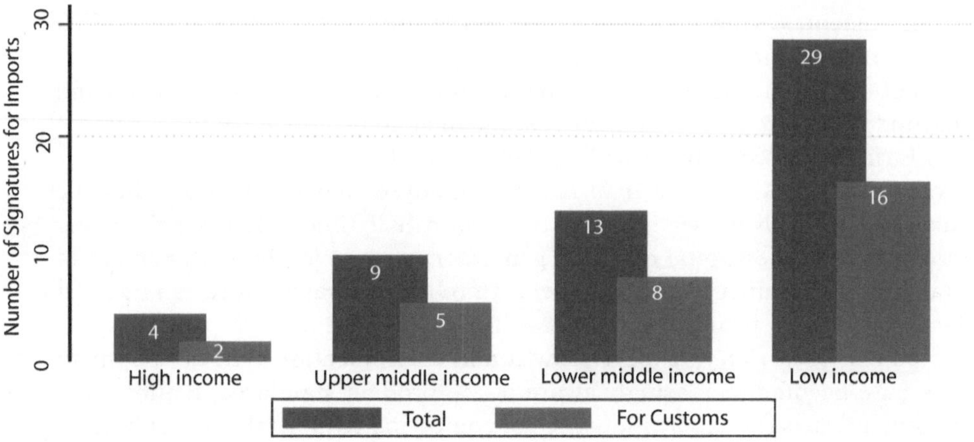

Figure 1.1. More complex and costly procedures in the poorest countries. (*Source:* Doing Business.)

services are all factors determining trade performance. They are also areas in which development assistance can help support the reform efforts of governments and enhance the capacity to trade.

For example, enterprises in Tanzania report that on average it takes about twelve days for exports and nineteen days for imports to clear customs.[9] In comparison, it takes only two and three days for exports and imports to clear customs in the Philippines. It takes 116 days to move an export container from the factory or farm in Bangui (Central African Republic) to the nearest port and fulfill all the customs, administrative, and port requirements to load the cargo onto a ship. It takes seventy-one days to do so from Ouagadougou (Burkina Faso). In contrast, it takes only twenty days in China, Malaysia, or Chile. Overall, it takes fifty-eight days for a typical import transaction in Africa, while it is only fourteen days in the OECD countries. On average it takes three times as many days, nearly twice as many documents, and six times as many signatures to trade in a poor country as it does in rich countries (Figure 1.1).

A major dimension of facilitating trade is action to reduce the incidence of internal tax/customs/police controls. Addressing this source of operating cost – which increases the time needed for transport (an indirect cost) and often requires bribes to officials – would have a high return. Djankov, Freund and Cong (2006) conclude that each day of delay reduces export volumes by 1 percent on average. For example, if Uganda reduced its factory-to-ship time from fifty-eight days to twenty-two (the average for the world), exports could increase by 36 percent. This is equivalent to bringing Uganda 3,600 kilometers closer to its trading partners, the distance from Kampala to Dubai. The delays just discussed are due to administrative hurdles – customs and tax procedures, clearance requirements and cargo inspections – often before the containers even reach the port. In addition to dealing with red tape, the trade agenda spans actions to improve access to finance, telecommunications and power, as well as transportation infrastructure. Currently, the road transport

[9] All data are from World Bank (2006).

network is so poor in much of Africa that its diverse regions remain largely isolated from one another. Overland trade between West Africa and South Africa is practically nonexistent. Within many countries, fertile soil lies fallow because hauling produce to market is too expensive, time-consuming, and difficult.

Much of the behind-the-border competitiveness agenda is services-related and goes beyond transport. Power outages cost the median firm in Tanzania 5 percent of sales. Firms try to cope by providing their own infrastructure: in Nigeria, over 90 percent of firms with more than twenty employees have generators. But the marginal cost of such power is about two and a half times higher than power from the grid, and the capital cost of a generator is equal to about 20 percent of the total cost of machinery and equipment. Unreliable infrastructure can be most problematic for small firms, which are less likely to be able to cope.

One potential barrier to export growth and diversification that development agencies have become increasingly aware of are product standards. Estimates of the investment costs for export industries of complying with market product standards can be as high as 1 to 3 percent of the value of the trade flows concerned. Firms in Africa report that product quality standards rank just behind freight and transport charges as the most important factor blocking export success. Case studies focusing on the costs and benefits of health and safety standards come to similar conclusions, but also demonstrate that the overall gains from making the associated investments can be significant (World Bank, 2005). This is another area where Aid for Trade can have a major impact on the ability of countries to benefit from trade opportunities: by helping firms to upgrade so as to satisfy prevailing market standards. One response to this agenda was the creation in 2004 of the Standards and Trade Development Facility (STDF), a joint venture between the UN Food and Agriculture Organization (FAO), the World Organization for Animal Health (OIE), World Bank, World Health Organization (WHO), and the WTO. The STDF aims to assist developing countries implement and satisfy sanitary and phytosanitary measures through projects and capacity building programs in the areas of food safety and plant and animal health.

4 Progress and Challenges in Moving Forward

The factors discussed in the preceding section all have had a role in building support for an effort to expand Aid for Trade. The IF, JITAP, and the STDF were three small-scale efforts to move forward, the first two largely driven by Geneva agencies, the third primarily the initiative of the World Bank. The WTO hosted both the IF and the STDF, and was an active participant in JITAP (which includes only the three Geneva-based trade agencies). In addition to these initiatives, increasing donor support came to be allocated to capacity building efforts, especially for negotiations and for supporting institutions based in Geneva (for example, the International Centre for Trade and Sustainable Development (ICTSD), which publishes the informative newsletter series *Bridges*). Missing, especially from the perspective of developing countries, was a substantial expansion in the magnitude of resources allocated to the trade agenda.

Arguments for increased attention to, and resources for, the national trade agenda in low-income countries were developed in a number of major reports and related task forces. These included: the UN MDG Task Force on Trade (UN 2005); a follow-on project supported by the UK Department for International Development (DFID) focusing on the global trade architecture (Zedillo et al., 2005); the Commission for Africa (2005) report; a report commissioned by Sweden on developing countries and the WTO (Page and Kleen, 2005); and a study by the Commonwealth Secretariat (Grynberg and Silva, 2004).

An important step towards mobilizing additional resources to bolster trade capacity was the commitment by the G-8 heads of government in May 2005 to increase aid to developing countries to build physical, human, and institutional capacity for trade, and to grant additional support to build developing countries' capacity to take advantage of the new opportunities for trade that would result from a positive conclusion of the Doha Round (G8, 2005, para. 22a). At the September 2005 IMF/World Bank annual meetings, agreement was reached on expanding the Integrated Framework by providing it with additional resources to analyze trade needs, and, further, to ensure that governments and donors consider such needs through existing development assistance mechanisms, for example, Poverty Reduction Strategy Papers and the consultative groups/donor roundtables. There was also agreement to consider extending the approach to span additional low-income countries that are not LDCs, and recognition of the need to consider whether there should be a mechanism to address requirements related to regional integration, rather than just country-specific actions.

Prospects for mobilizing the needed assistance increased with the support expressed for allocating additional aid to support trade capacity at the 2005 Hong Kong Ministerial meeting of the WTO. That meeting called for the establishment of a Task Force on Aid for Trade to recommend how to move forward in operationalizing this agenda. In its report (WTO, 2006), which is discussed at greater length in other chapters of this book, the Task Force sketched out a number of key elements for making a concerted effort to expand aid in order to strengthen trade capacity and performance. This will include mechanisms to better define priorities and to ensure that there are funds and expertise made available to address demands. The Task Force also stressed the importance of more regular monitoring of the development assistance for trade that is provided to developing countries.

Much remains to be done to define and put in place the modalities for moving forward on Aid for Trade. This is important whatever the ultimate outcome of the Doha Round. More effective mechanisms through which additional resources can be made available to developing countries to help them implement their trade strategies and benefit from trade opportunities will have a high return independent of the WTO process. Indeed, in the event of a Doha failure, a very similar trade agenda is likely to be pursued by WTO members in the context of preferential trade and regional integration agreements.

The challenges revolve around three broad questions: identification of the trade agenda at the national and regional level; responding to this through assistance and financing (with a sub-theme being determining the appropriate role of the WTO/trade community in the management and delivery of assistance, and the role of regional cooperation and related instruments); and effective monitoring and evaluation of both process and outcomes. All three of these challenges are identified in the WTO Aid for Trade Task Force report (WTO, 2006).

4.1 Defining the national (and regional) trade agenda

The key challenge in operationalizing Aid for Trade is at the national level. There must be constituencies that push for *their* trade agenda and work to make this a priority for the government and the private sector. These groups should encompass both exporters and importers, since they have common interests when it comes to the various factors that affect the cost of trade transactions. They need to organize and to have an interlocutor, either in the government or one that will work with the government to identify the priority areas for action, cost them, and make the case that these are *national* priorities. Once priorities have been identified and accepted by the government and/or parliament, help is needed to ensure that the case is made to the donor community, and that projects are developed and financed. Monitoring of the follow-up process and continued engagement is important.

An effective system at the national level is by far the most important dimension of operationalizing Aid for Trade. It is critical to solving a host of subsidiary issues related to the delivery of assistance, such as: who (which agency or firm, for example) should do what; ensuring that suppliers of aid work together and complement each other; ensuring coherence with actions at the regional level, be it through North-South cooperation (such as EPAs) or South-South arrangements (such as the regional economic communities in Africa). The importance of this national challenge is recognized in both the Aid for Trade Task Force report and the effort to create the Enhanced Integrated Framework. The latter justifies the creation of an earmarked fund of up to US$400 million for the Integrated Framework in part to finance the activities of national-level entities that will defend trade interests in national fora, work with trade constituencies to identify priorities for action, and follow up on the action plans that are agreed. Assuming that the Enhanced IF becomes operational during 2007, some of the preconditions for moving forward on the trade agenda in LDCs will have been put in place. But leveraging the IF to deliver on the ground will depend critically on the extent of engagement by not just the national "focal points" working with the IF secretariat, but also by the private sector – the trade constituency in each country.

Much of the trade agenda at the country level will be sector- or activity-specific and revolve around enhancing competitiveness and bolstering the "supply side." As numerous reports and statements by developing countries have emphasized, there is also an adjustment dimension to the Aid for Trade agenda. Here, the needs revolve around both ex ante identification of possible vulnerable groups that may be negatively affected by liberalization – whether external liberalization or a country's own reforms – and the design/financing of assistance, and ex post monitoring of impacts.

A potential source of adjustment pressure at the national level stems from erosion of preferential access to protected markets. Such erosion has been argued to be relatively small in terms of overall effects for most affected countries, but may be significant for specific sectors in specific countries. Although proposals to put in place a mechanism to compensate countries for such erosion have been rejected by the donor community, it is important that this source of adjustment costs be considered in the identification of priority areas for action. In addition to national responses and actions, this is a matter that can be raised in bilateral discussion with donors, especially those that have granted preferential access in the past. As mentioned previously, in principle there is much that the EU can do in the process of reforming its agricultural policies to assist affected producers in developing countries as well as farmers in the EU.[10]

Since many countries are active members of regional trade agreements, it is important that in the process of setting trade priorities at the national level attention also be given to identification of regional trade priorities. Perhaps and possibly more important, it is necessary to ensure that regional activities or projects are consistent with national priorities. In practice this will only be the case if there is a conscious effort to integrate the regional agenda – including both North-South and South-South arrangements – into the national priority-setting process. Regional cooperation is an instrument and can and should be used to enhance the competitiveness of enterprises that operate in a region, but this will only happen if the focus is on the competitiveness agenda.

A final challenge that plays at this national agenda-setting level is implementation of WTO agreements. As argued by Finger in Chapter 3, implementation audits are an appropriate method for defining what the government of a country should do and what will be needed from the donors to assist the government. This approach should also apply to regional trade agreements. This will ensure that there is a linkage between enforcement of trade agreements and prior assistance on implementation. While implementation is important to ensure that trade agreements are meaningful, this is, and should be, only a small part of the broader Aid for Trade agenda.

4.2 Financing the identified priority areas

Credibility and predictability of funding is critical to induce the level of engagement that is needed to identify national trade-related priority areas for action. Previous "best endeavor" promises to provide assistance for trade were only partly realized, and more promises provide little assurance to low-income countries that their concerns will be addressed. Various options have been proposed for financing Aid for Trade, of which only the Enhanced IF is close to becoming reality.[11] While the IF will have more funding available to support the process of identification and follow-up activities, much of the funding for trade-related projects and programs will come from and through existing mechanisms through with aid is allocated. Thus, there is no guarantee that once projects and priorities have been identified, the financial resources needed for larger trade-related investments will be available.

While this is often a major concern of proponents of Aid for Trade, if the national level process works, this should not be a problem. That process should be able, in principle, to work with the various agencies and actors that provide assistance, be

[10] The IMF and World Bank offer facilities to help countries finance adjustment shocks. The IMF's Trade Integration Mechanism (TIM) was created to provide for assistance in meeting balance of payments needs that might arise from multilateral trade liberalization. An Exogenous Shocks Facility was recently created by the IMF to provide policy support and financial assistance to low-income countries facing exogenous shocks, including sudden trade-related shocks.

[11] See Zedillo et al. (2005), Page and Kleen (2005), Grynberg and Silva (2004) and Prowse (2006). See Basu (2006) for a particularly ambitious proposal to generate funding for adjustment programs, arguing for the introduction of an equity tax that would be redistributed to workers hurt by globalization. As noted by Basu, such a tax would need to be coordinated at the global level, as adoption of such a tax by a country unilaterally would lead to capital outflows, lower wages and higher unemployment.

it bilateral or multilateral. Clearly managing and controlling this process is a major challenge that requires dedicated resources at the recipient country government level, but as long as this can be done, existing instruments can deliver. In the case of the World Bank, for example, there has been a significant increase in financing for trade projects in response to demand from developing countries. World Bank trade-related lending has almost trebled since 2002, rising to US$1.6 billion in 2005 from about US$550 million in 2002 (see Table 1.1).

It remains an open question whether there will be sufficient local capacity to manage and control the various potential suppliers of assistance and ensure that it is the national priorities that drive the agenda. While additional funding to support this activity will in principle be available for the LDCs (as a result of the Enhanced IF), no IF-type mechanism exists for other low-income developing countries. This implies that national governments in these countries – and, as important, their private sectors – need to pursue this autonomously, and/or request bilateral assistance from donors to support the needed "upstream" activities.

As noted previously, the trade policy and competitiveness agenda is being pursued to an increasing extent through regional integration and cooperation efforts. The World Bank and IMF (2005a) argue that existing instruments to support regional cooperation are inadequate, resulting in the under-provision of financing and assistance for multi-country trade-related projects. Existing support mechanisms, including the IF, center on countries. For many developing countries, regional cooperation is an important objective. It is also high on the agenda of the European Union and the United States, which are increasingly negotiating reciprocal free trade agreements with developing countries. The EU sees these agreements as instruments to encourage the formation of economic integration arrangements among subsets of African, Caribbean, and Pacific (ACP) countries.

A dedicated fund to support regional cooperation, covering both software (regulatory institutions, policy changes) and hardware (infrastructure to support cross-country flows of goods, services, and people) could help to fill the gap that currently exists. A concerted focus on identifying and financing regional projects that would help to address national priorities could also help overcome resistance to beneficial regional market integration (beneficial in the sense of helping to attain the competitiveness objective). Given donor opposition to the creation of new funds,[12] a practical way forward would be for a proportion of donor funds for Aid for Trade to be allocated to regional development banks, as well as to multilateral agencies for regional projects. Most regional and multilateral institutions already have trust funds through which such resources could be channeled. The regional agenda can in principle also be met through existing instruments such as the EDF.[13]

[12] While proposals for earmarked funds are controversial, as earmarking can be inconsistent with aid effectiveness (the activities for which funding is earmarked may not be a priority in individual countries), the creation of a mechanism that earmarks an overall amount for trade does not need to imply that countries must identify trade as a priority; it simply provides greater credibility to countries that if they decide that trade projects are a priority, development assistance will be available.

[13] For ACP countries, the 9th European Development Fund (EDF) was to provide a total of EUR20 billion through 2007. While this is intended for all types of development programs, the EDF offers a potential vehicle to address specific trade capacity concerns. Thus, the EDF could be an appropriate vehicle through which to address preference erosion, especially as such erosion will in large part be the direct consequence of policy reforms undertaken by the EU (Francois, Hoekman and Manchin, 2006).

Table 1.1. World Bank trade-related lending FY03-06

Regions	Approved FY03		Approved FY04		Approved FY05		Approved FY06	
	Projects	Commitment (US$ mil)	Projects	Commitment (US$ mil)	Projects	Commitment (US$ mil)	Projects	Commitment (US$ mil)
AFR	8	37	15	441	17	232	17	414
EAP	2	138	4	83	6	126	5	112
ECA	10	131	4	183	17	424	14	227
LCR	5	60	11	365	7	233	11	720
MNA	1	4	3	158	–	–	–	–
SAR	3	197	2	53	2	64	4	139
Total Trade lending	29	566	39	1,282	49	1,080	51	1,611
Including								
LDC	9	74	15	415	20	276	14	396
LIC	11	237	17	507	22	328	22	572

4.3 Monitoring and evaluation of Aid for Trade

As donor commitments to increase Aid for Trade will not be implemented through a multilateral fund or through other forms of pooling funds for this purpose, effective monitoring of delivery of Aid for Trade and the extent to which it responds to national priorities as defined by recipient governments is important. Effective monitoring is also important to allow accurate assessments and evaluation of outcomes. The WTO Aid for Trade Task Force (WTO, 2006) called for multilateral monitoring of donor "performance" – the delivery of resources to fund the priority trade projects identified by developing countries. Concretely, it suggests the WTO organize an annual review of Aid for Trade.

While aid and the aid business is not an area of WTO expertise, as the world's trade body the institution does have a clear interest in monitoring and discussing what its high-income members have done to support trade competitiveness of lower-income members. It therefore seems appropriate that the WTO take on this role, working with international development agencies and bilateral donors to compile and report data on Aid for Trade projects. Much of the required data is already collected by the Development Assistance Committee of the OECD and reported in a joint DAC/WTO database. In order to be able to monitor effectively, agreement must be reached on how to define Aid for Trade, and on a common classification of types of assistance/projects. At present the database is imperfect, with regional-level activities and support, for example, not being recorded very well, if at all.

Although much emphasis has been put on the need to agree on a common classification and monitoring of Aid for Trade flows, a Geneva-based process of annual summaries and scrutiny of aid delivery can only be of limited utility if it does not engage national government agencies, local donor representatives, and the private sector. Data must be complemented by analysis of outcomes and assessments of impacts. To be most useful, the information on aid must be related to the priorities and objectives that were identified by governments. Is the aid going to address those needs? Was the aid effective in helping to attain the objectives? If not, why not? The payoffs to such scrutiny will be at the national level, suggesting that monitoring and evaluation needs to take place locally and feed into the process and deliberations that inform the national prioritization processes. There is a major role here for local and regional think tanks and research networks. The funding of such bodies should be a priority in the allocation of Aid for Trade.

5 Concluding Remarks

It is remarkable how rapidly the concept of Aid for Trade has been adopted by both the trade and development communities. One reason for this may be that the rationale and objective is greater trade; the aim is to maximize/leverage trade opportunities by enhancing competitiveness. While the substance of the Aid for Trade agenda is certainly not a new one – indeed, all of the areas for potential intervention have been pursued by developing country governments and donors over many years – what is new about the recent focus on this agenda is the recognition that these are matters that concern both the international trade and development communities.

As with all types of international cooperation, the implementation of the concept is less than ideal in that it builds on existing mechanisms, in this case for the delivery of assistance. Although conceptually a strong case could be, and was, made for dedicated financing for Aid for Trade through a multilateral fund, what is emerging is a combination of smaller earmarked funds – most notably the Integrated Framework – and bilateral assistance and funding from the international financial institutions. One can argue with the benefit of hindsight that it was unfortunate that the initial response of the trade community to the need for Aid for Trade was the IF, as this instrument is limited to the LDCs. The reason for this is that the LDC group is the only subset of developing countries that is accepted in the WTO, and that this therefore was seen as the only practical way of targeting assistance to a set of countries that needed it the most while allowing other more advanced countries that did not have a similar need to be excluded. This is clearly imperfect, as the result was that many countries that do need assistance are excluded. The resulting gap can be filled through bilateral action to support similar activities in non-LDCs, but the coverage of such assistance is unlikely to be comprehensive. In principle, the matter could be resolved by expanding the mandate of the Enhanced IF to include additional countries, but to date this has been resisted by the LDCs.

A major implication of the emergence of the concept of Aid for Trade is that the WTO membership has recognized that trade liberalization alone is not enough to benefit poor countries, and that promises to provide technical assistance are an inadequate response to concerns regarding adjustment and implementation costs. The emergence of Aid for Trade is also a signal that the development community is according greater importance to the role of trade in fostering higher growth rates in low-income countries. The result is a move in the direction of greater policy coherence.

Achieving such coherence between trade and aid policies is obviously still a major challenge. Looking forward, one aspect of dealing with that challenge is to determine more clearly what the respective roles of the trade and development communities should be in the delivery of Aid for Trade. Implementation of aid projects is not an area of comparative advantage of the WTO; this is what the development agencies were created for. There is a tendency to make the WTO the fulcrum of Aid for Trade processes. While understandable given that this is where the trade interests are concentrated, it would be an example of policy *in*coherence if the WTO were to get in the business of defining and delivering aid. While there will be – and are – specific trade areas where the WTO may agree that there needs to be an explicit linkage between aid and the implementation/enforcement of agreements – for example, in the sphere of trade facilitation – delivery of assistance in such areas should continue to be through other specialized agencies or firms.

REFERENCES

Balat, Jorge F., Irene Brambilla, and Guido G. Porto. 2007. "An Analysis of the WTO Development Round on Poverty in Rural and Urban Zambia," in B. Hoekman and M. Olarreaga (eds.), *Impacts and Implications of Global Trade Reform on Poverty*, Washington D.C.: Brookings Institution.

Bhagwati, Jagdish. 2004. "In Defense of Globalization," New York: Oxford University Press.

Candau, Fabien and Sébastien Jean. 2006. "What are EU Trade Preferences Worth for Sub-Saharan Africa and Other Developing Countries?," prepared for the International Symposium on "Preference Erosion: Impacts and Policy Responses," Geneva, 13–14 June 2005.

Commission for Africa. 2005. "Our Common Interest – Report of the Commission," UK: Commission for Africa.

Dean, Judith and John Wainio. 2006. "Quantifying the Value of US Tariff Preferences," prepared for the International Symposium on "Preference Erosion: Impacts and Policy Responses," Geneva, 13–14 June 2005.

Djankov, Simeon, Caroline Freund, and Cong Pham. 2006. "Time Costs as a Barrier to Trade," Policy Research Working Paper 3909, Washington, D.C.: World Bank.

Finger, J. Michael and Philip Schuler. 2000. "Implementation of Uruguay Round Commitments: The Development Challenge," *The World Economy*, 23: 511–25.

Francois, Joseph, Bernard Hoekman, and Miriam Manchin. 2006. "Quantifying the Magnitude of Preference Erosion due to Multilateral Trade Liberalization," *World Bank Economic Review*, 20(2): 197–216.

G8. 2005. *Declaration*, Gleneagles: 8 July. http://www.g8.gov.uk/.

Gómez, Ania I. and Isidro Soloaga. 2007. "Nicaragua," in B. Hoekman and M. Olarreaga (eds.), *Impacts and Implications of Global Trade Reform on Poverty*, Washington, D.C.: Brookings Institution.

Grynberg, Roman and Sacha Silva. 2004. "Preference-Dependent Economies and Multilateral Liberalization: Impacts and Options," London: Commonwealth Secretariat.

Hertel, Thomas and L. Alan Winters. 2006. Eds. "Poverty and the WTO: Impacts of the Doha Development Agenda," London and Washington: Palgrave Macmillan and World Bank.

Hoekman, Bernard. 2002. "Strengthening the Global Trade Architecture for Development: The Post-Doha Agenda," *World Trade Review*, 1(1): 23–46.

Hoekman, Bernard. 2005. "Operationalizing the Concept of Policy Space in the WTO: Beyond Special and Differential Treatment," *Journal of International Economic Law*, 8(2): 405–28.

Hoekman, Bernard and Caglar Ozden. 2007. Eds. Trade Preferences and Differential Treatment of Developing Countries, Policy Research Working Paper 3566, Washington, D.C.: World Bank.

Hoekman, Bernard and Susan Prowse. 2005. "Policy responses to preference erosion: from trade as aid to Aid for Trade," Policy Research Working Paper 3721, Washington, D.C.: World Bank.

IMF/World Bank. 2005a. "Doha Development Agenda and Aid for Trade," DC2005-0016, Washington, D.C.: IMF and World Bank.

IMF/World Bank. 2005b. "Global Monitoring Report 2005 – Millennium Development Goals: From Consensus to Momentum," Washington, D.C.: IMF and World Bank.

Işık-Dikmelik, Aylin. 2005. "Implications of Doha Round on Rural and Urban Poverty in Vietnam," in B. Hoekman and M. Olarreaga (eds.), *Impacts and Implications of Global Trade Reform on Poverty*, Washington, D.C.: Brookings Institution.

Johnson, Harry G. 1967. "Economic Policies Toward Less Developed Countries," Washington, D.C.: Brookings Institution.

Lara, Gabriel and Isidro Soloaga. 2007. "Bolivia," in B. Hoekman and M. Olarreaga (eds.), *Impacts and Implications of Global Trade Reform on Poverty*, Washington, D.C.: Brookings Institution.

Low, Patrick, Roberta Piermartini, and Jürgen Richtering. 2005. "Multilateral Solutions to the Erosion of Non-Reciprocal Preferences in NAMA," Staff Working Paper ERSD-2005-06, Geneva: WTO.

Low, Patrick, Roberta Piermartini and Jürgen Richtering. 2006. "Non-Reciprocal Preference Erosion Arising From MFN Liberalization in Agriculture: What Are the Risks?," Staff Working Paper ERSD-2006-02, Geneva: WTO.

Maskus, Keith E. 2000. "Intellectual Property Rights in the Global Economy," Washington, D.C.: Institute for International Economics.

Nicita, Alessandro. 2007a. "Ethiopia," in B. Hoekman and M. Olarreaga (eds.), *Impacts and Implications of Global Trade Reform on Poverty*, Washington, D.C.: Brookings Institution.

Nicita, Alessandro. 2007b. "Madagascar," in B. Hoekman and M. Olarreaga (eds.), *Impacts and Implications of Global Trade Reform on Poverty*, Washington, D.C.: Brookings Institution.

Olarreaga, Marcelo and Caglar Özden. 2005. "AGOA and Apparel: Who Captures the Tariff Rent in the Presence of Preferential Market Access?," *The World Economy*, 28(1): 63–77.

Oxfam. 2002. "Rigged Rules and Double Standards: Trade, Globalization and the Fight against Poverty," Oxford: Oxfam International.

Özden, Caglar and Gunjan Sharma. 2006. "Price Effects of Preferential Market Access: Caribbean Basin Initiative and the Apparel Sector," *World Bank Economic Review*, 20(2): 241–60.

Pack, Howard and Kamal Saggi. 2006. "Is there a Case for Industrial Policy? A Critical Survey," *World Bank Research Observer*, 21(2): 267–97.

Page, Sheila and Peter Kleen. 2005. "Special and Differential Treatment of Developing Countries in the World Trade Organization," Global Development Studies No. 2, Ministry of Foreign Affairs, Sweden.

Prowse, Susan. 2006. "'Aid for Trade' – Increasing Support for Trade Adjustment and Integration – a Proposal," in S. Evenett and Bernard Hoekman (eds.), *Economic Development and Multilateral Cooperation*, New York and Washington: Palgrave Macmillan and World Bank.

Rodrik, Dani. 2004. "Industrial policy for the twenty-first century," CEPR Discussion Paper No. 4767, London: CEPR.

Rodrik, Dani. 2005. "The global governance of trade as if development really mattered," in P. King and S. King (eds.), *International Economics and International Economic Policy*, New York: McGraw-Hill.

Sapir, André. 2000. "Who Is Afraid of Globalization? The Challenge of Domestic Adjustment in Europe and America," CEPR Discussion Paper No. 2595, London: CEPR.

Soloaga, Isidro. 2007. "Doha's Development Agenda: Implications for Poverty Reduction in Cambodia," in B. Hoekman and M. Olarreaga (eds.), *Impacts and Implications of Global Trade Reform on Poverty*, Washington, D.C.: Brookings Institution.

Stiglitz, Joseph E. 2000. "Two Principles for the Next Round or, How to Bring Developing Countries in from the Cold," *The World Economy*, 23(4): 437–54.

Sutherland, Peter et al. 2004. "The Future of the WTO: Addressing Institutional Challenges in the New Millennium," Geneva: WTO.

Verdier, Thierry. 2005. "Socially Responsible Trade Integration: A Political Economy Perspective," in F. Bourguignon, B. Pleskovic and A. Sapir (eds.), *Are We on Track to Achieve the Millennium Development Goals?*, Washington, D.C.: World Bank.

UN Millennium Project. 2005. "Trade for Development," *Task Force on Trade*, New York: UNDP.

World Bank. 2005. "Food Safety and Agricultural Health Standards: Challenges and Opportunities for Developing Country Exports," Report No. 31207. Washington, D.C.: World Bank. 10 January.

World Bank. 2006. *Doing Business 2006*. Washington, D.C.: World Bank.

WTO. 2006. *Recommendations of the Task Force on Aid for Trade*, Aid for Trade Task Force, WT/AFT/1, 27 July.

Zedillo, Ernesto et al. 2005. "Strengthening the Global Trade Architecture for Economic Development: An Agenda for Action," GTA Policy Brief, http://www.ycsg.yale.edu/focus/gta/GTA_policy_brief.doc.

2 Aid for Trade: An Essential Component of the Multilateral Trading System and the WTO Doha Development Agenda

FAIZEL ISMAIL

1 Introduction

The concept of "Aid for Trade" has gained momentum since early 2005, culminating in an agreement at the WTO Hong Kong Ministerial Conference for the WTO Director-General to establish a Task Force on "Aid for Trade." As official development assistance (ODA) began to fall in the mid 1990s,[1] the slogan "Trade *not* Aid" gained currency. As donor fatigue grew, developed countries argued that developing countries needed to reduce their dependence on aid. In the WTO, developing countries were cautious about placing emphasis on aid in the Doha Round, launched in 2001. They felt that developed countries would use offers of additional aid as a substitute for providing genuine market access for products of interest to developing countries, especially in agriculture and textiles, and in place of fairer and more balanced trade rules. However, the development needs of the poorest countries gave rise to new demands for increased development aid. At the United Nations Millennium Summit in New York in September 2000, world leaders pledged to increase development aid as a means of realizing the Millennium Development Goals (MDGs), a main target of which is the reduction of extreme poverty by half by 2015.

Goal 8 of the MDGs has as one of its targets the further development of an "open, rule- based, predictable, non-discriminatory trading and financial system." In Monterrey, Mexico, world leaders met in March 2002 at the International Conference on Financing for Development, and agreed to increase development assistance and forge a framework for a global development partnership in which developed and developing countries would take joint action to reduce poverty in line with objectives set by the MDGs. The Monterrey Consensus recognized that both aid *and* trade are important for the development efforts of the poorest countries, and that there is a need to focus on both improved market access and supply-side competitiveness through increased investments in infrastructure and trade facilitation. A commitment to the realization of the MDGs was again reaffirmed by the World Summit on

[1] ODA levels had begun to fall in the mid-1990s from 0.34 percent of GNI to a low of 0.22 percent of GNI in 2001.

This chapter is written in the author's personal capacity. It has benefited considerably from comments made on an earlier draft by Sheila Page. Parts of the chapter have been adapted with the permission of the publisher from Ismail (2005).

Sustainable Development held in Johannesburg in 2002 (UN Millennium Project, 2005a).

At the WTO, the Doha Declaration adopted on 14 November 2001 confirmed that "technical cooperation and capacity building are core elements of the development dimension of the multilateral trading system," and recognized that "sustainably financed technical assistance and capacity building programs have important roles to play."[2] While aid or Aid for Trade are not specific negotiating issues in the Doha Development Agenda (DDA) (that is, not linked to the "single undertaking"), the commitment by WTO members to address the need for increased aid for trade-related capacity building (TRCB) is part of the DDA. Indeed, there are several areas of the Doha Work Programme in which this commitment is linked to specific parts of the negotiations, including trade facilitation, cotton, special and differential treatment (SDT), and provisions in favor of Least Developed Countries (LDCs). Thus the WTO Doha Development Agenda has been challenged to address both trade *and* aid.

Developing countries have placed the issue of aid in the form of trade-related technical assistance and capacity building (TRTA/CB) on the agenda of the multilateral trading system since the earliest days of the General Agreement on Tariffs and Trade (GATT). The need for technical assistance was recognized by the Contracting Parties of the GATT in early GATT agreements as part of the SDT offers made by developed countries to facilitate the integration of developing countries into the trading system. The concept of SDT, which emerged early on in the GATT system, calls for the interests of developing countries to be given special consideration. This concept remains essential to ensuring that there is proportionality in the commitments undertaken between developed and developing countries, reflecting their different levels of development and gains from the trading system. It is important that SDT not be confused with the broader development dimension of the trading system nor become a substitute for it. SDT is only one aspect of the broader development dimension. I have argued elsewhere that TRTA/CB is not only an aspect of SDT, with which it has been associated historically, but is also a core element of the development dimension of the multilateral trading system (Ismail, 2005).

I have also argued previously that the development dimension of the multilateral trading system needs to be mainstreamed. Four core elements can be seen as constituting the development dimension in the context of the multilateral trading system: (i) fair trade; (ii) capacity building; (iii) balanced rules; and (iv) good governance (Ismail, 2005). First, a fair trading system would remove the obstacles that developing countries experience in exporting their products to developed country markets and create opportunities for them to advance their development. Second, increasing the capacity of developing countries to develop their comparative advantage to produce and export would provide them with the necessary institutional, productive, and export capabilities needed to level the playing field in the trading system. Third, establishing rules that ensure a fair balance between the costs and benefits of new agreements, and that provide appropriate flexibility for developing countries to implement development policies, would contribute to the legitimacy and sustainability of the rules-based system. Fourth, by building a transparent and inclusive system of decision-making in the WTO, members will be contributing

[2] See paragraphs 38 and 2 of WTO (2001a).

to the capacity of developing countries to participate effectively in the decision-making process.

There is a vast range of issues that arise in the discussion on Aid for Trade, including predictability, effectiveness, policy coherence and coordination at global level, mainstreaming trade in national development strategies, country ownership, delivery mechanisms, and the role of the private sector. These issues fall outside the scope of this chapter and are covered elsewhere in this volume. This chapter focuses on the relationship between aid and trade in the WTO specifically.

Section 2 begins by developing a conceptual framework on the trade and development debate that provides a context for the discussion on Aid for Trade. Section 3 provides a brief historical perspective of the main trends identified in the multilateral trading system to address the development needs of developing countries, including through SDT provisions and TRTA/CB more specifically. Section 4 reviews progress made in the Doha Round on issues related to technical assistance and TRCB. Section 5 assesses the evolution of the concept of Aid for Trade since 2005 until the end of July 2006. Section 6 describes the trends and trajectory of ODA flows and the potential for additionality of ODA. Section 7, the conclusion, revisits the rationale for increased aid for development and Aid for Trade in the WTO, arguing that increased Aid for Trade is an essential component of a development-friendly multilateral trading system and of a successful DDA.

2 Mainstreaming development in the WTO

2.1 Introduction

It has been widely recognized by academic observers and civil society groups that there is an important development dimension to international trade (CUTS, 2004). The arguments for the interests of developing countries to be given special consideration in trade negotiations can be traced back to the earliest days of the formation of the GATT (Low and Keck, 2004). First, these arguments relate to the significant differences in economic power of the major developed countries and the relatively minor share of developing countries – and in particular of the LDCs – in global markets. Second, the major distortions in global markets caused by the protectionist policies of developed countries that continue to disadvantage developing countries have been another reason for developed countries to agree to provide SDT to developing countries in the GATT and WTO.

These SDT measures include aspects such as: preferential market access; longer tariff phase-down periods and flexibility in the implementation of GATT/WTO disciplines and rules for developing countries; and offers by developed countries to provide technical assistance and capacity building to developing countries to facilitate the implementation of GATT/WTO agreements.

However, according to many observers, these measures have not succeeded in addressing a number of fundamental issues in the trading system. First, developed countries have continued to distort global trade and protect their markets, stifling the development prospects of developing countries. Second, the costs to developing countries of implementing unbalanced rules from the Uruguay Round have been far higher than the benefits, with most benefits going to richer countries. Third, there is a persistent lack of capacity of many developing countries to participate effectively in the trading system. This is compounded by the lack of responsibility of developed countries for the negative development impact of unfair trade rules (for example, cotton and other agricultural subsidies) and the relatively high cost of adjustment experienced by many developing countries (for example, through preference erosion). Fourth, the WTO lacks transparency and inclusiveness in its decision-making processes. The perceived imbalances in the power structures of the WTO have also raised questions about the legitimacy of WTO agreements and decisions.

The debate about development in the WTO is often assumed to be about increasing the effectiveness of SDT for developing countries in the organization. This perception relegates the debate about development to the margins of the WTO. Development is thus regarded as an afterthought, as a "nice to do," or at worst an "optional extra." This perception of the development dimension is misconceived. This chapter argues that developing countries have fundamental interests in the WTO that are at the core of the trading system and its functioning. These interests are unpacked and described below in the four elements of the development dimension of the multilateral trading system: fair trade; capacity building; balanced rules; and good governance.

In developing the above conceptual framework, this chapter draws on the work of Amartya Sen, who defines development as "the removal of unfreedom" (Sen, 1999). In Sen's perspective, development is the process of expanding human freedoms. These substantive freedoms include elementary capabilities such as being able to avoid such deprivations as starvation and enjoy freedoms such as political participation. Human freedom is seen as the pre-eminent objective of development. It is also seen as the means of achieving development. The focus on rights, opportunities, and entitlements, he argues, contributes to the expansion of human freedom and promotion of development. Thus, for Sen, development is understood as the process of removing these unfreedoms.

Four types of unfreedoms, or deprivations, from Sen's work are relevant to the discussion of development and the multilateral trading system. First, Sen argues that deprivations can result when people are denied the economic opportunities and favorable consequences that markets offer and support. Second, he argues that poverty should be understood not so much as low incomes but as a deprivation of basic capabilities. Third, while Sen argues for government regulation to enable markets to work more effectively, he states that a system of ethics is required to build vision and trust for the successful use of the market mechanism. Sen urges policy makers to base these values on social justice. Sen recognizes that individuals would assert their "prudent and material concerns" but argues that policy makers can balance these concerns with the values of social justice through public discussion. Fourth, Sen argues against the view that the denial of political liberty and basic civil rights is "good" for rapid economic development and states that the deprivation of the opportunity to participate in crucial decisions regarding public affairs is to deny people the right to develop and strengthen a democratic system. The latter is seen as an essential part of the process of development.

In applying the above definition of development to the trading system, it could be argued that fair trade would remove the obstacles that developing countries experience in exporting their products to developed country markets and create opportunities for them to advance their development. This could happen in a variety of ways. Increasing the capacity of developing countries, especially the poorest and most marginalized, to develop their comparative advantage to produce and export would provide the necessary, human, institutional, productive, and export capabilities needed by these countries to level the playing field in the trading system. Establishing rules that ensure a fair balance between: (i) the costs and the benefits of new agreements; (ii) the values and interests of developed and developing countries; (iii) appropriate flexibility for developing countries to implement development policies; and (iv) the need to strengthen the rules-based trading system, would ensure both the legitimacy and sustainability of these rules. Finally, by building a transparent and inclusive system of decision-making in the WTO, members would contribute to the capacity of developing countries to participate effectively in the making of decisions that are both democratic and consistent with the foregoing three dimensions of development.

In this context, SDT could be a tool to ensure the proportionality of trade agreements, commensurate with the levels of development of developing countries and their capacity to manage the burdens of the adjustment process. There remain significant differences in economic power and benefits gained by developed and developing countries from international trade. A World Bank study, for example, points out that the top thirty countries export about 80 percent of world products (World Bank, 2002). However, it is argued in this chapter that SDT on its own is an inadequate concept to promote development objectives in trade. It will need to be part of a broader approach that recognizes that the fundamental interests of developing countries in the trading system are to seek fair trade, capacity building, balanced rules, and good governance in the WTO. This broader approach mainstreams the development dimension of trade and recognizes SDT as an important aspect of the development dimension. Advancing the development dimension in the WTO is of systemic interest to all – including developed and developing countries – who seek to build and advance a legitimate and strengthened multilateral rules-based system.

In developing this approach to development and the multilateral trading system, it is recognized that the WTO is essentially a trade negotiating body and not a development institution. However, the WTO cannot be understood in simple mercantilist terms. Most members of the WTO, developing and developed, locate these narrow mercantilist interests within the broader context of their strategic objectives in the WTO.[3] These broader objectives include the need to build greater equity in the trading regime, greater capacity for developing countries to benefit from trade, more balanced trade rules, and more inclusive and transparent decision-making in the WTO. If the trading system is insensitive to the lack of capacity of developing countries to benefit from trade, if the rules are imbalanced, and if the decision-making system is not transparent and exclusive, then SDT will not be effective and will be seen as a palliative for an unfair and unjust system. SDT, then, is of secondary importance for developing countries in the trading system – their primary concern is to ensure that the broader development dimension of the trading system is advanced.

Each of the four proposed elements of the development dimension in the WTO are discussed further below. The section concludes by locating this debate within

[3] See, for example, Government of Sweden (2003).

the broader context of the commitments made by world leaders to increase development and reduce poverty.

2.2 The four elements of the development dimension

2.2.1 *Fair trade*

A number of studies have demonstrated that the gains from globalization and international trade are not equal, and that the lion's share of benefits is enjoyed by the developed countries (World Bank, 2002/2004). While this is due partly to the vast differences in economic power and levels of development of WTO members, it is also due to the inequitable trade and economic policies of developed countries. In order to allow the theory of comparative advantage to work and stimulate increased growth and global economic welfare, developed countries will need to remove the distortions in global markets caused by their domestic trade policies and create greater coherence in global economic policy. These changes to their domestic and international policies could contribute significantly to the effective and sustainable integration of developing countries into the world economy. Moreover, a vast literature suggests that the protectionist policies of developed countries in agriculture, for example, are inefficient and ineffective in providing support to their own farmers and in correcting market failure (Tangermann, 2005; Messerlin, 2001).

The devastating negative development impacts of rich countries' agricultural policies have been widely criticized (Oxfam, 2002), and have prompted former World Bank President James Wolfensohn to remark that they are "crippling Africa's chance to export its way out of poverty." Thus the WTO needs to ensure that the policies of the developed countries that are the major beneficiaries of globalization and that dominate global trade are consistent with the WTO objective of liberalizing global markets and allowing the exports of developing countries fair access to these markets, thereby creating opportunities for them to grow and develop.

2.2.2 *Capacity building*

It has long been established that for many developing countries, especially the most marginalized, increased market access will not contribute significantly to export-driven growth. Their capacity to export is constrained by a range of supply-side factors, including lack of infrastructure, low research and innovation capacity, lack of access to finance, and a poor investment environment. Poor institutional capacity and human resources contribute to this lack of supply capacity. The poor fiscal base of these countries, combined with their overwhelming health, education, and welfare needs, reduces the capacity of the state to intervene to build these capabilities. In addition, the high adjustment costs and fiscal impact of trade liberalization make these governments reluctant to reduce their tariffs. In several cases, unilateral liberalization as part of International Monetary Fund (IMF) structural adjustment criteria may have already incurred severe adjustment and social costs. For a significant number of countries, the loss of existing dependence on trade preferences into developed country markets make them reluctant to support multilateral liberalization.

The multilateral trading system thus cannot ignore these development challenges[4] – the building of institutional, productive, and export capabilities – that are vital for the effective integration of developing countries into the global economy. The need for a global trade adjustment fund to contribute to TRCB is thus essential. Increased financial support for trade policy capacity building has to come from additional sources of funding, including additional ODA. Gordon Brown, as British Chancellor of the Exchequer, called for the creation of an International Finance Facility (IFF) – long-term donor aid to be securitized to front-load the funding available – that could generate an additional US$50 billion a year for donor aid to fund the Millennium Development Goals, including TRCB. In the spirit of the Marshall Plan (the U.S. program to finance the development of a ravaged post-war Europe), Gordon Brown has urged that other forms of funding also be considered, including the proposed Tobin Tax on currency transactions, to fulfill the promises made by world leaders at the United Nations in 2000 to meet the MDGs.[5]

An effective WTO would need to build greater coherence with the Bretton Woods institutions and with other multilateral and bilateral development agencies. In addition, a more equitable distribution of the gains from trade within developing countries is possible with greater integration of trade policies and broader development and poverty reduction strategies.

2.2.3 *Balanced rules*

The argument put forward by the European Union (EU) that globalization – which has created increased and rapid flows of trade and finance – requires increased regulation to protect the environment, consumers, animal and human health, and food safety, is a cogent one and worthy of serious consideration. Indeed, the report of the World Commission on the Social Dimensions of Globalization, established by the International Labor Organization (ILO), responded to this concern by calling for "fair global rules applied fairly" (ILO, 2004). Any new rules in this area would need to ensure that at least three conditions were met. First, that the relative costs and benefits of new rules for developed and developing countries are taken into consideration, and appropriate levels of flexibility are built into any agreement. Second, the interests and norms of developed countries and developing countries may not converge entirely, and thus the creation of new standards would need to be negotiated, with their development impact made transparent and linked to the implementation capacity of developing countries. Third, while developed countries have had recourse to a range of development instruments that allowed their judicious intervention in the market to enhance their economic development, this opportunity should not be unfairly denied to developing countries.

However, the calls by developing countries for increased flexibility, or "policy space," need to be balanced against the equally important need to ensure that the **multilateral rules-based trading system is strengthened** to enable all countries,

[4] There are several good reasons for the international community to take responsibility to address these challenges. Amongst these reasons is the impact of developed country (OECD) agriculture protection, responsible for a loss by developing countries estimated at US$100 billion a year (Oxfam, 2002). This is equivalent to twice the total amount of development aid (US$50 billion a year) that developing countries receive per year.

[5] See speeches by Gordon Brown (2004a; 2004b).

particularly weaker economies, to be treated fairly in trade disputes. A weakened rules-based trading system will allow the stronger and more powerful countries to resort to unilateral measures, discriminating against the interests of the weaker developing countries.[6] Multilateral rules that are not balanced will not be perceived to be in the interests of developing countries and will lack legitimacy.[7] Thus it is in the interests of all that WTO rules are balanced, taking account of the need for flexibility for the less developed countries without weakening the effectiveness of the rules-based system.

2.2.4 *Good governance*

Since the creation of the GATT in 1947 and the WTO in 1995, the multilateral trading system has been recognized as a vital part of the architecture of global governance – together with the IMF and World Bank. The WTO has been relatively more successful than its Bretton Woods counterparts in building a more democratic decision-making system. However, this has been a slow and painful growth process. Propelled by some major setbacks (Seattle and Cancún), the WTO has continued to learn and improve its decision-making system. The failure of Cancún propelled the then-EU Trade Commissioner (and subsequent WTO Director-General) Pascal Lamy, to argue that the WTO process was "medieval" and needed major reforms.

The emergence of stronger developing country alliances and negotiating groups has begun to provide a more effective counterbalance to the power of the EU and the United States, and provides opportunities for shared leadership.[8] The legitimacy of the WTO and the sustainability of its decisions require it to build on its experience and develop a more inclusive and democratic decision-making system that would contribute to better global governance.

2.3 Conclusions

Having made an argument for the development dimensions of the multilateral trading system to be addressed as a systemic issue by both developed and developing countries, this section concludes by cautioning that the WTO is "no panacea, and in particular, no guarantee for development" (Engammare and Lehmann, 2004). While trade polices may be a necessary condition for the development of many countries, they are not a sufficient condition, and a successful development strategy

[6] The United States accepted with reluctance the strengthening of the GATT/WTO dispute settlement system negotiated in the Uruguay Round, with many U.S legislators and academics arguing that the U.S. should not cede its right to act in the best interests of the country to a multilateral institution. See Jackson (1997).

[7] Developing countries have called for a review and renegotiation of several of the Uruguay Round agreements, such as those on Trade-Related Intellectual Property Rights (TRIPS), Anti-Dumping and Countervailing Duties, and Trade-Related Investment Measures (TRIMS). In addition, they have made about 88 proposals to review the application of SDT provisions of the WTO, arguing that these have not been effective. See paragraph 44 of WTO (2001a) and paragraph 12 of WTO (2001b).

[8] The emergence of the G20 group of agriculture-exporting developing countries since Cancún and the inclusion of India and Brazil in the "Non-Group" of 5 countries that negotiated the agriculture deal in the WTO's 'July 2004 Package' was largely successful in providing developing countries with leadership and negotiating leverage. This type of small group negotiations, however, was criticized by most WTO members as being untransparent and exclusive.

at a domestic level will require a range of other polices that are implemented in an integrated manner, especially to ensure that the gains from trade are distributed more evenly and contribute to poverty reduction. However, it is also recognized by many policy-makers that long-term initiatives to halve hunger and poverty will fail without fundamental restructuring of the global trading system – particularly in agriculture – that includes rich countries dismantling subsidies, lowering tariffs, and leveling the playing field."[9] Others have argued that "the Doha Round could provide a framework that could contribute to reducing poverty" (Engammare and Lehmann, 2004).

3 The GATT/WTO, special and differential treatment (SDT), and capacity building

This section begins by providing a schematic account of the historical origins of development provisions in the GATT/WTO,[10] and then provides an assessment of the main trends that are relevant to the discussion on Aid for Trade.

As the GATT developed, the need to assist developing countries increase their production and exports was gradually recognized by the GATT member countries (Contracting Parties). While there is a general reference to this need in the revised Article XVIII of GATT in 1955, the 1961 Declaration of the Contracting Parties makes specific reference to the need for technical assistance programs to assist developing countries with production and marketing. In 1964, the creation of the UN Conference on Trade and Development (UNCTAD) and the International Trade Centre (ITC) by the United Nations was a significant step in support of the TRTA/CB needs of developing countries to enable their fuller participation in international trade. The relationship between trade and aid is further mentioned in GATT Part IV (Trade and Development), added in 1965.[11]

The 1982 Ministerial Conference of the GATT subsequent to the Tokyo Round again recognized the need to strengthen developed country technical assistance programs. But it was only in the Uruguay Round (1986–1994), when developing countries were required to become part of all the multilateral agreements of the GATT through the concept of the "single undertaking," that more specific provisions on TRTA were added to individual Uruguay Round agreements to assist developing countries implement these new obligations.

There are *six main trends* that can be identified in the process of the unfolding development provisions of the GATT, including the specific references in these provisions to the TRTA/CB needs of developing countries.

First, while a number of positive provisions in favor of developing countries were included in the GATT Framework from 1955 to 1979, there was at the same time

[9] See Mark Malloch Brown in UNDP (2003, pg. vi).

[10] This section draws largely on the detailed account of this process in WTO (1999).

[11] GATT part IV para. 6 states that, "Because of the chronic deficiency in the export proceeds and other foreign exchange earnings of less-developed contracting parties, there are important inter-relationships between trade and financial assistance to development. There is, therefore, need for close and continuing collaboration between the CONTRACTING PARTIES and the international lending agencies so that they can contribute most effectively to alleviating the burdens these less-developed contracting parties assume in the interest of their economic development."

a steady increase in the protection and support for temperate zone agricultural products in industrialized countries. To a large extent, this was also due to the existing rules of GATT, which either permitted these protective and trade-distorting measures, or contained disciplines that were not clearly defined in the GATT. In the area of textiles and clothing, a multilateral framework was adopted, in derogation of GATT rules, for the imposition of discriminatory restrictions on low-wage or low-cost imports causing market disruption. This began in 1961 as the Short-Term Arrangement Regarding International Trade in Cotton Textiles, and was followed in 1962 by the Long-Term Arrangement Regarding International Trade in Cotton Textiles. The Long-Term Arrangement, which lasted twelve years, was replaced by the Multi-Fibre Arrangement (MFA) in 1974 and extended to man-made fibers and wool.

This trend of continued protection by developed countries of the products of interest to developing countries continued during and after the Uruguay Round. In the area of agriculture, protection levels in developed countries remained extremely high, creating a significant barrier to developing country exports. High levels of export and domestic support subsidies in developed countries continued to distort global agricultural prices and trade. Even in the area of textiles and clothing, the agreement reached in the Uruguay Round to eliminate quotas was backloaded to the end of the phase-out period in 2005, reducing its commercial significance for developing countries.

Second, these measures were largely of a best endeavor nature in that they did not impose mandatory obligations on industrialized countries, but instead encouraged the implementation of these provisions.

Third, the TRTA needs of developing countries were explicitly recognized by the GATT Contracting Parties as early as 1961, encouraging developed countries to address the production and marketing needs of developing countries in their technical assistance programs.

Fourth, the formation of UNCTAD and the establishment of the ITC (later to become a joint agency of UNCTAD and GATT) were significant steps in addressing the trade-related development concerns of developing countries, including technical assistance and capacity building.

Fifth, Part IV of the GATT specifically provided for greater coherence in trade and aid policies. It called for an examination of the trade and development policies and plans of developing countries in collaboration with international financial organizations "so that trade and aid relationships might be examined and the need for further action in the fields of trade and aid brought into focus." It also called on the GATT "to collaborate with the United Nations and its organs and agencies in matters of trade and development policy."

Sixth, developing countries complained of the difficulties they experienced in their attempts to implement the Uruguay Round agreements. The costs of implementing the Uruguay Round agreements were estimated to be onerous for many developing countries. World Bank estimates show that in only three areas of implementation – intellectual property rights, sanitary and phytosanitary standards (SPS) in health, and customs valuation – costs to a developing country could amount to about US$150 million, more than a full year's development budget in many LDCs (Finger, 2002).

4 The WTO Doha Round, special and differential treatment (SDT), and capacity building

This section sets out the various mandates provided in the 2001 WTO Doha Declaration for TRTA/CB to be addressed, including the more specific mandates on the issues related to trade facilitation, cotton, SDT, and LDCs.

4.1 The Doha Development Agenda

The Doha Ministerial Declaration made commitments in the mandate to address the development interests of developing countries. Paragraph 2 of the Doha Declaration set the tone for the rest of the document in stating that

> The majority of WTO Members are developing countries. We seek to place their needs and interests at the heart of the Work Programme adopted in this Declaration.... In this context, enhanced market access, balanced rules, and well targeted, sustainably financed technical assistance and capacity-building programmes have important roles to play.

Based on this and on other development-focused provisions in the Declaration, the Doha Work Programme was subsequently dubbed the "Doha Development Agenda" (DDA).

4.2 Technical assistance and capacity building

The Doha Declaration confirmed that "technical co-operation and capacity building are core elements of the development dimension of the multilateral trading system."[12] The WTO has made considerable advances on providing technical assistance, particularly in support of information and training for the Doha Round.

The July 2004 WTO General Council Decision that became known as the July 2004 Framework Agreement, while recognizing these efforts, calls for "developing countries and in particular least developed countries to be provided with enhanced TRTA and capacity building to increase their effective participation in the negotiations, to facilitate their implementation of WTO rules and to enable them to adjust and diversify their economies."[13] In addition, the section on "Other Development Issues" commits the WTO to ensure that "special attention shall be given to the specific trade and development related needs and concerns of developing countries, including capacity constraints."

4.3 Trade facilitation

The July 2004 Framework Agreement on modalities for trade facilitation committed members to provide "support and assistance for developing countries" to "implement the commitments resulting from the negotiations," and links this to their implementation obligations.[14] These are bold and positive commitments and would require additional donor support. This issue forms part of the overall Doha single

[12] See paragraphs 38 and 2 of WTO (2001a).
[13] See the section on "Other Development Issues" in WTO (2004a).
[14] See Paragraph 2 of Annex D of WTO (2004a).

undertaking, and further clarity is needed with regard to how it might best be tied into the wider Aid for Trade initiative.

4.4 Cotton

With a promise to ensure that the issue of cotton would be dealt with "ambitiously, expeditiously and specifically" (WTO, 2004a), the WTO General Council in July 2004 decided to negotiate the cotton issue within the context of the agriculture negotiations, not as a stand-alone issue that would be fast-tracked, as the four West African countries pushing the issue[15] had initially demanded. In addition, the July General Council Decision recognized the "complementarity between the trade and development" aspects of the cotton issue. The WTO Secretariat was urged to work with the "development community," namely multilateral and bilateral agencies. While the fundamental issue for West African countries was the need to eliminate the trade-distorting subsidies of developed countries in the cotton sector, the WTO did take a bold step forward in recognizing the complementarity between the trade and development aspects of the cotton issue.[16] Furthermore, it recognized that it would need to work closely with the development community, including multilateral and bilateral agencies. The Hong Kong Declaration went further, and called on the Director-General to intensify his consultative efforts with bilateral donors and with multilateral and regional institutions. The Declaration also urged the donor community to scale up its assistance, and called on the Director-General to set up a follow-up and monitoring mechanism. Thus the WTO has recognized that it has a role in the building of institutional, productive, and export capabilities. In addition, the WTO has recognized some responsibility for these development impacts of trade and that it needs to play a role in building coherence between the various levels and bodies responsible.

4.5 Negotiations on SDT

At the outset of the DDA negotiations, developing countries raised concerns with several existing WTO agreements negotiated in the Uruguay Round (TRIPS, TRIMS, and Anti-dumping, for example), arguing that many of these were against the interests of developing countries. They pointed out that the SDT provided by the Uruguay Round agreements and GATT meant to offset the cost of implementation was ineffective and needed to be reviewed.[17] These issues have been referred to as "implementation issues." A subset of these are proposals in the Doha Round calling for SDT provisions to be reviewed with a view to making them more precise, mandatory, and operational.

Developing countries have called for a review of these issues and a re-negotiation of the Uruguay Round agreements to provide greater flexibility in the rules so as to create more balanced rules that are consistent with the development dimension, referred to above. The implementation issues have not yet gained any real traction in the negotiations since the onset of the DDA. However, discussions on these issues

[15] Benin, Burkina Faso, Chad, and Mali.
[16] See 1b and Annex A 4 and 5 of WTO (2004a).
[17] See paragraph 44 of WTO (2001a) and paragraph 12 of WTO (2001b).

have taken place in some detail in the negotiations on SDT in the WTO's Committee on Trade and Development Special Session (CTDSS). The following section focuses on this debate, setting out the background of the negotiations and providing some insights into the issues and state-of-play.

A group of developing countries (mainly the Africa Group and India) tabled 88 proposals prior to the Doha Ministerial Conference in 2001 to review existing SDT provisions of the GATT/WTO and to make them more "precise, mandatory and operational." Following extensive consultations around the proposals, members eventually agreed prior to Hong Kong to focus on five relating specifically to LDC SDT concerns.

4.5.1 *LDCs*

In the CTDSS, LDCs had prioritized five proposals for members to consider. By the time of the Hong Kong Ministerial Conference, WTO members had made significant progress on these proposals. The most important of these five proposals was the commitment for developed countries – and those developing countries able to do so – to provide duty-free, quota-free market access to 97 percent of all products from LDCs (WTO, 2005).

There were three SDT LDC agreement-specific proposals that were agreed to in Annex F of the Hong Kong Declaration that are of relevance to the Aid for Trade agenda. The first of these (proposal number 36) urged "all donors and relevant international institutions to increase financial and technical support aimed at the diversification of LDC economies, while providing additional financial and technical assistance through appropriate delivery mechanisms to meet their implementation obligations, including fulfilling SPS and Technical Barriers to Trade (TBT) requirements and to assist them in managing their adjustment process, including those necessary to face the results of most-favored nation (MFN) multilateral liberalization."

The second proposal (proposal number 38) called on donors, multilateral agencies and international financial institutions to "coordinate their work to ensure that LDCs are not subjected to conditionalities on loans, grants, and official development assistance that are inconsistent with their rights and obligations under the WTO Agreements." A third agreement (proposal number 88) re-affirmed that LDCs will only be required to undertake commitments and concessions to the extent consistent with their development needs and capabilities, and directed the WTO to co-ordinate its efforts with donors to "significantly increase aid for trade-related technical assistance and capacity building." While the language of these proposals is not binding, the agreements do provide LDCs with some leverage in their efforts to secure greater Aid for Trade and to negotiate greater coherence of their obligations and commitments in the WTO and the conditionalities imposed by the Bretton Woods institutions.

5 Concept of increased Aid for Trade gains momentum in 2005/06

This section sets out the background on the development of the concept of Aid for Trade since 2005. The discussion traces the debate on the concept, its scope, and the modalities for delivery in the period before the Hong Kong Ministerial Conference.

The decisions made at the Hong Kong Ministerial Conference are then discussed, and the Report of the Task Force on Aid for Trade that was presented to the General Council of the WTO in July 2006 is briefly summarized.

The year 2005 was eventful for the debate on increased ODA to developing countries in general. The Commission for Africa issued a report in March that focused on the development needs of the African continent, and called for a substantial increase in aid by donors to sub-Saharan Africa. Tony Blair, the UK Prime Minister at the time, took the initiative forward to the G8 group of developed countries, where as chair he made the issue of Africa's development one of the main areas for discussion. Thus leaders at the G8 Summit, held at Gleneagles in July 2005, made pledges for substantial increases in ODA. In addition, the UN World Summit held in September 2005 in New York to review the Millennium Development Goals reaffirmed the commitments by donors to scale up aid commitments to ensure that the MDGs could be met. The concerns about the delivery and management of aid also gained prominence at a High Level Forum on Aid Effectiveness held in Paris in March of 2005. It is in this context that the debate on increasing Aid for Trade and its effectiveness should be seen.

Together with the focus on ODA in general, the concept of Aid for Trade began to gain support in the year 2005.[18] For instance, the Millennium Project Task Force on Trade (UN Millennium Project, 2005b) called for "a temporary aid for trade fund"; the report of the Director General's Consultative Board (UN Millennium Project, 2005a) stressed the need for adjustment assistance for developing countries to help them cope with trade liberalization; and EU Trade Commissioner, Peter Mandelson called for the richest countries to establish a special "Trade Adjustment Fund" (2005). The most ardent proponent of the proposal for additional aid for development was the UK's former Chancellor of the Exchequer (and subsequent Prime Minister), Gordon Brown,[19] who led the formation of the Commission for Africa and presented the case for Africa at the Gleneagles G8 Summit. In the period before the Hong Kong Ministerial Conference, UNCTAD called for a "Trade Marshall Plan" for LDCs. The proposal advocated a US$1 billion fund for LDCs, to be utilized to support adjustments arising from trade reform, trade-related infrastructure, and competitiveness capabilities.

There has been a persistent call by a large number of developing countries for the WTO to address the development challenges arising from the negative impact of trade liberalization. These include the need to address the loss of revenue, the increased cost of food imports, and the adjustment and diversification costs associated with preference erosion. In addition, many developing countries have argued that their access to developed country markets is further denied by the high costs associated with meeting health and technical standards (SPS and TBT).

In response to this call, discussions were held by a group of donor country and developing country experts based in Geneva, resulting in a "non-paper" written for the annual September meetings of the IMF and World Bank (Rugwabiza, 2005). The authors of this non-paper argue that the poorest countries need support to realize benefits from their membership of the WTO. The trade-related needs of

[18] The argument for increased Aid for Trade has been made most cogently in the work of Prowse (2006).
[19] Gordon Brown, in a speech to the UN General Assembly in December 2004, called for the creation of an International Financing Facility (IFF) to provide additional financial aid for development.

these members are numerous, and include aspects such as: enhanced negotiating capacity; increased investment in productivity; competitiveness and infrastructure; in-country institutional capacity; facilitation of adjustment that could arise from preference erosion; increased costs for food for net food-importing countries; loss of fiscal revenue, and social adjustment costs. The authors argue that measures that provide additional Aid for Trade should not be a substitute for, but a complement to, an ambitious outcome from the Doha Round.

5.1 Strengthening the Integrated Framework (IF)

The IMF/World Bank non-paper called for the strengthening of the six-agency Integrated Framework for Trade-Related Technical Assistance to LDCs (IF), an initiative geared at assisting LDCs to expand their participation in the global economy through increased trade. The IF's main purpose and approach since its inception in 1996 has been to assist LDCs to develop a broad trade development agenda with prioritized needs to which donors could respond. The non-paper pointed in particular to three possible options, at varying levels of ambition. The first envisaged enhancing the IF's current work program. The second level of ambition was to provide enhanced financing to respond to the prioritized trade-related needs of LDCs. The third level of ambition is for the IF to create a fund to manage adjustments arising from multilateral trade liberalization, and especially for the purposes of alleviating the costs of preference erosion. This formed the basis for the later emergence of an enhanced IF, which will serve to structure much of the forthcoming Aid for Trade for LDCs.

Many reasons have been advanced for developed countries to increase aid for TRTA/CB (Prowse, 2006). Developing countries have argued that any funds forthcoming under Aid for Trade should not be provided at the expense of aid for other areas of development such as health care and education, a provision that will need to be monitored closely to avoid donors shifting funds from other critical areas. Officials have generally concluded that developing countries do have the necessary capacity to absorb enhanced aid (IMF/World Bank, 2004) – indeed, the non-paper discussed above suggested some concrete ways in which this additional aid could be utilized, with increased co-ordination and coherence between the WTO, the IMF, World Bank, and the United Nations development agencies. Further country and regional input will be critical in maintaining effective follow-up.

5.2 The 2005 World Bank/IMF annual meetings

The World Bank and IMF at their spring meetings (April 2005) supported the calls for additional aid (IMF/World Bank, 2005b) and agreed to work with other institutions to prepare proposals for "additional assistance to countries to develop their trade and ease adjustment in their economies." The September 2005 World Bank/IMF annual meetings subsequently recognized the importance of the Doha Round for development. Their Development Committee communiqué stated that without a timely and ambitious outcome for the DDA, developing countries will not achieve the economic growth needed to meet the MDGs (IMF, 2005). In addition, it emphasized the importance of "major reform of agricultural trade policies to expand market access and eliminate trade-distorting subsidies" and the need for "increased aid for trade to address supply-side constraints and enhance the capacity of developing countries to take advantage of expanded trade opportunities."

However, in response to the proposals put forward by the non-paper, the World Bank and IMF document prepared for the meeting focused on the first level of ambition only, and "endorsed the proposal for an enhanced Integrated Framework for Trade-related Technical Assistance, including expanding its resources and scope and making it more effective." On the second level of ambition (enhanced financing to respond to LDCs' trade-related needs), the World Bank/IMF simply proposed to "examine further the adequacy of existing mechanisms to address regional or cross-country aid for trade needs and explore new mechanisms as appropriate". The institutions arguably did not adequately respond to the challenge proposed by the non-paper. In addition, the World Bank and IMF rejected the proposal for the creation of a trade adjustment fund envisaged by the third level of ambition of the non-paper. In this regard, the World Bank communiqué simply "supported a strengthened framework for assessing adjustment needs so that International Financial Institution and donor assistance mechanisms can be better utilized."

The stance taken by the international institutions elicited strong criticism from some observers. Writing in *The Financial Times*, Professors Jagdish Bhagwati (2005) and Bimal Ghosh (2005), in separate articles, argued that "an aid fund for trade provides the financial flexibility needed to ease the transitional difficulties of the countries that are genuine losers and have them on board, while equipping them to benefit from market openness over time". World Bank and IMF officials responded to these criticisms and argued that such a fund is unnecessary, as "any sensible governance structure of a dedicated fund would end up replicating already existing facilities available through the IMF, World Bank and other institutions that have not so far been hampered by funding constraints" (Dadush and Lankes, 2005). Developing countries have been critical of existing IMF facilities to fund adjustment, including the new Trade Integration Mechanism (TIM) facility, as these tend to be based on loans rather than grants and as a result are debt-creating.

This debate about the desirable and appropriate mechanisms to provide for the different TRTA needs of developing countries in the WTO is timely. The increasing support and recognition for additional Aid for Trade could provide a valuable contribution towards achieving the necessary balance in the Doha Round to assist many developing countries to support the round's ambitious liberalizing goals. However, this concept needs to be developed further and owned by the developing countries that are most in need of these resources themselves, and not be solely defined by multilateral institutions.

5.3 Hong Kong Ministerial Conference

The Hong Kong Ministerial Declaration (WTO, 2005) recognized the importance of "Aid for Trade" and called on the Director-General of the WTO to (a) create a Task Force that "provide recommendations on how to operationalize Aid for Trade", and (b) consult with members as well as the IMF and World Bank and other relevant international organizations "with a view to reporting to the General Council on appropriate mechanisms to secure additional financial resources for Aid for Trade."

This Task Force[20] was constituted by the WTO General Council in February 2006 and submitted its recommendations to the General Council at the end of July 2006 (WTO, 2006a). A large number of proposals were submitted to the Task Force by WTO members during its consultation period (ICTSD, 2006).

The African Group submitted proposals[21] addressing the scope of the Aid for Trade initiative and the need for additional resources. On the scope, the African Group proposed that the initiative should include "supply-side capacity and infrastructure, assistance to improve productivity of African economies and bolster their competitiveness, and assistance to deal with adjustment costs associated with trade liberalization." In a second proposal, the African Group emphasized that the funds provided under this initiative should be additional, predictable, and sustainable, after the current levels of Aid for Trade have first been identified. However, measuring the amount of new aid will first need an insight into how much of total ODA is currently provided, and how much of this is provided for the purposes of Aid for Trade. More complex is the definition of what constitutes Aid for Trade and how this is measured. These issues are considered further below, and are also taken up in other chapters of this volume.

5.4 The Aid for Trade Task Force Report of July 2006

The WTO Task Force on Aid for Trade tabled its final recommendations at a meeting of the General Council on 27–28 July 2006; they were formally adopted in October 2006. The report takes a broad view, and states that Aid for Trade is about "assisting developing countries to increase exports of goods and services, to integrate into the multilateral trading system, and to benefit from liberalized trade and increased market access." The objectives of Aid for Trade are also outlined, and include enhancing growth prospects, reducing poverty, and distributing the benefits of globalization more equitably across and within developing countries. The recommendations stress the need for additional, predictable, and effective financing. On the issue of scope, the Task Force took the view that Aid for Trade must be defined in a way "that is both broad enough to reflect the diverse trade needs identified by countries, and clear enough to establish a border between Aid for Trade and other development assistance of which it is a part." The Aid for Trade Task Force stated that building productive capacity and trade-related infrastructure in developing countries should be a major part of Aid for Trade efforts, in addition to assistance aimed at helping countries negotiate and comply with trade agreements.

The report emphasizes the need to mainstream trade-related issues into national development strategies. It identifies a number of challenges involved with doing so, such as the lack of private-sector involvement in identifying trade needs, the limited absorptive capacity of recipient countries, ineffective monitoring, and the slow, duplicative and bureaucratic processes in the assessment and delivery of trade-related assistance.

[20] The Task Force was composed of 13 members – Barbados, Brazil, Canada, China, Colombia, the EU, Japan, India, Thailand, the US and the coordinators of the ACP (African, Caribbean and Pacific) Group of States, the African Group and the LDC Group – plus the Chair. Ambassador Mia Horn of Sweden chaired the Task Force in her personal capacity.

[21] See WTO (2006d).

The recommendations also address the implementation of Aid for Trade at the national, regional, and global levels. They emphasize the need for national coordination, suggesting that "national aid for trade committees" could be created to coordinate development assistance, data collection and analysis, and cooperation between agencies, donors, regional banks, and governments. At the regional level, the Task Force recommends strengthening processes to identify cross-border and regional needs, as well as the ability of donors and agencies to respond to them. It asks countries to explore the merits of establishing "regional aid for trade committees," since cross-border infrastructure and regional policy cooperation are necessary to trade effectively.

The panel recommends convening a monitoring body in the WTO to conduct a global review of Aid for Trade based on reports from stakeholders, including those from recipients, the donor community, regional and multilateral agencies, and the private sector. It also recommends that mechanisms to facilitate reporting should be enhanced, including notification processes for WTO members.

The Task Force called on WTO Director-General Lamy to make reference to the report during his consultations aimed at securing "additional financial resources for Aid for Trade." The panel also requested the Director-General to set up an "ad hoc consultative group" to follow up on its recommendations.

5.5 Report of the Task Force on an Enhanced IF

The IF was created at a High Level Meeting of the WTO in response to the Plan of Action for Least Developed Countries agreed to by the first Ministerial Conference held in 1996. The main objective was to improve the capacity of the LDCs to formulate, negotiate, and implement trade policy so as to be able to fully integrate into the multilateral trading system (WTO, 2006c).[22]

The World Bank/IMF annual meetings in September 2005 had supported the proposal for an "Enhanced Integrated Framework for Trade Related Technical Assistance to LDCs, including its resources and scope and making it more effective," and proposed that a task force be created to make recommendations in this regard. At the Hong Kong Ministerial Conference in December 2005, WTO Ministers reaffirmed their commitment to effectively and meaningfully integrate LDCs into the multilateral trading system and supported the urgent need to make the IF more effective.

The report of the chair of the Enhanced Integrated Framework (EIF) Task Force, Ambassador Don Stephenson of Canada, was presented to the WTO General Council on 27 July 2006 (WTO, 2006b). The report recognized that while the IF had provided a good framework for helping LDCs enhance their trade development capacity and facilitate adjustment and integration into the multilateral trading system, it suffered from at least three major shortcomings. First, the IF has generally failed to mainstream trade into the PRSP process and has not provided adequate financial and human resources to the LDCs to deliver the intended outcomes. Second, country ownership of the IF processes has been weak. Third, the donor community has generally not responded adequately to the needs identified in the Diagnostic

[22] For a more thorough description of the IF see the Introductory Chapter to this volume.

Trade Integration Studies (DTIS), which outline priorities and actions for LDCs to undertake in trade through action matrices.

The Task Force decided to retain the IF for LDCs only, and made four main recommendations to build on the strengths of the IF and to improve its effectiveness and efficiency. First, it called on donors to provide more support to strengthen the ownership of the IF by the LDCs, and that agencies, donors and beneficiaries need to work together through local processes. Second, it stated that the gap between the diagnostic process and the submission of "bankable projects" needed to be filled, with Action Matrices being updated on a regular basis. Third, a much clearer management structure for the effective implementation of the IF was proposed, with a new Governing Board, Secretariat and full time CEO, still located in the WTO, but independent of the WTO. Fourth, the Task Force stated that the current level of funding of approximately US$35 million was inadequate, and proposed that the IF should mobilize around US$400 million over five years through the multilateral trust fund and bilateral cooperation.

The recommendations of the Task Force were accepted by the General Council in July 2006. Speaking on behalf of the LDCs, the Ambassador of Bangladesh, Toufiq Ali, stressed that the work was not yet over, as the recommendations of the Task Force still had to be implemented. He stated that the IF had remained a diagnostic tool thus far and needed to be more active in implementing the Action Plans of the DTISs.

There is no doubt that the recommended ten-fold increase in funding would provide a major boost to the IF, providing it with the capacity to address many of the weaknesses identified by the Task Force and its critics.[23] The fact that several LDCs[24] were represented in the Task Force ensured that the real concerns of LDCs were addressed in the Report, and gives credibility to the Task Force recommendations. The challenge now will be for the donors to implement the recommendations, including in particular its proposed funding increase.

6 Additional aid or additional Aid for Trade?

The issues related to the additionality of Aid for Trade are complicated by the lack of a commonly agreed definition of the scope of Aid for Trade (that is, whether it should cover supply-side issues and infrastructure in addition to support for trade policy capacity and implementation of WTO agreements). Different institutions continue to maintain different categories, and there is a need for harmonization of what exactly qualifies as Aid for Trade assistance. In addition, it is unclear whether the issue of additionality means that Aid for Trade will constitute a greater share of overall ODA or whether there will be an increase in the overall quantum of ODA, including support for Aid for Trade. This section thus attempts to provide background information that could assist this assessment. The trends in ODA growth and the future trajectory of ODA levels are first set out. The issue of additionality is discussed and the pledges made by donor countries in Hong Kong evaluated in

[23] There were a number of studies critical of the weaknesses of the current IF, including its poor funding. See ILEAP and German Marshall Fund (2006).

[24] The membership of the Enhanced IF Task Force included Benin, Lesotho, Nepal, Rwanda, Senegal, Tanzania and Zambia from LDCs. Other members were Canada (Chair), EC, Finland, Italy, Japan, Norway, Sweden, Switzerland, UK, and the USA.

this context. The complex issue of the scope of Aid for Trade and the consequent measurement of the increases in the share of Aid for Trade in overall aid flows is then discussed.

ODA levels are increasing but not fast enough to meet the MDGs...

Prior to 2001, total ODA levels had been falling since the early 1990s, when ODA had reached a high of 0.34 percent of gross national income (GNI) of the OECD donor countries. This trend continued up to 2001, at which time total ODA levels reached a low of 0.22 percent of OECD GNI. However, there has been a reversal of this trend since 2001, with a sharp increase in ODA reaching 0.33 percent of GNI in donor countries in 2005 (World Bank, 2006). According to the World Bank, this trend is likely to grow, with ODA levels expected to reach 0.36 percent of GNI in 2010. The UN Millennium Project estimated that financing the MDGs requires an increase in ODA (excluding debt relief) to 0.46 percent of GNI by 2010. At the current rate of increase of ODA (of about 0.017 percentage points per year on average over the period 2005–10), the World Bank estimates that the UN target of 0.7 percent will only be achievable in 2030, fifteen years after the target of 2015 set for the attainment of the MDGs.

At least five of the twenty-two OECD Development Assistance Committee (DAC) member countries have already exceeded the UN target of 0.7 percent (Norway, Denmark, Luxembourg, Sweden, and the Netherlands), and the EU as a whole has pledged to increase its contribution from 0.35 percent of GNI in 2004 to 0.56 percent in 2010 and 0.7 percent by 2015. At the Gleneagles Summit in 2005, Japan pledged to increase its ODA spending by US$10 billion over the next five years. In contrast, ODA spending by the United States is projected to decline from US$27 billion (US$23.4 billion excluding debt relief) in 2005 to US$24 billion in 2006 and remain at this level until 2010.

Increases in ODA are mainly due to increased debt relief to Iraq and Nigeria... and an increased share of special purpose grants

The DAC grouping of major donors has estimated that net ODA disbursements by DAC member countries increased by a record US$27 billion in 2005 to reach a total of US$106 billion (World Bank, 2006). However, a significant amount of this total was due to an increase in debt relief totaling US$23 billion (up from US$4 billion in 2004). The major part of this debt relief (US$14 billion) was provided to Iraq and Nigeria. However, the increase in overall ODA levels can also be attributed to an increased share of other (in addition to debt relief) special purpose grants, which include technical cooperation, emergency and distress relief, and administrative costs. Thus total ODA in 2005 net of special purpose grants totaled US$45 billion. This figure was the same in 2004, but did improve significantly from a low of US$30 billion in 2001. However, ODA net of special purpose grants remained the same as a percentage of OECD GNI between 1996 and 2005, averaging 0.14 percent and declining from the 0.23 percent figure of the early 1990s.

Sub-Saharan Africa's share of ODA has increased substantially...

Sub-Saharan countries have increased their share of total ODA from 25 percent in 1999 to 40 percent in 2004. At the G8 Summit in Gleneagles, donors pledged to increase ODA by US$50 billion by 2010 (in real terms from 2004 levels), with at least half of this pledged for Africa. This would double the amount of aid to the region by 2010, and raise its share of total ODA from 40 percent in 2004 to almost 50 percent in 2010.

Although aid to Sub-Saharan Africa is rising, much more will be needed to support the effort to achieve the MDGs. While about one-sixth of sub-Saharan countries have ODA/GDP levels that are over ten percent, an almost equal number have bilateral ODA/GDP levels under one percent. In addition, most of the US$8.5 billion increase in net ODA to the region during 2002 and 2003 was in the form of debt relief (US$5.6 billion) and emergency and disaster relief and food aid (US$1.5 billion) (IMF/World Bank, 2005a). Aid flows still represent the largest source of foreign finance to sub-Saharan Africa, constituting about 60 percent of external flows to the region in 2003, with FDI and remittances constituting a small but significant source of finance to the region. Sub-Saharan African countries have seen a decline in ODA flows to rural/agricultural development and infrastructure (Ibid, 2005a). Thus, much more substantial increases will be needed in program and project assistance to support the needs of the MDGs in the oncoming years.

Additionality of ODA is unlikely before 2010...

The OECD takes a somber view of whether there will be "additional new money over and beyond the level that has already been projected to 2010." In a submission made to the WTO, the OECD sates that this type of additionality is "unlikely... as most DAC members have already made commitments for their total aid levels to at least the year 2010" (OECD, 2006). However, the OECD submission does envisage an increase in the relative share of Aid for Trade, with this share rising faster than that of overall aid. Thus in Hong Kong, the EU and its member states pledged to provide EUR2 billion a year by 2010, the United States announced grants of US$2.7 billion a year by 2010, and Japan committed US$10 billion over the next three years for trade-related infrastructure, production, and distribution (though much of Japan's pledges appear to be directed toward loans). At the G8 St. Petersburg Summit in July 2006, the G8 stated that it expected "spending on Aid for Trade to increase to US$4 billion, including through enhancing the Integrated Framework" (G7/G8, 2006). In light of these statements, it can be assumed that the pledges made by the donors at both the Hong Kong Ministerial and the St. Petersburg G8 Summit are not new or additional pledges, but are in line with commitments already made in 2005 to increase their overall aid spending to 2010.

The scope of Aid for Trade... and share of total ODA

The OECD recognizes that it is difficult and in practice not feasible to draw a line between the assistance provided to trade capacity in particular and to support for economic growth in general (OECD, 2006). However, for the purposes of estimating spending on Aid for Trade, the OECD has established three categories. Category one is TRTA/CB; category two is Trade-related infrastructure; and category three is Building productive capacity. The latter two categories refer to supply-side constraints. The OECD does not address adjustment support separately, as this is assumed to be included in the given categories of support. The OECD recognizes that what falls outside these categories could include social safety nets, balance of payment support, compensation for preference erosion, and reductions in government revenues due to multilateral liberalization.

The World Bank estimates that as far as Aid for Trade is concerned, the share of trade-related assistance has risen over the past few years from 3.6 percent of total aid commitments in 2002 to 4.4 percent in 2003. If infrastructure (transport, energy, telecommunications) is included, then this amount should increase by a further 25 percent (World Bank, 2006). However, in the OECD estimates, the current share of category one support is 2.8 percent (US$2.6 billion), and if category two is added, this would raise the share of Aid for Trade to 14.5 percent of total ODA (or US$15.5 billion). While the share of both categories one and two is expected to remain the same by 2010, there is projected to be an increase in volume to US$4.3 billion in 2010 of category one, and US$21.9 billion in category two. If category three is added to the above two categories, this will increase Aid for Trade's share of total ODA to 22.4 percent (US$22.8 billion). The OECD projects the share of this broader Aid for Trade to remain constant up to 2010 (but increasing in volume to US$33.7 billion) and to increase to 30.2 percent (US$45 billion) by 2010 (if commitments to double spending are maintained). This would be part of projected total aid flows of US$150 billion by 2010.

6.1 Assessment

From the foregoing discussion, four broad trends in the trajectory of ODA and Aid for Trade can be observed:

First, while ODA levels reflect an increasing trend since 2001, and pledges have been made to increase the size of individual developed country (OECD) contributions by 2010, these pledges still fall far short of the target required to meet the Millennium Development Goals. Furthermore, when debt relief and special purpose grants are subtracted, the observation is that ODA levels have remained the same for the past ten years (1996–2005) – an amount of US$45 billion recorded in 2005 – averaging 0.14 percent of OECD GNI, a decline from the 0.23 percent figure of the early 1990s.

Second, in the case of sub-Saharan Africa, both the quantum and the overall share of total ODA, including the amount available for Aid for Trade, are scheduled to increase significantly. However, this additional funding will still fall far short of the needs of the sub-Saharan countries to meet the MDGs. In addition, this increase in ODA levels needs to recognize that most of the US$8.5 billion increase in net ODA to the region during 2002 and 2003 was in the form of debt relief (US$5.6 billion) and emergency and disaster relief and food aid (US$1.5 billion dollars) (IMF/World Bank, 2005a). The World Bank thus estimates that substantial increases in aid, particularly, program and project assistance, will still be required to fund shortfalls in agricultural/rural development, infrastructure investment, and support measures to improve the environment for investment in sub-Saharan Africa (World Bank, 2006).

Third, there is increasing support for the need to broaden the concept of Aid for Trade to include trade-related infrastructure and productive capacity. However, differences over the precise definition of the concept will make an evaluation of an increased share of Aid for Trade in overall ODA levels more difficult for policy makers and trade negotiators. As the definition and scope of Aid for Trade has been broadened to include supply-side issues and infrastructure investment, increases in Aid for Trade are thus inextricably linked with the need for increases in overall aid flows.

Fourth, according to the OECD, additionality of overall ODA levels is unlikely before 2010, as pledges by the major donors have already been made and are unlikely to change, though the share of Aid for Trade in total ODA levels could increase. Developed countries will, however, need to respond to the demands made by developing countries for additionality in their Aid for Trade offers. In addition, there are a number of specific mandates in the Doha Work Programme where the need for additional aid is part of the mandate of the Doha Round that will need to be addressed. The reasons for additionality of Aid for Trade over and above existing pledges on ODA, rather than a mere increase in the share of Aid for Trade from existing ODA pledges, will now be discussed.

7 Conclusion

In the introduction, this chapter argued that increased trade *and* aid are both essential to advance the development of many poorer countries. Several global summits since the Millennium Summit have reinforced the commitment of world leaders to increase overall ODA levels to meet the Millennium Development Goals. The DDA and the call for increased Aid for Trade that gained momentum in 2005/06 must be seen in this context. SDT, of which trade-related technical assistance and capacity building is an essential component, has often been relegated to the margins of the development debate in the WTO by developed countries, or sometimes incorrectly regarded as the main issue for development by developing countries. However, this chapter has presented a conceptual framework that argues that TRTA/CB is not only an essential element of the concept of SDT, but is also a core element of the development dimension of the multilateral trading system. The chapter thus calls for the development dimension and SDT (which is an important aspect of the development dimension) to be mainstreamed in the WTO.

The chapter proceeded to provide a schematic overview of the history of the GATT/WTO, with a specific focus on the provisions that provide for the interests of developing countries to be addressed. The section concluded that, while many provisions have been added to the GATT/WTO that seek to address the needs of developing countries (including on trade-related capacity building), since the formation of the GATT these provisions have generally been "best endeavor" provisions and have not been effective. It is for these reasons that the Doha mandate sought to specifically address the need to make SDT provisions more effective, mandatory, and operational. In addition, the Doha negotiations have specifically called for increased aid and greater coherence of WTO rules with donor agencies, including in the negotiations on trade facilitation, cotton, SDT, and LDCs.

The chapter also provided an overview of developments in 2005 and 2006 that have contributed to the momentum for increased Aid for Trade. The Commission for Africa initiated by the UK prior to the Gleneagles G8 Summit and the decisions of the Gleneagles Summit provided the momentum for commitments by developed countries to increase overall levels of ODA and increased Aid for Trade. The Report of the WTO Aid for Trade Task Force was in general positively received by members. The Report took on board the proposals of developing countries for Aid for Trade to be additional, predictable, and effective. The recommendations of the Enhanced IF Task Force were also considered. The Task Force recognized the criticisms that have been made of the IF and proposed a ten-fold increase in its budget and the strengthening of the IF's institutional capacity. This has also been generally supported by the WTO membership. The chapter argues that this is a positive development and needs to be further supported by donors.

In the final section of the chapter, the issue of additionality of overall ODA and Aid for Trade was considered. Four broad trends in the trajectory of ODA and Aid for Trade were observed. First, while ODA levels reflect an increasing trend since 2001, and pledges have been made to increase the size of individual developed country (OECD) contributions by 2010, these pledges still fall far short of the target required to meet the Millennium Development Goals. Second, in the case of sub-Saharan Africa, both the quantum and the overall share of total ODA, including the amount available for Aid for Trade, are scheduled to increase significantly. However, this additional funding will still fall far short of the needs of the sub-Saharan countries to meet the MDGs. Third, there is increasing support for the need to broaden the concept of Aid for Trade to include trade-related infrastructure and productive capacity. Fourth, additionality of overall ODA levels is unlikely before 2010, as pledges by the major donors have already been made and are unlikely to change, though the share of Aid for Trade in total ODA levels could increase.

Finally, this conclusion provides three reasons for developed countries to increase their overall aid commitments and provide additional Aid for Trade to developing countries as a contribution to the multilateral trading system and to the successful conclusion of the Doha Round.

First, *TRTA/CB is an essential complement to increased market access to help integrate developing countries into the world economy.* This chapter argued that TRTA/CB is not only a part of the concept of SDT, but a core element of the development dimension of the multilateral trading system. The history of European economic development provides some valuable insights. The post-World War II Marshall Plan for European reconstruction was partly instigated to "neutralize the forces moving Western Europe permanently away from multilateral trade" (Foreman-Peck, 1984). In addition, European integration itself was facilitated by economic assistance provided to weaker countries and regions (through structural and cohesion funds) (Tsoukalis, 2003). Some studies indicate that while a successful Doha Round could lift at least 140 million people out of poverty, these reforms would need to be accompanied by complementary actions being taken in low-income countries to support much-needed supply response and adjustment (Prowse, 2006). Several diagnostic studies undertaken in the past few years in low-income developing countries by the IF and the Joint Integrated Technical Assistance Program (JITAP) have identified actions that need to be taken by these countries to improve their trade and investment environment. These countries require additional financial resources to implement these recommendations.

Second, *additional Aid for Trade will be necessary to compensate a large number of the poorer developing countries that are likely to suffer significant losses from trade liberalization, thus requiring resources for adjustment and diversification.* Recent studies (Anderson, 2005) have pointed out that while an ambitious outcome of the DDA promises significant gains for both developed and developing counties, the poorest countries, including the LDCs and other small, weak, and vulnerable, economies will make fewer gains and could even experience significant losses from the round. There are a number of reasons for this result, including significant preference erosion for some countries and the lack of supply capacity to take advantage of new opportunities in global markets. Several studies have also revealed that there will be additional preference erosion under different scenarios of the possible outcomes of the DDA, causing a negative impact on LDCs and other small and vulnerable economies (World Bank/OECD/WTO, 2005). One study that focused on the impact of trade liberalization by the Quad (United States, EU, Japan, and Canada) on LDCs concluded that the potential losses for LDCs amount to 1.7 percent of total LDC exports (WTO, 2003).

Some individual LDCs, however, may suffer a more significant loss due to the concentration of their exports in products that enjoy strong preferences. The study finds that the losses predicted for Malawi are 11.5 percent of exports, with Mauritania, Haiti, Cape Verde, Sao Tome and Principe to be the next worst cases, with losses of between 5 and 10 percent of exports. A study (Alexandraki, 2005) that focused on the impact of trade liberalization on middle-income developing countries found at least six small island economies are most exposed to preference erosion. In the cases of Mauritius, St Lucia, Belize, St Kitts and Nevis, Guyana and Fiji, preferences add around one-quarter or more to the value of exports. Sugar and banana preferences account for three-quarters of the preferences, with textiles featuring as a distant third.

For the WTO's poorest members and other small, weak, and vulnerable economies, these challenges of preference erosion are compounded by the existing challenges of commodity dependence and volatility, poor trade facilitation infrastructure and supply capacity, and increased marginalization, reflected by a declining share in the global markets and increasing levels of poverty. A range of measures may be needed to assist these countries to manage their adjustment and diversification strategies. These could include funding from the Bretton Woods institutions, but without immersing these countries into more unsustainable debt. Thus, additional finance to fund supply-side and diversification strategies will be required to compensate these countries for the losses that they will sustain from the round.

Third, ***while it is argued here that the rationale for increased Aid for Trade goes beyond the Doha Round and is an essential element of the multilateral trading system, increased Aid for Trade will also be required as part of the "grand bargain" required for a successful Doha Round.*** At a meeting of the WTO's Trade Negotiations Committee in March 2006, Director-General Pascal Lamy stated that in his view there is a triangle of issues that need to be unlocked to advance the Doha Round. This triangle requires the EU to move on agricultural market access, the United States on domestic support, and the G20 on non-agricultural market access and services. He argued that the level of ambition established in these three legs would establish the level of ambition for the rest of the issues in the DDA, and provide momentum for progress on the rest of the issues in the round. However, there remain a number of issues that are of great importance to the majority of the poorer and smaller members of the WTO, and that are a crucial component of the Doha "grand bargain." Without successful resolution of these issues, a Doha deal or grand bargain will simply not be struck. These issues relate to addressing the trade-related development challenges faced by LDCs and the so-called "small, weak, and vulnerable developing countries." The specific development issues raised by these countries include the need to provide duty-free, quota-free market access to LDCs; cotton; preference erosion; special flexibilities for small, weak, and vulnerable economies; and development aid. There is thus a need to ensure that the LDCs and other small, weak, and vulnerable countries are provided with the necessary support through Aid for Trade as part of the "grand bargain" that is required to ensure a successful conclusion of the Doha Round that benefits all members.

REFERENCES

Alexandraki, Katerina. 2005. "Preference Erosion: Cause for Alarm?," *Finance and Development*, Washington, D.C.: IMF.

Anderson, Kym, Will Martin, and Dominique van der Mensbrugghe. 2005. "Would Multilateral Trade Reform Benefit Sub-Saharan Africans?," Washington, D.C.: World Bank.

Bhagwati, Jagdish. 2005. "World Bank funds should be used to lubricate trade liberalisation by developing countries," *Financial Times*, 26 September.

Brown, Gordon. 2004a. Speech by Chancellor of the Exchequer Gordon Brown at Seminar on "Poverty and Globalization: Financing for Development, including the Millennium Development Goals," Pontifical Council for Justice and Peace of the Holy See, Vatican City, 9 July.

Brown, Gordon. 2004b. Speech by the Chancellor of the Exchequer Gordon Brown at Conference on "Making Globalization Work for All – The Challenge of Delivering the Monterrey Consensus," HM Treasury and Department for International Development, London, 16 February.

CUTS International. 2004. "From Cancún to São Paulo: The Role of Civil Society in the International Trading System," Afro-Asian Seminar, New Delhi.

Dadush, Uri and Peter Lankes. 2005. "Dedicated multilateral fund may not always be desirable," *Financial Times*, 3 October.

Engammare, V. and J. P. Lehmann. 2004. "Does the Multilateral Trading System Promote the Interests of the Poor?," in *From Cancún to São Paulo: The Role of Civil Society in the International Trading System*, CUTS International, Afro-Asian Seminar, New Delhi.

Finger, J. Michael. 2002. "The Doha Agenda and Development: A View from the Uruguay Round," ERD Working Paper Series No. 21, Manila: ADB.

Foreman-Peck, James. 1984. "A History of the World Economy: International Economic Relations since 1950," Harvester: Barnes & Noble.

General Agreement on Tariffs and Trade (GATT). 61 Stat. A-11, T.I.A.S. 1700, 55 U.N.T.S. 194, 30 October 1947.

G7/G8. 2006. "Trade," St. Petersburg Summit Documents, G8 Information Centre, http://www.g7.utoronto.ca/summit/2006stpetersburg/trade.html.

Ghosh, Bimal. 2005. "Difficult to see why aid fund proposal was opposed," *Financial Times*, 3 October.

Government of Sweden. 2003. "Shared responsibility: Sweden's policy for global development," Government Bill 2002/03: 122, The Riksdag, 23 May.

ICTSD. 2006. "Comparative Table of Recommendations, Proposals, and Views on Aid for Trade," http://www.ictsd.org/dlogue/2006-11-14/Matrix_A4T.pdf.

IISD. 1999. *Report on the WTO's high-level symposium on trade and development*, International Institute for Sustainable Development, 17–18 March.

ILEAP and German Marshall Fund. 2006. "Aid for Trade after the Hong Kong Ministerial: An Introductory Guide," *ILEAP Background Brief No. 8*, prepared by Claire Healey, Dominique Njinkeu, and Hugo Cameron.

IMF. 2005. "Development Committee Communiqué," Washington, D.C.: IMF.

IMF/World Bank. 2004. "Aid Effectiveness and Financing Modalities," Development Committee Background Paper, DC2004-0012/Add.1, Washington, D.C.: IMF and World Bank.

IMF/World Bank. 2005a. "Global Monitoring Report 2005 – Millennium Development Goals: From Consensus to Momentum," Washington, D.C.: IMF and World Bank.

IMF/World Bank. 2005b. "Development Committee Communiqué," Development Committee, Washington, D.C.: IMF and World Bank.

Ismail, Faizel. 2005. "Mainstreaming Development in the World Trade Organization," *Journal of World Trade*, 39(1): 11–21.

Jackson, John H. 1997. "The Great 1994 Sovereignty Debate: United States Acceptance and Implementation of the Uruguay Round Results," *Columbia Journal of Transnational Law*, quoted in Ann Chen, 2004, "The Three Big Rounds of US Unilateralism Versus WTO Multilateralism during the Last Decade," Geneva: South Centre.

Keck, Alexander and Patrick Low. 2004. *Special and Differential Treatment in the WTO: Why, When, and How?*, Staff Working Paper ERSD-2004-03, Geneva: WTO.

Mandelson, Peter. 2005. Speech at the London School of Economics – "An action plan for trade and development in 2005: the EU, the WTO, the G8," MEMO/05/39, Brussels, 07 February.

Messerlin, Patrick A. 2001. "Measuring the costs of protection in Europe: European Commercial Policy in the 2000s," Washington, D.C.: Institute for International Economics.

OECD. 2006. "Aid for Trade: Making it Effective," *The Development Dimension*, preliminary version. Paris: OECD.

Oxfam. 2002. "Rigged Rules and Double Standards: trade, globalization, and the fight against poverty," Oxford: Oxfam International.

Polaski, Sandra. 2006. "Winners and Losers: Impact of the Doha Round on Developing Countries," Carnegie Endowment Report, Washington, D.C.: Carnegie Endowment for International Peace.

Prowse, Susan. 2006. "'Aid for Trade' – Increasing Support for Trade Adjustment and Integration – a Proposal," in S. Evenett and Bernard Hoekman (eds.), *Economic Development and Multilateral Cooperation*, New York and Washington: Palgrave Macmillan and World Bank.

Rugwabiza, V. and M. H. Rantzien. 2005. "'Aid for Trade' Initiative – Options to Enhance Support," non-paper presented at the 2005 annual meetings of the IMF and World Bank, Washington, D.C.

Sen, Amartya. 1999. "Development as Freedom," New York: Random House Inc.

Tangermann, Stefan. 2005. "How to Forge a Compromise in the Agricultural Negotiations?," in Ernst-Ulrich Petersmann (ed.), *Reforming the World Trading System: Legitimacy, Efficiency, and Democratic Governance*, Oxford: Oxford University Press.

Tsoukalis, Loukas. 2003. "What Kind of Europe?," Oxford: Oxford University Press.

UNDP. 2003. "Human Development Report 2003 – Millennium Development Goals: A compact among nations to end human poverty," New York: Oxford University Press.

UN Millennium Project. 2005a. "Investing in Development: A Practical Plan to Achieve the Millennium Development Goals," Report to the UN Secretary-General, New York: United Nations Development Programme.

UN Millennium Project. 2005b. "Trade for Development – Achieving the Millennium Development Goals," Task Force on Trade, New York: United Nations Development Programme.

World Bank. 2002. "Global Economic Prospects and the Developing Countries," Washington, D.C.: World Bank.

World Bank. 2004. "Global Economic Prospects – Realizing the Development Promise of the Doha Agenda," Washington, D.C.: World Bank.

World Bank. 2006. "Global Development Finance – The Development Potential of Surging Capital Flows," Washington, D.C.: World Bank.

World Bank/OECD/WTO. 2005. "Report of International Symposium on Preference Erosion: Impacts and Policy Responses," Geneva, 13–14 June.

World Commission on the Social Dimension of Globalization. 2004. "A Fair Globalization: Creating Opportunities for All," ILO, Geneva, http://www.ilo.org/public/english/wcsdg/docs/report.pdf.

WTO. 2001a. *Doha Ministerial Declaration*, Ministerial Conference Fourth Session, Doha, 9–14 November 2001, WT/MIN/(01)/DEC/1, 20 November.
WTO. 2001b. Implementation-related issues and concerns, Ministerial Conference, Fourth Session, Doha, 9–14 November 2001, WT/MIN(01)/17, 20 November.
WTO. 2003. *Communication from the International Monetary Fund*, WT/TF/COH/14, 14 February.
WTO. 2004a. *Decision Adopted by the General Council on 1 August 2004*, Doha Work Programme, WT/L/579, 2 August.
WTO. 2004b. *The Future of the WTO: Addressing institutional challenges in the new millennium*, report by the Consultative Board to the Director-General Supachai Panitchpakdi, Geneva: WTO.
WTO. 2005. *Hong Kong Ministerial Declaration*, Ministerial Conference Sixth Session, Hong Kong, 13–18 December 2005, WT/MIN(05)/DEC, 22 December.
WTO. 2006a. *Recommendations of the Task Force on Aid for Trade*, Aid for Trade Task Force, WT/AFT/1, 27 July.
WTO. 2006b. *Proposed Agenda*, General Council 27–28 July 2006, WT/GC/W/568, 25 July.
WTO. 2006c. *An Enhanced Integrated Framework*, Report of the Chairman of the Task Force on an Enhanced Integrated Framework, WT/IFSC/W/15, 29 June.
WTO. 2006d. *Communication from Benin on behalf of the African Group*, Aid for Trade Task Force, WT/AFT/W/21, 21 June.

3 Aid for Trade: How We Got Here, Where We Might Go

J. MICHAEL FINGER

1 Introduction

In the Declaration issued at the World Trade Organization (WTO) Ministerial Conference in Hong Kong in December 2005, trade ministers agreed on the need for a new initiative to help developing countries use the trading system as an effective vehicle for development and poverty reduction:

> We invite the Director-General to create a task force that shall provide recommendations on how to operationalize Aid for Trade (WTO, 2005c).

Why is there *in the WTO* an initiative on aid?[1] From the recipient country's perspective, the rationale could be additional resources for development and poverty reduction. From the donor's perspective, the rationale may be commercial, strategic or foreign policy interests; or simply that some taxpayers in donor countries would be gratified to know that assistance is provided to people in poorer countries.

This paper focuses less on aid than on the WTO as a venue for managing aid. The objectives of this paper are to examine the origin of the WTO Aid for Trade initiative, its rationale, and in particular the potential effectiveness of the WTO as a vehicle for motivating and managing development aid.[2]

The chapter examines three interrelated reasons for a WTO role in Aid for Trade:

- Market access concessions by developing countries would buy additional aid;
- It is a response to two issues of particular interest to developing countries: the problem of implementation of unfulfilled commitments by developed countries

[1] This chapter takes poverty reduction to be one of the paramount elements in development. The reader should keep in mind that "development" should be taken to include "development and poverty reduction."

[2] A tone of institutional rivalry often enters into discussions of Aid for Trade; for example, the WTO versus the World Bank. It is important to keep in mind that all of these are instruments created by the international community. The issue is not "Which of these institutions is best?" The issue is "How can we best use these institutions to advance our common objectives of development and poverty reduction?" Thus the WTO should be seen as an instrument rather than as an actor. The actor is the international community. The issue is what the international community can do through the WTO, not what the WTO can do. Similarly, the multilateral trading system comprises all the activities and entities involved with commerce that cross international borders. The WTO is a part of that system – a particular institution the international community has created to promote and to regulate international commerce so that this commerce advances our economic, social and moral goals.

in the Uruguay Round preceding the establishment of the WTO; and the unbalanced outcome that emerged from this process; and
- Existing aid mechanisms undervalue the development impact of resources applied to trade-related uses relative to their impact in other uses.

The first of these reasons has been widely rejected as part of the Doha negotiations and is somewhat moot now that negotiations have been suspended. However, it remains a lurking element in the two other rationales.

It is unlikely that any of these rationales suggest more than limited potential for the WTO to be useful in this area.

First, implementation and imbalance of outcomes are real issues, but, as explained later, the Doha negotiations have ineffectively addressed them. Second, as to the point of existing mechanisms undervaluing trade-related aid, this can be linked to a partisan assertion in the trade community's effort to win increased aid, as opposed to an objectively-structured and scientifically-tested hypothesis.

These conclusions, however, should not be causes for alarm. In the recent past, trade-related aid provided through other mechanisms has increased markedly. While little has been accomplished through the WTO, the international community has taken up these issues through national and international development agencies. These agencies are better suited to ensure that aid resources are productively applied than are multilateral negotiations. Moreover, the project design and cost-benefit analysis of such institutions are the appropriate tools – rather than multilateral negotiations – to test the hypothesis that trade-related aid is more productive than aid allocated to alternative uses.

Indeed, on Aid for Trade, one might interpret suspension of the Doha negotiations as cutting a laboring horse out of its harness – so as to allow the rest of the team to move forward more expeditiously.

2 Uruguay Round outcome – developing country concerns

The commitment of WTO members to pay particular attention to issues raised by developing countries in the Doha negotiations reflected two widespread perceptions of the Uruguay Round outcome:

- It was unbalanced and more favorable to the interests of developed country members than to developing country members; and
- It created an "implementation problem" more severe than any created previously under the General Agreement on Tariffs and Trade (GATT).

2.1 The unbalanced outcome

As Sylvia Ostry (2002) has explained, when the Uruguay Round Agreements were accepted, their implications were poorly understood and certainly not quantified. So what have developing country WTO members gained from the Uruguay Round?

- After a ten-year phase-in period, quantitative restrictions on imports of textiles and clothing from developing countries were removed, but tariffs continue to remain high on these products.

- The newly tariffied schedules of protection of agriculture have not proven to be less restrictive than the hodgepodge of non-tariff measures they replaced.
- Less noted is the impact of the WTO Agreement on Trade-Related Aspects of Intellectual Property Rights (TRIPS) that dominated the economics of the Uruguay Round Agreements. For the United States and other intellectual property providers, the value of the claims that TRIPS generates is several times larger than the gain to them from all the merchandise trade liberalization agreed upon, including the liberalization of their own restrictions. For countries that use intellectual property established elsewhere, the TRIPS-generated obligation entailed payments several times larger than the gains they were to enjoy from the Uruguay Round package of merchandise import liberalization.[3] Thus there emerged a concern that the basic GATT/WTO norm of reciprocity, or balance, had been violated – developing country members had given more than they received.

2.2 The implementation problem

The Uruguay Round brought into the GATT/WTO system challenges that the original GATT had not taken on. While the politics of agreeing to tariff reductions is difficult, implementing such an agreement does not pose any particular challenge. New tariff schedules are printed and distributed to customs houses.

The Uruguay Round, however, pushed past regulations aimed specifically at international trade into areas of behind-the-border institutions and regulations such as technical and sanitary standards and the protection of intellectual property. While these matters *are* "trade-related," they are much more. They provide the institutional structure of the domestic economy. Moreover, agreements in these areas took a form different from that of traditional agreements to reduce or eliminate barriers. They require that countries' regulations be harmonized to a common standard. For instance, under TRIPS, every WTO member must apply the same standard for defining and protecting intellectual property, and they must vigorously apply that standard to foreign-owned property. The standards required in these new agreements were generally similar to those already in place in developed countries; hence the obligation to change fell most heavily on developing countries.[4]

The implementation of the obligations undertaken in these agreements requires significant institution building, not just removing restrictions. This form of institution building would demand, as expected, significant investments in areas such as facilities, equipment and staff training.

Comparison of these agreements with development project experience has revealed that significant investments would be needed to meet their obligations – easily more than a year's development budget in many of the poorer WTO members. It also revealed that the demands of these agreements – taken in large part from the current practice in the more advanced economies – are not always good development advice. In fact, the expenditures demanded often are not those that maximize trade impact, much less the development or poverty reduction impact of the resources (Finger and Schuler, 2001).

[3] Finger (2002) provides details.
[4] This fact added to the sense of an unbalanced outcome.

The implementation problem also raises the "one-size-fits-all" question. Are multilateral rules, particularly those that are shaped significantly by the interests of more developed countries, a constructive blueprint for development and developing countries?

3 Implementation and Aid for Trade taken up in the WTO

The commitment by WTO members to pay particular attention to issues raised by developing countries – signaled by referring to the negotiations as the "Doha Development Agenda" or DDA rather than the "Doha Round" – is a reflection of how widespread the perception is that the Uruguay Round outcome was unbalanced. As to the implementation of Uruguay Round commitments, WTO ministers agreed at the 2001 Doha Ministerial Conference that they "attach the utmost importance to the implementation-related issues and concerns" (WTO 2001a, para. 12). They provided that, for subjects on which there is a negotiating mandate, implementation would be part of the Doha round negotiation, and that, on other subjects, the relevant WTO bodies would take up implementation issues as a matter of priority.

3.1 Defining the implementation issue

In a separate decision on "*Implementation-Related Issues and Concerns: Decision of 14 November 2001*" (WTO, 2001b), ministers elaborated their conception of the implementation issue. The content of the decision is summarized in Table 3.1.

Table 3.1. Doha Decision on Implementation: Table of Contents by Subject

Subject	Number of items
Use or extension of special and differential treatment provisions:	16
• less discipline on developing country policies	9
• more favorable access for developing country exports	7
Lengthen phase-in or phase-out (for example, sanitary and phyto-sanitary regulations, export subsidies)	10
Review to clarify certain points of the antidumping, subsidies, and TRIPS agreements	8
Technical assistance:	10
• to participate in the WTO or in standards-related international bodies	4
• to implement WTO obligations	6
Reminder that developed countries have a legal obligation under TRIPS Article 66.2 to provide incentives to enterprises and institutions to promote and encourage technology transfer to Least Developed Countries.	1
Total	**37**

As the tabulation indicates, WTO ministers at Doha framed the implementation issue within traditional conceptions of special and differential treatment: market access concessions by developed countries on products of export interest to developing countries; less-than-full reciprocity from developing countries in market access;

lesser application to developing countries of some of the system's generic rules – or at least longer phase-in periods for developing countries to implement such obligations; and expanded trade-related assistance for developing countries. Thus, as the Doha Declaration takes it up, "implementation" becomes "special and differential treatment." Moreover, the Doha Declaration responds to the unbalanced nature of the Uruguay Round outcome rather than to the need to make obligations specific to circumstances and assistance specific to need.

As the Doha negotiations evolved, concerns to make the WTO system more development-supportive sparked a discussion of the possibility that the dimensions of time and place be introduced into WTO obligations. Rather than one-size-fits-all (softened a bit by phase-in periods based on no particular criteria), members began to consider that perhaps obligations could be tailored to objective indicators of situation and need.

Within the traditional bounds of the WTO, this issue offered a considerable challenge. Legal obligations (technically, applicable only to the trade-related dimensions of things) would not only have to spell out the structure of such institutions when the economy achieved development, they would also have to map out the steps and the schedules for building them. Awareness of the difficulty of this challenge is evidenced more by what the international community has decided ***not*** to do through the WTO than by what it has taken on there. The Doha Ministerial Declaration had announced agreement to undertake preliminary work on four new subjects for possible multilateral agreements: investment, competition policy, government procurement, and trade facilitation. These would be taken up as negotiating issues only if the Members reached agreement to do so at a future meeting. The Doha Work Program agreed in July 2004 (WTO, 2004) dropped all but trade facilitation from the negotiating agenda and limited coverage of the negotiations on trade facilitation to "clarify and improve relevant aspects of Articles V, VIII and X of GATT 1994." (These articles take up *Freedom of Transit*,[5] *Fees and Formalities connected with Importation and Exportation*, and *Publication and Administration of Trade Regulations*.[6])

3.2 Obligation linked to assistance

Though implementation of new rules in the multilateral trading system is a bound obligation, implementation assistance had been urged but not provided for in several of the Uruguay Round Agreements. This imbalance fostered a discussion of how the legal obligation to implement might be linked to a legal obligation or other concrete commitment to provide assistance. It prompted former Secretary-General of the UN Conference on Trade and Development (UNCTAD) Rubens Ricupero (Ricupero, 2000) to suggest that future proposals include an "implementation audit" that would identify the specific investments needed to meet new

[5] This is a matter of particular importance to landlocked countries, whose surface shipments of exports and imports must transit through other countries.

[6] The July 2004 Work Program furthered the shift of WTO attention toward dealing with the implementation requirements of future negotiations rather than resolving those created by the Uruguay Round Agreements. The Work Program devotes only eight lines in a 778 line document to "those elements of the Work Program which do not involve negotiations." (paragraph 1.h)

obligations – so that any agreement could include bound commitments to provide the needed support.

Such audits would do more than identify the implementation costs. They would face up to the reality of the one-size-fits-all issue and they would carry the implementation challenge into the domain of project identification and design, where the question of introducing the dimensions of time and place into multilateral rules would have to be faced.

Perhaps the tightest link relates to "commitments whose implementation would require support for infrastructure development." This language was agreed as part of the language on trade facilitation in the WTO's 2004 Work Program. This further specifies that "developed-country Members will make every effort to ensure support," but "where required support and assistance for such infrastructure is not forthcoming, and where a developing or least-developed Member continues to lack the necessary capacity, ***implementation will not be required***." (WTO 2004, Annex D, para. 6, emphasis added) To the extent that the Doha negotiations addressed the issue of tying implementation assistance to implementation obligations, they did so by relaxing the obligation to implement rather than by tightening the obligation to provide assistance.

3.3 Hong Kong Ministerial Declaration

The work program agreed at Hong Kong in December 2005 (WTO, 2005c) continued the emphasis on issues of interest to developing countries. As to how these issues are perceived, "special and differential treatment" is particularly prominent; the phrase appears 23 times in the 45-page Declaration (including the annexes). By comparison, "liberalize" or "liberalization" appears nine times.

The substance of such treatment includes liberalization of trade in products of export interest to developing countries, including agriculture with an emphasis on cotton, and the commitment by developed country members to provide duty- and quota-free access to imports of most products from LDCs by 2008. Less liberalization by developing countries is also prominent. Examples are smaller coefficients for developing countries on the formulas by which tariff cuts will be determined, and LDCs will be given an additional seven years grace period on meeting the obligations of the existing agreement on Trade-Related Investment Measures (TRIMS).

The word "assistance" appears in the Declaration 34 times. The Declaration continues the consideration of aid or technical assistance to help developing countries participate in negotiations and implement obligations. It also broadens considerably the scope of assistance taken up:

> Aid for Trade should aim to help developing countries, particularly LDCs, to build the ***supply-side capacity and trade-related infrastructure*** that they need to assist them to implement and benefit from WTO Agreements and ***more broadly to expand their trade***. (WTO 2005c, para. 57, emphasis added.)

The same paragraph invites the WTO Director-General to appoint a task force on how to make Aid for Trade operational, and to consult with other relevant organizations and agencies on these matters.

3.4 The negotiations on trade facilitation

The Hong Kong Ministerial Declaration reports that some sixty written submissions have been submitted to the Negotiating Group on Trade Facilitation. These include:

- National Experience papers describing reforms undertaken;
- proposed or suggested measures to improve and clarify the GATT articles covered by the negotiating mandate;
- proposed or suggested provisions for effective cooperation between customs and other authorities on trade facilitation and customs compliance; and
- proposals or suggestions for enhancing technical assistance and support for capacity building on trade facilitation, and for the practical application of the principle of special and differential treatment.

The proposals to clarify and improve the GATT articles provide useful suggestions. For example:

- China (WTO, 2005e): There should be a reasonable interval (for example, at least thirty days) between the publication of regulations and their implementation or enforcement.
- Korea (WTO, 2005f): Much of this paperwork and document-related costs can be reduced if the following suggestions are implemented:
  - Acceptance of commercially available information and copies of documents;
  - Harmonization and standardization of document formats;
  - Use of a "single window" where traders can submit all the necessary documents and data to a single agency (paragraph 7); and
  - Accepting copies of documents in lieu of originals for import and export can also greatly streamline the customs process. Customs can, if necessary, always request the original documents at a later time (paragraph 10).
- Bolivia, Mongolia and Paraguay provided suggestions for streamlining transit trade into landlocked countries, for example by standardizing the documentation requirements for transit through different countries and for different routes through the same country.

3.5 Identifying concrete implementation needs/support

None of the proposals has yet been the subject of an implementation audit. Several members, however, have offered proposals on arrangements to determine the assistance needs of individual developing countries with regard to proposed new obligations.

One of the more elaborate of these is from the European Union (WTO, 2005d). The EU suggests that the WTO and other organizations (the World Bank, World Customs Organization, UNCTAD, Organization for Economic Cooperation and Development (OECD), regional development banks, and others) could establish and operate a "platform" for international cooperation on the provision of technical assistance and capacity building for trade facilitation. The platform would help WTO members take stock of trade facilitation needs in relation to the provisions/obligations emerging from negotiations. It would also help each eligible member identify if and what kind of technical assistance and support for capacity building would be needed to support implementation over what time frame.

The United States has offered a similar suggestion without mention of a specific platform:

> The unique situation of each individual Member regarding implementation of the proposed commitment could be addressed early in the negotiations through the use of diagnostic tools providing an assessment of specific needs, which can lead to appropriate and workable transition periods combined with assistance targeted at individual situations (WTO 2005g, Section V).

Switzerland and Pakistan have proposed a system under which each developing country, in cooperation with a bilateral or international agency of its choice, would develop an action plan for implementing new WTO rules. After a 'pledging session,' the action plan and pledged assistance would be reviewed by the WTO Trade Facilitation Committee. Endorsement by the committee would mean acceptance of the rules as legal obligation by the developing member, and the assistance pledges would likewise become legal obligations. If the assistance was not provided, the developing member would be freed of its obligation to implement (WTO, 2005b).

The proposal focuses on making assistance a legal obligation, but implicitly an implementation audit would be part of the preparation of the action plan. The developing member would not want to take on legal obligation to implement until it was confident that implementation of the rule would be a constructive use of resources, the implementation plan was workable, and that the funding was adequate.

So, as far as negotiations were concerned, the flaw in the schemes to conduct implementation audits was not in the underlying ideas; *it was that they were not executed*. The Doha negotiations were under way from 2001 to mid-2006, but no such platform has been created and no such implementation audits were conducted or even proposed – for *any* of the proposals.[7]

Development bank experiences suggest that it would not have been feasible to conduct implementation audits in time to accommodate the Doha Round calendar. The Hong Kong Ministerial Declaration asked that the round be completed in calendar year 2006. But World Bank experience shows that even after project identification, the process of project design and appraisal usually requires 18 months to complete (World Bank, 2005).

Moreover, project identification and preparation presupposes the existence of an overall development strategy (for poorer countries, a Poverty Reduction Strategy Paper or PRSP). Also in the background will be a Country Assistance Strategy (CAS). The CAS, produced by the Bank in co-operation with the government and stakeholders in the country, outlines a program of Bank Group support linked to the country's development strategy; it provides the guidelines for maintaining coherence among the various parts of a development plan.[8] Thus, the U.S. suggestion to examine the unique situation of each individual Member regarding implementation of the proposed rules came too late to be practical.

[7] Perhaps the negotiations work program should have required that each proposal include such an implementation audit.

[8] The World Bank webpage on "The Project Cycle" provides information on the steps in the process and links to information about particular projects. From the Bank's home page, http://www.worldbank.org, click "Projects and Operations," then "Project Cycle."

Box 3.1. Summary of African Group communication on Trade Facilitation (TN/TF/W/33 28 April 2005)

For the African Group, enhanced special and differential treatment, technical assistance, capacity building, and implementation assistance are critical components (paragraph 5).

Trade facilitation needs are enormous; intensive work is needed on how to:

- Reduce transport and communications costs;
- Enhance capacities of customs administrations;
- Better integrate African enterprises and economies into international payments and insurance systems (paragraph 6).

Cost implications of proposals for new commitments should be fully addressed (paragraph 7).

Technical assistance and capacity building should be provided during negotiations to support:

- Identification of research and capacity building proposals;
- Needs assessments and prioritization; and
- Travel for capital-based experts to participate in the negotiations (paragraph 9).

Special and differential treatment should:

- Be legally binding, precise, effective, operational;
- Provide policy space and flexibility;
- Condition implementation on provision by developed countries of assistance that is – in the view of the recipient country – effective, long-term, sustainable, and adequate to implement the new commitments.

The only available alternative would have been to accept the fact that the rules written into a Doha Development Agenda agreement would be unaudited when the negotiations were completed. Members would have had to take decisions on new rules *before* they knew how implementation would be undertaken, how much it would cost, or even if use of such resources made development sense.

Looking to future negotiations, unless each proposal is accompanied by an implementation audit, there are only two possibilities for creating a link between obligation to implement the new rules and obligation to provide assistance:

- The African Group proposal (WTO 2005h, summarized in Box 3.1). Implementation would not be an automatic legal obligation. Acceptance of the new rules or standards as legal obligations would be taken up as a follow-up negotiation of review of usefulness and cost, conditioned on provision by developed countries of assistance that is – in the view of the recipient country – effective, long-term, sustainable and adequate to implement the new commitments.
- Make implementation of unaudited obligations, as in the Uruguay Round Agreements, a legal obligation. A developing country member would be able to request an extension of implementation deadlines; discussion of that request would include an implementation audit and take up the provision of assistance.[9]

[9] This would be to allow for requests for permission from the WTO membership for extension of deadlines for implementation.

The first of these, the African Group proposal, follows the thrust of the July 2004 Work Program. The second parallels the Uruguay Round outcomes that have already proven unsatisfactory.

3.6 The Aid for Trade Task Force Report

The WTO Task Force on Aid for Trade tabled its final recommendations at a meeting of the General Council on 27–28 July 2006, the same meeting at which the General Council voted to temporarily suspend the Doha round negotiations. The mandate of the Task Force was to "provide recommendations on how to operationalize Aid for Trade" (WTO 2006b, para. 57). Their recommendations are listed in summary form in Annex A to this chapter.

The Task Force repeats familiar exhortations: recipients and donors should pay more attention to trade; donors to be guided by priorities identified by recipient countries; beneficiary country ownership; mainstreaming of trade into aid and development plans; coordination and harmonization among donors; South-South cooperation; attention to regional as well as country needs; accountability; results-based management; assignment of responsibilities; and monitoring and evaluation.

The Task Force recommends an annual debate in the WTO General Council on Aid for Trade. This debate is to be supported by a published global review of Aid for Trade by a WTO monitoring body. The global report should draw on Aid for Trade reports from recipient and donor countries, regional entities, international agencies, and the private sector. The recipient country reports should cover mainstreaming, formulation of trade strategies, needs assessments, donor responses, implementation, and impact of Aid for Trade programs and projects. Donor reports should cover mainstreaming, amount of funds dedicated to Aid for Trade, how they intend to meet Aid for Trade announced targets, and Aid for Trade categories covered by their programs. The information required should be mandated – "possibly," the Task Force qualifies – by WTO notification requirements.

Perhaps the major shortcoming of the Task Force is that it did little to "operationalize" its recommendations. The Task Force also does no more than to suggest that "mainstreaming" and "coordination" be "strengthened" or "made effective." In a document that provides 32 bulleted recommendations, the words "effective" or "effectively" occur 21 times; the word "strengthen" occurs 18 times.

Similarly, the recommendations for WTO monitoring of Aid for Trade are rich in "What," lean on "How" or even "Who" is to execute each of them. As a step toward "operationalizing," in Annex A, I have attempted to identify the "Who" – on whom responsibility for executing each recommendation might fall. For some, the "Who" is obvious; "recipient countries," for example, should mainstream trade into their development strategies. For others, it is difficult to identify the "Who". Who, for instance, should "establish a system of data collection and analysis at country level"?

Identifying the "Who" for the elements in the WTO monitoring of Aid for Trade suggests that a lot of work is implied.[10] There are, for example, 174 recipient countries and 28 donors (listed in a database of trade-related projects run by the

[10] There is no indication in the report that the Task Force examined even this elementary dimension of making its recommendations operational.

WTO and the OECD – see WTO/OECD, 2007) that would be obligated to provide country-level reports, 33 regional trade agreements (listed on the WTO web page) that might be expected to provide reports, plus international organization reports, and private sector reports. Though not listed by the Task Force, it would likely prove difficult to refuse inclusion of civil society reports. A WTO monitoring body would pull together information from all these reports in order to provide a global report – this to support an annual debate on Aid for Trade in the WTO General Council.

The Task Force report displays the dominance of intermediaries'[11] values. These values have also heavily influenced the Integrated Framework, which in turn has suffered from a lack of ownership by either donors or beneficiaries. In the report's list of thirteen "major challenges/gaps,"[12] the first twelve are administrative matters such as mainstreaming, linking mechanisms, monitoring, coordination, and coherence. (To take the most politically correct of the list, "mainstream" is an intermediary's value – something intermediaries insist developing country governments must do in order to correctly manage their people's interests.) "Resources for infrastructure and enterprise capacities" comes twelfth; only "uneven country coverage" comes lower. Aid for Trade requirements must satisfy a dozen or so administrative criteria that the intermediaries specify, while also displaying beneficiary country ownership and minimizing administrative costs. Other stipulations, such as "focus, *inter alia*" (WTO 2006b, p. 10), are non-sequiturs.

4 Aid for Trade: progress and contributors

The international community has recently expressed considerable concern over support for implementation of WTO obligations. As a result, the general level of Aid for Trade has substantially increased. Table 3.2, compiled from the WTO/OECD Trade Capacity Building Database, shows, however, that the increase in Aid for Trade amounts has not reached the Least Developed Countries (LDCs) – both the percentage of the total Aid for Trade and the absolute amount has declined for LDCs since 2001.

An analysis of the WTO/OECD Database brings out many important dimensions:

(a) Aid for Trade has increased significantly for the more advanced developing countries and less rapidly for sub-Saharan countries. For the LDCs, Aid for Trade was less in 2004 than in 2001.

(b) There are many providers. The Database lists 26 regional and multilateral international funding agencies and 28 donor countries, including four developing and transition economies.

(c) Aid for Trade covers a wide range of activities, many involving complex processes and requiring specialized knowledge. Activities are listed in Table 3.3. The two major categories are Trade Policy and Regulations, and Trade Development. A large part of aid that falls in the former relates to the capacity to participate in the WTO and in regional trade organizations. The latter includes a wide range of activities intended to help traders identify markets and develop attractive products, communicate with other businesses, and generally become a part of the international business network.

[11] Generally taken to mean multilateral and bilateral development agencies.
[12] The Task Force does not identify "To whom" or "In what" these challenges/gaps apply.

Table 3.2. Aid for Trade: Amounts and Growth 2001–04

Developing countries except sub-Saharan Africa	US$ millions				Percentage change 2001 to 2004 (%)
	2001	2002	2003	2004	
Trade Development	991	1,117	1,545	1,744	76
Trade Policy and Regulations	595	590	814	685	15
Trade Development, Policy and Regulations	1,587	1,707	2,359	2,428	53
Infrastructure	7,008	7,921	7,230	12,123	73
Sub-Saharan Africa					
Trade Development	363	215	503	440	21
Trade Policy and Regulations	55	67	120	127	133
Trade Development, Policy and Regulations	418	282	623	567	36
Infrastructure	2,138	1,306	2,100	2,680	25
Developing countries except LDCs					
Trade Development	987	1,106	1,699	1,870	89
Trade Policy and Regulations	524	586	778	716	37
Trade Development, Policy and Regulations	1,511	1,693	2,476	2,586	71
Infrastructure	7,196	7,751	6,620	11,507	60
Least Developed Countries					
Trade Development	368	226	349	314	–15
Trade Policy and Regulations	126	71	157	96	–24
Trade Development, Policy and Regulations	494	297	506	410	–17
Infrastructure	1,951	1,476	2,710	3,295	69

Source: WTO/OECD Doha Development Agenda Trade Capacity Building Database. http://tcbdb.wto.org/

(d) It is difficult to draw a line between Aid for Trade and other forms of assistance. Improved roadways, for example, may be intended to support rural development, but will also increase the likelihood that products will reach distribution centers that are connected with international trade. Because it is difficult to draw this line, the WTO/OECD Database also tabulates assistance for infrastructure – transport, storage, communications, and energy – without attempting to isolate what will support increased trade and what will not directly relate to trade. It is hard to separate trade facilitation from economy-wide improvements of transport and communications infrastructure. Moreover, infrastructure includes improvements of ports and airports and of roads and railways that connect directly to trade-related activities. Hence a significant but unidentifiable amount of support for infrastructure is directly trade-supportive.

(e) Assistance to Least Developed Countries for infrastructure increased 2001–2004 – by almost 70 percent. Twenty-two percent of assistance for infrastructure went to LDCs in 2004, as compared with less than 15 percent in the other two categories.

(f) Improvements in the areas of trade facilitation that the Doha Work Program includes are often a part of larger projects. As complements to broader improvements of facilities and enterprise capacities, they are more effective than they would be as stand-alone efforts.

Table 3.3. Activities reported in WTO/OECD capacity building database

Trade policy and regulations	Trade development
• Trade mainstreaming in PRSPs/development plans	• Business support services and institutions
• Technical barriers to trade (TBT)	Public-private sector networking
• Sanitary and phytosanitary measures (SPS)	• E-commerce
• Trade facilitation procedures	• Trade finance
• Customs valuation	• Trade promotion strategy and implementation
• Tariff reforms	• Market analysis and development
• Regional trade agreements (RTAs)	• Infrastructure
• Accession	• Transport and storage
• Dispute settlement	• Communications
• Trade-related intellectual property rights (TRIPS)	• Energy
• Agriculture	
• Services	
• Tariff negotiations – non-agricultural market access	
• Rules	
• Training in trade negotiation techniques	
• Trade and environment	
• Trade and competition	
• Trade and investment	
• Transparency and government procurement	
• Trade education/training	

With more than fifty providers, there are a large number of programs for Aid for Trade. The following section reviews three of the key existing multilateral programs that can provide lessons for how Aid for Trade could be administered. These are the Joint Integrated Technical Assistance Programme (JITAP), the Integrated Framework for Trade-Related Technical Assistance to LDCs (IF), and the Standards Trade Development Facility (STDF). The WTO has been an active partner in each of these initiatives. The first two programs cover a wide range of trade-related needs, while the STDF deals specifically with product standards.

4.1 JITAP

JITAP is a joint endeavor of the WTO, UNCTAD and the International Trade Centre (ITC), focused on responsibilities associated with WTO processes and obligations. It was created in response to a call from African trade ministers, in October 1994, for help to strengthen their capacity to participate in the WTO and to take advantage of trade opportunities. The program also provides support to develop strategies to help potential exporters.

One function of JITAP is to facilitate communication within the beneficiary country among the parties that have responsibilities for trade-related matters. This responds to a perception that Geneva delegates would benefit from closer contact with ministries and other interested parties at home who have operational responsibility in those areas in which the international community is considering rules, for example, the agriculture and health ministries and authorities responsible for sanitary and phyto-sanitary regulations. The effort involves organizing groups of interested parties and facilitating communication among them. For example, the

Botswana National Committee on Trade Policy and Negotiations has twenty-two members from the public sector, private and para-statal enterprises and organizations, academia, trade unions, research organizations, and consumer organizations. To support wider discussion, JITAP supports seminars and the training of trainers on WTO and trade-related issues. It also helps to create national Reference Centers for trade and WTO information: trade-related publications, and on-site links to trade-related websites and databases.

Another way in which JITAP helps a country to manage its WTO-related affairs is through the creation of Enquiry Points required by the agreements on Technical Barriers to Trade (TBT), Sanitary and Phytosanitary Standards (SPS), TRIPS, and General Agreement on Trade in Services (GATS), and similarly to meet the notification requirements of WTO agreements.

Kenya's assessment of its participation in JITAP (presented at UNCTAD XI) reports that trade issues are now widely discussed in government, private sector and civil society. This networking has provided widespread sharing of positions taken, contributed to Kenya's active participation in the third, fourth, and fifth WTO Ministerial Conferences, and strengthened linkages between the Geneva delegation and at-home ministries. Though the government's report was perhaps too modest to add the point, this constructive participation begins with capable persons – where these are present, the information-gathering and networking that JITAP supported proved to be supportive and productive.

4.2 Integrated Framework

The IF was inaugurated in October 1997 by six multilateral institutions: International Monetary Fund (IMF), ITC, UNCTAD, UN Development Programme (UNDP), World Bank and the WTO. Its original purpose was to help least developed countries identify their needs for trade-related assistance and to bring the governments together with potential donors to develop a program of support. It has since been modified to include support to help LDCs "mainstream" trade into national development plans such as Poverty Reduction Strategy Papers (PRSPs).

One of the IF's major instruments is the preparation of Diagnostic Trade Integration Studies (DTIS). These identify needs for trade-related assistance and link the trade support program to the country's overall development and poverty reduction strategy. The DTIS for Lesotho, for example, covers a wide range of issues, from macroeconomic policy to constraints on the expansion of the local garments industry. It pointed out many problems. The small sampling below illustrates the range of the issues covered:

- The government does not maintain a centralized inventory of ongoing support projects;
- The analytical capacity of some donors' local representatives does not include trade issues; and
- Expansion of the local garments industry depends on improved infrastructure – including electricity, telecommunications, and water. But Lesotho is a small, landlocked country whose infrastructure must necessarily be integrated with that of South Africa. Hence improved trade is complicated by the need for international arrangements.

Before a DTIS is undertaken, the country organizes a Steering Committee that brings together trade-related interests in the country. In Cambodia, for example, the DTIS was discussed at a national workshop. Based on the discussions at the workshop, in which the major public and private stakeholders participated, a program of technical assistance was formulated. The main areas in which Cambodia requested technical assistance included macroeconomic policy and trade policy. Areas identified in the latter included WTO accession, institutional capacity, customs and transport, and sectoral activities in agriculture, handicrafts, fisheries, garments, tourism, and labor services.

An IF Trust Fund was created in 2001 with two funding instruments, Window I and Window II, with voluntary contributions from multilateral and bilateral donors. Window I finances the preparation of the DTIS, while Window II provides "bridging money" for small assistance or capacity building activities that are part of the DTIS Action Matrix. Funding of the Action Plan comes primarily from bilateral donors as part of the overall response to national poverty reduction strategies.

In September 2005, the World Bank-IMF Development Committee endorsed a proposal for an enhanced Integrated Framework, including expanding its resources and scope and making it more effective. Subsequently, a task force made up of donors and LDCs was set up to develop proposals for such an enhancement. The recommendations of the task force were adopted in July 2006.[13] The task force recognized the lack of LDC ownership and the failure of the IF to follow its extensive diagnostic work with financial support. Chief among its recommendations were (a) the creation of a new independent executive secretariat in Geneva, administratively housed in the WTO Secretariat, which would take operational decisions; (b) significant strengthening of capacity in each LDC recipient country, funded by the IF, to manage the IF process; and (c) increased funding.

The output of the Integrated Framework program is listed in Annex B.

4.3 Standards Trade Development Facility

Market access programs such as the U.S. African Growth and Opportunity Act (AGOA) and the EU's Everything But Arms (EBA) initiative have provided opportunities for poorer countries to expand their exports of food products. However, lack of capacity to certify food products as meeting international standards has sometimes prevented such opportunities from being exploited. To complement such market access initiatives, five international agencies (UN Food and Agriculture Organization (FAO), World Organization for Animal Health (OIE), World Bank, World Health Organization (WHO), and WTO) in 2002 established the Standards Trade Development Facility (STDF) to assist developing countries augment their public and private capacities to implement sanitary and phytosanitary standards, particularly for agricultural products destined for international markets. The WTO accepted to serve as the executing institution. The philosophy behind the program is that meeting the demands of international trade will not only increase export earnings, it will also help to elevate the standards of human and animal health at home.[14]

[13] WTO 2006a.

[14] This discussion is based on information from the STDF website (2007).

The STDF website[15] lists 18 projects that the facility has supported. The larger part of them are for project preparation, for example, to assist the government of Cameroon in the preparation of a project on the basis of technical assistance needs identified by the government and submitted to the WTO's SPS Committee (WTO, 2003b). The project is intended to use FAO-developed guidelines to evaluate the food control system in Cameroon and to design an enhancement project.

Another example includes the STDF supporting the development of a regional and national training program for delegates to the World Organization for Animal Health (OIE) and to deliver this training through the regional offices of the OIE. The project aims to ensure greater coordination at the regional level between STDF partners, both in regular activities and in the delivery of technical assistance. A pilot workshop was held in April 2005 and the training program was subsequently integrated into WTO regional workshops in 2005 and 2006.

4.4 Pluses and minuses

The JITAP and the STDF have been generally well-received; the Integrated Framework less so. Interviews conducted with users of these programs raised the following points:

JITAP's efforts to bring together trade ministries and other parties with an interest in trade, and specifically the trade-related areas that WTO agreements now regulate, was welcomed – and met a perceived need. People in government found it useful to draw together the interested parties, to collect information and to form their own positions in light of the information and the inputs from interested parties. Likewise, the focus of support on requirements in the WTO agreements (such as enquiry points and notifications) was welcomed. In some cases, the notifications required by the WTO agreements spurred the tabulation of needed information on the government's own actions that had not previously been collected. Respondents pointed out that JITAP's scope did not extend into the much-needed areas of building enterprise capacities and infrastructure.

Comments on the Integrated Framework also indicated that the creation of steering committees of trade-related interests had been valuable, as it had broadened awareness of potential donors. Less favorable comments pointed to the complicated management structure: an overview Steering Committee with representatives from agencies, donors and Least Developed Countries; an Integrated Framework Working Group chaired by the WTO and made up of the six participating agencies and of each least developed country. (The DAC/OECD Secretariat is an observer.)

Others acknowledged that while the DTIS assembled information well, the studies have added little to information already available, such as the problems listed above that were reported in the Lesotho study.[16] LDC governments have valued the networking that resulted from bringing together ministries and other interested parties in the DTIS process and in the national workshops and follow-up discussions that were part of the process, though the JITAP accomplished this with a much

[15] As of 24 March 2006.

[16] A somewhat cynical comment from a person with country responsibilities in a development agency: "The Integrated Framework has been a good way for consultants to learn their business; it has not added much to what I know about [country name]."

smaller administrative overhead. The impact here was more to bring trade interests together than to communicate links between trade reforms and the national development strategy.

These comments are consistent with the tabulation in Annex B of the output of the Integrated Framework. For instance, the provision of assistance for supply capacity of $333,300 to support the cultivation of citrus and patchouli in Burundi was allocated for activities that were already on the government's program when the DTIS was conducted.

As to the nature of the projects supported, of the sixteen projects listed on the Integrated Framework website, ten provided support for negotiating capacity, information and networking, and two supported the development of export plans for particular sectors – again the sort of support the JITAP furnished with a smaller administrative overhead. Four IF Window II projects were to augment the supply capacity of enterprises.

5 Evaluation – negative points

The Aid for Trade discussion spans two objectives: first, to motivate sources of funds, and second, to ensure the effective use of these funds. We should keep in mind that the two objectives are related, but different.

5.1 Uruguay Round outcome

The development issues that resulted from the Uruguay Round stem from the following characteristics of the Round's outcome:

- Imbalance, measured in real economics as well as in the mercantilist concessions given and received between developed and developing countries.
- Implementation of new areas of agreements requires significant amounts of money.
- The demands of the agreements – taken in large part from current practice in the more advanced economies – are not always good development advice.

The third point is sometimes labeled as the "one-size-fits-all" problem. It arises because the international community has applied regulations through the WTO to institutions that constitute the basic structure of the economy, not just the interface between the domestic economy and the international economy.

5.2 The Doha negotiations have not faced the one-size-fits-all issue

The one-size-fits-all problem has received minimal attention. There are proposals for platforms or processes at which the legal obligation to implement new rules would be matched with the obligation to provide assistance. However, little attention has been paid to determining if such rules can in reality be tailored to a specific time and place, so that the investments they demand for implementation will have a reasonable development payoff.

Though there were proposals for the required implementation audits, given what we know from development institution experience, it would have been impossible to conduct these within the agreed Doha Round calendar. Whether or not the agreed rules make development sense, or how they might make development sense in each developing member's situation, could only have been taken up after the rules were written. If the WTO negotiations resume in this manner, decisions on which reforms will be mandated will not be informed by needs assessments or cost estimates. Each developing country would have to take decisions on what it accepted as mandated reforms without knowledge of the usefulness of the reforms and the cost implications for implementation.

The Task Force recommendations for operationalizing Aid for Trade did not address how WTO obligation and implementation assistance might be linked. They did not examine how to make operational the implementation assistance specified in WTO agreements.

5.3 What has gone before? Or what happens outside of Geneva?

The proposals in the Doha negotiations display inexperience concerning what development institutions do and a lack of knowledge of what has gone before. These proposals for platforms and process include the following steps:

- Inventory of WTO proposals for trade facilitation rules;
- Assessment of countries' needs and priorities;
- Inventory of trade-related assistance under way or committed;
- Determination of the appropriate sequencing of the needed measures;
- An Action Plan – including appropriate special and differential treatment; and
- Pledging meeting with donors.

The revised Action Plan expresses commitments by the member who will implement the plan and the donors who will provide assistance.[17]

Not surprisingly, these are identical to the steps agreed in 1997 when the Integrated Framework was created. The owners of the Integrated Framework have already revised it once and are currently doing it again – to expand it and to make it more effective. Its lack of performance may be related to its structure rather than its execution or money. And, as explained above, the mode that negotiations have followed means that decisions as to which obligations will be included in an agreement must be made before their usefulness and costs can be assessed.

5.4 Needs assessments

A major flaw in these proposals is that they include "needs assessment" as a basic element. Experience with the Integrated Framework and other Aid for Trade instruments suggests that (i) needs assessments are not needed; (ii) are impossible to do; (iii) duplicate what development institutions do; and (iv) that when these assessments are done, they are ignored.

5.4.1 *Not needed*

Development institution staff with country responsibilities commented that the needs assessments provided by the Integrated Framework DTIS provided them

[17] The Switzerland-Pakistan proposal would take up the legal obligation of the matter by submitting the Revised Action Plan and Pledges to the WTO Trade Facilitation Committee for review. After TFRC review, the obligations – Action Plan and Pledges – become binding.

with no new information. They are already aware of many needs and the more important step was project identification and design. The operations that the Integrated Framework Window II financed were not newly identified by the Integrated Framework needs assessment; in fact, twelve of the sixteen were projects similar to those supported by JITAP, which had no needs assessment component.

The self-examinations of implementation of the WTO TBT and SPS agreements have brought to light a number of things that need fixing. The next important step is project identification and design. To the extent that "needs" are to be identified, any person with operating responsibilities can provide immediately a long list. The issue, therefore, was not to determine where money is needed, but to determine how the limited funds can be put to use in the most productive and efficient way. Project design and cost-benefit analysis therefore become relevant tools for this allocation.

5.4.2 *Impossible to do*

World Bank staff have attempted to work from the perspective of identifying "gaps" between needs and resources available. These people are dedicated to development and poverty reduction, and by technical competence they are at the top of their field. To determine a dollar amount, they resorted to "gap" models and these models have been shown, by their own research, to misrepresent the development process.[18] Negotiating proposals pass over this problem by stating that "in-depth analysis" is needed. But experience indicates time and again that the resources and technology to do this do not exist.

5.4.3 *What development institutions do*

The challenge that negotiators face is to write these multilateral rules and obligations and tie them down to the specifics of each individual country's situation. Though some proposals acknowledge the need for "in-depth analysis," the discussion at the WTO has made no progress as to how to fit obligations to specific country situations.[19]

Development institutions, on the other hand, do this on a regular basis – apply legal obligations to the specifics of the individual countries. To a development institution, legal obligation is always country and project specific. For example, the World Bank may support education in both Senegal and in Mali. However, in Senegal, it is used to train teachers, while in Mali, support is for building schoolhouses. Or the World Bank may have an education project in one country but not in the other.

Each loan contract will impose obligations on the receiving country. It will include measures that the government and the Bank have agreed are appropriate to monitoring the progress and the effect of the project. It is always the result of a long process of project identification and design in which both the Bank and the government have taken an active role together.

18 These experiences are reviewed by Easterly (2005).

19 Consider the following exercise in geometry: *Given line segment A-B and point C (that does not lie on line A-B), construct a perpendicular bisector to A-B that passes through C.* Generally speaking, you can construct a perpendicular bisector to A-B, or a bisector to A-B that passes through C, but not a line that satisfies both conditions. The GATT drew perpendicular bisectors, the development banks pass bisectors through point C. Negotiation is not likely to find a way to do both, simultaneously.

For trade negotiations to work, the "platforms" that the WTO might create will have to duplicate the day-to-day work of these development institutions.

5.5 The WTO is not a development institution

Or is it? That statement has become a cliché – a mantra recited to pre-empt criticism as one proposes another extension of WTO rules beyond the management of trade policy further into institutions and regulations that are primarily about the structure of the domestic economy.

Trade facilitation is, of course, "trade-related." Major components of trade facilitation – such as public service efficiency, transportation, and communications – are more about institution-building than about "restriction-removing." Moreover, these are part of the basic structure of an economy; their development dimension is broader than their trade dimension. The ***"more than trade-related"*** nature of these policies and institutions challenges the capacity of the WTO to act as a development institution.

A hopeful reader might want to interpret the Task Force report as a plea for the international community to get serious about building in poorer countries the enterprise capacities and the infrastructure important to doing international business. The Task Force report, however, emphasizes WTO review of other organizations' work. It prominently arrays all the concerns of intermediaries but pays no attention to donor interests. That attitude is not likely to be read as encouraging by institutions and agencies that do have the expertise and the resources needed in this area.

6 Evaluation – positive points

According to data through 2004, the amount of Aid for Trade has increased (see Table 3.2). The amount of assistance for infrastructure, which is impossible to separate from Aid for Trade, has also increased. Have developed countries honored their Uruguay Round commitment to provide implementation assistance in exchange for developing countries taking on new obligations? It is impossible to answer the question. Because there have been no implementation audits on the Uruguay Round obligations, it is impossible to say if the amount of Aid for Trade provided has been sufficient to finance the investments needed to meet these obligations.

For sub-Saharan African countries, the amount of Aid for Trade increased in 2001–2004, but less so than Aid for Trade to other developing countries. For LDCs, the amount of Aid for Trade has not increased, but the amount of assistance for infrastructure has increased. It is not possible to isolate the amount of this investment in infrastructure that solely increases the countries' capacities to produce tradable goods and services.

6.1 Sorting out trade facilitation proposals where a multilateral rule might be helpful

The WTO Secretariat has compiled a useful list of proposals made in the Doha negotiations on trade facilitation (WTO, 2005i). The tabulation summarizes some 60 submissions and covers 82 pages.

For some of the items on the list, binding commitments might be workable and useful; publication of laws and regulations, and establishment of enquiry points, for example.[20] In other instances, such as training facilities and preparation and dissemination of a code of conduct for officials, the benefit will be from the effect of these actions rather than from the actions themselves. A single window for customs clearance should reduce clearance time and cost. It would not, however, do so if, behind that window, the same inefficient processes existed as before. The relevant performance measures here are time and cost of overall improvement in efficiency, not performance of a mandated action.

In a recent paper, Jean Christophe Maur has provided the beginnings for sorting proposals where binding commitments might be workable and useful (Maur, 2006). It might be productive to carry on such work.

6.2 Is there a need for legal obligation to spark reform?

The GATT legal system has been a useful mechanism for developed countries to reduce their trade barriers. It provided a mechanism to organize export interests as an effective force against the import-competing interests that had dominated trade politics.

Liberalization in developing countries has been in great part sparked by the realization, country-by-country, that integrating their economies would provide a needed stimulus and source of discipline for their economies to achieve the levels of productivity that other countries had achieved. There is already interest in developing countries in improved trade facilitation. The Aid for Trade provision in the Hong Kong Ministerial Declaration was a developing country initiative, put forward to advance their integration into the international economy rather than to retard it. This means that whatever multilateral rules the international community might apply should be judged only by their usefulness to guide the construction of useful institutions – not rationalized by the assertion that without *some* rules no reform will be undertaken.

6.3 Ownership

Aid administration has taken on seriously the idea of "ownership." The word conveys a complex meaning, not only of the aid receivers seeing their own interests advanced by the reforms or construction being supported, but that the receivers see – in the actions, the problems and the solutions – something which they are doing for themselves rather than something that is being done for them. Mobilizing local groups to help with project identification, design, and monitoring are critical parts in the programs of bilateral and multilateral institutions.

For the sake of analysis, separate the parties involved in aid as donors, receivers, or intermediaries. The donors are the legislators who provide funds, and behind them the taxpayers who pay the money or ultimately would cover with their taxes

[20] In a recent study of a different subject, Latin American governments' use of safeguards and antidumping to support their recent trade liberalization, my colleague Julio Nogués and I found that the notification requirements of the WTO agreements provided a useful push toward keeping systematic records that were useful for policy managers to direct performance toward their objectives. See (Finger and Nogués, 2005).

the guarantees their national governments provide for the borrowings of development banks. Receivers are the governments of receiving countries, and behind them are the people and enterprises whose lives should be made better by the projects that aid helps to provide. Everyone else involved is an intermediary, including the staffs of the World Bank, UNDP and bilateral development agencies.

Less often noted than receiver ownership is the idea of donor ownership. It is, however, particularly important in motivating the provision of resources. It can also be important for their effective use, such as in the promotion of business-to-business contacts. France, for example, has identified support for the private sector as one of its assistance priorities (WTO/OECD, 2005). The US Trade and Development Agency (USTDA) provides engineering and investment consultants to foreign companies to help them to develop plans for new products, production lines, and other investments (USTDA, 2007).

6.4 Public goods

In its first decades after 1948, the GATT was an institution driven in significant part by systemic interests. Preventing another European war, and later resisting the expansion of the Soviet Union, were important means for the governments who were the GATT's members to gain the authority from their peoples (in the United States, through the formality of a vote by Congress). The WTO, however, is an institution driven by constituent interests. U.S. trade negotiators are guided by seventeen "United States Industry Advisory Committees," mandated by the U.S. Congress because representatives viewed other countries' negotiators as more closely tied to their business interest than were U.S. negotiators.[21]

The WTO is not about "public goods;" it is about bargains that serve constituent interests on both sides. Support for trade-related assistance can more readily be built on identifying reforms that have constituent support in both the donor and the receiver country than on appeals to the need for public goods.

6.5 Mutual interest

Developing countries do not have to depend on accepting WTO legal obligations to motivate assistance for trade facilitation and capacity building. Developed countries do not have to depend on WTO legal obligations to motivate developing countries to reform. Mutual interest is sufficient to motivate both, and is perhaps the best guide for effective use of resources.

6.6 Identify needs

Needs, experience shows, are evident. "Needs assessments" need only focus on making a list. After that, project identification and design are needed. Self-assessment of performance is often sufficient to identify further needs (WTO, 2001c). A 400-word self-assessment from Cameroon of its TBT capacities (WTO, 2000), for instance, has been the basis for a project preparation grant from the STDF.

[21] The transformation from a public or systemic orientation to a constituent orientation is explained in Finger (2005b).

In a recent WTO communication, the government of Egypt reviewed its current transit procedures, its approach to the determination and assessment of fees and formalities connected with importation and exportation, and its rules and procedures for publication and administration of trade regulations (WTO, 2005a). The communication also outlined the government's vision of how these services would be improved in the future. Indeed, the communication indicates that the government in Egypt is aware of its needs and has in hand a program of improvement. The next step should be project identification – design, not more needs assessment.

6.7 Monitoring, evaluation, and coordination

What is needed for this? A new "platform" or increased capacities country by country? Experience suggests the latter. Where JITAP and the Integrated Framework have been judged to be effective are in their contribution to help competent officials in the receiving countries to pull together needed information and to establish networks with interested parties inside and outside of government. The success of the self-assessments of implementation of the TBT Agreement indicates that this is a workable approach.

That aid will often be motivated by the interests of commercial constituents in the donor countries is not a negative. It is, however, a reason to ensure that the capacities exist in receiver countries to determine when the proposed assistance is in the interests of all parties as well. The JITAP and Integrated Framework experiences provide an example of where this can start. Trade Policy Reviews might be undertaken more frequently, with more emphasis on self-assessment and support for such capacity. Outside evaluation (particularly a dispute settlement process in which the complaint came from outside) promotes defensive ownership, not constructive ownership.

As mentioned earlier, there are twenty-six international and twenty-eight bilateral agencies that provide Aid for Trade. That certainly suggests a need for coordination. Again the question is: Should this coordination be provided by a new "platform" or by increased capacities country-by-country? Again, experience suggests the latter as the better alternative. A new platform would not lift national governments from the burden of coordination. Instead, it would provide one more agent that national officials would have to deal with.

Suppose Toyota, in building a new truck factory, was approached by a large number of interested suppliers. Should Toyota tell them to get together and decide which should supply what and let Toyota know what they had decided? Dealing with the suppliers is a management problem that Toyota must take on for itself. Likewise, aid coordination demands building the relevant in-country capacities – resources, sustained commitment, and patience. The Tanzanian Ministry of Finance has an annual "quiet time," April-August of each year, in which it will receive only urgent missions (Birdsall et al., 2006). This fact is often cited as evidence of a coordination problem; one can also see it as part of a solution – a home-grown solution. They are usually the best kind.

7 Putting things together

In discussing how the foregoing relates to a possible agreement on Aid for Trade, I will begin from the recent proposal submitted by Mauritius on behalf of the ACP

Group of WTO members (WTO, 2005j). It is perhaps the most complete of the proposals submitted.

The document starts from a crucial premise. Trade facilitation for the ACP countries is about institutional development: systems, technology, equipment, personnel training, and changes in management culture. It is more about such things than about new trade rules.

The proposal calls for:

- An inter-agency coordinating mechanism and trust fund that would (a) support developing country participation in negotiations; (b) help them to identify their needs and priorities for improved systems, infrastructure, regulations, and so forth; and (c) help them to design improvement projects and to put such things in place.
- A study by the WTO Secretariat that would compile an inventory of available trade facilitation measures and tools, the physical and policy infrastructure needed to put these in place, the costs and time frames for such tasks.

Implicit in the proposals are two interrelated functions for an Aid for Trade agreement: (a) to provide generalized support for developing countries, as in the first point; and (b) to craft a bargain of bound obligations accepted by developing countries in exchange for bound assistance from developed countries.

The latter part of the agreement – a bargain of obligations and assistance – must both isolate proposals that will be productive for developing countries[22] *and* reflect a reliable determination of the costs of putting these reforms in place. Each of these challenges is taken up below.

7.1 Identifying useful reforms

Before the Doha Round negotiations were suspended, the trade facilitation negotiations were moving toward the sorting phase in an effort to identify those proposals that would be useful for *all* members. For example, a communication from Australia, Canada, and the United States tagged proposals on the issue of advanced rulings on customs issues that in their analysis are common to all proposals on this topic; that is, where WTO members who have submitted proposals appear to be agreed (WTO, 2006c). A similar communication from eight members (WTO, 2006d) covers the range of proposals on freedom of transit, again with the purpose of moving toward matters on which agreement is emerging.

7.2 Implementation audits

Less progress has been made in identifying the structures and costs of implementation.

For some of the proposals, the steps needed for compliance (such as publication and periodic review) can be readily determined. Here, the stated obligation is expressive of what must be done to meet the obligation.

The content of the other section, on reduction and simplification of procedures, is more guideline than mandate: "the progressive establishment of a single window,"

[22] Concessions by developing countries in the mercantilist language of negotiations, but beneficial reforms in real economics.

"the use by traders of commercially available information," "Members shall use risk management techniques," "Members shall promote bilateral and regional transit agreements or arrangements."

The bonded transport regimes paragraph provides another example:

> *Bonded transport regime and guarantees:*
> Members shall operate bonded transport regimes that allow the transit of goods through the territory of Members without payment of customs duties or other charges subject to the provision of an appropriate guarantee. Members shall ensure that guarantees required from transit operators are:
> - Reasonable having regard to the conditions of transit and the nature and value of the consignment in question, and limited to the amount of customs debt or other charges which may be incurred in respect of the goods;
> - Designed and applied on a regional or international basis to as great an extent as possible;
> - Released promptly after the completion of the transit operation; and
> - Released in full after the completion of the transit operation (WTO, 2006d).

To determine what must be done to meet an obligation so stated and what it will cost to do so is not a simple matter. If an obligation were worded as these proposals are, operational content might have to be added through dispute settlement process.[23] An additional difficulty is that WTO rules approach what they regulate from the perspective of reducing barriers to sales of foreigners' exports. They provide a means by which foreigners, through their governments, can provide pressure for reforms that will advance their interests, but they do not provide a means for identifying the interests of domestic enterprises, say, in better facilities for moving their exports out of the country.

A quick WTO Secretariat review of reform experiences is not likely to provide the needed information on the structures and resources needed for implementation. Philip Schuler and I, in 1995, spent several months going through World Bank project experience to pin down the implementation costs of the Uruguay Round Agreements (Finger and Schuler, 2001). (This was our initial work on implementation.) We found it impossible to find project experiences that exactly matched the legal obligations in the agreements. The basis for our calculations was that the Uruguay Round Agreements, generally speaking, required countries to upgrade to established international practice. In a general way, the projects the World Bank supported had the same objective. The results provided a reasonable indication of costs, but nothing precise enough to approach the demands of a legal contract; *I will do ___ if you will provide ___ in support*.

As negotiations proceeded, delegates did constructively move toward sorting out proposals on which agreement seemed near. They were remiss, however, not to have begun the more difficult part of a possible obligation-assistance bargain, the implementation audits: What has to be done and what will it cost? If dealing effectively with the implementation issue had meant bound commitments to provide appropriate implementation assistance in exchange for bound obligations,

[23] There have been complaints that, where the dispute settlement process has had to take up the ambiguities of the safeguards agreements, the process has not clarified what a member must do to meet its obligations under the agreement – this being as lesser standard than interpreting the agreement in a way that guides members toward applications that are economically productive. The best sources are Sykes (2003; 2004).

implementation would have been another issue that prevented completion of the round.

7.3 A constructive obligation-assistance bargain

An obligation-assistance bargain will be, of course, only part of a program of Aid for Trade. Trade capacity and infrastructure include much more than the Doha trade facilitation agenda. Moreover, there is no realistic possibility of having reliable implementation audits even for the tabled proposals that members will agree provide useful development guidelines.

An immediate task would be for negotiators to focus on identification of proposals whose operational content is evident, such as the publication and notification rules taken up above. This would be a sorting, in addition to the sorting now going on, among proposals which most members accept as useful versus those on which serious questions remain. Of course, implementation audits should be conducted.

Given the time-frame of the negotiations, negotiators will have to recognize that many of the proposals are unaudited guidelines and treat them as such. Here, the African Group proposal becomes relevant. Acceptance of obligations that add operational specificity to these guidelines will be a country-by-country process, in which implementation audits determine the specificity of what will be done as well as the resource needs.

7.4 Broader commitment to assistance and to development

Even if every proposal on the table had attached a full implementation audit, the scope of an Aid for Trade agreement would have to be much broader than the Doha Round trade facilitation agenda. Beyond the Doha trade facilitation agenda, the Aid for Trade agenda involves building negotiating capacity – capacity for developing countries to manage their affairs with trading partners through the WTO and regional agreements. It also involves infrastructure and enterprise capacities.

Many international and bilateral agencies now provide technical assistance and financing to build such capacities. The problem for developing countries is more to manage their relationships with these agencies than to motivate them to provide assistance.

It might therefore be useful to think of the broader element of a WTO agreement on Aid for Trade as an approach to building this capacity to manage. Recent experience indicates that the most useful support helped government officials responsible for trade-related decisions gather information and build networks of interested parties.

Assessments of what needed to be done that stemmed from in-government reviews of how agreements were being used and to satisfy information requirements likewise proved to be useful – more useful than elaborate "needs assessments" that were often conducted by outsiders and generated no new information.[24] A new platform seems unnecessary. In the end, the responsibility for decisions and for coordination among the many agencies that provide support rests with national

[24] A commentator on an earlier draft pointed out that, if these assessments had been done by local analysts, they would have served to broaden the accessible base of human resources that are knowledgeable on the issues.

officials. A government might want to draw on a particular agency to help it to craft the tools needed for coordinating the inputs from many agencies, but no government will be satisfied with an outside "platform" that takes upon itself or is given the responsibility for such coordination.

A WTO agreement on Aid for Trade would be an expression of the international community's commitment to support development and poverty reduction. This commitment, however, has many other expressions: the Millennium Development Goals, the existence of the development banks, the various national assistance policies, the recent increase in trade-related assistance, and many others. Given the ineffectiveness of the WTO as a venue for addressing even the development problems created by the Uruguay Round Agreements – most recently demonstrated by the matter not being addressed by the WTO Task Force charged to find ways to operationalize Aid for Trade – the development community should perhaps focus elsewhere its efforts to expand trade-related assistance.

ANNEX A: SUMMARY OF WTO AID FOR TRADE TASK FORCE RECOMMENDATIONS (see Section 3.6 in text)

Strengthening the "demand side"

What	Who
A commitment to country ownership and approaches driven by recipient countries	Donor countries, recipient countries, international agencies
Mainstream trade into national development strategies	Recipient countries
Establish national coordination	Recipient countries
Explore the necessity (sic) of establishing an agency for non-LDCs like the IF – but separately funded	Everyone
Urge agencies, donors and governments to work together	Aid for Trade Task Force, the WTO Director-General, everyone?
Urge donors, agencies, regional banks, organizations, to step up efforts to identify regional needs	Not clear
Establish a country-level system of data collection and analysis	Not clear

Strengthening donor "response"

What	Who
Pay more attention to trade issues, strengthen trade expertise	Donor countries, international agencies
Greater donor coordination and harmonization	Ditto
Be guided by priority projects and programs identified by developing countries; follow developing country needs assessments	Ditto
Supply targeted funds for infrastructure and enterprise capacity, but not by shifting funds from WTO implementation or training country officials to manage WTO issues	Ditto

Strengthening the bridge between "demand" and "response"

What	Who
Country level	
Mainstream trade into national development strategies	Recipient countries
Strengthen in-country structures to identify trade-related needs and link to donors; for example, establish a "National Aid for Trade Committee" of stakeholders such as government ministries, private sector, civil society	Recipient countries
Partners commit to contributing to the implementation of recipient country strategies	Donor countries, international agencies
South-South cooperation	Recipient countries, donor developing countries
Promote the involvement of local, regional and private-sector actors	Everyone
Results-based management framework, accountability	Everyone
Regional level	
Strengthen diagnosis, project design for regional, sub-regional, cross-border issues:	Regional organizations, everyone?
Coordinate donor response	Not clear
Assign responsibility for the above	Not clear
Explore the merits of establishing a Regional Aid for Trade Committee among regional organizations and financial institutions to report on needs, monitor and evaluate responses and impacts	Regional organizations and financial institutions?
Global level	
Data collection	OECD/WTO Database(?)
Results-based evaluation	Everyone(?)
Knowledge creation and sharing; e.g., on project impacts, best practice guidelines	Not clear
Some donors might wish to direct contributions through multilateral channels – this could include an IF-type organization for non-LDC	Not clear
Clearing house sessions on particular Aid for Trade themes and groups of countries – to connect needs to donors willing to contribute	Not clear

Strengthening monitoring and evaluation

What	Who
Annual debate on Aid for Trade in the WTO General Council	149 WTO Members, 32 Observer Governments
Periodic global review of Aid-for-Trade by a monitoring body in the WTO, based on reports from: • country level • donors • regional level	174 recipientcountries 27 countries and the European Union All regional organizations and financial institutions?

(continued)

What	Who
Relevant multilateral agencies Private sector	The WTO web page lists 33 regional trade agreements (13 September 2006) WTO/OECD Database lists 26 agency providers
Recipient countries report on: • mainstreaming; • formulation of trade strategies; • Aid for Trade needs; • donor responses; • implementation and impact	174 recipient countries
Donors report on: • funds dedicated to Aid for Trade; • how they intend to meet announced Aid for Trade targets; • Aid for Trade categories covered; • mainstreaming trade into aid programs	27 countries and the European Union
Include assessment of Aid for Trade in donor and recipient Trade Policy Reviews	149 WTO Members
Promote and fund mainstreaming, needs identification, donor response, impact	Potentially everyone
Possibly a notification process for WTO members (legal obligation to submit the reports?)	149 WTO Members, 32 Observer Governments

ANNEX B: INTEGRATED FRAMEWORK ACTIVITIES[25]

Countries are grouped by the most advanced stage of the Integrated Framework process reported: (i) Technical assistance or capacity building activities funded; (ii) DTIS completed; (iii) Concept paper or preliminary mission aide memoire completed; (iv) Mission planned or Integrated Framework process suspended. All amounts are shown in US dollars.

(i) Technical assistance or capacity building (Window II) funded (11 countries):

Burundi
US$215,500 to install an ISO 9000 system among Burundi enterprises.
US$333,300 to support the cultivation of citrus and patchouli.
US$150,000 to support production of PVC tubes.

Cambodia
US$500,000 to establish a team of experts on WTO, ASEAN and related affairs, particularly on intellectual property, commercial law development, trade promotion,

[25] Source: Integrated Framework web page (http://www.integratedframework.org), accessed 14 February 2006.

website development and management. Conduct an export quality fair, training in trade policy and trade negotiation skills inside and outside government.

Djibouti
US$335,000 to develop a strategy and action plan to further expand the tourism industry.

Ethiopia
US$350,000 to augment the government's capacity in trade policy analysis and formation, including creation of a trade documentation and information center.
US$300,000 to develop an export diversification plan with emphasis on laboratories and other requirements to meet export market standards; includes networking among producers, government.

Guinea
US$250,000 to train trainers on WTO and related affairs, conduct workshops for government and non-government interested parties.

Madagascar
US$679,000 to train experts and conduct workshops to improve the capacity of the government to participate in trade policy formation and negotiations.

Malawi
US$524,000 to build capacity for trade policy analysis and negotiation including training, review of existing agreements, website construction.

Mali
US$150,000 to fund a study of the potential of the music industry.
US$500,000 to improve the quality of mangos produced in Mali
US$165,000 to create a unit in the government to administer these projects and to conduct a roundtable on the DTIS.

Mauritania
US$183,000 to develop a plan and pilot project to further develop the fisheries industry.

Nepal
US$665,000 to establish a national trade advisory board, train customs officials, computerize entry points, strengthen TBT and SPS enquiry points.

Yemen
US$350,000 to assist establishment of a Yemen-Saudi Arabia exchange of expertise to build Yemenis' capacity in food standardization and quality control, including food laboratories, for fruits and vegetables.

(ii) DTIS completed (5 countries):

Rwanda: DTIS Final Draft, 1 November 2005.
Lesotho: DTIS completed 20 November 2003.
Senegal: DTIS completed 12 March 2003, Action Matrix 9 June 2003.
Mozambique: DTIS completed; national workshop September 2004.
Zambia: DTIS completed 10 October 2005.

(iii) Concept Paper or Aide Memoire (8 countries):

Benin: Concept note for DTIS, dated April 2004.
Lao PDR: Undated concept paper is the last entry.
Burkina Faso: Aide memoire, 2 July 2005.
Sao Tomé & Principe: Concept paper second draft, 10 June 2004.
Sierra Leone: Aide memoire mission, 4–8 July 2005.
Chad: Aide memoire, 2 June 2004; concept paper undated.
Tanzania: Concept paper undated.
Uganda: Concept paper, mission July 2005.

(iv) Mission planned or Integrated Framework process suspended (3 countries):

Angola: Mission planned for September 2005.
Niger: Mission planned for September 2005.
Eritrea: 16 January 2003, government decided to suspend the Integrated Framework process.

REFERENCES

Anderson, Kym, Will Martin, and Dominique van der Mensbrugghe. 2006. "Doha Policies: Where are the Payoffs?," ch. 3, pp. 43–57 in Richard Newfarmer (ed.), *Trade, Doha and Development: A Window into the Issues*, Washington, D.C.: World Bank.

Birdsall, Nancy, Stewart Patrick, and Milan Vaishnav. 2006. "Reforming US Development Policy: Four Critical Fixes," Washington, D.C.: Center for Global Development.

de Wulf, Luc. 2004. "Ghana," ch. 3, pp. 19–32 in Luc de Wulf and José B. Sokol (eds.), *Customs Modernization Initiatives: Case Studies*, Washington, D.C.: World Bank.

Easterly, William. 2005. "How to Assess the Needs for Aid? The Answer: Don't Ask," paper prepared for the Third AFD/EUDN Conference on "Financing Development: What are the Challenges in Expanding Aid Flows?," Paris, 14 December.

Escobar, Flavio. 2004. "Bolivia," ch. 1, pp. 7–18 in Luc De Wulf and José B. Sokol (eds.), *Customs Modernization Initiatives: Case Studies*, Washington, D.C.: World Bank.

Finger, J. Michael. 2002. "The Doha Agenda and Development: A View from the Uruguay Round," Manila: ADB.

Finger, J. Michael. 2005a. "A diplomat's economics: reciprocity in the Uruguay Round negotiations," *World Trade Review*, 4(1): 27–40.

Finger, J. Michael. 2005b. "The Future of the World Trade Organization: Addressing Institutional Challenges in the New Millennium – A Review," *Journal of World Trade*, 39(4): 795–904.

Finger, J. Michael and Julio J. Nogués. 2005. "Safeguards and Antidumping in Latin American Trade Liberalization: Fighting Fire with Fire," New York and Washington: Palgrave Macmillan and World Bank.

Finger, J. Michael and Phillip Schuler. 2001. "Implementation of Uruguay Round Commitments: The Development Challenge," ch. 7, pp. 115–130 in Bernard Hoekman and Will Martin (eds.), *Developing Countries and the WTO: A Pro-Active Agenda*, UK: Blackwell Publishers.

Hathaway, Dale E. and Merlinda Ingco. 1996. "Agricultural Liberalization and the Uruguay Round," ch. 2, pp. 30–58 in L. Allan Winters and Will Martin (eds.), *The Uruguay Round and the Developing Countries*, Cambridge: Cambridge University Press.

Hudec, Robert E. 1970. "The GATT Legal System: A Diplomat's Jurisprudence," *Journal of World Trade Law*, 4: 615–670.

Hudec, Robert E. 1987. "Developing Countries in the GATT Legal System," London: Trade Policy Research Centre.

Hudec, Robert E. 1999. "The New WTO Dispute Settlement Procedure: An Overview of the First Three Years," *Minnesota Journal of Global Trade*, 8(1): 1–53.

Integrated Framework. 2007. "Homepage," http://www.integratedframework.org/.

JETRO. 2002. "Report on Market Access to Japan: Single Windows for Trade and Port-related Procedures," (in Japanese), Tokyo.

Maur, Jean-Christophe. 2006. "Trade Facilitation: What is the scope for capacity building in the WTO?," Manuscript, UK: Department for International Development.

OECD. 2003. "Quantitative Assessment of the Benefits of Trade Facilitation," TD/TC/WP(2003)31/FINAL, Paris: OECD.

OECD. 2005. "OECD/DAC Project on Trade Facilitation Phase 1: Review of Technical Assistance and Capacity Building Initiatives for Trade Facilitation," Preliminary Draft, Paris: OECD.

Ostry, Sylvia. 2002. "The Uruguay Round North-South Grand Bargain: Implications for Future Negotiations," ch. 10, pp. 285–300 in Daniel M. Kennedy and James D. Southwick (eds.), *The Political Economy of International Trade Law: Essays in Honor of Robert E. Hudec*, Cambridge and New York: Cambridge University Press.

Ricupero, Rubens. 1999. "Integration of Developing Countries into the Multilateral Trading System," pp. 9–36 in Jagdish Bhagwati and Mathias Hirsch (eds.), *The Uruguay Round and Beyond: Essays in Honor of Arthur Dunkel*, Ann Arbor: The University of Michigan Press.

Ricupero, Rubens. 2000. "A Development Round: Converting Rhetoric into Substance," paper presented at the Symposium on "Efficiency, Equity and Legitimacy – The Multilateral Trading System at the Millennium," John F. Kennedy School of Government, Harvard University, Cambridge, Massachusetts, 1–2 June.

Standards and Trade Development Facility. 2007. "Homepage," http://www.standardsfacility.org/.

Sykes, Alan O. 2003. "The Safeguard Mess: A Critique of WTO Jurisprudence," *World Trade Review*, 2(3): 261–95.

Sykes, Alan O. 2004. "The Persistent Puzzle of Safeguards: Lessons from the Steel Dispute," *Journal of International Economic Law*, 7(3): 532–564.

United States Trade and Development Agency. 2007. "Homepage," http://www.tda.gov/.

Yeuter, Clayton. 1999. "Bringing Agriculture into the Multilateral Trading System," pp. 61–77 in Jagdish Bhagwati and Mathias Hirsch (eds.), *The Uruguay Round and Beyond: Essays in Honor of Arthur Dunkel*, Ann Arbor: The University of Michigan Press.

Wilson, John S. 2003. "Trade Facilitation: New Issues in a Development Context," World Bank International Trade Department Trade Note No. 12, Washington, D.C.: World Bank.

Wilson, John S., Catherine L. Mann, and Tsunehiro Otsuki. 2005. "Assessing the Benefits of Trade Facilitation: A Global Perspective," *The World Economy*, 6(06): 841–871.

World Bank. 2005. "Implementation Completion Report (SCL-44440) on a loan in the amount of US $71 million to the People's Republic of China for a container transport project," Report No. 33620, http://www.wds.worldbank.org/external.

World Bank. 2007. "Projects – Project Cycle," http://web.worldbank.org/WBSITE/EXTERNAL/PROJECTS/0,contentMDK:20120731~menuPK:41390~pagePK:41367~piPK:51533~theSitePK:40941,00.html.

WTO. 2000. *Communication from Cameroon on Technical Assistance on TBT*, Committee on Technical Barriers to Trade, G/TBT/W/146, 3 October.

WTO. 2001a. *Ministerial Declaration*, Ministerial Conference, Fourth Session, Doha, 9–14 November 2001, WT/MIN(01)/DEC/1, 20 November.

WTO. 2001b. *Implementation-Related Issues And Concerns*, Ministerial Conference, Fourth Session, Doha, 9–14 November 2001, WT/MIN(01)/17, 20 November.

WTO. 2001c. *Philippines Experience in the Implementation of the TBT Agreement*, Committee on Technical Barriers to Trade, G/TBT/W/166, 26 June.

WTO. 2003a. *Communication from Japan*, G/C.W/465, 10 June.

WTO. 2003b. *Technical Assistance – Communication from Cameroon*, Committee on Sanitary and Phytosanitary Measures, G/SPS/GEN/401, 20 May.

WTO. 2004. *Decision Adopted by the General Council on 1 August 2004*, Doha Work Programme, WT/L/579, 2 August.

WTO. 2005a. *Communication from Egypt*, Negotiating Group on Trade Facilitation, TN/TF/W/75, 15 November.

WTO. 2005b. *Communication from Pakistan and Switzerland on Development-Related Issues in Trade Facilitation*, TN/TF/W/63, 19 September.

WTO. 2005c. *Draft Ministerial Declaration*, Ministerial Conference, Sixth Session, Hong Kong, 13–18 December 2005, Doha Work Programme, WT/MIN(05)/W/3/Rev. 2, 18 December.

WTO. 2005d. *Communication from the European Communities*, Negotiating Group on Trade Facilitation, TN/TF/W/46, 9 June.

WTO. 2005e. *Communication from the People's Republic of China*, Negotiating Group on Trade Facilitation, TN/TF/W/26, 21 March.

WTO. 2005f. *Communication from Korea*, Negotiating Group on Trade Facilitation, TN/TF/W/18, 16 March.

WTO. 2005g. *Communication from the United States*, Negotiating Group on Trade Facilitation, TN/TF/W/13, 4 February.

WTO. 2005h. *Communication from the African Group*, Negotiating Group on Trade Facilitation, TN/TF/W/56, 22 July.

WTO. 2005i. *WTO Negotiations on Trade Facilitation – Compilation of Members' Proposals*, Negotiating Group on Trade Facilitation, TN/TF/W/43/Rev.4, 31 October.

WTO. 2005j. *Communication from Mauritius on behalf of the ACP Group*, Negotiating Group on Trade Facilitation, TN/TF/W73, 10 November.

WTO. 2005k. *Communication from the African Group*, Negotiating Group on Trade Facilitation, TN/TF/W/33, 28 April.

WTO. 2006a. *An Enhanced Integrated Framework*, Report of the Chairman of the Task Force on an Enhanced Integrated Framework, WT/IFSC/W/15, 29 June.

WTO. 2006b. *Recommendations of the Task Force on Aid for Trade*, Aid for Trade Task Force, WT/AFT/1, 27 July.

WTO. 2006c. *Communication from Australia, Canada, and the United States*, Negotiating Group on Trade Facilitation, TN/TF/W/80, 17 February.

WTO. 2006d. *Communication from Armenia, Canada, the European Communities, the Kyrgyz Republic, Mongolia, New Zealand*, Negotiating Group on Trade Facilitation, TN/TF/W/79, 23 February.

WTO/OECD. 2005. "2005 Joint WTO/OECD Report on Trade-Related Technical Assistance and Capacity Building," http://www.oecd.org/dataoecd/27/4/11422694.pdf.

WTO/OECD. 2007. "Doha Development Agenda Trade Capacity Building Database," http://tcbdb.wto.org/

4 Financing International Public Goods: A Framework to Address Aid for Trade

DIRK WILLEM TE VELDE

1 Introduction

Aid for Trade has rapidly emerged as an important topic for those interested in both aid and trade.[1] It became firmly established as a concept when the World Trade Organization's (WTO) Sixth Ministerial Conference in Hong Kong in December 2005 led to the set-up of a Task Force on Aid for Trade.

The Task Force reported to the WTO membership in July 2006. Part C of its recommendations reads:

> Additional, predictable, sustainable and effective financing is fundamental for fulfilling the Aid for Trade mandate. The effectiveness of the following recommendations for operationalising Aid for Trade requires substantial additional targeted resources for trade-related programs and projects as pledged at the WTO's Hong Kong Ministerial Conference,[2] and against the background of the broader international commitment at the UN's Monterrey Conference and the G8 Summits in Gleneagles and St Petersburg to significantly scale up development assistance by 2010. The Task Force urges the Director-General to seek confirmation from donors and agencies that funds are readily available for the implementation of the Aid for Trade initiative and as part of his mandate to consult on "appropriate mechanisms to secure additional financial resources for Aid for Trade". In order to measure additionality and the adequacy of funding available to meet the Aid for Trade needs of developing countries, including those associated with a successful completion of the DDA, an account of what is being done today needs to be established as part of that process. The Task Force urges donors and agencies to provide the necessary information in order to make it possible for the Director-General to fulfil his mandate (WTO, 2006).

[1] See ODI (2006) for references to the literature.

[2] In Hong Kong, Japan announced spending on trade, production and distribution infrastructure of US$10 billion over three years, the U.S. announced Aid for Trade grants of US$2.7 billion a year by 2010, and the EU and its member states announced trade-related spending of EUR2 billion per year (up by EUR600 million) by 2010.

The author is grateful to Massimiliano Calì, Martina Garcia, Sheila Page, Lauren Phillips, and Keith Noble-Nesbitt for their comments and contributions to this chapter. The chapter is based on a paper funded by ILEAP (ILEAP, 2006), which benefited from comments by Hugo Cameron and Dominique Njinkeu.

Despite the laudable results of the Task Force, little is known about the precise operationalization of Aid for Trade. This chapter addresses the issue of "additional targeted resources for trade-related programs and projects" from an international public goods perspective. In particular, while it is important to consult on "appropriate mechanisms to secure additional financial resources for Aid for Trade," a key issue will also be to understand the purpose of these additional funds and how they will be allocated and spent (often a pre-condition for generating new, additional pledges).

While the literatures on Aid for Trade and (financing) international public goods (IPGs) have largely developed separately, linking both areas has implications for the way we think about Aid for Trade, both in terms of justifying the allocation of resources on trade-related programs and in terms of the financial architecture for Aid for Trade. In this context, it is important to differentiate between the types of trade-related projects and programs. Such projects will have different degrees of international "*publicness*," which, therefore, need different types of approaches.

The literature on IPGs has developed concepts, definitions, and examples of activities that contribute to IPGs (Kaul,1999; Mody and Ferroni, 2002; Kaul, 2003), and justified the use of aid to provide such IPGs on the basis that developing countries would not be in a position to supply these goods from their own resources. The aid financing literature developed the principles of aid systems (OECD Paris Declaration; Rogerson, 2005). The emphasis here is entirely on country-based aid strategies and how they are owned by the host, harmonized across donors, and aligned with developing country programs, with little regard for challenges that span borders.

The current aid system is a hybrid of national aid programs, some of which contribute to IPGs and global funds. Recently, te Velde, Morrissey and Hewitt (2006) suggested that aid for financing needs to take into account the Paris aid principles[3] before aid for public goods initiatives become more entrenched in aid agencies. In contrast, this chapter will suggest that aid programming *will* have to take into account international challenges such as the development of global trade rules, and that these challenges cannot necessarily be solved by fragmented and uncoordinated national aid programs.

The discussions surrounding Aid for Trade can be seen as useful ways to raise the importance of trade in country-based development programs. Thus, those interested in Aid for Trade and public goods need to take into account aid principles in order to get this type of aid to resonate with aid agencies. In contrast, aid agencies concentrating much of their efforts in bilateral programs need to take into account challenges posed by international public goods.

Neither aid nor public goods literatures have considered individual sectors and activities, while the WTO Aid for Trade Task Force recommendations are more explicit, and deal with the "sector" of trade. This chapter applies an IPG financing framework to the specific example of Aid for Trade to inform a possible Aid for Trade architecture. What makes this task challenging is the fact that the currently

[3] The Paris Declaration, endorsed on 2 March 2005, is an international agreement to which over one hundred ministers, heads of agencies and other senior officials adhered and committed their countries and organizations to continue to increase efforts in harmonization, alignment and managing aid for results with a set of monitorable actions and indicators. See OECD (2007).

accepted definition of Aid for Trade is deliberately wide-ranging and does not correspond easily to what the IPG literature has so far covered in terms of health, environment, security, governance, and knowledge.

The report of the International Task Force on Global Public Goods, *Meeting Global Challenges: International Cooperation in the National Interest*, in September 2006 referred to the need for an Aid for Trade fund. The report argued that:

> the Quad members,[4] given their pre-eminence as providers of official development assistance, could also take the first clear steps [to restart the stalled WTO negotiations and strengthen the international trading system] to constitute an 'Aid for Trade' fund to compensate the poorest countries for their loss of trade preferences and support them to improve their infrastructure and develop their export capacity.

Despite the suggestion of a new fund, the report does not address financing implications nor the specific activities a fund would focus on.

The Aid for Trade literature has included several references to the need for the establishment of a (global) Aid for Trade fund, albeit for different reasons. For instance, the Millennium Project Task Force on Trade suggested the establishment of a (temporary) Aid for Trade Fund. In January 2005, Page (2005) called for the establishment of a preference erosion fund. The Zedillo report (2005) recommended an Aid for Trade fund in August 2005. Subsequently, Joseph Stiglitz presented the idea for an Aid for Trade fund in February 2006 (Stiglitz and Charlton, 2006). One of the aims of this paper is to unpack these ideas and provide a basis for why certain activities would benefit from an international approach by applying an international public goods framework to the range of activities covered by Aid for Trade.

The structure of this chapter is as follows. Section 2 discusses key concepts in the literature on international public goods and how Aid for Trade relates to the aid financing of international public goods in definitional terms. Section 3 provides some practical examples of global programs that have addressed public goods-type concerns, and considers the advantages and disadvantages vis-à-vis national programs. Section 4 provides a public goods framework for conceptualizing Aid for Trade, suggesting that the financial architecture of Aid for Trade is likely to consist of a hybrid of international and national approaches. Section 5 offers some concluding reflections.

2 Financing international public goods

2.1 Review of key issues in the literature on IPGs

2.1.1 *Definition*

A pure public good must exhibit two characteristics. First, the good must be *non-excludable*: that is, once it has been provided, no one can be excluded from enjoying its benefits. As long as it is difficult or costly to exclude, private providers will not find the market attractive – they cannot exclude non-payers from deriving benefit and therefore cannot recover the costs of production. Consequently,

[4] Canada, the EU, Japan, and the United States.

there is a role for the public sector in providing the good. Second, the good must be *non-rival in consumption*: consumption by one person does not prevent someone else from consuming the same amount; therefore extending consumption to more users creates benefits for zero marginal costs. As the private sector would under-supply a non-rival good, there is a role for the public sector to increase its provision.

In practice, most goods are impure public goods, as they exhibit neither of the two characteristics completely. For example, a road is, in principle, non-rival, but access to a road is rival or excludable if the road is congested or if it is a toll road. Developing a rules-based system is another example. The benefit of global rules is both non-rival and non-excludable. However, the method of providing the public good may be both rival and excludable (for instance, if private consultancies were contracted to draft trade rules). The discussion about public goods and providing them is, therefore, often one about degree of excludability and rivalry.

Reflecting these practical difficulties, different researchers use different definitions. The UNDP approach is quite broad, using the concept of global public goods to encompass a broad range of development activities (Kaul et al., 1999; 2003). Other researchers use narrower definitions of what constitutes a global public good (Kanbur et al., 1999; Ferroni and Mody, 2002).

2.1.2 *Spillover range*

Traditional discussions on public goods have tended to be national in scope (for example, the provision of national security by the government within its borders). However, the spillover or spatial range can extend from the local to the global level, such that we can distinguish between national and international public goods. The term "international public good" is used when the benefits of a good extend beyond national boundaries. Conversely, a national public good (NPG) is one where the benefits are enjoyed mainly within national borders. NPGs may be needed to contribute to providing the associated IPG. For example, to provide the IPG for eliminating a contagious disease, each country must have a health system in place, or an NPG, to administer the cure or prevention.

Within international public goods, one can distinguish between truly global and regional public goods. A significant part of the literature covers regional public goods (Arce and Sandler, 2002; Ferroni, 2002). The regional reach of the spillovers depends on a host of factors, and contiguity of countries and area is not a precondition (in the case of preferential trade rules, for example). However, often a public good is regional precisely because its neighbors are affected by the provision of the public good. For some issues, a regional spillover range is more likely than global.

The World Bank (2001) distinguishes further between core and complementary activities associated with the provision of IPGs. Core activities aim to produce international public goods. Complementary activities, in turn, prepare countries to consume the international public goods that core activities make available – while at the same time creating valuable national public goods (World Bank, 2001). Core refers to the provision of the global benefit or, in other words, the production of the IPG. Similarly, a core activity helps to provide NPGs, which is complementary to providing IPGs. Complementary refers to helping in providing the good or assisting in the ability to derive a benefit from the presence of the public good.

2.2 Options for providing international public goods

The general rule is that public goods will not be supplied in the optimal quantity when supply is left to the market alone. This does not mean that the public sector must supply the good itself, but it could intervene to correct market prices and hence provision, including through setting rules and regulation to reach a socially more optimal supply. In general, if non-excludability is the core feature of the good, direct public provision may be the most effective solution. If, however, non-rivalry is the core feature, public intervention would help to increase the level of private provision. In both cases, it could require public provision using public financial resources.

Morrissey and te Velde (2005) distinguish three levels of intervention. First, there is *direct provision* when the government finances and provides the good, usually financed by taxes. Security public goods are typically provided directly, with perhaps some private sector involvement. Activities with significant positive externalities, where provision is excludable, and rival because of congestion, typically have public and private provision. Examples include infrastructure, such as toll roads (rival and excludable) and telecommunication or broadcasting services (non-rival but excludable using scrambling). Part of the externality derives from the fact that new infrastructure reduces congestion on older infrastructure, but generally if one firm helps to build a road others would benefit as well.

Second, public goods can be provided by *regulation or agency*, at the national or international level. In practice, this is related to governance, as an agency or regulatory body undertakes the intervention. Many of the market failures associated with economic development can be addressed through agencies that, in doing so, provide a public good. Agencies coordinating training or providing information on adopting technologies are examples. As in the case of direct provision, the agency is usually publicly financed. However, charges, at a subsidized rate, can be levied for the service provided so that costs are shared. For example, the International Trade Centre (ITC) charges for its services.

Third, public goods can be supplied by altering the price or cost of production, either through taxes or subsidies. The intervention can be made by an agency or by a direct public provider. Subsidies can encourage activities with positive externalities with regard to health or education, or for adopting cleaner technologies, while taxes could discourage activities with negative externalities associated with polluters.

These three levels of intervention may apply to both IPGs and NPGs. Since international agencies such as the WTO play a coordination and monitoring role at the global level, one could consider such agencies as direct *providers* of governance IPGs. However, the institutions themselves are not public goods. International bodies are required to coordinate the provision of the core IPG, and have a role in assisting national providers of complementary NPGs. It does not necessarily require an international body to provide the IPG. For example, national or international trade research centers are, in principle, equally competent to deliver knowledge, but the latter may be better able to benefit from research economies of scale. It is important to coordinate national programs related to the provision of some IPGs, for example in the case of knowledge public goods related to trade policy research, so single countries do not need to reinvent the wheel of trade policy research.

The literature on financing the provision of IPGs is complex (Sandler, 2002), and depends on such issues as the aggregation of technology for the provision of public goods. Some international public goods can best be provided at the point of the weakest link, such as polio eradication in those few countries doing the least about it but which are crucial in the fight against a communicable disease. Some countries will derive more benefits from provision than others. An effective multilateral trading system and national trade development contribute to global economic stability, but this is likely to benefit some countries more than others (including differential benefits for those that are or are not committed to the rules). The poorest countries tend to be the least stable, both politically and economically, with relatively low levels of capacity, and are least able to pay. For these reasons, financing IPGs is often justified in terms of aid allocations by rich countries to poor countries (te Velde et al., 2002). It would also justify grants rather than loans. In addition, it would not be easy to provide loans to regional bodies; and most financing instruments and loans are at national not international level (World Bank, 2006).

The private sector can support the financing of public goods. The principal source of private sector contributions is charitable organizations such as the large Bill and Melinda Gates Foundation on health, the Ford Foundation on research, or World Wildlife Fund on environmental issues. Another factor that can increase the role of the private sector is the focus on corporate social responsibility (CSR), which initially included voluntary contributions and community investment by corporations. Movements to put CSR into practice include the promotion of socially and environmentally responsible behavior by corporations.

2.3 Mapping Aid for Trade activities onto the provision of international public goods

The Aid for Trade Task Force suggested that the scope of Aid for Trade include support for the following activities:

- Trade policy and regulations
- Trade development
- Trade-related infrastructure
- Building productive capacity
- Trade-related adjustment
- Other trade-related needs.

Public goods use a different classification, and are normally divided into the following (World Bank, 2001):

- Governance
- Knowledge
- Health
- Security
- Environment

There are several links between the two types of categories. Aid for Trade activities can contribute to the provision of public goods, but not all categories do. Projects in one Aid for Trade category may contribute to the provision of different types

Table 4.1. Mapping Aid for Trade and IPG classifications

Task force classification of Aid for Trade	GPG classification
Trade policy and regulations	**Governance IPGs** in the area of establishing global trade rules. **Knowledge IPGs** (for example, trade policy analyses would benefit from international expertise and coordination).
Trade development	**Knowledge NPG** when related to knowledge activities to support trade development.
Trade-related infrastructure	These activities do not provide pure public goods, and are often rival and excludable.
Building productive capacity	Features externalities and the provision of **knowledge public goods (IPGs and NPGs)**, such as raising the level of knowledge on technological development.
Trade-related adjustment	Not specified.
Other trade-related needs.	Not specified.

of public goods (that is, once the Aid for Trade project has been provided, the benefits are close to being non-rival and non-excludable), or none at all. While several activities have externalities that cross borders, this does not necessarily mean they contribute to public goods.

A simple mapping of individual activities is as follows (summarized in Table 4.1). Activities contained in *trade policy and regulations* contribute to governance IPGs in the area of establishing global trade rules. The benefits from trade rules may confer "benefits" to countries even if they are not directly part of a trade rules agreement, although the utility derived from those trade rules will not be the same across all countries. Activities in this category can also contribute to knowledge IPGs – support for trade policy impact assessments, for instance. NPGs, on the other hand, would benefit from international expertise and coordination. Activities contained in *trade development* contribute to knowledge NPGs, insofar as they relate to knowledge activities to support trade development. *Trade-related infrastructure* activities do not provide pure public goods, since they are often rival (toll roads) and excludable (through scrambling). The building of *productive capacity* can feature externalities and the provision of knowledge public goods (IPGs and NPGs), for instance through raising the level of knowledge of technological development and adoption. *Trade-related adjustment* activities are not further specified, though certain adjustment measures could contribute to the provision of public goods, depending on how the adjustment aid is spent. *Other trade-related needs* are also not specified.

Aid for Trade activities fall into at least three different categories with varying public goods aspects: 1) knowledge international and national public goods; 2) governance international and national public goods; and 3) international or national provision of infrastructure. This will have implications for operationalizing Aid for Trade, particularly if an issues-based, public goods approach to aid financing will be prevalent.

Table 4.2. Providing public goods for trade and development – examples by activity

	Core activity	Complementary activity	
Public goods sector and spatial range	**Provision of public goods**	**Production of public goods**	**Consumption and utilization of public goods**
KNOWLEDGE			
Research, transfer, dissemination, skills	Policy research	Research and knowledge transfer; training	Facilitating and disseminating
International	Trade policy research	Policy development, statistics evidence, training provision	Policy transfer, advice and experience.
National	Analysis to support trade in services	Policy development, national statistics, training	Disseminating local advice and providing support to be receptive to new knowledge.
GOVERNANCE			
Regulation and coordination	Policy coherence and global trade rules	Institutions (e.g., WTO)	Implementation of trade rules
International	Coordinating research, policy and rules setting	Research and policy networks	Support for adapting and adopting research and policy
National	Adapting and coordinating policy and research	Policy and research agencies, national export promotion agencies, regulatory agencies	Support for adapting and adopting research and policy

Source: Adapted from te Velde and Morrisey (2005).

There is another, more general point. One could regard all of these activities as being required to secure progress on the development of global trade rules, and that all activities contribute to the provision of international governance public goods. There is a further argument that would regard the discussions on Aid for Trade as international knowledge public goods. The discussions themselves raise the profile and knowledge of trade issues. This is helpful in at least two ways: (i) for aid agencies to understand the importance of trade, and hence Aid for Trade; and (ii) for developing countries to act strategically about trade in the economy and trade in country assistance programs, such as national and regional indicative programs between the EU and ACP countries (see Chapter 12 by Sunassee in this volume). As such, a global forum to discuss trade issues can inform national development programs, which may otherwise not sufficiently take global challenges into account.

Table 4.2 provides a public goods lens of Aid for Trade activities, distinguished by core and complementary activities. This is useful for designing a strategy and the appropriate roles of government and the international community in supporting trade in developing countries. One could consider the core activity as the aim of policy or the objective to which an organization contributes. Core activities are those that are directly required to provide the public good, whereas complementary activities are those that contribute to the production and facilitate the consumption of the public good. For instance, the core is knowledge on trade policy. Specifically, under knowledge it is shown as policy research and under governance it is shown as policy coordination on trade policy. The core activity is able to provide the public good only if the complementary activities are undertaken, ensuring that full benefits are derived from the public good. Complementary activities that are needed to produce research include training, statistics and a conducive research environment, while complementary consumption activities include education and dissemination or transfer of information and experience, so the research results can be used.

2.4 Aid financing of Aid for Trade and public goods: how much?

There have been several estimates of how much aid is already going to Aid for Trade (see ILEAP, 2006) and how much aid is used to provide IPGs. The share of aid allocated to IPGs has risen since the early 1980s (see Raffer, 1998; te Velde et al., 2002 for the first estimates). Te Velde et al. (2002) estimate the share of aid allocated to IPGs and NPGs – in total and by individual donors – since the 1980s, and show that by the late 1990s donors allocated at least 10 percent of aid to IPGs and 30 percent to NPGs. They also show that using CRS (OECD Creditor Reporting System) data may underestimate the share of aid allocated to IPGs by some 50 percent, so one can assume that 15–20 percent of aid by bilateral donors in the late 1990s was allocated to providing IPGs.

Chart 4.1 presents new evidence on the share of aid going to different spending categories. Using public good definitions as in te Velde et al. (2002), it shows that there was a doubling in the share of aid allocated to financing public goods over the past two decades, and this has been broadly true for both IPGs and NPGs. There was a marked increase in aid commitments in 2003 in all categories (IPGs,

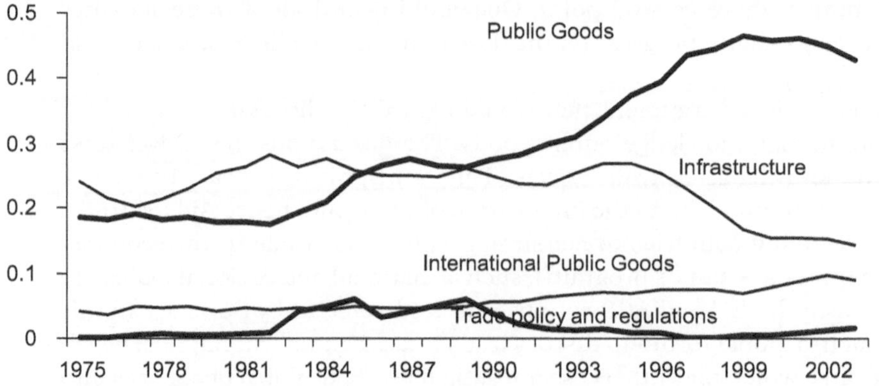

Chart 4.1. Share of Aid to Public Goods (all, international), Infrastructure, and Trade Policy (last 3 yr average). (*Source:* OECD Creditor Reporting System (commitments).)

NPGs, other aid), but while the share of IPGs in aid increased, the share of NPGs in aid actually declined. This is in part due to the boost in aid due to debt relief and spending on infrastructure (Chart 4.2). According to these data, Aid for Trade policy and regulations was much higher (in percentage terms) in the 1980s than currently. This is an interesting finding, given that the WTO/OECD Trade Capacity Building Database has recorded data only over the past few years (though we need to acknowledge that measurement and definitions may have changed).

In the past two decades, increased aid spending on public goods has been undertaken at the expense of other types of aid spending.[5] Some of these other types of spending may be desirable in their own right (schemes targeted directly at poverty reduction, for example) or may generate externalities and benefits that contribute to growth and development (such as capital infrastructure projects excluded from the definition of public goods). Chart 4.2 shows that aid going to "economic infrastructure" stabilized in the 2000s after decreases in the 1990s, but has increased in the last few years.

3 Examples of past financing mechanisms relevant to Aid for Trade

The purpose of this section is to review a number of funds, multilateral and bilateral, general and specific (or "vertical") trade- and non-trade-related, created mostly over the past decade.[6] This is done in order to analyze their advantages and disadvantages, and determine whether the fund or the experience derived from it can be applied to designing the architecture for Aid for Trade. The information in this section is based on a common set of criteria, including basic facts about the funds as well as their general effectiveness and relevance to Aid for Trade. This section will summarize the relevance of each fund to Aid for Trade.

5 Primarily because total aid spending did not increase much; of course, this has changed dramatically more recently.

6 There is a longer discussion of this material in ILEAP (2006). The additional information was compiled mainly by Lauren Phillips and Sven Grimm; the discussion on the relevance of funds to Aid for Trade discussions owes much to Sheila Page. This section adds an assessment of which type of public good each fund might contribute to.

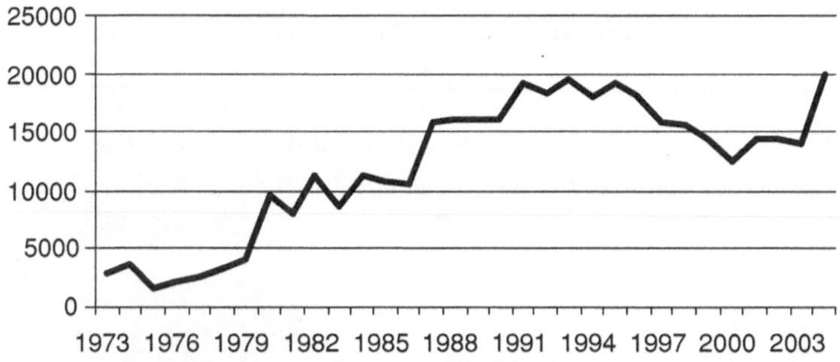

Figure 4.2. Aid to Infrastructure (US$ millions). (*Source:* OECD Creditor Reporting System (disbursements).)

We focus on bilateral, regional, and multilateral funds. However, national aid programs can also be useful in delivering international public goods. For instance, we discuss the role of national indicative programs (NIPs) in trade-related assistance that the EC has put in place in discussion with African, Caribbean and Pacific (ACP) countries. Poverty reduction strategies are another way, though we know that trade is not sufficiently included in Poverty Reduction Strategy Papers (PRSPs) – see Box 4.1 on recent comments on this by multilateral agencies. See also Hewitt and Gillson (2003) on the trade content of first-generation PRSPs, and Prowse (2006) on weaknesses of trade ministries in developing countries as a factor behind this.

3.1 Multilateral

The Integrated Framework (IF) is relevant to Aid for Trade because an enhanced IF can be considered to be part of Aid for Trade. Its Diagnostic Trade Integration Studies (DTIS) can only identify needs, not meet them, so it contributes to a knowledge public good. There has been criticism that the IF is highly administration-intensive for little or no return, and reduces the interest of potential recipients in participating in it, thus weakening its status (in aid policy terms) as a country-led program based on countries' own identification of needs. Its limited funding makes it unlikely that it will go beyond funding studies to actually implementing what the studies recommend for LDCs (see Box 4.2).

The Joint Integrated Technical Assistance Programme (JITAP) is also highly relevant to Aid for Trade, but like the IF is small in scale. Its size effectively restricts it to small projects, particularly capacity building, and in this respect it contributes to a governance IPG.

WTO technical assistance is a form of Aid for Trade, though the initiative has a small budget and is primarily designed to do training-type activities. The present structure, based on unbound contributions from member countries, could not be massively scaled up and there is no capacity to determine needs for trade-related supply-side assistance (based on demand for training courses). It has a direct link with articles in WTO agreements calling for greater assistance in implementing trade agreements. It has been criticized by recipients because its relationship to the WTO means that it is not able to offer advice on how to minimize compliance with WTO rules. The fund contributes to a governance IPG.

Box 4.1. Trade and PRSPs: Selected submissions to the Aid for Trade Task Force

One set of questions raised in Aid for Trade Task Force submissions concerns the trade content of PRSPs: Has trade been adequately addressed in countries' development plans and poverty reduction strategies? If not, what are the main reasons and how could this be corrected? What are the lessons learned?

World Bank
Focus on trade is correlated to focus on growth in PRSPs; however, trade strategies are not operational because of lack of capacity and intra-ministry coordination. The Enhanced IF should be undertaken at the same time as PRSPs to maximize results.

ITC
No, for three reasons: links between trade, development and poverty reduction have not been proven to national policy makers (economic vs. social goals); lack of link between development programs and trade expertise; insufficient awareness of trade opportunities for small and medium enterprises.

IMF
Focus on trade is correlated to focus on growth in PRSPs; however, trade strategies are not operational. Diagnostic Trade Integration Studies (DTIS) can have a positive impact on the quality of the trade information included.

UNIDO
Have not incorporated trade sufficiently, in part because donor agencies have a hard time justifying aid for private sector development.

UNCTAD
Needs to be better integrated into development strategies. Lack of capacity to articulate in-country trade policy formulation. The Integrated Framework (IF) should be linked to national development strategies.

UNDP
Shortcomings with the analytical approach – there are projections but no follow through with trade strategies. These are more short-term than long-term strategies.

Source: Phillips, Lauren. 2006. Summary of Aid for Trade positions. ODI. http://www.odi.org.uk/IEDG/Projects/Aid4trade_files/aid_for_trade_multilat_orgs_views.pdf.

The United Nations Conference on Trade and Development (UNCTAD) is the organization with the longest history of relating trade to development and has major current capacity building functions. It may also offer evidence on how to ensure that developing countries participate actively and believe that they are involved in making decisions. UNCTAD is mainly an implementing agency, so it provides technical cooperation on the basis of projects planned by donors. The main areas of activities are in trade policy and regulations.

Box 4.2. The Integrated Framework (IF)

The Integrated Framework is one possible example of how the Aid for Trade architecture might look. However, in order to fit the criteria for an Aid for Trade fund, the IF would have to be empowered to provide funding of its own, separate from other lending and aid processes. This has started to a limited extent with the creation of an IF Trust Fund. This is for trade, so it is an example of a trade-specific fund. It is relevant to the Broad types of Aid for Trade, but it can only identify needs through DTIS, not meet them. The IF has not been able to solve the problem of ensuring that the commitment in principle to meet identified needs is translated into actual aid flows, and has instead focused on mainstreaming trade in PRSPs on the basis of DTISs, which unfortunately have often come later than PRSPs.

Recent attempts to enhance the IF in the context of Aid for Trade have resulted in three broad changes: (i) the establishment of an Integrated Framework Steering Committee; (ii) a group to help coordinate donors (the IF Working Group); and (iii) the establishment of an IF Trust Fund to give the mechanism its own funding and encourage improved coordination amongst donors in trade policy aid.

LDCs do not want the Integrated Framework extended to non-LDCs because it provides a very limited amount of money. It is not a suitable model for Narrow Aid for Trade because its main purpose is to identify countries' needs (through the Diagnostic Studies), and Narrow needs are already identified. It is unlikely to be a model for Broad Aid for Trade because the funding is only sufficient for the studies, not for implementing what the studies recommend. Do non-LDCs need a diagnostic process? There may be elements of the IF administrative process that agencies may wish to copy in designing programs to spend Aid for Trade money.

If the DTIS process has already identified projects under the IF, then Broad Aid for Trade may be able to start from these. Several WTO papers have suggested the IF infrastructure as a vehicle to access Aid for Trade funds.

Source: ILEAP (2006).

The International Trade Centre (ITC) offers trade-related aid. The main areas of intervention are concentrated in trade development and business participation in the global trading system. The ITC has developed a role related to global products and networking of trade support institutions that is complementary to the *trade development* trade-related technical assistance of the bilateral donors that support larger projects in developing and transition economies. Some of these activities fall under knowledge national and international public goods.

The Trade Integration Mechanism (TIM) of the IMF is close to the Aid for Trade concept in its purpose, and type of analysis of needs for adjustment. It was established explicitly to deal with preference erosion, as implementation of the commitments made by the IMF and the World Bank before and at the WTO Cancún Ministerial 10–14 September 2003. It is the clearest recognition by an international agency outside the WTO that there is a legitimate aid problem as a consequence of WTO obligations. The facility offers loans, not grants. It is impossible to say what the ultimate aims of the funds would be.

The World Bank's Highly Indebted Poor Country (HIPC) initiative is an example of how funds can be allocated to some broad areas, such as education and health) but not to specific initiatives. Governments have to decide on priorities within these sectors, an approach that is considered less distorting than narrower funds.

The Standards and Trade Development Facility (STDF) is an example of a program (run by the WTO) created to tackle one of the main non-tariff barriers to developing countries' access to developed regions' markets: meeting and implementing international sanitary and phytosanitary standards (SPS).

The Global Environmental Fund (GEF) is an example of a fund established to meet international objectives outside the normal scope of national aid programs. It contributes to the provision of environmental public goods.

The Montreal Protocol Fund is an example of a vertical fund established, after widespread consensus about the causes and effects of the issues addressed, to implement an international agreement that imposes obligations on developing countries, outside normal national aid programs. It contributes to the provision of environmental public goods.

Global Fund to Fight Aids, Tuberculosis and Malaria is an example of a fund established because some donors felt that a specific need was not being met as part of normal aid programs. There is criticism that even where a country had a health plan that was well costed, but not funded, donors came in and over-funded spending on AIDS, while everything else was under-funded. The Global Fund is quite different from other vertical funds reviewed in this section as it disburses money through a competitive proposal process. It contributes to the provision of health public goods.

Global Alliance for Vaccines and Immunisation (GAVI) is an example of a vertical fund established to meet a need identified outside the aid community, but not one that is the result of an international convention. It contributes to the provision of health public goods.

The Consultative Group on International Agricultural Research (CGIAR) is a research network with very flexible funding for members, which determine the level of earmarking. It is potentially a pick-and-choose approach to a (research) menu set by the institutions. It is not quite clear how the funding covers all institutes, but it seems there are preferred partners to some. It contributes to the provision of knowledge public goods.

3.2 Regional schemes

A particularly interesting example is the *trilateral scheme* by the Inter-American Development Bank, the UN Economic Commission for Latin America and the Caribbean, and the Organization of American States to provide Latin American and Caribbean countries with assistance for negotiations and for regional integration. This was initially put in place only for the FTAA negotiations, but was subsequently extended to other needs. If meeting regional needs is one of the "gaps" identified, there could be a role for regional organizations. The range of programs has allowed the IDB to provide support to all the types of trade needs identified here, and it is one of the few multilateral donors with a regional focus.

In the **European Cohesion and Structural Funds**, the funding rules are relatively straightforward; country ownership and planning is required. This might be due to the relatively recent date of establishment.

3.3 Bilateral schemes

The EU-ACP Project Management Unit could be a precedent for country-by-country identification of costs of adjustment to an agreement. It is like the IF, with its DTISs, in identifying needs, but the methods and criteria include some similar to those used by TIM to calculate transition costs of liberalization. There is no commitment by any donor to supply additional money to meet identified costs, but as the studies are to be completed before the end of the negotiations, countries have the option of not signing an Economic Partnership Agreement if the costs are too high and are not met. Although it is bilateral and funded by a donor that is also the relevant trader, the organization operates in a way that ensures that country assessments are not seen by the EC. It contributes to the provision of knowledge public goods.

The EU special fund for rum was intended to help a sector damaged by trade reform in the EU. It was unusual in its direct assistance to the private sector. It attracted a high degree of regional ownership (private sector) and because of this showed some success. It was transitional and ended after its scheduled end date.

The EU special framework for assistance for bananas is an example of an assistance program designed to meet the costs of countries damaged by trade reforms that could assist other developing countries. It demonstrates the potential difficulties of choosing the most appropriate means of adjustment. Initially, the Commission specified that funds be used for investments in the affected industry; later, it insisted on diversification. The low share of assistance funds spent on diversification has been raised as an important factor in the low levels of growth experienced in traditional ACP banana-producing countries, despite substantial financing. The Commission and member states explicitly cited the precedent of the banana program as an example of a badly designed program. A major failure has been its tendency to support banana production in those countries that have limited potential to become competitive. It will not have contributed to the provision of public goods.

The EU Action Plan for Sugar, which from the beginning allowed for adjustment through increasing productivity, finding related production, or a total change in production, attempted to avoid the problems of the banana scheme. Like the rum and banana schemes, it is an example of aid to provide adjustment assistance for countries that suffer losses because of trade reforms. It is an interesting precedent because compensating ACP countries for changes in European sugar policy is treated differently from aid by giving it a separate budget line additional to the European Development Fund (EDF) (see te Velde et al., 2006). It uses grants, and it bases eligibility on adjustment needs, not on need for infrastructure.

The Proinvest scheme for ACP countries provides direct support for the private sector and for intermediary organizations. The mechanism interacts with the private sector. Support may consist of a technical or financial diagnostic study of the enterprise, market surveys, feasibility studies, partner searches, financial forecasts for a project, assistance for project implementation, marketing assistance, training of enterprise staff, training of enterprise management, or other technical assistance. The scheme also finances financial intermediaries, such as investment promotion agencies, and as such might contribute to the provision of governance public goods.

Other EU trade-related assistance is provided as part of regional and country programs when the EC and partner countries have decided on this as a priority. The ACP assistance (through EDF) tends to be delivered through National (such as Namibia, Kenya, Zambia, Ethiopia, Jamaica, Suriname, Dominican Republic, Rwanda, Ghana) or Regional Indicative Programmes (NIPs and RIPs), where trade and development or regional integration is a priority, or through All-ACP programs. The interpretation of Aid for Trade by the EC is a fairly broad one, encompassing assistance to individual companies and institutions but also sectors, national governments and regions (the trade component in RIPs can be much higher than 50 percent).

Trade assistance under **USAID** is an example of a bilateral program that has grown as new areas have been identified. It has combined general support with specific assistance in taking advantage of U.S. trade programs such as the African Growth and Opportunity Act (AGOA). It has assisted both the public and the private sectors. African private sectors have found this aid more active and more useful than programs from other trade partners in helping them to access trade preference schemes. It has provided extensive support to ministries in their trade work. The U.S Millennium Challenge Account (MCA) is an example of a growth/trade-related vertical fund that has emerged alongside traditional USAID programs.

3.4 Conclusion

This section has identified a number of vertical initiatives, both trade- and non-trade related, some of which address the provision of (international) public goods. Funds differ not only in purpose, but also in eligibility criteria and geographic implementation. Some funds have emerged out of specific concerns: for example, the Montreal Protocol addresses ozone depletion, and the Sugar Action Plan provides payments to ACP Sugar Protocol countries that need to adjust after sugar sector reform. Other initiatives are more general in their focus: the Millennium Challenge Corporation (MCC) focuses on growth and poverty reduction. This range corresponds well to the discussions on Aid for Trade, with different solutions possible for different components along the Aid for Trade spectrum.

There are quite a few funds that address the type of trade measures required at the national level and that contribute to national knowledge public goods. Examples are the IF, part of EC TRA, and JITAP. However, far fewer programs address regional constraints or supply-side constraints directly (though the MCC could do some) or implementation costs of trade agreements (though current WTO assistance might fit with this, and so does the EC Sugar Action Plan for adjustment away from preferences). Indeed, reviews of PRSPs uncover very few direct regional links. Thus, there are significant gaps that the Aid for Trade debate can address, particularly in relation to governance and knowledge public goods. Of course, budgeting procedures must allow for the setup of such funds. In this context, te Velde et al. (2006) discuss the budgeting difficulties in the European Parliament in financing Aid for Trade programs.

Different funds have different ways of operating. Some take time to reach the disbursement point, while others can come to fruition more quickly. EC procedures tend to be slow; bilateral funders tend to be faster. The EC integrates much of its TRA in country programs, (through country strategy papers), but other funds, such as the MCC and GAVI, do this to a lesser extent. The disadvantage of integration with country programs is that it is difficult to secure quick and targeted disbursement for immediate trade or supply needs if this is required by developing countries.

In some instances, vertical funds are well placed to deal with important global and specific issues. First, they may help to focus attention on important issues (for example, protection of the thinning ozone layer through the Montreal Protocol, or the current adjustment to sugar sector reform, and indeed the lack of trade support generally). There might be some rigidity and potential distortion in vertical funds, but where an issue has been neglected by donors, imposing rigidity and reversing past distortions may be required. In the case of the Montreal Protocol, quick agreement was found to fund a specific problem (the elimination of ozone depleting substances), according to certain timetables and based on national implementation programs. The success of that effort demonstrated also that global initiatives that contribute to international public goods are required as a means of informing national programs.

Second, some issues require global coordination and involvement of a pool of expertise. For instance, research (and the CGIAR) is often seen to benefit from economies of scale. UNCTAD relies on expertise in the area of trade negotiations, the Global Fund relies on health expertise to create breakthroughs in the area of vaccines. The GAVI approach is helpful in bringing funders and private sector expertise together.

Any conclusions on the merits of different aid architectures must be evaluated in the context of the most important lesson derived from work on aid, which is that good plans and participation by recipient governments are the most important determinants of what works. It may be that a compromise is needed between special funds and general assistance so as to ensure that the special funds have broad aims (HIPC, for example) and align their rules with the government and with other programs (such as common rules for government procurement). There are high risks but also many benefits associated with the provision of direct budget support. One example of such a compromise is the Sector-Wide Approach (SWAp). A SWAp is a process in which donors give significant funding to a government's comprehensive sector policy and expenditure program. A SWAp tends to have a joint review mechanism and performance monitoring system relying on the government's own performance assessment framework. It might be a means to ensure increased aid to a sector, improve coordination in-country, and reduce the fungibility of aid funds by setting clear sectoral program objectives, but it should not lead to additional administrative requirements.

The SWAp is normally a hybrid form of funding (Foster and Leavy, 2001). At one extreme, it involves budget support to a sector when donors are confident that implementation and accountability concerns are being met. Where weaknesses exist, financing may be more mixed in the form of funds earmarked for specific purposes or project support – some of this could come from vertical funds. In practice, sector programs (and thus SWAps) have centered around lead implementation ministries, while it has been more difficult to fund activities that involve other ministries or NGOs or the private sector. This has implications for the debate on Aid for Trade, where there are different categories of needs that may require several SWAps; the Broad definition of Aid for Trade (see Chapter 5 by Page in this volume) presents a challenge in that it includes too many things: capacity building, infrastructure, and private sector development, among others.

4 A public goods framework to address Aid for Trade

While a disadvantage of any framework is that one has to frame a complex issue starting sometimes from an arbitrary point, an advantage is that it provides a clear structure for separating out key issues. In this particular instance, we take various elements in the Aid for Trade discussion and then consider how these elements can best be provided. The results can then be compared with the current situation and gaps identified.

A framework to address the provision of Aid for Trade is based on four general questions:

1. *What is the rationale for providing the good in terms of its publicness?*

It is important to classify the activities under discussion by their degree of publicness. The more public good aspects an activity has, the less likely it is that a private firm can be solely responsible for providing it, because of the reasons given in Section 2. On the other hand, a public body may provide a private good, but needs a justification for why it does not let the private market take its place.

2. *How does the provision of public goods link to development?*

Both public and private goods can contribute to development by overcoming market failures. But not all market failures require the provision of public goods; other types of government interventions include the use of taxes and subsidies and setting of rules and standards. Section 2 argues that many market failures are most appropriately addressed through tax and subsidy policies – "correcting" distortions in the structure of incentives – or through specific regulatory measures, rather than taking the approach that providing a public good is necessary to address a specific market failure.

While public goods by definition benefit everybody, because everybody has the chance to consume the same public goods, it does not follow that certain groups or the country as a whole benefit in terms of economic development. The provision of public goods will have different effects in different areas.

Table 4.3 provides a mapping of how certain public goods may address challenges linked to economic development. Practical cost-benefit analyses and other impact studies will need to accompany such theoretical mappings (the Copenhagen Consensus[7] is one such approach, though some will question the outcomes).

3. *What are the current gaps in the provision of the good?*

Theoretically, public goods are underprovided. From a public point of view, it is important to understand the size of the gap. Assessing this is not straightforward,

[7] See the project sponsored by The Economist and Bjorn Lomborg, ("Copenhagen" 2007).

Table 4.3. Trade development, market failures, and responses

Type (sources of failure)	Examples of market failures	Responses: policies and activities	Relevant Aid for Trade public goods
Coordination	Externalities ignored Linkages not exploited No policy coherence Complementarities	Capacity building for trade policy to identify linkages and externalities National trade strategy	Governance Knowledge
Technology: developing, adapting and adopting	Incomplete and imperfect information Network externalities	Promoting technology transfer and adoption Support for standardization and quality control	Knowledge
Skills formation	Externalities (in training workers) Imperfect information	Coordinate and/or subsidies for training	Knowledge
Capital markets, access to finance	Rationing and/or high interest rates	Micro-credit schemes or formal sector subsidy based on rational information about borrowers	Knowledge

Source: Adapted from te Velde and Morrissey (2005).

as it depends on comparing what is already provided with what is needed in an optimal situation, an assessment that is difficult to obtain from interviews with key stakeholders alone.

4. *What are the financing mechanisms to address the gaps (country programs, regional and global initiatives)?*

We need to first establish the case for aid, and, then second, the type of aid mechanism. There are three building blocks underpinning the case for aid financing of IPGs. First, the private sector will not provide a sufficient amount of public goods, as it will consider private rather than social benefits. This calls for some public sector engagement. Second, individual countries have insufficient incentives to make an optimal contribution to IPGs, given that some of the benefits accrue outside the country. This calls for a form of cooperation between countries. Finally, poor countries lack the resources to make a full contribution to the provision of IPGs. This justifies aid finance of IPGs in poor countries (te Velde, 2002; Mascarenhas and Sandler, 2005).

However, the argument is more complex in practice. In particular, the following three issues are important. First, aid financing does not necessarily imply implementation or actual provision by donor agencies. Coordination with and subcontracting to other actors, including the private sector, can be part of providing the public good. Second, even if a pure public good can be identified, it is difficult to verify what the exact current contribution is to the provision of the good or how much the good is underprovided. Finally, there are several sources of financing IPGs. For instance, there are proposals for a Tobin tax on currency flows, an air travel tax, a carbon tax on carbon dioxide emissions, all of which can raise finance for the provision of IPGs. But there are also other, existing sources of finance, such as regular contributions by the private sector, donations by private firms, NGOs and charities, in addition to national sources.

With all the discussion that has taken place on the need for finance, there has been very little emphasis on how exactly funds would be collected and disbursed. National programs are funded through PRSP exercises or EDF cooperation cycles between the EU and ACP countries. But it is different for global causes. The International Finance Facility proposed by the United Kingdom (and operational in the area of health) is an example of how funds could be raised from capital markets and of frontloading aid on the basis of long-term commitments. There are also certain public-private groups that work together to fund development of vaccines.

The aid architecture is changing and has to deal with major increases in aid over the coming few years, and this raises questions about the effectiveness of aid, including about such issues as harmonization, alignment and ownership (Rocha Menocal et al., 2006). The evolving architecture also has to deal with an increasing number of new initiatives and a large number of institutions providing IPGs. All this raises questions as to the general setup of donor agencies, departments and organizations, and the benefits they deliver vis-à-vis national programs.

The OECD Development Assistance Committee with donor and aid recipients agreed at a High Level Forum in Paris in 2005 to reform the delivery of official development assistance to make it become a less competitive and self-interested flow of public resources and more a system of delivery of aid.[8] It is not clear how the Paris reforms will deal with global challenges, in terms, for example, of allocating aid across issues and countries, though clearly global challenges have assumed greater importance than before (Kaul and Conceição, 2006). Unless the sums provided are genuinely additional (as aimed for in the Aid for Trade debate), the proliferation of special funds may divert real resources from other genuine development priorities, thereby harming or hampering the delivery of real IPGs. There is also the issue of substitution, whereby donors may sometimes claim IPG status in their development spending for activities that are not public goods. Some argue that the same increase in aid (as currently planned) has never been promised to so many different causes.

4.1 Applying the public goods framework to Aid for Trade activities

This section relates the public goods framework questions to the components of Aid for Trade, as summarized in Table 4.4. Two public goods are relevant: governance in the form of a global system of trade rules; and knowledge, nationally in the form of impact assessments and trade development studies, and internationally in the form of awareness-raising. Infrastructure is not a pure public good.

[8] Increasingly, support for social sector improvements having direct impact on the poor (and even the funding of their recurrent costs) has become the leading motive of post-debt relief assistance given to poor countries, even at the expense of support for economic development.

Table 4.4. A public goods framework for financing Aid for Trade activities

	Aid for Trade activities		
	Governance	**Knowledge**	**Infrastructure**
1. Rationale for the provision in public good terms (non-rivalry; non-excludability)?	Global trade rules contribute to the provision of governance IPGs and require global approaches.	Impact assessment studies, trade policy analysis contribute to knowledge IPGs, some of which are regional. Aid for Trade awareness-raising is a global activity	Tends to be described as a club good.
2. How does the public good relate to (economic) development?	Evidence suggests more stable and transparent rules will increase investment and growth.	Knowledge and development Trade helps to set an environment conducive to development.	Several studies find that infrastructure is crucial for investment and growth.
3. What are the current gaps in provision of the good and at what level (national, regional, global)?	Ongoing debate, regional networks important but mostly national level.	Lack of economic and trade policy knowledge. Lack of relevant trade impact assessment, and lack of knowledge on regional trade constraints.	Large gaps in infrastructure as aid decreased and private sector did not fill gap in the past decade. Commission for Africa recommended US$20 billion increase in aid for African infrastructure. NEPAD has a list of infrastructure projects.
4. What are the financing mechanisms to address the gaps (country programs, regional, and global initiatives)?	**Global** coordination local implementation (**beyond country** program) or **regional** implementation in the case of regional trade rules.	Knowledge (e.g., for trade policy) needs **national** approach, but **regional** is also needed to contribute to regional knowledge PGs. Awareness-raising needs to include a global approach.	**Regional** development banks and regional groupings, **national** development programs.

Some Aid for Trade activities will be more relevant for development than others. Infrastructure plays a key role. There is also evidence regarding the effects of knowledge and governance public goods.

The gaps are massive and clearest for infrastructure, but also significant for governance and knowledge activities contained in Aid for Trade. The gaps are smaller in diagnostics of national constraints to trade, and greater in the areas of regional constraints, impact assessments of changes to trade rules, and follow-up. Importantly, there are still gaps in awareness-raising at a global, regional, and national level.

As will have become clear, effective financing mechanisms are likely to differ substantially among key components of Aid for Trade activities. In this sense, it is unwise to speak of one "global Aid for Trade fund." On the other hand, solving these issues based on bilateral or national programs only will not work either. How does regional infrastructure get implemented? This probably needs some international co-ordination. How can knowledge on trade development policies be coordinated? How can a system of global trade rules be developed and sustained? How can the profile of trade issues be raised? These are mostly international challenges and may involve the provision of international public goods using global or regional approaches, global or regional funds, and global or regional co-ordination. The discussion in Section 3 indicated that there are varying experiences in the use of special or vertical funds. Several of these funds have been successful (or in any case not less successful than purely national programs or not addressing the challenge at all), so something can be learned.

The World Bank (2006) has also recognized regional constraints in delivering Aid for Trade. Multi-country programs constitute 2–6 percent of the portfolio of regional development banks. The trade-related parts of World Bank lending for regional projects in the past few years amount to around 1 percent of total lending. Regional projects face higher transaction costs and donor funds do not appear to be suited to regional projects; donor mandates and thinking tend to focus on national lines. Within developing countries themselves, there may be too few incentives to co-operate regionally due to the free-rider effect for non-participants. The World Bank argues that, "The national focus of development assistance makes it more difficult to realize the potential benefits of cross-country cooperation in trade-related areas." This is serious. The donors who came together to draw up the Paris Declaration did not fully appreciate the potential importance of regional projects. In the case of Aid for Trade, it is best if some of the activities are not programmed at the national level.

5 Conclusion

The currently used definition of Aid for Trade lumps together very different types of activities. We applied a public goods framework and argued that some Aid for Trade activities contribute more to public goods than others. This has implications for financing, as different activities are likely to need different approaches and solutions. In putting Aid for Trade into operation, now is the time to assess what is behind the notion of Aid for Trade funds, including the appropriate levels of financing.

We argued that it is important to examine the purposes of funds more closely in order to assess a possible Aid for Trade architecture. We suggested that there are already numerous special vertical funds, and that there are theoretical and empirical reasons why some of these work. Not all vertical funds are rational, and some will raise the transaction costs of aid. Despite this, the purposes and benefits of Aid for Trade involve the provision of *international* public goods, and we argued that some of these involve global approaches to complement and inform national approaches. The key point is that while the global/vertical funds need to take into account aid principles, national programs on the other hand will need to take into account global challenges and solutions, because relying on nationally-based solutions alone may not be the most efficient or effective way to address the challenges. Hence it is important to consider the use of regional and other international approaches to Aid for Trade directly to try to tackle international challenges.

REFERENCES

Arce, D. and T. Sandler. 2002. "Regional Public Goods: Typologies, Provision, Financing, and Development Assistance," Expert Group on Development Issues, Stockholm: Almkvist & Wiksell International.

Copenhagen Consensus Center. 2007. "Copenhagen Consensus 2004," http://www.copenhagenconsensus.com/Default.aspx?ID=158.

Ferroni, M. and A. Mody. 2002. Eds. "International Public Goods: Incentives, Measurement and Financing," Boston and London: Kluwer Academic Publishers for the World Bank.

Foster, Mick and Jennifer Leavy. 2001. "The Choice of Financial Aid Instruments," Working Paper 158, London: Overseas Development Institute.

Hewitt, Adrian and Ian Gillson. 2003. "A Review of the Trade and Poverty Content in PRSPs and Loan-Related Documents," London: Overseas Development Institute.

ILEAP. 2006. "The Financial Architecture of Aid for Trade," *Background Brief* no. 9. By Calì, Massimiliano et al., Toronto: International Lawyers and Economists Against Poverty.

Kanbur, Ravi, and Todd Sandler, with Kevin M. Morrison. 1999. "The Future of Development Assistance: Common Pools and International Public Goods," *Policy Essay* no. 25, Washington, D.C.: Overseas Development Council.

Kaul, Inge, Isabelle Grunberg, and Marc Stern. 1999. Eds. "Global Public Goods: International Cooperation in the 21st Century," New York: Oxford University Press.

Kaul, Inge, et al. 2003. Eds. "Providing Global Public Goods: Managing Globalization," New York: Oxford University Press.

Kaul, Inge and Pedro Conceição. 2006. Eds. "The New Public Finance: Responding to Global Challenges," New York: Oxford University Press.

Mascarenhas, Raechelle and Todd Sandler. 2005. "Donors' Mechanisms for Financing International and National Public Goods: Loans or Grants?," *World Economy*, 8(08): 1095–1117.

Mascarenhas, Raechelle and Todd Sandler. 2006. "Do donors cooperatively fund foreign aid?," *Review of International Organizations*, 2006 (1): 337–357.

Overseas Development Institute. 2006. "Aid for Trade References Database," http://www.odi.org.uk/iedg/aid4trade.html.

OECD. 2007. "Homepage," http://www.oecd.org.

OECD/DAC Working Party on Aid Effectiveness. 2005. "Harmonisation, Alignment, Results: Report on Progress, Challenges and Opportunities," prepared for the high level forum "Joint Progress Toward Enhanced Aid Effectiveness," Paris, 28 February–2 March.

Page, Sheila. 2005. "A Preference Erosion Compensation Fund," *ODI Opinions* 35, http://www.odi.org.uk/publications/opinions/35_preference_erosion_jan05.html.

Prowse, Susan. 2006. "Mega-coherence: The Integrated Framework," in S. Page (ed.), *Trade and Aid: Rivals or Partners in Development Policy*, London: Cameron May Ltd.

Raffer, Kunibert. 1999. "ODA and Global Public Goods: A Trend Analysis of Past and Present Spending Patterns," United Nations Development Programme background paper, New York: United Nations.

Rocha Menocal, Alina, with Simon Maxwell and Andrew Rogerson. 2006. "The Future of Aid: User Perspectives on Reform of the International Aid System," prepared for the Commonwealth Secretariat and La Francophonie Workshop, London: Overseas Development Institute.

Rogerson, Andrew. 2005. "Aid Harmonisation and Alignment: Bridging the Gaps Between Reality and the Paris Reform Agenda," *Development Policy Review*, 23(5): 531–552.

Stiglitz, Joseph E. and Andrew Charlton. 2006. "Aid for Trade: A Report for the Commonwealth Secretariat," London: Commonwealth Secretariat.

te Velde, Dirk Willem, Adrian Hewitt, and Oliver Morrissey. 2002. "Allocating Aid to International Public Goods," ch. 5, pp. 119–156 in Marco Ferroni and Ashoka Mody (eds.), *International Public Goods: Incentives, Measurement and Financing*, Boston: Kluwer Academic Publishers for the World Bank.

te Velde, Dirk Willem and Oliver Morrissey. 2005. "Supporting Industrial Development: Overcoming Market Failures and Providing Public Goods," report for United Nations Industrial Development Organization Research Programme, Vienna.

te Velde, Dirk Willem, Adrian Hewitt, and Oliver Morrissey. 2006. "Aid financing of International Public Goods – recent developments," paper prepared for United Nations Industrial Development Organization, Vienna, Overseas Development Institute.

te Velde, Dirk Willem et al. 2006. "A Critical Assessment of the EU's Trade-Related Assistance (TRA) to Third Countries – Lessons from the Past, Policy Options for the Future," study for the International Trade Committee of the European Parliament, Overseas Development Institute.

World Bank. 2001. "Effective Use of Development Finance for International Public Goods," *Global Development Finance*, Washington, D.C.: World Bank.

World Bank. 2006. "Doha Development Report and Aid for Trade," progress report for Development Committee Meeting, Washington, D.C.: World Bank.

WTO. 2006. *Recommendations of the Task force on Aid for Trade*, Aid for Trade Task Force, WT/AFT/1, 27 July.

WTO/OECD. 2005. *Report on Trade-Related Technical Assistance and Capacity Building (TRTA/CB)*, http://www.oecd.org/dataoecd/27/4/11422694.pdf.

Zedillo, Ernesto et al. 2005. "Strengthening the Global Trade Architecture for Economic Development: An Agenda for Action," http://www.ycsg.yale.edu/focus/gta/GTA_policy_brief.doc.

5 Aid for Trade: A New Issue in the WTO

SHEILA PAGE

The explicit recognition of a World Trade Organization (WTO) interest in, and responsibility for, aid at its Sixth Ministerial Conference in Hong Kong[1] raised high expectations that it would now be possible to ensure that no country lost from the Doha negotiations, and that developing countries would receive the assistance they needed to take advantage of any improved access to markets. But there was also concern due to disappointment at both the limited results of the technical assistance mentioned so frequently in the Uruguay Round Agreement and the failure of the Integrated Framework[2] to guarantee that donors responded to identified needs. After considering the scope and mechanisms for Aid for Trade from March to July, and receiving submissions from international organizations and WTO member countries, the WTO Aid for Trade Task Force[3] submitted its recommendations to the WTO General Council of 27–28 July 2006 (perhaps the only Doha Round deadline that was met). The General Council took note of them, and considered them formally in October 2006.

Everyone could agree in principle that Aid for Trade is a good thing. The problem was to move to specific proposals that observe the principles of both aid and trade and that could obtain consensus from all WTO members and the support of a range of other institutions, including the international financial institutions, regional organizations, and non-trade elements of the governments of both donor and recipient countries. This chapter will first review what types of aid would meet WTO-related needs, and the types needed more broadly to help countries use trade as part of their development strategies. Secondly, it will consider how to decide which needs and which countries or regions should receive Aid for Trade. It will then discuss how to apply some of the general principles for aid that any scheme should take into account. The final section analyzes what any Aid for Trade package should include, taking into account the different types of need identified, the

1 See WTO (2005a) paragraph 57, as quoted in the Introduction to this volume.

2 Integrated Framework for Trade-Related Technical Assistance to Least Developed Countries. Outlined in the Introduction to this volume.

3 The members of the WTO Aid for Trade Task Force were Barbados, Brazil, Canada, Chile, Colombia, EU, India, Japan, Thailand, U.S., and the coordinators of the African, Caribbean and Pacific (ACP), African, and Least Developed Country (LDC) groups. The chair was Ambassador Mia Horn af Rantzien, the Ambassador of Sweden.

The author is grateful to Massimiliano Calì, Dominique Njinkeu, and Dirk Willem te Velde for their comments and contributions to this chapter.

different timing of needs (adjustment to specific changes in the trading system and long-term development), and the different principles that tend to guide the aid and trade discourses, and consider how the proposals made by the WTO Aid for Trade Task Force meet these requirements.

1 Aid for Trade coverage and principles[4]

1.1 Possible components of Aid for Trade

The Hong Kong mandate gives examples of Aid for Trade in terms of infrastructure and supply capacity, but also implies a strong link between it and the Doha Round. The Concept Paper that the WTO Secretariat prepared to guide the Task Force on Aid for Trade (WTO, 2006b) went further, and said that developing countries "expect Aid-for-Trade to go well beyond the scope of the IF, and help them to cover the costs of implementing WTO Agreements, macroeconomic adjustment, training and institution-building, and supply-side capacity and infrastructure." Capacity building and infrastructure are familiar terms, but the "costs" of WTO agreements and contributing to "the development dimension of the Doha Development Agenda (DDA)" are less clear. This section will suggest some possible definitions of these terms in the Aid for Trade context. It is not clear whether "macroeconomic adjustment" is the best description of the type of adjustment that countries are expecting. Lower external income or higher import costs clearly can have macroeconomic costs, as could loss of fiscal revenue. The IMF's scheme, the Trade Integration Mechanism (discussed in Chapter 4 by te Velde) focuses on such costs because of the nature of the IMF's mandate. But in trade and normal trade assistance terms, what is required is switching to new types of production or new markets. This is production adjustment or even "structural" adjustment.

1.1.1 *Narrow definitions of Aid for Trade: WTO-related costs*

A. Implementation of existing commitments under the Doha Round.

The WTO's July 2004 Framework Agreement (WTO, 2004) included in its Annex on "Trade Facilitation" an explicit provision for making fulfillment of commitments under trade facilitation subject to receiving adequate technical and other assistance:

> Support and assistance should also be provided to help developing and least-developed countries implement the commitments resulting from the negotiations, in accordance with their nature and scope. In this context, it is recognized that negotiations could lead to certain commitments whose implementation would require support for infrastructure development on the part of some Members. In these limited cases, developed-country Members will make every effort to ensure support and assistance directly related to the nature and scope of the commitments in order to allow implementation. It is understood, however, that in cases where required support and assistance for such infrastructure is not forthcoming, and where a

[4] For a listing of official papers on Aid for Trade, and a bibliography of reports and research on it, see ODI (2007).

> developing or least-developed Member continues to lack the necessary capacity, implementation will not be required. While every effort will be made to ensure the necessary support and assistance, it is understood that the commitments by developed countries to provide such support are not open-ended.

Such support is thus a recognized potential cost of a Doha settlement, so there is expected to be an obligation on developed countries to provide it or to accept that some developing countries will not be obliged to implement the agreement.

Implementing trade facilitation may be of benefit to a country in the medium term, and it may benefit its trading partners, some of which will also be developing countries, but it is not necessarily an immediate priority for a cash-constrained government; accepting the commitment is therefore a "cost" of entering the WTO agreement. It can be argued (and World Bank officials have argued) that meeting WTO-related costs is not an appropriate use of official aid money, as it is for the benefit of the WTO system or of more advanced traders, not for the benefit of the developing countries. There are two possible reasons for including WTO-related costs in Aid for Trade funds in spite of this argument. First, a predictable and enforced system of international rules is a benefit for developing countries. Second, developing countries (even if not necessarily the ones incurring the implementation costs) will get benefits from a Doha settlement, so these are necessary costs for a development end (just as a road across a coastal country may have developmental benefits for a landlocked neighbor). But the indirect nature of the benefit may mean that even if it is financed as an obligation of the developed members of the WTO, it may not necessarily be as part of their aid budgets (such as in the precedents of a separate budget line for the EU Action Plan for Sugar or the cohesion objective in Swedish aid). Any Aid for Trade mechanism must therefore allow for non-traditional aid components.

B. *Implementation of the explicit commitments in the Uruguay Round that were left without an implementing mechanism. This would cover commitments under the Marrakech Declaration for the costs imposed by agricultural liberalization on Net Food Importing Developing Countries (NFIDCs).*

On covering these costs, there is a clear commitment.

The fact that countries have benefited from the previous, distorted, system of agricultural subsidies and other interventions is not in itself a welfare or development argument for helping them when the distortion is removed, but a shock from a major systemic change to a developing country is a potentially valid use for aid, and helping a country adjust to a long-term sustainable pattern of production and trade in food products is certainly a developmental aim.

Subject to the pattern of implementation (if there are any agreements they are likely to be phased in), the highest costs, of both higher imports and higher investment in adjustment, are likely to be early in the process, with the cost diminishing over time.

C. *The costs to developing countries of implementation by other countries of WTO agreements that benefit others – that is, the costs of preference erosion. (Higher food costs are also the result of reforms that benefit others, but they are treated separately because the status of the commitments is different.)*

This issue has been recognized in the July 2004 Decision and Hong Kong Declaration as a legitimate concern of the WTO. The first proposal to mention it was the Harbinson proposal on agriculture in 2003 (WTO, 2003), which suggested dealing with it by maintaining preferences "to the maximum extent technically feasible." As many preferences offered zero tariffs, this would have meant no liberalization, and was therefore clearly contrary to normal WTO principles and was unacceptable to those seeking liberalization. Liberalizing preferred products by less by either including them in sensitive products or delaying liberalization would be less damaging to non-preference-receiving countries, but would still impose costs on some developing countries. These arguments contributed to efforts to identify non-trade solutions, such as Aid for Trade.

The welfare or developmental arguments for including or excluding the costs of preference erosion are the same as for food import costs, and the pattern of costs over time is likely to be similar.

Reforming agriculture or lowering tariffs removes distortions that have damaged other economies. That the food-importing and preference-dependent countries have been gaining from these distortions can be used as a reason not to give them more special assistance. But the parallel arguments are often rejected within countries, especially when those affected are poor or have the political power to prevent reform. Calling the Doha Round "development" suggests that some solution should be found for losses to developing countries.

D. Other implementation costs.

The Uruguay Round is believed to have imposed important costs on developing countries, particularly the Trade-Related Aspects of Intellectual Property Rights (TRIPS), Sanitary and Phyto-Sanitary (SPS), and Technical Barriers to Trade (TBT) agreements. There was no formal WTO commitment to help countries meet the costs of these agreements, as there is expected to be for trade facilitation in this round, but there is an implied commitment from the promise to tackle implementation and from the "best endeavor" commitments on technical assistance that were frequent in the Uruguay Round. The arguments for helping countries to meet these are the same as for trade facilitation costs, and, like these, the costs are likely to be small. There have been large estimates for the costs of implementing Uruguay Round commitments, but these have included all costs related to the commitments, not just the legal commitments, and have been based on very limited country evidence.

A final direct cost of WTO agreements that is sometimes included is:

E. The fiscal costs of liberalizing a country's own imports.

The economic justification for including this element is weaker because this is not a cost to the country, but a transfer from the government to those who buy the imports. If there is not then an adjustment of taxes by which the government recoups the revenue, some groups within the country receive the income that the government loses. These may be the importing companies, commercial users of the product, or consumers. In principle, each of these could be taxed to recoup government revenue. Another reason for questioning whether this cost should be included is that it is a normal part of adjustment to a WTO settlement, not an exceptional one from the introduction of either new rules (like A and D) or major reforms to the system (bringing agriculture into it and taking preferences out of it, like B and C).

1.1.2 *Broad definitions of Aid for Trade: Aid to help countries use trade for development*

For all the elements that fall under a Broad definition, the developmental case is clear and not at issue: countries need infrastructure, institutions, technical capacity, investment, and so forth, in order to trade, both in general and in the specific case of new liberalization under the WTO. What is new and controversial is the implication that the WTO should have a role in this type of aid. One role that it has already had is in shifting aid agencies' attention back to trade after the emphasis on direct poverty reduction in the 1990s. Therefore, there has been and will be more Broad Aid for Trade (at least until the current support for this form of aid wanes), with or without a direct role for the WTO.

F. Support for conventionally-recognized trade policy capacity building.

This includes "mainstreaming" trade into Poverty Reduction Strategy Papers (PRSPs) and development plans; assistance in and training for trade negotiations; and other capacity building relevant to trade-related policies. Within this, assistance to negotiate, which has been a very conspicuous part of trade-related aid, may be particularly difficult to incorporate into a WTO-related program. This type of assistance can be very damaging to developing country bargaining if it is too closely related to negotiations. Emphasizing the donor-recipient relationship can distort trade negotiations.

G. Support for infrastructure and other measures to build countries' ability to trade.

Infrastructure may be needed at country or regional level. Improving public sector efficiency enables investment, by both public and private sectors, to respond to trading opportunities, whether from the Doha Round or more generally. There is a particular need for infrastructure based on regional needs because the country-based nature of most aid programs makes it difficult to identify and fund cross-country projects. This can include regional facilities such as ports, or bilateral arrangements such as a road from a landlocked country to a port.

There are practical and conceptual difficulties in separating trade-related infrastructure from other infrastructure, suggesting that purpose-driven definitions will be required.

H. Support for institutions that improve capacity to trade.

1. At country level
2. At regional and/or other country group level (for example, regional banks or the Advisory Centre on WTO Law)

This is closely related to capacity building, under F. As with infrastructure, there have been problems in getting support for multi-country projects.

I. Support for the supply-side in the sense of building up private sector enterprise in new export (or import-replacing) areas.

This may be what the WTO Concept Paper (WTO, 2006b) means by "supply-side." Arguably, this is normal adjustment to changes in trade opportunities (or to current opportunities), so it is not necessarily either exceptional in scale and type (as the Narrow categories are) or exceptionally concentrated on developing countries (as the Broad categories are). It is not clear how it would be possible to reconcile this support with aid modalities: aid to the private sector might involve picking some companies to benefit and not others. But current fashions in aid and development theory tend to distrust "picking winners." Such an approach might, however, be consistent with the support by some donors (notably the U.S.) and some NGOs for involving the private sector in aid. Infrastructure (G) also, of course, assists the private sector.

1.2 The interaction of Narrow and Broad Aid for Trade

Aid for Trade could cover a combination of Narrow and Broad Aid, including any or all of the categories of each. But it is not necessarily appropriate to estimate the needs or the supply of funds by adding them together. Broad aid can be discussed and implemented without considering the Narrow. However, the criteria for two of the categories under Narrow – the adjustment costs from food price increases or preference erosion (B and C) (and fiscal losses [E] if they are included) – can only be used to identify needs for support and, subject to the uncertainties in the estimates, the quantity of support needed. These do not define what the funds would be used for. The criteria under Broad, along with the specific WTO needs of implementation under A and D, could be used both independently and to define the purposes for which funds allocated under Narrow were used.

The way to solve the adjustment problems in the medium term is to increase capacity to trade. While a purely trade or reciprocity-based policy would imply offering countries cash payments to replace their lost gains from low food prices or preferences, the nature of aid relations suggests that the payments will be conditional on their use for an identified need. Grouping them in Aid for Trade suggests that this will be a trade need.

In the event that the pause in the Doha Round becomes a collapse, all the Broad needs would remain relevant. Some of the Narrow would cease to be relevant, and the legal or negotiating arguments for the others would also lapse.

Some donors do not view the needs identified under Narrow as directly related to development because, as was noted above for trade facilitation, there is no direct development effect or because they arise from a trade negotiation, not from a country-based assessment of priorities (as discussed below). Therefore, additional aid to cover them might need to come under a separate budget line. For this purpose, separate calculations of the amounts are needed (see Chapter 6 by Calì in this volume).

Acceptance of a role for the WTO in ensuring that needs are met, both in terms of commitments in 2006 in securing commitments in the medium term, may be stronger for the Narrow needs than the Broad, although the Hong Kong Declaration covers both. It might, however, be decided to use the Narrow criteria to identify countries in need of extra assistance, not to calculate exact needs, and this would require a coordinated approach. More important, any plan for assisting a country with building trade capacity would need to take account of funds from both types of assessment, and any country will be concerned to ensure that its total receipts are sufficient.

1.3 Alternative classifications

The classification suggested here is intended to divide Aid for Trade according to the relevance of each type of aid to the WTO and the acceptability of each type by normal aid criteria. The classification in the WTO Concept Paper, as already noted, follows a similar, although less explicit, model. In a summary of the debate on Aid for Trade in a World Bank publication, Nielson (2006) suggests that it covers technical assistance and capacity building (both of which would come under F), institutional reform (which would fall under H), infrastructure (G), and adjustment costs. This last is defined as for preference erosion (C), NFIDCs (B), and "major processes of trade reform," and there is some emphasis (p. 331) on loss of revenue (E), and supply in the private sector (I). It does not appear to cover implementation costs, whether for new or old commitments (A or D).

2 Eligibility criteria and allocation of funds

The question of which countries should be eligible for any special treatment is sensitive in both aid and trade. The only classification in current use that is the same for both areas is Least Developed Countries. This is the determinant of eligibility for the Integrated Framework and is used to offer more special treatment in the WTO – both in WTO rules (compliance with TRIPS, lack of obligations to make offers on goods in the Doha Round, for example) and in WTO-permitted derogations such as preferences. That these countries should be included in Aid for Trade is already determined in the Hong Kong statement, and they were all eligible to be included in NFIDCs.

Beyond this, the WTO gives special status in a few agreements to "developing countries," and specifies this as a condition for allowing preferences. Although this is conventionally described as "self-selecting," in practice the list is not open to all: the countries that have always been on it normally remain on it, but can be strongly encouraged to graduate themselves (for example, countries that have joined the EU), and countries joining the WTO have had to negotiate details of their rules, even if they have been allowed to call themselves developing.

While aid agencies can determine their own differentiations among recipients and define groups, the WTO can only differentiate by consensus of all members, and it is clear that there will be no new general categories adopted in this round. What has become the practice is to list, either positively or negatively, countries other than LDCs that may be eligible for particular treatment (such as in the agreement on agricultural subsidies in the Uruguay Round) or excluded from it (such as in the WTO agreement on importing pharmaceutical products of 2003). In legal terms, any eligibility for Aid for Trade specified by the WTO would have to follow this model.[5]

[5] The suggestion by the WTO Appellate Body that preferences could discriminate among developing countries if the categories were clear and relevant supports the view that *ad hoc* differentiation is emerging in the WTO.

For NFIDCs, there is already a list, although this could be revised once the Doha agricultural settlement is known. It is a simple list, not an assessment of the exact losses of each member, although it was based on such analysis. This could be one model for the other Narrow types of Aid for Trade. It might be particularly relevant for preference erosion, which shares the characteristics that the effect can be large, by any calculation, but where the numbers are not knowable with any certainty. The list model could also be used for countries likely to be in need of assistance for trade facilitation (A) or other implementation costs (D).[6]

For any adjustment-cost-based criterion for eligibility, it would be necessary to ask if it was the costs of a particular problem, total costs, or total net costs that made a country eligible. (A country might suffer a little preference erosion, have some food imports, but have sufficient gains on other products that its net result from a settlement was positive.) The discussion has normally been in terms of total costs, and this is consistent with treating the problem as an exceptional shock, not just a disappointing negotiating outcome, and also consistent with giving the Doha Round a development bias. If any scheme adopted for Aid for Trade uses adjustment costs as indicative, rather than as formulae, to determine the quantum of aid, it might not be necessary to agree on the way they were measured. But if it is decided that there must be certainty, then it would be necessary to choose which measure, and whether it was net or total. In either case, some minimum level of loss would need to be set, and some might argue for a maximum level of income per capita or other measure of development.

Alternatively, there has always been the possibility for any country to ask for the application of a particular rule to be postponed (often used, for example, of the rules for customs valuation). The July 2004 agreement suggests a similar model for trade facilitation, by which countries present evidence to an appropriate Committee that they have not had the necessary aid. This would be a more discretionary approach, and might therefore not meet the increased determination by developing countries to have clear and enforceable commitments for special and differential treatment. It has been supported by some commentators as a way of introducing a more flexible approach to determining development needs in the rules-based WTO system.

Identifying countries that need aid to build their general trade capacity and ability to respond to new trade opportunities is likely to need a broader development measure, and could include all developing countries or perhaps all except those who chose to exclude themselves, as in the TRIPS agreement on imports. As some of this assistance is likely to be for international institutions, such as the Advisory Centre on WTO Law, or to meet regional needs, introducing strictly differentiated eligibility requirements could restrict its usefulness (most regions, whether legal or geographical, include countries at different levels of income).

If implementation of Aid for Trade is through existing programs, then the rules of each donor and program will constrain what is offered to whom. As there is a strong argument for accepting that existing systems will work best if they work in their normal mode, and with their normal recipients, this may be effective for those

[6] One category implied by the presence of Barbados in the WTO Task Force could be "small and vulnerable economies" (SVEs), but if the SVEs really are exceptionally vulnerable, one of the numerical tests of eligibility would presumably ensure that they received support, and this would be more consistent with the trend towards defining particular needs (as in the rules on importing pharmaceuticals).

needs and those countries that are covered. But this suggests there will be a need to identify gaps, and to find ways of filling them. It is particularly important that the mechanism agreed for implementing Aid for Trade find a credible way of doing this, as failure to meet identified needs is one of the major perceived weaknesses of both the WTO's previous relationship to aid (the identification of the NFIDCs in the Uruguay Round) and of the Integrated Framework.

3 Reconciling Aid for Trade and programs and principles for aid

There are three basic problems in the relationship between the need- and purpose-based assessment of Aid for Trade that is presented here (and that underlies the inclusion of aid in the Hong Kong Declaration), and the normal discourse on aid: (i) mobilizing sufficient funds; (ii) coordinating multiple funds from multiple donors with multiple purposes; and (iii) reconciling aid criteria, including local participation in decisions, with ensuring that there is aid directed at specific trade purposes. The first of these problems is discussed by Calì in Chapter 6. The others are summarized here.

A. *Reconciling multiple funds from multiple donors, each covering some countries and/or some types of spending in order to secure adequate funding for all relevant countries and purposes.*

The different purposes and the large scale of what donors are now calling Aid for Trade, as well as the unwillingness of both donors and recipients to rely on a single existing institution, suggest that the way in which Aid for Trade will work will be mainly through existing funds, multilateral and bilateral. These will be augmented by the new commitments by donors to support Aid for Trade, and in some cases the changes in scale will require new administration and new types of spending. It is possible that some of the needs identified here will be so far from what donors and their rules of operation recognize as official development assistance that new funds or new sections of funds will be needed. The World Bank, for example, has stated that supporting a Doha outcome is not its responsibility. (The way in which the European Commission designated a new budget line for its support for ACP sugar producers is discussed in the chapter by te Velde). This suggests a complex and multi-player mechanism.

Ensuring that some mechanisms are available for all the needs will be the first problem to address. Securing the funds – that is, ensuring that the commitments are not only made, but are credible – will need to be done through the mechanisms that each agency or fund uses to set its program. It is unlikely that aid agencies will agree to have their funds bound in a WTO agreement, or that the WTO will agree to include such binding, but some agency, whether the WTO or a new overriding agency or committee, will need to ensure that such commitments are made.

The WTO or some other agency will then need to monitor implementation over a medium term period. There are various reporting mechanisms in place, such as the WTO/OECD Database (2007), country reports on donors by the OECD, reports on countries that are both donors and recipients through the WTO Trade Policy Reviews and the IMF country reports, and reports on recipient countries through the World Bank. These currently cover some of the information that would be required, and could be extended to include the rest. The commitment by the WTO and the international financial agencies to "coherence" suggests that reports on both overall results and individual countries could go from all these agencies to the WTO, perhaps through both the Committee on Trade and Development (to monitor total implementation), and the Trade Policy Review Mechanism (to cover individual countries). In some cases, most obviously for trade facilitation, the reports might have a legal WTO function in determining whether countries needed to comply with the rules.

B. Reconciling efficient and effective aid administration with ensuring that trade criteria are applied (ensuring that trade is raised from its frequent position as a low priority for conventional aid).

In policy discussions and the literature on aid, there have been conflicts between targeting specific areas for help and taking a broad view of a country's development process, and between donor- or internationally-determined priorities and country priorities. For example, the recent initiatives to deal with particular illnesses have been criticized for causing major distortions to health and total budgets. A discussion of the positive and negative effects of global health initiatives reveals a concern that global initiatives do not sit easily with existing national programs. Lele et al. (2005) observe a shift in the focus of global health interventions away from general preventative measures towards the prevention and treatment of specific diseases, leading to augmented financial resources to combat specific diseases. For these, there are clear advantages: coordination of aid, development of disease-specific strategies, mobilization of cutting-edge technical knowledge from diverse sources, increased efforts to address issues of global drugs, promoting global networking among professionals, development of technical guidelines and performance indicators, improved surveillance, support for epidemiological and operational research, and the development of incentive systems. But possible negative impacts include competition among different programs for the same resources, a lack of effort to develop a single-purpose staff among multipurpose health workers, the failure to integrate the single-disease campaigns into sustainable programs in developing countries, the fragmentation of multipurpose health services, distorted allocation of scarce human and financial resources, and the lack of evidence of cost effectiveness. It would be easy to envisage a similar conflict between expertise and coordination for trade-related activities.

In 2005, through the Paris Declaration on Aid Effectiveness, donors signed up to principles on harmonization, alignment and ownership that were subsequently cited in the Aid for Trade Task Force recommendations (section F.2). Rogerson (2005) summarizes the main elements in the aid effectiveness debate that donors are currently discussing (as part of the agenda set out in Paris and Rome before) as:

- *Ownership*, to respect the right – and responsibility – of the partner country itself to establish its development agenda, setting out its own strategies for poverty reduction and growth.
- *Alignment*, align development assistance with the development priorities and results-oriented strategies set out by the partner country and to progressively depend on partner countries' own systems.
- *Harmonization*, to streamline and harmonize donor policies.

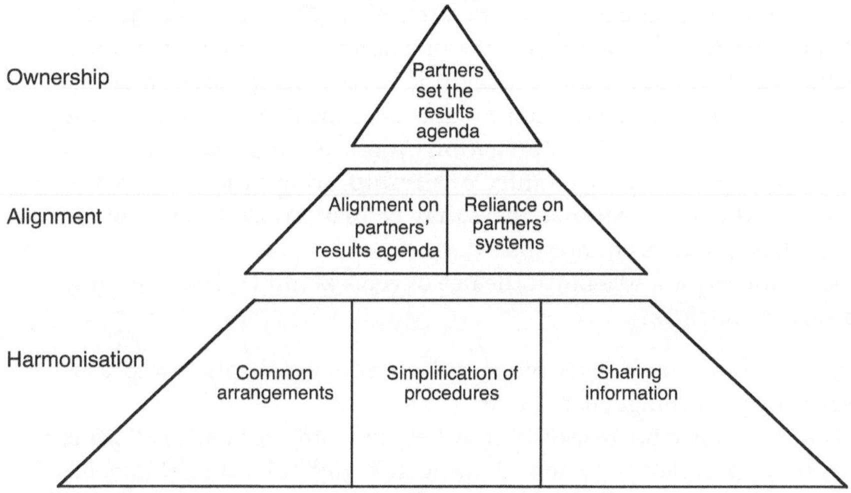

Chart 5.1. Aid effectiveness pyramid. (*Source:* Rogerson (2005))

These are set out graphically in Chart 5.1 above. But the conflict between country-determined agendas and international priorities may be more apparent than real. In practice, the degree of intervention by donors to assist countries to prepare their national assessments, to guide recipients in their choice of projects, and to limit recipients by specifying their own priorities and what they are willing to fund means that there is still *de facto* intervention to influence the allocation of aid among sectors.

Each of these aid points has led to the adoption of a set of objectives and suggested measurable targets and indicators in aid programs. It has also led to discussions by the major financing and donor agencies. Such discussions do not sit easily with the debates on aid for vertical funds. In fact, the two debates appear separate and often ignore each other. The premise behind any special funds, including the proposals on Aid for Trade, is that there is also a need for mechanisms to ensure that international obligations or national objectives that are identified outside the narrow focus of poverty-related aid are funded.

Indeed, Rogerson (2005) finds that there are systemic flaws in the aid architecture that cannot be remedied by the country-based coordination envisaged in Paris. These include:

- Lack of agreement on whether and how donors should balance aid allocations across countries.
- Lack of a road map from a top-level commitment to increase aid to more specific commitments, and how this gets allocated to different countries, purposes, and agencies.
- The conundrum between, on the one hand, achieving long-term predictable aid partnerships and, on the other, having multiple lock-in devices to rescind contracts.

It was then suggested by Rogerson that donors should reserve a portion of all aid to be given in the form of large-scale, long-term recurrent-cost support, linked only to specific sectoral outcomes such as primary education provision.

This has relevance for the debate on aid for vertical funds or for specific purposes, and for Aid for Trade in particular. On the one hand, current country-based programs are unlikely to balance aid for vertical funds across countries, but on the other hand the debate on Aid for Trade cannot ignore all the developments in the areas of ownership, alignment, and harmonization. At one extreme, vertical funds including Aid for Trade do not allow country ownership, so questions related to use might be raised. At the other extreme, there may be inappropriate levels of aid allocated to Aid for Trade if all is country-based.

There are several voices for and against the use of vertical funds. Those arguing in favor include reasons such as:

- Vertical funds may build up a level of expertise and specialization and thus create a comparative advantage in an area;
- Vertical funds (for instance for research) may benefit from economies of scale;
- Vertical funds may be better at co-coordinating at a global level solutions for global problems (co-ordination and harmonization); and
- Vertical funds can ensure that money is effectively distributed to a cause.

Arguments against include:

- Possible lack of ownership by receiving country;
- Prone to sudden shocks in donor tastes; and
- Challenges in aligning vertical funds with country programs (see problems of health funds).

A complicating element in the discussion of a possible vertical fund for trade is the significant level of distrust, occasionally even contempt, between aid and trade agencies and between their practitioners. Aid agencies fear that the ability of countries to exert pressure in the WTO could lead to these countries receiving more than an "objectively determined" share of aid funds. Trade people worry that aid programs are too focused on immediate poverty reduction and not enough on long-term production and trade (Page, 2006).[7] Although allowing countries to participate effectively in decisions is clearly an element of any definition of development, including the UN Millennium Development Goals (and there now seems to be a turning point in aid priorities towards growth and away from short-term poverty reduction), there is an inevitable conflict between a needs-driven and a negotiation-driven approach.

4 What Aid for Trade needs, and what the Task Force proposed

4.1 Scope

The needs identified here vary from low-cost technical assistance to major infrastructure investment. All discussion of Aid for Trade now assumes that there will be significant additional funding, and thus that it is reasonable to discuss new

[7] Hoebink (2005) shows that the share of "trade" in the distribution of programmed resources by the EC under the 9th EDF (in 58 country strategy papers) was a mere 0.1%, with structural adjustment, water supply, rural development, and health being major sectors (though infrastructure and regional integration are also important components). This share might be higher in the 10th EDF.

aid mechanisms for developing projects, disbursing funds, and monitoring what is achieved. (Chapter 6 by Calì discusses in detail estimates of past funding, funding needs, and funding commitments on Aid for Trade.) The recommendations of the Task Force state that they are dependent on the provision of "substantial additional targeted resources" (section C), but they do not set up a mechanism to secure this either in the immediate future or in the long run. They note that the Hong Kong Declaration gives the responsibility for consulting on these to the WTO Director-General. There is no discussion of how to secure continuing replenishment of funds in future, although the amounts will be monitored (see Section 4.3 below). There is no recommendation that donors should bind the funds that they have announced, even in terms of each agency rather than under WTO rules. Countries will need sufficient confidence in the pledges made in Hong Kong in 2006 to sign up to any Doha agreement with the assurance that their costs and adjustment needs will be met.

The identification here of possible needs for funding suggests that there are very different types of need. These are likely to require different types of organizations and programs to meet them. Some needs are small and easily defined (for example, assessments of new circumstances or institutional reform to meet particular implementation needs, often to a deadline). These require an organization able to offer quick disbursement, probably with a minimum of conditionality or planning. Others require longer term and more considered programs to ensure that building the supply capacity to trade is well integrated into a country's (and perhaps a region's) development program. This contrast is not an inconsistency, and there are examples of successful programs of both types. A third type, the costs of adjustment, requires a macroeconomic analysis of a country's overall eligibility, not assessment of specific needs. The possible relationship of aid under this heading to countries' willingness to allow other countries to make concessions in the Doha Round that will raise agricultural prices or reduce preferences means that this type may also require an approach to allocating money among countries that is not based on normal criteria of poverty or ability to use aid funds.

The Task Force recommendations could be interpreted as covering all the needs identified here. The Task Force report categorizes them, drawing on the WTO/OECD Database classification but explicitly extending them, as (section C):

- Trade policy and regulations
- Trade development
- Trade-related infrastructure
- Building productive capacity
- Trade-related adjustment
- Other trade-related needs.

The "adjustment" category could include adjustment to preference erosion, higher food prices, and loss of tariff revenue, as the objectives include helping countries to "adjust to trade reform and liberalization" (section F.1). So far, there has been no formal coordination between the work of the Task Force and negotiations on agriculture or non-agricultural market access so as to allocate some or all responsibility for dealing with preference erosion or food costs to Aid for Trade.

The Task Force recommendations follow the Hong Kong Declaration in specifying that Aid for Trade is for "developing countries, particularly LDCs" (section F.1). They do not suggest any categories other than this. They do not suggest any a priori allocation by country.

The Task Force placed particular emphasis on the need to consider regional needs, and thus meet one identified gap in current aid (sections F.3, F.5.2). It did not explicitly deal with the problem that some of the needs closely related to WTO agreements (such as the costs of implementing trade facilitation requirements) or some adjustment costs might not fit the mandates of aid donors, because their immediate purpose is to meet international obligations, not to promote a country's development in accordance with a nationally adopted plan. The Task Force dealt with this issue by implication by providing for "clearing house functions" to meet unfunded needs (see Section 4.3 below). The recommendations further emphasize the need for donors to reform their mechanisms to meet the demand for trade-related assistance more effectively.

The Task Force recommendations show a preference for defining trade needs through a general country or country/donor planning process (section F.5.1). Of the needs defined here, this seems more appropriate to the longer term than to those requiring immediate disbursement of small sums. Although the recommendations note the need to minimize administrative costs, they seem to assume that a program approach will normally be appropriate. This contrasts with the emphasis on targeted, quick-disbursing funds in some other vertical funds (see Chapter 4 by te Velde) or in successful precedents for trade-related aid by the regional development banks.

4.2 Aid or trade principles?

As discussed above, there is a potential conflict between country-led and problem-led criteria for aid. The first sees aid as a means of providing general support for all of a country's needs, with choices made within this by the country (or donor) in response to its own identification of priorities, suitable for that country at a particular time. But the premise behind both the donor commitments of increased trade-related aid and the inclusion of paragraph 57 in the Hong Kong Declaration was that there has been insufficient Aid for Trade, not just because of general constraints, but because it has had too low a priority in donor and country programs. The existing vertical funds for environment, health, and other needs show that trade is not the only area where those outside the aid process have identified a need for more aid, and show both the advantages and the disadvantages of solving the problem by providing finance "tied" to a particular subject. There is increased knowledge, clear identification of needs, and concentration of resources; but also distortion and negative effects on other programs. There is now an additional problem: once some vertical funds exist, there is an argument that other general needs require their own vertical fund in order to avoid being "crowded out" by the subjects that have their own facilities.

The Task Force report reflects the irreconcilable trade and aid approaches. The Task Force recommendations formally look only at aid principles, and emphasize the need for a "country-driven" approach based on the Paris Declaration principles. But the report's emphasis on ensuring that there are clear definitions of what is to be included under Aid for Trade (as described above), and its provision for agencies to identify cross-border needs, could provide some assurance that there will be pressure to spend on trade needs. Its compromise is two apparently inconsistent recommendations (section F.4), that donors and agencies should:

- Move towards a program/sector/budget approach, if country-owned, if mainstreamed in national development strategies and if a robust system of financial accountability is in place; and
- Make targeted funds available for building infrastructure and removing supply-side constraints – over and above capacity building and technical assistance – perhaps as co-financing with multilateral development banks.

These recommendations do not resolve the problem of whether Aid for Trade should be offered to countries identified as needing particular types of spending by some external process in addition to that identified as needed by the countries themselves. For regional or multi-country programs, where action by one country is needed to help another to trade (transit infrastructure or trade facilitation, for example), there is a potential conflict between externally and nationally identified needs.

The importance given to regional needs, and in particular to the regional development banks, may mean an implicit shift towards a more sectoral rather than a country-program based approach. Both the Inter-American Development Bank and the Asian Development Bank have experience in such lending, and have been less committed to the PRSP/country strategy approach. They and the International Trade Centre emphasized this type of assistance in their presentations to the Task Force.

4.3 Securing implementation

The fact that trade-related aid has increased in recent years, without a "Global Trade Fund" could suggest that normal, horizontal, donors agree that there is a need to spend more on trade, and perhaps therefore that a specific "trade" fund is not needed. But the history of aid flows shifting from one priority to another suggests that those who support more Aid for Trade may justifiably feel a need to ensure that the increased shares to trade are sustained. The commitment in the WTO Hong Kong Declaration, and the identification of increased costs that countries will face because of new WTO obligations, also suggest that some formal way of guaranteeing a continued priority for trade needs to be found.

WTO member countries will not forget that the World Bank, although now showing interest in Aid for Trade, retreated from its pre-Cancún commitment to support trade-related adjustment needs (IMF, 2003), and rejected the support among countries in Geneva for a new initiative in its paper of September 2005.[8] At Hong Kong, the World Bank stated that the "Bank and Fund also plan to further assess the nature and magnitude of adjustment needs of countries facing external shocks associated with multilateral liberalization. We stand ready to coordinate with other donors to bring complementary packages of assistance, in the form of grants or loans as appropriate in these cases" (WTO, 2005b). This implies that

[8] The Bank published the Geneva analysis on Aid for Trade as an appendix to its report, but did not accept it (IMF/World Bank, 2005).

the Bank and the IMF want a coordinating role, but won't deal with adjustment themselves.

There are two elements in the needs for Aid for Trade identified here that could require some form of guarantee, or legal commitment, plus continuing monitoring, in addition to the informal donor-by-donor commitments already recorded. The first is that some countries will face exceptionally high costs (in relation to their economies) from the implementation of any reasonably ambitious agreement. These are what we have called the 'narrow' needs. Experience since the Uruguay Round shows that while small costs, particularly those easily tied to a need for specific spending (customs rules, for example) did attract additional aid, those which require a macroeconomic approach both to calculate them and to find a way of meeting them (adjustment needs following on the terms of trade change in agriculture) were left to one side. It is not possible to argue that this is simply because they were too small: they may have been small, but no calculations of need were done, in either the WTO or aid contexts. As discussed above, some donors even question whether either type of implementation cost should receive aid money if it is imposed by external commitments, not derived from a country's own development program.[9]

The second element is the growth in 'broad' Aid for Trade: how to ensure that the increase that has occurred in the last five years will in fact be repeated, as the pledges made in 2005 promised? The increase in the past has been the result of changes in individual programs, although responding to a general increase in interest in trade. Will this continue, or, if other interests emerge, will trade fall back into neglect? A case in point is the large increase in infrastructure expenditure between 2003 and 2004 (see Chapter 6 by Calì), which has been entirely driven by U.S. foreign policy interests in rebuilding Iraq and Afghanistan.

The first problem suggests that there may be a need for new funds, with new criteria, either as designated parts of individual donors' programs (the EU Action Plan for Sugar, for example) or in a new multilateral form (for example, the Highly Indebted Poor Countries Initiative (HIPC) or the vertical funds in health). In addition, there may be a need for a new assessment process (such as the IF for trade in PRSPs, TIM for balance of payments costs, or the EU-ACP assessment of the costs of EPAs, as discussed in Chapter 4 by te Velde) to provide an agreed definition and calculation of macroeconomic adjustment needs. The IF precedent suggests that an assessment process divorced from any commitment to provide finance can be inadequate and disappointing. TIM provides both assessment and funding, although it then offers loans not grants. The EPA assessments are coming before binding trade commitments, not after as is suggested for Aid for Trade, so countries retain a choice not to make the trade commitment if the costs are too high.

There is an additional reason for believing that a special fund or special terms within normal funds may be needed. Although any financing provided on the basis of the adjustment costs of trade liberalization (B and C), could be used for purposes and in countries that might normally expect loan, not grant terms, the fact that countries need this additional finance for reasons of benefit to others, and as a

9 This suggests a limited view of what a country's program should include, as accepting an external obligation in implicit or explicit return for other benefits from the international trading system could be considered a proper decision for a country to make, not one to be questioned by a donor.

replacement for previous transfers, suggests that there is a need for at least some of this to be on concessional terms. Paragraph 57 suggests that Aid for Trade should be "where appropriate through grants or concessional loans." The "narrow needs" are all additional costs imposed on countries by changes in the international trading system, not investments that can be expected to have a long-term return, permitting the servicing of a debt. In the case of NFIDCs and preference erosion (B and C), the "cost" is the loss of a de facto transfer payment. For these, both equity (the countries themselves do not gain from the cost) and financial considerations (there is no identifiable return) suggest that the financing should be on grant terms for any developing country incurring significant costs.

The "broad needs" are for funding to enable a country to trade (or produce) more or more efficiently. In some instances, such as assistance to private sector production or for infrastructure of a type that can recover its costs, there may be a clear source of returns to repay a loan. For others, such as assistance to government capacity to negotiate or to build new institutions, there can be expected to be a return to the country as a whole, but not an identified income stream. For these, whether loans or grants are appropriate should be decided in the context of normal aid criteria. It will depend on the income level of the country and on the use of the funds.

Both these problems suggest that a new way is needed to monitor both the overall supply of funds and their allocation to countries' needs, in order to ensure that the new types of need are appropriately met and that the overall allocation to trade remains high and growing. Paragraph 57 outlined a role for the Task Force, in making recommendations, and for the Director-General, in consulting other organizations and reporting on appropriate mechanisms. These roles for the Task Force and Director-General seem to go beyond the suggestion in the WTO Concept Paper that the "main role the WTO can play this year is one of advocacy." Now that the WTO has accepted that meeting the costs of adjustment and providing for what countries "need to assist them to implement and benefit from WTO Agreements" are legitimate concerns, it will need to take responsibility for identifying the procedures that will be needed and "ensuring" that all of them take place. Some are required in the beginning to set out the programs; some in subsequent years to implement them. There is a need to check that donors have committed ("bound" in trade terms) the funds that they have announced, in terms of the rules of each agency. This needs to be sufficiently credible that countries can take on WTO-bound commitments with confidence that their needs for aid will be met. In subsequent years, the WTO will need to monitor that the commitments are kept.

The Task Force proposal follows the aid model of not imposing any reciprocal obligations on donors to fund identified needs. Insofar as peer pressure can be a substitute, its proposed set of monitoring mechanisms will provide information and opportunities to assess their compliance. In section F.6, the Task Force argued that, "Monitoring and evaluating progress is essential in building confidence that increased Aid for Trade will be delivered and effectively used. It will also provide strong incentives to both donors and recipients to advance the Aid for Trade agenda."

Under the Task Force proposals, there will be "clearing house functions" to identify needs that do not fit conventional categories or donor objectives, and with perhaps some role in ensuring that the needs are met. These could develop into a central role in coordinating aid, and solve the problem of needs that are not met by current aid programs. But the fact that proposals on this were weakened in the course of the Task Force's deliberations suggests that they will face resistance from established donors.

At the regional level, the Task Force suggested (section F.5.2), "a Regional Aid for Trade Committee, comprising sub-regional and regional organizations and financial institutions, to oversee the implementation of the sub-regional and regional dimensions of Aid for Trade, to report on needs, responses and impacts, and to oversee monitoring and evaluation."

At the global level, it suggested (section F.5.3) that, "While a clearing-house function should in most cases be performed at the country and the regional level, sessions dedicated to specific themes and groups of countries could be periodically organized to provide a platform for donors and developing countries to discuss specific gaps which may occur in the implementation of Aid for Trade. One important function could be to connect outstanding Trade-Related Assistance (TRA) needs to donors willing to contribute to their fulfillment." Its recommendations are to:

- Strengthen the following functions in relation to global issues:
  - the collection and analysis of data on trade policies and their impact, the facilitation of knowledge sharing, and the development of guidelines. Funding for such activities needs to be secured;
  - provision of information on existing Aid for Trade instruments and expertise; and
  - matching and brokering unfunded TRA-needs and available donor funding for such projects and programs.
- Assign responsibility for these functions. In doing so, priority should be given to improving and strengthening existing mechanisms before considering the establishment of a new clearing house at the global level.

But the Task Force did not clearly assign responsibility for these functions to a specific organization. Its only specific recommendation (section G) was, "after the completion of the Doha Development Agenda (DDA), that the Secretariat conduct an assessment of associated Aid-for-Trade needs in developing countries, particularly those most affected, including LDCs, and of how Aid for Trade can contribute to the development dimension of the DDA."

Finally, there is to be monitoring of aggregate Aid for Trade at country, regional, and global level by the various institutions involved, by donors, and by countries (and also by the private sector, although the mechanism for this is not explained). The OECD Development Assistance Committee (DAC) will supply data using definitions revised to be consistent with those proposed here for Aid for Trade. Reports will go to a "monitoring body in the WTO," with the possibility of requiring notification from member countries, all leading to an annual debate in the WTO General Council. The General Council is to "give political guidance on Aid for Trade." At the country level, there would be reviews in-country and by the WTO Trade Policy Reviews (section F.6).

Although the Trade Policy Reviews (TPR) would assess donor and recipient performance, it is never, of course, the function of the TPR to determine compliance with WTO commitments (much less, non-WTO commitments). But it is its function to provide the information on which such judgments can be made. A country being reviewed could use its response to the Secretariat TPR report to draw attention to any gaps in funding relative to what it had anticipated, and, if appropriate, relative to what had been identified as necessary for it to comply with WTO requirements on trade facilitation. This would then be discussed by the Trade Policy Review Body (equivalent to the General Council, but meeting to discuss a TPR). It could also be raised in the General Council meeting to discuss aggregate Aid for Trade.

The General Council discussion does not, on these suggestions, have an explicit function of approving or censuring performance. It might ask the Director-General and the Secretariat to include in the annual report on trade a chapter on the level, direction, and types of trade-related aid. This would, like the Trade Policy Reviews, allow users to reach their own conclusions on whether the aid was sufficient and appropriate to meet the commitments made.

The Task Force argued (section G) that "Aid for Trade is important in its own right." But the WTO General Council view of Aid for Trade as "an important element in the Doha Development Agenda" (WTO, 2006a) probably helps to explain why the recommendations were not approved in July 2006. The report of the Director-General to the December 2006 General Council, however, took it for granted that Aid for Trade will go ahead.

5 Assessment

The set of recommendations from the Task Force does not fully cover all the problems and needs identified in this chapter, and it does not provide the legally enforceable reciprocal commitments that would make Aid for Trade a full part of the WTO system. But the establishment of a mechanism to identify and find funding for unmet aid needs and the strong role of a non-aid agency, the WTO, in monitoring aid performance go far beyond any previous aid programs. If countries and the international agencies are all committed to a coherent international system, including a contribution of aid to promote greater trade, and where trade in turn is regarded as an important contribution to development, the proposals by the Task Force may be sufficient to ensure that the World Trade Organization can monitor the establishment and functioning of an effective system of Aid for Trade.

The Task Force justified the role of the WTO in Aid for Trade in terms of the "coherence mandate" (section H). It will be important that the international financial agencies, in particular the World Bank, also take coherence seriously. The IMF has done this with its Trade Integration Mechanism, but the World Bank has not yet altered its position that it has no responsibility for WTO-related needs.

REFERENCES

Hoebink, P. 2005. "European Development Aid in Transition," in O. Babarinde and G. Faber (eds.), *The European Union and the Developing Countries: The Contonou Agreement*, Leiden: Koninklijke Brill NV.

IMF. 2003. "IMF and World Bank Announce Plans to Support Developing Countries with Trade-Related Adjustment Needs in WTO Round," Press Release 03/140, 21 August.

IMF/World Bank. 2005. "Doha Development Agenda and Aid for Trade," prepared by the staffs of the IMF and World Bank, Washington, D.C.

Lele, U., Ronald Ridker, and Jagadish Upadhyay. 2005. "Health System Capacities in Developing Countries and Global Health Initiatives on Communicable Diseases," background paper prepared for the International Task Force on Global Public Goods, 22 April.

Nielson, J. 2006. "Aid for Trade," in Richard Newfarmer (ed.), *Trade, Doha and Development: A Window into the Issues*, Washington, D.C.: World Bank.

Overseas Development Institute. 2007. "Aid for Trade References Database," http://www.odi.org.uk/iedg/aid4trade.html.

Page, S. 2006. "Bringing Aid and Trade Together," in S. Page (ed.), *Trade and Aid – Partners or Rivals in Development Policy?* London: Cameron May.

Page, S. 2007. "The Potential Impact of the Aid for Trade Initiative," *G-24 Discussion Paper* no. 45, Geneva: UNCTAD.

Rogerson, A. 2005. "Aid Harmonization and Alignment: Bridging the Gaps Between Reality and the Paris Reform Agenda," *Development Policy Review*, 23(5): 531–552.

WTO. 2003. *Negotiations On Agriculture First Draft Of Modalities For The Further Commitments*, Committee on Agriculture, TN/AG/W/1/Rev.1, 18 March.

WTO. 2004. *Decision Adopted by the General Council on 1 August 2004*, Doha Work Program, WT/L/579, 2 August.

WTO. 2005a. *Draft Ministerial Declaration*, Ministerial Conference, Sixth Session, Hong Kong, 13–18 December 2005, Doha Work Program, WT/MIN(05)/W/3/Rev.2, 18 December.

WTO. 2005b. *World Bank – Statement by Mr. Danny Leipziger – Vice President and Head of Network (Speaking as an Observer)*, Ministerial Conference, Sixth Session, Hong Kong, 13–18 December 2005, WT/MIN(05)/ST/15, 14 December.

WTO. 2006a. *Recommendations of the Task force on Aid for Trade*, Aid for Trade Task Force, WT/AFT/1, 27 July.

WTO. 2006b. *Aid-For-Trade Concept Paper and Timeline for 2006*, prepared by the WTO Secretariat, Geneva, 17 January.

WTO. 2006c. *General Council Meeting of 27–28 July 2006*, http://www.wto.org/english/thewto_e/gcounc_e/meeting_july06_e.htm.

WTO/OECD. 2005. *Report on Trade-Related Technical Assistance and Capacity Building (TRTA/CB)*, http://www.oecd.org/dataoecd/27/4/11422694.pdf.

WTO/OECD. 2007. "Doha Development Agenda Trade Capacity Building Database," http://tcbdb.wto.org/.

6 Scale and Types of Funds for Aid for Trade

MASSIMILIANO CALÌ

1 Introduction

Despite the fact that Aid for Trade is widely recognized as an essential component of a successful World Trade Organization (WTO) Doha Round (WTO, 2005), there is as yet no agreement on the exact rationale and scale of the funds required for this type of assistance to take form.[1] Moreover, there is a paucity of analysis of whether past Aid for Trade spending was in types of aid relevant to the potential needs of recipients, which should form the basis of the allocation of Aid for Trade.[2] The object of this chapter is to contribute to the analysis of these issues in two main ways: (i) by providing some possible estimates of the scale of funds that may be needed on the basis of a Narrow definition of Aid for Trade; and (ii) by analyzing past Aid for Trade spending[3] and assessing possible ways in which this may (or may not) match current needs. The latter is important as it shows the scale of funds previously available for Broad trade-related needs as well as the priorities set by donors in allocating funds across various types of Broad Aid for Trade activities.

2 Defining trade-related needs

Defining what Aid for Trade should cover is a controversial task. On the one hand, there is the view that it should only cover the adjustment costs following the implementation of the commitments made under the various WTO rounds. On the other hand, there is the view that Aid for Trade should be used to help countries reap the benefits of the integration of the global market, for instance by strengthening their capacity for competitively supplying world markets.

The (preceding) chapter by Sheila Page in this volume offers a functional classification of these two alternative views by dividing the types of assistance into two categories: Narrow and Broad Aid for Trade. The former refers to the assistance

1 Note that this chapter refers to Aid for Trade and trade-related aid interchangeably.
2 "Past Aid for Trade" generally refers here to the 2001–04 period, for which data is readily available and which represents a period of sustained levels of Aid for Trade.
3 The references to Aid for Trade spending in this chapter follow the definition of the WTO/OECD Database (2007), which includes infrastructure projects as well as the more directly trade-related forms of aid.

The author is grateful to Sheila Page, Hugo Cameron, Dominique Njinkeu, and Dirk Willem te Velde for their comments and contributions to this chapter, and to Genevieve Matthews for editorial assistance.

required to cover the expected costs of adjustment following the implementation of the Doha round; the latter refers to the assistance needed by countries to strengthen their supply capacity so to maximize the benefits from multilateral trade liberalization (for example, by improving their infrastructure and strengthening the capacity of trade negotiators). Adopting Page's classification, this section tries to quantify the potential narrow costs on the basis of the (scant) evidence available. As the Broad type of assistance is based on needs rather than costs, estimation of the Broad needs is a much more complex task than that of Narrow costs. What is, for example, the "right size" of assistance to strengthen supply capacity for each country? More fundamentally, what is the "right" or minimum acceptable level of supply capacity that countries should reach? And how is it possible to guarantee equitable assistance to all countries, given the limited resources available?

One way of estimating these needs could be based on assuming that every developing country should face the same level of unit cost for trade-related activities (after controlling for natural factors, including geography and resource endowments). For example, a firm in location A should have the same cost of transportation as a firm in location B, to move a unit of good X to location L – after controlling for the distances A-L and B-L and for the modes of transportation. Such a criterion clearly requires a huge amount of information that is not readily available for most developing countries. Moreover, it is often hard to address country-specific constraints that may raise the cost of the activity via aid flows (for instance, what is the amount of aid needed to address the problem of corruption in processing the goods for export in a specific port?).

Another way of approaching the issue of Broad needs could be to rely on countries' own (or external) assessment of their needs to trade effectively. This type of evaluation could be similar in spirit to the Diagnostic Trade Integration Studies (DTIS) carried out under the Integrated Framework, although it should specifically estimate the resources needed to address the constraints identified. One problem with this approach is that it may create incentives for countries to inflate their real needs to obtain more aid. Therefore, donors may need to ensure that countries have the appropriate incentive to estimate realistic needs.

Given the limited data available and the lack of consensus on an appropriate methodology, this chapter does not attempt a calculation of the Broad needs of Aid for Trade. Rather, it estimates how much aid during the 2001–04 period has been channeled to activities that aim to cover such needs. This type of calculation is important for two reasons: first, it shows the scale of the funds previously available for broad trade-related needs; second, it shows the priorities that donors have set in allocating the funds across various types of Broad Aid for Trade activities.

3 Estimating the narrow costs of adjustment

Following the categorization developed in Chapter 5 by Sheila Page, the following section provides a rough estimate of Narrow costs on the basis of various studies that assess specific types of costs.

A. Implementation of existing commitments under the Doha Round.

It is difficult to make estimates of this cost because trade facilitation commitments are not yet known. In the summary table (Table 6.1), we have used a rough estimate based on a calculation for Jamaica made by Hoekman et al. (2002 – quoted in Kleen and Page (2005)). They estimate that the cost of implementing sanitary and phytosanitary (SPS) measures and new rules on customs (not part of trade facilitation, but used to represent all other possible costs) would amount to about US$7 million in Jamaica. Starting from this figure, we adopt a combined method in order to obtain a rough estimate of the cost for all developing countries. First, we consider the total cost for developing countries by multiplying the US$7 million by the number of the main developing countries (60). Then, given the fact that this type of cost is not completely fixed (there may be a variable part related to the size of a country's general adjustment following the implementation of the Doha Development Agenda), we also calculate the ratio of this cost (US$7 million) to the estimated preference erosion costs for Jamaica (about 10 percent) and apply it to all developing countries (using the upper and lower bounds of the preference erosion estimation – see *C.* below). We then take the average between these two calculations and obtain the upper and lower bound figure.

The total numbers are small, in aid terms, at around US$0.3 billion, and these are one-off, not continuing, costs. This calculation clearly represents a gross approximation of what the potential implementation costs may be, based on partial information available for one country. As individual countries have better information about their own potential costs of implementation, it would be useful to include this if it were available to improve the reliability of the estimation. Many countries that are members of regional groupings may be already making reforms of this type, so it is the marginal cost that would need to be included.

B. Implementation of the explicit commitments in the Uruguay Round, which were left without an implementing mechanism (including the costs imposed by agricultural liberalization on Net Food Importing Developing Countries (NFIDCs) under the Marrakech Declaration).

To calculate these costs, we have used the upper and lower bounds from a recent World Bank study (Mitchell and Hoppe, 2006). However, these numbers are sensitive to the size and exact composition of any eventual Doha settlement on agriculture. (If reforms are very limited, as proved to be the case in the Uruguay Round, the negative consequences will be equally limited.) Mitchell and Hoppe (2006) partially address the issue of the estimates' sensitivity by considering the results from studies that use different sets of assumptions. Table 6.1 reports both the upper and lower bound of these estimates. The costs are likely to be under US$1 billion and these are in principle annual costs. The cost of adjusting to a new pattern of trade is not, however, necessarily directly related to the income lost, and the actual costs will depend also on how well and how fast a country is able to adjust. The highest costs both in terms of higher costs of imports and adjustment of the production structure are likely to be faced early in the process, with the cost diminishing over time.

C. The costs to developing countries of implementation by other countries of WTO agreements that benefit others: the costs of preference erosion.

There are many estimates of these costs available, with those by the IMF and WTO probably the most consistent across countries and products (see Annex A to this chapter). Gillson et al. (2004) has more detailed ones for sugar and bananas. As with any trade effect estimates, it depends on a number of factors: (i) what is taken as the base year, in particular the choice between end-Uruguay Round in 1995, or end-Agreement on Textiles and Clothing in 2005, since exemption from Multi-fibre Arrangement (MFA) quotas was an important preference for several countries; (ii) what is included (UNCTAD estimates exclude sugar because these effects are the result of domestic support, not tariffs); (iii) what liberalization is assumed; and (iv) which effects are included (that is, only the loss of rents from a change in tariff, or losses in market share, or losses from price changes as well). As with NFIDCs in the Uruguay Round, if there is little or no liberalization, there will be no problem. If all pre-Doha erosion is excluded (in particular, textiles and clothing), the only major losses are in agriculture. There are small potential losses for countries with preferences on textiles and clothing into the EU, but for most these are offset by gains into the United States, which has excluded these from most preferences. Countries with free trade areas lose, whether these are with developed or other developing countries, but these are not the "long-standing preferences" that the WTO is committed to take into account, and are not included in our analysis. Previous rounds have not treated members of regions as special cases and members of regions have not made a case for compensation in this round.

We use various studies to estimate the preference erosion figures reported in Annex A. The lower bound is obtained by adding two sets of estimates from WTO studies: Low et al. (2005) estimation of costs for non-agricultural products due to preference erosion and Low et al. (2006) estimation of costs for agricultural products due to preference erosion. The upper bound is computed by including additional estimates that use the highest figures for each country among the lower bound estimate, Gillson et al. (2004), IMF (2003) and Alexandraki and Lankes (2004).

Different assumptions (regarding the liberalization process and the methods of calculation) produce different rankings of losers (and gainers). Our central estimates are mainly based on WTO studies, as they employ the most up-to-date methodology in terms of the assumptions about what may be in the settlement. An important part of that methodology is related to the adjustment of preference margin for competition and for utilization rates (where available). The first type of adjustment accounts for the competition effect deriving from other exporters benefiting from the same preferential scheme or other forms of preferences, implying that estimates will be lower than those that do not take such competition into account. If there is significant liberalization, leading to entry into the market by countries that are currently completely excluded, this will under estimate preference erosion. The latter type of adjustment considers the actual rate of utilization of preference by exporters from developing countries (which can be low). This adjustment is computed only for access of non-agricultural products to the U.S. market.

The IMF estimates are not comparable to the WTO estimates, as they use different methodologies, so some caution is required in comparing these.

Note that all estimates are based on partial information and static calculation; thus, they are potentially subject to various types of biases. One such bias is due to the fact that we do not know the share of benefits of preferences that accrue to the exporter (this share is likely to be less than the 100 percent assumed by the studies, except for sugar where the quota scheme ensures that countries receive the rents). Other issues are due to the lack of consideration of elasticities of substitution and of dynamic interaction.

Table 6.1. Estimated narrow total costs of implementing the Doha Round (US$ millions)

	Upper bound	Lower bound	Estimate
A) Implementing existing WTO commitments	305	279	300
B) NFIDCs costs	1,236	329	800
C) Preference Erosion	2,362	1,069	1,150
D) Implementation of TRIPS, TRIMS, etc.	348	318	350
Total Narrow (A + B + C + D)	**4,251**	**1,995**	**2,600**

Note: based on 2003 data – different sources (see below). A and D are costs to be faced once. Estimation of B and C refers to costs potentially faced as if a country fully implemented the Doha Round.
Source: Author's calculations on various sources (see text).

The calculations relying only on WTO studies give total estimates, including textiles and clothing and sugar, of about US$1.1 billion (lower bound) on current maximum expectations for the Doha round; taking an upper bound estimate would give a loss of US$2.3 billion a year.

D. Other implementation costs.

Because of the uncertain nature of these costs and the poor availability of in-country data, we have only a few limited estimates of them. As for A-type costs, again the only estimations of TRIPS-related implementation are provided by Hoekman et al. (2002) – which calculate US$6 million for Jamaica. Mattoo (2005) offers the calculation of a further implementation cost, in the order of US$ 2 million, for the Organization of Eastern Caribbean States (OECS) telecommunications regulatory authority. The total cost of US$8 million thus obtained is then compared to the US$7 million of point A and proportionately scaled up, obtaining average total costs of around US$330 million.

E. The fiscal costs of liberalizing a country's own imports.

We have not included estimates for this because for LDCs the cost would be 0 (as they are not expected to reduce their tariffs in this round) and for most developing countries, of the type expected to be included, the cost will also be 0 (bound tariffs are sufficiently high that any reduction is likely to merely remove some water in the tariffs, not reduce revenue). Moreover, these should not be thought of as costs to the country as a whole, as they represent in principle a transfer of resources from governments (in terms of less revenue) to consumers (in terms of lower prices) within an economy.

All Narrow costs

The costs outlined above give a sum for all the Narrow costs ranging from US$2 billion to US$4.2 billion, depending on assumptions (see Table 6.1). The central estimate of all costs, US$2.6 billion, is probably too high because the size of a settlement is likely to be less than these calculations assume. Of these, about US$2 billion are in principle annual costs (from food imports and preference erosion) and US$0.6 billion are one-off costs of implementing agreements.

Table 6.2. Aid for Trade – share by WTO/OECD category (% and US$ thousands)

	2001	2002	2003	2004
Trade Policy and Regulations	6%	6%	7%	5%
Trade Development	13%	13%	18%	10%
Infrastructure	82%	82%	74%	85%
TOTAL	11,214,732	11,312,734	12,524,404	17,372,650

Source: WTO/OECD (2007).

D is the only one of the "Narrow" costs for which we have estimates of past aid. A, C, and E will only happen, and their size will only be known, if and when the Doha Round is completed. No aid seems to have been made available specifically for B (NFIDCs). Using WTO/OECD data (see below for a description of those), we estimate spending on Uruguay Round implementation costs at around US$0.4 billion per annum. Our estimates for the future are lower for D because the Uruguay Round imposed more new types of costs than the Doha Round is likely to require and because some of the implementation costs will fall under A. Our estimates for A plus D are in the order of US$0.6 billion, so financing at the level seen in recent years (between 2001 and 2004, for example) for D would cover these.

4 Estimates of past spending on Broad needs

As argued above, past Aid for Trade has been predominantly channeled towards such aims as building infrastructure, developing institutions, strengthening technical capacity, and promoting investment. The value of these Broad activities in the 2001–04 period can be approximated by analyzing trade-related aid projects classified in a database set up jointly by the WTO and the OECD (henceforth WTO/OECD Database). The Database aims to track funded trade-related and capacity building projects collecting information directly from the donors. Trade-related aid as classified by the Database appears to fall into both Narrow and Broad categories: direct costs of implementation of WTO commitments (Narrow category D) and Broad support to enhance developing countries' capacity to reap the benefits of trade integration (Broad categories F-I, see below).

The WTO/OECD Database groups trade-related aid into three Broad categories: Trade Policy and Regulations (TPR), Trade Development (TD), and Infrastructure, which are in turn classified into various sub-categories. As is apparent from Table 6.2, Aid for Trade activities as defined by the Database have been rising at increasing rates over the 2001–04 period from US$11.2 billion to US$17.4 billion. Most of this increase (especially between 2003 and 2004) is explained by the rising contribution of infrastructure related activities, which represent 85 percent of total trade-related aid in 2004.[4] The average value of the first two categories in 2003–04 was higher than in 2001–02, although the values in 2004 are lower than in 2003.

[4] This category includes three types of infrastructure: communication, transport and energy. The accuracy of this analysis is limited by the usual problem of classifying projects that have broad scope and aims as trade-related activities.

Table 6.3. Trade policy and regulations and trade development – share by sub-category (%)

	2001	2002	2003	2004	Our category
Dispute Settlement	0.5	0.4	0.4	0.2	D
Customs Valuation	0.6	2.5	1.9	5.4	D
Technical Barriers to Trade	4.4	4.2	6.4	5.1	H
Sanitary and Phytosanitary Measures	15.2	5.2	6.8	3.1	D
Trade Mainstreaming in PRSPs/Dev. Plans	18.8	11.1	15.3	15.3	F
Trade-Related Intellectual Property Rights	2.0	1.4	1.4	1.6	D
Agriculture	1.6	0.6	1.0	1.6	I
Services	0.7	2.7	0.6	0.5	I
Tariff Negotiations – NAMA	1.0	0.5	0.3	0.3	F
Rules	1.5	0.4	0.1	0.2	F
Trade and Environment	12.8	5.0	3.0	3.4	F
Trade and Investment	1.4	1.8	0.8	0.2	G
Trade and Competition	6.3	4.8	3.0	4.7	G
Trade Facilitation	15.5	20.4	28.3	40.6	D
Transparency and Government Procurement	0.3	0.4	0.8	0.9	F
Accession	2.0	3.8	2.9	1.0	D
Tariff Reforms	0.0	0.0	0.1	0.1	D
Trade-Related Training Education	5.6	8.7	7.8	3.8	F
Negotiation Training	1.3	1.3	1.3	0.1	F
Regional Trade Agreements (RTAs)	8.6	24.8	17.9	11.8	H
Trade Policy and Regulations (TPR)	**100.0**	**100.0**	**100.0**	**100.0**	
Trade Promotion Strategy Design and Implementation	16.2	22.1	33.3	37.3	I
Market Analysis and Development	17.6	24.3	24.8	10.6	I
Business Support Services and Institutions	35.0	24.0	18.4	21.9	H
Public-Private Sector Networking	1.9	3.6	5.2	3.8	H
E-commerce	0.1	2.6	1.4	3.0	H
Trade Finance	29.1	23.5	16.9	23.3	H
Trade Development (TD)	**100.0**	**100.0**	**100.0**	**100.0**	

Source: WTO/OECD (2007).

Table 6.3 reports the evolution of the composition of the TPR and TD categories. *Trade Facilitation*, *Trade Mainstreaming in PRSPs/Development Plans* and *Regional Trade Agreements* sub-categories represent over 50 percent of the total funds allocated to the TPR category, with a substantial increase in the concentration of spending, in particular towards trade facilitation. The allocation of trade development funds is dominated by *Trade Finance*, *Trade Promotion* and *Business Support* categories. A couple of methodological notes of caution are in order. First, the classification of the activities into categories in the WTO/OECD Database is performed by the donor countries according to their interpretation of categories that are not always clearly defined; thus, the interpretation is not necessarily homogenous across donors. Second, for those projects, which include some non-trade related activities, donors do not always separate out the trade-related part of the project, therefore potentially overstating the actual size of Aid for Trade.

The last column of Table 6.3 also shows the way in which we match each of these WTO/OECD sub-categories in TPR and TD respectively with the needs as identified in Page's chapter. Infrastructure-related activities fall entirely under G – type of need. This reclassification of the data according to our Broad groupings allows us to assess the relative importance that donors and countries have attributed to the various Broad categories, and within these to understand what activities donors have concentrated on. Table 6.4 presents the 2001–04 WTO/OECD data according to our classification.

Table 6.4. Past Aid for Trade spending on narrow and broad categories (US$ thousands)

Category	2001	2002	2003	2004
D	232,470	222,127	388,248	421,199
Total Narrow	232,470	222,127	388,248	421,199
F	268,136	179,888	265,474	194,731
G	9,196,584	9,270,297	9,366,025	14,842,632
H	1,021,976	957,172	1,174,338	1,054,434
I	495,566	683,250	1,330,319	859,654
Total Broad	10,982,262	11,090,607	12,136,156	16,951,451

Source: WTO/OECD (2007).

While this matching exercise may be useful to understand the scale of different trade-related assistance activities carried out by donors so far, it is limited by the possible overlap between categories. The distinction between Narrow and Broad categories appears to be less problematic. This is the most relevant to our analysis.

F. Support for conventionally recognized trade capacity building.

Notwithstanding the important role that capacity building activities have been playing in trade-related aid, their value has been fluctuating around US$0.2 billion, representing the category with the lowest Aid for Trade spending. This may be explained by the nature of the activities under this heading, which are often tailored only to a handful of bureaucrats within ministries and do not involve any provision of expensive assets.

G. Support for infrastructure investment, other measures to build supply capacity.

Aid to support infrastructure has increased sharply in recent years, from US$9.2 billion a year in 2001 to US$14.8 billion by 2004.[5] A closer look at these figures indicates that almost the entire rise in expenditures has been driven by U.S. spending to rebuild infrastructure in Iraq and Afghanistan. However, many donors (bilateral and multilateral) have announced their intention to increase aid for infrastructure.

H. Support for institutions that improve capacity to trade.

Aid for this type of support has been about US$1.1 billion a year, and, like F, has not shown an increase.

[5] We use here a general definition of infrastructure, without trying to separate infrastructure that helps trade from other types of infrastructure.

Table 6.5. Pledges by donors

	Original pledge	Annual amount (US$ millions)	Additional
EC	€1 billion	1200	The current level of TRA is around €800 annually so that around €200 mn is additional
Japan	US$10 billion in total	3300	The OECD DAC report treats this as additional, but doubts exist
UK	£100 million	185	£50 mn
USA	US$2.7 billion	2700	US$1.35 billion
France	€33 million	39	Nothing additional; estimate is based on WTO/OECD (2005)
Total pledges		5036	
Narrow costs		3038	
Left for Broad		2001	

Sources: Different public statements made by donors.

I. Support for the supply side in the sense of building up private sector enterprise in new export (or import-replacing) areas.

This category has moved up with infrastructure, from about US$0.5 billion in 2001 to US$0.9 billion in 2004.

Total Broad support

The support for Broad categories has risen from US$11 billion in 2001 to US$17 billion in 2004, mainly driven by expenditure in infrastructure. However, some rising trends since 2001 are discernible for virtually all Broad categories.

According to our calculation, new implementation needs (A and D) are likely to require about the same financing as past aid for implementation, and the costs of NFIDCs and preference erosion (B and C) on realistic expectations for the outcome of the Doha round are at most US$1 billion each. As a result, the value of current trade assistance would ensure that the narrow costs of adjustment could be easily covered. However, in as much as Broad support to trade is necessary for a successful Doha Round, one may want to consider aid to cover adjustment costs as additional to those already spent on trade-related activities. The Concept Paper that the WTO prepared to guide the Task Force on Aid for Trade (WTO, 2006) suggests that the target is an extra US$2 billion by 2007, "rising to US$5–6 billion by 2010," such that trade-related aid would receive about 10 percent of the pledged additional aid of US$50 billion.

In the second half of 2005, including at the WTO Hong Kong Ministerial, increases in trade-related aid were announced by several donors (Table 6.5). Despite the fact that they would not represent an acceleration of recent spending on trade-related aid, these funds would cover the costs of the Round (B and C) plus a continuing increase in Broad Aid for Trade, if they are additional to the 2004 levels of spending.

Table 6.6. Aid for Trade by type of flow (2001–04)

	Total (US$ 000)	Equity investment	Grant	Loan
Trade Policy and Regulation	3,053,371	0%	92%	8%
Trade Development	6,918,408	0%	85%	15%
Infrastructure	42,506,577	1%	38%	61%
Total Aid for Trade	**52,478,356**	1%	47%	52%

Note that shares may not add up to 100% due to rounding.
Source: WTO/OECD (2007).

Several questions that remain open on the basis of this analysis will have to be addressed if Aid for Trade is to be effective: Does the allocation of aid across the various Broad categories reflect the real needs of the developing world? Is the level of Broad support enough to help developing (and in particular least developed) countries to effectively integrate into the world economy? Will the level of Broad trade-related aid keep rising?

Answers to these questions will have to wait for a proper definition and analysis of the Narrow and (more importantly the) Broad needs of countries. They will need to be complemented with analyses of other crucial dimensions of Aid for Trade, such as the type of support available, the allocation of funds across recipients, and the commitments of donors to such form of aid. The following section offers an exploratory analysis of these issues on the basis of past trade-related aid spending.

5 Scale of past aid by type of flows

As different needs require different modes of assistance, we describe the type of flows (grants versus loans) through which trade-related aid has been channeled so far. Table 6.6 describes the share of Aid for Trade in grants or loans according to the WTO/OECD Database's categories. Most aid for both Trade Policy and Regulation and Trade Development categories has been channeled through grants over the period 2001–04. Around 92 percent of US$3 billion spent on the former category and 85 percent of US$6.9 billion spent on the latter category were channeled through grants by the donors. As expected, the situation is different for infrastructure aid, most of which has come about in the form of loans rather than grants (with a tiny share of equity investments). These results seem to be consistent with an inverse relation between the extent to which a precise financial return of the projects is identifiable and the share of non reimbursable funding. Projects with no clear identifiable financial return, such as those aimed at strengthening the process of trade policy making and its regulation, would be financed mostly through grants. Some sub-categories of Trade Development, such as assistance to trade finance, have more precise returns and appear to more suitable to loan arrangements. Finally, infrastructure investments usually have more identifiable financial returns and are particularly suitable to project financing given the large size of funds involved. However, the share of grants for aid for

Table 6.7. Narrow and broad categories, by type of flow (2001–04)

Category/ Type of flow	Total (US$ 000)	Equity investment	Grant	Loan
D	1,264,247	0%	84%	16%
Total Narrow	**1,264,247**	0%	84%	16%
F	918,591	0%	100%	0%
G	42,673,758	1%	38%	61%
H	4,258,065	0%	83%	17%
I	3,363,695	0%	90%	10%
Total Broad	**51,214,109**	1%	46%	53%

Note that shares may not add up to 100% due to rounding.
Source: WTO/OECD (2007).

infrastructure has been constantly increasing since 2001, reaching a record 49 percent in 2004.

Using the matching procedure between categories as above, Table 6.7 shows that the grant component dominates aid in the Narrow categories, while the loan part is slightly more important for the Broad categories. Such prevalence of grant over loan in the Narrow categories may be viewed as a sign of donors' willingness to interpret this part of aid as covering pure costs, from which recipient countries do not gain in net terms.

6 Donors' structure of Aid for Trade

A second important dimension to analyze is donors' structure of Aid for Trade. This may help assess the relative importance that donors attach to this type of assistance and the scope for future contributions towards a potential fund. All major donors have either maintained or increased their spending on trade-related assistance over the period 2001–04 (Table 6.8). The United States registered a major increase, which has made it the country with the highest contribution in Aid for Trade in 2004. This increase is entirely explained by infrastructure spending for the rebuilding of Iraq and Afghanistan. France, Denmark, Australia and Belgium have also raised the level of their spending. Japan has been the largest donor over 2001–04, mainly due to its large assistance in infrastructure investments. The EC is the largest donor in the categories more strictly related to trade (Trade Policy and Regulation and Trade Development), with a relatively lower spending on infrastructure (though the level of aid for infrastructure is still high relative to the other donors). The rise in bilateral spending has not crowded out multilateral aid, which has been constantly increasing over the period, following the larger contribution of the World Bank to infrastructure investments.[6]

In order to understand the relative importance that donors attach to Aid for Trade, we estimate the extent to which countries are specialized in this type of assistance by constructing a simple *index of specialization* for all major aid donors.

[6] Contrary to the WTO/OECD Database, for the purpose of the analysis, we consider the EC as a bilateral rather than a multilateral donor.

Table 6.8. Total Aid for Trade by donor and by year (US$ thousands)

Years (Commitments)	2001	2002	2003	2004	2001–04
Japan	4,076,888	3,541,488	3,380,556	4,077,637	15,076,570
EC	2,259,363	2,364,378	2,179,817	2,594,250	9,397,809
United States	982,630	1,446,475	1,261,755	5,067,599	8,758,458
Germany	635,743	408,412	482,782	656,377	2,183,314
France	197,215	231,778	332,122	452,672	1,213,788
United Kingdom	187,195	179,715	444,264	206,237	1,017,411
Netherlands	191,413	279,033	177,310	200,109	847,865
Spain	98,806	196,170	293,738	161,953	750,667
Denmark	25,993	128,879	155,135	210,128	520,136
Norway	166,199	68,886	118,553	88,767	442,404
Switzerland	63,514	98,049	136,733	117,797	416,092
Sweden	103,078	56,487	154,116	74,922	388,602
Canada	96,318	52,243	129,952	95,230	373,744
Australia	78,006	17,855	40,586	148,650	285,097
Belgium	39,391	44,754	96,188	97,913	278,246
Italy	29,379	45,747	166,626	35,504	277,256
Others	46,705	128,921	96,704	134,720	407,050
Total Bilateral	9,277,836	9,289,270	9,646,937	14,420,465	42,634,509
Total Multilateral	1,873,654	1,926,861	2,665,412	3,377,921	9,843,847
Total Donor	11,151,490	11,216,131	12,312,349	17,798,386	52,478,356

Source: WTO/OECD (2007).

The index is the ratio of the share of a country in total Aid for Trade and the share of the country in total Official Development Assistance (ODA):

$$S_i = \frac{AT_i / \sum_{j=1}^{n} AT_j}{A_i / \left(\sum_{j=1}^{n} A_j\right)} \tag{6.1}$$

where AT_i and A_i are Aid for Trade (in US$) and total ODA for country i respectively, and n is the total number of donors.[7] A value of the index greater than one indicates that the donor is spending proportionally more on Aid for Trade. Table 6.9 shows that the EC and Japan are the only donors with a relative specialization in Aid for Trade over the entire period 2001–04, although the intensity of this specialization has been somewhat declining. The value for the EC is mainly driven by expenditure on trade policy and regulation and trade development, while Japan's value is the result of the focus on infrastructure in its development assistance strategy. The United States has an index greater than 1 only in 2004, because of the shock in its aid pattern mentioned above. All other donors are spending relatively little on trade-related assistance, with UK, Canada, France and Italy at the bottom of the list.

Relatively high spending on Aid for Trade by the major donors is likely to cause a high level of concentration of funding relative to the entire ODA sector. We use the *Herfindhal index* (H_{AT}) to verify whether Aid for Trade is more concentrated than

[7] Data for ODA are obtained by the OECD/DAC database on aid flows.

Table 6.9. Index of Aid for Trade specialization (by donor and year)

	2001	2002	2003	2004	2001–04
EC	2.3	2.5	1.8	1.6	2.0
Japan	1.7	2.1	1.6	1.6	1.7
United States	0.5	0.6	0.5	1.2	0.8
Spain	0.3	0.7	1.1	0.4	0.6
Switzerland	0.4	0.7	0.8	0.4	0.6
Denmark	0.1	0.6	0.8	0.5	0.5
Germany	0.6	0.4	0.5	0.4	0.5
Australia	0.5	0.1	0.3	0.7	0.4
Norway	0.7	0.3	0.5	0.3	0.4
Netherlands	0.3	0.4	0.6	0.4	0.4
Belgium	0.3	0.4	0.4	0.3	0.3
Sweden	0.5	0.2	0.5	0.2	0.3
United Kingdom	0.2	0.2	0.6	0.2	0.3
Canada	0.4	0.2	0.4	0.2	0.3
France	0.2	0.2	0.3	0.3	0.3
Others	0.1	0.3	0.2	0.2	0.2
Italy	0.1	0.1	0.4	0.1	0.2

Note: the index is obtained by dividing the share of a country in total Aid for Trade over the share of the country in total ODA. An index greater than 1 means relative specialization in Aid for Trade.
Source: Author's calculation on WTO/OECD (2007).

general aid and whether there has been any changes in concentration over the time considered. The index is simply the sum of the squares of each country's share in total Aid for Trade:

$$H_{AT} = \sum_{i=1}^{n} \left(\frac{AT_i}{\sum_{j=1}^{n} AT_j} \right)^2 \tag{6.2}$$

As Table 6.10 shows, both the Herfindhal index and the share of spending of the major three donors are higher in the trade-related assistance sub-sector than in the general ODA sector. However, whereas the latter sector displays a relative stability

Table 6.10. Donors' concentration of Aid for Trade expenditure relative to other ODA

	2001	2002	2003	2004	2001–04
Herfindhal Index Aid for Trade	0.187	0.164	0.123	0.158	0.146
Herfindhal Index total ODA	0.114	0.104	0.119	0.116	0.112
Share first 3 donors Aid for Trade	65.6%	65.6%	55.4%	66.0%	63.3%
Share first 3 donors total ODA	49%	45%	51%	48%	48%

Note: the Herfindhal index is calculated as the sum of the squares of each country's share in total Aid for Trade; the higher the Herfindhal Index the more concentrated is the sector.
Source: Author's calculation on WTO/OECD (2007).

Table 6.11. Aid for Trade by recipient country/region and year (US$ thousands)

	2001	2002	2003	2004	2001–04	Rank*
Total Aid for Trade	11,151,490	11,216,131	12,312,349	17,798,386	52,478,356	
1. Far East Asia	**3,247,649**	**2,982,697**	**2,958,317**	**3,474,778**	**12,663,441**	
Vietnam	716,339	992,886	767,227	1,066,953	3,543,405	1
Indonesia	464,332	123,506	1,143,825	1,242,666	2,974,329	3
China	1,005,238	655,597	606,128	382,171	2,649,134	4
Philippines	668,005	595,666	110,687	116,406	1,490,764	6
Thailand	47,018	393,344	18,791	427,664	886,817	11
2. Sub-Saharan Africa	**2,556,546**	**1,587,703**	**2,723,313**	**3,246,941**	**10,114,503**	
Ethiopia	179,886	247,894	197,040	234,745	859,565	12
Tanzania	392,666	34,741	47,909	356,105	831,421	13
Mozambique	278,741	98,145	218,876	170,992	766,754	15
Kenya	128,781	5,066	113,660	447,553	695,060	17
Ghana	275,816	56,870	193,050	104,017	629,753	18
Uganda	340,422	62,900	72,657	148,960	624,939	19
3. South & Central Asia	**1,330,671**	**2,123,079**	**2,406,415**	**3,108,523**	**8,968,688**	
India	319,768	710,666	801,953	1,353,725	3,186,112	2
Bangladesh	151,804	355,547	598,291	324,103	1,429,745	7
Afghanistan	378	40,424	271,584	771,716	1,084,102	–
Sri Lanka	288,434	429,116	220,819	107,642	1,046,011	9
4. Europe	**1,647,466**	**2,307,528**	**1,340,546**	**1,975,460**	**7,271,000**	
Russia	276,060	522,627	396,987	630,673	1,826,347	5
Serbia & Montenegro	88,038	148,814	200,497	360,486	797,835	14
Romania	339,378	128,648	20,257	211,770	700,053	16
5. Middle East	**152,742**	**96,491**	**173,027**	**3,396,974**	**3,819,234**	
Iraq	4	5	60,828	3,257,910	3,318,747	–
6. North Africa	**497,575**	**834,683**	**803,957**	**710,042**	**2,846,257**	
Egypt	93,221	204,883	456,164	292,520	1,046,788	8
Morocco	174,648	171,970	276,884	268,777	892,279	10
7. Central America	**576,907**	**281,135**	**393,600**	**558,451**	**1,810,093**	
Nicaragua	123,104	38,130	36,038	146,744	344,016	29
8. South America	**233,253**	**295,186**	**290,723**	**227,447**	**1,046,609**	
Bolivia	11,688	103,367	106,259	46,269	267,583	38
9. Oceania	**154,170**	**60,476**	**113,454**	**290,460**	**618,560**	
Papua New Guinea	59,190	8,626	34,747	159,261	261,824	39

* *Countries are ranked according to the cumulative 2001–04 spending.*
Source: WTO/OECD (2007).

over time, the former shows some declining patterns, which is the consequence of the increases in Aid for Trade below the average by the largest donors.[8]

7 The allocation of Aid for Trade and its potential determinants

Finally, we describe the allocation of Aid for Trade among receiving countries, in order to identify those countries and regions that have benefited from higher levels of trade-related assistance in the past. A description of aid by recipient (Table 6.11) shows that the funds are fairly equally spread across regions, with Asian regions

[8] The sudden increase between 2003 and 2004 can be explained mainly through the large jump in Aid for Trade spending by the US.

Table 6.12. Destination of Aid for Trade by income group, shares in total, and specialization index

	2001	2002	2003	2004	2001–04
LDCs (share)	22%	16%	26%	21%	21%
LDCs (index)	1.07	0.7	1.04	0.83	0.88
Other Low Income Countries (share)	25%	24%	29%	28%	27%
Other Low Income Countries (index)	0.84	1	0.97	1.3	1.04
Low-Middle Income Countries (share)	28%	35%	23%	35%	31%
Low-Middle Income Countries (index)	1.09	1.34	0.92	1.15	1.14
Upper-Middle Income Countries (share)	3%	3%	3%	1%	2%
Upper-Middle Income Countries. (index)	1	0.84	0.69	0.39	0.59
Others and unallocated (share)	21%	22%	19%	15%	19%
Others and unallocated (index)	1	0.94	1.23	0.74	0.97
Total Aid for Trade (million US$)	**11,151**	**11,216**	**12,312**	**17,798**	**42,507**

Note: the index is obtained by dividing the share of an income group in total Aid for Trade over the share of the income group in total ODA; an index greater than 1 means that a country is receiving Aid for Trade more than proportionally with respect to ODA
Source: WTO/OECD (2007).

(Far East, South and Central Asia and Middle East) all receiving over US$3 billion in 2004, the same amount as sub-Saharan Africa. However, the allocation of spending over time varies widely across these regions: the Far East has enjoyed stable inflows of Aid for Trade, while flows into sub-Saharan Africa have been increasing steadily, and the Middle East and South and Central Asian regions have benefited from investments in Iraq and Afghanistan. Slightly less goes to Europe (US$2 billion), while less than US$1 billion is spent in North Africa, the Americas and Oceania. The largest recipient countries were all Asian: Vietnam, India, Indonesia, and China.[9] The first sub-Saharan recipient, Ethiopia, is in the 12th position, confirming a different (less trade-related) model of development assistance for sub-Saharan Africa compared to Asia.

As argued above, trying to identify a precise rationale for allocating Aid for Trade across countries is a hard task, but this analysis could already provide some reflections on the allocation of past funds. To the extent that Narrow costs of adjustment provide a part of the rationale for Aid for Trade, it is somewhat surprising to notice very little relation between countries' potential costs (as from Annex A) and past allocation across recipients (Table 6.11). Most of the largest potential losers, including Mauritius, Dominican Republic, Tunisia, Guatemala, Honduras, Jamaica, Cambodia, Guyana, Fiji, and Malawi, rank well below 20th place in terms of trade-related aid received between 2001 and 2004. Among the ten largest recipients of Aid for Trade only Bangladesh (7th) and Morocco (10th) are likely to experience potentially significant adjustment costs.

While we do not deny that other types of (Broad) needs may have driven the allocation of past assistance, the analysis of the distribution of trade-related aid across income groups seems to contradict this hypothesis. As reported in Table 6.12, Low-Middle Income countries (LMIs) and non-LDC low-income countries (OLICs)

[9] In this analysis by rankings we do not take into account Iraq and Afghanistan as the very large trade-related aid flowing into these countries is driven by a specific non-development related shock.

Table 6.13. Aid for Trade spending relative to total ODA – by region of destination

	2001	2002	2003	2004	2001–04
Europe	2.38	2.19	1.89	2.89	2.32
Far East Asia	1.13	1.5	1.63	1.46	1.44
North Africa	0.72	1.36	1.91	0.82	1.14
South and Central Asia	0.75	1.12	0.95	1.17	0.98
North and Central America	0.8	0.54	1.06	0.63	0.76
Oceania	0.77	0.33	0.66	0.79	0.69
Sub-Saharan Africa	0.93	0.45	0.78	0.58	0.66
Middle East	0.2	0.15	0.11	0.99	0.58
South America	0.38	0.37	0.56	0.22	0.36

Note: the index is obtained by dividing the share of a region in total Aid for Trade over the share of the region in total ODA; an index greater than 1 means relative specialization in Aid for Trade
Source: Author's calculations on WTO/OECD (2007).

have received the highest share of trade-related funds over 2001–04. This result is in line with the analysis of spending relative to total ODA, which shows that LDCs receive the lowest level of spending in trade-related assistance relative to total aid among the large aid recipients (which include LMIs and OLICs as well). This is confirmed by the presence of only one LDC (Bangladesh) in the list of the first ten recipients of past Aid for Trade in the period 2001–04. Such a figure may be a cause for concern to the extent that LDCs are likely to face the highest relative costs in the trade integration process. Moreover, in as much as the levels of trade-related needs tend to be (inversely) related to the income of countries, this allocation by income group seems to have been driven by determinants other than trade-related needs.

Table 6.13 complements these findings by calculating the regional indices of relative specialization in Aid for Trade (obtained as for the donors' index above). Europe and the Far East appear to be the regions with the highest level of trade-related aid relative to the total aid they receive, while sub-Saharan Africa, the Middle East and South America have the lowest values of the index. Investment in infrastructure in the context of post-cold war reconstruction of Eastern Europe and the influence of Japan's (trade-oriented) mode of development assistance may account for the large weight of Aid for Trade in those two regions. On the other hand, a more social-related mode of spending, for instance on health and education, seems to have prevailed in the other regions, particularly in sub-Saharan Africa and in the Americas.

A brief analysis of the largest recipients of Aid for Trade seems to confirm the importance of non trade-related determinants in driving this allocation among countries. In fact, these determinants appear to be closely related to those of general ODA rather than being specific to Aid for Trade. For example, Japan's pattern of giving large amounts of (investment and trade-related) aid in Asia to countries that are well-governed and not poor (Dollar and Levin, 2004) is in line with the fact that eight of the largest eleven recipients of past Aid for Trade are Asian countries. By the same token, United States and EU foreign policy interests[10] may explain the large

[10] See Alesina and Dollar (2000) for empirical evidence on the relevance of political and strategic considerations as the main determinants of ODA allocation among recipient countries.

allocation of trade-related assistance to Egypt and Russia, despite their relatively competitive position in world markets. Of course including Iraq and Afghanistan in such analysis would only reinforce the hypotheses that trade-related needs have not been the major drivers of aid allocation.

8 Concluding remarks

Such potential lack of meaningful economic rationale in allocating trade-related assistance may undermine the effectiveness of any future Aid for Trade spending, even if, as it seems to be the case, this were potentially sufficient to cover both Narrow and Broad needs (as shown in Table 6.5).

A reliable identification of trade-related costs and needs and an allocation of funds that follows from such identification are features as crucial as securing sufficient funds of the "right" type to cover all the Narrow and Broad categories. As it would appear from this analysis, ensuring the former seems to be more problematic than guaranteeing the latter.

ANNEX A: ESTIMATED COSTS BY COUNTRY OF AGRICULTURAL LIBERALIZATION AND PREFERENCE EROSION

		C) Pref. Erosion NAMA – WTO est.	C) Pref. Erosion Agriculture – WTO est.	C) Total Pref. Erosion – lower bound	Banana & sugar Pref. Erosion – high lib.	Pref. Erosion (IMF estimates)	C) Total Pref. Erosion – upper bound
All figures in US$ millions	B) NFIDCs	Low et al. (2005)	Low et al. (2006)	Low et al. (2005); Low et al. (2006)	Gillson et al. (2004)	IMF (2003) & Alexandraki et al. (2004)	All sources
LDC	All						
Angola	x	0.3	0	0.3		21.1	21.1
Bangladesh	x	61.6	0.1	61.7		222.4	222.4
Benin	x			0		0.3	0.3
Burkina Faso	x		1.6	1.6		0.3	1.6
Burundi	x			0		1	1
Cambodia	x	18.8		18.8		53.6	53.6
Cape Verde	x			0		0.9	0.9
Central African Republic	x			0		0.7	0.7
Chad	x			0		0.1	0.1
Comoros	x			0		0.3	0.3
Congo, Dem. Rep.	x		0.1	0.1	0.7	0.8	0.8
Equatorial Guinea	x			0		1.3	1.3
Ethiopia	x			0		15.4	15.4
Gambia, The	x			0		0.3	0.3
Guinea	x	0.2		0.2		1.6	1.6
Guinea Bissau	x			0		0.2	0.2
Haiti	x	21.7		21.7		3.9	21.7

(continued)

All figures in US$ millions	B) NFIDCs	C) Pref. Erosion NAMA – WTO est.	C) Pref. Erosion Agriculture – WTO est.	C) Total Pref. Erosion – lower bound	Banana & sugar Pref. Erosion – high lib.	Pref. Erosion (IMF estimates)	C) Total Pref. Erosion – upper bound
		Low et al. (2005)	Low et al. (2006)	Low et al. (2005); Low et al. (2006)	Gillson et al. (2004)	IMF (2003) & Alexandraki et al. (2004)	All sources
Lesotho	x	30.1		30.1			30.1
Liberia	x			0		3.4	3.4
Madagascar	x	19.1		19.1	5.6	8.6	19.1
Malawi	x	2	0.8	2.8	13.9	48.6	48.6
Maldives	x			0		2.8	2.8
Mali	x			0		0.1	0.1
Mauritania	x	1.7		1.7		40.4	40.4
Mozambique	x	5.5		5.5		5.7	5.7
Myanmar	x	8.3		8.3		2.2	8.3
Nepal	x			0		17.8	17.8
S T and P	x			0		1.1	1.1
Senegal	x	3.6	0.5	4.1		23.6	23.6
Sierra Leone	x	0.2		0.2		2.5	2.5
Solomon Islands	x	0.1		0.1		2.5	2.5
Sudan	x			0		6.9	6.9
Tanzania	x	1.2	1.4	2.6	5	28.9	28.9
Togo	x	0.2	0.1	0.3		1.3	1.3
Uganda	x	0.7	0.5	1.2		9.1	9.1
Vanuatu	x			0		1.9	1.9
Zambia	x	0		0	5.5		5.5
Total LDCs Other		**175.3**	**5.1**	**180.4**	**30.7**	**531.6**	**602.9**
Albania		1.2		1.2		10	10
Barbados	x	0.1	1.2	1.3	18.4		18.4
Belize		0.7	9.5	10.2	32.7	18	32.7
Bolivia			0.7	0.7			0.7
Botswana,	x	0.8	5.8	6.6			6.6
Cameroon		1	29.8	30.8			30.8
C d'Ivoire	x	25.3	22.1	47.4	3.7	69	69
Cuba	x			0			0
Dominica	x		1	1	14.6	2	14.6
Dom Rep	x	139.2	21	160.2		100	160.2
Egypt	x		1.4	1.4			1.4
El Salvador		110.5	2.5	113			113
Fiji			6.7	6.7	55.5	41	55.5
Ghana			0.6	0.6			0.6
Guatemala		141.7	1.9	143.6			143.6
Guyana			6.6	6.6	69.3	41	69.3
Honduras	x	167		167			167
Jamaica	x	6.4	8.5	14.9	80.5	46	80.5
Jordan	x			0			0
Kenya	x	14	5.8	19.8	1.3		19.8
Mauritius	x	31	23.4	54.4	205.6	201	205.6
Morocco	x			0		152	152
Namibia	x	10.7	6.5	17.2			17.2
Nicaragua		31	1.2	32.2			32.2
Nigeria		1.3	0.1	1.4			1.4
Pakistan	x		2.7	2.7			2.7
Papua			4.9	4.9			4.9
Peru	x		8.4	8.4			8.4

		C) Pref. Erosion NAMA – WTO est.	C) Pref. Erosion Agriculture – WTO est.	C) Total Pref. Erosion – lower bound	Banana & sugar Pref. Erosion – high lib.	Pref. Erosion (IMF estimates)	C) Total Pref. Erosion – upper bound
All figures in US$ millions	B) NFIDCs	Low et al. (2005)	Low et al. (2006)	Low et al. (2005); Low et al. (2006)	Gillson et al. (2004)	IMF (2003) & Alexandraki et al. (2004)	All sources
Serbia and M				0		45	45
Seychelles				0		10	10
Sri Lanka	x		0.1	0.1			0.1
St K and N	x		0.5	0.5		3	3
St Lucia	x	0.3	3.1	3.4	30.5	4	30.5
St V and the Gren			1.9	1.9	22	5	22
Swaziland		11.9	5.6	17.5	41.1	21	41.1
T&t	x		1.8	1.8	16.7		16.7
Tunisia	x			0		146	146
Venezuela	x	3.7	0.5	4.2			4.2
Zimbabwe		1.9	3	4.9	22.7		22.7
Total Others		**699.7**	**188.8**	**888.5**	**614.6**	**914**	**1759.4**
Total Costs	**329 < X < 1236**	**875**	**193.9**	**1068.9**	**645.3**	**1445.6**	**2362.3**
Total Pref. Erosion lower bound		**1,069**	Cumulative value of countries' estimates from Low et al. (2005) and Low et al. (2006)				
Total Pref. Erosion upper bound		**2,362**	Obtained by using the highest estimates for each country among the lower bound estimate, Gillson et al., IMF and Alexandraki and Lankes.				
Total of implementing WTO – upper bound		**305**	Average between method using fixed cost of implementation (US$7 million) times 60 countries and method using percentage (10% – calculated on Jamaica) of total pref. erosion cost-upper bound				
Total of implementing WTO – lower bound		**279**	Average between method using fixed cost of implementation (US$7 million) times 60 countries and method using percentage (10% – calculated on Jamaica) of total pref. erosion cost -lower bound				
Total for NFIDCs – upper bound		**1236**					
Total for NFIDCs – lower bound		**329**					

REFERENCES

Alesina, A. and D. Dollar. 2000. "Who Gives Foreign Aid to Whom and Why?," *Journal of Economic Growth*, 5(1): 33–63.

Alexandraki, K. and H. P. Lankes. 2004. "Estimating the Impact of Preference Erosion on Middle-Income Countries," IMF Working Paper, Washington, D.C.: IMF.

Dollar, D. and V. Levin. 2004. "The Increasing Selectivity of Foreign Aid, 1984–2002," Policy Research Working Paper 3299, Washington, D.C.: World Bank.

Gillson, I., A. Hewitt, and S. Page. 2004. "Forthcoming Changes in the EU Banana/Sugar Markets: A Menu of Options for an Effective EU Transitional Package," Report to DFID, London: Overseas Development Institute.

Hoekman, B., A. Mattoo, and P. English. 2002. Eds. "Development, Trade and the WTO: A Handbook," Washington, D.C.: World Bank, quoted in P. Kleen and S. Page. 2005.

"Special and Differential Treatment of developing countries in the World Trade Organization," Global Development Studies No. 2, Ministry for Foreign Affairs, Sweden.

Low, P., R. Piermartini, and J. Richtering. 2005. "Multilateral Solutions to the Erosion of Non-Reciprocal Preferences in NAMA," Staff Working Paper ERSD-2005–05, Geneva: WTO.

Low, P., R. Piermartini, and J. Richtering. 2006. "Non-reciprocal Preference Erosion Arising from MFN Liberalization in Agriculture: What Are the Risks?," WTO Working Paper ERSD-2006-02, March 2006.

Mattoo, A. 2005. "Services in a Development Round," Policy Research Working Paper Series 3718, Washington, D.C.: World Bank.

Mitchell, D. and M. Hoppe. 2006. "From Marrakesh to Doha: Effects of Removing Food Subsidies on the Poor," in Richard Newfarmer (ed.), *Trade, Doha and Development: A Window into the Issues*, Washington, D.C.: World Bank.

OECD/DAC, 2007. International Development Statistics online database, http://www.oecd.org/dataoecd/50/17/5037721.htm

WTO. 2005. *Draft Ministerial Declaration*, Ministerial Conference, Sixth Session, Hong Kong, 13–18 December 2005, Doha Work Programme, WT/MIN(05)/W/3/Rev.2, 18 December.

WTO. 2006. *Aid-For-Trade Concept Paper and Timeline for 2006*, prepared by the WTO Secretariat, Geneva, 17 January.

WTO/OECD. 2005. *Report on Trade-Related Technical Assistance and Capacity Building (TRTA/CB)*, http://www.oecd.org/dataoecd/27/4/11422694.pdf

WTO/OECD. 2007. "Doha Development Agenda Trade Capacity Building Database," http://tcbdb.wto.org/.

7 An African Perspective on Aid for Trade[1]

DOMINIQUE NJINKEU ET AL.

1 Introduction

For low-income countries, particularly the least-developed among them, trade negotiations will promote development only if there is a balanced market access package in agriculture and in industrial goods and services, complemented by adequate trade-related assistance – or Aid for Trade. Such Aid for Trade, intended to enable low-income countries to take advantage of market access opportunities emerging from trade negotiations, requires a mix of policy reforms and significant investments in infrastructure, training, and institutional development. As expected recipients of Aid for Trade funding and projects, African countries have a significant role to play in articulating how an Aid for Trade initiative can be structured in order to build their competitiveness so that they may engage productively in regional and global markets. Toward this end, this chapter presents an African perspective on Aid for Trade.

As a starting point, it is worthwhile noting the position of the African Group leading into the WTO Hong Kong Ministerial in December 2005:

> We reiterate the centrality of adequate and predictable development assistance for trade capacity building for African countries. We emphasize the need for a firm commitment to expand development assistance for trade capacity building in all African countries. The proposed Aid for Trade Initiative should focus not only on the capacity to negotiate, adjust, produce and trade, but also lead to better market access, improved infrastructure and address supply-side constraints. Such aid should come in grant form without compromising on Members' negotiating positions.[2]

As African countries are expected to be the primary beneficiaries of increased Aid for Trade, it is imperative that their voices are heard in the articulation and implementation of an Aid for Trade agenda. While it is a relatively new focus on donor assistance, Aid for Trade needs to be seen in the context of previous endorsements at the highest political levels, such as the New Partnership for Africa's Development

[1] This study represents the work of a team led by Dominique Njinkeu, comprising Hugo Cameron, Emmanuel Douya, Prisca Koncy Fosso, Thomas Dakayi Kamga, Babatunde Lawal, Bede Lyimo, Francis Mangeni, Iba Mar Oularé, Ademola Oyejide, Amanda Sunassee, and Edward Sungula. The team met in Douala, Cameroon on 22–26 February 2006 to contribute the views from African experts on Aid for Trade.

[2] African Union Arusha Trade Ministers' statement, 22–24 November 2005.

(NEPAD),[3] the Monterrey Consensus,[4] the Report of the World Commission on the Social Dimension of Globalization (ILO, 2004), the report by the Commission for Africa (2005), and the reports on the Mid-term Evaluation of the Millennium Development Goals (MDGs) and the Millennium Project Task Force (UN, 2005).

These issues are also being considered in the development cluster of Economic Partnership Agreement (EPA) negotiations between the European Commission (EC) and four geographical groupings in sub-Saharan Africa. To ensure a coherent approach, it is crucial for a constructive interface between the WTO and EPA negotiations to be maintained. Opening up first at the regional level can be a useful learning ground for the eventual integration of African countries into the international trading system. As such, the Aid for Trade initiative should seek to build on regional economic communities and strengthen trade links between them.

Section 2 of this chapter clarifies the concept of Aid for Trade within the broad spectrum of existing related activities. This clarification, based on a three-pillar approach, seeks to highlight the range of issues that a holistic trade capacity building program under Aid for Trade would encompass. Section 3 then reviews selected trade capacity building programs, with a view to identifying gaps in current delivery mechanisms. In particular, we note that regional issues – whether in the context of negotiations or in the range of supply-side constraints and competitiveness enhancement – have not received adequate attention. Further emphasis is also needed on private sector development. Section 4 explores delivery mechanisms. On this, we argue that the architecture of Aid for Trade needs to build on the experience of previous trade capacity building efforts that have benefited Africa. We further emphasize that adequate coordination and involvement of African WTO members should drive the entire process from the design phase to its implementation, monitoring, and evaluation.

2 Definition and scope of Aid for Trade

For many potential Aid for Trade stakeholders, there is a great deal of confusion and some skepticism as to what Aid for Trade is, who it is for, how it might work, and where the money will come from. This section proposes a "pillar"-based approach of defining how Aid for Trade might be categorized in order to help better envision what this concept could include. However, it is important to note that there are many different ways of subdividing Aid for Trade, depending on the perspective being used (see, for instance, Chapter 5 by Page in this volume). The pillar-based approach used here aims to structure discussions in a meaningful way for African officials (ILEAP and German Marshall Fund, 2006).

2.1 Pillar 1: building supply-side capacity

African countries lack the necessary infrastructure, technology, and knowledge to get goods to market in a competitive manner or meet product standards prevailing in the high-value markets of Europe or North America. This lack of supply capacity

[3] See NEPAD (2007).

[4] The International Conference on Financing for Development was held from 18–22 March 2002 in Monterrey, N. L., Mexico. At the meeting, countries adopted a plan that calls for the resources to meet the Millennium Development Goals and the conditions that will enable freer trade, more foreign investment, debt relief, and efficient government.

limits the opportunities offered by market access and hence acts as a barrier to trade. Aid for Trade therefore becomes a necessary complement to the core market access issues pursued in agriculture, non-agricultural market access (NAMA), and trade in services. It does so by creating effective market access through the removal of internal barriers to trade, by promoting value-added exports, by diversifying export products and export markets, and by creating an environment conducive for increased investment. Given the central role of the private sector in these areas, a coherent trade development strategy must also include the development of infrastructure that facilitates such activity. The first Aid for Trade pillar therefore addresses the need to improve competitiveness and alleviate supply-side constraints.

Paragraph 57 of the Hong Kong Declaration explicitly requires Aid for Trade to "help developing countries, particularly least developed countries (LDCs), to build the supply-side capacity and trade-related infrastructure that they need to assist them in implementing and benefiting from WTO Agreements and more broadly in expanding their trade." This pillar is crucial for African countries and regions if they are to expect meaningful benefits from participation in international trade. At its heart, this pillar is about building productive capacities by enhancing the regulatory, human resource, and physical infrastructures that businesses need to produce goods competitively and to move and export these goods efficiently. It can be broadly grouped into two categories: The first deals with private sector development, while the second includes investment in infrastructure more broadly. It should be noted that there is scope for some crossover between these two categories.[5]

2.1.1 *Private sector development*[6]

For many African exporters, the costs imposed on them by tariffs, quotas, or rules of origin are relatively small compared to the transaction costs associated with a hostile business environment and inadequate local financial resources. Support for private sector development in this sense would encompass activities to help expand exports by enabling domestic firms to exploit opportunities existing in export markets. Areas covered would include export promotion activities aimed at improving competitiveness, and thus expanding the volume of exportable goods and services. It would further include support for market intelligence, such as requirements for accessing new export goods or new markets and niche markets, and networking with international business communities. These would lead to the removal of impediments to business that drive up costs for exporters, such as costly and inefficient transit and border crossings, customs delays, delivery uncertainty, lack of export and market analysis skills, weak institutional support, standards compliance, excessive business regulations, and lack of access to capital and finance.

Assistance toward helping countries diversify away from primary products would also fall into this category. Value chain analysis is one mechanism that could

[5] See ILEAP (2006a).

[6] Listed as "Trade Development" under the WTO OECD Doha Development Agenda Trade Capacity Building Database (2007), this category includes a wide range of activities intended to help traders identify markets and develop attractive products, communicate with other businesses, and generally become a part of the international business network.

be used to help prioritize strategies in order to remove constraints encountered in production, marketing, distribution, and transport chains.

If they are to be effective, improvements to the business environment in African countries must be coupled with sound policy frameworks and regulations. Implementation of a regional telecommunications policy, for instance, could help the competitiveness of the sector within African regions. Conversely, the value of investment in private sector development is easily eroded by inefficient and corrupt customs services.

2.1.2 *Infrastructure*

Inadequate infrastructure is a major impediment to trade in sub-Saharan African countries. Poor trade-related infrastructure such as dysfunctional ports, roads, and telecommunications can add up to 40 percent to the cost of overseas-bound products in some African countries. Costs related to improvements in transport, communications, and energy infrastructure all fall under this category. Investments in infrastructure can serve directly or indirectly to facilitate trade. Improved roadways, for example, may be intended to support rural development, but will also increase the likelihood that products will reach distribution centers that are connected with international trade.

Large cash investments are needed to build appropriate infrastructure, but over the past two decades, public spending on this area in many low-income countries has declined due to fiscal requirements under structural adjustment programs (Stiglitz and Charlton, 2006). Some sources suggest that public investment in infrastructure has fallen to less than 1 percent of GDP in many African countries, whereas in order to service their infrastructure needs, these countries must spend at least 5 percent to 6 percent of GDP. The situation has been exacerbated by the fact that anticipated private-sector participation in improvement to infrastructure has for the most part failed to materialize.

The winds have recently shifted back toward multilateral interest in funding for infrastructure. However, much of this is being forwarded as low-interest loans rather than grants, a consideration that has serious implications for debt sustainability in low-income countries that are already highly indebted. For instance, in January 2006, the World Bank issued a package of loans and grants of US$199 million to improve trade and transport services in East Africa. Only US$15 million of this was given in the form of grants, which means US$184 million sits as debt.

Support for infrastructure can be divided into three subcategories (Brewster, 2006). The first covers assistance for infrastructure planning. This subsumes a range of primarily administrative activities, such as project identification, the preparation of programs, plans, and projects for funding, feasibility studies, and project design. The second category covers technical assistance in setting up systems for the efficient operation of infrastructure, including the legal and regulatory framework in priority sectors such as transportation or public utilities. The third category is support for the actual hard infrastructure itself, such as financing, construction, rehabilitation, or upgrading of transport, communications, and energy facilities.[7]

[7] Brewster argues that this third component is best noted in the Aid for Trade debate and addressed separately, particularly by development banks. See Brewster (2006).

2.2 Pillar 2: Trade system costs: adjustment and implementation

The second pillar of Aid for Trade refers to the alleviation of costs incurred as a result of trade reforms, including those undertaken as a means of implementation of international trade agreements. While trade reforms may bring long-term benefits, they typically generate winners and losers in the short run. Developing countries generally lack sufficient resources to provide the necessary safety nets, retraining, and other programs necessary for compensating those negatively affected by liberalization undertaken at the national, regional, and multilateral levels. Grouped under this category are costs incurred from the implementation of trade rules; food price increases to net food importers; preference erosion; reductions in tariff revenues; and other economic and social costs related to adjustment in specific sectors.

Implementation costs are of central concern for Africa. The costs of implementing multilateral commitments are twofold: (1) macroeconomic adjustment costs; and (2) technical requirements, obligations to accept new standards, rules systems, and reporting obligations for individual governments. Implementing these commitments may require the creation of new institutions and the employment or redeployment of scarce skilled personnel, all of which can be costly to governments.[8]

Short-term difficulties could also arise from food price increases to net food importers. Liberalization of agricultural trade through a phaseout of export subsidies and the substantial reduction of domestic support in food-exporting countries would lead to an increase in the price of food for those who import it. Developing countries that rely heavily on imports of one or two products could suffer disproportionately from threats to food security in the event of price increases related to trade policy reform.

Deteriorating terms of trade are also a concern for those countries that have relied on preferential access to markets. If the Doha Round succeeds in its aspirations for the nondiscriminatory reduction of tariffs in developed countries, a number of African countries will suffer losses from the erosion of preferences they previously enjoyed. Major African exporters of bananas and sugar are expected to suffer the most significant impacts.

2.3 Pillar 3: trade policy development and participation in rule-making

The third pillar outlines assistance needed to address the human resource capacity gap in trade policy making and implementation. If African governments are to formulate trade policy and trade negotiating positions that promote development and poverty reduction, they require a range of expertise at many different levels.

First and foremost, there is a need for a versatile core of trade officials with prior advanced-level training and long-term experience on the job. Such a cadre allows for the assessment of domestic and regional priorities and provides informed negotiators at the regional and multilateral levels. There must be a sufficient quantity and quality of these analysts to allow negotiation of winning outcomes and strategic alliances on a needs or issue basis. They must further be able to update

[8] This is further elaborated in ILEAP (2006a).

capitals promptly, request specific policy guidance, and understand instructions from capitals when provided. These officials need to be supported by a domestic private sector that is able to articulate commercial interests that shape market access concessions. Dynamic research and civil society communities in turn can help to combine business interests and long-term development objectives based on robust evidence, and feed this into the policy-making process. To enable the effective integration of these diverse perspectives, there must be an overall decision-making infrastructure to consolidate and identify the trade-offs that would be in the overall interest of the particular country.

Unfortunately, African countries and regional economic communities lack the staff, finance, and the depth of skills that would enable them to formulate their own development-supportive trade policies or represent their interests adequately in trade negotiations. Existing Aid for Trade programs tend to focus narrowly on enhancing participation in negotiations and implementing trade agreements that may not necessarily be aligned with countries' own development objectives. There is a limited supply of aid programs that promote independent thinking about trade policy and negotiations or that take a holistic and long-term perspective. Most current programs are funded on an *ad hoc* basis over a short time span and are subject to changing priorities from donor agencies.

Well-coordinated assistance in this area would include training of trade negotiators and experts, together with capital-based officials and staff in relevant regional bodies. It also would involve establishing a policy dialogue and consensus-building framework to facilitate the consolidation of trade policy and identification of negotiating positions that would overall be in the interest of beneficiary countries. Examples include training of trade negotiators (based in Geneva, Brussels, and in capitals), support for institutions such as research centers or universities, and programs to increase the quantity and enhance the quality of trade professionals. There is also a need for secure, long-term funding to keep salaries of such officials at a competitive level to ensure that they remain in post. To ensure overall long-term impacts, the training of future generations of trade diplomats and other stakeholders should adequately integrate trade issues and address how these can best promote African interests.

3 Building on existing trade-related assistance delivery mechanisms

Most trade-related assistance (TRA) tends to be disbursed through national and regional projects, and through multilateral initiatives such as the Joint Integrated Technical Assistance Programme (JITAP) and the Integrated Framework (IF). The Aid for Trade initiative needs to be looked at in the context of these existing projects and programs. In Africa, it would be best to build on them for reasons of efficiency and convenience. This section reviews existing TRA delivery mechanisms, highlighting some of their strengths and weaknesses, with a view to recommending what would be the most effective means of providing Aid for Trade, and what elements would constitute a strong and effective Aid for Trade architecture. We then look at which instruments currently serve the three aforementioned pillars most effectively, while attempting to identify the main gaps that the Aid for Trade initiative would best fill.

3.1 Multilateral level

3.1.1 *JITAP*

As covered in the introduction to this volume, JITAP is a trade capacity building (TCB) program for selected least-developed and other African countries.[9] It channels TCB support from various donors into one program to help African country partners benefit from the multilateral trading system (MTS).

Strengths and weaknesses of JITAP

An evaluation of JITAP undertaken in 2002 points to a number of strengths and weaknesses of the program (De Silva and Weston, 2002). Three of its key strengths are its innovative design; its high profile (which raised awareness on WTO trade negotiations at a time when most countries' technical capacity for the MTS was very low); and its successful development of governmental human resources in trade capacity.

However, JITAP has also suffered from at least four shortcomings. In general, the program's weaknesses stem from the fact that it aimed to address a portfolio beyond its financial and managerial means – evidenced by the less than full implementation of its five modules. First, because of its narrow focus on trade policy, the program provides only a limited approach to TRA. As such, a number of key TRA programs, notably those related to supply-side constraints, have received little coverage under JITAP.

Second, a recent evaluation of JITAP for Burkina Faso and Tanzania undertaken by the Netherlands Ministry of Foreign Affairs (Lanser and Wijmenga, 2004) shows that, after nearly seven years of operation, there are clear signs of poor sustainability and anchoring of institutional memory within beneficiary country ministries of trade. This finding is also common to other country evaluations. Due to the lack of longer-term planning, when the first group of countries was to be phased out from the first phase of JITAP, nothing had been designed to ensure continuity of program activities.

Third, according to JITAP country evaluations, IITCs (see footnote 9) did not function effectively due to budgetary constraints (Abugattas, 2001). In Tanzania, for instance, it was noted that mobilizing resources for regular JITAP activities, such as holding workshops, was often a very lengthy process. This can result in postponed actions, and forces recipients to seek out alternative funding sources. However, in some countries, such as Uganda, national trade negotiations structures have been highly successful. This is due to strong government commitment and the ability of governments to continue funding such structures in the absence of ongoing JITAP funding.

9 JITAP is implemented by three multilateral trade agencies: the International Trade Centre (ITC), the UN Conference on Trade and Development (UNCTAD) and the WTO. It relies on inter-institutional committees (IITCs) that act as platforms for analyzing negotiating strategies, preparing and supporting trade negotiations, and coordinating and undertaking consensus building among governmental institutions. It posits itself between governments and the private sector, academia, and other stakeholders. JITAP is funded through a Common Trust Fund (CTF) supported by a number of donor countries. For further information see the Introductory Chapter, this volume.

A fourth shortcoming relates to JITAP's insufficient linkages with participating countries. The program is highly centralized in Geneva and poorly connected to country governance and decision-making systems, as well as to in-country development partners. It tends to be dominated by the UNDP in-country, and there has been poor coordination at the country level with other donors involved with trade-related assistance at the bilateral level.

How can JITAP be used in the context of Aid for Trade?

When assessing the lessons of JITAP for Aid for Trade to African countries, there are a number of issues to bear in mind. First, the fact that JITAP is an instrument that could be available to all African (developing and least-developed) countries makes it a tool that could be adapted to channel part of an Aid for Trade package to countries in the region. This also makes it suitable for regional programs, which are likely to address problems of both LDCs and other countries. Its focus on building capacity for countries to engage with the multilateral trading system makes it a useful model for addressing government-level aspects of the third pillar proposed in this chapter – "Trade Policy Development and Participation in Rule Making" (though it would not help in addressing capacity building in trade policy research centers, for instance). Building on the modules of the JITAP, and assuming the Doha negotiations will be successfully concluded, the focus of a "New JITAP" program could be expected to be on compliance and implementation of WTO rules as well as on notifications. However, despite the potential of such a model to meet some (but not all) of the Pillar 3 requirements, JITAP would not be the most appropriate tool to handle the Aid for Trade package in its entirety, particularly not in the areas involving infrastructure or more complex adjustment-funding mechanisms.

It is important to bear in mind that the volumes of funds that have been handled by JITAP in the past have been quite modest. On average, beneficiary countries have received approximately US$1.5 million over five to eight years. The flows of aid required under the Aid for Trade initiative, however, are much larger, especially given the focus on addressing supply-side constraints and infrastructure.

3.1.2 *Integrated Framework*

Also outlined in the Introductory Chapter, the Integrated Framework for Trade-Related Technical Assistance for Least Developed Countries (IF), established in 1997, is supported by six agencies – ITC, IMF, UNCTAD, UNDP, the World Bank, and WTO. When the IF was launched, its main objective was to increase the benefits LDCs derive from trade by coordinating technical assistance provided by the six agencies. The IF aimed at enhancing LDCs' trade capacities to better respond to market opportunities and to work toward full integration into the multilateral trading system (UNCTAD, 2005). After three years of only modest results, the IF was relaunched with a renewed focus on two major objectives: (i) mainstream trade into national development plans, notably the Poverty Reduction Strategy Papers (PRSPs); and (ii) assist and coordinate technical assistance addressing the needs identified by LDCs.

The IF is built on in-country and international structures. The in-country structure goes further than JITAP by placing stronger emphasis on being embedded in existing national institutions and by ensuring wider and stronger participation of other donors. Unlike JITAP, which only maintains an in-country focal point, IF secretariats are in principle set up within ministries of trade. The IF's emphasis on mainstreaming trade in PRSPs further helps to embed it within host governments. IF stakeholders are also expected to set up a local project appraisal committee that includes the government and donors in order to vet TRA deliverables.

Strengths and weaknesses of the Integrated Framework[10]

Like the JITAP, the IF has features that could be built upon or emulated in designing an Aid for Trade delivery framework. Indeed, as a key part of the Aid for Trade initiative, at Hong Kong the WTO also endorsed the establishment of an "Enhanced" IF (EIF), which members are considering alongside the wider Aid for Trade initiative (see Introductory chapter to this volume). First, the most important strength of the existing IF framework is the implementation structure that links countries' PRSP and DTIS matrices with existing government/donor coordination mechanisms (consultative groups and round tables) and the budgetary process. The existing setup offers the potential to use in-country instruments such as budget support, sector wide approaches (SWAps), and bilateral projects.[11] A second useful feature is the degree of increased awareness of trade policy potential for growth and development. The IF may have heightened national, international, and donor awareness of the role played by trade in growth and development, although attribution of this to the IF is difficult. Third, the IF has enhanced coordination not only among agencies providing TRA but also among ministries or others receiving it, for instance, among the ministries of trade, finance, and planning and between the public and private sectors. Fourth, the IF structures are strongly embedded in country structures and the DTIS. Although criticized by some countries as not bringing any new element into the identification of national trade-related priorities, the IF does have the power to mobilize both governments and donors behind a consolidated matrix and action plan.

Set against these strengths are four key weaknesses. First, by focusing largely on public expenditures and social sectors, PRSPs have not explored the full range of policy options to achieve growth and development. While donors have improved the PRSP process, they have not changed the content of their assistance. Second, the IF focuses mainly on studies, and provides only a small amount of follow-up technical assistance as bridging finance until other funding materializes. Window II bridging funding of US$1 million per country is dwarfed by the needs identified by the IF studies themselves and by the demands prompted from recipient countries. Third, there is limited evidence on the mobilization of additional investment resources based on the DTIS. Fourth, country support strategies and PRSPs still largely do not address trade issues.

[10] Observations based mainly on the World Bank Operation Evaluation Department (OED). See Agarwal and Cutura (2004).

[11] Donors are increasingly using SWAps and budget support programmes (for instance in Mozambique, Tanzania, Uganda, and Ethiopia) particularly for the social sectors. These programmes are characterized by direct donor support for government-executed activities, and donor funding is directly transferred into the government budget. They are usually linked to certain conditions (for example, with regard to the public finance management system) and performance indicators. In most cases, donors are jointly involved in providing budget support (UNCTAD, 2005).

How can the IF be used in the context of Aid for Trade?

At the September 2005 IMF and World Bank Development Committee meeting, a proposal was made for setting up an Enhanced IF, as mentioned previously. The main aim of the Enhanced IF is to help mitigate some of the identified weaknesses of the current IF by: (i) supporting the creation of strong country leadership on trade; (ii) promoting the development of a coherent strategy for trade and competitiveness; (iii) sustaining this push via a multiyear rolling program of capacity building; and (iv) promoting increased donor coordination on Aid for Trade via both multilateral and bilateral channels. It is also envisioned that an enhanced IF would entail a window for regional issues.

The IF – and more specifically the Enhanced IF, once it materializes – represents a potentially strong aid delivery mechanism, given its emphasis on country leadership, its planned link to countries' national development plans and PRSPs, and its promised sustainability. The IF's robust government/donor coordination mechanism and the fact that it is already deeply embedded in country systems is a further benefit. The structure of the IF and its past track record are such that it could provide a useful basis for addressing certain elements of Pillar 1: "Building Supply-Side Capacity."

However, since the current IF is not set up to transfer large amounts of money, in its current form it lacks the structures to transfer large sums to recipients. This is a key concern in using the IF as a mechanism for delivering aid under Pillar 2: "Trade System Costs: Adjustment and Implementation." Negotiations around an Enhanced IF could be useful in addressing this challenge.

The IF may be less suited for supporting macroeconomic adjustment, which has to date been mainly undertaken in African countries via the IMF and the European Development Fund (EDF). However, the IF suffers from one key limitation: it is restricted to LDCs; presumably this would apply to an Enhanced IF as well. Because of this limitation, alternative or parallel structures will need to be established for non-LDCs. When creating these structures, the IF and the Enhanced IF could be used as models for part of this work.

Standards and Trade Development Facility

The Standards and Trade Development Facility (STDF) is a World Bank mechanism set up in 2004 to assist countries to conform to SPS regulations and other standards requirements. It is centrally managed by the IF Secretariat as a separate fund and program, and is organized in the form of quarterly calls for proposals. The project is not yet widely used by WTO members, for two key reasons. One is due to the central management structure and low visibility and awareness of the project, even though the WTO has written to countries informing them of the fund and how to apply. Second is the difficulty that countries face in assessing their required adjustments and standards conformity.

The STDF was in part a response to a donor shortfall in addressing SPS issues. The World Bank estimates that in 2002, the total funds spent by donors on SPS standards compliance support was US$53 million. This is dwarfed by the estimated US$1.75 billion of exports from developing countries disrupted by SPS standards in the same year. In addition, ACP countries face an estimated US$140–700 million of annual investment to meet the current level of SPS regulations (CTA, 2003).

The EC has initiated two related programs on SPS for ACP countries – one for agricultural goods (Pesticide Initiative Programme) and another for fisheries (Strengthening Fishery Products Health Conditions Programme).

How can the STDF be used in the context of Aid for Trade?

Given the heavy adjustment costs associated with compliance and implementation of standards and SPS regulations, this facility potentially has the scope to address part of Pillar 2, that is, the cost of implementing technical requirements, and also the private sector development element of Pillar 3. However, given the sheer size of the funding required to assist Africa adequately in the area of SPS, additional specific focus on SPS under Pillars 2 and 3 should be included in any further Aid for Trade package.

3.2 Bilateral and regional projects

3.2.1 *The importance of the EC*

The European Commission has been one of the driving forces of TCB programs at both the global and regional levels. TCB support is featured throughout the EC's development cooperation agenda, and over the past three years some US$2 billion has been spent on TCB or related program. For the last fifteen years, the EC has been implementing in parallel to the National Indicative Programmes (NIPs) what is commonly know as Regional Indicative Programmes (RIPs). These RIPs are managed by the six regional integration secretariats in the ACP regions. These projects have focused strongly in assisting each region with its market integration agenda (i.e., setting up free trade agreements and/or customs unions), pooling resources in the area of regional standard setting, and heavy infrastructure development. There are also a number of regional EPA negotiations projects.

A number of EPA negotiations projects are being delivered at the regional level, as well as EPA-focused projects implemented under the RIPs. These include:

- PAIRAC – "Support Programme for Regional Integration in Central Africa." This program is implemented by the Secretariat of CEMAC and comprises five major activities: support to EPA negotiations, macroeconomic convergence/multilateral monitoring, customs union, common market, and strengthening of regional institutional capacities (EUR16 million).
- SADC EPA Negotiations Support Facility (EUR7.5 million).
- "COMESA – Regional Integration Support Programme" (EUR30 million) and "Support for EPA Negotiations" (EUR2 million).
- ECOWAS economic integration and trade support (EUR118 million).[12] In this framework, two projects have already been decided in 2005: the "RIP follow-up mechanism" (EUR6 million) and "support to regional integration and EPA negotiations" (EUR7 million).

[12] Its objectives are the consolidation of the ECOWAS and WAEMU customs unions, the elimination of barriers to the free movement of goods, services, and capital and the creation of a common market in the region; the reinforcement of economic stability and of the institutional framework of ECOWAS and WAEMU; reinforced participation of the citizens in the integration process; and support to the private sector and the preparation of multilateral negotiations in the framework of EPAs and the WTO.

Looking at Aid for Trade in the context of the EDF is particularly relevant for Africa, given the ongoing programming exercise for the 10th EDF NIPs and RIPs. The ongoing EPA negotiations are also critical in the current debate on Aid for Trade. The EPA negotiations will open up discussions on (a) how to prioritize TRA in the context of the EDF; and (b) the appropriate level of funding to be allocated to TRA. The EPAs and EDF also present an important window of opportunity to help African countries address erosion of preferences, particularly those associated with sugar and bananas.

In the context of the EPAs, it is worth noting that Regional Preparatory Task Forces (RPTFs), which are joint EC-ACP bodies, have been set up in each of the EPA regions with the aim of bringing together the key decisions on EDF programming and to ensure the linkage between the negotiating process and the programming of development cooperation. Together, the 10th EDF programming, the ongoing EPA negotiations, and the newly established RPTFs offer ACP countries and the African Group a formidable window of opportunity to leverage changes and improve the current management and implementation of the EDF and particularly Aid for Trade.

3.2.2 *New trends in EC-ACP relations*

Over the past five years, EC-ACP relations have undergone a critical transformation, resulting in the EC reviewing its mode of operation in the ACP regions. This transformation was spurred on by the evolving nature of EC development policy; the changing nature of its external trade relations, particularly in the case of the ACP regions; and the lessons it learned from its overall development cooperation. Based on these key changes and the internal restructuring undertaken by the Commission, a number of pan-African initiatives are under consideration, such as basket funds and regional compensatory mechanisms. We also note a dramatic increase in TRA within RIPs. While such projects are likely to become more prominent under the 10th EDF, there remains much scope for greater focus on trade in the NIPs, where trade content under the 9th EDF was only 0.1 percent.

At the regional level, there are a number of trade adjustment mechanisms being developed, such as the Regional Trade Integration Budget Support (RTIBS) facility, which will act as a mechanism for regional budget support. Also in line with the revamped spirit of donor coordination and harmonization, captured in the 2005 Paris Declaration on Aid Effectiveness, the EC and major development partners such as the World Bank and the African Development Bank (AfDB) are pooling resources for the setup of a Basket Partnership Fund for the East African Community (EAC) region.

There has been an emergence of "New Generation" project/program funding, in the form of trade compensation mechanisms and sectoral adjustment and market restructuring projects. One prominent example is the EC-ACP Sugar Action Plan. It was launched in July 2005, with an initial accompanying financial package of EUR40 million, to assist the ACP sugar sector to diversify for the year 2006. This is to be increased to approximately EUR170 million per year for the following eight years. However, the EC has resisted qualifying this money specifically as compensation, saying it is rather for "adapting to new situations." The critical issue will be to ensure that these funds are directed to structural reforms in the sector, including to R&D. This fund has emerged as a direct response to the EC sugar reform and its associated erosion of preferences for ACP sugar exporting countries. Notably, the Sugar Action Plan has been allocated a separate line in the EU budget and is thus additional to existing EDF monies. It can be concluded that there are important windows of opportunity to address preference erosion and adjustment costs under EDF funding or funding from the EC budget.

By 2008, EPA negotiations may transform EC-ACP trade relations. As part of adjusting to and implementing the new EPAs, ACP countries would have to undertake a number of critical reforms. But if these countries are to benefit from the EPA negotiations, substantial investments in infrastructure and productive capacity will be needed. Although a number of these costs may be attributable to other ongoing trade liberalization processes such as the WTO and other regional and bilateral agreements, there will be certain associated costs directly attributable to the EPA negotiations. This is most apparent in the case of LDCs, which under the WTO Doha round are required to make few commitments, yet must comply with reciprocity requirements under EPAs.

3.2.3 *How can African countries maximize the effectiveness of bilateral and regional projects/programs in the context of Aid for Trade?*

To date, most TRA and TCB has been provided through bilateral and regional projects. Given the potential for increased Aid for Trade, it is imperative that bilateral and regional projects and programs be structured in a manner that maximizes the effectiveness of this new funding.

Using regional channels for delivering Aid for Trade creates a number of advantages for African countries. Most importantly, regional integration initiatives have real potential to strengthen and deepen regional integration processes, and by doing so prepare regions and their member states for integration into the multilateral trading system. Another important advantage to a regional approach is its positive effect on building competitiveness. The following points are some of the strategic and operational steps African countries can take to maximize the effectiveness of bilateral and regional projects and programs in the context of Aid for Trade. While it would be problematic to use the current IF to implement regional projects due to its exclusive focus on LDCs, there may be potential to consider a "regional window" under the Enhanced IF that could include both LDCs and non-LDCs.

It is important that projects are anchored in national development strategies, with priority given to growth enhancing and productive activities, in order to ensure that TRA, particularly in the area of overcoming supply-side constraints and increasing capacity to produce, is funded as a priority or focal area. There is need for greater coherence from the EC with respect to their demands from ACP group under the EPA and WTO negotiations. The African Group needs to make a substantiated request for additional Aid for Trade funds to cover EPA associated-adjustment costs. Where feasible, budget support or basket funds should be the preferred means of aid delivery, paying particular attention to establishing a balance between projects and programs.

3.2.4 *Operational Response*

At the operational level, there are critical steps that African countries and regions could consider. First, there is a need for coordination at the continental level as part of an overall ACP-wide coordination. The African Union Commission, for instance, could help coordinate training for African countries on EDF procedures. This should also be extended to other ACP beneficiaries. EDF procedures are known to be a formidable hurdle for ACP countries trying to access EC funds. This is a particular problem in the area of project implementation, and it needs to be addressed as a priority under each region's Joint Regional Preparatory Task Force (RPTF).

The second key operational response is the need for development partners to honor commitments to improve aid delivery systems, harmonize donor policies and procedures, and implement principles of good practice in development cooperation. The African Group should make several concrete recommendations in this area. First is the establishment of an EC road map depicting the key goals to be achieved in the area of harmonization and coordination of aid. This should be based on the March 2005 OECD Paris Declaration on Aid Effectiveness, which lays out a strategy for improving the quality of aid and its impact on development.[13]

Second, the EC and its respective delegations in-country, together with EU member states, should establish a joint financial agreement favoring the harmonization of procedures around the country system. The EC should be encouraged to move swiftly toward joint programming with member states and ensure that an EC road map is established in every country.

The third response is to create a beneficiary-led review of development partner assistance. This could be done through the creation of a Joint Assistance Strategy (JAS). African countries need to prioritize the setup of the JAS, laying out clear indicators for assessment of donor effectiveness and harmonization efforts, through which development partner assistance would be jointly reviewed. Global and pan-African initiatives should be anchored in in-country aid delivery mechanisms, in order to minimize the possible inefficiencies common in such instruments. ACP countries themselves need to proactively strengthen their public finance management systems in order to prepare for channeling the scaled up Aid for Trade funds through national budgets.

4 Aid for Trade architecture

4.1 Costing and funding an Aid for Trade package

After years of historic declines in official development assistance (ODA), there has gradually been a pickup in foreign aid, though the level remains far from the 0.7 percent GDP target pledged by developed countries nearly fifty years ago in the first UN Development Decade.[14] The recent boost in aid emerges from the 2002 Monterrey Consensus (UN, 2003), and has picked up strength as the deadline for meeting the UN Millennium Development Goals (MDGs) in 2015 closes in. On the basis of the joint WTO/OECD Trade Capacity Building Database (TCBDB), from 2001 to 2006 more than forty bilateral donors and multilateral agencies have funded close to 15,000 activities. According to a joint report by the WTO and the Organization for Economic Co-operation and Development (OECD), aid for TCB has grown to 4.4 percent of total aid commitments (WTO/OECD, 2005). The OECD Development Assistance Committee (DAC) Secretariat has projected that following commitments

[13] See OECD (2007).
[14] The ODA target of 0.7% of developed country GDP was established by the United Nations in 1969.

by the G8 and the EC at the UN 2005 Summit, total ODA is projected to increase from US$80 billion in 2004 to US$130 billion in 2010, that is, an increase of US$50 billion, of which half is destined for Africa (WTO, 2005).

Having a sense of the scale of required assistance will help determine the extent to which committed Aid for Trade funds meet the needs of the continent and of individual countries. Getting the right mix of grants and loans is particularly relevant for Africa, given that the majority of the supply-side constraints faced by these countries lie in the area of heavy infrastructure, which tends to be funded via loans and public–private partnerships.

There are several key elements which could guide African countries in estimating their Aid for Trade requirements:

- An Aid for Trade package should not be designed as a one-off initiative. Instead, it must be provided in the context of a recurrent cycle, preferably multiples of four to five years, with an inbuilt midterm review mechanism.
- At the national level, trade must be anchored in countries' Poverty Reduction Strategies/National Development Plans, and linked to the budgetary process. Where possible, direct budgetary support or basket funds should be encouraged. This will assist countries in their needs assessment and budget estimation exercise at a later stage, and is critical in building ownership in, and sustainability of, the process.
- Any estimation needs to be carried out based on a common set of agreed criteria. It will have to be credible, verifiable, and justifiable.
- Aid for Trade should avoid the crowding-out effect that a scaled-up Aid for Trade scheme could have on other sources of grants and loans.
- Particular attention should also be paid to the mix of loans and grants used to fund Aid for Trade.

4.2 Architecture and operational modalities

In addition to estimating Aid for Trade requirements, it is essential that African countries focus on how an Aid for Trade package can be delivered in a way that benefits their economies to the greatest extent possible. Several guiding principles could be kept in mind when undertaking this task:[15]

- Aid for Trade should be based on the needs and priorities of African countries, and rooted in these countries' own development strategies.
- Where feasible, Aid for Trade needs to be embedded in existing aid delivery systems. There should also be reliance on government mechanisms (i.e., direct budgetary support), where these provide reasonable assurance that resources will be used for agreed purposes and where it is likely to enhance achievement of sustainable improvements in government performance.
- To ensure additionality of resources, there is a need for a vertical fund[16] which could channel funds through SWAps, for example, through sector budget support.

[15] See ILEAP (2006d) for more elaboration of ideas presented in this section.

[16] "Vertical funds" are those that focus on a particular issue or a small number of related issues, typically financing programs and projects encompassing all aspects of the issue. Also see ILEAP (2006b).

- Weaknesses in institutional capacity or other constraints in existing aid delivery mechanisms need to be addressed so as to ensure effective use of the Aid for Trade package. However, it is important to note that the development of appropriate systems will often be a medium-term process. Until donors can rely on these systems, they should simplify and harmonize their own procedures to reduce the burden placed on partner countries.
- Aid for Trade cannot be managed by a single donor or institution; no single approach is suitable for all countries. The manner in which harmonization is implemented needs to be adapted to local circumstances and institutional capacities.

The different purposes and the large scale of what falls under Aid for Trade, as well as the unwillingness of both donors and recipients to rely on a single existing institution, suggest a need to find a way of reconciling multiple funds from multiple donors, each covering some countries/regions or some types of spending addressing specific purposes. Furthermore, there is a need to ensure secure mechanisms based on the legal structures of each funding scheme. One option would be for the WTO secretariat to monitor the implementation over a medium-term period. Reports on both overall results and individual countries could go from all implementing agencies to the WTO, perhaps through the Committee on Trade and Development (to monitor total implementation) to the Trade Policy Review Mechanism (to cover individual countries).

Vertical funds may help countries build up a level of expertise and specialization and benefit from economies of scale. They tend to be easier to coordinate at a global level than horizontal funds that address a range of cross-cutting issues. Against this is the possible lack of "ownership" by the receiving country, the difficulties of aligning vertical funds with country programs, and the risk of shocks due to changes in donor priorities. A survey of twenty-three funds, some horizontal, others vertical, both trade and nontrade, suggests that there are a number of funds that include diagnostics of what trade measures are required (IF, part of EC TRA, JITAP, the PMU, etc.). However, far fewer programs address supply-side constraints directly or the implementation costs of trade agreements. Thus, new funds will be needed for supply-side and implementation, which are two critical areas for Africa.

The examination of existing programs and the discussion of how trade-related aid has increased in recent years demonstrate that there is no need to design Aid for Trade from scratch. Existing mechanisms have been able to sustain an increase of US$6 billion in trade-related aid. But the analysis suggests that some types of needs are not being well met. While there is reasonable capacity to determine new types of needs, the means for translating these assessments into new financing are less satisfactory. It also suggests that there are very different types of needs, and, on the basis of both analysis of institutions and the precedents in aid, these are likely to require different types of organizations and programs to meet them. Some needs are small and easily defined. These require an organization able to offer quick disbursement, probably with a minimum of conditionality or planning. Others require longer term and more considered programs in order to ensure that building the supply capacity to trade is well integrated into a country's (and perhaps a region's) development program.

Alternative components of Aid for Trade have very different implications for the design of an Aid for Trade mechanism. There may be a need for new funds, with new criteria, either as designated parts of individual donors' programs (the EU Action Plan for Sugar, for example) or in a new multilateral form. In addition, or possibly as an alternative, there may be a need for a new assessment process to provide an agreed definition and calculation of macroeconomic adjustment needs. This could take the form, for instance, of the IF for trade in PRSPs, the IMF's Trade Integration Mechanism (TIM) for balance of payments costs, or the EU-ACP assessment of the costs of EPAs. The IF experience suggests that an assessment process divorced from any commitment to provide finance can be inadequate and disappointing.

There is an additional reason for a special fund or special terms within normal funds. Some forms of assistance are justified under concessional terms, others under a loan scheme, and cases of combinations of both loans and grants cannot be ruled out.

4.3 Delivery mechanisms

Since trade capacity building deals with a multiplicity of problems and objectives, it tends to be provided through a patchwork of different mechanisms and agencies. Aid for Trade should operate under the full ownership of the recipient countries, and its activities should be demand-driven and aim at promoting local development priorities.

An ideal approach is for a comprehensive Aid for Trade package that supports all relevant aspects using more efficient assistance mechanisms, which recognize individual recipient-country characteristics and ownership and target priority trade areas defined in development plans and strategies. In addition, there is a need for coordination and harmonization of different trade-related assistance arrangements and appropriate alignment of the management and implementation with the policies and programs of individual recipient countries.

The mobilization of the resources for a comprehensive Aid for Trade initiative raises several important questions. for instance, what sources and through which mechanisms would the additional funds be mobilized? What impact would the funding of enlarged trade-related assistance schemes have on the availability of resources for more general development assistance?

For analytical convenience, it is useful to decompose the elements of Aid for Trade assistance by type and source of problem in relation to the financing of the corresponding compensation. In the case of negative impacts of countries' own trade liberalization, for instance, the adopted approach would have to meet the urgent needs of countries, both to adjust to trade reforms that are already happening and to build up their infrastructure. For compensation for losses incurred as a result of developed-country trade policies, it is preferable to build from the principle that those imposing the costs should bear the burden of offsetting them. As such, there should be bound commitments in the WTO by preference-granting countries to provide adequate compensation funds related to benefits withdrawn. A similar line of argument could provide the basis for mobilizing compensation funds in respect to losses imposed by developed-country domestic support and export subsidies in agriculture on both low-income country exporters and net food importers.

With respect to allocation among the eligible low-income countries, African countries should bear in mind that allocation of any "free" fund tends to generate a "race for aid" that could threaten the solidarity of the group of recipients. To avoid such a situation, the following considerations should be taken into account:

- Access to assistance for relaxing supply response capacity constraints should be open to all low-income countries, rather than being restricted only to the LDCs.
- Recipients of Aid for Trade funds in respect of adjustment costs related to countries' own trade liberalization will, by and large, be self-selected.
- Compensation for preference erosion, export revenue losses and increased food import bills will be for countries that suffer from these specific problems. What they receive is not aid but entitlement.

4.4 Governance issues

Multiple funds from multiple donors characterize current TRA delivery; each initiative covers some countries and/or some types of spending in order to secure adequate funding for all relevant countries and purposes. There is a need to harmonize the funds themselves as well as the procedures of each separate fund, and ensure ownership and accountability. A first step will be to establish coherence between aid and trade agencies and practitioners.

There is a potential conflict between country programs and a vertical approach to aid. Vertical funds for health, education, and other needs show that trade is not the only area where those outside the aid process have identified a need for more aid, and show both the advantages and the disadvantages of solving the problem by providing finance 'tied' to a particular subject. The fact that trade-related aid has increased in recent years suggests that traditional donors agree that there is a need to spend more on trade, but the commitment in the WTO Declaration and the identification of increased costs that countries will face because of new WTO commitments suggest that some formal way of guaranteeing a continued priority for trade needs to be found.

An attractive feature of dedicated funds is the guarantee that the problem identified will be addressed. One option to consider for an Aid for Trade delivery mechanism would be to consolidate the main features of the IF and JITAP into a special facility with its own governance structure. Africa could ensure representation proportionate to the level of aid that is likely to be earmarked to the continent.

There are two elements of Aid for Trade that could require some form of guarantee or legal commitment that would be additional to existing donor commitments. The first is that some countries will face exceptionally high costs, and may need assurance that their efforts to build capacity would be supported in the longer term. Experience since the Uruguay Round shows that while small costs, particularly those easily tied to specific spending (i.e., reform of customs procedures) have attracted additional aid, those that require a macroeconomic approach both to calculate them and to find a way of meeting them (i.e., adjustment needs following on the terms of trade change in agriculture) have been left to one side. The second element relates to announcements by some countries to support further growth in Aid for Trade – it may be of benefit to establish rules that guarantee such commitments such that they carry forward the trend that has occurred in the last five years. Ongoing monitoring could also be worked into this process.

There is a need for a new way to monitor both the overall supply of funds and how they are allocated to ensure that new country needs are appropriately met and that the overall allocation to trade remains high and growing. Now that the WTO has accepted that meeting the costs of adjustment and providing what countries "need to assist them to implement and benefit from WTO Agreements" are legitimate concerns, members will have to take responsibility for identifying what procedures are needed and ensuring that they are implemented. The WTO could check that members have committed ("bound," in trade terms) the funds that they have announced. In subsequent years, the WTO will need to monitor that the commitments are kept, for instance, through the TPR mechanism.

4.5 Role of specialized agencies

Building on the experience of the Integrated Framework and JITAP, all the institutions involved in these programs should provide advisory and technical assistance support to the Aid for Trade initiative. To properly address the Aid for Trade priorities, at least three new agencies need to be included: the African Development Bank, the UN Food and Agriculture Organization (FAO), and the World Customs Organization (WCO). In the case of the AfDB, given the centrality of supply-side constraints and the competitiveness agenda of Aid for Trade in Africa, it could play a role drawing on its close links with the global trade and finance community. Its operational expertise with African policy issues and global competitiveness is another attribute. With respect to the FAO, given the high priority placed on agriculture by African countries in the area of trade, the institution could help to build competitiveness and assist countries meet product standards for agricultural exports. Similar arguments hold for the WCO on helping countries implement initiatives in trade facilitation.

5 Conclusion

Building on the experience with and lessons from existing trade capacity building, the Aid for Trade initiative at the WTO should be in the form of a comprehensive new mechanism that could have the following components:

- Existing multilateral Aid for Trade structures consolidated under a new Global Aid for Trade Facility.
- Specialized agencies, including those participating in the Integrated Framework, operating in an advisory capacity.
- A stream of funding (additional to existing aid commitments) to the facility, agreed to as part of binding Doha Round agreements.
- Commitments subsequently enforceable within the WTO.
- A broad mandate for the facility to finance technical assistance, trade-related capacity building, enterprise development, and infrastructure projects through a combination of grants and concessional loans.

On balance, while there have been some constructive examples of TRA for African countries, major gaps remain. JITAP and the IF have proven useful for increasing participation of African countries in the trading system and in helping to define trade-related priorities. The EDF provides some elements for addressing preference erosion, adjustment costs, and infrastructure. However, major gaps still exist in funding for trade-related infrastructure and private-sector development (Pillar 1). At the same time, African countries face further challenges in meeting regulatory requirements (both in export markets and domestically), in implementation of WTO agreements, and in dialogue, negotiations, and skill enhancement at the regional level.

African countries should pursue their hard infrastructure issues in a program led by the African Development Bank, the World Bank, and relevant bilateral programs (EU, Japan) and the private sector. Funding will come as a mixture of grant and loans.

Preference erosion is important but should be included in Aid for Trade in a way that does not crowd out the core priority issues. Adjustment costs associated with preference erosion could be borne by the former preference granters, preferably in a binding fashion. Bilateral programs such as the EDF or U.S. Millennium Challenge Account (MCA) could be useful existing mechanisms for this goal.

REFERENCES

Abugattas, Luis. 2001. "Negotiating Strategies for the East African Community Countries in Multilateral Trade Negotiations: Including Implementation Aspects of the WTO Agreements and Implications of the Transitional Periods and Special and Differential Treatment," Consultancy Final Report, elaborated for UNCTAD-JITAP Project, UNCTAD/ITC/WTO.

Agarwal, Manmohan and Jozefina Cutura. 2004. "Integrated Framework for Trade-Related Technical Assistance – Addressing Challenges of Globalization: An Independent Evaluation of the World Bank's Approach to Global Programs," Washington, D.C.: World Bank.

Brewster, Havelock R. 2006. "Challenges Faced by the Private Sector in Taking Advantage of the New Trading Opportunities under the International Trading System," prepared for the COMSEC / UNCTAD meeting on "Aid for Trade," Geneva, 21–22 March.

Commission for Africa. 2005. "Our Common Interest – Report of the Commission," UK: Commission for Africa.

CTA. 2003. "Study of the Consequences of the Application of Sanitary and Phytosanitary (SPS) Measures on ACP Countries," prepared by Cerrex Ltd., UK.

De Silva, Leelananda and Ann Weston. 2002. "Report of the Summative Evaluation of the Joint Integrated Technical Assistance Programme," Geneva: ITC.

ILEAP. 2005. "Aid for Trade: Why and How?," *Negotiation Advisory Brief* No. 10, Aid for Trade prepared by Dominique Njinkeu and Hugo Cameron.

ILEAP. 2006a. "Aid for Trade: How We Got Here, Where We Might Go," *Background Brief* No. 10, prepared by Michael J. Finger.

ILEAP. 2006b. "The Financial Architecture of Aid for Trade," *Background Brief* No. 9, prepared by Massimiliano Calì, Sven Grimm, Sheila Page, Lauren Phillips, and Dirk Willem te Velde.

ILEAP. 2006c. "Aid for Trade Facility: Lessons for the Tanzanian Experience on Trade-Related Assistance," *Background Brief* No. 12, prepared by Bede Lyimo and Edward Sungula.

ILEAP. 2006d. "Operational Modalities for the Aid for Trade Initiative," Background Brief No. 11, prepared by Ademola Oyejide.

ILEAP and German Marshall Fund. 2006. "Aid for Trade after the Hong Kong Ministerial: An Introductory Guide," *Background Brief* No. 8, prepared by Claire Healey, Dominique Njinkeu, and Hugo Cameron.

ILO. 2004. "A Fair Globalization: Making it Happen," http://www.ilo.org/public/english/fairglobalization/index.htm.

Lanser, Piet and Paul Wijmenga. 2004. "Evaluation of the Joint Integrated Technical Assistance Programme Country Report of Burkina Faso and Tanzania," The Hague: Ministry of Foreign Affairs, The Netherlands.

NEPAD. 2007. "Homepage," http://www.nepad.org.

OECD. 2007. "Homepage," http://www.oecd.org.

Stiglitz, Joseph E. and Andrew Charlton. 2006. "Aid for Trade: A Report for the Commonwealth Secretariat," London: Commonwealth Secretariat.

UN. 2003. "Monterrey Consensus of the International Conference on Financing for Development," report from the International Conference on "Financing for Development," Monterrey, Mexico, 18–22 March 2002.

UN. 2005. "UN Millennium Development Goals," http://www.un.org/millenniumgoals/.

UNCTAD. 2005. "Integrated Framework (IF) for Trade-Related Technical Assistance for Least Developed Countries – An IMF Manual: Integrating LDCs into the International Trading System," New York and Geneva: United Nations.

WTO. 2005. "Aid for Trade capacity in poorer countries up by 50 percent since Doha" Press Release, 12 December, http://www.wto.org/english/news_e/pres05_e/pr427_e.htm.

WTO/OECD. 2005. "2005 Joint WTO/OECD Report on Trade-Related Technical Assistance and Capacity Building," http://www.oecd.org/dataoecd/27/4/11422694.pdf.

WTO/OECD. 2007. "Doha Development Agenda Trade Capacity Building Database," http://tcbdb.wto.org/

PART TWO

Aid for Trade in Action

8 Lessons from the Tanzanian Experience in Trade Capacity Building

BEDE LYIMO AND EDWARD MATHEW SUNGULA

1 Introduction

This paper reviews the implementation of the Integrated Framework for Trade-related Technical Assistance for Least Developed Countries (IF) and the Joint Integrated Technical Assistance Programme (JITAP) in Tanzania, with a view to assessing the lessons thereof and how to ensure beneficiary leadership and ownership of the Aid for Trade agenda.

A review of these lessons has to be based on the objectives and premises on which the two programs were designed and are being implemented. At the outset, it is noted that whereas JITAP was created to build capacity for low-income African countries to participate in the multilateral trading system (MTS), the mandate of the IF is confined to addressing the concerns of Least Developed Countries (LDCs) exclusively.

JITAP was designed as a generic program to be implemented through a multiplicity of agencies at the international, regional, and national levels. Its implementation (JITAP Phase I) started in 1998 with a group of eight African low-income countries. JITAP Phase II, launched in 2003, brought in eight more countries to implement a set of activities around five modules.[1]

The main objectives of JITAP include: building understanding of the MTS, based on knowledge of WTO agreements; participation in negotiations; implementation of the agreements; and effective utilization of market access opportunities resulting from the negotiations. Initially, management and control of the implementation process was vested in three international agencies operating from Geneva: the World Trade Organization (WTO), International Trade Centre (ITC) and the UN Conference on Trade and Development (UNCTAD), with national governments and private sector stakeholders as co-implementers and beneficiaries. Eventually, increasing elements of ownership shifted partially first to the regional level and

[1] The eight initial JITAP Phase I implementing countries were Benin, Burkina Faso, Ghana, Ivory Coast, Kenya, Tunisia, United Republic of Tanzania, and Uganda. Countries involved in the second phase, in addition to the original eight, are Botswana, Cameroon, Malawi, Mali, Mauritania, Mozambique, Senegal and Zambia. The modules comprise: Multilateral trading system (MTS) institutional support; Compliance, policies and negotiations; Strengthening MTS reference centre and National Enquiry Points on standards; Enhancing MTS knowledge and networks; Product and services sector strategies; and Networking and programme synergy.

eventually to national stakeholders. This was based on decentralization of resources to local UN Development Programme (UNDP) offices and increased flexibility in implementation.

The IF was launched in 1998–99 in most of the twelve pilot scheme LDCs. Each country designed its own program, reflecting national needs based on an approach of tripartite consultations between the public and the private sectors as well as development partners. The process was primarily left in the hands of actors at the national level, with the Geneva agencies playing a largely marginal role, thereby avoiding problems of ownership that were initially prevalent under JITAP. A revamped program with more generic features was introduced in 2000. It was based on a diagnostic review of the economy that in turn served as the basis for agreeing on priority intervention measures. The cornerstone of the revamped scheme is the Diagnostic Trade Integration Study (DTIS) and the Action Matrix that is the blueprint for measures to address constraints identified as impeding trade.

2 The conceptual framework for trade-related assistance

Consensus building on the role, nature and structure of an Aid for Trade facility has to start with a common understanding of the nature and coverage of "trade-related assistance" (TRA), as reflected in three concepts that underpin the recent literature on trade development. The three concepts are: trade-not-aid, trade-related technical assistance (TRTA), and TRA. The usefulness of the lessons of JITAP and the IF in influencing such a facility also depends on a common understanding of the role and place assigned to the JITAP and IF programs in meeting the demands for TRA in target countries. Apart from JITAP and the IF, Tanzania has also been implementing bilateral tradecapacity building programs that have provided much-needed complementarity to the multilateral programs.

2.1 From trade-not-aid to Aid for Trade

Recent literature on economic growth and development has highlighted a shift in thinking from increasing aid flows to provide the momentum for growth and development towards highlighting the expansion of trade flows as an engine of growth. According to the school of "trade rather than aid" for development, the transmission mechanism between trade and development is preferences. Preferential trade arrangements can stimulate transfer of technology, new investments that lead to the creation of employment and income generation, and higher levels of productivity and competitiveness.

The empirical evidence confirms that preferences can lead to growth for developing countries that are able to produce competitively for the global market, and that such growth can lead to poverty reduction if it is broad-based and inclusive of the majority. However, the empirical evidence also shows that many countries that have received unilateral preferences have not been able to utilize them because of a number of supply-side constraints whose resolution requires enhanced aid inflow as the stimulant of expanding trade. Ideally, the genesis of Aid for Trade should be seen in the context of the need to break a vicious cycle, whereby developing countries are expected to take increasing recourse to expanding trade as the engine of growth, but where such expansion cannot materialize without increasing the competitiveness of the private sector to make effective use of preferences. In practice, for most developing countries, and in particular for countries in sub-Saharan Africa, the transmission mechanism does not work unless there is a catalyst in the form of increased aid to build the capacity to trade. The need for special attention to factors that link trade with poverty reduction is also important.

The salient message is that there are a number of other factors that must be addressed for preferences to become an effective tool for trade development. Often this has been identified as a package of appropriate complimentary policies to be implemented in unison with trade liberalization measures. In the course of identifying the critical minimum resources necessary for building the requisite capacity, the role for aid targeting capacity building for trade has inevitably come back into the broad picture.

2.2 The trade policy process and TRTA

One aspect of Aid for Trade focuses on addressing countries' capacity for handling the process around trade policy formulation. The trade policy process itself is comprised of two main elements: trade policy formulation and implementation, and integration into the MTS. The first includes economic and trade policy analysis; trade policy and trade strategy formulation and implementation; and mainstreaming trade into the national development agenda. The second includes enhancing understanding of the MTS, effective participation in negotiations, and implementing WTO agreements.

To a large extent, JITAP is a TRTA program that primarily seeks to address issues relating to the "trade policy process". Although the program includes a component on export readiness, this takes the form of building technical capacity to design and implement "export development strategies." In the case of JITAP I in Tanzania, lack of counterpart resources to implement such strategies reduced this aspect to an academic exercise. Phase II has met with more practical success in this area in view of the allocation of considerable resources from the poverty reduction budget as well as the availability of bilateral donor support. A pilot project on horticulture is under implementation in the Morogoro region.

2.3 Trade development, supply-side issues, and the concept of TRA

TRA includes two categories of interventions: "Trade Policy Process" and "Trade Development and Supply-side Issues." This means that TRA is broader in scope and coverage than TRTA. Whereas TRTA focuses solely on technical capacity building on issues under the trade policy process, TRA brings in other issues related to production and delivery capacity. For its part, supply-side capacity can be very broad and includes economic and social infrastructure.

The "Trade Development and Supply-side Issues" perspective seeks to address the broad range of issues affecting the direction of trade and is divided into three categories: (i) inside-the-border (border-in measures); border-level measures; and outside-the-border measures. Border-in measures include a wide range of national-level measures on the supply side such as those that negatively affect investment climate, productive sectors, and delivery networks.

2.4 Trade Development Index (TDI)

UNCTAD in 2005 published work introducing a single figure index outlining major factors that influence the process of trade and development. The TDI identifies three "dimensions" that influence trade: structural and institutional; trade policies and processes; and the level of development. The TDI places emphasis on the reality that although openness to trade remains the major factor in export performance, there are other, equally important factors that have to be addressed through appropriate complementary policies.

(i) The structural and institutional dimension includes:
- Human capital (education and health);
- Physical infrastructure (transportation and ICT);
- Financial environment (access to finance);
- Institutional quality (public administration quality and government effectiveness as well as good governance);
- Environmental sustainability (based on access to water and access to improved sanitation facilities);
- Economic structure (as an indicator of level of development based, for instance, on contribution of agriculture to GDP); and
- Market access.

(ii) The trade policies and processes dimension includes:
- Openness to trade (trade liberalization in terms of tariff barriers and NTBs); and
- Effective access to foreign markets, defined in terms of low trade barriers in destination markets as well as the structure of the export sector of the receiving country.

(iii) Components of the level of development dimension include:
- Level of economic development as reflected in GDP per capita;
- Social development, reflected by a combination of adult literacy, gross school enrolment, and life expectancy at birth;
- Education and health improvements; and
- Gender development as measured by the UNDP gender development index.

The power and potential of the TDI lies in highlighting and sensitizing stakeholders in the MTS and in developing countries on the essential factors that must be addressed in strategies for export-led growth and growth driven by trade expansion. By implication, the TDI is a useful tool for generating lasting support for the wider concept of TRA that includes supply-side constraints.

3 The problem

Prior to the launching of the Doha Round, developing countries and LDCs consistently called for assistance to build their capacities to benefit from market access opportunities emerging in the MTS. In response, capacity building has tended to focus on institutional and human capacities for two broad categories: the trade policy process, and supply-side constraints. While the first has received some attention, there has been limited support for addressing supply problems.

The launching of the Doha Round as a development-oriented round, in a context in which many LDCs and other developing countries have not been able to make effective use of preferences, further strengthened the call for measures to assist developing countries to address supply-side constraints. LDCs' difficulties in fulfilling quotas under the EU's Everything but Arms (EBA) and the United States' African Growth and Economic Opportunity Act (AGOA) schemes has driven home the message that there are supply constraints that mitigate against low-income countries' capacity to trade, and that, for such countries, preferences will not work unless the binding constraints are addressed.

Furthermore, preferences have become a temporary tool that is being phased out. Many countries that benefited from this instrument in the past now face the prospect of painful adjustment as preferences come to an end. This highlights the need for a dramatic shift toward building capacities in the trade development agenda in terms of raising productivity and competitiveness in producing and delivering higher quality goods and services. In short, the clarion call is for capacity building based on the broad concept of TRA, targeting the wide range of factors that impede trade. Intuitively, Aid for Trade should respond to this call, apart from addressing other specific issues relating to adjustment.

4 Tanzania's experience with JITAP, the IF, and the National Growth and Poverty Reduction Strategy

As noted earlier, JITAP seeks to develop the capacity for low-income African countries to better understand the MTS and engage more effectively in its operations, including the ability to participate in negotiations and comply with obligations. It further seeks to build countries' capacities to benefit from the rights of WTO membership through designing strategies for export development. However, implementation of such strategies was left to national resources or bilateral programs that have not necessarily been forthcoming.

The IF, although targeting LDCs only, seeks to address the wider range of constraints that impede competitive production and delivery of goods and services into the global market. Tanzania's experience with both programs suggests that there is a need to increase capacity development and orient it toward the broader trade development agenda, particularly tackling supply-side constraints. The experience emerging from other bilateral programs implemented concurrently with JITAP and the IF reinforces arguments for an effective Aid for Trade facility that will address the binding constraints – by incorporating the broad coverage inherent in TRA.

4.1 JITAP

JITAP, launched in Tanzania and seven other African countries in 1998, primarily sought to raise awareness of the issues involved in the MTS, to help countries implement the WTO agreements, and to facilitate participation in negotiations based initially on the mandate built into the Uruguay Round Agreements and later the Doha Development Round. To a large extent, JITAP addressed issues under the trade policy process, focusing on the narrow concept of tariff policy and its implications. In this regard, emphasis was on issues relating to "integration in regional trading schemes and the MTS," with a focus on tariff reforms, negotiation of trade agreements, implementation of such agreements, and obligations to comply with rules and recourse to dispute settlement.

The formal review of the performance of the first phase of the Tanzanian JITAP highlighted mixed results. While seen as generally successful in raising knowledge of the MTS among trade professionals, problems emerged due to the concentration of management power in Geneva and the regional coordinating office for East Africa (then located in Kampala, Uganda), and due to slippages based on poor responses at the national level. For instance, the total lack of provision of counterpart funding by Tanzanian implementing agencies meant that only activities with adequate funding from the Common Facility Fund administered in Geneva could be implemented. Consequently, there was greater success in activities relating to the trade policy process (that is, concerning integration in the MTS through raising awareness of the MTS and participation in negotiations), rather than in activities relating to trade development. Even in this area, the focus of training on short-term delivery instruments, such as two- or three-day workshops and seminars, had its limitations in terms of putting in place effective capacity for undertaking economic and trade policy analysis and implementing the agreements.

Toward the end of JITAP Phase I, Tanzania allocated US$300,000 of the resources it had received from the old IF program to bridge the shortfall in counterpart funding, and thus managed to reverse the negative trend that had prevailed across the implementation of the whole program, as revealed during a mid-term review undertaken in 2002–03. This enabled the national implementing agencies responsible for the country's Export Development Strategy (EDS) to initiate implementation of the EDS for horticulture development.

Implementation of JITAP Phase II has met with some success, but its impact has not been as far-reaching as one would have anticipated after the hard lessons emerging from Phase I. Delays in program take-off meant that actual implementation for countries that had to exit the program in December 2005 was effectively reduced to one year. The effective implementation period of one year (January to December 2005) and differences with the Tanzanian fiscal calendar have meant that substantial counterpart resources are available for use only after the country's exit from the international program.

Nevertheless, Tanzania is implementing an exit strategy in which most of the programs initiated under JITAP on continued implementation are being placed under its Diagnostic Trade Integration Study (DTIS), combined with the National Growth and Poverty Reduction Strategy (NGPRS) process and bilateral donor programs. Activities undertaken under JITAP on their own have not been sufficiently comprehensive to ensure success. Even on those measures that have targeted the trade policy process, there is evidence that a training approach based largely on workshops and seminars – while useful in providing an "academic" portrayal of the WTO agreements and their implications – develops very limited capacity for handling the practical aspects involved in implementation. Experience emerging from the bilateral programs highlights the positive benefits of both training schemes that are longer in duration as well as highly specialized postgraduate programs that cover the full range of trade development issues in building effective technical capacity for economic and trade analysis.

4.2 The Integrated Framework

The Integrated Framework focuses largely on the trade development and supply-side issues of TRA. Under the old IF, Tanzania designed and began implementation of a large program addressing the totality of issues involved in the investment climate. The result is the Programme for Strengthening the Business Environment of Tanzania (BEST). BEST is financed by a basket fund with initial contributions coming from the Danish International Development Agency (DANIDA), the UK Department for International Development (DFID), the Swedish International Development Agency (SIDA), and the Government of the Netherlands. The World Bank is also joining the basket through its Micro, Small and Medium Enterprises (MSME) Project for private sector development.

BEST seeks to undertake a wide range of legal and regulatory reforms, including: putting in place the institutional framework and mechanisms for transforming the labor laws; implementation of market-oriented land policies based on establishment of the appropriate legislation and regulations; updating the business licensing and registration systems; and taxation reforms for MSMEs. The size of the interventions is reflected in the budget of more than US$40 million. The objective is transformation of the legal and regulatory framework inherited from the planned economy into a business-friendly investment climate.

As a tool for implementing the revamped IF, the DTIS has identified interventions needed to develop a competitive private sector. These interventions are based on two core factors: (i) the ability to comply with quality standards and competitiveness, based on higher productivity; and (ii) more efficient delivery systems. Hence, the IF seeks to tackle the constraints that impede private sector productivity and competitiveness in a global environment, and takes on a wider perspective than JITAP.

4.3 Other bilateral programs and national initiatives

The process of mainstreaming trade – based on the National Growth and Poverty Reduction Strategy – seeks to improve awareness of issues involved in trade development within the lead public institutions responsible for the productive and services sectors. These include programs funded by SIDA, DANIDA, DFID, and the European Union.

(a) SIDA bilateral support. From 2000, Tanzania, with support from SIDA, implemented a capacity building project that included, among other things, a component on "Trade Policy/Strategy Formulation and Implementation." A major outcome of this activity was the adoption and publication of a National Trade Policy document and the National Trade Policy Background Papers, which detail the major elements of a trade development strategy for Tanzania. These two documents have become the blueprint for a comprehensive set of measures aimed at tackling the totality of Tanzania's trade development agenda. The documents look at a range of factors included in the TDI dimensions of trade development outlined in section 2.4 in this chapter.

(b) DANIDA Market Access Programme. Capacity development for effective integration into regional and multilateral trading systems, initiated under JITAP, is being supported by DANIDA. The "Market Access" module is a component of Tanzania's Business Sector Development, a program being implemented over a five-year period starting from July 2003. DANIDA's support includes the establishment of a master's degree program at the University of Dar es Salaam to provide training for

those working in the public and private sectors on both the trade policy process and on trade development and supply-side issues. It is envisaged that the degree program coverage will eventually be broadened to include an "International Business Management" option to meet the needs of the private sector.

(c) EU support for EPA negotiations. The EU is supporting major initiatives on capacity building for the trade policy process, focused on capacity for analysis of trade issues and participation in negotiations. This includes economic analyses of the impact of changes in major trade policy variables such as tariff reduction and its impact on revenue generation.

(d) Other programs. Other bilateral programs include DFID support under the African Trade and Poverty Program (ATPP), and support by the Swiss Ministry of Economic Cooperation (SECO) for a six-week training program on the WTO agreements. SECO is also providing support to address supply-side capacity issues in the areas of infrastructure for quality standards.

At first glance, it might appear that there has been duplication in program implementation. However, the magnitude of the required interventions, an intervention time-frame of more than six years, and a large turnover in core stakeholder institutions account for the need for repeated undertaking of similar capacity building activities to a certain extent. The DFID program financed two detailed studies on the trade policy institutional set-up in Tanzania as well as the links between poverty and trade. The reports from these studies underscore the magnitude of interventions required to address supply-side constraints.

5 The Tanzanian experience and lessons for an Aid for Trade facility

An effective trade development strategy that involves well-coordinated Aid for Trade is a medium- to long-term objective. Tanzania's experience with the totality of multilateral (JITAP and IF) and bilateral programs supporting trade development highlights the importance of implementing programs that complement each other.

The Tanzanian experience confirms that none of the Aid for Trade programs implemented so far has successfully targeted the major supply-side impediments. However, there has been some success working with existing programs to ensure their complementarity; BEST, for instance, highlights the benefits of a basket fund approach in terms of broader program coverage and coordination.

Findings emerging from the Tanzanian experience confirm the need to adopt a broad-based perspective to ensure that any Aid for Trade facility addresses the full spectrum of interventions required. These fall broadly into the following groups, outlined below: trade policy formulation and implementation; technical capacity for analysis of economic and trade issues; training for technical capacity building and institutional reforms; addressing supply-side constraints; addressing adjustment problems; and ownership, transaction costs and basket funding.

5.1 Trade policy and strategy formulation

Tanzania started its initiatives on trade development with the formulation of a trade policy and strategy that was adopted by the Government in 2003 and is now providing guidance for implementing trade development programs and measures.

Implementation of some of the more important measures, such as legal and regulatory reforms, was initiated even before the policy and strategy had been formally approved. It is important for countries that seek to embark on the road of growth through trade to have a concrete strategy that clearly portrays a comprehensive picture of the actions required on each of the major underpinning factors as identified in the TDI. Countries must also be realistic about the status of each of their TDI factors and about the measures required to change that status. The process of developing a trade policy and strategy does require considerable resources and can take time if it is to be accomplished in a manner that responds to the needs for ownership by stakeholders from the beginning.

5.2 Technical capacity for analysis of economic and trade issues

This is the most important element after putting in place the capacity to formulate and implement a trade policy and strategy. Indeed, capacity for analysis is critical in coming up with programs for implementing the trade strategy. The typical strategy would cover the issues of shifting from trade based on comparative advantages to trade based on competitive advantages through higher productivity resulting from innovation and technology. Such economic analysis must also take into consideration the social issues of poverty, where the poor are located, and how to include them in a trade strategy. Clear understanding of and responses to the linkages between poverty and trade, how the poor tend to lose out from trade liberalization, and how to mitigate against such effects, are critical for a poverty-reducing process of growth through trade. Measures for addressing this capacity remain in the offing in Tanzania, and are due to be implemented as part of a new initiative on crafting a "Private Sector Development Strategy" supported by the World Bank. Such processes tend to be outside the remit of JITAP.

5.3 Training for technical capacity building and institutional reforms

Capacity building has to address both the human factors as well as the organizational aspects of the institutional framework for trade. In this regard, the need for reorienting institutions such as the conventional trade promotion agency in order that they focus more on trade development while continuing with their promotional role, is critical. Simultaneous with institutional reforms, it is necessary to develop a new cadre of technical experts capable of undertaking rigorous analysis of the wide range of specific issues involved in the trade and development agenda. Tanzania has not been able to address these requirements through JITAP or the IF. As noted earlier, the bilateral program supported by DANIDA has partially bridged the gap by financing a graduate degree program on international trade at the University of Dar es Salaam, with the intention of broadening the curriculum later to provide more coverage of international business management for the private sector. There is a provision under the IF to look into the institutional framework for the trade policy process.

5.4 Addressing supply-side constraints

While JITAP does not cover supply side constraints per se, the IF is geared more towards these issues. However, there has been little involvement in this area due to a dearth of IF resources. Furthermore, interventions under the IF are limited to LDCs. Clearly, there is a need for an instrument to accommodate developing countries other than LDCs and to supplement the inadequate resources that LDCs receive under the IF. For the majority of African countries, supply-side constraints remain the most important issue, and an Aid for Trade facility must address this element first and foremost.

5.5 Addressing adjustment problems

In addition to supply-side constraints, African countries experience problems of adjustment to revenue losses due to trade liberalization as well as adjustment due to preference erosion. These are issues that should be considered under an Aid for Trade facility, although care should be taken to ensure that support for adjustment to revenue losses is not seen as a temporary carrot to stimulate abandonment of longer-term policy flexibility.

5.6 Ownership, transaction costs, and basket funding

One of the experiences emerging from Tanzania is the volume of work and costs involved in administering and managing a multiplicity of donor programs targeting essentially the same issue. A basket funding approach to bilateral and multilateral resources would reduce transaction costs and time as well as ensure ownership in program implementation by the government and the private sector. Available information suggests that Ghana may be the only African country with a basket-funded trade development program (closely linked with a private sector development program). Thus, lessons from Ghana are bound to be useful in this regard.

6 Conclusion

In the final analysis, the structure and objectives of an Aid for Trade facility should channel support for LDCs and other developing countries to address impediments inherent in the most critical factors that have been identified in the Trade Development Index. The key is to give a name to the complementary policy package that should be put in place in tandem with trade liberalization measures and to channel resources into the areas concerned. Of particular importance to Africa remains the issue of increasing support to the establishment of wider social and economic infrastructure. Social infrastructure is critical for development of the human capital which fuels the process of trade development.

Economic and physical infrastructure is critical for enhancing the productivity and competitiveness of economic agents. These are areas that the UK's Commission for Africa Report (2005) has identified as absolutely central to releasing the energies and potential of African economies through more effective linkages with the multilateral trading system.

An Aid for Trade facility should be bold enough to target this wide array of factors and extend the substantial resources necessary to make the difference between the status quo and the minimum critical mass for shifting economies to higher trajectories of growth. The lessons that have emerged from Tanzania in terms of ongoing interventions, first under JITAP and now envisaged under the enhanced IF and the National Growth and Poverty Reduction Strategy, confirm the validity of this approach and augur well for the future.

REFERENCE

Commission for Africa. 2005. "Our Common Interest – Report of the Commission," UK: Commission for Africa.

9 Lessons from the Cambodian Experience in Trade Capacity Building

SOK SIPHANA

1 Introduction

From the notorious "Killing Fields" in the 1970s to the successful UN peacekeeping process in the 1990s, Cambodia came to be well known for its misery and its attempts to rebuild its shattered economy and society. World news coverage of the country abounded with stories of mine victims, HIV/AIDS, and the reconstruction process. This was followed by diplomatic reengagement with the West and with international financial institutions in the mid-1990s. To a great extent, the advent of the revamped Integrated Framework (IF)[1] and the World Trade Organization (WTO) Doha Development Agenda (DDA) in 2001 shaped the course of Cambodia's economic future. Cambodia was selected by the Integrated Framework Steering Committee in May 2001 as one of three countries to implement a pilot scheme to put into effect the new approach for the IF in order to enhance the participation of Least Developed Countries (LDCs) in global trade and investment. Cambodia has not looked back since.

Cambodia turned the IF pilot scheme into a success story for itself, and by extension made a positive contribution to the global trading system. Cambodia surprised skeptics by becoming the first ever LDC to accede to the WTO. Its export sectors continue to thrive, with its services sector, particularly tourism, exhibiting dramatic growth.

The overall objective of this chapter is to examine the experiences of low-income countries in dealing with trade-related capacity building (TRCB), with a particular focus on Cambodia. In this vein, we will examine the case of Cambodia as a pilot country of the revamped IF, and its recent pioneering effort to move toward a full trade Sector-wide Approach (SWAp)[2] in 2006 as an effective tool for trade

[1] The IF is the outcome of a commitment made by six multilateral Agencies (IMF, ITC, UNCTAD, UNDP, World Bank, and WTO) to coordinate their assistance in the area of trade and investment integration into the global economy. Following a six-month review process in 2000, the IF was revamped into a mechanism for mainstreaming trade into national economic plans and poverty reduction strategies.

[2] Sector-wide Approaches, or SWAps, bring together governments, donors and other stakeholders to deliver aid in a specific sector (such as trade or health), characterized by a set of operating principles rather than a specific package of policies or activities. They comprise one of several relatively new aid

The views expressed herein do not necessarily reflect the views or position of the International Trade Centre (ITC) or the Royal Government of Cambodia. The author expresses thanks to his former assistant, Mr. You Mab, for the overall research and his contribution to the trade SWAp section.

mainstreaming as well as a new mechanism for aid delivery. Cambodia is also a good example of a post-conflict country, juxtaposed on to which we could learn the lessons of trade-related capacity building (TRCB) over a spectrum of time starting from the post-conflict period to pre- and post-economic re-integration periods.

The chapter begins with an overview of the political and economic history of Cambodia (Section 1). This is followed by a section on the challenges of trade development in the post-conflict period, in which there was a tentative emergence of Cambodia's trade policy and capacity development (Section 2 – Post-conflict period). The chapter introduces the revived IF initiative, depicting its evolution both in the global arena and in Cambodia. Soon after the selection of Cambodia as an IF pilot country, there was a rapid evolution of its "trade mainstreaming" efforts from a conceptual stage to full integration of trade into the national development strategy. This was reflected in the country's five-year plan and ultimately in its Poverty Reduction Strategy Paper (PRSP) (Section 3 – Pre-Integration). The chapter examines difficulties associated with Cambodia's accession to the WTO, particularly focusing attention on problems related to the weak capacity of the government in understanding complex global trade rules, on the one hand, and the challenges facing Cambodia in their bilateral negotiations, on the other. In this context, the chapter highlights lessons learned from the process related in particular to the efficient and coordinated delivery of trade-related capacity building.

Cambodia garnered renewed attention when it moved toward designing a SWAp in trade-related assistance, once again testing the imagination and commitment of Cambodian policy-makers as well as the will and good faith of the donors in implementing the Paris Declaration on Aid Effectiveness. Covering the post-integration period, Section 4 highlights the efforts of the Cambodian government in furthering its trade SWAp as an example of an aid delivery mechanism. Because of the novelty of SWAps, the paper provides detailed coverage of its concept and targets, policy guidelines and priority actions, as well as strategy and actions to implement it.

Section 5 summarizes the lessons learned from Cambodia's TRCB, addressing, among others, the issues of country ownership, policy coherence, and an institutional implementation mechanism with substantive focus on partnership mechanisms for consultation among key stakeholders. The chapter concludes with recommendations for improving capacity building for development that could be adopted by other regions. It highlights the complementarity of a few TRCB initiatives in three main areas of trade capacity building, namely: trade rules compliance capacity; trade competitiveness capacity; and trade readiness capacity.

2 A snapshot of the Cambodian political economy

Since the mid-1950s, the impact of the Cold War on Cambodia led to the unfolding of a disastrous era for the country. In the mid-1970s, a catastrophe struck. In just three years, a genocidal regime destroyed the country's long-established traditions, as well as its political, financial and social institutions. The intelligentsia – the

modalities that have emerged as a means of overcoming the lack of sufficient recipient ownership and the fragmentation of many individual projects, which, even when taken as a whole, have not necessarily resulted in adequate support for a country's identified development priorities. Also see Box 9.3, below.

educated, trained and skilled workforce – was systematically wiped out. Emerging from this dark period, yet still caught in the clutches of the Cold War, Cambodia faced international neglect and isolation for more than another decade.

Subsequent to the peace accord of 1991, general elections were held in 1993 followed by the establishment of the Royal Government of Cambodia later that year. Cambodia was thus reborn. After the elections, the country entered a new period of development.

Cambodia became a member of the Association of Southeast Asian Nations (ASEAN) in 1999 and a member of the WTO in 2003 (WTO, 2004). Joining the WTO marked the final step in bringing Cambodia back into the major regional and international organizations that govern international economic relations.

2.1 Initial economic conditions: the legacy of Cambodia's genocidal past

The breakdown of Cambodian society as a result of decades of war and the Khmer Rouge genocide resulted in several major development challenges for the country, including in human resources, demographics, infrastructure, and economic reconstruction. Among the many tragic consequences of the conflict was a depletion of many of Cambodia's most skilled people, leading to a severe shortage of qualified personnel – *the human resources challenge*. The country's demographic structure was also severely impacted, to the extent that approximately 43 percent of its population is under the age of fifteen – *the demographic challenge*. Beyond human and social capital, physical infrastructure was also lacking. After nearly thirty years of war, Cambodia's infrastructure was left in ruins. This included transportation, communication, and access to sources of energy, such as electricity and water. The absence of public services resulted in extremely high levels of self-provision of services at high cost, while the absence of a quality road network in particular excluded the rural areas from taking up market opportunities in domestic and non-domestic markets, and hampered access to goods and services – *the infrastructure challenge*.

Cambodia's needs for reconstruction and development represented probably the biggest challenge of all – *the economic reconstruction challenge*. During the Khmer Rouge regime, its economy reverted to an agrarian barter system, the industrial base and infrastructure were destroyed, and the banking system and domestic currency were abolished. Rebuilding began after 1979, initially within the framework of a centrally planned economy and a monobank system, supported by the Soviets and other communist countries. Market-oriented reforms were introduced in 1985–86, including liberalization of prices, privatization of certain state enterprises, and the formal adoption of a two-tier banking system. However, the economic situation remained difficult given the withdrawal of external assistance and continued civil conflict. The Paris Peace Accord of 1991 and the subsequent establishment of the United Nations Transitional Authority of Cambodia (UNTAC) finally paved the way for Cambodia's renewed access to international financial assistance, including from the International Monetary Fund (IMF).

2.2 Overview of economic performance

Cambodia is a small economy and an LDC, with real gross domestic product (GDP) in 2004 of around US$4.5 billion and per capita income of US$328 ("National

Accounts" 2005). While GDP growth has averaged around 6.6 percent per annum in recent years, GDP per capita growth has only averaged around 4.6 percent. The economic base is shifting away from agriculture, fisheries and forestry, with these sectors accounting for around 33 percent of GDP. The manufacturing sector continues to grow strongly and now accounts for around 31 percent of GDP, with the textiles, garments and footwear industries accounting for 56 percent of the sector. The services sector, the largest sector in the economy, accounts for 36 percent of GDP and is largely driven by the tourism industry. Most of the economic growth since 1995 has been due to the growth in the textiles, garments and footwear industries.

3 Challenges in trade development in the early post-conflict stage (Stage I)

3.1 General observations of the trade sector

Starting from a zero base, following a seventeen-year complete trade and economic embargo, Cambodia claimed quick successes in rebuilding its private sector and export base. Five years after the 1991 peace process, the trade sector began to emerge rather timidly, competing against other post-conflict rehabilitation and development priorities.

The characteristics of Cambodia's exports during the early post-conflict era reflected the relatively nascent export base that the country had rebuilt over the previous several years, and suggested there was plenty of room for improvement. Four general observations could be made of the economic situation during that period.

First, Cambodian exporters struggled to remain competitive. The high costs of doing export-oriented business in Cambodia were due, in part, to weaknesses in physical infrastructure and productive capacities, an incomplete macro-economic and legal framework, misplaced political priorities, and misdirected investment incentives.

Second, the multiplier effect of exports on Cambodia's economy remained low. Most of the garment sector operated on a Cut, Manufacture and Tailor (CMT) basis. Fabric and accessories were imported and financed overseas, and the purchase of local inputs was limited to transportation and freight clearing services, utility-type services to run factories, and construction to build factories. There was very little processing of exported wood or rubber and little processing of agricultural exports. Of all exports, tourism was the one with the greatest multiplier effect: typically, hotels and restaurants must purchase local food, and other inputs including electricity and telecommunications.[3]

Third, Cambodia needed both to boost the productivity of its exports and to move up the value chain. For example, improvements in rice seeds, irrigation, and farming methods went a long way in increasing both labor and land productivity and strengthening Cambodia's export capacity in rice. Likewise, a shift to higher

[3] See "Cambodia's Tourism" (2001). For example, large foreign tourist hotels in Phnom Penh and Siem Reap are said to be importing nearly half of the food they serve their customers. Large hotel projects (such as the construction of the new Sofitel and the renovation of the Grand Hotel in Siem Reap) have had to rely on extensive (and expensive) imports of construction materials from Thailand and elsewhere.

value agricultural production (spices, nuts and seeds, fruits, for example) and more processing (such as milling of exported rice, extraction of essential oils, and processing of wood) also brought more value from Cambodian exports.

Fourth, the geographical impacts from Cambodian exports were limited. The country's export sector was overwhelmingly located in three centers, namely the capital city of Phnom Penh, the tourism mecca of Siem Reap, and the deep port city of Sihanoukville. The concern then was that, notwithstanding its positive contribution to national income, the export sector was also aggravating the wealth gap between the three areas and the rest of the country. The need for regionalizing and decentralizing Cambodia's export production was a major issue in mitigating the growing wealth gap between a few cities and the rest of the country.

3.2 General situation of trade capacity: post-conflict period characterized by a lack of capacity to manage the trade development process

The institutional setting in Cambodia in the post-conflict period was hampered by the lack of a global vision for the development of the trade sector. The responsibilities of the Ministry of Commerce (MoC) were relatively new and concentrated on domestic trade and control. Ministry officials were more absorbed by day-to-day work routines,[4] leaving little remaining time and resources for analytical and strategic thinking about how best to enhance the country's gains from trade.

Poor knowledge of the main international languages – which affected the quality of communications with external partners – together with insufficient or inadequate skills were common weaknesses for the majority of the ministry's staff. Low salaries and unclear prospects for career advancement for mid-level management were also major impediments to staff performance. Working conditions were exacerbated by insufficient office space, inadequate operational budgets, and scarcity of or non-access to equipment, in particular information technology facilities.

Very little emphasis was placed on turning policies into practice and on enforcing laws and regulations. Intra-government consultations were held as a matter of bureaucratic formality, while government-private sector dialogue was on an ad hoc and reactive basis. Lack of mutual trust and confidence between the government and private sector stakeholders was a further impediment. The absence of private sector involvement in the policy-making process, both local and international, resulted in superficial identification of trade needs, resulting in weak support for trade projects and programs. The clear absence of consultation with civil society organizations was striking.

While government-donor coordination received regular and systematic attention in the post-conflict era, trade sector development did not emerge as a priority until the late 1990s. Up until that time, donor agencies attached low attention to trade as a tool of development, thus explaining their inadequate and uncertain responses to trade priorities. As a result, there was no systematic effort to gather available information on existing TRCB instruments and expertise, nor to undertake analysis of trade polices and their impact. Technical assistance provided to the trade ministry to build its capacity was neither sufficient nor integrated in the relevant structure. Technical assistance tended to favor capacity substitution rather

[4] Routine tasks included issuances of export licenses, registrations of companies, and similar tasks.

than capacity building. Salary supplements provided by donors within externally funded projects, while they had an evident advantage in ensuring the motivation of a small cadre of staff, also created some distortion and dysfunction within the ministry.

For the most part, the emphasis of donors since 1993 has been on governance and government institution-building, macro-economic structural reform, legal reform, ending internal strife, removal of mines and other ordinance, and food security. To a large extent, the business community has been left to fend for itself.

4 Trade development in the pre-integration stage: raising the profile of trade

4.1 Trade mainstreaming: pro-poor trade strategy, the IF, and the PRSP

4.1.1 *Pro-poor trade strategy and the IF*

The pre-integration stage in Cambodia could be characterized by its pioneering trade mainstreaming efforts in response to the evolving development of the global trade agenda. The period was remembered for its pro-poor trade strategy formulation, catalyzed by the advent of the IF, the PRSP, and the emergence of TRCB initiatives.

In September 1998, following the IF High-Level Meeting for LDCs in October 1997, the Cambodian government prepared and presented to the IF its trade-related needs assessment report. In late 2000, the government requested the assistance of the IF agencies to update its needs assessment and to begin work on the formulation of a pro-poor trade sector strategy. A mission was organized to Phnom Penh by three of the six agencies on behalf of the IF in October 2000. Following that mission, the International Trade Centre (ITC) assisted the government in its initial efforts to launch the process of formulating the pro-poor trade sector strategy in consultation with the other IF Agencies.

Parallel to these national developments, the IF was undergoing some restructuring, leading to the creation of an Integrated Framework Trust Fund (IFTF) and the adoption of a Pilot Phase Work Program in late March 2001 (WTO, 2001a). The Pilot Phase Work Program was to be implemented by the IF agencies under the leadership of the World Bank in a small number of countries using IFTF and other resources. In May 2001, Cambodia was selected by the IF Steering Committee as one of three countries – the others being Madagascar and Mauritania – to implement the pilot scheme.[5]

The mainstreaming process involved five steps, starting with a country Diagnostic Trade Integration Study (DTIS). The DTIS looked at a number of issues that included establishing the link between trade development and poverty reduction; the impact of trade reform on the country's economic growth and development; the complementary policy agenda necessary to support successful trade reform; and market access issues. The DTIS outcomes provided the basis for identification of

[5] In a nutshell, the IF Pilot Phase Work Program seeks to provide financial and technical support to selected countries for the formulation of a full-fledged pro-poor trade sector strategy that is fully mainstreamed into the PRSP. See WTO (2001b).

prioritized TRCB and technical assistance needs that were linked to the country's overall development strategy.

The second step involved the organization of a national workshop to review the findings and policy recommendations of the DTIS, including identification of a technical assistance action plan. Cambodia did this in November 2001, followed by the third step, the endorsement by government and other stakeholders of the policy recommendations and a Technical Assistance Action Plan, or TA Matrix. Cambodia adopted the TA Matrix in January 2002, and it was subsequently endorsed by the OECD's Development Assistance Committee (DAC).

The fourth step involved the submission of the TA Matrix to donors for financing. Within the six-month period leading to the Consultative Group (CG) meeting in June 2002, Cambodia worked with the core agencies and bilateral donors to secure funding for activities identified in the TA Matrix. Cambodia tabled its TRCB requirements at the formal CG meeting in Phnom Penh. The last step of the mainstreaming process related to the responses of donors and the six core agencies to follow up on the specific TA projects identified in the TA Matrix.

4.1.2 *The IF and the PRSP Process*

During the same period as the development of Cambodia's participation in the IF, the government together with the World Bank and the IMF began preparation of a country PRSP. This involved both process and substance.

On the process side, the PRSP placed a great deal of emphasis on country ownership of the strategy, meaning not only ownership by the government, but by a range of national stakeholders – including the poor. The PRSP also emphasized mechanisms of partnership between government and national stakeholders on the one hand and donors on the other. On the substantive side, the PRSP was based on a poverty diagnosis, clear and achievable medium- and long-term poverty reduction targets, including monitoring of achievements, as well as a set of priorities to achieve those targets.[6]

The early efforts of the government to formulate a pro-poor trade sector strategy – initially under the umbrella and with the support of the IF – coincided closely with the PRSP effort. As the IF consultation process with key stakeholders evolved, there was an emerging recognition of the need to embed the trade agenda into the country's overall development strategy, in this case the PRSP.[7] The expectation then was that the PRSP process, which formed the basis for the World Bank's Country Assistance Strategies, would assist Cambodia to formulate a poverty reduction strategy that would include efforts to benefit from integration into the global economy.

Efforts to mainstream trade into the PRSP were centered on developing a trade chapter. The chapter included a trade policy matrix that identified poverty reduction

[6] See Mbida-Essama (2001) and IMF/World Bank.

[7] The formulation of the interim PRSP, which highlighted the government's policy framework, comprehensive strategies, and commitment to pull Cambodia and Cambodians out of poverty, did not identify trade as a policy priority. The main concept behind the interim PRSP was that the government had responded to poverty by taking various measures to accelerate economic growth, improve the distribution of income and wealth, and promote social development. Nonetheless, trade was only sporadically mentioned as a sub-component of other measures.

objectives, defined strategies to achieve these objectives, and outlined measures to monitor outcomes in order to evaluate impacts and to adjust the process as needed.

Building on the success of the PRSP, the government went on to mainstream the trade sector strategy into various other national policy documents.[8] These documents outlined a clear strategy of support to the national poverty reduction initiative through upstream poverty-focused policy advisory support to the government, and strengthening government's ownership of the development agenda and leadership of the development process.

4.2 General observations of the trade sector

A number of observations can be made regarding the Cambodian trade sector in this pre-integration stage. Generally, the ability of Cambodia as an LDC to participate more fully in the global economy was constrained by bottlenecks and limitations arising from three main areas: (1) border barriers to trade;[9] (2) "behind the border" barriers;[10] and (3) barriers in accessing global markets.[11]

The first observation is that the government, in more active consultation with trade sector stakeholders, began tackling issues related to improving the overall enabling environment for the private sector and export development. Some of the key highlights of this process included bringing the trade regime in line with WTO rules, lowering the costs of trade facilitation, strengthening trade promotion capacity, improving the investment environment, and launching macro-economic and legal reforms.

The second observation is that the government, with the UN Millennium Development Goals (MDGs) commitments in mind, began a collaborative campaign to bring export opportunities to the poor, as indicated by at least three important policy measures:

- Investment and entrepreneurship in rural-based sectors were encouraged, attracted, and developed. These included developing specialty non-traditional export crops (spices, fruits, nuts and seeds), freshwater fish and seafood, handicrafts, labor service exports, and other activities.
- Work was initiated to decentralize the current export base toward new regions, including developing new Cambodian destinations for tourism and creating export and industrial processing zones in new areas to attract investment in new sectors.

[8] The documents include the following: the Second Socio-Economic Development Plan (SEPD-II); the country's ten-year Plan of Action tabled at the UN LDC-III Conference in Brussels in May 2000; the United Nations Development Assistance Framework (UNDAF 2001–2005); and the UNDP Country Co-operation Framework (2001–2005).

[9] "Border barriers" issues may include, for example, export procedures, customs procedures, infrastructure bottlenecks, and certification services.

[10] "Behind the border" or "border-in" issues may include increasing product competitiveness, creating new products for export, developing new exporters, and improving competency to manage the export process; Among "border-in" issues, one could also consider technology-related issues such as quality, product and environmental standards; level of process technology; health and safety; "organic" production, and other issues.

[11] "Barriers in accessing global markets or "border-out" issues may include, for example, market access, export promotion, market supporting services for existing products, and the like.

- The value-added of exports was increased through improved productivity and increased processing. The latter included, for instance, strengthening rice milling capacity, processing spices, canning fruits and fruit juices, extracting essential oils, processing and packaging cashew nuts, and developing and strengthening a furniture manufacturing sector for export.

The third observation is that there was more emphasis than in the recent past on energizing export enterprises and export sectors through a sharper focus on the delivery of capacity building support at the level of product sectors and enterprises. However, success has been limited due to the country's limited human, institutional, and financial resources.

The fourth observation is that supply bottlenecks rather than market access were a major constraint for trade development in Cambodia.

The fifth observation is that the government started to realize the effects of not having a broad range of trade support services (trade information, trade promotion and marketing, trade financing, and others) to assist exporting enterprises as well as fostering a range of export skills within those enterprises. The institutional and human capacity in Cambodia in this broad area was clearly inadequate.

4.3 Early responses to institutional strengthening and capacity building to support trade development

The critical challenges facing the government during the pre-integration stage were those related to weak human and institutional capacity. If Cambodia was to improve its trade performance, it needed to overcome many of these challenges. Capacity gaps had to be addressed in a wide range of areas, often simultaneously, and an unusually diverse array of stakeholders needed to be engaged.

Developing new export products and markets also required an entrepreneurial capacity that was weak in Cambodia. Even if domestic savings were mobilized for investment in the trade sector, there was a shortage of "soft" capital – the know-how that entrepreneurs needed if they were to succeed. How to promote the transfer or development of this know-how into the country became a concern of the government and the business community. Without the technical and financial support to upgrade the various areas where there were capacity gaps, the country's domestic supply response capability would remain weak and would in turn negatively affect the competitiveness dimension of Cambodia even within its own borders.

The following sections detail the key responses made by the government to tackle the capacity issues:

Response 1: Strengthen the capacity of the Ministry of Commerce (MoC) to lead and manage. The first response was to use the IF initiative as an opportunity to strengthen the ability and capacity of the MoC to lead and manage the formulation and implementation of the trade sector strategy through robust partnerships with all key trade stakeholders and with development partners. The goal was to create strong ownership of the process.

Capacity building approaches were introduced and tailored to specific Cambodian circumstances. The MoC, like many government institutions, had limited human and institutional resources, owing to the country's level of development and its recent history. These "internal" resources were strengthened in parallel with the development of a network of "external" resources (local and international consultants and NGOs). In the process, the MoC learned to become a good "manager" and "user" of external resources while pursuing the delivery of its trade mainstreaming mandate.

The concept of a dedicated trade core team: the response to the lack of absorptive capacity. From the beginning there was a clear recognition that the success of the trade mainstreaming process would depend on the existence of strong national implementation arrangements. The work of the IF Focal Point person and of the Steering Committee relied on this support structure. The need for such an arrangement was identified very early on in the process, and a dedicated core team was envisaged and put into action.[12]

One of the selection criteria was sustainability of the core team, with emphasis placed on selecting officials from within the ministry who were already involved in the WTO accession and the trade mainstreaming process. This approach offered the possibility for a limited number of ministry officials to spend a one-year period acquiring in-depth knowledge on specific trade issues and eventually to ensure efficient follow-up upon their return to their original posts (see Box 9.1).

The main functions of the core team were to provide operational and substantive support to the IF Focal Point and the Steering Committee in the performance of their respective mandates at the strategic and policy level. These included trade advocacy and mainstreaming; trade policy formulation and implementation; intra-governmental and donor coordination; and public-private sector dialogue. At the operational level, their tasks were, among others: to formulate, implement, and monitor specific trade-related projects as a follow-up of the DTIS TA matrix; to ensure active engagement, coordination, and synergies with stakeholders; and to engage in advocacy activities to create awareness of trade issues at the national and provincial level.

Response 2: Creation of a network of stakeholders. Another response, the creation of an informal network of trade stakeholders, was consistent with the government's objective of sustainability, as it ensured that capacity was developed broadly and did not rest within a single institution. The rationale was that, while leadership was needed to manage the trade agenda, that agenda was too large to be managed by a single government institution and should be supported by a wide range of stakeholders. The network members benefited to a large extent from enhanced access to international knowledge and best practices pertinent to trade and poverty outcomes. Little did anyone know in those days that this network, with its modest beginnings, would evolve to become one of the most dynamic and influential forums of government, business, academia, and civil society organizations in Cambodia.

[12] The team was created with US$500,000 provided by the Government of Japan as part of the first IF post-DTIS project. UNDP's Cambodia country office provided US$49,000 of complementary assistance. The project was nationally executed under the direct leadership of a MoC Secretary of State who served as IF Focal Point and National Project Coordinator, with technical assistance provided by the ITC.

Box 9.1. Training of trade policy professionals

The Cambodian Ministry of Commerce envisaged that a dedicated core team would receive substantial training inside and outside the country, so as to boost their general trade-related capacity and sharpen their ability to support their work.

- **General training.** General capacity building to support trade mainstreaming was provided to the core team and other MoC personnel. This included advanced English language training with a focus on trade, trade policy, and trade promotion terminology; computer skills training, and website management training.
- **Specific capacity building on project management.** Training was provided in areas which required greater expertise related to project identification, formulation, implementation and coordination. This was considered critical in light of the government's keen desire to follow up on the development of TRTA projects deriving from the DTIS action matrix. Ad hoc training for relevant core members included the use of different tools for program/project development and implementation (such as logframe, project cycle, financing, budgeting, and implementation schemes).
- **Capacity building on specific trade-related issues.** The core team was provided with extensive advisory services and training on how to mainstream trade into the country's development agenda, in particular understanding various national policy instruments and donor frameworks, such as the five-year development plan, the PRSP, the World Bank Country Assistance Strategy (CAS), and the United Nations Development Framework (UNDAF).

The capacity of the core team was further strengthened through an on-the-job training approach where they were required to engage in various day-to-day activities. Team members interacted with ministerial staff, local institutions, business associations, and private entrepreneurs as well as IF development partners on project activities. Their substantive participation was also expected at various trade events. Over the months, as their capacities improved, they were expected to act as local trainers or presenters, obviating on many occasions the need to hire externally paid consultants.

The core team benefited extensively from the availability of a functioning secretariat well-equipped with IT infrastructure, Internet connection, and essential reference materials. Specific pedagogical material and other ad hoc training materials aimed at enhancing the capacities of the core team to implement and respond to the different phases of trade development, including export development and promotion, UNCTAD's TRAINFORTRADE methodology, value chain analysis, and formulation of trade strategies and trade policies.

Gradually, the process enabled the formalization of a specialized network of trade support institutions from the private and public sectors. The network was able to provide several types of services to exporters, including trade policy information and commercial intelligence; export promotion and marketing; product development; financial services; and training. This was a departure from the traditional approach, in which the MoC attempted to meet most of the trade support service needs of exporters.

Response 3: Trade mainstreaming awareness campaign – building partnerships, one partner at a time. In its preliminary stages, the trade mainstreaming exercise was difficult due to the conceptual novelty of the initiative and the embryonic effort to promote a broader national constituency on trade and poverty.[13]

The MoC realized that its success in trade mainstreaming would depend to a large extent on its ability to convince its stakeholders of the strategic importance of trade. As such, it felt the necessity to launch an all-encompassing awareness campaign to promote a broader national constituency on trade and poverty. The awareness strategy was geared towards engaging key trade stakeholders in the consensus-building process. It also aimed at facilitating the sharing of experiences and best practices on trade mainstreaming among the various beneficiaries, and enhancing access to trade-related information and issues.

The core team produced a series of trade research newsletters to keep all stakeholders informed of progress on the trade mainstreaming process. A website was established to enable posting of information on policies, trade issues, laws, and development studies. A national and provincial resources database was constructed and used as a support tool for promoting trade and investment. A number of trade-related documents were translated into Khmer and disseminated to final users through inter-ministerial workshops, including information-gathering missions to the provinces. The systematic translation into Khmer of key IF and trade-related documents provided for additional opportunities to strengthen the partnership framework and to allow for informed dialogue with grassroots non-English-speaking stakeholders.

Further to this, the core team organized a wide range of awareness-raising events targeting national stakeholders, including key ministries with a lead role in the poverty reduction process, such as finance and planning ministries, as well as the private sector. Other interventions were made, inter alia at: annual government conventions for senior government and MoC officials; dialogue sessions with the business community under the umbrella of the Business Forum; and presentations in the national media and public workshops. More ambitious activities, such as TV and radio talk shows, were undertaken and aimed at the general public.

Last, the MoC used similar awareness campaign opportunities to reach out globally to gain the support of the international community. These efforts were successful, providing a basis for deepening trust and developing synergies with donors.

Generally, the MoC acknowledged the positive effects of its campaign effort, as reflected by a gradual and steady increase in the number of requests from various stakeholder groups interested in the trade mainstreaming agenda and its pro-poor aspects.

4.4 Specific lessons learned from Cambodia's WTO accession process[14]

4.4.1 *Facing the challenges of accession*

Cambodia's WTO accession is unique, for both political and economic reasons; and lessons from it have to be drawn with extreme care. If there is an important lesson

13 Experiences in other countries have shown that poor country ownership of the IF was partly due to the country stakeholders' limited knowledge of the IF process, actors, and framework. To anchor ownership and participation in the IF, the flow of IF-related information would therefore need to be stimulated.

14 For a full analysis of Cambodia's accession to the WTO see Siphana (2005).

to be drawn, it is that each accession case, and Cambodia is no exception, involves a different negotiation, with different dynamics. This makes it difficult to generalize. In sum, there is really no miracle prescription that would render the accession process easy. While the process of WTO accession is and will likely continue to be lengthy, complex, and challenging for all countries, especially LDCs, the experiences drawn from Cambodia's accession process do reveal, nevertheless, a few recurring themes which some acceding economies could learn and benefit from.

It was clear that difficulties existed, and delays occurred, during Cambodia's accession process due to the following:

(i) Policy issues, consistency with development strategies, and domestic reforms: Resolving substantive policy issues relating to internal adjustment shocks takes time. They would have to be taken into account in Cambodia's development strategies and implementing instruments – which were all necessary if Cambodia were to be in compliance with the multitude of WTO rules and disciplines. Cambodia would need to carry out serious legislative reforms to achieve conformity with the WTO requirements.

(ii) Capacity issues: Insufficient knowledge, inadequate experience, limited resources, and shallow analytical capacities were also recurrent sources of delay. The scope of negotiations was very broad, ranging from the consistency of Cambodia's policies and institutions with various aspects of the WTO agreements, to specific tariff bindings and commitments in agriculture and services. To top it off, Cambodia was required to prepare voluminous and complex documentation regarding its trade regime for goods and services, and had to engage in lengthy negotiations with other WTO member countries, both at the bilateral and multilateral level.

4.4.2 *The crucial role of capacity building and technical assistance*

The process of accession represents a great opportunity for local capacity building in this respect. Cambodia has made active use of technical assistance and consultancies from international organizations, in particular the IF agencies, specialized UN agencies, and from governments of WTO member countries in the preparation of required documentation and human resource development. Within the context of the IF, developed nations have extended their technical assistance to Cambodia on a fast-track basis in some specific areas where immediate compliance with WTO rules is needed. The target beneficiaries encompassed both categories of public sector and private sector decision makers and civil society stakeholders.

5 Maximizing trade opportunities in the post-integration stage – Introducing the Trade SWAp: a national commitment to trade mainstreaming from within

5.1 The challenges of post-accession

The accession of Cambodia to the WTO in 2003 offered enormous opportunities for trade and investment in the economy and stimulated the export potential of the country. Trade now contributes nearly 10 percent of GDP and accounts for about 14 percent of the total work force. It has stimulated linkages with other productive and service sectors, and its multiplier effect can be seen across a wide spectrum of the economy.

The National Strategic Development Plan (2006) provides a sound statement regarding the crucial role of trade:

> Linking production to consumption or producers to consumers, trade is a powerful and important catalyst for socio-economic development. Promotion of trade for Cambodian products has been among top priorities. If market outlets are available, investments would flow to encourage and enhance production of goods and services using the country's natural advantages as has happened in the garment industry, and as could be achieved in agriculture, agro-processing, handicraft and other areas.

Within this context, and in order to take full advantage of the new trade opportunities, the government has embarked on a long process of economic, financial, institutional, and legal reforms to establish a solid foundation for increased investment and diversified trade. The government has continued to push its economic integration process further in the context of regional and bilateral trade arrangements, in particular with ASEAN Dialogue Partners (U.S., China, India, Australia, New Zealand). Significant efforts have also been deployed in order to secure additional gains from the Doha Round negotiations, in particular on obtaining quota-free/duty-free market access. Tackling its WTO commitments, probably the most difficult and time-consuming process of all, the government has been pursuing the drafting and enactment of legal and regulatory instruments aimed at further facilitating trade, investment, and private sector development. Significant progress has been made in completing the legal framework, but much more remains to be done due to the limited capacity of concerned institutions both at the executive and legislative levels.[15]

Overall progress and achievements to date in the area of trade facilitation and private sector development, although having made substantial progress since accession days, are far from being adequate. The Trade Facilitation and Competitiveness Program, funded by a US$10 million grant from the World Bank, was implemented by the government in 2005, incorporating a broad range of cross-cutting reforms. A decree implementing a risk management strategy was put into effect on 1 March 2006, mandating the utilization of a Single Administrative Document and establishment of a Single Automated Window for trade transactions clearance at the borders, and further simplifying and streamlining regulations and procedures regarding customs and taxation.[16]

[15] Cambodia has promulgated or adopted the following trade- and investment-related rules and regulations: (1) Law on Marks, Trade Name and Acts of Unfair Competition; (2) Law on Patents, Utility Models and Industrial Designs; (3) Law on Copyright and Related Rights; (4) Law on the Management of Quality and Safety of Products and Services; (5) Law amending the 1995 Law on Commercial Rules and Register; (6) Amendment of the Law on Investment; (7) Law on Commercial Arbitration, (8) Law on Business Enterprises; (9) Sub-Decree on the establishment and management of Special Economic Zones; and (10) Sub-Decree on the Facilitation of Trade through Risk Management.

The government is also developing other key legal structures to promote trade and investment that are at different stages of preparation or awaiting ratification: Commercial Court; Insolvency; Secured Transactions; Commercial Contracts; Commercial Leasing; Commercial Agency; Industrial Standards; Metrology; and Geographical Indications.

[16] Already, the government achieved noticeable results in reducing transaction costs and processing times. According to an independent survey, the average cost has decreased from US$2,477 per import transaction in 2003 to US$673 in 2005, and for exports, from US$942 in 2003 to US$598 in 2005. The private sector perception of the amount of time required to process transactions has also improved,

Box 9.2. ITC's export potential assessment for Cambodia

This study assessed the export potential of some twenty sectors in Cambodia, which can be broadly grouped in fishery products, agricultural products, industrial products, and arts and crafts. It aimed to provide a systematic, comprehensive, and reliable assessment method to compare and rank sectors according to several dimensions, including the international environment (for example, world demand and market access conditions), Cambodia's current export performance, and domestic supply conditions in the sectors.

Statistical analysis and a literature survey were complemented by interviews with local stakeholders in Cambodia from both public and private sectors, to gain first-hand insights into the domestic business environment that affects enterprises in Cambodia in the various product sectors. The report also includes an in-depth analysis of individual industries, including an assessment of strengths, weaknesses, opportunities and threats (SWOT analysis), and identifies possible target markets for diversification for each industry. It also identifies key areas of intervention and related policies that can promote future export growth.

As such, the report may serve as a reference for policy-makers, export support organizations, business associations, and interested academics. Cambodia's export potential appears highest for fisheries, organic rice, garments, handicrafts, rubber, beer, corn (maize), cassava, mango, black pepper, cashew nuts, livestock, medicinal herbs, palm sap products, pulp and paper, tourism, light manufacturing, packaging and outsourcing. Measuring the export potential of sectors and identifying industry-specific policies can only be part of a much larger undertaking that tackles the real issues at stake in Cambodia.

The government has moved ahead to deepen the analytical dimension of its key policy and strategy documents, providing further clarity on the direction and approaches to trade and investment development and promotion. Of particular relevance is the initiative of the government to update its DTIS, the first iteration of which was completed in 2001. The revised DTIS, along with its TRTA Action Matrix, feeds into the national trade development agenda.[17] The government took the lead in the updating process by tapping into local expertise as well as looking to exploit new trade analysis and competitive tools of the IF core agencies. The chapter on Trade has benefited from a new tool of ITC called the Export Potential Assessment (see Box 9.2). The Assessment argues that Cambodia's best option is not to pick winners on export markets, but to provide a business environment that is conducive to risk-taking, entrepreneurship, creativity and innovation.

Another important development is the National Export Strategy (NES), undertaken by a team comprised exclusively of nationals with the technical support of

with respondents reporting a reduction in processing time of over 20 percent from 2003. In addition, 84 percent and 91 percent of respondents said they were at least adequately informed about fees and documentation respectively.

17 The main objectives of the revised DTIS are to: (i) identify existing and needed legal and institutional capacity for implementation of trade policy and export sector development strategies; (ii) review employment, income, GDP, trade and trade diversification, investment and FDI data; and (iii) identify poverty-reduction needs through trade development, employment generation, productivity growth, export base diversification, and employment creation in rural areas.

ITC. The NES is based on a realistic assessment of national capacities, competitive position, resources available to devote to the export priority, and a clear understanding of what generally works and what does not. It provides detailed parameters for the preparation of sector-level strategies. It also includes support services such as trade information, trade finance, quality management, and competency development.

Reaching out to the United Nations Development Programme (UNDP) as the institution with expertise and leadership on human development and poverty, the government has begun an assessment of the impact of WTO accession on human development and poverty, targeting key sectors such as the garment industry and agriculture, as well as vulnerable groups, particularly women, who form a large part of the formal and informal trade and production sectors.

5.2 The need to consolidate and prepare a comprehensive trade development strategy

Encouraged by the new paradigm in international aid, Cambodia in 2006 decided to pursue a trade SWAp in developing its comprehensive trade development strategy and program (see Box 9.3 for a description of a SWAp).[18] While the focus of the program is to improve the governance environment of the trade sector and thus to facilitate the effective implementation of ongoing reforms, its aim is more ambitious. The government aims to achieve better functioning of existing coordination and consultation mechanisms, to improve resources management systems, and to facilitate harmonization and alignment of increasing donor operations and resources in the sector, in line with the OECD/DAC guidelines and the Rome and Paris Declarations.[19]

5.3 Why the SWAp as a framework to improve trade management and coordination?

(i) A response to the limits of the IF: the promises of trade mainstreaming with no assurance of predictable funding. Cambodia is recognized as an IF success story. Its success has stemmed from its drive to mobilize support to implement downstream activities. Cambodia has used the IF as a tool and as a means to an end. It has integrated the process into the broader framework for donor support and programming. However, there is no guarantee that donors will come through under the funding umbrella of the existing IF framework. Downstream activities as identified in the Action Matrix, such as trade infrastructure and trade facilitation, were financed from mechanisms outside the IF Trust Fund, for example through the World Bank Consultative Group meeting or directly through bilateral cooperation. While recognized as a sound framework for trade capacity building and donor coordination, the IF still suffers from weak in-country implementation

[18] Technical assistance was provided by ITC under an EC regional trade assistance program called the Asia Trust Fund.

[19] In this respect, the Rome Declaration on Harmonization (2003) and the Paris Declaration on Aid Effectiveness (2005) have placed an emphasis on national ownership of the development process by recipient countries, as well as harmonization of donors' practices to avoid duplication and overlapping of activities and to minimize the burden on implementing institutions.

Box 9.3. What is a SWAp?

Concept: A SWAp is a management and coordination framework comprising the following components and steps:

- A sector development strategy defining priority objectives, targets, reforms, and the supporting expenditure framework encompassing projects and defining resources for investment and capacity building.
- A strategy for implementation, all of which must be properly designed and fully operational, including: (i) detailed action plans and benchmarks; (ii) arrangements for coordination, procedures for resources management and joint monitoring; and (iii) modalities for the harmonization and alignment of donors' operations and practices within the sector.

The establishment of a SWAp follows a lengthy and gradual process. By early 2007, the MoC in Cambodia had completed some of the steps, namely: the formulation of a sector program comprising key policy and governance issues, an expenditure framework to support the implementation of priority policies, arrangements to strengthen coordination and management of resources, as well as the initiation of the trade mainstreaming process. Setting up subsequent components for a wider scope of trade policies and strategies, further defining linkages with the country's overall planning and budgeting process, and operationalizing the SWAp are next steps at the top of the ministry's work.

Principles and objectives: The basic principles of a SWAp consist of the following elements: (i) government leadership and accountability regarding the sector strategy design and implementation, and national ownership of the sector activities and outcomes; (ii) integration and mainstreaming of the sector policy and strategies into the country development agenda and overall management systems; (iii) inclusive participation of national stakeholders and external development partners in policy setting and implementation monitoring; and (iv) the sector being considered in its widest scope to encompass all related aspects.

The SWAp's target objectives are to (i) ensure the national ownership of the sector management; (ii) improve the effectiveness of development resources; and (iii) achieve increased and sustained impact on the sector development.

Expected outcomes: The successful implementation of a SWAp can result in the following: (i) coherent development policies and strategies; (ii) enhanced management capacity of stakeholders' institutions; (iii) strengthened participation of national stakeholders in the sector development process; (iv) improved coordination between the government and external development partners; (v) harmonized and aligned donors' policies and operations; and (vi) reduced transaction costs attached to ODA delivery.

Conditions of success: As a SWAp is a comprehensive answer to concerns related to lack of national ownership and weak effectiveness of resources, two major conditions should be achieved to ensure the success of the SWAp: (i) strong government and civil society willingness and capacity to apply and comply with the SWAp principles; and (ii) substantial financial and technical support from external partners to facilitate the implementation of the SWAp components.

capacity and ownership. Increasing the funding envelope for implementation, as proposed through the "Enhanced IF," would go a long way to respond to these shortcomings.

(ii) The SWAp in the global development agenda and ODA policies. The trade SWAp is becoming the new paradigm for managing and coordinating Official Development Assistance. OECD/DAC has adopted the SWAp to achieve better aid efficiency and is encouraging LDCs and donors to move in this direction.[20] Other donors and multilateral organizations are supporting SWAps in various countries and sectors.[21]

(iii) The SWAp has already been incorporated in the government vision and strategies. The SWAp is not new to Cambodia. Several government initiatives aimed at translating the OECD/DAC guidelines into concrete operational actions provide additional strength to the implementation of program-based approaches.[22]

The National Strategic Development Plan (NSDP) considers the SWAp as a sound and relevant instrument for better management, coordination, and effectiveness of resources and has encouraged core and line ministries to adopt and implement this new approach. At the 2006 Consultative Group Meeting, the government as well as its external development partners showed strong interest in supporting the SWAp and widening its sector coverage.[23]

This type of program-based approach is currently being applied in education, health, public finance management, and now in the trade sector. Similar initiatives for other sectors are also under consideration.

5.4 Financing aspects

5.4.1 *Expenditure framework*

The MoC has updated the TRTA matrix and developed it into a medium-term expenditure framework incorporating updated information on ongoing projects as well as integrating new TRTA and trade-related investment needs and requirements, as identified by the trade support institutions. The objective is to ensure that ongoing and future trade and trade-related interventions match needs, that duplication is avoided, and that new commitments or possible future funding from bilateral and multilateral donors are reflected.

[20] In November 2002 the Task Force on Harmonization of Donors Practices established by OECD/DAC, produced "Good Practices Papers" as guidelines for the management of development cooperation. These guidelines were endorsed by the Rome (2003) and Paris (2005) declarations on aid effectiveness, which encourage donors and recipient countries to adopt program-based approaches and consider budget support, program aid, and pooling of funds as good practices to support and operationalize SWAps, and to facilitate national leadership and ownership, as well as harmonization and alignment of development assistance policies and programs with those of recipient countries.

[21] For instance, the European Commission has issued in February 2003 detailed guidelines for EC support to sector programs.

[22] See the government's Action Plan on Harmonization and Alignment endorsed by the Council of Ministers on 19 November 2004 (and updated on 14 February 2006), and the Strategic Framework for Development Cooperation Management approved on 27 January 2006.

[23] "Delegates agreed with the government's request to aim for the development and implementation of more sector-wide programs . . . " Excerpt from the Consultative Group Meeting press release, 3 March 2006.

Table 9.1. Expenditure framework for 2006–08

Project status	Institutional support to MoC (US$)	Other trade support institutions (US$)	Initial estimation of support to supply-side capacity (US$)
Ongoing projects	3,699,000	9,728,667	9,856,000
New-planned-proposed projects	5,800,760	1,196,667	2,615,000
Total	**9,499,760**	**10,925,333**	**12,471,000**

The expenditure framework was prepared on the basis of a bottom-up participatory approach and went through a lengthy process of scrutiny and validation.[24] The expenditure framework, being an integral part of the trade sector program, constitutes its implementation instrument. It is a multi-year plan for resources allocation and mobilization, with clear identification of sources of required funding, whether they be the government, external partners, or other national stakeholders.

5.4.2 *Program cost*

The total financial outlay of the program is US$33 million for the three-year period 2006–08, giving an annual average of US$11 million (see Tables 9.1 and 9.2). This amount incorporates development activities for institutional strengthening of trade support institutions, including the MoC and other ministries and national organizations, and an initial estimation of external assistance requirements in supply-side capacity.

The expenditure framework distinguishes three types of external assistance, namely: Technical Assistance for Capacity Building, Budget Support to accompany reforms, and Investment-Related Technical Assistance and Capital Investment, mostly for strengthening supply-side capacity. The terms of external assistance provided to or sought for trade and trade-related activities are very favorable, as 96 percent of this assistance is in the form of grants and the remaining 4 percent in the form of concessional loans. The total cost of the present program is to be covered by ODA earmarked for trade and trade-related matters.

5.4.3 *Resource mobilization and management*

Financial and technical resource mobilization is crucial for the implementation of trade and trade-related activities. Resources include public and private funding in different forms and for various targets. Private investment, domestic and FDI, in

[24] The principles guiding the selection and prioritization of the needs considered in the expenditure framework are based on the following criteria: (i) no stand-alone projects: each proposal must be linked to the relevant policy, problem to be solved and objectives to be achieved, and must be integrated in the expenditure plan; (ii) projects that aim principally to develop institutional and human capacities must be favored; (iii) existing assistance in the concerned department, institution or area of intervention must be taken into account to avoid duplication or overlap; and (iv) absorptive capacity must be taken into consideration.

Table 9.2. Ongoing and required assistance by clusters of actions and domains

Presentation of needs and assistance by clusters		
	Projected level of assistance 2006–08 (ongoing and new projects)	
Cluster	Amount	%
Legal framework	1,349,000	4%
Trade facilitation reform	7,025,000	21%
Capacity of relevant institutions in SPS and food safety	1,220,000	4%
Domestic and external trade promotion	3,964.000	12%
Trade support services	3,053,000	9%
MoC reform and restructuring	1,400,000	4%
Other institutional support	2,415,000	7%
Supply-side capacity	12,471,000	38%
Total	**33,000,000**	**100%**

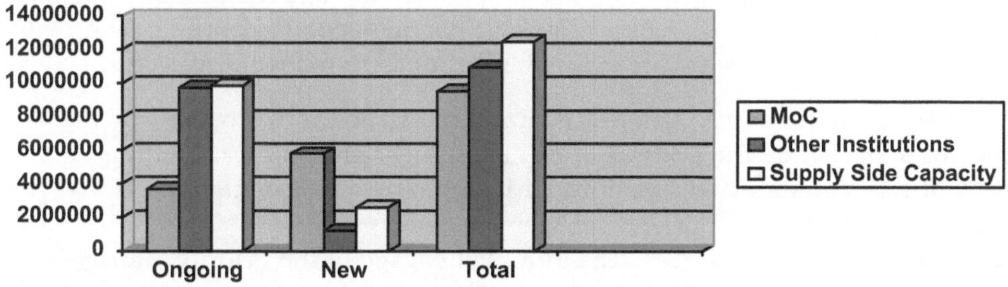

infrastructure and supply-side capacity is of crucial importance for the growth of the trade sector and its contribution to employment and income generation.

The focus of this program is on public resources. Public resource mobilization was facilitated by the strong interest shown by several donors over the past few years. About twenty multilateral and bilateral donors are active in various trade and trade-related areas, in particular with WTO pre- and post-accession commitments. The bulk of financing is provided by ten main donors, with other partners intervening either with modest financial contributions or as implementing agencies contributing through policy and operational support.

For the short term, and while the ministry's management instruments are being put in place, external financing will be guided by three modalities. First, pooling resources in multi-donor trust funds and 'common baskets' managed by a single multilateral agency agreed upon by the government and donors concerned is the preferred modality from the government's perspective, especially for financing reform packages and the Priority Management Groups/Merit-Base Pay Initiatives (PMGs/MBPI). Second, separate resources and management will be implemented only when common baskets cannot be envisaged. Third, ultimately, most external support will be channeled through the government financial systems.[25]

[25] Budget support – in the form of grants – is essential for the implementation of the program. In the Rome and Paris Declarations cited earlier, it is stated that donors are encouraged to provide sectoral

5.5 Institutional mechanism

5.5.1 *Coordination and monitoring mechanism*

The MoC will ensure the implementation and monitoring of the trade SWAp through the following mechanism:

- A national implementation body (NIB) will be formed with representatives from key ministries and government agencies and chaired by a high-ranked official from the MoC at the level of Secretary of State.
- A core team formed by officials from relevant departments within the ministry and managed by a high-ranked official at the level of Under-secretary of State will ensure the day-to-day coordination and follow-up of work activities. A Planning and Research Unit created under the direct supervision of the minister's office will provide the necessary secretarial support.

5.5.2 *Reinforcing the absorptive capacity to manage the SWAp*

High on the agenda of the program is the reform of the MoC and the strengthening of its management capacity to become more efficient in managing the trade SWAp. Envisaged actions in this regard are articulated around the following aspects:

- *Institutional strengthening*: A new organizational structure[26] proposed by the MoC for adoption by the Council of Ministers envisages the restructuring of the ministry's mandate and functions with emphasis on accountability, transparency, and efficiency as its key management principles.
- *Human Resources Management*: The MoC will engage in the Priority Management Groups/Merit-Based Pay Initiatives in line with the government policy and modeled after the successful initiative piloted by the World Bank in the area of Public Finance Management.[27] On-the-job skills upgrading will be undertaken systematically in accordance with specific needs and job requirements in the areas of management, policy analysis, trade negotiations, trade flow analysis, communications and language skills, project proposal designs, and so forth.

6 Lessons learned from Cambodia's trade capacity building for development

Overall, the technical support to boost the capacity of the MoC to actively manage the trade mainstreaming process has borne fruit. While systematic measurement

budget support. This type of support would be used partially to accompany the implementation of the institutional reforms such as the restructuring of the MoC, and specifically for the merit-based payments and operational expenditures. Another part of the budget support could be utilized – at a later stage within the expanded versions of this program – for offsetting possible negative impacts of trade liberalization and for promoting supply-side capacity.

26 This structure – together with detailed description of functions for each department – was discussed at a MoC meeting in April 2006. Staff from Chief of Office to Secretary of State and Senior Minister participated in the discussions and design of the new structure.

27 PMG allowances are regulated by Sub-Decree 98 of August 2005. PMG and MBPI are being implemented gradually. A first PMG/MBPII is operational in the sector of Public Finance Management. Others are being developed in other sectors.

of the impact of TRCB initiatives in Cambodia might not be possible without in-depth research and analysis, there have been concrete indications that those actions initiated under the IF have had positive impacts, the most visible and significant being Cambodia's accession as the first LDC to the WTO in 2003. Other tangible evidence of successes included concrete results in deepening the understanding of the linkages and potential impacts of trade reform on the poor, the inclusion of trade into the national development and poverty reduction policies, and the recent initiation of a trade SWAp.

From this experience it is possible to draw a few lessons from the process and identify key drivers of success. The main lesson from the implementation of TRCB initiatives in Cambodia is that they should be holistic and encompassing enough to support the trade policy framework of the country, and include at a minimum the following elements: (i) a coherent trade strategy closely integrated with the country's overall development strategy; (ii) effective mechanisms for intra-governmental policy coordination, and for consultation among the three key sets of stakeholders: government, the private sector and civil society; and (iii) a network of trade support institutions. To be successful, TRCB initiatives need to be anchored with firm country ownership and backed by strong political commitment.

6.1 First lesson: country ownership of the process

Government ownership of the process was a sine qua non condition for the success of the pilot scheme in Cambodia. The success of the trade mainstreaming process rests to a great extent on the government being able to provide the right leadership at both the formulation and implementation stages. The Cambodian Commerce Minister and his deputy were closely involved, on both the domestic and international fronts, to earn the respect and support of the key stakeholders and to assert their leadership in this vital initiative. This leadership was, in fact, one of the key determinants of Cambodia being selected in the IF pilot scheme and its successful accession to the WTO.

Had it not been for the strong political will of the government, the accelerated pace of the mainstreaming process would not have been achieved – from the preparation for accession to the WTO, to the successful completion of the diagnostic study, to the integration of pro-poor trade policies and programs into the PRSP. Throughout the entire process, this political commitment, support, and participation of the Cambodian leadership, so needed to materialize the country's ambitious long-term vision, were visibly felt. On numerous occasions the Cambodian Prime Minister reiterated his commitment to accelerate the various reforms and render them more effective.[28]

6.1.1 *Government as local partner with local knowledge*

The government believed that substantive achievements could be achieved provided it and its partners could develop an efficient, collaborative and synergistic

[28] Conversely, a case study commissioned by the government of the Netherlands in 2005 confirmed that one of the main reasons for the poor performance of the IF was linked to both the limited TRTA absorption capacity of the LDCs and the lack of means and political commitment at the country level.

partnership drawing on each other's strengths and making up for each other's shortcomings. Metaphorically speaking, the partnership contribution of the government would be in the form of "sweat equity" and local knowledge. More often than not, most technical missions were comprised of highly qualified international consultants, most of whom, regrettably, had never been in Cambodia and thus lacked insight into the local realities. This deficiency was compensated by extensive exchanges with local Cambodian consultants and official counterparts. Research materials and other policy documents were conveniently made available to the missions, saving a great deal of research time and resources.

6.1.2 *Capacity building to ensure policy coherence*

Mainstreaming trade into a national development strategy requires a coherent policy framework.[29] Ultimately, mainstreaming trade means giving greater visibility to the linkages between trade and all other related economic policy areas. Capacity building provided to the government should aim at helping it reconcile two distinct cultures: *trade culture* (which is legalistic and highly centralized, including negotiation and implementation of the WTO Agreements) and *development culture* (which is decentralized, demand-driven, and based on a country-owned process). The latter involves a host of complementary policy reforms in areas outside the purview of the WTO, together with costly investments in trade-related institutions, infrastructure, and human resources. For that purpose, the government took bold measures to restructure and rationalize key ministerial functions under the MoC, including investment, regional and global economic integration, and intellectual property protection. Regional organizations, including regional banks, were requested to play a proactive role in assisting Cambodia to respond to needs at the regional level.

Over the longer term, there is a need to develop and consolidate mutually supportive policies, and to connect the trade, development, and finance communities. Financing is critical in mainstreaming efforts, in the absence of which efforts to mainstream are likely to dissipate. This requires effective coordination across government institutions and development partners (donors and agencies), as well as partnership between the government and private sector participants in the economy, a common view shared by developed and developing countries at the 2002 Monterrey Conference on Financing for Development. The recognition of this need led to further reflection by the government and the seed for the trade SWAp was planted.

6.2 Second lesson: Cambodia's partnership mechanisms for consultation and coordination

The implementation of a national trade sector strategy is not likely to be successful without a large measure of support from all key stakeholders: government policy-makers, bureaucrats, business sector actors, development partners, and civil society. To achieve such support requires an inclusive process that engages the key stakeholders throughout the various stages of the cycle. It is only in this manner that stakeholders can identify realistic goals, take full measure of their respective

[29] "Coherence" is one of the WTO's five core functions. See WTO (1994), Article III: 5; and WTO (1993).

commitments, and become true "owners" of the strategy.[30] This inclusiveness can significantly contribute to bringing trade needs into the policy arena and ultimately seeing them reflected in the country's development strategy.

For Cambodia, identifying key issues and broad approaches to the trade sector strategy was not necessarily the most difficult part of the exercise. What was more demanding was the formulation of a plan of action that was the result of a true process of consultation among all stakeholders, in which each partner is able to contribute ideas and inputs. Cambodia ensured that continuous support of the stakeholders was secured through an effective multi-pronged coordination mechanism.

6.2.1 *Intra-governmental policy co-ordination*

The government designated the MoC as the focal point for the implementation of TRTA, including the IF program in Cambodia. A broad-based Steering Committee was also established to guide and monitor formulation and implementation of a "mainstreamed" trade sector strategy.

The Council for Social Development was the government agency mandated with poverty-focused policy and program design and monitoring of implementation. Its work was central in steering the preparation of the national poverty reduction strategy as well as the monitoring of process, inputs, intermediary outputs, and outcomes in close co-ordination with sectoral and local-level monitoring systems. The work of the IF closely contributed to the process by providing critical trade policy-level inputs in the preparation of the PRSP and the five-year plan.

6.2.2 *Government and private sector coordination*

Institutionalizing systematic consultations between private and public sector institutions can have positive, long-term effects. As actors in the field, private enterprises are well-placed to identify trade-related problems and bottlenecks. An increased dialogue between the public sector and private entrepreneurs would improve effectiveness in assessing TRTA needs, in implementing as well as evaluating the effectiveness of assistance. Importantly, the private sector believed that actions did result from their participation in the process.

Together with the trade mainstreaming process, Cambodia supported – and continues to support – an engagement policy that strongly favored national partnerships with the private sector. It has a formalized procedure through which the government and private sector are able to hold dialogue. It is headed by a high-level Government-Private Sector Forum established in late 1999, chaired by the Prime Minister and supported by a high-level Steering Committee for Private Sector Development, chaired by the Senior Minister and Minister of Economy and Finance).[31] In support of the development of specific sectors, seven sectoral working groups

[30] An IF simulation exercise led by USAID in September 2005 revealed that the main vulnerable points of the IF are the inadequate country ownership, the lack of broader national stakeholders' participation, and the weak involvement of the local private sector and the international business community.

[31] The Committee is composed of three sub-committees: a Sub-Steering Committee on Trade Facilitation (chaired by the Senior. Minister and Minister of Commerce); a Sub-Steering Committee on Investment Climate and Private Sector Participation in Infrastructure (chaired by the Senior Minister and Minister of Economy and Finance); and a Sub-Steering Committee on SMEs (chaired by the Minister of Industry, Energy and Mines).

identify issues and bottlenecks on an ongoing basis.[32] Each sectoral working group is run by a committee of ten members, six of whom come from the business community under the auspices of the Phnom Penh Chamber of Commerce, and the remaining four from the government. The sectoral working groups were extensively consulted on the formulation of the pro-poor trade sector strategy, including (but not limited to) the formulation of product-sector action plans.

Capacity building of business community representatives, many of whom were involved with trade support institutions (TSIs), has proven to be critical in strengthening their advocacy capacity.[33] Through their access to government decision makers and their active participation in coordination meetings with the government – namely the Private Sector Forum and the Sectoral Working Groups – these TSIs could finally ensure, on the one hand, that the constraints faced by private enterprises were correctly understood and taken into consideration for the definition of a coherent development strategy and, at the same time, the resources and potential of the private sector could be appropriately tapped.

6.2.3 *Government and donors' coordination*

Cambodia has developed an intensive system of consultations with donors. This includes the formal Consultative Group (CG) meetings and the bi-annual post-CG consultations. The CG process included working groups involving donors and government focusing on specific reform areas. These mechanisms were critical in ensuring that national stakeholders and donors at all times develop and work from a shared vision of objectives and goals. The CG formally integrated trade in its work process.

Since Cambodia's accession to the WTO, an increasing number of donors have been prepared to support more pointed efforts for trade sector development, provided that a solid framework existed to ensure overall coherence of individual donors' interventions. They have expressed a strong interest in the IF, and now in the SWAp, as promising platforms that, if implemented as a shared responsibility among donors, recipients, and multilateral agencies, could promote mainstreaming of trade and improved donor coordination within a country-owned poverty reduction framework.

6.2.4 *The role of civil society stakeholders*

In recent years, civil society groups have been very proactive in shaping the trade development process, despite the lack of a formal dialogue mechanism. Besides

[32] The specific sector focuses are: export processing, manufacturing and distribution, agriculture and agro-processing, tourism, infrastructure, financial services, and governance and tax.

[33] Examples of emerging trade support institutions have begun to appear in Cambodia, such as the National Codex Committee, created to help enterprises meet the technical standards and packaging requirements of export markets; formation of the Provincial Rice Millers' Associations and the National Federation of Cambodian Rice Millers' Associations, the Brick and Tile Manufacturers, Rural Electricity enterprises, and other business development services. Sector-specific private business associations were also formed, including farmer producing and marketing associations for tobacco, fragrant rice, bananas, soybeans, and castor seed production. In the tourism sector, the Tour Guide Association in Siem Reap, the Hotel Owners Association, and the Cambodian Association of Travel Agents were also established.

contributing to positions and supporting, technically and financially, specific trade events, they have by and large shed their adversarial character and gradually earned the respect of society and the government. For its part, the government has initiated extensive awareness campaigns with civil society stakeholders, including the holding of international conferences, seminars and focused lectures within national academic circles. These initial efforts provided a basis for deepening the synergies thus far developed among trade sector stakeholders under the leadership of the MoC.

6.3 Third lesson: Institutional implementation mechanisms to bridge "demand" and "response"

The third lesson to be derived from successful TRCB initiatives is the necessity of having a solid implementation mechanism championed by a focal point and supported by a dedicated core team. To improve the implementation of TRCB initiatives, the focal point should be strengthened and empowered as the driver of the process. Resources should be provided as appropriate to strengthen this capacity, including the creation of a national implementation unit, the provision of secretariat resources and adequate capacity building support in trade-related issues.

The success of Cambodia's process was largely attributed to the creation of a strong national implementing body whose active operational involvement boosted the mobilization and delivery of TRTA. A senior policymaker at the Secretary of State level was appointed to act as the focal point for the entire exercise. It is interesting to note that Cambodia did not have a local donor facilitator. Much of the implementation of the DTIS and projects identified in the TA action matrices materialized from the work of the focal point and his core team.

Ultimately, due to the enhanced capacity of the focal point, Cambodia was able to take advantage of considerable trade opportunities through its ability to translate and elaborate the findings of the DTIS into concrete projects and supportive policies and reforms.

7 Conclusion

Should the Doha Round be concluded, it will significantly alter the rights and obligations of WTO members, requiring changes in domestic policies and leading to alterations in markets and the flow of benefits. In this context, the ability of governments and trading communities in LDCs and other lower income countries, African and non-African alike, to address the post-Doha challenges and opportunities so as to promote development, reduce poverty, and contribute to the realization of the MDGs, will depend to a large extent on their knowledge, understanding, and ability to deal with the complex rules being put in place.

The ability of these countries to address this new environment will also depend on their effective participation in shaping and adapting to these rules, and on their capacity to adopt the necessary policies and establish the institutions, infrastructures and enterprises that will contribute to developing their supply capacities to take advantage of new market access opportunities.

TRCB initiatives have proven to be of great importance in supporting and strengthening these much-needed capacities. For its part, Cambodia has benefited enormously from various TRCB initiatives, in particular the revamped IF. A few lessons could be shared from the Cambodian experiences:

a. Country ownership is needed at all levels: government, private sector, and civil societies;
b. Policy advocacy should be backed by tangible interventions;
c. Quick and timely responses are essential to sustain the momentum;
d. Continuity of activities over the long term will be necessary to produce visible results;
e. TRCB activities should be organized as part of a systematic, long term plan;
f. A clear understanding of the roles and expectations among the various stakeholders needs to be reached prior to the launch of any initiative;
g. Stakeholder participation is empowering and should be further encouraged;
h. Partnerships are key to the success and efficient use of any TRCB resources; and
i. Efforts of the trade ministry, to be effective, should always be fully supported and backed by the finance ministry.

While the efforts expended to ensure that Cambodia succeeded as an IF pilot country were difficult, it is now facing even more pressure in embarking in a new form of aid delivery under the trade SWAp. The SWAp is an attempt to consolidate earlier achievements under the IF. It involves promoting a national constituency on trade and poverty through a strategic partnership development approach, enhancing opportunities for effective allocation of ODA towards trade, strengthening supply-side responses. Cambodia is in the process of updating its DTIS, which should feed into its national trade development program. With the SWAp in place, Cambodia will have completed a major chapter of its "trade mainstreaming process". The measure of its success will be in the extent to which the country benefits from its integration with the global economy.

But Cambodia can only go but so far on its own. Donor support, committed under the Paris Declaration on Aid Effectiveness, will help ensure that the necessary elements linking demand and supply responses are in place, such that Cambodia can ultimately achieve the Millennium Development Goals. Until then, the road ahead will be long and winding.

At the global level, while the WTO Director-General is busy with finding ways and means to support the expansion of global TRTA programs, particularly supply-side capacity and infrastructure, the LDCs and other developing countries for their part should be strengthening their capacity to attract and absorb increased quantities of new funds, whether under the Enhanced IF or the Aid for Trade initiative, and allocate them to viable trade-related projects. The successful development of well-trained human resources equipped with a sound knowledge base of international trade will be crucial. The political commitment of their policymakers at the highest level will be needed to send a clear signal that trade matters.

In this context, it becomes imperative that LDCs and non-LDC developing countries – for those that have not done so – work to mainstream trade into their development planning. They should formulate or readjust their trade strategies through broad-based consultation processes to reflect the realities of the rapidly evolving trade world and develop a comprehensive and coherent TRCB program to assist them build the necessary response capacities.

Donors and agencies also need to do a better job at integrating trade into their planning and programming. They should seek to further harmonize and optimize returns from various trade-related technical assistance programs they are funding, be they multilateral or bilateral. The success of the Enhanced IF, the JITAP, and other ongoing multilateral programs should be further improved and capitalized upon to build an integrated approach to provide TRTA covering all aspects of trade-related matters, particularly the three prongs of trade capacity: (i) trade rules compliance capacity, (ii) trade competitiveness capacity, and (iii) trade readiness capacity at the enterprise level. This "systemic" capacity building versus a "free-standing" approach should be encouraged so as to ensure that the capacities established are synergistically sustainable for the benefits of the respective beneficiary countries.

REFERENCES

Far Eastern Economic Review. 2001. "Cambodia's Tourism Industry," *Far Eastern Economic Review*, 5–12 May.

IMF/World Bank. "Guidelines for Joint Staff Assessment of a Poverty Reduction Strategy Paper," http://worldbank.org/transport/training/arms_01/klug_gl.pdf.

Mbida-Essama, Bonaventure. 2001. "Opening Remarks by Mr. Bonaventure Mbida-Essama," Chief of Country Office of the World Bank, Poverty Strategy Reduction paper (PSRP) Workshop, Phnom Penh, Cambodia, 25–26 April.

National Institute of Statistics. 2005. "National Accounts of Cambodia, 1993–2004," Phnom Phen: National Institute of Statistics.

"Paris Declaration on Aid Effectiveness – Ownership, Harmonisation, Alignment, Results and Mutual Accountability," High Level Forum, Paris, 28 February – 2 March 2005, http://www.oecd.org/dataoecd/11/41/34428351.pdf.

Royal Government of Cambodia. 2006. "Cambodia: National Strategic Development Plan (NSDP) 2006–2010 – Formulation, Monitoring and Evaluation Process," for Forum on "National Plans as Poverty Reduction Strategies in East Asia," Vientiane, 4–6 April.

"Rome Declaration on Harmonization," Rome, Italy, 25 February 2003, http://www.who.int/hdp/publications/1b_rome_declaration.pdf.

Siphana, Sok. 2005. "Cambodia Enters the WTO: Lessons learned for Least Developed Countries," ADBI Research Policy Brief No. 16, Tokyo: ADBI.

WTO. 1993. *Declaration on the Contribution of the World Trade Organization to Achieving Greater Coherence in Global Economic Policymaking*, 15 December, http://www.wto.org/English/docs_e/legal_e/32-dcohr.pdf.

WTO. 1994. *Marrakesh Agreement Establishing the World Trade Organization*, 15 April, http://www.wto.org/English/docs_e/legal_e/04-wto.pdf.

WTO. 2001a. *Report on the 26th IAWG Meeting*, Integrated Framework, 17 April.

WTO. 2001b. *Integrated Framework: Pilot Phase Work Program, presentation by the World Bank on behalf of the IF core agencies at The First IF Steering Committee Meeting*, 15 March.

WTO. 2004. Cambodia raises WTO membership to 148, WTO News: 2004, 13 October, http://www.wto.org/english/news_e/news04_e/cambodia_148members_13oct04_e.htm.

10 Lessons Learned Delivering Aid for Trade in Latin America and the Caribbean: The Role of the Inter-American Development Bank[1]

ANTONI ESTEVADEORDAL, PAOLO GIORDANO, ANNEKE JESSEN, JESSICA LUNA, AND KATI SUOMINEN

1 Introduction

The Inter-American Development Bank (IDB) is the main source of multilateral development finance in Latin America and the Caribbean (LAC).[2] From 2000 to 2005, total financing for economic, social and institutional development projects amounted to US$38.7 billion, of which close to US$35 billion was ordinary capital, US$2.7 billion was concessional lending, and US$1.1 billion was grant funding.[3] Concomitant with emerging demands in its borrowing member countries, the IDB has in recent years devoted a growing share of its financing to trade-related assistance, echoing a broader trend in aid flows across the world. Trade-related assistance, or Aid for Trade, encompasses both traditional trade-related capacity building and broader forms of assistance aimed at enhancing a country's capacity to trade.

At the Sixth Ministerial Conference of the World Trade Organization (WTO), held in Hong Kong in December 2005, Ministers called for the establishment of a WTO Task Force to examine ways in which Aid for Trade could be made operational and might contribute to the development dimension of the Doha Development Agenda. The 13-member task force was created in February 2006. Half of its members were also member countries of the IDB (Barbados, Brazil, Canada, Colombia, Japan and the United States, with European Union (EU) countries

1 This chapter is based in the document WTO (2006), which was prepared by the IDB's Integration and Regional Programs Department (INT) as a contribution to the work of the WTO Task Force on Aid for Trade. It was prepared in collaboration with an inter-departmental working group comprising the Bank's various operational departments. For questions regarding this report please contact Mr. Antoni Estevadeordal (antonie@iadb.org).

2 The IDB has 47 member countries: ***Borrowing member countries*** are: Argentina, The Bahamas, Barbados, Belize, Bolivia, Brazil, Chile, Colombia, Costa Rica, Dominican Republic, Ecuador, El Salvador, Guatemala, Guyana, Haiti, Honduras, Jamaica, Mexico, Nicaragua, Panama, Paraguay, Peru, Suriname, Trinidad & Tobago, Uruguay, and Venezuela. ***Non-borrowing member countries*** include: Austria, Belgium, Canada, Croatia, Denmark, Finland, France, Germany, Israel, Italy, Japan, Korea, Netherlands, Norway, Portugal, Slovenia, Spain, Sweden, Switzerland, the United Kingdom and the United States.

3 Total funding approved for new loans and grants, including Multilateral Investment Fund (MIF). Another US$1.1 billion in loans was provided by the IDB's sister organization, the Inter-American Investment Corporation (IIC).

holding a joint seat).[4] Based on interventions from a number of parties, including the IDB, the Task Force provided recommendations to the WTO General Council in July 2006, subsequently adopted in October 2006 (see Introductory Chapter).

The IDB is well placed to provide contributions to the current discussion around Aid for Trade. Since its creation more than forty years ago, the Bank has actively supported the development of trade-related infrastructure and supply-side capacities in its LAC member countries. Over the last decade, moreover, the Bank has built a solid track record in trade-related capacity building in LAC, developing both country-focused and region-wide approaches to the provision of such assistance. Through regular interaction with government authorities, the private sector and other non-state actors, it has developed a sound reputation in the LAC trade community, based on technical expertise, working experience and mutual trust.

LAC is a diverse region comprising mostly middle-income countries, many of which no longer have access to concessional IDB or World Bank financing. Most LAC countries are moreover excluded from recent trade-related cooperation initiatives that target the Least Developed Countries (LDCs) – such as the Integrated Framework (IF) or the EU Everything But Arms (EBA) initiative.[5] Trade, however, is crucial for their development, and despite their relatively more advanced levels of development, LAC countries continue to face serious challenges in this area. For many of them, trade liberalization has been at the center of a significant structural reform process spanning the last two decades, but it has not yet delivered the expected results in terms of stronger export growth and economic development.

The challenges facing LAC in the area of trade are briefly reviewed in Section 2 of this document. Section 3 provides an overview of IDB support to trade in the past decade, examining institutional developments, efforts to integrate trade into the Bank's programming process, and innovations in the types of instruments and mechanisms used to deliver trade-related assistance. Section 4 examines lessons learned and, based on these, highlights existing gaps in the provision of trade-related assistance. Section 5 looks to the future, offering some recommendations on how the IDB could contribute to global efforts at delivering Aid for Trade more effectively.

2 Trade challenges in Latin America and the Caribbean

Among developing regions, LAC has been one of the most active participants in multilateral, regional and bilateral trade initiatives. LAC countries recognize that trade can be a powerful engine of growth and that liberalization affords them many opportunities for expanding economic welfare. Because many LAC countries are relatively small, they depend crucially on trade for their economic development. Even in larger economies, domestic market size is constrained by low income levels across large sections of the population. LAC countries need export income

4 The remaining members of the Task Force were China, India, Thailand, Mauritius, Benin and Zambia. The latter three acted as coordinators, respectively, of the African, Caribbean and Pacific (ACP), African, and Least-Developed Country (LDC) groups in the WTO.

5 In February 2001, the EU Council adopted the Everything But Arms Regulation (Regulation (EC) 416/2001), granting duty-free access to imports of all products from LDCs without any quantitative restrictions, except to arms and munitions.

to create and sustain jobs, finance imports, pay off foreign debt, and maintain a healthy balance in their external accounts, all of which is necessary to achieve sustainable levels of economic growth. LAC countries also depend on the supply of competitively priced imports to support local production and satisfy consumer demands. In a global context marked by the emergence of new trade powerhouses such as China and India, LAC countries need to preserve their trade competitiveness to secure continued access to international markets and the associated welfare gains.

In the 1980s and 1990s, LAC countries undertook significant structural reforms to facilitate economic growth and development. Trade liberalization featured prominently in the reform process and was pursued through a multi-polar integration strategy (IDB, 2003). Unilateral trade liberalization helped raise efficiency in domestic markets, while reciprocal multilateral liberalization (through the General Agreement on Tariffs and Trade (GATT) and WTO) and bilateral free trade agreements opened new markets for exporters and provided the means for establishing effective rules governing trade with external partners. Regional integration, meanwhile, offered easier access to neighboring markets and an opportunity for businesses to prepare for further global market integration. Import protection declined substantially during this period: the region's average tariff fell from 40 percent in the mid-1980s to 10 percent in 2000. However, liberalization was not systematically accompanied by complementary policies to help countries maximize the benefits of reform. A comprehensive strategy aimed at making trade work for development is even more urgent as the scope of global trade integration broadens.

Increase Welfare through Trade Performance. Despite the structural reforms, the region's trade performance displays some weaknesses and needs to be improved in most countries. Trade openness, measured as the ratio of a country's external trade to its gross domestic product (GDP), is below levels prevalent in other regions of the world.[6] Some of the smaller Central American and Caribbean countries do have high levels of trade openness, but in these and most other LAC countries, the quality of trade integration presents vulnerabilities. Exports are not very diversified, and consist mostly of commodities or resource-based manufactures with low technology content. In addition, several LAC countries – prominent among them the smaller Caribbean islands – have been exposed to significant preference erosion in recent years, adding to their difficulties of maintaining a competitive presence in world markets. After a decade of sluggish growth, the region needs stronger trade performance to achieve and sustain higher levels of economic growth.

Equitably Distribute the Gains from Trade. In the reform process, efficiency considerations overshadowed concerns regarding the distributional aspects of trade liberalization. As a result, trade opening was only rarely accompanied by mechanisms for compensating inevitable losers in the process and boosting the opportunities of potential winners. Few countries implemented broad adjustment programs to address the disruptions to local industries and labor markets resulting from

[6] For example, Colombia has roughly the same GDP as the Philippines, but its trade/GDP ratio is less than half that of the Philippines. Similarly, Venezuela's population and GDP are close to those of Malaysia, but its trade/GDP ratio is less than one fourth of Malaysia's.

trade liberalization. Such disruptions – along with rapid import growth unmatched by similar export performance, pressures on national trade balances and current accounts, and widespread perceptions of insufficient public consultation during the reform process – have tested LAC countries' continued support for trade liberalization and reform. In some countries, a certain "reform fatigue" has heightened the risk of a backlash to further trade liberalization. Partly as a result of these developments, trade issues have assumed a much more prominent role in the public debate. At a time when further reform is needed to boost competitiveness, waning support for trade opening is a serious challenge.

Adapt to the Complexity of Modern Trade Agreements. For LAC countries, trade liberalization is not a linear process starting with negotiations at the bilateral, regional or multilateral level, then moving to implementation of commitments and, finally, to adjustment to a more open trade regime. Rather, it is a circular and continuous process in which implementation and adjustment often raise the need for further negotiation and liberalization. In addition, LAC countries are often at various stages of implementing multiple agreements with different trade partners, which requires careful planning and adequate resource allocation across all stages of the reform process. Finally, trade agreements themselves have become more complex, increasingly covering behind-the-border issues in addition to traditional border issues such as customs tariffs and rules of origin. Behind-the-border issues such as investment, intellectual property, competition and standards are becoming standard features in modern trade agreements. To fulfill commitments in these areas, governments are often required to make significant changes to long-standing institutional, legal and administrative practices in their countries.

Promote Ownership of Trade Reforms. The combination of a more complex reform agenda and growing public debate about trade means that governments must increasingly involve multiple actors in the formulation and implementation of trade policy, with a view to creating a sense of public ownership of the reform process. This requires the development of efficient consultation mechanisms among relevant government departments, and between these and prominent civil society groups such as labor and the private sector.

Further Expand Trade-related Institutional Capacity. Technical capacity is crucial to managing a complex trade agenda, and is not always readily available in the region. There are significant variations in capacity and experience among LAC countries with respect to the negotiation and implementation of trade agreements. While several countries were actively involved in the GATT Uruguay Round negotiations, others were less involved, their participation often constrained by the lack of permanent representation in Geneva. The speed of implementation of Uruguay Round commitments has also varied greatly across the region. On the regional and bilateral front, Chile and Mexico started liberalizing early and are now implementing complex North-South trade agreements with the United States, Canada, the EU, and Asian countries. Other LAC countries have gained most of their experience through less ambitious South-South agreements with neighboring countries, and have only recently begun to negotiate and implement bilateral trade agreements with developed countries (for example the U.S.-Central America-Dominican

Republic Free Trade Agreement, CAFTA-DR). Some countries are fairly new members to the WTO and one – The Bahamas – has not yet joined.

Secure Adequate Funding for Trade-related Assistance. LAC countries have limited financial resources to manage their trade agenda, particularly as the agenda expands to respond to emerging needs. Severe debt overhangs, sluggish economic growth during most of the past decade, loss of tariff revenue, difficulties in establishing alternative revenue sources, and growing social demands have all put severe pressure on fiscal resources to fund the various stages of trade-related policymaking. The concentration of some recent trade-support programs on LDCs has not been helpful for LAC countries, which are mostly middle-income countries. In some cases, such as the EU Everything but Arms Initiative, such programs have placed additional strain on LAC export efforts because they have affected relative market access conditions for many of the region's exporters. In others, such as the Integrated Framework, most of them are simply not included.

Implement Complementary Domestic Policies. Against this background, LAC governments increasingly recognize that trade policy can no longer be treated as a sectoral issue isolated from other aspects of economic policy. First, trade liberalization can induce macroeconomic shocks and thus requires broad-based macroeconomic responses to address the fiscal impact of liberalization and preserve price competitiveness through sustainable exchange rate policies. Second, trade liberalization is a necessary, but not sufficient, condition for generating equitable economic growth. It opens doors and provides new opportunities for growth, but to help economic actors seize those opportunities, governments must create an enabling environment for enhanced productivity and competitiveness, particularly through the removal of red tape and other impediments to business development. This requires action in many areas of economic policy, both at the macro and micro level, and investments in infrastructure and related services. Finally, efforts to boost economic efficiency should be accompanied by policies that promote equity. Specific trade-related social policies aimed at protecting the most vulnerable and facilitating the transition of labor to expanding sectors of the economy should form an integral part of trade reform.

3 A decade of IDB trade-related assistance in LAC

For the IDB, as for its clients in Latin America and the Caribbean, 1994 marked a milestone in the area of trade. It was the year in which the Uruguay Round of multilateral trade negotiations was concluded, with LAC countries binding their tariffs for the first time in GATT history and agreeing to a comprehensive agenda of complementary, behind-the-border trade reforms to be implemented under the newly established WTO. It was also the year the North-American Free Trade Agreement (NAFTA) entered into force between Canada, Mexico and the United States. In South America, Mercosur countries signed the Ouro Preto Protocol, consolidating the group's institutional structure and moving it toward a customs union, the second largest in the world. Also in 1994, thirty-four countries in the western hemisphere, all of them IDB members, decided to negotiate a Free Trade Area of the Americas (FTAA). Since then, LAC countries have concluded thirty-nine bilateral and regional trade agreements with each other and with countries outside the hemisphere.

For the IDB, responding to this upsurge in trade policy developments in the region was an urgent priority. The Bank faced three challenges in this regard: how to adapt its institutional strategy and structure to growing demands for trade-related assistance; how to integrate trade into its programming process; and how to deliver trade-related assistance effectively through traditional and new instruments.

3.1 Institutional adjustments to meet client needs

Trade and the IDB Institutional Strategy. In 1994, the IDB's Board of Governors increased the Bank's financial resources and reaffirmed regional integration as an important strategy for enhanced global integration and one of the institution's foremost operational priorities. These priorities are developed in greater detail in the Bank's Institutional Strategy, approved in 1999. The strategy defines sustainable economic growth, poverty reduction and promotion of social equity as the institution's overarching goals. These goals are advanced through action in four priority areas: modernization of the state, regional integration, competitiveness, and social development.

Trade is deeply embedded in each of these four areas. Modernization of the state includes trade-related capacity building and institutional reforms in the public sector aimed at fostering more efficient trade policymaking and implementation. Regional integration covers support to regional trade agreements and institutions, the development of regional infrastructure, and the fostering of regional public goods. Competitiveness operations target supply-side capacities and adjustment, infrastructure and trade finance, and support to business development activities that improve a country's ability to compete in the global economy. Social development encompasses the creation of safety nets as well as compensatory programs such as re-training of displaced workers.

In 1994, major changes aimed at improving the IDB's lending operations and enhancing its capacity to respond to rapidly changing circumstances in its borrowing member countries.[7] The restructuring included the creation of the Department for Integration and Regional Programs (INT) and, within that Department, a Bank unit dedicated exclusively to trade and integration issues – the Integration, Trade and Hemispheric Issues Division (ITD). As part of the restructuring, the Bank's Buenos Aires-based Institute for the Integration of Latin America and the Caribbean (INTAL) was made part of the new Integration Department. The aim was to bring together the Bank's headquarters and field-based expertise in the area of trade.

A Bank Unit Specialized in Trade. The Bank's Trade Division, ITD, was given three mandates: (i) to deliver trade-related technical assistance directly to LAC countries and sub-regions; (ii) to provide technical support services to the Bank's main operational units and departments (both its public and private sector lending windows);

[7] The IDB Group comprises the Inter-American Development Bank (IDB), the Multilateral Investment Fund (MIF), and the Inter-American Investment Corporation (IIC). For information regarding the Bank's organizational structure see IDB (2007).

and (iii) to act as the Bank's focal point of contact and coordination with other organizations working on trade:

i. *Provision of technical assistance to governments.* One of the Trade Division's most important initial tasks was to provide assistance to the launching of the FTAA process in 1994. ITD provided significant technical support in the areas of market access, agriculture and government procurement, both in the preparatory phase (1994–1998) and during the actual trade negotiations, which began in 1998. More recently, ITD has also provided direct technical support to LAC countries in their multilateral, sub-regional and bilateral negotiating processes, including WTO, CAFTA and U.S.-Andean free trade negotiations, and to implementation of resulting agreements.
ii. *Technical support services to Bank operational departments.* The Division assists the Bank's operational departments in the design and implementation of trade-related operations, ranging from comprehensive programs of institutional strengthening spanning several ministries and trade-related agencies, to more specific interventions in areas such as customs, technical standards, and trade-related fiscal reform. The Division also provides non-operational support in the form of regional papers and national trade and integration sector studies that feed into the Bank's regional and national programming cycles (see below). Over the years, the Trade Division has established close links with the Bank's operational departments in all stages of the programming process.
iii. *Coordination with other agencies.* The Trade Division is a focal point for the Bank's contacts and coordination with other institutions in the area of trade. Collaboration between the IDB and the WTO was formalized through a Memorandum of Understanding between the two institutions in 1999, and covers such areas as training, research and support to the preparation of WTO Trade Policy Reviews in Latin American and Caribbean countries. Other institutions with which the Bank collaborates in the area of trade include the Asian Development Bank (ADB), the World Bank, International Monetary Fund (IMF), European Commission, Organization of American States (OAS), UN Economic Commission for Latin America and the Caribbean (ECLAC), and UN Conference on Trade and Development (UNCTAD).[8] Over the years, the Bank has conducted many joint research, outreach and training activities with these agencies.

To help fulfill its mandate, ITD launched a comprehensive research program aimed at providing the basis for informed policy recommendations and decisions. The Division produced numerous policy-relevant studies on a broad range of trade and regional integration issues, including market access negotiations (tariff, non-tariff measures and rules of origin); analysis of major trade agreements (e.g., FTAA, Mercosur bilateral free trade agreements); economic impact of trade liberalization and regional integration (computable general equilibrium modeling and sector studies); the interplay between regional and multilateral trade negotiations; regional cooperation; and regional public goods.

A Revitalized field-based Integration Institute. In 1995, the Bank gave INTAL additional resources to support its trade and integration-related work in the region.

[8] ITD has represented the IDB on the Tripartite Committee of Technical Support to the FTAA process, comprising the IDB, the OAS and ECLAC.

Since then, ITD and INTAL have partnered on a wide variety of activities and initiatives supporting trade in the region, combining ITD's technical expertise with INTAL's field experience, operational skills and know-how in the areas of training, publications, and outreach. In 1997, INTAL began to collaborate with the WTO in the organization of training courses for trade negotiators in the region. To date, the two institutions have jointly organized over 100 training events in LAC countries, often with direct participation by the Bank's Trade Division. INTAL has also been instrumental in executing regional projects and disseminating Bank research on trade and integration-related issues.

New IDB Institutional Strategy. Since global economic conditions and the participation of the region in the globalization process have substantially changed, the Bank faces new significant opportunities and challenges. In order to better serve the region, the Bank started in 2006 a process of realignment. The realignment has two main objectives: i) increase the development effectiveness of Bank activities by means of a greater country focus, deeper sector expertise and improved management based on risk management and attainment of results; and ii) increase organizational efficiency through better corporate integration of operations and scaling up the various functions. The vision of the Bank as the region's partner in development is one that: (i) facilitates poverty reduction and reduction of inequality by promoting growth and supporting sustainable development; (ii) fosters social cohesion by creating opportunities for the majority; (iii) supports private sector development and job creation; and (iv) furthers regional integration.

Under the Bank's new structure, the **Integration and Trade Sector Department** (INT) will lead the Bank's integration and trade agenda and provide technical support to INTAL. The Trade and Integration sector Department will focus, among others, on the following areas of knowledge: general integration and trade sector, trade facilitation, customs, standards, trade capacity building, export promotion and foreign investment attraction, global productive chains, trade agreements (negotiation, implementation and adjustment), regional integration and cooperation, and policy coordination. Through the Integration and Trade Sector Department, the Bank is in an excellent position to provide to the countries of the region the technical and financial assistance needed to successfully put the Aid for Trade agenda into motion. Indeed, the renewed mandate to support the countries of the region in their efforts to adapt to a more open trading environment is closely aligned with the wide scope of the Aid for Trade initiative.

3.2 Integrating trade into the Bank's programming process

Beyond building institutional capacity in the area of trade, the Bank has made efforts to integrate trade more strongly into its policy dialogue with governments and the programming of its regional and country-specific operations. This has required attention to the various stages of the programming process, and the provision of specific trade-related inputs in each stage. The Bank's programming process is increasingly based on technical analysis. This feeds into policy dialogue with governments and other relevant partners, which, in turn, informs the development of a Bank strategy and related project pipeline. This is then followed by the design and implementation of specific interventions. The process is circular in that lessons learned from programming and the delivery of development finance feed into new technical analysis and policy dialogue. The Bank conducts two types of programming: regional and national, with the latter proving to be the more challenging in terms of integrating trade into the various stages of the process.

Regional Programming focuses on the four main integration groups within LAC: the Andean Community, Caribbean Community (CARICOM), Central American Common Market, and Mercosur. Approximately every five years, the Bank prepares new strategies for support to regional integration in each of the four groups. Because of the importance of trade in these integration processes, and the multiple initiatives of regional cooperation in this area among LAC countries, trade has always dominated the Bank's regional strategies. In coordination with the operational departments, the Integration and Regional Programs Department undertakes diagnostic studies to identify the key challenges in each sub-regional integration process, as well as in the group's trade integration with the rest of the world, and on the basis of this assessment proposes priority areas for Bank support. Policy dialogue with regional secretariats, national authorities and relevant non-state actors is crucial throughout the process. The regional strategy facilitates the formulation of regional programs and activities, which are then implemented mainly through grants and direct non-financial support. Regional secretariats and other regional agencies often act as executing units for these programs, and over the years the IDB has developed close working relationships with them. Lending for regional programs is very limited owing to the difficulties in securing appropriate guarantees for multi-country loans.

National Programming is the Bank's main programming instrument. It follows a similar process as regional programming, but the focus is not necessarily on trade. Rather, trade is one of several issues analyzed in the preparation of the Bank's country strategies. The challenge of mainstreaming trade into national programming has been three-fold: first, to support Bank country teams in their efforts to focus more on trade integration in their diagnostic work; second, greater emphasis is needed on trade issues in the Bank's policy dialogue with governments and relevant non-state actors; and third, subsequent to approval of country strategies, trade specialists must provide technical support to the Bank's operational units during the development and implementation of trade-related operations. To address these challenges, ITD began in the late 1990s to provide specific inputs to the national programming process. Over time, these contributions have evolved into comprehensive trade and integration sector studies (or Diagnostic Trade and Integration Studies, DTIS) that serve as a basis for policy dialogue and feed into the formulation of country strategies. Trade specialists from the Bank have increasingly participated alongside country teams in the Bank's high-level, closed-door policy discussions (*encerronas*) with newly elected governments in the region. ITD has also assigned some of its trade specialists to work exclusively on operations, helping the Bank to translate technical expertise into operational benefits for its clients.

Efforts to integrate trade into national programming have already yielded results. Whereas country strategies produced by the Bank in the mid-1990s contained few specific references to trade, today many strategies devote significant attention to trade and global market integration and to strengthening of related institutions. This also reflects the fact that trade is increasingly mainstreamed into the national development agendas of the Bank's client countries. Requests for trade-related

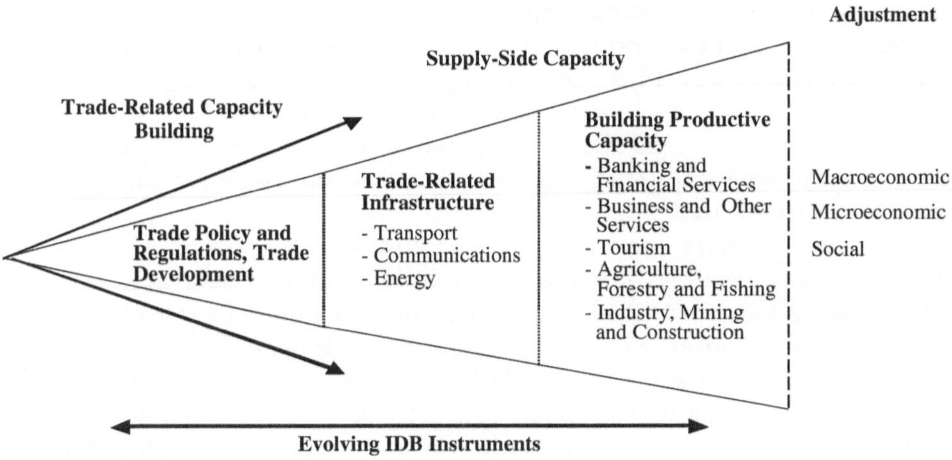

Figure 10.1. Aid for Trade: The Expanding Agenda. (*Source:* IDB adaptation of figure presented in OECD (2006).)

assistance have increased as a result, and the Bank has used both existing and new instruments to respond to this growing demand.

3.3 Adapting the Bank's instruments to a more complex trade agenda

Aid for Trade is not new for the IDB: many of the Bank's traditional lending instruments were designed to support the very elements of what is today perceived as the broader Aid for Trade agenda, including infrastructure development (transport, energy and communications) and strengthening of countries' productive capacities. The Bank also has a long track record of providing adjustment-related lending, some of which has been directly related to trade. What was new in the 1990s was that the Bank began to build institutional capacity and deepen its operational support in the area of trade-related capacity building (Figure 10.1). The Bank also began to explore ways of better linking the various components of trade-related assistance (capacity building, supply-side development and adjustment), and to design new grant and lending instruments to this effect.[9]

Traditional Financial and Non-Financial Support. During the 1990s, the IDB relied on existing lending and grant instruments to deliver trade-related assistance. The Bank's most important *lending instruments*, investment and policy-based loans, continue to finance the vast majority of the Bank's operational activities in LAC, including operations to improve *trade-related infrastructure and supply-side capacities*. Investment loans are the Bank's most widely used lending instrument and span the whole range of the expanded Aid for Trade agenda.[10] Policy-based loans

[9] The section provides a broad overview of the Bank's trade-related operations; specific projects are mentioned only for illustrative purposes.

[10] Examples of such loans include Productivity Support and Development of New Livestock Products in Uruguay (US$19.8 million), Improvement of the Competitiveness of Tourism in Argentina (US$56 million), SIEPAC Central American Electric Interconnection (US$50 million), Rural Roads National Program II in Paraguay (US$89.5 million), Northern Coastal Highway Improvement in Jamaica

disburse against the implementation of agreed policy changes.[11] While most loans are non-concessional, some are provided on a concessional basis from the Bank's Fund for Special Operations (FSO). Only five countries – Bolivia, Guyana, Haiti, Honduras and Nicaragua – have access to this type of financing.[12] The Bank lends to both the public and private sector. The latter operations are managed by the Bank's Private Sector Department (PRI) and its sister organization, the Inter-American Investment Corporation (IIC).[13]

Grants and non-financial support were the main instruments for the Bank's assistance to *trade-related capacity building* during this period. Grant funding came from the FSO and the various trust funds managed by the Bank on behalf of its non-borrowing member countries. None of these funds was dedicated exclusively to trade. The Multilateral Investment Fund (MIF), established in 1993 and administered by the IDB, focused its assistance on private sector development, using both grant and investment mechanisms to undertake small, targeted development projects to build the capabilities and skill standards of the workforce, broaden the economic participation of smaller enterprises, and strengthen the environment for doing business – but the connection to trade, and trade policy, was still precarious. During the 1990s, the Bank moreover maintained a limited Export Finance Program, which, however, was terminated in 2001 amidst calls for alternative, more efficient mechanisms to address the continuing and growing need for trade finance in the region. Assistance provided directly by the Bank through its administrative budget (defined as non-financial support) was delivered mainly through the Bank's Trade Division and INTAL.

The majority of trade-related capacity building programs funded during this period were regional projects. The Bank's main instrument for regional grant projects is the *Regional Technical Cooperation (RTC) Program*, which uses both FSO and trust fund resources to finance a wide range of initiatives that span the entire Aid for Trade agenda, including supply-side capacity and adjustment. In the area of trade-related capacity building, RTC projects and non-financial support were used to finance the Bank's significant support to the FTAA process.[14] The Bank also

(US$85 million), Program for Institutional Strengthening of the Tax and Customs Administration in Nicaragua (US$12.5 million) and Modernization of the National Customs Bureau in Uruguay (US$1.1 million).

11 The Bank has developed a number of policy-based loans to help strengthen the institutions in charge of competitiveness and trade negotiations, simplify trade and customs procedures, enhance business and labor productivity, and improve the regulatory framework for the provision of infrastructure services. An example of a PBL is the Peru Competitiveness Reform Program (US$300 million), which is based on three areas of action: (i) long-term approach to addressing and resolving impediments to competitiveness; (ii) policy and institutional reform to improve the climate for private sector investment as well as reduce costs and improve efficiency at the enterprise level; and (iii) public-private cooperation activities at the local level through the development of clusters.

12 The FSO has US$9.8 billion in paid-in contributions from all Bank member states. The net income of the FSO enables the IDB to approve on average over US$400 million per year in grants and concessional lending.

13 Examples of PRI projects include support to Ecuador's Quito International Airport (US$610 million) that includes the construction of a connector road to the new airport and the Inter-oceanic highway, and the development of a free trade zone in the area; and six highway concession projects in Brazil since 1996 (nearly US$1.7 billion) as part of the IDB contribution to Brazil's highway concession program.

14 RTC projects financed the FTAA Secretariat and the Bank's technical support to three of nine FTAA negotiating groups. Further technical support to the process was provided directly by the Bank's Trade

provided grant funding for a number of sub-regional trade initiatives.[15] The Bank moreover stepped up its non-financial support in the areas of policy research, technical workshops, and other outreach activities. Many of these initiatives were also regional in nature.

New instruments. As LAC demands for trade-related assistance increased, it became clear that new instruments were needed to respond rapidly and efficiently to those demands. More funding was needed for policy research, policy dialogue and direct assistance to governments. Grant funding alone was not adequate to meet the demands, and the Bank's existing loan instruments were tailored more toward large-scale investments (requiring a substantial preparation process) than to urgent needs for technical cooperation to assist in ongoing negotiations and implementation of trade agreements. The region's private sector also needed more targeted assistance to cope with a rapidly changing external environment. Starting in 2000, therefore, the Bank developed a number of new instruments and mechanisms to strengthen its trade-related assistance. Some are designed for national interventions, while others focus on regional support; several instruments can cover both types of intervention. Seven are outlined below:

i. Starting in 2000, the Bank instituted a regular **Regional Policy Dialogue** on trade as part of a broader program that also includes other thematic areas. The objective was to create a trade forum or network through which LAC countries could share experiences, learn about practices outside the region, and explore opportunities for regional cooperation in areas related to trade. The regional policy dialogue meetings bring together vice-ministers and other senior trade officials from LAC countries to explore pressing trade issues, based on a previously-agreed agenda and technical work prepared by the Bank.[16]
ii. In 2000, the IDB created a **Trade Sector Facility** that provides fast track approval for ordinary or concessional loans up to US$5 million to strengthen the capacity of trade ministries and other trade-related institutions to formulate, negotiate and implement trade policy. By 2007, ten of the Bank's borrowing member countries had accessed the facility, with approved funds totaling US$46.6 million.[17]

Division; meanwhile, a MIF grant financed implementation of customs-related business facilitation measures agreed by the countries in 1999.

15 In the Andean Community, for example, the Bank financed several border development initiatives, while in CARICOM it supported the creation and operation of the Caribbean Regional Negotiating Machinery (CRNM) and implementation of member states' Uruguay Round commitments. In Central America, the Bank provided assistance in such areas as services trade liberalization and customs. In Mercosur, the Bank supported institutional strengthening of the Mercosur Secretariat, as well as the building of a computable general equilibrium model to measure the impact of various trade liberalization scenarios on the group's economies.

16 The last two regional meetings focused on the negotiating agenda for the December 2005 WTO Hong Kong ministerial meeting and on macroeconomic implications of trade liberalization, respectively, while sub-regional meetings have covered such issues as bilateral negotiations with the United States and special and differential treatment.

17 The ten countries are: Bolivia, Chile, Dominican Republic, Ecuador, Guatemala, Nicaragua, Panama, Peru, Suriname and Trinidad and Tobago. Although each project is tailored to the specific needs of the client, these operations typically comprise the following components: (i) institutional reform to improve trade policymaking; (ii) implementation of effective information and communications systems for the Ministry of Trade and other trade-related agencies; (iii) technical support to negotiations

iii. In 2002, MIF launched its **Facilitation of International Trade and Investment** project cluster, the aim of which is to foster greater participation of smaller enterprises in international trade and investment. Projects in this cluster support trade facilitation activities related to customs reform, technical standards and certification, as well as strengthening the private sector's participation in the formulation of trade policy. Many projects are regional, rather than national in scope. As of 2007, the MIF had approved seventeen grant projects under the cluster, with a total contribution of US$28.2 million.[18] The cluster is supported by technical experts who regularly visit projects, facilitate project implementation, and foster the sharing of experiences among beneficiary agencies.

iv. In 2002, the Bank created the **Special Initiative on Trade and Integration**, providing additional funding to the Trade Division over a four-year period (2003–2006). The aim was to (i) strengthen the Bank's capacity to influence the policy debate on trade and integration; (ii) provide technical support to governments, particularly in response to urgent, time-sensitive requests; and (iii) conduct more public outreach.[19]

v. In 2003, responding to growing needs for adjustment-related assistance, the Bank established a **Lending Program for Trade, Integration and Competitiveness**, which allows a country to combine components of the Bank's policy-based, investment and technical assistance lending into a single loan operation to address the broader range of sectoral adjustments that it must make in the transition to freer trade. This program, coupled with the availability of loans focused on competitiveness, provides support for all the critical issues in the transition to free trade, including infrastructure, labor market adjustment, worker re-training, rural agriculture, small and medium enterprise development, tax reform, customs modernization, and trade-related capacity building.[20]

vi. In 2003, the **International Trade Finance Reactivation Program** (TFRP) was approved, allowing the Bank to commit up to US$1 billion for projects, programs and other actions aimed at supporting the availability of trade finance in LAC countries. Initially created on a two-year trial basis, the program was made permanent in 2005. The Bank's private sector department, PRI, has developed several instruments to implement the TFRP. In 2005, it launched one such instrument, the Trade Finance Facilitation Program (TFFP). Under the TFFP,

and implementation of trade agreements, and training in all areas related to trade; (iv) sector-specific support in such areas as agriculture, sanitary and phytosanitary standards and intellectual property rights; (v) modernization of export promotion and investment attraction agencies; and (vi) support for outreach activities and stakeholder consultations.

18 Project examples include a US$1.1 million regional grant to support the private sector's participation in CARICOM's external trade negotiations; a US$2.48 million grant to support small rural producers in Argentina in overcoming technical barriers to trade; and a US$2.14 million regional grant to raise awareness and facilitate application of sanitary and phytosanitary standards in Mesoamerica.

19 The Special Initiative has allowed the Bank to expand its trade-related research, technical assistance and outreach activities substantially. For example, it has enabled the Bank to provide direct support to Central American and Andean countries in developing and implementing national action plans for trade-related capacity building. It has also facilitated the Bank's policy research into crucial areas such as rules of origin; asymmetries and distributional effects related to trade liberalization, and the implications for LAC of China's emergence as a major trading power. Finally, it has helped expand the Bank's outreach activities, for example by funding orientation workshops on trade for parliamentarians and civil society.

20 Costa Rica was the first to develop a multi-sector loan under the program, comprising foreign trade, science and technology and rural roads rehabilitation. The US$116.8 million investment loan was approved in 2005.

the IDB extends guarantees to cover risks associated with trade-related instruments (e.g., letters of credit, documentary collections, promissory notes) issued by banks in the financing of international trade transactions.[21] The Bank has also approved several loans to investment funds that provide trade financing to under-served exporters and importers in the region.

vii. Bilateral donors have increasingly channeled trade-related assistance through the IDB. The **IDB-Canada Trade Fund**, established in 2003, provides grants to relevant ministries or regional agencies to support trade-related capacity building programs agreed by LAC countries under the FTAA Hemispheric Cooperation Program. The Fund has expanded the Bank's possibilities of offering grant assistance at the national level. So far, ten countries and one regional agency have accessed the fund, for total financing of CAN$1.65 million (US$1.5 million). The **Trade and Poverty Trust Fund**, established in 2005 as a multi-donor trust fund from the United Kingdom (DFID), supports Bank efforts to respond to increased demands for analysis of the distributional effects of trade integration, as well as the formulation and implementation of strategies, policies and instruments aimed at enhancing the impact of trade integration on the poor.

Beyond specifically trade-related instruments, several broader initiatives launched by the IDB in recent years support the institution's efforts to deliver Aid for Trade more effectively. Noteworthy are three infrastructure initiatives aimed specifically at supporting the region's intra-regional and global integration.

i. **Initiative for the Integration of Regional Infrastructure in South America** (IIRSA). Launched in 2000, IIRSA supports the development and integration of energy, transport and telecommunications infrastructure across twelve South American countries to facilitate trade integration both intra-regionally and with the rest of the world. The IDB, along with the Andean Development Corporation (Corporación Andina de Fomento, CAF) and the Financial Fund for the Development of the River Plate Basin (Fondo Financiero para el Desarrollo de la Cuenca de Plata, FONPLATA) forms part of IIRSA's technical coordination committee, which provides support to countries in all IIRSA-related topics. IIRSA has developed physical infrastructure requirements for eight integration hubs in the region, and identified 335 related projects with an estimated value of US$37.5 billion.[22] From this portfolio, governments have selected thirty-one additional priority projects worth US$5.9 billion for implementation over the next five years.[23] Under the IIRSA initiative, the IDB has so far financed seven strategic infrastructure projects for a combined value of US$515 million. In 2005, moreover, the IDB created a US$20 million fund for the Financing of Technical Cooperation Operations for Regional Infrastructure Integration Initiatives under IIRSA.

[21] The TFFP currently comprises a network of over sixty confirming banks belonging to twenty-six different international banking groups in twenty countries, and eleven issuing banks in seven LAC countries with over US$270 million in approved credit lines. To date, the IDB has issued guarantees for over US$30 million in support of approximately fifty international trade transactions totaling over US$66 million.

[22] To date, twenty-nine projects with an estimated value of US$3.8 billion have been approved or are under financial planning by IDB-CAF-FONPLATA.

[23] One example of an initiative directly related to trade is the four-country project to pave the Carmelo Peralta-Loma Plata route and build the Carmelo Peralta-Porto Murtinho bridge, which will interconnect productive areas in Chile, Bolivia, Brazil and Paraguay and ensure access for isolated, landlocked regions to Pacific ports.

ii. The **Puebla-Panama Plan (PPP)**, launched in 2001, seeks to improve the trade, growth, and economic development potential of southern Mexico and Central America. The PPP focuses on a number of areas, including trade facilitation, infrastructure development (roads, energy, telecommunications), and tourism services. The core PPP structure is comprised of the IDB, the Central American Bank for Economic Integration (CABEI), and ECLAC, as well as national governments. IDB acts as financial coordinator of the program and is also a member of its technical committee. Envisioned as a multi-billion, multi-year program with stated goals until 2020, the PPP is financed by contributions from participating countries, the private sector, and bilateral and multilateral donors, including the IDB.[24]
iii. The Bank approved a new US$20 million **Infrastructure Project Preparation Fund** (InfraFund) in early 2006. The fund, which is not exclusive to either IIRSA or the PPP, supports the preparation of pre-investment studies (e.g., financial and environmental assessment) for infrastructure projects.
iv. The Bank has also supported improved provision of infrastructure services for trade with technical cooperation grants in areas such as port security, institutional strengthening of port authorities, and strengthening of border crossing logistics.

The Bank's **Business Climate Initiative (BCI)**, launched in 2003, aims to identify and then reduce or eliminate critical barriers to growth, promoting the expansion of private sector activities through legal and regulatory changes in the institutions and policies that affect the investment climate. The BCI seeks to identify areas where there is consensus among public officials and private business leaders that significant barriers to private sector-led growth exist, and to define priority actions to address those barriers. The initiative has three phases: (i) signature of an aide-memoire between the IDB and the government reaffirming the importance of a sound environment for private sector development, and defining the scope of action for identifying the appropriate reform agenda and support program; (ii) diagnostic assessment based on consultations with a broad range of stakeholders to identify issues that should be addressed as a matter of priority to maximize the impact of any policy action on the country's business climate; and (iii) business climate reform financing. Once identified in the country strategies, the specific action plans are then supported through the IDB's operational programs.

Not exclusively linked to trade, but important for its potential to facilitate larger-scale regional interventions, is the Bank's new **Regional Public Goods** Initiative, launched in 2004. This initiative aims to support the development of goods, services, rules systems or policy regimes that generate shared benefits for the participating countries as a result of cooperation and collective action by those countries. The Bank provides non-reimbursable resources of up to US$10 million a year to finance demand-driven projects that develop regional public goods in LAC. Based on a competitive selection process, the IDB approved US$8.9 million in grants in 2005 and in 2006 had a pipeline of eleven projects for twenty-three borrowing member countries in areas such as environmental protection, education, modernization of the state, financial markets, information and communication technologies,

[24] Two recent IDB operations are a US$50 million loan to Honduras and two loans for a total of US$80 million to Nicaragua in 2004 to support PPP-related road projects.

agriculture, health, and social development. The Bank has already approved several trade-related projects under this initiative, and there is good potential for developing more such projects in the future. Importantly, this instrument could be used to provide seed money and as an incentive for countries to cooperate around larger regional projects that also require lending for the implementation of national components.

3.4 Addressing future challenges in trade-related assistance

A Regional Development Bank Positioned to Deliver Aid For Trade. As the above demonstrates, both the Bank's institutional structure and its support for trade-related assistance have evolved over time to meet growing demand in LAC countries, for which global trade integration is emerging as a priority. Historically a supplier of technical and financial assistance to what are perceived today as the broader components of the Aid for Trade agenda, the Bank has also established a solid track record in the delivery of assistance for trade-related capacity building. The combination of a critical mass of technical expertise in trade-related issues, operational know-how to deliver development assistance, and a presence in each country of the region, along with a wide representation of donors in its shareholding structure, put the Bank in a good position to contribute to the delivery of trade-related assistance to LAC.

A "New Lending Framework" to Improve Development Effectiveness. In 2005, the IDB adopted a New Lending Framework (NLF) to support the region's need for more effective spending and higher returns on investment within the context of narrowing fiscal space. The NLF favors a programmatic (rather than individual project) approach to lending, more flexibility in terms of lending criteria, increased reliance on national fiduciary and evaluation systems, and greater focus on results. The NLF includes the use of Sector-wide Approaches (SWAps), new lending instruments such as programmatic policy-based loans (PBLs) and performance-driven loans (PDLs), and a wide range of other measures to make lending more flexible and execution of projects more efficient.[25] In 2006, moreover, the Bank relaxed its conditions for lending to the private sector. Several elements of the NLF may prove to be critical for delivering trade-related assistance more effectively.

A Dynamic Institution Aligned with Client Needs. Along with upgrading its operational instruments and procedures, the Bank is currently engaged in a process of institutional realignment to increase its effectiveness in the delivery of development finance. With Bank operations now covering the whole range of trade-related assistance, and using many different instruments to deliver such assistance, the

[25] A *Sector-wide Approach* (SWAp) can be supported by any type of investment loan. In a SWAp, all development partners involved in a sector collaborate to support a single government-led sector policy and expenditure program, relying increasingly on government procedures to disburse and account for all funds. A *programmatic policy-based loan* comprises a series of individual operations set within a medium-term framework of reform, approved on a phased basis to support a country's reform program, with specific triggers for moving from one operation to the next. A *performance-driven loan* is an investment loan that disburses once the program's actual developmental results or outcomes are achieved and after the Bank has verified the expenditures incurred by the borrower to reach the outcomes.

challenge is to ensure that all interventions are closely linked with and complement each other, and that the region's trade concerns are effectively addressed in all areas of Bank intervention, and through all available instruments. The Bank's proven capacity to adapt to changing demands in its borrowing member countries, its New Lending Framework, and its long-established presence in the region provide good tools for addressing this challenge. So do the lessons learned from its past experience in providing trade-related assistance.

4 Lessons learned and gaps in the delivery of Aid for Trade

4.1 Recognizing the context and defining the scope of assistance

The ultimate objective of Aid for Trade is broad-based economic growth and development. Achieving this outcome requires, first, recognizing the context in which such aid is being delivered, particularly if it involves further trade liberalization as envisaged by the Doha Development Agenda or other trade negotiations. While trade has assumed a much more prominent place in the public debate and on the policy agenda of LAC governments, trade is not yet sufficiently mainstreamed into national development agendas in the region. Past experience has moreover shown that to sustain support for trade liberalization, adequate attention must be paid to supply-side capacity and adjustment issues in conjunction with future liberalization efforts. Finally, most LAC countries are highly indebted and face serious fiscal constraints. All this has implications for what kind of trade-related assistance LAC countries now need, and how it should be delivered.

Demand for traditional trade-related capacity building continues to be acute in many LAC countries, but there is also a growing need for trade-related assistance to address the broader Aid for Trade agenda. In particular, such assistance should increasingly help countries eliminate supply-side constraints that inhibit them from realizing the opportunities of trade liberalization and that weaken their capacity to respond efficiently to trade-related adjustment shocks.[26] The IDB has provided such assistance for decades both at the national and regional level, but is now making efforts to link it more effectively with countries' trade agendas. At the same time, trade-related assistance must seek to address the distributional effects of liberalization and the problems of asymmetry, which, if left unsolved, can intensify as a result of liberalization. Aid for Trade could make an important contribution toward changing attitudes about trade liberalization and mitigating the risk of a backlash against further trade reform in LAC.

4.2 Delivering Aid for Trade: experiences and lessons learned

Technical Analysis and Diagnostic Work. The best way to identify a country's trade-related needs is through comprehensive and broad-based technical analysis. The preparation of Diagnostic Trade Integration Studies (DTIS) presents several challenges. First, developing countries often lack the capacity for doing their own

[26] Overcoming supply-side constraints requires both physical investments and regulatory reform. In the area of infrastructure, for example, it is important not only to focus on building roads, ports or communications systems, but also on related policy and regulatory improvements. For trade-related infrastructure, it is moreover important to address questions of policy consistency across countries, and to prioritize cross-border linkages.

diagnostic work, and their action plans tend to be somewhat narrow, focusing on short-term capacity building rather than *considering trade challenges within a broader, long-term development perspective*. Lack of sufficient data and adequate methodologies for preparation of DTIS often contribute to this outcome. Second, and as a consequence of the above, trade and integration are often supply-driven, prepared by international financial institutions (IFI) or other development agencies. Here, however, is another challenge in that staff, time and budget constraints in these agencies may prevent them from conducting the kind of in-depth analysis that is needed to prepare a comprehensive diagnostic study. Effective coordination in the preparation of analytical work, both at the country level (inter-agency) and within the development agency (inter-departmental) is crucial to ensure that trade strategies encompass all relevant sectors and aspects of the economy. This, too, may present a challenge. The way forward is to support the preparation of diagnostic studies that are demand-driven, have local ownership, and are effectively integrated into national development plans.

Policy Dialogue and Programming. Analytical work feeds into policy dialogue with governments and other relevant stakeholders. Here, the challenge is to *move beyond traditional constituencies in the trade community* to target decision-makers in the country more broadly. It is important to expand dialogue on trade issues with finance and planning ministries, who have crucial responsibilities in deciding future macroeconomic and development policy and prioritize funding requests for external assistance. Ideally, policy dialogue should encompass all relevant ministries (for example finance, planning, trade, and agriculture) as well as the legislative branch of government (Congress, Parliament), the private sector, and other important civil society groups, including labor. Without such dialogue, trade strategies run the risk of being unbalanced and unsustainable (because of insufficient political support and lack of "ownership").

Broad-based dialogue is also necessary to *mainstream trade into national development agendas*. Trade ministries are often aware of the significant challenges that lie ahead, but finance or planning ministries may be less attuned to the specifics of those challenges given their much broader policy mandates. As a result, they may undervalue the importance of trade for economic development, and of well-functioning institutions for trade development. Continued efforts to integrate trade into country dialogue and programming are urgently needed.

Identification and design of operations. For IFIs and other development agencies, one important challenge in the design of operations is to ensure efficient coordination between staff engaged in strategy and policy formulation on trade for a specific beneficiary country or region, and the operational staff that will design and help implement programs in the field. In other words, it is important to establish a close working relationship or *link between "trade practitioners" and "aid practitioners"* in the identification, design and development of trade-related assistance. The Bank has made efforts in recent years to strengthen this link, aiming to ensure that policy research feeds seamlessly into operational support.

Implementation. One challenge related to the implementation of trade-related operations is the *limited absorptive capacity* of local executing or "beneficiary" agencies in LAC, some of which execute multiple donor projects at the same time. Donor coordination can go some way toward easing the pressure on these agencies, but capacity problems will remain a serious issue for the foreseeable future, particularly in the region's smaller and/or poorer countries. Trade ministries and other relevant agencies in these countries are often inadequately staffed and too weak to implement operations without outside technical and administrative assistance.

To help countries execute projects, donors often establish specific project implementation units in trade agencies, staffed by consultants. The availability of a broad pool of international experts who can assist in implementation is crucial to achieving beneficial outcomes. However, it has sometimes been difficult to attract such expertise, particularly for longer-term assignments in the region; language has also been an issue. The problem of limited implementation capacity could become even more pronounced with the planned increase in Aid for Trade. There is thus urgent need to *build local expertise in all areas of trade* as a first step in expanding such aid. This is also crucial to ensure the consolidation and sustainability of Aid for Trade development outcomes over the long term.

In terms of the Bank's own processes, it is worth noting that IDB operations, similar to those of other IFIs, are developed by staff in headquarters and, once approved, are administered by field-based staff. In the IDB, trade specialists from headquarters provide regular advice on the technical aspects of implementation, but field office staff is in day-to-day contact with local executing agencies. The *presence of field offices* in each of the IDB's borrowing member countries provides a good opportunity for the Bank to participate in the delivery of expanded Aid for Trade flows. Their responsibility in the administration of such flows also highlights the importance of further developing technical expertise on trade in these offices, and of ensuring effective coordination between headquarters and field offices.

Instruments for delivering Aid for Trade. As mentioned earlier, most LAC countries are highly indebted and face serious fiscal constraints. This places limits on how much they can borrow to facilitate trade integration and adjustment.[27] In such a context, the *limited availability of grant funding for trade-related assistance to middle-income countries is a serious challenge*. In the IDB, for example, 21 of the 26 borrowing member countries have no access to Bank grant funding beyond trust fund, MIF and regional FSO resources, which are scarce. The Bank's specialized trust funds for trade-related assistance have emerged as important instruments for channeling resources to countries engaged in trade reform; expanding their scope could help LAC countries overcome their binding financial constraints in addressing trade-related adjustment.

Grant funding is not only limited, but often also programmed on an annual basis. This makes it difficult to *support programmatic, long-term approaches to trade-related assistance*. The scarcity of grant funding also limits the scope of activities that can be undertaken. There has been a significant amount of support for short-term training in LAC countries, perhaps crowding out other important trade-related priorities. Coordination among donors has not always been optimal and

[27] The Caribbean countries are a good example of this dilemma: they have relatively high per capita income levels, but their high debt ratios limit the amount of borrowing they can do. These countries, nevertheless, are highly vulnerable to further multilateral trade liberalization and are struggling with the consequences of preference erosion in their main export markets.

short-term training also raises the question about the sustainability of its outcome. Grant funding is sometimes tied to specific nationality requirements for consultants, country eligibility criteria, and thematic priorities, limiting the flexibility of its use. Grant funding, of course, must also grapple with the question of ownership – some counterpart funding may be warranted to ensure that beneficiary countries have sufficient incentives to work toward optimal outcomes of such aid.

As regards specific lending instruments, one lesson learned is that *a multi-sector approach to trade-related assistance is crucial*. Hybrid programs covering multiple sectors and combining multiple lending instruments and executing agencies have all the requisites for addressing the complexity of the Aid for Trade agenda. They can, however, be difficult to design, implement, monitor and evaluate. Meanwhile, *sector-wide interventions involving multiple donors could provide significant benefits* to a country if implemented effectively (through SWAps or similar mechanisms). They could also provide a vehicle through which to combine loans with technical assistance grants. The grant element could be used for purposes of strengthening local execution capacity, which, as noted above, has been a serious challenge in some LAC countries. SWAps, meanwhile, present their own challenges in terms of donor coordination and attribution of development outcomes.

There is a clear *gap in financing for large-scale regional interventions*, particularly those involving the public sector. The Bank has a lot of experience working with LAC governments at the regional and sub-regional level, but its regional interventions are necessarily small owing to the scarcity of funding for such programs. The current level of grant funding that is available to LAC countries cannot cover the cost of large-scale regional infrastructure or public goods initiatives in the region, and lending instruments continue to focus almost exclusively on national interventions. It may be worthwhile for development banks to explore the possibility of combining national loans with a regional grant component that provides incentives for countries to approach problems from a regional perspective. To a certain extent, the Bank's IIRSA experience suggests that regional infrastructure projects can be financed through separate national projects, but perhaps the provision of grant funding could facilitate greater use of such regional approaches. The Bank's Regional Public Goods Initiative, by providing seed money for the development of new regional public goods, presents one possibility to foster greater use of regional approaches in the delivery of Aid for Trade. At the national level, a combination of grant and loan financing could be used to lower the effective cost of borrowing for countries.

Finally, in terms of instruments, the Bank's experience also points to the *need for a flexible "rapid response" facility* to address short-term, urgent requests from governments. When countries are already negotiating, and need urgent technical assistance within a week or two, there is little time to develop even a small grant-financed project. Flexible funds would also allow timely identification and execution of pilot projects that could subsequently be scaled up and replicated in other countries or regions. To date, the Bank has sought to address urgent, very time-sensitive requests through deployment of its own staff and administrative budget resources.

Monitoring and Evaluation. There is much need to strengthen this aspect of Aid for Trade delivery. In the current context of serious fiscal constraints, many LAC countries are reluctant to borrow for projects that do not have an immediate or easily measurable development outcome. However, *measuring outcome is very difficult in trade-related assistance*, particularly assistance related to institutional strengthening and capacity building. This partly owes to the difficulty of establishing baseline indicators for measuring progress in trade-related assistance that is not related to physical infrastructure or investment. It also owes to the difficulty of establishing attribution in countries where many donors are involved in trade-related assistance.

One area where donor coordination could be very effective would be in the development of well-designed *results-based frameworks for trade-related assistance*. A "Results Framework" comprises goals, objectives, baseline indicators, target indicators, and an assessment of identified risks and mitigation efforts. Common frameworks, agreed and used across IFIs and donor agencies for the various types of trade-related assistance (ranging from training and institutional reform in trade ministries, to improved customs procedures, export promotion, infrastructure development, business development and adjustment efforts) would strengthen monitoring and evaluation capacities in individual institutions, and would also make it easier to monitor trade-related assistance at the regional and global level.

Role of the Private Sector. The private sector should play an active role in identifying countries' trade-related needs and in implementing adequate responses. The Bank has been active in this area with its MIF project cluster and Trade Finance Facilitation Program. In 2006, moreover, the Bank relaxed its conditions for lending to the private sector. Previously, such lending was limited to infrastructure, capital markets and trade finance. The Bank can now lend to private companies in any sector, and can also support public-private partnerships, where public sector involvement can be at both the national and sub-national level. This expanded mandate could substantially strengthen the Bank's role in supporting Aid for Trade, particularly as it relates to infrastructure and supply-side capacity.

In an effort to expand and better coordinate its support to private sector development in LAC, the Bank has recently launched the *preparation of private sector development strategies* for all its countries. These strategies, which feed into the Bank's country programming, guide the activities of the Bank's public and private sector lending departments and seek to provide a more coordinated approach to the Bank's support to the private sector. One challenge in the area of trade is that private sector agents in many LAC countries lack awareness of the benefits and consequences of trade liberalization. Particularly in the smaller countries of the region, they are often inadequately informed about public sector initiatives in the area of trade, and have little influence on the development of national trade policy. *Outreach activities and awareness building* for the private sector are therefore important activities that should be covered in trade-related assistance. This would naturally lead to improved capacity for preparing private sector needs assessments in the area of trade.

Donor coordination. Donor coordination in the delivery of Aid for Trade must be strengthened to *avoid duplication of efforts, streamline reporting requirements for executing agencies and facilitate greater use of SWAps*. The IDB has taken a number of steps to coordinate its trade-related assistance, not least in conjunction with the FTAA Hemispheric Cooperation Program and the donor meetings organized during the bilateral trade negotiations between the United States and Central American and Andean countries. In delivering Aid for Trade, donors should adhere to the principles outlined in the 2005 Paris Declaration on Aid Effectiveness – ownership, harmonization, alignment, managing for results, and mutual accountability. These principles are particularly relevant in view of the trade challenges outlined above and the planned expansion of Aid for Trade in the future.

5 Looking ahead: LAC, Aid for Trade, and the IDB

One of the most important lessons learned by the IDB in its efforts to supply trade-related assistance to its borrowing member countries is that there is overwhelming need for such assistance in LAC. Despite being mostly middle-income, LAC countries face serious resource constraints that have created significant gaps in their capacity to respond to trade-related challenges and to exploit the opportunities of more open markets. Aid for Trade, appropriately tailored to their more advanced levels of economic development (relative to other developing regions) could make an important contribution toward closing those gaps.

In the past decade, the IDB has made significant efforts to align its institutional structure, technical expertise and financial and non-financial instruments with client needs in the area of trade. It has established a solid reputation for the delivery of trade-related assistance to LAC countries and can draw on valuable lessons learned in designing its future interventions in this area. Along with new instruments for trade-related assistance, the Bank has also added greater flexibility to its overall lending process, making it easier and faster for countries to access its resources. Perhaps most importantly, working with trade-related assistance has given the Bank a keen sense of where the current bottlenecks to the provision of such assistance lie, and what gaps need to be filled to make Aid for Trade a truly effective instrument for helping developing countries participate more effectively in the multilateral trading system and, ultimately, to achieve stronger and more sustained economic growth.

This experience makes the Bank a natural partner for LAC – and for the wider global trade community – in the design and implementation of an expanded Aid for Trade package under the Doha Development Agenda. In developing its own expertise in trade-related assistance, the Bank has grappled with many of the issues that now confront the WTO Task Force on Aid for Trade: identifying the gaps, finding effective means of delivery, involving the private sector, and strengthening monitoring and evaluation mechanisms, to name just a few.

As the previous section on lessons learned showed, there is clearly a need to develop better analytical tools and diagnostic capacities, more effective dialogue and programming, more appropriate operational instruments and stronger monitoring and evaluation mechanisms for trade-related assistance. But in terms of institutions for managing additional aid, the existing global and regional architecture appears to be adequate, at least on the supply-side. Regional development banks, in particular, should play a prominent role in the future delivery of Aid for Trade. They offer a number of advantages in this respect, regional experience and proximity to clients being among the most important ones, not least because trade is often a politically sensitive issue. On the demand side, greater efforts should go into strengthening the absorptive capacity and sustainability of institutions that implement trade-related assistance. In fact, this aspect of managing Aid for Trade may be the most important issue for ensuring effective delivery of aid, and it deserves greater attention in the current debate on Aid for Trade. The efforts of the WTO will therefore be crucial in ensuring a balanced debate between the supply and demand sides of Aid for Trade on how best to operationalize this important initiative in order to contribute to the development dimension of the Doha Development Agenda.

REFERENCES

IDB. 2003. "Beyond Borders: The New Regionalism in Latin America – Economic and Social Progress Report," Washington, D.C.: IDB.

IDB. 2007. "Homepage," http://www.iadb.org.

OECD. 2006. "Aid for Trade: Support for an Expanding Agenda," Paris: OECD.

WTO. 2006. *Communication from the Inter-American Development Bank Integration and Regional Programmes Department*, Aid for Trade Task Force, WT/AFT/W/13, 24 May.

11 Mainstreaming Development in Trade: Lessons from the Caribbean's Experience with the FTAA Hemispheric Cooperation Program

DERYCK R. BROWN

1 Introduction

The submission of the report of the WTO Task Force on Aid for Trade in July 2006 marked a qualitative shift in the debate over the relationship between aid and trade. For the first time, the WTO became involved in trade-related assistance beyond the provision of technical assistance. For a combination of reasons, including richer countries' aversion to providing funds for adjustment and compensation, there has been an acceptance that developing countries require further assistance to overcome supply-side constraints in order to make the most of the opportunities created for them through trade liberalization. This includes investments in trade-related infrastructure, and is a quantum leap from the Doha Declaration, which envisaged only "technical cooperation and capacity building." Moving from a commitment to providing strictly technical assistance to broad acceptance of the need for trade-related infrastructure required considerable efforts on the part of developing countries and equally considerable accommodation on the part of developed countries.

Whereas many developing countries, in particular the least-developed, had previously called for "trade, not aid" in a plea for fair conditions of international trade instead of further injections of Official Development Assistance (ODA), the new mantra had become "Aid for Trade". This new mantra recognizes not only the centrality of trade in promoting economic growth and development, but also the need for explicit support to assist countries develop the capacity to competitively produce and trade in goods and services.

Aid for Trade has been defined broadly as any assistance intended to help countries to trade and, in particular, to help them take advantage of WTO agreements (Phillips, Page and te Velde, 2005). It represents the latest stage in the evolution of a concept that emerged in the mid-to-late 1990s, variously termed trade-related technical assistance, trade-related assistance and trade capacity building.[1] All of these

[1] A recent study carried out for the European Commission uses the term "trade-related assistance" and defines it to include support for trade policy and regulation, trade development, adjustment to trade, and supply-side measures. See te Velde et al. (2006) and Kostecki (2001).

The views expressed herein are personal and do not reflect the official positions of either the Commonwealth Secretariat or the Caribbean Regional Negotiating Machinery (CRNM).

terms were used to refer to the effort to build human and institutional capacity through training, enhanced research skills, meeting policy makers' demands for studies or negotiating proposals, and specialized expertise. The Doha Declaration recognized technical cooperation and capacity building to be core elements of the multilateral trading system, and acknowledged that "sustainably financed technical assistance programs have an important role to play" (WTO, 2005).

The standard mode of delivery for this technical assistance (TA) or trade capacity building (TCB) is projects bringing together donors, service providers, trade policy makers, the business community, mass media and civil society, with limited, if any, involvement of other government ministries or public institutions. Such technical assistance projects typically take the form of:

a) Seminars, workshops, courses and technical missions;
b) Manuals, guides, documents, data, software and hardware;
c) Assistance to online networks to facilitate access to information and dialogue;
d) Research and consulting services; and
e) Support in the development and management of trade policy and related organizations in developing countries.

Despite being launched in 2001, only belatedly has the WTO's Doha Development Agenda (DDA) begun to reflect a pro-development approach – an important element of which is Aid for Trade. The DDA's pro-development possibilities, particularly as it relates to Aid for Trade, were slow in resonating with the international development community. Beginning with the run-up to the Gleneagles G8 Summit in July 2005, and accelerating during the months leading up to the preparation of the Aid for Trade Task Force report, there was considerable activity and discussion as institutions involved not strictly in trade, but in development, weighed in on the discourse. These institutions included governmental, inter-governmental, and non-governmental actors such as the UK's Department for International Development, the Organization for Economic Cooperation and Development (OECD), the World Bank, the International Monetary Fund (IMF), Oxfam, and a host of other international civil society organizations (see, for example, IMF, 2004; Prowse, 2005; Hoekman and Prowse, 2005; IMF/World Bank, 2005; Inter-American Development Bank (IDB), 2006; OECD, 2006). The inclusion of Aid for Trade on the WTO's agenda around the December 2005 Hong Kong Ministerial effectively served as a catalyst for bringing the international development community into the DDA, bridging the divide between trade and diplomatic officials, on the one hand, and aid and development practitioners on the other.

This chapter examines some of the issues that small developing countries need to take note of in the Aid for Trade discussion currently unfolding. It draws lessons from another negotiating arena, the Free Trade Area of the Americas (FTAA), which was an attempt to create a free trade zone among 34 countries in the Western Hemisphere. Like the Doha Declaration, the FTAA negotiating text recognized the need for technical assistance as a form of special and differential treatment (S&DT) to assist countries participate effectively in the negotiations and to enable weaker countries to meet the obligations of an eventual FTAA. In 2002, trade ministers proposed the establishment of a Hemispheric Cooperation Program (HCP), not unlike the Aid for Trade facility proposed in the context of the WTO. While the FTAA negotiating process stalled in 2004, and has been in hiatus ever since, there are important parallels that can be drawn between the HCP and the Aid for Trade process that this chapter will highlight. The chapter reviews the genesis of the HCP and the experience of the Caribbean Community (CARICOM) countries in negotiating it.[2] Key lessons are drawn on the challenges of mainstreaming trade in development, based on CARICOM's experience in the HCP. These lessons may be relevant to the Aid for Trade agenda as it continues to unfold.

2 Genesis and Development of the FTAA/HCP

The FTAA negotiating process experienced resistance around the inclusion of S&DT for "small and vulnerable economies."[3] It was eventually, grudgingly, taken into account. There was always an implicit recognition and acceptance by larger participating countries that some countries would be winners and others losers in the context of any hemispheric free trade undertaking. Indeed, by 2002 it was obvious that many countries required assistance even to keep up their participation in the negotiations. Thus, in November 2002 at their meeting in Quito, Ecuador, hemispheric trade ministers proposed the creation of the HCP. The program was aimed primarily at providing technical assistance to help the so-called smaller economies respond effectively to the obligations and challenges of negotiating trade liberalization in general, and the implementation of the FTAA in particular. The objectives of the HCP, as defined by the trade ministers, were to:

a) Strengthen the capacity of countries to implement and participate fully in the FTAA in order to contribute to growth with equity and broad-based economic development;
b) Assist countries to effectively address and overcome the challenges and maximize the benefits associated with trade liberalization in the FTAA;
c) Promote greater inter-relationships between the objectives and requirements of development and those of trade liberalization;
d) Complement current and future multilateral, sub-regional, and national programs aimed at:
   - strengthening productive capacity and fostering the competitiveness of the economies;
   - encouraging the development of innovation capacity and the transfer of appropriate technology; and
   - improving mechanisms for responding to economic shocks;
e) Enhance institutional strengthening and capacity building for policy making, development of negotiating strategies, and implementation of the FTAA; and
f) Increase coordination among donors and between donors and recipients with the objective of maximizing cooperation and technical assistance.

From the above, it can be inferred that FTAA trade ministers were aware of the need to "mainstream" trade into overall development policy and strategy with a view to improving prospects for economic growth and, by extension, poverty reduction.

[2] CARICOM consists of fifteen full members and five associated members. The full members are: Antigua-Barbuda, The Bahamas, Barbados, Belize, Dominica, Grenada, Guyana, Haiti, Jamaica, Montserrat, St. Lucia, St. Kitts-Nevis, St. Vincent & the Grenadines, Suriname, and Trinidad & Tobago.

[3] The FTAA terminology was "smaller economies" and there was recognition of "broad differences in the levels of development and size of economies."

In terms of the modalities for implementation of the HCP, the following, inter alia, were originally contemplated:

a) Establishment of a mechanism to receive, disseminate, evaluate and consider possible financing of specific project profiles submitted by FTAA countries and groups of countries or negotiating groups;[4]
b) Establishment of a mechanism to enable countries to define, prioritize, and articulate needs related to strengthening capacity for: (i) preparing for negotiations; (ii) implementing trade commitments; and (iii) adjusting to integration; and
c) Interaction between countries seeking assistance to improve their trade-related capacities and those countries and institutions that are in a position to provide assistance, through, for example, roundtable meetings focusing on specific areas of need, including the preparation of studies related to fiscal scenarios, socio-economic impact and competitiveness analysis.

These modalities suffered from a lack of specificity. With respect to (a) above, it is doubtful that trade ministers had any specific thoughts on what kind of "mechanism" would be required. Certainly, no financing mechanism was created by the time the FTAA negotiations succumbed to stalemate in 2004. Insofar as (b) is concerned, the mechanism established so-called "trade capacity building strategies and action plans." Countries and/or regions seeking assistance under the HCP were required to develop such strategies and action plans defining, prioritizing, and articulating their needs in respect of the strengthening of capacity for negotiations (short term or immediate needs relating to actual participation in the negotiations themselves), implementing trade commitments (medium term needs relating to compliance) and adjusting to integration (longer-term needs relating to economic competitiveness and survival). In relation to (c), there was officially only one interaction in October 2003 geared towards the matching of needs with potential donors before the FTAA negotiating process became unhinged in 2004.[5]

The notion of three categories of support in the HCP, each representing a distinct phase in the process around trade reform, was reproduced in the WTO arena when the July 2005 Framework called for extending enhanced trade capacity building to developing countries in order to:

a) increase their **effective participation** in the [WTO] negotiations;
b) facilitate their **implementation** of [WTO] rules; and
c) enable them to **adjust and diversify** their economies.

3 CARICOM Experience with the HCP

The responsibility of conceptualizing and developing the HCP was delegated to the FTAA Consultative Group on Smaller Economies (CGSE). However, the process

[4] The Quito Ministerial Declaration went on to say that the support offered under the HCP, both financial and non-financial, should be secure, predictable and multi-faceted.

[5] This is not to say that there were no interactions. The Central American countries had regularly-scheduled meetings with USAID and the Tripartite Committee on the wings of the Central American Free Trade Agreement (CAFTA) negotiations.

was very much driven by the Tripartite Committee[6] and the United States (as represented on the CGSE by the U.S. Trade Representative), with CARICOM as *demandeurs*.[7] The HCP process involved an extensive diagnostic and consultative exercise intended to identify and prioritize needs and prepare project profiles that could be considered for funding. However, as it evolved, the process became more and more elaborate and demanding on the scarce human and financial resources of small states. In the end, the strategies were produced by external agencies – specifically by members of the Tripartite Committee and contractors from the U.S. Agency for International Development (USAID) – with inputs from country governments, in concert with intergovernmental organizations such as the Caribbean Regional Negotiating Machinery (CRNM).

The process of preparing the strategies revealed critical weaknesses in trade policy capacity and, for that matter, about the overall governance *problematique* facing the Caribbean. Specifically, it revealed the lack of policy coherence that is characteristic of most Caribbean countries and the poor coordination both between the public and private sectors, and within the public sector itself. In a nutshell, the countries were spectacularly unprepared for such an exercise; basic steps needed to be taken before comprehensive trade capacity building strategies and action plans could be drawn up.

Following the preparation of the strategies, a meeting was convened among all FTAA countries seeking assistance under the HCP and potential bilateral and multilateral donors in October 2003.[8] The pressure to complete at least draft strategies and convene such a meeting came from the U.S., which was determined to have something positive to report back to trade ministers at the Miami meeting in December 2003, and from agencies such as CRNM. This "Initial Roundtable Meeting," as it was called, received the usual billing associated with such encounters: one could almost visualize donors' representatives arriving, cheque books in hand, on the lookout for interesting and bankable projects. Of course, not unlike most other such "pledging" meetings, representatives of donor agencies listened almost ritualistically to countries presenting their strategies, but in the end committed to nothing.

Caribbean countries were subsequently asked to meet among themselves and review their strategies in order to identify areas of common need and define regional (as opposed to purely national) priorities and projects. Such a meeting was convened in June 2004 and a summary document of "CARICOM Priority Areas for Trade-related Assistance under the Hemispheric Cooperation Program" was agreed.

[6] The Tripartite Committee consisted of the three major hemispheric multilateral or inter-governmental organizations, namely, the Inter-American Development Bank (IDB), the Organization of American States (OAS), and the United Nations Economic Commission for Latin America and the Caribbean (ECLAC). It was set up to support the various negotiating groups in the FTAA, and provided technical support to the Consultative Group for Smaller Economies (CGSE) in particular.

[7] One iinteresting argument was that, by burdening the CGSE with the development of the HCP, the U.S. actually succeeded in distracting attention away from the issue of special and differential treatment, which was the main preoccupation and *raison d'être* of the CGSE before the HCP.

[8] The Initial Roundtable Meeting was restricted mostly to Washington-based donors (World Bank and IDB), along with the major bilateral donors in the hemisphere (USAID and Canadian International Development Agency – CIDA). The United States was adamant that outside donors who were active in the hemisphere should not be involved at that stage. In the case of the Caribbean, for example, this meant that the European Commission and the UK Department for International Development, which are major donors to the region, were excluded.

The meeting sought to distill the most important regional priorities from all the national strategies, with the following results:

Participation in Negotiations
- Specialized training for public as well as private sectors;
- Public education and awareness programs;
- Economic and statistical data collection and analysis; and
- Assistance to participate at negotiations.

Implementation of Commitments
- Strengthening of national enquiry points;
- Trade facilitation and related activities; and
- Legislation and regulations.

Very little could be discerned from the strategies in relation to longer-term needs of adjustment and diversification, for reasons discussed below. Meanwhile, the donors active in the region undertook to carry out an audit or inventory of ongoing trade-related projects, ostensibly to get an overview of what each donor was already doing, to identify existing projects that could accommodate additional activities to meet the needs articulated in the strategies, and to help avoid duplication. This was all meant to be in preparation for a regional roundtable meeting with donors operating in the Caribbean. By the time the regional roundtable was arranged on the margins of the 2005 Caribbean Forum for Development (CFD), it was clear to most that the FTAA was in an intractable stalemate.[9]

4 Key Lessons Learnt

The experience of CARICOM countries with the HCP – both in terms of its construction and outcomes – is important because it has a bearing on how the region approaches Aid for Trade in the WTO. Lessons learnt in the FTAA are readily transferable to the wider multilateral stage and are especially relevant in the context of another arena of negotiations CARICOM is involved in – the Economic Partnership Agreement (EPA) talks with Europe.

Five key lessons learnt from CARICOM's experience negotiating the HCP are relevant to the WTO and EPA Aid for Trade contexts. These are presented and discussed in the following sections.

4.1 There is a wide chasm between the trade and development communities, both nationally and within the donor community

The process of developing trade capacity building strategies and action plans revealed the deep divide between national trade officials in the Caribbean, on the one hand, and their finance, planning and development counterparts, on the other. In order to "mainstream" development in trade, the strategy development exercise required a "joined up" approach: it should ideally have been a collaborative effort

[9] The Caribbean Forum for Development is the successor to the World Bank-coordinated Caribbean Group for Cooperation in Economic Development (CGCED), which met biennially in Washington. In 2001, the World Bank transferred responsibility for this activity to the Caribbean Development Bank (CDB), who hosted the first CFD meeting in Barbados in 2005.

involving not just trade ministries, but also other areas of government affected by trade. In reality, however, it was largely left to trade or foreign affairs officials whose remit and capacities did not extend to broad-based economic development. Trade officials were preoccupied with the issues immediately confronting them or those perceived as challenges, such as knowledge gaps and human resource shortages, and not with "bigger picture" issues such as broad-based economic growth, wealth- and employment-creation and poverty reduction; while the finance and development officials were less informed of the issues being confronted by their trade colleagues, and were naturally more concerned with fundamental macroeconomic policy issues.

To illustrate the point, consider the concern consistently expressed by trade officials over the loss of government revenue as a result of tariff reduction. This was consistently presented as a stumbling block to negotiating tariff reduction. Most CARICOM countries, and particularly the smallest (Organization of Eastern Caribbean States – OECS), rely heavily on trade taxes for a large proportion of public revenue, varying from 22 percent to almost 75 percent in some cases (ECLAC, 2003). They were therefore concerned by the effects of trade liberalization on fiscal revenues. Yet, while trade officials complained about the absence of detailed studies on potential revenue losses and either alternative sources of revenue or alternative tax regimes, finance officials were already considering at least five such studies and were actively pursuing the introduction of a value-added tax to replace revenue lost from border taxes decreases.[10]

Another aspect of the divide had to do with the fact that while trade officials could propose all manner of projects in the context of the HCP, it is finance and development planning ministries that are the repositories of project planning expertise and the formal conduits to international financial institutions (IFIs). Many donors will only act on the authority of designated officials in finance and/or development planning ministries. The requests of trade officials often fell on "deaf ears" within their own finance ministries, as they had failed to bring the latter on board at an early stage in the process.

The chasm referred to is not limited to trade and finance/development planning ministries. Government ministries and departments in other key sectors were also unfamiliar with the pressures confronting their trade colleagues, even where these pressures affected them directly. For instance, a minister responsible for public works and transport, when asked about ongoing FTAA negotiations in the area of government procurement, had no knowledge that procurement was being negotiated in the context of a free trade agreement. A similar situation was encountered with a tourism minister who saw no connection between services negotiations and the industry he represented.

As suggested above, the problem was not peculiar to Caribbean countries. Donor agency country offices or headquarters-based operational staff were in some cases unaware of developments on the trade front, unable to appreciate the likely impacts of trade liberalization on the economies of CARICOM countries, and therefore unlikely to see the relevance of stand-alone trade-related projects. As a result, they were unsympathetic to the needs expressed by countries for trade-related technical

[10] See CARICOM (2002); ECLAC (2003); OECS Tax Reform and Administration Commission (2003); IDB (2004); CARTAC (2004).

assistance.[11] Even in the CGSE, where the HCP was being discussed and developed, the representatives of FTAA countries were predominantly diplomats from ministries of trade and foreign affairs, and not development practitioners. Yet the subject matter required a far deeper understanding of project design and financing issues than of diplomacy.[12]

4.2 It is far easier to identify immediate needs and compliance or implementation issues, but far more difficult to envisage longer-term needs relating to economic adjustment and diversification

The CARICOM strategies developed for the HCP were very long on immediate needs and compliance issues, but extremely short on longer-term projects that could be considered either adjustment to liberalization, addressing supply-side constraints, or in any way related to economic diversification. Certainly very little – if any – attention was given to major infrastructural works that might be contemplated to boost trade and development. This assessment was confirmed by Parsan (2006) and underscores the point made above regarding the divide between trade and development communities. Trade officials cannot forecast infrastructure needs any better than planning and development officials can forecast immediate negotiating requirements. It also highlights the difficulty that trade officials can have in standing back and seeing the wood from the trees, to think strategically, and to mainstream longer-term development into the national trade agenda (and vice versa).[13]

An examination of the CARICOM strategies developed under the HCP reveals an abundance of immediate needs and a preoccupation with the "here and now," particularly in connection with the training of officials in new areas where the region lacks expertise. This could be anything from the analysis of trade data to the assessment of market access offers; generic training in the negotiation of services to specific training on standards, safeguards, sanitary and phyto-sanitary (SPS) measures, and technical barriers to trade (TBT). Improvement in economic data collection and analysis through the strengthening of national and regional statistical offices was also identified as crucial. Until these parts of government functioned effectively, it was impossible to develop evidence-based trade policy and even to prepare adequate offers and requests.

The tendency among donors was to respond to these immediate needs by financing workshops and consultancies aimed at producing technical studies or providing policy advice. Donors and other development agencies excel at this type of technical assistance, as it is easy to supply, despite its many proven shortcomings (see, for example, Nelson, 2006). Unfortunately, having financed a two-to-five-day workshop

[11] The IDB had restructured itself since the 1990s to give trade and integration a greater profile. The World Bank, however, set up a trade department very late in the context of multilateral trade negotiations, whether at the WTO or in the FTAA. See IMF/World Bank (2005) and IDB (2006).

[12] The majority of representatives attending CGSE meetings came from ministries of foreign affairs and international trade. Only Canada and CARICOM were represented by officials from development agencies – CIDA and the Caribbean Development Bank, respectively. The U.S. delegation, though led by the office of the U.S. Trade Representative (USTR), always included a USAID representative.

[13] The lack of clear national development plans and strategies in most Caribbean countries made it difficult to integrate trade into a development strategy per se. Integrating trade into poverty reduction strategies was even less likely, as the latter are typically handled by social or community development ministries that have even less of a relationship with trade ministries.

for officials from across the region, donors considered that they had discharged their obligations and were no longer expected to assist. Indeed, as far as they were concerned, capacity had been built as reflected in the number of persons trained and, more importantly, a dollar value could be assigned to it.[14] But no amount of training could overcome the disabilities of small size and the absence of sufficient numbers of qualified personnel.[15] Generalists cannot be transformed into specialists only by attending workshops.

Even if the training were to somehow transform CARICOM officials into specialists, there is little point to being well-prepared if countries are unable to articulate their positions because they are absent from the negotiating table. It is instructive to note that almost every developing FTAA country – including CARICOM countries – without exception, identified support for travel to FTAA negotiating group meetings as a top priority. If financing travel to Mexico for Caribbean officials was unaffordable, then, in the context of Aid for Trade, financing travel for developing country delegates to Geneva and the many exotic locations selected for WTO meetings will be even more difficult. Safadi (2005) makes the point that influence in the WTO is shaped largely by whether a country has resident or non-resident representation and whether it is active in the "WTO network." He also observed that the number of proposals on special and differential treatment put forward by developing countries is limited by their lack of technical capacity and their absence from the negotiating table.

The strategies produced for CARICOM countries also reveal a preoccupation with compliance or implementation issues – not so much in relation to the FTAA itself but, rather, in relation to their obligations under the Uruguay Round agreements such as the GATS and TRIPS. Many countries were struggling to get their houses in order by establishing or strengthening the most basic of institutions such as national standards bodies and TRIPS and SPS enquiry points. In some cases, the items listed in the trade capacity building strategies and action plans were "brick and mortar" projects involving the construction of buildings to house standards offices, supply of metrology and other vital equipment, and training of staff.

The strategies put forward by Caribbean countries were notably thin on detail about longer-term projects that could potentially improve economic competitiveness and help in overcoming supply-side constraints. Once again, this was a result of the chasm between trade and development officials. Trade officials are not capable of envisaging what roads, bridges, power plants, ports, and other infrastructure would be required to capitalize the most as regards a free trade agreement. What new crops or industries could be introduced, what innovations could be developed, what trade-related infrastructure and human resource development

14 While it may appear to some a rather cynical interpretation of what passes for development assistance, there is compelling evidence to suggest that the United States, particularly, was less concerned about genuine and effective capacity building and more concerned about being able to show a dollar value to both their own domestic constituency and the beneficiary countries as a way of stemming criticism. If a country later complained about lack of capacity in any area, USAID would be able to produce statistics to show how much money had been devoted to capacity building in that area.

15 For an assessment of human and institutional capacity in one part of CARICOM, see Stewart, Francis and Rigobert (2005). This audit of trade policy capacity and technical resources in the OECS demonstrates that most trade ministries are inadequately staffed, in most cases comprising only three professionals who are generalists, overwhelmed by the volume and variety of the workload, and frequently traveling.

programs would be needed to support these new initiatives in the liberalized world of the future were all questions that trade officials proved themselves incapable of answering.

It also highlights the gulf between the public and private sectors. If, as modern economic theory postulates, it is the state's responsibility to create the right environment and stimuli for private investment, then it is the private sector's role to respond to those stimuli. It is not possible to accurately predict how the private sector might respond to free trade agreements in any given situation. All this suggests that attempts at estimating the likely costs of adjustment or Aid for Trade requirements are futile.

4.3 Because of the inability to predict the future and identify adjustment requirements, there is a need for the creation of an enduring financing mechanism whose existence is not linked to the negotiations

Precisely because no one has perfect knowledge of the future and longer-term needs could not all be neatly anticipated well in advance and included in a strategy, the issue of predictability of financing becomes very important. The FTAA negotiations originally had a completion date of 2004, with the expectation that implementation would begin following the Agreement's ratification in respective national legislative bodies. With the exception of Canada (which contributed the sum of CAD$24 million at a very early stage in the HCP), no other country or donor – including the U.S. – came forward with a firm pledge or commitment to provide funding under the HCP. It was therefore necessary to give consideration to a financing facility whose life transcended the negotiations themselves.

Seven main issues are to be considered. First, beneficiary countries felt there should be some guaranteed funding for projects. They were being encouraged to embrace the FTAA and offered technical and financial assistance to overcome any difficulties or challenges they might have in meeting their obligations. As in the WTO, the offer of technical and financial assistance was used by the larger, wealthier countries – principally the United States – to provide an incentive to encourage countries skeptical about the advantages of the FTAA to continue with the negotiations and eventually sign on to the agreement. However, while concessions and commitments made during the negotiations are reflected in the final agreement, and become legally binding and enforceable through the dispute settlement mechanism, technical assistance provisions are "best endeavor" clauses. Failure to deliver on promised technical assistance would attract no sanctions; nor, for that matter, would there be any avenues for complaint. The provision of Aid for Trade needs to be, at a minimum, predictable and as legally binding and enforceable as the obligations and commitments made in the trade agreement itself.

Second, quite apart from the predictability of funding, there was a related issue of what institutional mechanism could be created or adapted to administer the HCP. To whom would a country seeking assistance turn after the negotiations were completed and the agreement was being implemented? On the one hand, some suggested that the FTAA Secretariat that would be set up to superintend the agreement and countries' compliance with it could administer the HCP. On the other hand, a convincing argument was put forward that an administrative secretariat would not be equipped to perform the functions of a financial institution. To the extent that the HCP was to be a financing facility, it was suggested, it should be housed in either a new or existing financial institution. Without doubt, this argument would apply equally to the WTO.

Third, there should be additionality. Not only should there be funds specifically earmarked for trade, but these funds should also be additional, in the sense that they are not a reallocation of previously-committed funds. In other words, "new" money needed to be introduced. The apparent reluctance on the part of the United States to state categorically what new money it would contribute to the HCP created apprehension among potential beneficiary countries. Their demand that the United States "put their money on the table" revealed a deep distrust of the major hemispheric power that could easily spill over into the multilateral (that is, WTO) context.[16]

Fourth, the funds should be made available on a non-reimbursable (grant) basis rather than as loans. The difficulty with some of the facilities set up, for example, by the IMF and the IDB to assist with trade-related activities has to do with the fact that they are loan and not grant facilities. From the countries' standpoint, already heavily indebted countries were being asked to borrow to implement policies that would, in the short term, enable compliance but, in the longer term, reduce their revenue intake and compromise their ability to service these very loans. This is why the IDB, for instance, could report that grants and non-financial support were the main instruments of assistance to trade-related capacity building in its borrowing members. A total of ten countries – only two of which were CARICOM countries – had sought assistance under the Bank's Trade Sector Facility that provides fast-track approval for ordinary or concessional loans of up to US$5 million to strengthen the capacity of trade ministries and other trade-related institutions to formulate, negotiate, and implement trade policy (IDB, 2006).[17]

Fifth, there was a need for transparent and unambiguous criteria to be established to govern access to the funds dedicated to the HCP. These included the procedures for project preparation and submission, a typology of acceptable projects, and an ex ante definition of which countries, regions, sectors, companies or projects would be eligible for financing under the facility. The fundamental contradiction in the conceptualization of the HCP was that, although it was intended to provide technical assistance, it was clear that the third category of assistance – adjustment to integration – transcended technical assistance and could include major investments in human resource development, private sector development, and large infrastructure projects. This issue raised some major questions: What would qualify as trade-related and what would not, and how would the line be drawn between the two? How could one distinguish between so-called trade-related and other infrastructure projects of the type that governments are expected to undertake in the normal course of promoting growth and development in their countries?

Previous experience – not least with the European Commission – has taught the CARICOM region to be circumspect about promises of assistance that never

[16] The mistrust was mutual, and led to a Catch-22 situation. On the one hand, some CARICOM countries had little or no commitment to the FTAA but expected to benefit from the HCP. On the other hand, the U.S. government was reluctant to pledge resources to countries whose commitment to the FTAA was questionable at best.

[17] The Hong Kong Declaration speaks of grants and concessionary loans, but most developing countries expect that Aid for Trade should take the form of grants only.

materialize because of lengthy and unnecessarily onerous procedures for accessing the funds (see Chapter 12 by Sunassee in this volume). In addition, many countries at the FTAA negotiations viewed themselves as potential beneficiaries of some form of assistance. Even Venezuela, a country classified by the IDB as one of the four "most developed" Latin American economies, found it possible to justify including itself among the "smaller, weakest economies" in the hemisphere (Brewster, 2004). Indeed, of the 34 countries negotiating the FTAA, as many as 25 were categorized as "smaller."[18]

Sixth, there was a major issue relating to the source and quantum or volume of resources that would be needed to support the HCP. While efforts to estimate adjustment costs have already been commented upon, the estimates that did exist varied into the billions, and most countries looked towards their richer neighbors in the north to provide the funding.

Finally, it was felt that there should be some system set up to monitor performance. While the FTAA negotiations were in progress, this responsibility rested with the CGSE, the Trade Negotiations Committee (TNC – the Vice-Ministerial level that met quarterly) and ultimately the trade ministers themselves. Once the negotiations were completed, however, the agreement signed, and the ink dried, the CGSE along with all other negotiating groups would cease to exist. How, then, would it be possible to ascertain that the promised assistance would be actually getting to the countries in need?

For the reasons outlined above, CARICOM proposed the creation of a Regional Integration Fund (RIF), conceived as a financing mechanism that would mobilize resources for investment in projects to enable participating countries to overcome supply-side constraints. The CARICOM proposal was premised on the understanding that the level of development, and thus the capacity to benefit from and make effective use of the opportunities offered by the FTAA, should be the principal rationale for a RIF. The most revealing, practical, and least contentious measure of the level of development is per capita Gross National Income (GNI). GNI correlates well with the level of infrastructure, transportation, energy, telecommunications, human resource development, health, and education – which are among the most crucial explanatory variables of the level of development. CARICOM proposed a fund of US$2.17 billion, representing about 0.017 percent of the hemisphere's total GDP (US$12.649 billion) or 0.020 percent of the combined GDP of Canada and the United States. The fund proposed would be a loan-based revolving fund offering differentiated interest rates and maturity periods according to the country/project being supported.[19] Significantly, the proposal also set out beneficiary/eligibility criteria, possible terms of assistance, modalities of disbursement, the likely sources of financing and contribution formula, and suggested that the fund be housed within the IDB rather than establishing a new financial institution (Brewster, 2004).[20]

[18] It should also be recalled that the HCP was originally intended to be a technical assistance facility and neither a compensatory facility (as Venezuela referred to it) nor a development facility to support investments in infrastructure and private sector development. This issue of which projects were eligible and which were not was always bound to be contentious.

[19] There was no consensus on whether the fund should be grant only or loan based. The more pragmatic acknowledged that an entirely grant-based fund was not feasible. However, for political reasons, others upheld their position that the fund should provide non-reimbursable financing.

[20] CARICOM's was not the only proposal. The United Nations Economic Commission for Latin America and the Caribbean (ECLAC) had also tabled a proposal as early as 1997, and other countries such as Venezuela had proposed a Regional Cooperation Fund. See Arrocha (2003).

The FTAA was derailed after the 2003 Miami ministerial meeting, and the CARICOM RIF proposal fell by the wayside. Had it been developed further, it might have been an experiment from which the Aid for Trade initiative at the WTO could have learnt. There are, nevertheless, certain clear parallels and principles to be gleaned from the experience to avoid old disappointments and baggage carrying over into the WTO. Those involved in developing the Enhanced Integrated Framework and Aid for Trade could benefit from revisiting the RIF proposal. On the surface, the proposal advanced by Stiglitz and Charlton (2006) for a special facility to be set up within the World Bank seems consistent with the CARICOM proposal on the RIF, as the World Bank works at the global level while the IDB operates at the hemispheric level.

4.4 National needs, priorities and projects have to be balanced against regional ones

The participants in the FTAA process were the 34 countries of the Americas. These were organized into several trading or political blocs, namely, the parties to the North American Free Trade Agreement (NAFTA), MERCOSUR, the Andean Community, the Central American countries, and CARICOM. Although the trade capacity building strategies developed in the context of the HCP were intended to be country-driven and nationally-focused, donors had an expressed preference for regional projects. CARICOM was thus asked to review all 14 national strategies to establish common problems and needs that could be addressed by way of regional projects, an exercise that was more for the convenience of the donor community than in the countries' interests.

It is true that many of the trade-related weaknesses affecting one CARICOM country affect most, if not all, of the others. But there is an inherent contradiction in having both national strategies and regional approaches. Even in the presence of an active regional integration process – the creation of the CARICOM Single Market and Economy (CSME) – countries were more concerned with national as opposed to regional development. It is perfectly understandable that national governments should look inward and seek to secure resources for their countries' national development rather than identify a set of regional public goods to be supplied through regional organizations. Put simply, if mainstreaming trade into national development strategies is challenging, it would be virtually impossible to mainstream trade into a non-existent regional development strategy requiring extensive coordination among countries. To take one example from the infrastructure sector, although many CARICOM countries might envisage the need for access roads, power plants, airport, or seaport improvements as part of the adjustment phase of the HCP, no country identified cross-border transportation as a trade-related infrastructure need, when it very clearly is.

4.5 Avoid elaborate diagnostic and project identification exercises

As Parsan (2006) points out, the Caribbean region is suffering from "needs assessment fatigue," and will not respond favorably to yet another attempt to identify and prioritize needs. Some method will have to be devised to gather information on needs and priorities, but too much of this has gone on in the past decade with no tangible results. Despite the Rome and Paris Declarations on donor coordination and harmonization, each donor agency continues to demand its own assessment, and assessments done in the context of one set of negotiations are not transferable to another set of negotiations. For example, after all the effort and resources that went into preparing the FTAA trade capacity building strategies and action plans, and despite their deficiencies, it would not surprise anyone to find that an Aid for Trade program would require entirely new assessments to be carried out. Not only is this wasteful, but it is taxing on small bureaucracies, and leads to frustration and disenchantment with the process. In any Aid for Trade initiative, including the EU-funded Trade.com program to support African, Caribbean, and Pacific (ACP) countries' EPA-related adjustment, it would be important to demonstrate seriousness and commitment by seeking to build on existing action plans and delivering some quick results so that beneficiary countries could believe it is real.

A second aspect to this is the role of the United States as both negotiator and major donor. In the context of the FTAA, most countries looked to the United States to provide the resources for trade capacity building. But the United States as a party to the FTAA negotiations could manipulate the entire process by providing its aid selectively. In the final stages of the FTAA negotiations (2002–04), there was an alarming expansion in the U.S. Trade Representative's (USTR) power over USAID – to the extent, one might argue, that the latter's aid program in the Caribbean and Central America was largely driven by the USTR's agenda. USAID assisted several countries with the preparation of their trade capacity building strategies and action plans, and fed information directly back to USTR on a regular basis. This constituted a conflict of interest in which the major negotiating power had also devised and funded a process that gave them ready access to detailed assessments of negotiating strengths – and, more importantly, weaknesses – of other countries at the table.[21]

5 Conclusion

Two broad conclusions may be drawn from the discussion presented in this chapter. The first relates to the lessons learnt from the HCP that might inform our approach to Aid for Trade. The second relates more generally to the goal of mainstreaming trade in development.

On the first point, one might reasonably argue that aid really has no business in trade negotiations. CARICOM's experience with the HCP, as outlined above, was disappointing. Some territories made a genuine effort to get their strategies prepared in the expectation that development assistance would be forthcoming. Others went through the motions to see how, if at all, they could benefit, but lacked any real commitment to or interest in the FTAA. To cynical observers, the HCP was nothing more than a carrot dangled before smaller countries by the United States to maintain their interest and keep them at the negotiating table. In the final analysis, the HCP collapsed because FTAA negotiations collapsed. Without the FTAA process, developing countries in the Americas had no basis to demand

[21] In terms of assisting CARICOM countries with the development of their trade capacity building strategies and action plans, the work was shared around the members of the Tripartite Committee and USAID. Jamaica was initially assigned to USAID but refused to allow the bilateral to render the assistance, arguing that there was a clear conflict of interest.

trade-related assistance from the larger hemispheric powers, and the larger powers had no incentive to provide any assistance to these countries. Developing countries should remain aware of similar tactics in the context of Aid for Trade at the WTO.

The five lessons identified here are relevant to those who still hold out hope for the resuscitation of the WTO talks. They should also inform a Caribbean approach, should the WTO negotiations resume, as well as the region's approach to the EPA negotiations with Europe, which are also intended to be developmental and to have financing of development at their core. Indeed, what exactly is meant by a developmental EPA has proved a thorny issue in the negotiations thus far.

The lessons learnt on mainstreaming trade into development or vice-versa are equally disappointing. Based on CARICOM's experience with the development of trade capacity building strategies and action plans, no link could be discerned between trade and development, nor between trade policy and poverty reduction strategies. Different ministries are responsible for Poverty Reduction Strategy Papers (PRSPs), Public Sector Investment Programs (PSIPs) and trade capacity-building strategies. Much more will have to be done to persuade national development planners to mainstream trade, and to enable trade officials to play a more meaningful part in national development planning. Nevertheless, the strategies developed for the HCP remain valuable, as they are, perhaps, the only comprehensive needs assessment ever carried out in all CARICOM countries. In any future effort at national-level diagnosis, these strategies could be updated, improved upon, and better integrated into overall development policy.

REFERENCES

Arrocha, William. 2003. "Study on the possible structure of a regional cooperation fund taking into account the FTAA Hemispheric Cooperation Program," paper presented at the Association of Caribbean States seminar on "The Greater Caribbean in International Trade Negotiations," Port of Spain, Trinidad, 14–15 July.

Brewster, Havelock R. 2004. "Proposal for an FTAA Regional Integration Fund," prepared for the Caribbean Regional Negotiating Machinery, Bridgetown: CRNM.

Caribbean Community Secretariat. 2002. "The fiscal effects of tariff reduction in the Caribbean Community," Georgetown: CARICOM (with support from the IDB).

CRNM. 2004. "CARICOM priority areas for trade-related assistance under the Hemispheric Cooperation Programme," Bridgetown: CRNM.

CARTAC. 2004. "CARICOM: Survey of the Caribbean tax systems," Barbados: CARTAC.

ECLAC. 1997. "A Regional Integration Fund of the Free Trade Area of the Americas," New York: ECLAC.

ECLAC. 2003. "Fiscal trends and policy: issues and implications for the Caribbean," Port of Spain: ECLAC.

Franco, Santiago Apunte. 2003. "Hemispheric Cooperation Programme," paper presented at the Association of Caribbean States seminar on "The Greater Caribbean in International Trade Negotiations," Port of Spain, Trinidad, 14–15 July.

Hoekman, Bernard and Susan Prowse. 2005. "Policy Responses to Preference Erosion: From Trade as Aid to Aid for Trade," paper presented at the OECD Global Forum on Trade – "Special and Differential Treatment: Thinking Outside the Box," Bridgetown, Barbados, 28–29 June.

IDB. 2004. "Fiscal impact of trade liberalization in the Americas," *Periodic Note*, Washington, D.C.: IDB.

IDB. 2006. "Aid for Trade in Latin America and the Caribbean: the Inter-American Development Bank's experience," Washington, D.C.: IDB.

IMF. 2004. "Fund support for trade-related balance of payments adjustments," Washington, D.C.: IMF.

IMF/World Bank. 2005. "Aid for Trade: competitiveness and adjustment," joint note by the staffs of the IMF and World Bank, Washington, D.C.

Kostecki, Michel. 2001. "Technical assistance services in trade policy: a contribution to the discussion on capacity-building in the WTO," *Resource Paper* No. 2., Geneva: ICTSD.

Nelson, Mark. 2006. "Does training work? Re-examining donor-sponsored training programs in developing countries," *Capacity Development Briefs* No. 15, Washington, D.C.: World Bank Institute.

OECD. 2006. "The Development Dimension – Aid for Trade: Making it Effective," Preliminary Version, Paris: OECD.

OECS Tax Reform and Administration Commission. 2003. "New approaches to taxation and tax administration in the Eastern Caribbean Currency Union," Basseterre: Eastern Caribbean Central Bank.

Parsan, Elizabeth. 2006. "Aid for Trade: a Caribbean perspective," prepared for the Caribbean Regional Negotiating Machinery, Bridgetown: CRNM.

Phillips, Lauren, S. Page, and Dirk Willem te Velde. 2005. "Aid for Trade: What does it mean? Why should aid be part of WTO negotiations? And how much might it cost?," *ODI Opinions*, London: Overseas Development Institute.

Prowse, Susan. 2005. "Aid for Trade: increasing support for trade adjustment and integration – a proposal," proceedings of the OECD Global Forum on Trade – "Special and Differential Treatment: Thinking Outside the Box," Bridgetown, Barbados, 28–29 June.

Safadi, Raed. 2005. "Comments on SDT and the Doha Development Agenda: beyond tariffs preferences," proceedings of the OECD Global Forum on Trade – "Special and Differential Treatment: Thinking Outside the Box," Paris: OECD.

South Centre. 2006. "Elements for the architecture of Aid for Trade," Draft Working Paper, Geneva: South Centre.

Stewart, T., A. Francis and G. Rigobert. 2005. "Audit of OECS technical resources," St. Castries: OECS Secretariat.

Stiglitz, Joseph E. and Andrew Charlton. 2006. "Aid for Trade: A Report for the Commonwealth Secretariat," London: Commonwealth Secretariat.

te Velde, Dirk Willem et al. 2006. "A critical assessment of the EU's trade-related assistance to third countries: lessons from the past, policy options for the future," study for the International Trade Committee of the European Parliament, London: Overseas Development Institute.

WTO. 2005. *Draft Ministerial Declaration*, Ministerial Conference, Sixth Session, Hong Kong, 13–18 December 2005, Doha Work Programme, WT/MIN(05)/W/3/Rev.2, 18 December.

WTO. 2006. Summary of contributions from inter-governmental organizations, *Aid for Trade Task Force*, WT/AFT/W/17, 9 June.

12 Aid for Trade and the European Development Fund

AMANDA SUNASSEE LAM

1 Introduction

Over the past five years, trade has moved increasingly to center stage in the relationship between the European Union (EU) and the group of African, Caribbean and Pacific countries (ACP). In the process, the spotlight has shifted away from a focus on Official Development Assistance (ODA) towards negotiating new trade policy frameworks between the EU and the ACP regions. However, the World Trade Organization (WTO) Aid for Trade initiative (WTO, 2006) has introduced a more balanced view of the complementary nature of aid and trade, as opposed to the "either/or" approach that has until recently dominated international discourse on trade, growth, and poverty reduction.

There has been a recent major shift in mindset among European countries and the development community at large around providing aid for trade-related areas; Aid for Trade is increasingly being seen as the missing link that will help to make trade a true engine of growth for poorer countries. Putting the Aid for Trade initiative forward and gaining commitment internationally on the subject is by no means a small feat. Indeed, in the early 1990s the widely held view was that trade liberalization would generate sufficient "gains from trade," and that this would in itself be sufficient motivation for developing countries to engage in the multilateral trading system. This argument has lost its appeal over time, as the international community has come to recognize and witness first-hand that, although "international trade is vital for poverty reduction, the links between trade expansion and poverty reduction are neither simple nor automatic" (UNCTAD, 2004).

The rationale for Aid for Trade is now widely accepted, and hinges on at least three arguments. First, developing countries face serious supply-side constraints that prevent them from taking advantage of market access benefits conferred by trade liberalization. Second, productivity and competitiveness are stifled by poor market conditions such as access to finance, access to knowledge and technology, poor regulatory frameworks, and poor business environments. Third, adjustment costs and preference erosion confer immediate macro-economic shocks and can temporarily destabilize sectors that are not properly buttressed (such as sugar and bananas). These can disproportionately affect certain countries, such as net food importers and small island states. There have also been some serious questions raised about the real gains from trade. The World Bank, for instance, has revised its initial 2003 projection on potential welfare gains from a successful Doha round from US$832 billion to US$287 billion (Wise and Gallagher, 2005).

An important element to consider when discussing Aid for Trade and EU development assistance is how it relates to the ongoing negotiations on establishing Economic Partnership Agreements (EPAs) with the ACP by 2008. In the context of the European Commission's (EC) negotiations with six ACP regions on establishing Economic Partnership Agreements (EPAs), there has been discussion between the parties for provision of additional funding through an "EPA Facility."[1] For the EU, much Aid for Trade is provided from particular funding mechanisms with a regional focus. In 2004, 29 percent of the EU's Aid for Trade was funded by the European Development Fund (EDF) for ACP countries. Another 24 percent was for an aid program for the Western Balkans (CARDS). The EU, which already counts as the largest funder for trade related assistance (TRA),[2] has committed to scale up its aid contribution to trade. In July 2005 at the G8 summit in Gleneagles, the EC pledged EUR1 billion per year from 2007 to support the trading capacity of developing countries. It further committed an additional EUR1 billion by 2010 at the WTO Hong Kong Ministerial in December 2005, taking the EU contribution up to EUR2 billion a year, which also includes the EU member states' commitment of around EUR400 million per year in TRA.

The pledge to step up the efforts of the EU member states and institutions on trade-related development assistance was formalized with a decision by the EU General Affairs and External Relations Council (GAERC) in October 2006 to address EPA-related adjustment needs under the broader framework of Aid for Trade (GAERC, 2006). The GAERC conclusions show that development support to EPAs and Aid for Trade are closely intertwined (ECDPM-ICTSD, 2006). Although EU policy makers decided that there would be no additional financial envelope specific to EPAs, EU member states agreed to provide bilateral funds for Aid for Trade on top of the EC-administered EDF. A substantial share of this TRA (EUR1 billion each by the EC and collectively by member states) was earmarked for Aid for Trade, including support for the EPAs (ECDPM, 2006a). However, what remains a grey area is how much of the "additional funding" will in fact be funds additional to those being allocated by the EU under the 10th EDF or the Integrated Framework (IF)[3] and other trade-related regional and multilateral initiatives.

It is important to recognize from the outset that the Aid for Trade initiative may bring an additional layer of development assistance to the existing myriad of EC funding instruments, projects and initiatives. Operationalizing Aid for Trade in an effective manner will require that EU member states and the EC adhere to the Paris Declaration on Aid Effectiveness,[4] and that new and innovative collaborative

1 The revised Cotonou Agreement Article XX makes provisions for the setup of an EPA-specific funding instrument.

2 Since 2001, the EU has contributed an average of EUR700 million per year for trade related assistance (trade policy and trade development, not including infrastructure).

3 The Integrated Framework for Trade Related Technical Assistance for LDCs is a multi-agency, multi-donor program that assists the least developed countries expand their participation in the global economy by integrating trade with their poverty reduction strategies. See the Introduction to this volume for further details.

4 The Paris Declaration, endorsed in March 2005, is an international agreement to which over one hundred Ministers, Heads of Agencies and other Senior Officials adhered and committed their countries and organizations to continue to increase efforts in harmonization, alignment and managing aid for results with a set of monitorable actions and indicators.

arrangements are explored and piloted at country and regional levels. The EU is already actively involved in trade-related aid delivery at the multilateral level (via the IF and the Joint Integrated Technical Assistance Programme – JITAP[5]) and bilaterally (via TRA through the EDF). The EU's effectiveness in implementing the new Aid for Trade framework will depend on its ability to adapt its existing procedures so as to allow any additional Aid for Trade funding to sit coherently with existing EDF programs and projects. This in turn will need to be harmonized with the Enhanced Integrated Framework. Aid for Trade will need to be channeled through an aid architecture that promotes the key principles of the Paris Declaration and which supports the key recommendations put forward by the WTO Aid for Trade Task Force (WTO, 2006), namely:

- Coordination between development partners;
- Harmonization of government and donor procedures and their bilateral and multilateral efforts;
- Alignment of TRA with countries' national development priorities, via Poverty Reduction Strategy Papers (PRSPs) and Diagnostic Trade Integration Studies (DTIS);[6] and
- Enhanced collaboration between development partners and agencies, together with regional banks and organizations, to identify and collaborate on regional, sub-regional and cross-border projects.

To achieve these objectives will require the use of existing mechanisms as far as possible, and an enhancement of these mechanisms to ensure overall efficiency in the delivery of trade capacity building and funding of trade-related infrastructure. Various proposals on an Aid for Trade delivery mechanism, such as those from the World Bank and the UK's Department for International Development (DFID),[7] have the merit of focusing on well-defined and coordinated structures. A strong case has been made in favor of an Enhanced IF as a delivery mechanism, though its impact is limited in that it is only applicable to LDCs. In the context of ACP-EU development cooperation, stronger coordination between EU member states to ensure coherence and complementarity between their TRA and that of the EC will also be needed.

Any "EPA Facility," be it through additional funding or existing funding, will need to be defined in a way that is both broad enough to reflect the diverse needs identified by countries and clear enough to establish a border between Aid for Trade and other TRA (WTO, 2006). Various sources of funding are expected to come onstream in the context of the EPAs, including through the EDF's National and Regional Indicative Programmes, EU member states' trade-related bilateral funding, and Aid for Trade. As this happens, it will be imperative that an internal EC and EU member state committee be established at country level to track and monitor EU TRA. This would help to ensure at the EU level that funding dedicated

[5] JITAP aims to build and strengthen the capacity of selected African countries to integrate into the multilateral trading system by building capacity in trade policy negotiation and formulation, and by promoting supply capacity and market knowledge of exporting enterprises. See the Introduction to this volume for further details.

[6] A key part of the IF, the DTIS evaluates internal and external constraints on a country's integration into the world economy, and recommend areas in which technical assistance and policy actions can help the country overcome these barriers.

[7] See IMF/World Bank (2005) and Hoekman and Prowse (2005).

to trade respects the principle of the "three C's" – coordination, coherence and complementarity. Such committees should be included in trade-related coordination mechanisms and Joint Assistance Strategies (JAS)[8] being set up in a number of countries as part of the OECD Development Assistance Committee's (DAC) aid effectiveness efforts.

2 Fifty years of EU-ACP cooperation

The post-colonial relationship between the European Union and the ACP countries is characterized by a web of agreements, from the Yaoundé agreements to the Lomé Convention and currently the Cotonou Partnership Agreement. The next generation of agreements will be the EPAs, set to enter into force in 2008. The ACP/EU relationship has since the 1960s undergone major changes, which have been captured in these various agreements. These changes have been shaped by various external forces and by shifting geopolitical priorities such as EU enlargement and WTO rules on regional trade agreements. The three cornerstones of these EU-ACP agreements have been political dialogue, trade relations, and development cooperation. The most radical changes to the ACP/EU relations were set in motion through the signature of the Cotonou Agreement in 2000. The Cotonou Agreement was adopted for a twenty-year period, with allowance for revision every five years, and a financial protocol for each five-year period. It contains a reformed aid package to support development and poverty reduction policies, plans for new economic partnerships to harness regional growth, and a political commitment to promote democratic principles and good governance. Under Cotonou, new principles were introduced such as greater aid selectivity, linking aid to performance, ensuring closer involvement of civil society and the private sector, and, probably the most challenging of all, making the trade regime "compatible" with the WTO. This last element entails changing the ACP non-reciprocal trade relationship with the EU into a reciprocal one.

The EDF is the main instrument for EC aid for development cooperation in the ACP countries and the Overseas Countries and Territories (OCT). The development aid provided by the EDF forms part of a broader European framework within the European Union and is supplemented by funds from the Community's general budget. The first EDF started in 1959, and the fund is still in operation. Since Lomé I in 1975 to date, close to EUR53 billion have been committed though the EDF. These funds are managed through the EC Headquarters in Brussels and EC delegations based in ACP countries, in collaboration with the National Authorising Officer[9] appointed by the respective ACP government. The EDF also channels

[8] For example, a JAS has been set up successfully in Tanzania, where it is expected to specify all modalities and arrangements of development support to Tanzania and replace individual and multilateral country assistance strategies. In this way, it will eliminate multiple development partner processes and requirements and allow for more efficient and effective use of donor resources. The JAS initiative is in line with international initiatives for aid effectiveness, such as the Monterrey Consensus on Financing for Development and the Rome and Paris Declarations on Aid Harmonization.

[9] The NAO, in close collaboration with the Head of Delegation, is responsible for the preparation and submission of projects/programs and examination and completion of tenders for approval by the Head of Delegation. The NAO is also responsible for: (i) coordination, monitoring, and assessment of projects and programs funded through the European Development Fund; and (ii) ensuring the proper execution of projects, programs, and disbursements of EC funding in the country.

projects to regional integration organizations, such as the Common Market for Eastern and Southern Africa (COMESA), the Southern African Development Community (SADC), CARIFORUM, and the Economic Community of West African States (ECOWAS). When looking at the EC and ACP's past experience in managing the EDF, it is important to keep in mind the major ongoing reforms launched by the Commission in 2000. These reforms aimed at streamlining EDF procedures and at providing more autonomy to EC delegations, while ensuring stronger "coherence, complementarity and coordination" (3C's) among the EU member states' external aid policies.

3 The European Development Fund as a major player in trade-related assistance and private sector development

Over the last fifty years, the EDF has been the main instrument for channeling EU funds to the ACP. At country level, EDF funds are disbursed through National Indicative Programmes (NIPs), organized in complex project set-ups, with a number of parallel management structures put in place to oversee the implementation of projects, often referred to as Project Management Units (PMUs). A large volume of funds is also channeled through "All ACP/intra ACP" Projects, with central PMUs based in Brussels. At the regional level, EDF funds are channeled through Regional Indicative Programmes (RIPs), which come with their own set of complex regional projects, which are not always coordinated with EDF national projects. In addition to this maze of projects, there are the EC budget line projects, the SYSMIN and STABEX[10] (now replaced by the FLEX), and projects managed by specialized institutions such as the Centre for Development and Enterprise, which focuses on private sector development. The European Investment Bank (EIB) also operates in the ACP regions, providing loans from its own resources,[11] and under the 9th EDF manages close to EUR2.2 billion though the investment facility. Under the 9th EDF, which spans a seven-year period from 2000–07,[12] a total of approximately EUR2.5 billion has been allocated to TRA, capacity building, and private sector development, channeled via intra-ACP instruments and Community institutions such as:

- ProInvest (CDE): EUR101 million
- Centre for Development & Enterprise: EUR90 million
- Private Sector Enabling Environment Facility: EUR20 million
- Microfinance Framework contract: EUR15 million
- Investment Facility EIB: EUR2.2 billion
- EPA PMU: EUR20 million
- WTO PMU: EUR10 million; and
- Trade.Com: EUR50 million

[10] The SYSMIN and STABEX instruments were designed to provide support for countries affected by fluctuations in commodity prices (minerals and agricultural commodities), through a system of compensation of foreign exchange earnings.

[11] The European Investment Bank (EIB) has provided ACP countries under the EDF a total of EUR1.7 billion in loans. The total financial resources allocated to ACP countries for the period 2000–2007 is EUR25 billion.

[12] The financial protocol under the Cotonou agreement is for a five-year period. However, exceptionally, the 9th EDF financial protocol extends for seven years, so as to coincide with the end of the WTO waiver for the extension of the Cotonou Agreement through 2008.

Under both the 8th and 9th EDF, very few ACP countries included trade as a focal area of intervention in their NIPs.[13] As the EPA and WTO negotiations have progressed, a number of ACP countries have responded by reallocating funds from other areas of their NIPs to address trade issues.[14] However, given the central role held by trade in regional integration initiatives, at the regional level the reverse seems to hold. For example, under the 9th EDF RIP for SADC, close to 45 percent of the financial envelope was allocated to TRA. This trend is on the rise, especially given the EU's focus on EPAs and the regional dimension of the ongoing EPA negotiations. However, disbursement and commitment rates under regional projects tend to be among the lowest in the EDF. This is due to the complexities involved in coordinating among countries in the regions and to the nature of the projects, which are often large infrastructure initiatives requiring extensive feasibility studies and coordination among member states. The situation is often further compounded by the under-staffed and under-funded regional integration organizations responsible for identification, formulation, and implementation of regional projects. This point is particularly relevant to the Aid for Trade initiative, since it is foreseen that sizeable funds will be channeled through the regional integration organizations, with a view to strengthening regional integration processes and fostering South-South trade – actions that will help prepare the ACP regions integrate into the multilateral trading system.

3.1 The key bottlenecks

The picture depicted above presents a highly complex aid delivery mechanism, used to deliver approximately EUR56 billion (53 EDF + 3 EIB) to seventy-nine ACP countries[15] over a thirty-year period (a rough average of EUR23 million per country per year). However, commitments and disbursement rates of EDF programs have been plagued with low performance. The 8th EDF, for instance, experienced low commitment and disbursement rates amounting to *EUR9.5 billion* in uncommitted funds, while in the case of the 6th EDF (1985 to 1990), the last payment made was in 2002, sixteen years after it had been signed (Grimm, 2004). It is not surprising that beneficiaries have often described the overall EDF aid delivery as poorly coordinated with an overly complex management structure. On a positive note, the woes of the past are gradually being phased out by the EC, and reforms undertaken in 2000 are slowly bearing fruit. The 2005 annual report on the EC's development policy states that the European Court of Auditors has reported signs of improved speed and quality of project management at delegation level. We are also seeing the

[13] National and Regional Indicative Programmes are five-year arrangements under which the EC and ACP countries set out the key areas of intervention.

[14] The National Indicative Programme is split into focal and non-focal sectors of intervention. Under the 9th EDF, very few countries allocated funds to trade and regional integration as a focal sector. However, ACP countries have either used the non-focal sector envelopes for funding TRA or, after the mandatory country strategy mid-term review, have reallocated unused funds for TRA and capacity building activities.

[15] The initial EDF did not comprise seventy-nine countries. These figures are used to show an overall trend and are in no way an exact representation of the volumes disbursed over time, but they convey an idea of volumes being channeled through the EDF mechanism.

emergence of innovative funding arrangements in the form of "basket funds" and initiatives such as the COMESA fund.[16]

Identifying and understanding the real causes of the current bottlenecks in EDF funding are the first steps in addressing problems with the EDF and in improving EU aid effectiveness. It is critical that this begin for at least two reasons. First, the scaling up of European aid to Africa will undoubtedly exert added pressure on the already limited aid administration resources in ACP countries in the context of Cotonou. Second, the "sunset clause"[17] under Cotonou means that any unused funds will be lost after the expiry of each financial protocol signed under the Cotonou Agreement. This means that as of December 2007, any uncommitted funds under the 9th EDF will be lost. This will exert enormous planning and implementation pressures on government agencies, regional bodies, and non-state actors.

Often, bottlenecks are simply a result of poor understanding of procedures, which can be overly complex from a beneficiary standpoint. However, procedures are a necessary evil in development cooperation. They help to ensure both accountability to taxpayers and transparency in the allocation of resources. Ideally, they should be conceived so as to ensure that development programs are implemented smoothly and efficiently (ECDPM, 2003). But often this is not the case, and the EU is not the only development partner to err in this area. In the last few years, there has been a renewed dialogue in the context of the EC reforms and the Paris Declaration to lighten these procedures. Some major changes have been made in contractual procedures with the setup of what are called "framework contracts," which have significantly reduced the time required to mobilize technical expertise. There is also a greater emphasis on providing direct budgetary support to governments, as opposed to project-based funding. This greatly reduces the need to use external procurement procedures, and rather favors the use of harmonized government/donor procurement procedures.

While the concept of "aid effectiveness" has now gained general endorsement among donors and governments, it is unlikely that there will be much improvement in aid delivery until donors and agencies overhaul their own procedures, and are given flexibilities from headquarters to find home-grown solutions for harmonizing and aligning donor procedures. Donors who have attempted to find innovative solutions on the ground by setting up pool funding schemes come up repeatedly against a wall of obstacles that in many cases emanate from the bigger agencies such as the World Bank, which in some countries are not able to participate in common delivery of aid. Yet in some countries, donors have found solutions to their administrative bottlenecks. As we move away from conceptualizing the principles of aid effectiveness to actual implementation, it will be critical for donors and agencies

16 The COMESA Fund has two components, namely, the COMESA Infrastructure Fund and the COMESA Adjustment Facility. The Secretariat has also been developing the COMESA Fund Adjustment Facility. This has been done by developing a regional integration surveillance mechanism, which should act as a "trigger mechanism" for budgetary support.

17 The overall financing period of EDFs used to be open-ended: the fund was open until the last money was paid. In 2003, the EC introduced a "sunset clause n+3": all contracts (excluding audit and evaluation measures) have to be signed at the latest three years after the date of adoption of the budgetary commitment. With the 9th EDF, a general sunset clause for the entire fund will have to be decided upon before 2007.

to provide the required positive incentives to encourage innovation and changes in the current blueprint of procedures. For too long, the reward has been directed to those who were able to respect procedures to the letter. Making aid effectiveness a reality will require a total change in mindset that will reward innovation in project design and encourage a leaning-by-doing approach.

3.2 Positive signs on the horizon

The weaknesses identified in the context of the EDF are not exclusive to the EC, but are often common to other bilateral and multilateral development partners' funding practices. These shared problems have prompted the donor community to review its way of doing business. In the process, a number of key principles on delivery of development aid have emerged. These include: (i) anchoring development aid in beneficiaries' national development policies (such as PRSPs); (ii) ensuring that PRSPs are built along the lines of the UN's Millennium Development Goals (MDGs) (UN, 2005) and that growth is included as a main cluster; (iii) ensuring that trade is mainstreamed into PRSPs; and (iv) ensuring that aid delivery systems are in line with the Paris Declaration on Aid Effectiveness, which has prompted a move towards general budget support and sectoral budget support.

In November 2006 the Council of the European Union and the European Commission adopted a new EU development policy statement, the "European Consensus on Development." The statement provides, for the first time, a common vision that guides the action of the EU, both at its member state and Community levels, in development cooperation. It reflects the changed circumstances since the previous strategy was published in November 2000, and shows a stronger commitment to the Millennium Development Goals. The European Consensus supports the need for increasing development aid and strengthening coordination, harmonization and improved aid effectiveness along the lines of the Paris Declaration. The EC's new development policy and its 10th EDF guidelines on programming of aid to ACP countries are faithful to these principles, which today constitute the key benchmarks of good practice in development cooperation (see Box 12.1 below).

Internal EC reforms both in Brussels (with the creation of EuropeAid, which will implement the EC's external aid instruments) and the devolution process at country level[18] have begun to show some signs of improvement in EDF management. The 2005 Annual Report on EC development policy and the implementation of external assistance in 2004 point to some important findings, namely that:

- At national level, the EC continues to devote a large share of its aid to ACP countries in the form of budget support (30 percent of programs approved in 2004) and sector programs.[19]

[18] Namely, devolution of responsibilities and resources to the EC's offices in the field (delegations). Devolution increased the role of the delegations in matters such as policy dialogue with authorities on complex public service and governance-related reforms, and in coordination with other donors.

[19] In 2004 alone, the EC approved new macroeconomic budget support programs in ten countries, as well as eight new sector policy support programs (SPSPs). Four of the latter – for education, health, rural growth, and infrastructure – are to be funded using budget support, while the remaining four will finance projects.

Box 12.1. EC benchmarks for good practice, as applied to Aid for Trade

- Aid for Trade should be based on the needs and priorities of African countries and needs to be a country-driven process.
- Aid for Trade should be provided in ways that build, and do not inadvertently undermine, African countries' sustainable capacity to develop, implement and account for Aid for Trade to their people and legislatures. The Aid for Trade initiative needs to be embedded in countries' existing aid delivery systems.
- There should be reliance on government systems, where these provide reasonable assurance that Aid for Trade resources will be used for agreed purposes, and where it is likely to enhance achievement of sustainable improvements in government performance.
- African Governments should address weaknesses in institutional capacity or other constraints in existing aid delivery mechanisms so as to ensure effective use of the Aid for Trade package.
- The development of appropriate systems will often be a medium-term process. Until donors can rely on these, they should simplify and harmonize their own procedures to reduce the burden placed on partner countries.
- No single approach is suitable for all countries. The manner in which harmonization is implemented needs to be adapted to local circumstances and institutional capacities.

- Disbursements and commitments, though still not at the level of other regions (including the Euro-Mediterranean Partnership and Asia and Latin America) have been improving, reflecting a better performance of the EDF. Nevertheless, the ACP countries missed their commitment targets in 2004.
- The first sign of efficiency gains due to the devolution from EC headquarters to delegations at country level have been confirmed. However, the ACP region scores lower than other regions.
- Education, health, and other social welfare programs received by far the highest proportion of EC commitments and payments to ACP countries, reflecting the importance the EC attaches to helping achieve the UN's MDGs. The EC also continued to devote considerable resources to infrastructure programs, in which it has many years' experience and expertise, and to budget support to fund government-led initiatives to tackle poverty and promote growth.
- The European Union has been at the forefront of international efforts to harmonize donor practices. An EU pilot initiative on harmonization was launched in 2002 in Mozambique, Morocco, Nicaragua and Vietnam (see Box 12.2 below).

4 How can the ACP maximize the effectiveness of the EDF?

2007 is an important year for the ACP for identifying how the EDF will be delivered in future. Over this period, the ACP countries and their six regional integration organizations are drawing up their Country Strategy Papers and National and Regional Indicative Programmes for the next (10th) EDF disbursement period of 2008–2013. During this time, the ACP and the EU will also finalize the EPAs, under which development finance figures as an area for discussion under the newly-established

Box 12.2. EU harmonization initiatives in Vietnam

Vietnam (along with three other countries) is an EU harmonization pilot. In this country, EC donors consist of twelve active EU member states and the EC. These donors (i) have established joint guidelines for financing of local costs in development cooperation; (ii) use Vietnam's PRSP (Comprehensive Poverty Reduction and Growth Strategy) as a central reference point for cooperation activities; (iii) draft and deliver joint statements at major events such as Consultative Group (CG) meetings; and (iv) offer combined pledging at CG meetings.

Some EU member states are represented in Vietnam's Like-Minded Group of bilateral donors which works closely with the Ministry of Planning and Investment (MPI) as mandated by the Government of Vietnam for harmonization issues. Some are involved with the harmonization activities undertaken by development banks (five-bank group). All groups are coordinating their activities through the CG meetings and, between meetings, through the government-led Partnership Group for Aid Effectiveness chaired by MPI/DFID. However, there is still scope for harmonization across a range of issues. EU coordination and harmonization in Vietnam is at two levels: strategic/policy and operational. At each level, the EU plans to intensify coordination and harmonization across the board, and focus harmonization activities in the following five sectors of co-operation: health, education, private sector development, trade, and governance, and on one geographical area: the Central Highlands (one of the poorest regions in Vietnam).

An EU Action Plan for harmonization and coordination was agreed among EC donors in Vietnam in May 2003 and presented to the government and the other development partners at the mid-term CG meeting in Sapa in June 2003. As a result, there has been enhanced cooperation among EC donors in education, private sector development, and health. Particular focus is on the introduction of sector approaches and budgetary support.

Regional Preparatory Task Forces (RPTFs).[20] These two ongoing parallel processes are unique windows of opportunity for ACP countries to address some of the key bottlenecks that have plagued the implementation of the EDF.

2007 is also important for ACP countries to make fresh and innovative suggestions on how to improve coordination and coherence between the EDF and other instruments such as Aid for Trade and any possible funding that may be available specifically in the context of EPAs. In recent years, ACP countries – through the secretariat of the African Union, the ACP Secretariat, and respective regional organizations – have lobbied strongly for increased funding. Moving forward, the ACP will need to focus on defining with the EC improved, innovative, and efficient aid delivery mechanisms under the 10th EDF. Aid programming and negotiations processes share a common feature, which is that once the processes are over, stakeholders are left with inflexible timelines, projects, and agreements, so preparation is key.

[20] RPTFs have been formed for the EPA negotiating regions in order to cement the strategic link between EPA negotiations and development cooperation. They include representatives from both the EC and EPA countries.

With respect to the EDF programming exercise, the starting point should invariably be countries' national development strategies and/or PRSPs. The programming process should feed from existing national initiatives and make use of existing tools such as implementation plans embedded in PRSPs and DTIS. Anchoring country strategy papers to national development plans is essential to ensure overall coherence between governments and development partners and coordination of aid.

Linking national and regional development projects, especially in the area of trade and infrastructure, could play a catalytic role in strengthening regional trade and integration. The previous NIPs and RIPs have suffered from a lack of coordination, and have been managed in most regions as separate entities. This has prevented the build-up of synergies between projects at regional and national level. Establishing coordination mechanisms that will create a bridge between regions and member states is key in ensuring coherence and complementarity among projects. Under the 9th EDF, the COMESA Secretariat initiated an inter-regional coordination mechanism – the Inter Regional Coordination Committee (IRCC) – that has played a significant role in coordinating COMESA member states not only at the level of programming but also within the context of the EPAs. This model has a number of virtues which could be replicated in other regions and that could also include coordination of Aid for Trade.

Since EDF procedures are known to be an important hurdle for ACP countries, particularly in the area of project implementation, the programming exercise and EPA negotiations through the respective RPTFs offer an opportunity to address this issue. In the spirit of the Joint Assistance Strategy and OECD DAC Working Group on Aid Effectiveness, the EC and other key development partners need to follow through on their commitments to align development assistance and improve systems, harmonize policies and procedures, and implement principles of good practice in development cooperation. A starting point for the EC would be to press for stronger coordination between EU member states. The 10th EDF Programming Guidelines proposed establishing a 'Road Map' which would identify the steps needed to improve harmonization. This Road Map should eventually lead to a coordinated EU approach in development assistance, with the ultimate aim of establishing joint programming among EU member states.

Concurrently, ACP governments must take on a more proactive role in the EDF programming process and demand more accountability from development partners. Being an 'aid recipient' today is no longer synonymous with being passive vis-à-vis the development community. In the context of the Cotonou Partnership, and particularly in setting up their NIPs, ACP countries must impress upon the EC and EU member states the need for a joint financial agreement favoring harmonization of procedures around the country system. To a certain extent, this is already being done in some countries through the set-up of budget support programs. The Joint Assistance Strategy, which is in operation in some ACP countries, is an appropriate tool to enhance coordination and should be implemented in all ACP countries. In the case of Tanzania, the Joint Assistance Strategy offers government and development partners a forum for exploring ways of enhancing aid effectiveness and monitoring commitments made by both sides. The Tanzanian experience offers lessons that could be useful for other ACP countries (see Chapter 8 in this volume).

The issue of absorptive capacity, or the ability of beneficiaries to effectively intake funds, is a problem related both to the ability of donors to disburse funds and to beneficiaries' (private sector and government ministries) ability to take them up. It is not sufficient to make funds available; the administrative and procedural requirements accompanying these funds must be adapted to recipients' capacities to use them effectively (recall that under the 8th EDF, EUR9.5 billion remained unused during the period 1995–2000). Absorptive capacity is not solely a recipient problem, but often lies in inappropriate design of projects and schemes that do not match the capacity of beneficiary countries. For their part, recipients need to be fully trained and provided with the skills and tools in project management. It is imperative that ACP countries address the absorptive capacity issue from both perspectives. Some of the major problems encountered at government level could be addressed by, for instance, improving the institutional linkages between ministries; reviewing management systems (i.e. linking information, human resources and training, salaries and reward systems with staff performance review); and fostering strong project management skills in-house, particularly in project formulation, implementation, and monitoring and evaluation.

5 New trends in EDF programming

In the 1960s, the EDF was the main external expenditure administered by the European Commission. Today, however, the EDF has lost importance as an EC instrument, accounting for less than one third of all EC external expenditure in 2000 (Grimm, 2004). Nevertheless, in absolute terms the EDF remains an important source of funding for ACP countries. The following section reviews some of the new trends in EDF and EC funding to the ACP and African countries. Recently, there has been a marked emergence of global and pan-African initiatives (see below); these need to be anchored in the ACP countries' national priorities. It is imperative that the National Authorising Officers (NAO) follow up on the management and implementation of such projects.

5.1 Global and Pan-African initiatives

EDF funds have increasingly been channeled through a number of new "Global Initiatives" and a "Pan-African Initiative". These new initiatives find their roots in the EU's recent strategy for Africa (Commission of the EC, 2005) and its new communication on development policy, "The European Consensus," which seeks to find new ways to increase the impact of its cooperation by consolidating African-led solutions to the continent's problems.

Global initiatives	Pan-African initiative
• EU Water Initiatives (EUR500 million) • EU Energy Initiatives • Global Fund to fight AIDS, Tuberculosis and Malaria • Education For All/Fast Track Initiative	• EUR250 million African Peace Facility • Trust Fund in Support of Infrastructure in Africa, EUR60 million in grants and EUR250 million in loans from the EIB

These new initiatives have much in common with the 'all ACP' projects and caution must be taken to avoid overlap. It is critical that such initiatives be strongly anchored in countries' national aid delivery mechanisms, lest they suffer the same implementation weaknesses which have previously been associated with other intra-ACP programs. Such an initiative offers the EC strong visibility and usually shifts large volumes of funding (which is also a key priority for the EC). However, if not well designed, these initiatives may confer only very small gains to African countries.

5.1.1 *Regional TRA – budget support and basket funds*

At the regional level, trade adjustment mechanisms already exist and can be used by the EU and ACP to improve regional integration in the context of expanded Aid for Trade. For instance, the Regional Integration Budget Support (RIBS) facility for the Eastern and Southern African EPA region provides direct budgetary support for regional projects. It is coordinated through the Regional Indicative Programme, and as such is linked to EC trade policy and ongoing EPAs and WTO negotiations. In Central and Western Africa, there has also recently been an increase in EU-funded EPA and regional TRA, through projects such as the Appui à l'intégration régionale en Afrique centrale (PAIRAC)[21] and the Programme Economique Régional (PER), a multi-donor program covering regional integration projects in the West African Economic and Monetary Union (UEMOA) zone.

In East Africa, EC delegations and development partners including the World Bank and the African Development Bank are pooling resources for setting up a basket fund for regional projects. The EC has indicated that such arrangements will increasingly be used to enhance donor coordination at regional and national levels.

5.2 EPAs and adjustment

The onset of the EPAs after 2008 is expected to radically alter the traditional framework of EC/ACP trade relations. As liberalization of ACP countries' trade regimes for European goods and services progresses, the ACP will have to grapple with adjustment costs and industry reforms in order to improve competitiveness. To do this will require serious investment in improving productive capacity and trade-related infrastructure. This will be most apparent in the case of LDCs. Under current WTO Doha Round proposals, LDCs would not be required to make any commitments on tariff reductions and services, whereas under the reciprocity requirements under EPAs they would be required to liberalize.[22] It should be noted that, to date, there

[21] The PAIRAC project has an overall budget of EUR16 million to support the Central African regional integration process though (i) support in setting up an EPA to assist in negotiations and activities, paving the way for the agreement; (ii) tightening up multilateral surveillance, so as to facilitate economic convergence of CEMAC member countries; (iii) support in strengthening customs union, especially via observance of existing regulations; (iv) support in strengthening the common market, especially in order to consolidate and develop procedures currently underway; and (v) institution-building (including program management), particularly of the institutions most involved in the regional integration process. The project covers all Central African countries.

[22] GATT Article XXIV holds that countries entering into free trade areas – such as the EPAs – should eliminate duties and other restrictive regulations on "substantially all the trade." Currently, this is

has been little mention of any form of special and differential treatment for LDCs under EPAs. To help mitigate some of the additional costs that ACP countries will have to face when implementing the EPAs, the ACP group has requested that an adjustment facility be established within the framework of the revised Cotonou Partnership Agreement. Uncommitted funds from the 10th EDF (approx. EUR400–700 million) could be used to set up such an adjustment facility.

In the same vein, a case for compensating ACP countries for preference erosion,[23] arising from eventual across-the-board reductions at WTO level and from reform of the EU's Common Agriculture Policy, could be made in the context of Aid for Trade. An October 2005 study by the UN Conference on Trade and Development (UNCTAD) found that the export revenue loss for preference-receiving African ACP States from a 36 percent cut in most-favored nation duties on agricultural products in the EU would lead to an aggregate loss of US$460 million annually, whilst the Commonwealth Secretariat estimates that US$1.7 billion will be lost annually in agriculture and textiles and clothing for preference-dependent countries (UNCTAD, 2005). While these figures are highly divergent, they do indicate that some ACP countries stand to lose significantly from reform in the EU.

5.3 Sectoral adjustment projects

As part of its "new generation" of project and program funding, and in the context of providing assistance to ACP members incurring losses through liberalization, the EU is making use of trade compensation mechanisms and sectoral adjustment/market restructuring projects for the ACP. One example is the EC-ACP Sugar Action Plan, launched in July 2005 with an accompanying financial package of EUR40 million to assist ACP sugar-producing countries diversify their economies in the context of lower guaranteed prices for sugar exports to the EU.[24] This project, which is funded from the EU budget and not EDF, emerged as a direct response to the EU's own sugar reform and its associated erosion of preferences on ACP sugar exporting countries. In the past, there have been similar projects for banana-exporting countries as a result of the collapse of the sector after the dismantling of the EU's banana regime.

5.4 What can we infer from these new trends?

The new trends in EU funding have been motivated by the evolving nature of EU development policy and external trade relations, particularly in the case of the ACP. These changes have been captured in more than forty political and policy commitments made by the EU since 2002, including on improving donor coordination and on coherence between the EC and member states (ECDPM, 2006b). The following are some of the key changes which are likely to affect the way in which EU aid,

interpreted to mean eliminating barriers on 90 percent of the products between parties. Since the EU allows duty- and quota-free market access to ACP countries, the EC has proposed that the ACP eliminate restrictions on 80 percent of EU goods. Phase-in periods and exceptions for special and sensitive products would still need to be defined.

23 It is important to point out that a number of studies on preference erosion indicate that, under the trade protocols, the problem is limited to a handful of countries – primarily small island states and those that have been major recipients of preferential trade agreements and quotas.

24 The EC explicitly clarifies that the EUR40m (2005/06, targeting eighteen ACP countries) is not for compensation but for adapting to new situations.

and for that matter Aid for Trade, will be channeled under the EDF, with some recommendations.

- There will be a stronger focus on RIPs; these should be built around existing regional arrangements and not the EPA configuration. The ACP countries should ensure that the NIPs and RIPs are programmed concurrently, to ensure linkages and complementarity between the two processes.
- A stronger focus on TRA, especially at regional level. There may also be a greater shift to budget support mechanisms and basket funding at regional level.
- Global initiatives and pan-African initiatives need to be anchored in country aid delivery mechanisms.
- ACP countries need to proactively strengthen their public finance management systems.
- Budget support should be the preferred means of aid delivery, leaving projects to private sector development and non-state actors.
- The ACP group needs to make a strong case for additional funds under EPAs, focusing on adjustment cost issues and supply-side constraints. ACP countries should ensure that funds pledged in the context of Aid for Trade be channeled to NIPs and RIPs.
- Encourage the EC to move forward swiftly towards joint programming with member states and ensure that an EU Road Map is established in every country.

It is critical that ACP countries be aware of the wave of change ahead so as to be in a position to prepare and strategize as a group on how best to capitalize on the positive trends and mitigate any negative trends. The 10th EDF programming exercise needs to be seen as more than a mere *fund allocating process*. The programming process provides the ACP countries with an opportunity to ensure that EDF funds are made more efficient, by focusing on coordination mechanisms that need to be put in place. In the same vein, particular attention should also be paid to capacity building and institutional building activities, which should go hand-in-hand with the set-up of the programs and projects. It is also an opportunity to review coordination among donors and in particular, in the context of TRA, to see how Aid for Trade can be incorporated in the 10th EDF process.

The EDF guidelines and framework have already been set in motion and the National and Regional Indicative Programmes will – as under the 9th EDF – be distributed between Envelope A (program funds) and Envelope B (non-program funds).[25] However, for the sake of coordination and complementarity, it could be envisaged that any "new funding" from the EC under either an EPA facility or Aid for Trade could be rationalized under a newly created Envelope C. Given that ACP countries and regions are well versed in the implementation of the NIPs and RIPs, and that systems are already in place for the management of such funds, this would help rationalize activities and minimize the need for countries and regional integration organizations to navigate a maze of facilities and complex implementation processes. The Envelope C could be dedicated to trade-related adjustment and could be seen as a more dynamic envelope that could be updated throughout the life cycle of the 10th EDF, depending on the flow of funding from the EC to TRA. Given that the 10th EDF process is already in motion, this proposal could still be introduced at the RPTF level by the ACP secretariat in the context of the

[25] Envelope B consists of funds put aside for unforeseen circumstances and emergencies.

EPA negotiations. It is worth noting that such an envelope may require a different accounting set-up, in the event that the funding on Aid for Trade or EPAs would come from a different source than the EDF. An Envelope C would greatly enhance coordination and complementarity between EDF funding and other sources of EC TRA. The following section will deal specifically with how Aid for Trade could be incorporated into the existing EDF architecture.

6 Articulating Europe's TRA in the context of Aid for Trade

The delivery systems available for TRA, capacity building, and trade-related infrastructure are common to the existing systems used for aid delivery in general. When discussing these systems, it is useful to make the distinction between Channels and Instruments (see Table 12.1). In the area of TRA,[26] the majority of aid tends to be disbursed through national and regional projects, and through the IF and JITAP at the global level. According to the joint WTO/OECD Trade Capacity Building Database (2007), from 2001 to 2006, donors funded close to 15,000 activities, provided by more than forty bilateral donors and multilateral agencies. Since the Doha Ministerial Declaration in 2001, total assistance to trade capacity building has increased by 50 percent. As donors become increasingly active in this area, Aid for Trade capacity has grown to some 4.4 percent of total aid commitments of the world's major contributors, according to a joint report by the WTO and the OECD.

Table 12.1. TRA delivery systems

Channel	Instruments	TRA delivery systems
Multilateral	Projects: Global	• IF contributions to the TRA / capacity building Trust Funds (JITAP, IF Trust Fund, the ITC and the WTO) increased from US$26 million in 2001 to US$45 million in 2003, and remained stable at that level in 2004. • JITAP • Doha Development Agenda Global Trust Fund
Regional	Projects and programs (budget support, SWAps,[27] basket funds)	At regional level, the focus is also on projects, with a few basket funds in the making.
Bilateral	Projects and programs (budget support, SWAps, basket funds)	At bilateral level, the focus to date has been on projects. However, we are seeing an emerging trend in basket funds and budget support in the area of compensation for revenue losses.

26 TRA in this context includes capacity building and trade-related assistance for infrastructure.

27 Sector-wide approaches, or SWAps, bring together governments, donors and other stakeholders to deliver aid in a specific sector (such as trade or health), characterized by a set of operating principles rather than a specific package of policies or activities. They comprise one of several relatively new aid modalities that have emerged as a means of overcoming the lack of sufficient recipient ownership and the fragmentation of many individual projects, which, even when taken as a whole, have not necessarily resulted in adequate support for a country's identified development priorities.

It is worth noting that the EC and EU member states' contributions to the IF Trust Fund[28] represent more than one third of total TRA contributions. This raises the question of how the EC's contribution to the Aid for Trade initiative should be coordinated with its existing national and regional projects, a question which is valid for all bilateral projects, and how this will fit into an overall Aid for Trade delivery mechanism. In the case of the EC, setting up an Envelope C, as proposed in this chapter, could help ensure that Aid for Trade and any potential additional funding for EPAs is synchronized and aligned with the existing EDF architecture.

7 What does the EU Aid for Trade mechanism currently look like, and how to articulate it in the broader national context of Aid for Trade?

The diagram below lays out a typical EDF aid delivery mechanism, including both national and regional levels. The EC has a number of options for channeling aid to TRA, capacity building, and infrastructure. The challenge, however, remains on how to include the Aid for Trade initiative in that existing framework without having to create new funding structures and new procedural rules that would add to the already impenetrable maze of projects and programs with which ACP countries have to grapple.

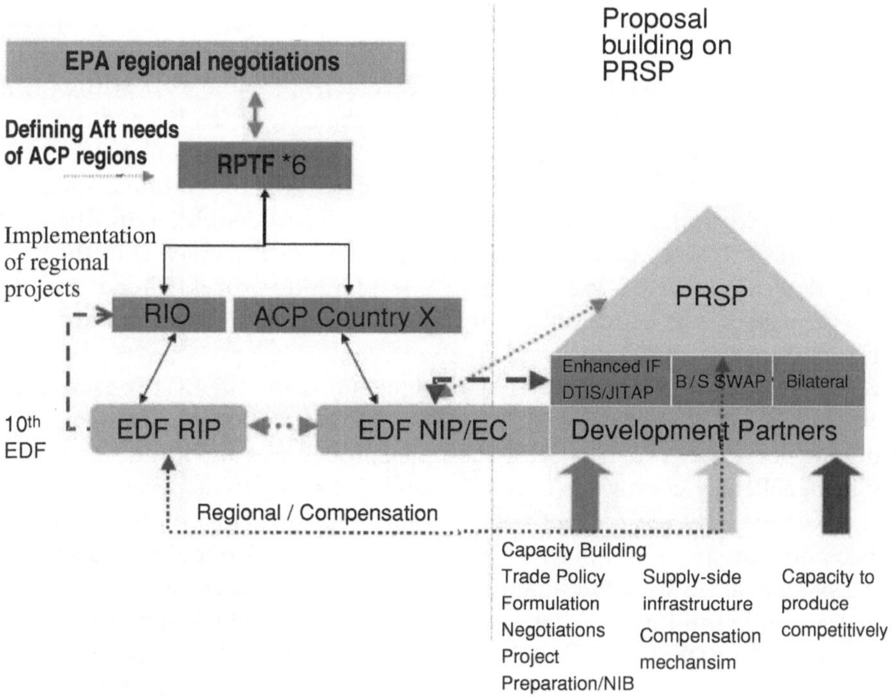

Figure 12.1. EDF aid delivery mechanism.

28 EU member states' contributions represent more than half of total contributions to the WTO Global Trust Fund; EC and member states' contribution to UNCTAD trade-related technical assistance is also significant. In addition, EU member states have contributed significantly to the creation of the Advisory Centre for WTO Law and to other programs, such as JITAP, IF, and the ITC.

Regional Level: The EC via the RPTF has a platform for discussing programming of TRA, capacity building, and infrastructure that could be channeled to the regional integration organizations and managed by the secretariats of the respective organizations, namely COMESA, EAC, SADC, ECOWAS, CARIFORUM and PACIFIC FORUM. The focus on Aid for Trade at this level would be on regional infrastructure, such as trade facilitation, roads, rail, information and communication technologies, and a compensation mechanism for tariff revenue loss resulting from liberalization.

National Level: Aid for Trade would be channeled to the NIPs and would be aligned to the priority areas identified in the PRSPs, national development plans, and DTIS action matrices (where available). Delivery of Aid for Trade will be anchored in existing mechanisms. In the case of the EC, given its preference for general budgetary support, SWAps and sectoral budget support, it is likely that these will be the preferred instruments for delivery of Aid for Trade.

Multilateral Level: The EC contribution to the Enhanced IF is likely to be increased in view of its pledged additional EUR1 billion a year to Aid for Trade.

Global Project: The EC has set up a number of global funds such as the Trust Fund for Infrastructure in Africa with the EIB. These will also constitute a growing share of the aid delivery mechanism.

8 Conclusions

If Aid for Trade is to be delivered effectively, it should as far as possible work within the existing architecture, especially at bilateral level. In the case of the EC and the ACP, this could be done though the joint programming and management of Aid for Trade via the existing EDF aid delivery infrastructure, particularly the National and Regional Indicative Programs. Any new funding from the EC under either an EPA facility or wider Aid for Trade could be rationalized under an Envelope C in the EDF specifically dedicated to TRA. With the 10th EDF planning process already in motion, such a proposal could be introduced by the ACP Secretariat in the context of the EPA negotiations.

Strong coordination is needed between EU member states and the EC to ensure coherence and complementarity in aid delivery. Such efforts will need to be reinforced by reducing bottlenecks such as overly-complex procedures and low absorptive capacity in beneficiary countries. This will require development partners to establish a fine balance between control and flexibility, whilst recipient countries will need to become more proactive players. In the case of LDCs, Aid for Trade also will need to be synchronized with the IF and the upcoming Enhanced IF.

Disbursement and commitment rates for regional projects, which tend to be among the lowest in the EDF, will definitely need to be improved. This is particularly relevant in the context of the push toward more regional integration and the expectation that many Aid for Trade funds will be directed at strengthening intra-regional trade capacity. Since sizeable funds are expected to be channeled through regional integration organizations, significant investments will need to be made in improving the staffing of these bodies that are responsible for identification, formulation, and implementation of regional projects. The COMESA IRCC, which has played a significant role in coordinating COMESA member states' programming on trade issues, is a useful model to consider in coordinating regional Aid for Trade delivery.

A final note on infrastructure, which remains a critical component of building supply-side capacity. Given the challenge ahead for the ACP countries with respect to funding in this area, it is imperative that more flexible collaboration be explored between development partners and development banks such as the African Development Bank. The current situation is that the entities tend to work separately, and that due to financial and institutional regulations co-funding is often difficult. Financing hard infrastructure in ACP countries will need new and innovative approaches that bring together development partners, development banks, and the private sector. This process could be catalyzed by ACP countries strategically opening up certain key services sectors with a view to enhancing foreign direct investment. The ultimate challenge will be for ACP countries to find the right balance of aid, loans, local private equity, and foreign direct investment to finance development and bring these partners to sit at the same table, and to supplement this with improved aid delivery systems and procedures.

REFERENCES

Commission of the European Communities. 2005. "EU Strategy for Africa: Towards a Euro-African pact to accelerate Africa's development," communication from the Commission to the Council, the European Parliament and the European Economic and Social Committee, SEC(2005) 1255, Brussels: Commission of the European Communities.

ECDPM. 2003. "InfoCotonou No. 3: Do procedures hamper policy ambitions?," Maastricht: ECDPM.

ECDPM. 2006a. "EPA Development Support: Consequences of GAERC conclusions for EPAs," *ECDPM InBrief 16A*, Maastricht: ECDPM.

ECDPM. 2006b. "The 10th European Development Fund – Negotiations, next steps and key issues," Maastricht: ECDPM.

ECDPM/ICTSD. 2006. "Suspension of Doha Round and EPAs: the case of Aid for Trade," *Trade Negotiations Insights*, 5(5), Maastricht and Geneva: ECDPM and ICTSD.

GAERC. 2006. "Aid for Trade – Draft conclusions of the Council and the Representatives of the Governments of the Member States meeting within the Council," Council of the European Union, 13882/06, Brussels: GAERC.

Grimm, Sven. 2004. "Aid disbursement and effectiveness," *European Development Cooperation to 2010*, London: Overseas Development Institute.

Hoekman, Bernard and Susan Prowse. 2005. "Policy Responses to Preference Erosion: From Trade as Aid to Aid for Trade," Policy Research Working Paper 3721, Washington, D.C.: World Bank.

IMF/World Bank. 2004. "Aid Effectiveness and Financing Modalities," Development Committee Background Paper, DC2004-0012/Add.1, Washington, D.C.: IMF and World Bank.

OECD. 2005. "Paris Declaration on Aid Effectiveness – Ownership, Harmonization, Alignment, Results and Mutual Accountability," High Level Forum, Paris, 28 February–2 March 2005, http://www.oecd.org/dataoecd/11/41/34428351.pdf.

UN. 2005. "UN Millennium Development Goals," United Nations, http://www.un.org/millenniumgoals/.

UNCTAD. 2004. "The Least Developed Countries Report 2004 – Linking International Trade with Poverty Reduction," prepared by the UNCTAD secretariat, New York and Geneva: United Nations.

UNCTAD. 2005. "Review of the Development and Issues in the Post Doha Work Program of Particular Concern to Developing Countries," note by the UNCTAD Secretariat, Geneva: United Nations.

Wise, Timothy A. and Kevin P. Gallagher. 2005. "The Hong Kong Ministerial: What's at Stake for the Poor?," *Bridges*, 9(10), December.

WTO. 2006. *Recommendations of the Task Force on Aid for Trade*, Aid for Trade Task Force, WT/AFT/1, 27 July.

WTO/OECD. 2007. "Doha Development Agenda Trade Capacity Building Database," http://tcbdb.wto.org/.

13 Services-Related Projects in Aid for Trade[1]

PIERRE SAUVÉ

1 Aid for Trade in services: the need for a tailored response

Aid for Trade is about assisting developing countries increase their exports of goods and services, better integrate into the multilateral trading system, and benefit from liberalized trade and increased market access. Effective Aid for Trade can be expected, alongside a range of domestic policies, to enhance growth prospects and reduce poverty in developing countries, as well as complement multilateral trade reforms and help distribute global benefits from liberalization more equitably across and within developing countries.[2]

The particular nature of services trade and of services liberalization – regulated by the World Trade Organization's (WTO) General Agreement on Trade in Services (GATS) – imparts a number of special features to the Aid for Trade debate in the sector. For starters, in the absence of tariff protection, there is no significant preference erosion agenda to speak of in services, and hence little need to foresee compensatory payments for countries or regions affected by MFN-based negotiating advances. The non-tariff nature of impediments to services trade implies that governments do not forego fiscal receipts when engaging in preferential liberalization in services trade (Mattoo and Fink, 2004).

The multiplicity of modes of supplying services and the ensuing regulatory intensity of services trade and of related factor movements raises a host of technical assistance challenges. The predominance of commercial presence as a mode of supplying services suggests that assistance directed at enhancing a host country's investment climate may be particularly important in enhancing the competitiveness of the service sector. At the same time, the rising salience of cross-border trade and of possibilities for remotely supplying services markets highlights the need for greater regulatory convergence, for the development and adoption of international standards, and the negotiation of mutual recognition agreements as various means of facilitating cross-border trade in services.

Moreover, the practice of market opening in services, where negotiated outcomes are far likelier to result in status quo commitments (that is, policy consolidation or less) than to generate *de novo* market opening, suggests that the scope for significant post-liberalization adjustment pressures is generally absent (or

[1] This paper draws on insights first developed in Sauvé (2006c).
[2] See the recommendations of the WTO Task Force on Aid for Trade (WTO, 2006).

minimal) in most negotiating settings. This implies that discussions of an Aid for Trade response in services can generally be divorced from concerns over the design and adequacy of compensatory financing for the potential "losers" from market opening.

This is not to say that market opening in services cannot produce distributional downsides. It most surely can, as with liberalization in any given sector. The main point, however, is that significant new market opening is rarely the norm.[3] Such opening can be sequenced (including through pre-commitments to future liberalization via GATS Article 18 commitments) in such a manner as to mitigate significant adjustment pressures. Little as they may be, any such adjustment pressures resulting from market opening initiatives in services could also be addressed through recourse to an operational emergency safeguard mechanism.[4]

2 Toward legally binding Aid for Trade commitments?

Managing service sector reforms requires that market opening be accompanied by a careful combination of competition and regulation, including pro-competitive regulation. Such a process can present important challenges to resource-constrained governments in many developing countries. It also highlights the need for progressive liberalization, a feature that trade agreements are generally well-framed to promote, and to the equally critical need, today fully acknowledged in the Doha Development Agenda (DDA), to invest in trade-related capacity building aimed at building sounder negotiating and regulatory regimes and implementing institutions in developing countries.

In the services area, an approach that combines Aid for Trade with additional trade and investment liberalization commitments could help promote progress in the negotiations, while also addressing the legitimate concerns voiced by many developing country governments and civil society organizations over the extent of asymmetries at the negotiating table. Because of the sheer diversity of the sectoral realities encompassed by services trade, a coherence-promoting Aid for Trade package in services requires close cooperation and coordination among numerous multilateral institutions, bilateral donors, and civil society actors (both private sector and non-governmental organization – NGO – representatives).

The DDA and other WTO ministerial declarations are replete with references to trade-related technical assistance and capacity building, none of which are legally binding. To guard against the very real risk that the absence of technical assistance may stymie needed reforms and unduly hold back liberalization commitments, consideration needs to be given to establishing a more formal link between enhanced market access commitments by developing countries and additional assistance on the part of developed countries and relevant multilateral agencies.

Such a link could lend greater credibility to both liberalization and technical assistance programs. Indeed, the development promise of the Doha Round, and the ubiquitous calls for coherence in policy-making, would be well served if one of the tangible dividends of a completed DDA would be up-front commitments by the

[3] With the notable exception of countries seeking accession to the WTO whose average level of GATS commitments in most instances is that scheduled by developed countries during the Uruguay Round. See Adlung (2004) and Adlung and Roy (2005).

[4] See Sauvé (2002; 2006a), Marchetti and Mavroidis (2004), and Pierola (2006) for a fuller discussion of emergency safeguard measures in services trade.

leading multilateral and regional lending agencies in support of a strengthening of regulatory institutions and of supply responses in developing countries.

3 Aid for Trade challenges in services trade

The question naturally arises of where additional assistance can best be directed in the services field. Developing countries face two central challenges in undertaking service sector reforms. First, that of identifying the elements of 'good' (economically sound) services policy. And second, that of assessing how the choice of good policy at the domestic level can be supported by multilateral (or bilateral/regional) negotiations (Mattoo, 2003).

Addressing the clear deficit in negotiating, enforcement, and supply-side capacities faced by most developing countries under the GATS requires that a fresh look be given in the Doha Round to the idea of linking scheduled commitments, now or in the future, to legally binding provisions on the supply of needed technical assistance. The latter should aim at the threefold strengthening of the:

(i) Ability to negotiate from a more informed position;
(ii) Capacity to better manage the process of market opening; and
(iii) Ability to supply newly-opened foreign markets.

3.1 Negotiating and analytical capacities

Despite its innate promise, the complexity of liberalizing services trade under the GATS cannot be underestimated, particularly in light of the limited administrative and negotiating capacities of many developing countries. A country needs to gather significant knowledge before it can submit informed market opening requests and offers. This includes identifying opportunities and challenges for its exporters; determining the capacity building needs of its negotiators, line ministries, and regulatory agencies; and assessing the likely economic and social impacts of various liberalization scenarios.

Preparing for negotiations thus requires that countries establish a multi-stakeholder approach involving all relevant governmental agencies (and negotiators), legislators, sectoral regulators, as well as civil society representatives (business and NGOs). Improved mechanisms for coordination and consultation are critical to putting forward a coherent view that identifies and pursues the national interest. This is particularly true for services, given the wide variety of sectors, modes of supply and regulatory spheres involved and the economy-wide influences that service sector reforms can impart.

Numerous developing countries have encountered recurring difficulties in identifying their specific sectoral interests in services negotiations, the barriers to their exports, or the impact of detailed requests by trading partners (particularly those from developed countries) on their services sectors. Such challenges are compounded when developing country administrations are stretched by several concurrent negotiations at the bilateral, regional, and multilateral level.[5] Not surprisingly,

[5] Djibouti offers a useful illustration. The country's sole services expert at the Ministry of Trade and Industry is expected to simultaneously lead negotiations on an Economic Partnership Agreement with the European Union alongside regional talks within COMESA and multilaterally at the WTO. Needless to say, there are not enough days in the week to carry out such tasks in an informed manner.

progress in tabling meaningful liberalization commitments has been slow, with several leading developing country services exporters advancing proposals that have to date failed singularly (albeit partly on tactical grounds) to lock in the regulatory status quo, let alone roll back new impediments to trade and investment in services.

Of particular concern to developing countries is the question of how to evaluate the requests received from trading partners, and the formulation of their own requests and offers. The latter is a particularly complex task, as countries need to determine their national policy objectives and the competitiveness of each sector or sub-sector. Such challenges are compounded by the need to determine, among other things, the optimal sequencing of the steps involved in liberalization, the capacity of domestic firms to provide the services in question and whether this capacity would be positively or negatively affected by further competition in the market, as well as the adequacy of domestic regulatory regimes and enforcement capacities.

Other elements of such an evaluation relate to the impact of market opening on investment, employment, and access to higher quality imports or more efficient foreign suppliers. While the adoption of plurilateral negotiating platforms (that is, collective requests and offers) could lessen some of these burdens, it would clearly not obviate the need for WTO members to be clear on the economic and regulatory implications of making new or improved commitments.

WTO members cannot participate meaningfully in services negotiations without first understanding how domestic reform is best pursued. This requires careful analysis informed through dialogue between national stakeholders, country negotiators, and independent researchers. A stocktaking exercise to consider national and cross-country experience with services reform could help identify areas where reforms can be fast-tracked, and those where uncertainties suggest greater doses of regulatory precaution.

Many capacity building efforts in services have so far focused on helping negotiators and policy officials master the legal provisions of the GATS. More pressing needs that are arguably more conducive to harnessing the pro-development potential of services liberalization include acquiring the analytical tools to determine a country's readiness to liberalize; developing government-wide negotiating strategies; and helping domestic service providers take full advantage of market access opportunities arising from regional and multilateral liberalization efforts.

Technical assistance directed to meet the above needs deserves greater attention on the part of multilateral agencies and the donor community. For the most part, this entails the dissemination of knowledge on best practice initiatives in countries – developed and developing – that have been successful reformers. Invariably, these countries will tend to be those that have developed efficient communication channels with the multiplicity of stakeholders that services negotiations entail.

An assessment of the effects of services liberalization is foreseen under the GATS. The donor community could lend credibility to such a process by setting up a group of internationally recognized experts to lead and direct such work. An initiative of this type could help ensure that WTO commitments reflect sound economic policy rather than the dictates of domestic or foreign pressure groups (Mattoo, 2003).

3.2 Implementation and enforcement capacities

The complexity of services sector reform can present formidable challenges to developing countries. These are compounded by the critical need for liberalization efforts to be rooted in, accompanied by, and, in some instances, preceded by sound regulation (including regulatory enforcement capacity). Low-income countries are also likelier on average to have weak regulatory regimes and enforcement capacities. There is, accordingly, a need for progressivity in liberalization, a feature the GATS is uniquely framed to promote. This is matched by the equally critical need, fully acknowledged in the DDA, to invest in trade-related capacity building aimed at remedying such institutional and regulatory weaknesses.

If there is one area where competent technical assistance can make a difference, it is in strengthening regulatory agencies and their staff in developing countries. Regulatory institutions are costly and require staff with sophisticated legal and economic skills. Yet sound domestic regulation is critical to realizing the full benefits of open services markets and responding to their potential downsides.

Helping developing countries improve domestic standards and qualifications for services, notably by strengthening their participation in regional or global standard-setting initiatives, is another area where more focused capacity building efforts can yield strong development dividends. Low standards and related inadequacies in domestic regulation can frustrate access of developing country services and service providers to foreign markets. It can also legitimize existing trade and investment barriers directed against such exports (Mattoo, 2003).

A further candidate for enhanced assistance in the post-negotiating/implementation phase relates to help in designing reforms that properly factor the impacts of liberalization on the poor, and improve their access to essential services. Such services run the gamut from sanitation to transport, health, telecommunications, small-scale finance, education and health. While most of these complementary policy challenges lie outside the realm of GATS negotiations, getting them right can help build needed support for reform efforts. However, implementing such policies in an economically sound manner can present numerous challenges to weak bureaucracies, and many developing countries, particularly the Least Developed Countries (LDCs), will require outside support in meeting them.

Services-exporting firms in industrial countries also have a stake in ensuring that markets are opened, that such opening is sustainable, and that it occurs in a stable regulatory environment. These objectives can be served by enhanced private sector support for improved regulatory institutions and universal access policies. Just as the private sector is often required to contribute, directly or indirectly (through taxation) to financing domestic regulatory agencies without compromising arms-length relationships, it should be possible for the private sector to contribute financial resources, people, and expertise toward enhanced regulatory reform and supply capacity in developing countries. The international development community should thus establish a mechanism, funded by public and private donors, to provide policy advice and to diagnose and remedy regulatory inadequacies for developing countries that are considering liberalizing commitments in services.

Facilitating regulatory cooperation could help deal with the genuine apprehensions about liberalization that are felt by many WTO members. For example, in financial services, confidence in cooperation by the home-country regulator could lead to openness to both commercial presence and cross-border trade.

3.3 Supply capacity[6]

The third pillar of a coherent Aid for Trade package in services needs to target the very real constraints that many developing country exporters face in attempting to contest newly-opened markets. Despite the many (and growing number of) success stories in the developing world in sectors such as energy, research and development, business process outsourcing, construction, or environmental services, there remain too few examples of companies from developing countries involved in export trade to a significant degree.

Several reasons may be put forward to explain this fact, starting with the large fixed costs of entering such capital-intensive sectors, as well as the global presence of some very large companies already in the market. Even in sectors where developing countries are exporting, studies reveal a number of key common problems facing their exporters, including: (i) lack of access to financing for export or business development; (ii) difficulties encountered in establishing credibility with international suppliers; (iii) lack of access to reliable and inexpensive infrastructure;[7] and (iv) lack of access to a range of formal and informal networks and institutional facilities necessary for trade.[8]

Because of its central focus on the private sector, capacity building in respect of supply-side constraints involves a different set of institutional actors than those concerned with the strengthening of trade negotiating or regulatory capacity. Such differences matter for assistance design and inter-agency coordination efforts. It is also an area in which greater private sector involvement from services exporting firms in industrial countries could usefully complement the efforts of bilateral donors and multilateral agencies such as the United Nations Industrial Development Organization (UNIDO) and the International Trade Centre (ITC). The contribution of private sector actors from the developed world may also be usefully harnessed in strengthening the regulatory compliance mechanisms of services firms in developing countries.

REFERENCES

Adlung, Rudolf. 2004. "The GATS Turns Ten: A Preliminary Stocktaking," Staff Working Paper ERSD 2004-05, Geneva: WTO.

Adlung, Rudolf and Martin Roy. 2005. "Turning hills into mountains? Current commitments under the GATS and prospects for change," Staff Working Paper ERSD 2005-01, Geneva: WTO.

6 For a fuller discussion, see OECD (2003).

7 Lack of reliable energy supply and inadequate transport or telecommunications infrastructure raises costs for all goods- and services-producing sectors. Poor infrastructure can thus exacerbate the credibility problems described above.

8 The latter absence can range from a sound domestic legal environment for business, to links to other exporters or export associations, or to broader business networks. For services in particular, given the close linkages and symbiotic relationships between services firms, particularly small and medium-sized enterprises, problems can arise from the unavailability of important ancillary or supporting business services in the home market.

Marchetti, Juan and Petros Mavroidis. 2004. "What are the main challenges for the GATS framework? Don't talk about revolution," *European Business Organization Law Review*, 5(3): 511–62.

Mattoo, Aaditya. 2003. "Services in a Development Round," *The World Trade Brief*, London: Agenda Publishing.

Mattoo, Aaditya and Carsten Fink. 2004. "Regional Agreements and Trade in Services: Policy Issues," *Journal of Economic Integration*, 19(4): 742–79.

OECD. 2003. "Services Liberalisation: Identifying Opportunities and Gains – Part II: Modelling the Benefits of Services Trade Liberalisation," TD/TC/WP(2003)23/Part2/Rev1, Paris: OECD.

Pierola, Fernando. 2006. "A Safeguard Regime for GATS," paper prepared for the World Trade Forum, World Trade Institute, Berne, Switzerland, 8–9 September.

Roy, Martin, Juan Marchetti, and Aik Hoe Lim. 2006. "WTO: Services Liberalization in the New Generation of PTAs: How Much Further than the GATS," paper prepared for the World Trade Forum, World Trade Institute, Berne, Switzerland, 8–9 September.

Sauvé, Pierre. 2002. "Services," *Regionalism and the Multilateral Trading System*, Paris: OECD.

Sauvé, Pierre. 2006a. "Services and the Doha Development Agenda: Southern Perspectives," in P. Van Dyck and G. Faber (eds.), *Completing the Doha Round*, London: Routledge (forthcoming).

Sauvé, Pierre. 2006b. "Adding Value at the Periphery: Aiming for GATS+ Advances in Regional Agreements on Services," *World Trade Review*, (forthcoming).

Sauvé, Pierre. 2006c. "Been There, Not [Quite] [Yet] Done That: Lessons and Challenges in Services Trade," NCCR Trade Regulation Working Paper No. 2006/18, Berne: World Trade Institute (Revised).

WTO. 2006. *Recommendations of the Task Force on Aid for Trade*, Aid for Trade Task Force, WT/AFT/1, 27 July.

14 Aid for Trade for Services in Small Economies: Some Considerations from the Caribbean

RAMESH CHAITOO

1 Introduction

Services comprise a significant proportion of the economies of the Caribbean Community (CARICOM).[1] This is particularly true of the smaller territories in the Eastern Caribbean. However, few countries in the region, if any, have a clearly-articulated services trade policy. The historical approach in government policy-making has been to focus on trade in goods and inadvertently ignore services, perhaps because the stakeholders in the manufacturing and agricultural sectors are much more organized and have traditionally enjoyed direct access to the government. Also, data limitations make it very difficult to get a grasp of activities in the "invisibles" sector.[2] As a result, little specific attention has been paid to fostering the development of services industries in CARICOM, with the exception of the tourism sector, and, to a lesser extent, offshore financial services. Furthermore, CARICOM states have not included rules or market access provisions regarding services in their bilateral trade agreements. This is true even in a recent free trade agreement negotiated with Costa Rica in 2003.

At the international level, Aid for Trade discussions have largely focused on support to facilitate and increase the export of goods or merchandise trade from developing countries. Furthermore, as te Velde points out, aid for services trade negotiations is quite low, at around three quarters of a percent (0.75 percent) of total aid for trade policy and regulation (te Velde, 2005). Secondly, there is a preoccupation with support to the public rather than the private sector; but while the former has policy constraints, the real commercial capacity constraints lie in the private sector. The focus on the public sector is partly due to the nature and mandates of multilateral agencies, which are really designed to serve national governments, or which see public rather than private stakeholders as their clients; but it is also due to a lack of appreciation of what is needed to really help developing countries expand their trade. While not downplaying the importance of support to governments for addressing "infrastructural" needs such as the regulatory framework for

[1] Antigua and Barbuda, Bahamas, Barbados, Belize, Dominica, Grenada, Guyana, Haiti, Jamaica, St. Kitts and Nevis, St. Lucia, St. Vincent and the Grenadines, Suriname, Trinidad and Tobago. Haiti joined CARICOM in 2002 but as of 2007 had not yet fulfilled all of its obligations under the CARICOM Treaty. The Bahamas is a member of CARICOM but not of the Common Market.

[2] While economists traditionally considered most services non-tradable because they have to be consumed where they are produced and to some extent lack mobility, technological changes and trade liberalization have led to phenomenal growth in trade in services.

services trade and policy development regarding the services sector, this paper will argue that in the case of small countries, it is critical that the constraints faced by services firms be urgently addressed if gains are to be made by developing countries in the short and medium term. While the World Trade Organization's (WTO) General Agreement on Trade in Services (GATS) Article IV aspires to increase the participation of developing countries in global trade in services, the mechanisms to do so have not been addressed by multilateral or plurilateral initiatives. With a view to shedding light on a way forward for Aid for Trade in services, this chapter first presents an overview of services trade in CARICOM states and the idiosyncrasies of services firms in the region. It then explores mechanisms to address their constraints and challenges through Aid for Trade initiatives.

The small countries of CARICOM face declining competitiveness in trade in their traditional products and relative decline in the value of preferences in their key markets for their mainly agricultural export commodities.[3] As Canada, the European Union, and the United States sign bilateral trade agreements with a host of different countries, the preferences that CARICOM states now enjoy in those markets are becoming less meaningful. Furthermore, all countries in the group except Trinidad and Tobago have been facing deficits in their trade accounts for the past decade at least. Therefore, it is imperative that CARICOM countries develop the full potential of their services industries to contribute to export growth and development. In light of this issue, it is critical for Aid for Trade discussions in the Caribbean context to focus on services industries rather than on the traditional preoccupation with manufactured and agricultural goods. There is also a need for close linkages between the regional process to create a single market in services and the need to attract foreign investment in order to take advantage of economic opportunities in the global economy.

Although the tourism and offshore financial services sectors are well developed in several CARICOM economies, foreign investment in other services sectors that have potential for exports have not grown significantly since 2000.[4] Most domestic services firms are small, and lack the capital base to develop into exporters. Also, Caribbean governments have apparently not focused on promoting the services sector through their industrial and trade policies.

2 Contribution of services to CARICOM economies

Table 14.1 shows the contribution of services to gross domestic product (GDP) and to exports respectively in CARICOM states. It is evident that services are by far the most important component of economic activity in most economies in the region.[5] Further, the smaller the economy, the more important is the contribution of services to exports. Nevertheless, services have traditionally enjoyed little political

[3] Except for Trinidad and Tobago, which is an oil and gas producer and has various petrochemical industries.

[4] The liberalization of some telecommunications services since 2000 in several CARICOM states has resulted in considerable foreign investment in the infrastructure for mobile or cellular telephone services.

[5] The situation is different in the strong manufacturing economy of Trinidad and Tobago, which has significant natural resources. In the case of Guyana and Suriname, the services sector is underdeveloped and this is reflected both in terms of its lower contribution to GDP and particularly to exports.

Table 14.1. Contribution of services to GDP and exports in CARICOM

	Services as % of GDP (2000)*	Share of total exports (%) (2002)	
		Goods	Services
Antigua and Barbuda	92.9	8.8	91.2
Bahamas	90.0	28.1	71.9
Barbados	84.1	19.5	80.5
Belize	62.4	62.8	37.2
Dominica	76.4	36.7	63.3
Grenada	83.9	30.6	69.4
Guyana	46.5	74.2	25.8
Haiti	61.8	66.9	33.1
Jamaica	71.1	40.5	59.5
St. Kitts and Nevis	84.2	41.6	58.4
St. Lucia	87.1	12.8	87.2
St. Vincent and the Grenadines	83.3	22.9	77.1
Suriname	61.5	90.6	9.4
Trinidad and Tobago	67.9	87.2	12.8
CARICOM		**52.8**	**47.2**
CARICOM (less Trinidad and Tobago)		**38.3**	**61.7**
OECS		**20.3**	**79.7**

* ECLAC, IMF and ECCB
Source: IDB/INTAL (2005, p. 82).

importance, and still appear to have very low priority in terms of Overseas Development Assistance to CARICOM states. This may be partly due to the fact that the national governments themselves do not pay sufficient attention to services sector development. There may be a clear case for reorientation of the focus of industrial and trade policy on the services sector in this region and a focus for the first time on the private sector, rather than on government agencies or trade ministries.

While services constitute a significant part of CARICOM economies, services exports for most CARICOM states are now concentrated in tourism and financial services. As the Economic Commission for Latin America and the Caribbean (ECLAC) has pointed out:

> An examination of services exports from the Caribbean reveals high dependence on tourism (travel receipts). For example, travel accounted for nearly 90 percent of the service receipts of the Dominican Republic and Bahamas and 67 percent of those of Jamaica and Barbados in 2000 (ECLAC, 2003).

The level of this dependence on tourism is clearly revealed in Figure 14.1. For the period 1997–2002, tourism comprised 70 percent of total services exports on average. However, CARICOM states import a much wider range of services, particularly business, finance, construction, and transport, among others; and the greatest concentration is in Other Business Services (24 percent) (see Figure 14.2). This pattern of the export of relatively low valued-added services (tourism) while importing higher value-added services is very much akin to the situation in merchandise trade, since the bulk of goods exports are commodities. But it is not a healthy formula

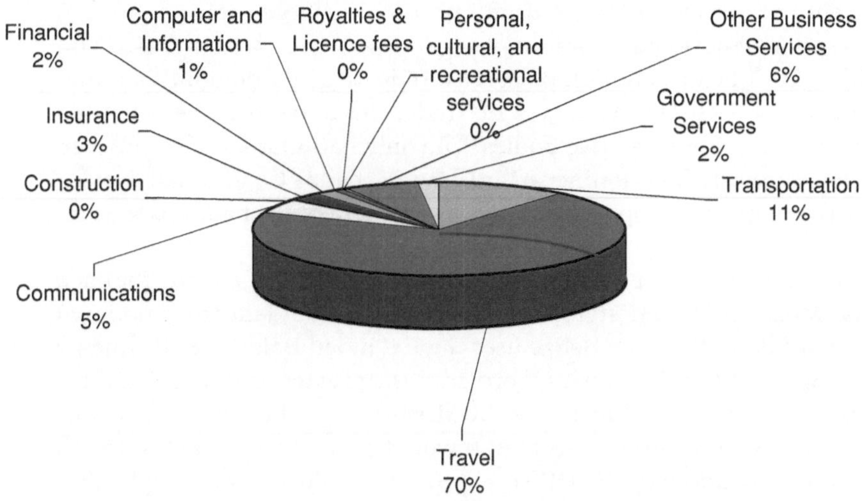

Figure 14.1. Composition of CARICOM service exports, 1997–2002. (*Source:* Based on balance of payment data for CARICOM states (Haiti not included).)

or strategy for the long term. As in goods, CARICOM economies need to urgently diversify their services export portfolio.

3 Constraints to the development of services industries in CARICOM

3.1 Inadequate information on services industries and trade

The lack of adequate information on services industries in CARICOM may be a major constraint to the development of appropriate policies to stimulate growth and exports. Services firms are not well represented in chambers of commerce in the region, and the diverse nature and small size of services companies make it difficult to have unified representation to government to seek policy initiatives

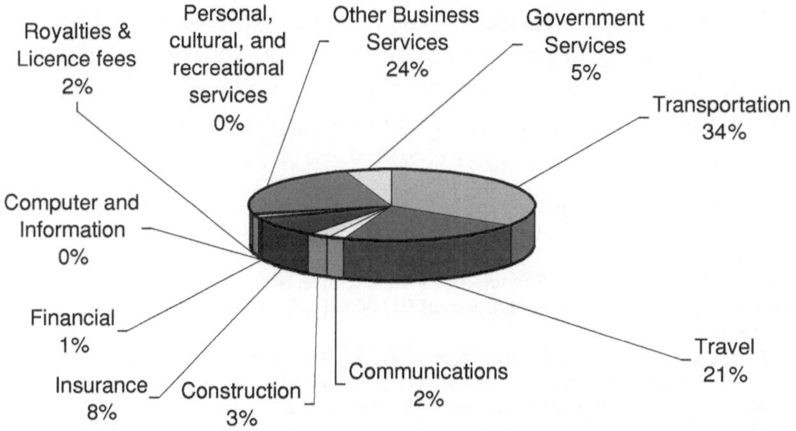

Figure 14.2. Composition of CARICOM service imports, 1997–2002. (*Source:* Based on balance of payment data for CARICOM states (Haiti not included).)

that would benefit the services sector. A useful proposal emerged some years ago regarding the creation of national coalitions of service industries in each CARICOM state along with a Caribbean Coalition of Service Industries. Although this initiative was endorsed by CARICOM Ministers of Trade, there has been very limited success in creating such representative bodies. The only national services entity to be established and properly functioning so far is the Barbados Coalition of Service Industries (BCSI), set up with support from the Government of Barbados in November 2002.[6]

In fact, trade in services is poorly understood in CARICOM due to the lack of reliable data. Most CARICOM states obtain services trade data from national balance of payments data. But only Belize uses the Extended Balance of Payments Classification of Services (EBOPS), which provides the greatest sectoral detail for services receipts and payments. Most CARICOM states use the BPM 5 system,[7] which is limited to only a few services sectors. It would be highly worthwhile for all countries in the region to adopt the EBOPS regime and to collect data through other means as well. This would provide a better indication of the composition of less traditional services in the overall trade of the region. Information on investment in service industries is also highly inadequate.

A study by the Organization for Economic Cooperation and Development (OECD) on concrete examples of services exports by developing countries highlights the importance of linkages between companies in developing export capacity, in particular, partnerships with companies from developed countries and also with companies in other developing countries. Furthermore, research indicates that few services exporters are single entrepreneurs (Nielson and Taglioni, 2004). This suggests that it is important for small countries (as in CARICOM) to provide the conditions for foreign firms to invest in their services markets, as well as seek the reduction of regulatory barriers in the larger economies in which small firms from developing countries have an interest.

4 The idiosyncrasies of services firms in CARICOM

Indigenous services firms in CARICOM, which is comprised primarily of small economies,[8] tend to be very small by international standards.[9] Apart from the financial services and tourism sectors, most services firms in the region have less than twenty employees and an annual turnover of less than US$500,000.[10] The majority are also family-owned businesses. This results in significant challenges for them in terms of exporting their services. Small service suppliers typically have limited

[6] However, at the sectoral level there are various services associations, particularly in professional and financial services – accounting, engineering, insurance, banking, among others – but they do not deal with trade negotiation issues.

[7] Classification of International Transactions in Services in the fifth edition of the BOP Manual.

[8] Note that ten CARICOM states have populations of less than 500,000. The smallest member, St Kitts and Nevis, has only 45,000 people.

[9] Interestingly, at the WTO the United States submitted a proposal in 2002 in which it defined small service suppliers as firms with up to 100 employees, total assets of up to US$3 million, and total sales of up to US$3 million. This would be a large firm in most CARICOM states.

[10] Across CARICOM a small firm may be considered to have capital of less than US$200,000, as defined by national legislation, usually Small Business Acts.

human resources to build referral networks, find local partners, identify market opportunities, and research regulations overseas. They therefore need to network to succeed. As Riddle (2002) points out, "Experience shows that human resources are the primary constraint, across all sectors and markets, as it is staff that actually creates and delivers any service."

The mainly small services firms in CARICOM also have market development constraints, since they have low brand name recognition outside their domestic markets. This makes it difficult for them to compete with larger well-known international services companies. As a result, they cannot market their services based simply on reputation. They have to find other means of demonstrating their capabilities to potential clients overseas, which usually means business trips to target markets. It is therefore not surprising that temporary entry or presence of natural persons (Mode 4 in GATS jargon) is the means of supply in which CARICOM firms are the most competitive. They are generally too small to invest overseas or establish a commercial presence.

The third major constraint to services firms is the lack of finance, since many of them have to rely mainly on internal working capital for export market development, which creates an often insurmountable limit for small companies with limited financial resources. As informed commentators have pointed out:

> Small service suppliers wishing to access external funds (e.g., bank financing) report having to invest considerable time to educate account managers regarding their businesses and their credit worthiness (Bruce, 2001; Riddle, 2000). For contractors, access to funding to post performance bonds may also be difficult. In most CARICOM countries, the usual financing mechanism for service suppliers of an overdraft secured by accounts receivable is not available (Riddle, 2002).

5 The role of infrastructure services

It is common knowledge that telecommunications and financial services are critical infrastructure services to manufacturing as well as many other service industries. In the Caribbean, neither of these services is now appropriately priced to foster the development of competitive exports from small service suppliers or from new service industries.

5.1 The attitudes of financial institutions

Capital markets are underdeveloped in the Caribbean, and most firms have to rely on debt financing for running and expanding their businesses. Since most firms are small, family-owned businesses, equity financing is not a viable option. The cost of loans varies from 20 percent in Suriname to about 10 percent in Trinidad and Tobago; even so, the mainly small services firms in CARICOM economies have difficulty in securing loans for investment. While there is no published data to demonstrate it, anecdotal evidence clearly indicates that banks in the CARICOM region are less willing to provide loans to services firms than they do to manufacturers. This is particularly acute in the case of new or "sunrise" services such as information and communication technologies (ICT) and potentially lucrative areas such as entertainment and music. The lack of access to finance is perhaps the biggest constraint to the development of new service industries in the Caribbean.

The reasons are partly due to the small size of services firms and the perception of greater risk by financial institutions. But there is clearly a deep-seated tendency for financial institutions to be over-conservative and not lend to firms that do not have physical assets (perhaps that can be appropriated in the case of loan default). In fact, commentators in the business community and in academic circles have argued that banks in CARICOM seem hesitant, unwilling or unable to value intellectual assets, and hence they avoid loans to services firms that typically do not have extensive physical assets. On the other hand, banks seem to be much more enthusiastic about providing consumption loans to private citizens.[11] This problem must be addressed, and mechanisms for the provision of both affordable working capital and capital for investment in small services firms should be put in place in order to foster the development of service companies that may eventually become exporters.

It would be worthwhile for governments and chambers of commerce to explore the possibility of creating special incubator-type facilities for small service firms and provide soft loans to facilitate the development of services exporters. But even at the global level, institutions such as the World Bank and others with a development focus need to explore new mechanisms for financing services firms that do not have physical collateral.

5.2 The cost and availability of telecommunications services

In spite of the much-touted liberalization of telecommunications across the Caribbean, the real liberalization in the CARICOM region has been timid so far and is largely limited to cellular or mobile services, and in some instances only to domestic cellular services. This may go a long way in reducing the cost of telephone charges to consumers, but it does little to stimulate the growth of commercial valued-added operations in telecommunications and a host of ICT services. Policy makers must be cognizant of this and see low-cost telecommunications as a requirement for facilitating the growth of other service industries, and act to ensure that effective competition is introduced in all areas of telecommunication services, especially broadband Internet services.

While new technologies have made it possible to deliver a wide and increasing range of services electronically, the cost of telecommunications in CARICOM states significantly limits such possibilities. For instance, during regular working hours, it is significantly cheaper to make a telephone call from North America to the Caribbean than vice versa, or even between Caribbean islands. More important, broadband or high speed Internet services are still prohibitive in terms of the cost to most small businesses in the Caribbean (Stern, 2006). However, the Internet holds out the prospect of providing opportunities for addressing some of the key limitations faced by small businesses by reducing transaction costs and giving them a global presence.

[11] Caribbean banks prefer to focus on consumption loans in which the returns are higher and risk is apparently less. See Henry (2003) and Chaitoo (2006).

6 Strategies to develop and export new services

In its report on *Prospects for Services Exports from the English-Speaking Caribbean* in 1996, the World Bank made the following recommendations, which are still valid:

> A public sector strategy to spur development of service exports should focus on enabling the private sector to achieve four objectives: developing capacity to produce service exports, increasing cost competitiveness, improving service exports quality, and building market linkages. . . .There is an inability to substantially expand service exports in many subsectors due to insufficient inputs (World Bank, 1996).

Various commentators have suggested that the Caribbean region should be able to make significant inroads in the development of services exports to the United States in non-traditional sectors (that is, other than tourism and finance). In 1996, the World Bank suggested that greater attention should be paid to ICT, valued-added telecommunications, professional services, health services, and entertainment services. There are also prospects for increased exports of ship repair and maintenance and maritime transport services. Culture and entertainment services also have great potential that can be developed with the right policy framework, including incentives.

Given the relative proximity of the region to the United States and Canada, there is potential for export possibilities through outsourcing contracts from North American companies in a range of back-office business services such as accounting, payroll administration, and processing of insurance claims, among others. While outsourcing is a highly controversial issue in the United States at the moment,[12] it will remain an area of significant activity due to the economic realities of modern business arrangements. As production systems continue to become more flexible with networks of production spread across various countries, CARICOM countries should actively position themselves and promote the capacity of Caribbean firms to provide valuable business and other services at competitive cost and in an efficient manner.

In any event, significant promotional efforts need to be put in place to facilitate and stimulate such outsourcing activities. But to date, little focused attention has been paid to this area either by government agencies or private sector organizations in CARICOM.

7 An Aid for Trade program for services for the Caribbean

For the purposes of this discussion, we assume that Aid for Trade involves the following: (i) increased market access for developing countries in the sectors in which they can become competitive in OECD markets; (ii) supply-side capacity building; and (iii) trade infrastructure. This is the broad definition that makes practical sense to all small, vulnerable economies in the context of Aid for Trade discussions in the WTO Doha Round.

[12] There have been attempts to introduce a bill in the U.S. Congress to penalize firms for outsourcing, while CNN runs a slot on its Lou Dobbs morning program that identifies firms that are "exporting American jobs."

A recent extensive inventory of completed and ongoing technical support initiatives for the CARIFORUM region[13] conducted for the European Commission (EC) revealed some interesting trends. Of about 200 trade-related projects or multi-year programs, only three specifically targeted services. The first was for the establishment of a Services Trade Unit in the Caribbean Regional Negotiating Machinery (CRNM) (US$600,000 from the UK Department for International Development (DFID) and Caribbean Development Bank (CDB)).[14] The second was for the creation of a Services Trade Unit in the Trinidad and Tobago Chamber of Commerce (CAD$100,000 from the Canadian International Development Agency (CIDA)); and the third was to allow the Caribbean Association of Industry and Commerce to inform Caribbean services firms of the implications of the GATS, the Free Trade Area of the Americas (FTAA) and the CARICOM Single Market (CAD$100,000 – CIDA). Furthermore, most of the programs were for the public sector.[15] The review included the following donors: CDB, CIDA, DFID, the EC, Inter-American Development Bank, Organization of American States, UN Development Programme, U.S. Agency for International Development, and some minor European bilateral donors.

In light of the structural and other challenges faced by services firms in the Caribbean, it is evident that the thrust of aid programs is inappropriately focused. This is particularly unfortunate, since it is really only services industries and diversification of services exports that can take the CARICOM economies out of the persistent deficit situations in their trade account which the majority of them have been facing for more than a decade.

In order to give credibility and substance to the development provision in GATS Article IV, we propose the following multi-faceted approach to address the special needs of service suppliers from the Caribbean. The first strategy is to address market access needs, and the second is to deal with supply-side and infrastructural needs for the development of services firms and industries. The latter, which is the substance of Aid for Trade, is critical, since no matter how generous the market access CARICOM states receive through the WTO or bilateral trade agreements, unless their capacity to export services improves, they will not be able to contest international markets.

7.1 Market access-related Aid for Trade requirements for services

The following are some key elements in terms of tangible market access concessions that are needed by Caribbean service suppliers in order to take advantage of opportunities in developed country markets.

- Developed countries should remove all economic needs tests for service suppliers from Caribbean states, since they are all small, vulnerable economies and their services trade is so miniscule that it has negligible impact on any OECD economy.

[13] CARICOM and the Dominican Republic.

[14] Incidentally, much of this amount was unspent by the end of the project cycle (2006) due to difficulties faced by CRNM in having to first spend on activities and then seek reimbursement. DFID subsequently reclaimed the unspent balances from its contribution.

[15] The CRNM manages an IDB-funded project aimed at helping the private sector prepare for trade negotiations. The EC also provides funding for the private sector through its PROINVEST program but most organizations and firms in the region consider the requirements for disbursement and accounting too onerous.

- Due to their very limited human, financial, and marketing resources, small services firms are unable to service markets through commercial presence. Temporary entry (Mode 4) for Caribbean service suppliers should be de-linked from the requirement to have commercial presence. In other words, service suppliers should be granted entry as individuals. There should also be further expansion in the scope of categories covered by horizontal commitments in developed WTO members' schedules to include middle and lower level professionals (that is, persons without university degrees), in the definition of "other persons" and "specialists."
- Developed countries such as Canada, the EU, Japan and the United States should grant market access to Caribbean countries in sectors and modes of supply in which they have particular market access interests and are competitive. Some broad indicative areas are: culture and entertainment; professional services; health tourism; tour operators; building cleaning and maintenance services; ship repair and maintenance; landscaping; and finishing work for buildings.

7.2 Incentives for services firms

Given the need to increase investment in and exports from services industries in the Caribbean, it is timely for CARICOM states to revise their incentives regimes and focus on services. Information on current incentives to promote the development of service industries in CARICOM is not readily available from national governments. However, Trade Policy Reviews conducted by the WTO shed some light on what is currently in place. In the case of tourism, it appears that most countries except Suriname have subsidies in the form of tax incentives for new investments, while duty is waived on inputs for businesses in free zones.[16] But incentives are limited in other service sectors. Jamaica has the most extensive incentive program for service industries covering the sectors of tourism, maritime transport, banking, other financial services, software/information technology, recreation, audiovisual services, and culture and sports. The incentives in CARICOM states that are considered services subsidies are mainly tax incentives and duty free inputs. No CARICOM government gives direct grants because they cannot afford to do so.

The development of better incentive schemes for services industries is an area that Aid for Trade programs should address. Very little work has been done in this field, and although the International Trade Centre (ITC) has been working with several countries around the world on promoting services exports, there is little information on best practices in terms of incentive schemes for service industries. In the context of the creation of the CARICOM Single Market for services and capital, it is timely to review and revise incentives regimes in the region. However, most governments do not have the technical capacity to do this on their own. They will need technical assistance and support from the international community.

7.3 Development of regulatory regimes and collection of services statistics

Most commentators have indicated that it is critical for developed countries to assist developing countries in developing their regulatory frameworks for many service sectors. The same applies to the Caribbean. In particular, it is important

[16] Tourism incentives are the most common across other WTO members as well.

to develop regulations in new services areas in which governments would like to attract foreign investment. Given the importance of an adequate regulatory framework to the liberalization of trade in services and more importantly implementation of commitments, there should be cooperation between the EU and the Caribbean on regulatory matters in the context of their negotiations towards an Economic Partnership Agreement (EPA). This cooperation could focus, among other matters, on addressing regulatory weakness, particularly of Caribbean states in new sectors of activity, while preserving the regulatory rights of governments.

A further need is to significantly improve the long-term capacity of CARICOM governments to collect information on their services industries and their imports and exports of services. As argued above, the BPM 5 system is sorely inadequate for planning purposes for service sector development or for trade negotiations. It is necessary to implement the necessary infrastructure to allow the small bureaucracies in the Caribbean to collect more detailed services production and trade data. This will require significant financial and human resources for the members of CARICOM and should be considered a key element of Aid for Trade in services.

7.4 Financing mechanisms for services firms

Given the critical role of finance for the development of new services companies in CARICOM and for the growth of existing firms, it is critical to establish a special mechanism to provide funds at affordable interest rates to services SMEs. In fact, this may be a sine qua non for the development of new indigenous services firms. The cost of capital is too high and it is even more difficult to obtain debt financing. One particular thrust in Aid for Trade for services programs should be the establishment of a major private fund for services sector development that is at rates lower than the existing interest rates in the Caribbean.[17] Given the vast difference in terms of the cost of finance to SMEs in the region compared to finance costs in developed countries, it is practically impossible for most services firms to compete with their counterparts in OECD markets.

Similarly, a program of education of financial institutions on financing instruments for firms without physical collateral and on valuing intellectual assets for the purposes of lending should be implemented. In this regard, best practices from other parts of the world should be highlighted and emulated. At the same time, creative approaches have to be taken to address the issue of under-developed capital markets in the Caribbean. A program of training should also be developed for services SMEs to educate them on mechanisms and options for financing their businesses through equity rather than debt in the medium term.

7.5 Facilitation offices for services trade in OECD countries

Much of the discussion on trade facilitation in international forums tends to address trade in goods issues. It is necessary to pay focused attention to facilitating trade

[17] The EU has provided funds under the Cotonou Agreement through the European Investment Bank (EIB) for lending to the private sector in ACP countries. However, while the EIB makes available funds at preferential rates (3–5 percent), the local intermediary institutions then on-lend at current and sometimes higher-than-market rates in countries in the region. In effect, it is a subsidy not to firms but to financial institutions. This is a somewhat perverse effect compared to what was intended for or is needed by Caribbean and ACP firms.

in services. The need for simplification of information on domestic regulatory procedures and the lack of market intelligence are the biggest commercial barriers to exports of Caribbean service suppliers. There is a need to implement mechanisms in OECD countries that will be better than simple Enquiry/Contact Points to really help the mainly small service suppliers from Caribbean states to effectively contest markets in rich countries.

Developed countries should give real meaning to the commitment in GATS Articles IV and XIX (and Articles 2, 3, 4 and 5 of the Cotonou Agreement) by giving relevant substance to the notion of facilitating the access of service suppliers from the Caribbean in their markets. Contact points are useful only if there is the capacity to access and use them. It would be more useful and practical for small service firms in Caribbean states if the developed countries established contact points for services trade in their missions in the Caribbean.

However, contact points per se are not enough. Special attention should be paid to assisting service suppliers from the Caribbean states. In that regard, we suggest that the OECD countries provide tangible market access support to Caribbean service suppliers to help them take advantage of opportunities in their markets. Some examples of useful programs for promoting trade in goods from developing countries are those of the Centre for the Promotion of Imports from developing countries (CBI) in the Netherlands and the Trade Facilitation Office of Canada. It is critical that Canada, the EU, Japan and the United States provide institutional mechanisms similar to the CBI for services trade and investment between the Caribbean and their economies. In the interim, it would be useful to expand the EC's Export Help Desk to include trade in services and initiatives such as those recommended below, which would assist in promoting services exports from Caribbean states and be of great benefit to service suppliers from this region.

Targeted support by the developed countries for service suppliers from the Caribbean should include the establishment of a formal agency in European capitals, the United States, Canada, and Japan for promoting services trade and investment. It should include the following initiatives, among others:

(a) Advice and training to assist in strengthening the services export capability of trade and investment promotion organizations and private companies in Caribbean countries (seminars and courses both in-country and in their home country);
(b) Detailed information on the regulatory regimes in specific service sectors in developed countries that are of interest to service suppliers from the Caribbean;
(c) The development of an on-line database and electronic meeting place to facilitate interaction between service suppliers from Caribbean states and service companies in the relevant developed countries that may be looking to outsource work or to find partners. The website should ensure that importers, buyers and agents in the particular developed country are aware of the services that suppliers in Caribbean states are seeking to export to their market. In addition, such a web site could also assist in the establishment of distribution channels, thereby helping to ensure market penetration;
(d) Funding for trade missions to OECD markets for services exporters from Caribbean states, and buying missions to client countries for services importers from the developed countries;

(e) Training and capacity building initiatives such as seminars, courses and exchange programs for service exporters, government officials, and export and investment marketing agencies from the Caribbean in the OECD markets. Also, sector-specific reports on the market for services in their countries that are of interest to Caribbean states;

(f) Assistance to enhance the research and development capacity of Caribbean states to improve their efficiency in the supply of services;

(g) Support for training of personnel and the expansion of regional/national standards bodies to address quality and standards requirements that would ensure easier access to the OECD markets and provide required quality assurance for services industries; and

(h) The establishment of mutual recognition agreements for the qualifications of nationals from the Caribbean in professional services and other areas of particular interest.

8 Conclusion

It is clear that there are opportunities for CARICOM countries to increase their trade in services. It is first necessary to further develop their services industries and to stimulate the development of new services. This requires not only a marriage of industrial and trade policies in the region, but also considerable external support. Given the resource and capacity constraints of most service suppliers in CARICOM, it is important for governments and multilateral agencies to play a facilitation role by actively promoting and supporting services firms. This will also address some of the information asymmetries faced by potential and actual service exporters. As well, structural impediments to the growth of services industries must be addressed. It is important to understand the linkages between trade and investment in services and the growth of the services sector and factor this into both national trade policies and Aid for Trade policies.

REFERENCES

CARICOM Secretariat. 2003. "CARICOM's Trade in Services, 1990–2000," Statistics Sub-Programme, Caribbean Community Secretariat, Georgetown: CARICOM.

Chaitoo, Ramesh. 2000. "Electronic Commerce and CARICOM Economies: Strategic Considerations for Governments," report prepared for the Caribbean Regional Negotiating Machinery, Barbados: CRNM.

Chaitoo, Ramesh. 2006. "Trade, Development and Financial Services Issues in CARICOM," paper presented at Second Biennial Conference on "Business, Banking and Finance," University of the West Indies, St. Augustine, Trinidad, 1–3 May.

Cleland, Celene and David Gomez. 2003. "Prospects for CARICOM Services Exports in Information and Communication Technology: Trade and Investment Issues," report prepared for the Caribbean Regional Negotiating Machinery, Barbados: CRNM.

Demas, Allison and Ralph Henry. 2001. "Entertainment Services with Special Reference to Music, Mas and the Film and Video Segments," report prepared for the Caribbean Regional Negotiating Machinery, Barbados: CRNM.

ECLAC. 2003. "The Development of Services in the Caribbean," Caribbean Development and Cooperation Committee, LC/CAR/G.717, Port of Spain: ECLAC.

ECLAC. 2006. "Economic Survey of Latin America and the Caribbean 2005–2006," ECLAC Economic Development Division, LC/G.2314-P/I, New York: United Nations.

Gonzales, Anthony, Logan Brenzel, and Jennifer Sancho. 2001. "Health Tourism and Related Services: Caribbean Development and International Trade," report prepared for the Caribbean Regional Negotiating Machinery, Barbados: CRNM.

Henry, Lester. 2003. "Implications for CARICOM Countries of Negotiations on Financial Services in the FTAA and GATS," paper prepared for the Caribbean Regional Negotiating Machinery, Barbados: CRNM.

IDB/INTAL. 2005. "CARICOM Report," *CARICOM Report* No. 2, Buenos Aires: IDB and INTAL.

Nielson, J. and D. Taglioni. 2004. "Services Trade Liberalisation: Identifying Opportunities and Gains," *OECD Trade Policy Working Papers* No. 1, Paris: OECD.

Parsan, Elizabeth. 2006. "Aid for Trade: A Caribbean Perspective," study prepared for the Caribbean Regional Negotiating Machinery, Barbados: CRNM.

Riddle, Dorothy. 2002a. "Issues Regarding Small Service Suppliers in the Context of the FTAA," paper prepared for the Caribbean Regional Negotiating Machinery, Barbados: CRNM.

Riddle, Dorothy. 2002b. "Services Export Capacity in Developing Countries," paper presented at WTO Symposium on Assessment of Trade in Services, 15 March 2002, http://www.wto.org/english/tratop/e/serv_e/symp_mar02_riddle_e.doc.

Schware, Robert and Susan Hume. 1996. "Prospects for Information Service Exports for the English-speaking Caribbean," Washington, D.C.: World Bank.

Stern, Peter A. 2006. "Assessment of the Telecommunications Services Sector in CARICOM: Convergence Issues at the Regional and International Level," paper prepared for the Caribbean Regional Negotiating Machinery, Barbados: CRNM.

te Velde, Dirk Willem. 2005. "Revitalizing services negotiations at the WTO: Can technical assistance help?," London: Overseas Development Institute.

World Bank. 1996. "Prospects for Services Exports from the English-Speaking Caribbean," Caribbean Group for Cooperation in Economic Development, Report No. 15301 CRG., Washington, D.C.: World Bank.

World Bank. 2005. "A Time to Choose: Caribbean Development in the 21st Century," Report No. 31725-LAC, Washington, D.C.: World Bank.

15 The Role of Local Researchers in Delivery of Aid for Trade: The Case of the African Economic Research Consortium (AERC)

WILLIAM LYAKURWA, OLUSANYA AJAKAIYE, AND OLAWALE OGUNKOLA

1 Introduction

The recommendations of the World Trade Organization (WTO) Task Force on Aid for Trade provide a comprehensive view of issues relating to scope, financing and operationalization of Aid for Trade, as well as a clear demarcation of responsibilities for different stakeholders (private sector, government, regional/continental organizations, WTO and development partners). The scope, according to the Task Force, should be broad enough to reflect the diverse trade needs identified by countries, "and clear enough to establish a border between Aid for Trade and other development assistance of which it is a part". This position points to the need for country/regional/continental economic communities, with the cooperation of relevant stakeholders, to come up with programs and projects that will assist them increase their export of goods and services and enable them to benefit from increased market opening in the multilateral trading system.

While the Task Force recommended that recipient countries should be responsible for identifying Aid for Trade programs and projects, it also suggested a broad categorization to guide the process. These categories include: (i) trade policy and regulations; (ii) trade development; (iii) trade-related infrastructure; (iv) building productive capacity; (v) trade-related adjustment; and (vi) other trade-related needs. Operationalizing Aid for Trade along the lines of the Task Force's recommendations and suggestions will require human and technical assistance capacity building activities in two main areas. First, and perhaps most importantly, is to carry out a correct diagnosis of trade-related needs. Second is the need to develop capacity to implement an Aid for Trade package and ensure that targeted interventions are effective. This chapter examines these issues with a focus on Africa and draws lessons on capacity building from the experience of a continent-wide research group – the African Economic Research Consortium (AERC).

The realization of the importance of supply-side issues and concerns in the process of making trade policy work for sustainable development is not new; various attempts have been directed at analyzing these issues.[1] From the African perspective, a partial list of issues includes special and differential treatment, preference erosion, market access conditions, and rules of origin. Thus to a reasonable extent,

[1] A partial list of studies in this area includes Oyejide (1989, 2004), Oyejide et al. (2004), Helleiner (2002), Amjadi and Yeats (1995), Bond (1983), and Elbadawi (1999).

analysis of concerns in trade and development from the African perspective is not lacking. However, making trade work for sustainable development and poverty alleviation goes beyond analysis; it must involve well-funded programs and projects directed at different constraints identified by detailed research analyses.

Only a few institutions in Africa have the mandate and ability to build the necessary capacity to understand and integrate development concerns into trade policy regimes.[2] AERC is one of the few such organizations that has consistently addressed issues in the area of trade and development for the continent. Its achievements over the years are a testimony to the Consortium's role in building trade capacity in Africa.

The Aid for Trade initiative as conceived in the WTO has recognized that it must build on existing mechanisms. Prominent among these are the Joint Integrated Technical Assistance Programme (JITAP) and the Integrated Framework for Trade-Related Technical Assistance for Least Developed Countries (IF). The experiences with JITAP and IF have much to offer in the process of ensuring proper design and effective implementation of any Aid for Trade package. As earlier chapters have pointed out (see Introductory chapter and chapters 8 and 9 in this volume), the two programs have a mixed track record of success from which lessons can be drawn in designing the next wave of Aid for Trade.

The IF, for instance, has been commended for linking Poverty Reduction Strategy Papers (PRSPs) and Diagnostic Trade Integration Study (DTIS) matrices with existing government/donor coordination mechanisms and the budgetary process. An important strength of the IF that the Aid for Trade initiative must preserve and possibly strengthen is the increased awareness of the role of trade policy in stimulating growth and development. The IF is also credited with enhanced coordination among agencies providing trade related assistance, among ministries and related government agencies, and between the public and private sectors. However, JITAP and IF are not sufficient to handle all the issues in Aid for Trade; such programs need to be supplemented with further initiatives on trade-related infrastructure, building productive capacity, and trade-related adjustment.

The purpose of this chapter is to chart a way forward for implementation of Aid for Trade by addressing some of the weaknesses of JITAP and IF, particularly in the area of poor sustainability and anchoring of institutional memory and insufficient linkages with participating countries. There is a strong need to involve local researchers in the process of promoting the sustainability of the different programs and projects under the Aid for Trade package as well as in ensuring institutional memory. The involvement of local researchers at different levels (design, implementation and evaluation) would help provide much-needed longer-term linkages with participating countries.

More specifically, this chapter examines the capability of AERC in assisting sub-Saharan African (SSA) countries build the necessary capacity for implementing the Aid for Trade initiative, as recommended by the WTO Task Force. Section 2 begins with a brief presentation of trade and development issues in SSA, with an

[2] A partial list of such institutions includes the African Economic Research Consortium (AERC), the African Capacity Building Foundation (ACBF), Trade Law Centre for Southern Africa (TRALAC), Southern African Regional Poverty Network (SARPN), International Lawyers and Economists Against Poverty (ILEAP), and Trade Policy Research and Training Programme (TPRTP).

emphasis on trade capacity building. Section 3 looks at the trade capacity building efforts of AERC. Possible ways in which institutions such as AERC could assist in the implementation of Aid for Trade is the focus of analysis in section 4. Section 5 concludes the chapter.

2 Trade and development challenges facing sub-Saharan Africa

Trade constitutes a large proportion of the typical African country's gross domestic product (GDP). According to the United Nations Economic Commission for Africa (ECA) (2004), the share of trade in GDP of African countries averaged about 59 percent between 1994 and 2000. Trade, for most African countries, generates a significant proportion of government revenue, mostly from tariffs on imports. Indeed, taxes on international trade transactions represented more than 20 percent of total revenue in twenty-six out of forty-two sub-Saharan African countries between 1985 and 1994. In the period between 2000 and 2003, trade taxes represented more than 50 percent of total revenue in Comoros, Gambia and Niger. They represented more than 40 percent of the total revenue in Benin, Lesotho, Madagascar, Mali, Sierra Leone, Togo and Uganda (Osakwe, 2007). This focus on trade predates the emergence of the current world trade order. Prior to the adoption of structural adjustment programs (SAPs) by most African countries in the 1980s and before the establishment of the WTO in 1995, Africa's development strategy rested on a foundation of regionally integrated markets with a view to achieving sustainable economic growth and eradicating poverty.

This traditional regionally-based development strategy has come across two key challenges. First, most of the African countries embarked on unilateral trade liberalization under SAPs without significant regional coordination. This has led to fragmented trade policies within regions as neighboring countries confront the challenge of maintaining diverse tariff rates while participating in one regional bloc. Second, at the multilateral level, the need for countries to negotiate at the WTO according to what suits their national development strategies can conflict with their need to coordinate positions both regionally and at the continental level.

While the level of participation of African countries in the Doha Round negotiations is superior to the Uruguay Round (where it was virtually non-existent), tremendous efforts are now required to improve their ability to undertake in-depth analysis of issues at national, regional and continental levels. The negotiating capacity of African countries has been stretched by the ever-expanding negotiating agenda in the WTO and further stressed by the Economic Partnership Agreement (EPA) negotiations with the European Union. Since the EPA negotiations are organized around regional groupings, they require a further step of strengthening regional integration. In an ideal world, the EPAs would be negotiated by regional customs unions with a common external tariff. However, since none of the African EPA regional groupings has developed to this stage, member states also find themselves engaged in simultaneous negotiations to strengthen their regional economic communities, further straining their limited capacities. In other words, since the end of the Uruguay Round negotiations, African countries have been faced with the arduous task of building capacity not only to be able to implement the agreements, but also to effectively negotiate the Doha Round, regional integration agreements, and the EPAs. The need to build capacity to implement various agreements is equally important, if not more important, than the capacity to negotiate.

Some elements of required capacity in the African context include capacity to effectively negotiate, comply and compete (Ohiorhenuan, 2005; Blackhurst et al., 2000; Ogunkola, 1999). Capacity to negotiate is required in the area of providing adequate and skilled professional capital-based staff, in coordinating domestic institutions, in monitoring and analyzing the trade policies of key trading partners, and in creating a pool of personnel with requisite knowledge in international trade law and economics. Effective participation in the multifaceted trading system further requires capacity for articulating, coordinating, and implementing trade policy at national level.

Looking forward, lack of effective supply response capacity is arguably the most important binding constraint to increased trade in Africa (Blackhurst et al, 2000). While various negotiations have the potential of improving market access conditions for traditional and non-traditional exports, efforts now need to be directed at addressing supply response constraints, without which developing countries would not be able to take full advantage of improved market access conditions. This is the central impetus behind the Aid for Trade initiative. This includes institutionalization and upgrading of trade legislation frameworks, introduction of new legislation, modification of existing ones, adoption of new tools and administrative procedures such as in the area of dumping, and integrating emerging trade policy with rest of the legal system to ensure internal consistency.

Trade-related capacity building issues in the context of SSA have been well summarized by Oyejide (2006b). The simultaneous and overlapping nature of the EPAs, and of regional and multilateral trade negotiations, confronts SSA countries with a variety of challenges in the area of human and institutional capacity building. There are several areas of pronounced weakness. For instance, the effective integration of trade and trade policy objectives into national development plans remains incomplete in most African countries, as does the capacity to derive appropriate trade negotiating objectives from each country's own development strategy and programs. Both the EPA and Doha Round negotiating processes call for a strengthening of the dialogue with stakeholders in the articulation of trade at the national and regional levels. By implication, this requires the capacity to articulate, aggregate and transform these into negotiating positions in various fora in ways that enable them to be mutually self-reinforcing. In addition, effective participation in the interlocking series of trade negotiations requires the consolidation of national and regional negotiating machineries.

In order to address these challenges, Oyejide (2006b) argues that African countries must generously invest in building strong analytical capacities and technical expertise for deployment at national, regional and continental levels. This should be complemented by supporting consultation, coordination, and harmonization mechanisms at the intra-government, intra-national, and intra-regional and interregional levels. In doing this, African countries must be wary of excessive reliance on the use of analytical and technical assistance provided directly and in kind by their negotiating partners, such as the EC for example. It may be more effective if such assistance is channeled through competent and more neutral regional and multilateral institutions (Ibid). Some of these elements of African trade concerns are listed in the recommendations of the Task Force on Aid for Trade; as such, African countries should express their interest in seeking further clarification with a view to ensuring that appropriate interventions are secured and that implementation is effective.

3 AERC's capacity building efforts

Efforts at addressing trade and development challenges facing SSA countries have resulted in the establishment of various trade capacity building institutions across the continent, including AERC. AERC is a network of researchers interested in issues relating to the development of the continent. The Consortium, established in 1988, aims at advancing economic policy research and training in SSA countries.

AERC's mission is to strengthen local capacity for conducting independent, rigorous inquiry into the problems facing the management of economies in SSA, with a view to promoting retention of such capacity and encouraging its application in the policy context. This is premised on the belief that development is more likely to occur where there is sustained sound management of the economy, and that such management is more likely to happen where there is an active, well-informed group of locally-based professional economists to conduct policy-relevant research. As such, AERC is uniquely placed to support many of the capacity building elements of the Aid for Trade initiative.

AERC's program revolves around the two primary components of research and training. The former uses a flexible approach toward improving the technical skills of local researchers, allowing for regional determination of research priorities and strengthening national institutions concerned with economic policy research. The research program also fosters closer ties between researchers and policy-makers. AERC's training program supports both masters and doctoral-level studies in economics, and helps improve the capacities of departments of economics in public universities across the continent.

While AERC's training program is general, some elements contribute directly and indirectly to trade and trade policy development on the continent. A number of methodological workshops that have been organized to sharpen research skills and expose members of the network to recent and relevant methods in the discipline have contributed to the high quality of AERC research. Beyond this, those who have passed through the various training programs (collaborative MA and Collaborative PhD programs) are in one way or another contributing to building the longer-term capacity needed for economic analysis that is so important for SSA economies.

Although the thematic research process employed by AERC is expected to generate policy relevant outputs either as AERC research reports and/or as publications in reputable journals, the main vehicle for producing policy-relevant research output remains the collaborative research process. The process starts with the selection of relevant areas for research. A team is put in place, usually composed of senior researchers within and outside Africa. In some cases, senior policy-makers are also involved in the process as either co-authors or at another level such as discussants at workshops. In all the research activities, the quality and relevance of research to policy are emphasized to enhance the credibility of the researchers as well as utilization of their outputs.

To date, four collaborative research projects have included analysis of trade and development concerns of SSA countries: (i) Regional Integration and Trade

Liberalisation in sub-Saharan Africa; (ii) Africa in the World Trading System; (iii) African Imperatives in the New World Trade Order; and (iv) Export Supply Response Capacity constraints in Africa. While the first three projects have been completed, the fourth was launched in the middle of 2006 and remained underway at time of writing.

It is noteworthy that AERC collaborative research projects are driven by the objective of ensuring studies remain relevant to African economies. An example is the project on 'African Imperatives in the New World Trade Order,' which was premised on the fact that the impact of macroeconomic and trade policies on various sectors of African economies is of considerable concern to economists and policy-makers alike. Recognition of this impact has influenced the nature and focus of policy reforms implemented by many African countries for more than two decades. In addition, the increasing shift towards export-oriented development strategies has generated concern about external market access opportunities and challenges faced by these countries in a new world trade order that is shaped by a mix of special preferential trade arrangements plus bilateral, regional and multilateral trade agreements. In effect, the structure and performance of various sectors of African economies are influenced not only by the domestic trade regime and macroeconomic policy environment, but also by the net incentives generated by external market access conditions.

AERC's thematic research program has a strong focus on capacity building as the entry point for junior researchers, but it has a limited scope in terms of number of researchers that can be accommodated at any point in time. For instance, between 1997 and 2003, the 303 new projects under this research program involved about 415 researchers. This translates to about sixty researchers per year (Wuyts, 2004). Collaborative research programs provide better coverage. In an evaluation of AERC research programs between 1997 and 2003, four collaborative research projects that were evaluated involved about 145 African researchers.[3] The 'African Imperatives in the New World Trade Order' project, for instance, involved about 98 African researchers.

The composition of researchers reflects not only the need to build capacity but also to ensure that the project is relevant to policy. While senior researchers both within and outside the continent are responsible for the framework and methodology aspects of projects, middle and junior researchers in collaboration with practitioners in relevant areas apply the framework to the domestic environment. Thus, researchers generally expand their capacities in at least two main directions: learning from senior colleagues on recent developments in their areas of specialization, as well as understanding and attempting to address important policy issues and concerns in these areas.[4]

Beyond the collaborative research projects and possibly in recognition of the capacity of the network of researchers in the continent, AERC has provided expertise at different levels: national, regional, continental as well as international. At national level, AERC members have served at in different capacities as convener

[3] These four projects are: (i) Managing the transition from Aid Dependency in SSA; (ii) Explaining African Economic Growth Performance; (iii) African Imperatives in the New World Trade Order; and (iv) Poverty, Income Distribution and Labour Market Issues.

[4] Thus the collaborative nature of the project is at two levels: collaboration between African and international institutions and researchers, on the one hand, and between researchers and practitioners in relevant fields, on the other.

of national workshops; resource persons, advisers to governments, members of the board of government agencies, and governor of central bank, just to mention a few. Members of the network are involved in the ongoing regional negotiations of the Economic Partnership Agreements between the EU and four groups of countries on the continent. Involvement of the research network members at continental level either as individual consultants or as groups of consultants to institutions such as the African Union Commission and the ECA is also common.

Members of the network have served as resource persons and in other capacities in various international organizations. They are prominent in the WTO's regional trade policy course, where they have been serving as resource persons since its inception in 2000. Some members have also assisted the World Bank in various capacities, including on specific projects (see Ingco et al., 2003). The collaboration and recognition of the Consortium members also contributed significantly to the UN Food and Agriculture Organization's (FAO) trade reforms and food security projects (see Thomas, 2006). Other organizations that have benefited from the capacity building efforts of AERC include the UN Conference on Trade and Development (UNCTAD) and numerous NGOs across the continent.

4 AERC's capacity building role in implementing the Task Force recommendations

The recommendations of the WTO Aid for Trade Task Force are structured into four sections: (i) strengthening the demand side; (ii) strengthening donor response; (iii) strengthening the bridge between demand and response at three levels; national, regional and global levels; and (iv) strengthening monitoring and evaluation. Some of the tasks, especially those relating to capacity building, cut across the different sections. For instance, the process of mainstreaming trade into national strategies (a recommendation under strengthening the bridge between "demand and "supply") is also an important step in the process of "strengthening the demand side". Specifically, efforts at mainstreaming trade into national strategies would require among other things including the establishment of an effective system of coordination at national, regional and multilateral levels. Such efforts would also involve a system of data collection and analysis.

Efforts at strengthening the "demand side" for Aid for Trade, according to the Task Force, should include strengthening trade capacity. This involves an array of activities, such as: identifying trade needs; proposing priorities to be supported by development partners; mainstreaming trade into national strategies; establishing broad-based consultation processes involving the private sector, civil society organizations and relevant government agencies to formulate trade strategies; formulating priority project proposals; and establishing a system of data collection. The Consortium has been engaged in most of these elements of capacity building, and thus is well-placed to continue its delivery in these areas in accordance with recommendations of the Task Force.

AERC's ongoing collaborative research project 'Behind-the-Border Issues and Export Supply Response Capacity Constraints in Africa' has much to offer on issues relating to Aid for Trade. The project addresses a range of relevant areas, including the nature, features and measurement of export supply response capacity; elements of trade-related infrastructure and its trade impact; elements of trade-related inputs and services and their impact on trade; transaction costs, competitiveness, and export supply response; macroeconomic environment, trade regime and export performance; and the impact of standards and technical regulations on export supply response capacity.

AERC has the capacity to train trade officials on a range of issues, with the objective of making trade work for sustainable development and poverty alleviation. In addition to its collaborative MA and PhD programs, AERC has organized dozens of special training workshops, including on methodological issues such as in econometrics and computable general equilibrium (CGE) models. In addition to introducing recent developments in these areas, participants are introduced to relevant computer software. The target groups for these workshops vary from junior researchers to senior researchers within the network. The content and rigor of the instruction are tailored to match the experience of the participants. The training activities of the consortium place it in an ideal position to train trade officials on issues relating to trade policy for enhancing Africa's development, with a view to providing reputable, locally-generated, evidence-based research.

4.1 Negotiations-based analysis

Another important element in the capacity building component of the recommendations by the Task Force relates to "analysis of proposals and positions and their impacts". As outlined in the previous section, AERC's experience is wide and rich in this area, including in preparing and presenting analysis for African negotiators in the context of WTO negotiations. A few examples include AERC's collaborative efforts with the ECA and the African Union in the preparation of policy briefs addressing issues in the WTO's Doha Development Agenda. These briefs cover issues in negotiations on agriculture, trade in services, trade-related intellectual property rights (TRIPS), Singapore issues, special and differential treatment, and governance issues in the WTO negotiations. Related activities of the Consortium include analysis of African countries' proposals and objectives in the WTO (see Oyejide and Njinkeu, 2002a), and African preparation for trade negotiations in the context of the ACP-EU Cotonou Partnership Agreement (see Oyejide and Njinkeu, 2006b).

AERC's assistance to African countries further includes participation at different meetings of stakeholders and providing technical assistance at such meetings. The Consortium has organized regional as well as national workshops with a view to assisting negotiators at these levels. The relevance of AERC's activities in ensuring effective understanding of issues in the negotiations is not in doubt. However, some challenges must be addressed for these efforts to be an appropriate fit for the Aid for Trade initiative.

A critical step in the implementation of Aid for Trade is to conduct assessments at national, regional and continental levels. AERC is well suited to assist stakeholders in this process by bringing its extensive research outputs and human capacity into play. Such assessments are expected to translate into concrete programs and projects. Since the Consortium has members of its network in virtually all countries in the continent, and since it has also established productive relationships with relevant government agencies at national, regional and continental levels, it is in a key position to assist these stakeholders in the task of translating priorities into concrete deliverables.

Under the category of 'capacity building for trade policy and regulations,' the Aid for Trade Task Force identified the need for support for national stakeholders to articulate commercial interests and identify trade-offs.[5] National stakeholders include a range of groups, such as consumers, producers, academic institutions, other government ministries, and civil society. While AERC has so far not been directly involved in this type of activity, it has provided critical services in linking its network members with various organizations, including national stakeholders. Given the expected demand for this type of service in the context of Aid for Trade, AERC could help to make linkages among these groups of stakeholders.

The effectiveness of any Aid for Trade package depends on many factors, among which are the need to conduct rigorous needs assessments/diagnoses, ensure effective implementation of identified projects, and evaluate the effectiveness of delivered projects. One important lesson to draw from the IF experience is its process, which places emphasis on comprehensive needs assessments (through the DTIS) together with stakeholder validation. While the IF – and its successor the Enhanced Integrated Framework (EIF) – may not be sufficient for meeting all LDC Aid for Trade needs (due primarily to limited funding and a focus on project identification rather than delivery), it nevertheless provides a good starting point. Additional efforts would be required to ensure effective implementation of the identified intervention programs; this could require significant increases in ODA as well as private sector investment.

The recommendations of the WTO Aid for Trade Task Force recognized the importance of technical cooperation among developing countries. Indeed, it is one of the guiding principles of Aid for Trade that technical experts from the South be used to implement projects through triangular schemes of cooperation.[6] The involvement of local expertise and stakeholders is a means to ensure that the project is owned locally. It would also help to ensure that administrative and processing costs are minimized and thus ensure that the bulk of the resources go to the actual implementation of projects. The comparative advantage of local experts is their strong understanding of the workings of their respective economies – an important factor when designing and implementing intervention programs such as those being envisaged under Aid for Trade. Indeed many local experts possess related experiences in different areas of their respective economies which could be applied to relevant issues in Aid for Trade delivery. Since some of the intended beneficiary countries are similar in structure, pooling of experts among these countries also has an added advantage of sharing experiences and comparing notes. As a network of researchers with strong linkages with the continents' policy-makers, AERC has experience in this area that could be useful on the implementation side.

4.2 Data collection and analysis

Another important Task Force recommendation in the area of strengthening the demand side is the call for the establishment of a system of data collection and analysis at country level. This important task was also part of the recommendations

5 See the Task Force recommendations (WTO, 2006) under strengthening the "demand side" and those under the strengthening the bridge between "demand" and "response."

6 See WTO (2006) paragraph F.2.

in strengthening the bridge between "demand" and "response". To us, the issue should go beyond data collection. It should include data processing, presentation, storing, and retrieval, which are important for local expertise and stakeholders in many respects. However, past experience with data and analytical tools should guide the implementation of this Aid for Trade task. First, local expertise should be assigned important roles in the design and collection and processing of necessary information. Second is the need to ensure that such tools are not only available but also affordable, as they are expected to serve as a critical input in the process of assessing the effectiveness of the implementation of the Task Force recommendations.

The diagnostic stage of priority identification requires needs assessment studies that relate and clearly show the areas where trade can increase growth and poverty reduction. For these exercises, in-depth knowledge of the structure of the economy and major constraints to trade (especially export) development are required. These studies are best conducted by local experts and stakeholders with a strong bias for analysis of sustainable development and poverty alleviation. Following diagnosis is the transition to implementation. This requires many actors[7] working together in a coherent manner. In both diagnosis and implementation, AERC can offer assistance through its expertise and through collaboration with regional trade policy-making bodies. To help meet the coherence objectives, the Consortium can offer many years of experience in organizing stakeholder meetings.

The Task Force further recommended that a number of activities would be best undertaken at the global level, with inputs and collaboration from regional institutions. Such tasks include data collection, knowledge creation and sharing (for example dissemination of Aid for Trade project and program evaluation results, development of best practices and guidelines, facilitation of information sharing); production of guidelines; provision of information on existing Aid for Trade instruments and expertise; and periodic review of Aid for Trade programs and projects. Given the scope of issues involved and the diversity of countries to be covered, a regional approach feeding into the global level would offer the right balance between efficiency and inclusiveness. Across all these areas, AERC could use its network to provide required technical assistance.

5 Conclusion

The recommendations of the Task Force on Aid for Trade are broad and general and thus require further elaboration at different levels: national, regional and global. Given the experience with similar existing initiatives such as IF and JITAP, and based on the guiding principles of the Paris Declaration, further elaboration is best undertaken by local experts and stakeholders. Involving locally-based researchers also builds longer-term capacity in the regions by building up a trained cadre of trade professionals. This chapter argued that involvement of these stakeholders

[7] At the international level, these include institutions such as the World Bank, the IMF, the African Development Bank, and other United Nations agencies and donors. At the national level, relevant government ministries such as Agriculture, Industry, Commerce, Finance, and government agencies such as Immigrations and Customs Services; Civil Societies including Academia are expected to be on board.

is an effective way of ensuring ownership of the Aid for Trade initiative by the beneficiary countries.

Research outputs from AERC network members such as those emerging from its various projects demonstrate extensive knowledge of the workings of SSA economies and the possible roles for trade and trade policy in promoting sustainable development and poverty eradication. This is coupled with an effective outreach program which has helped maintain a close relationship with government agencies. The Consortium has also established an effective training program. Given the wide diversity of issues involved in undertaking Aid for Trade, a multidisciplinary and multifaceted approach is required, involving collaboration with other institutions such as the Southern and Eastern African Trade Information and Negotiations Institute (SEATINI), Trade Law Centre for Southern Africa (TRALAC), and International Lawyers and Economists Against Poverty (ILEAP). Given its good standing with international donor agencies, AERC also has the ability to help link the "demand side" with the "supply response" of an Aid for Trade package. The effective utilization of the competence and skills of the human resources already created by the Consortium is an optimal means of ensuring that Aid for Trade addresses the supply response capacity of individual countries, regions and the continent.

However, the Consortium may also need to conduct its own needs assessment to decide on the best modalities for assisting in Aid for Trade, including in the generation of additional information, implementation at different levels, and evaluation. This is important given that the Consortium's mandate goes beyond trade issues.

REFERENCES

Amjadi, A. and A. Yeats. 1995. "Have Transport Costs Contributed to the Relative Decline of Sub-Saharan African Exports?," *Policy Research Working Paper* 1559, Washington, D.C.: World Bank.

Blackhurst, R., B. Lyakwwa, and A. Oyejide. 2000. "Options for Improving Africa's Participation in the WTO," *The World Economy*, 23(4): 491–510.

Bond, M. 1983. "Agricultural Responses in Sub-Saharan African Countries", *IMF Staff Papers*, 30(4): 703–726.

ECA. 2004. "Assessing Regional Integration in Africa," ECA Policy Research Report, Addis Ababa: ECA.

Elbadawi, I. A. 1999. "Can Africa Export Manufactures? The Role of Endowment, Exchange Rate, and Transaction Costs," Development Research Group and Africa Region, Washington, D.C.: World Bank.

Helleiner, G. K. 2002. Ed. "Non-traditional Export Promotion in Africa: Experience and Issues," New York: Palgrave Macmillan.

ILEAP. 2006. "An African Perspective on Aid for Trade," *Negotiation Advisory Brief* No. 11.

Ingco, M. D., J. D. Nash and D. Njinkeu. 2003. "Liberalising Agricultural Trade: Issues and Options for sub-Saharan Africa in the World Trade Organisation," Ibadan: Palgrave Macmillan.

Ohiorhenuan, J. F. E. 2005. "Capacity Building Implications of Enhanced African Participation in the Global Trade Rules-Making and Arrangements" ch. 11 in A. Oyejide and W. Lyakurwa (eds.), *Africa and the World Trading System Volume 1 Selected Issues of the Doha Agenda*, Trenton: Africa World Press.

Ogunkola, E. O. 1999. "African Capacity for Compliance and Defence of WTO Rights," paper presented at the Dissemination Workshop of the Collaborative Research Project on "Africa and the World Trading System" Yaoundé, Cameroon, 17–18 April.

Osakwe, P. N. 2007. "Emerging Issues and Concerns of African Countries in the WTO Negotiations on Agriculture and the Doha Round," in J. Morrison and A. Sarris (eds.), *WTO Rules for Agriculture Compatible with Development*, Rome: FAO.

Oyejide, T. A. 1989. "Supply Response in the Context of Structural Adjustment in Sub-Saharan Africa," *Special Paper* No. 1, Nairobi: AERC.

Oyejide, T. A. 2004. "African Export Supply Response Capacity: An Exploratory Analysis," mimeo, Nairobi: AERC.

Oyejide, T. A. 2005. "Costs and Benefits of 'Special and Differential' Treatment for Developing Countries in the GATT/WTO: An African Perspective," ch. 5 in A. Oyejide and W. Lyakurwa (eds.), *Africa and the World Trading System Volume 1 Selected Issues of the Doha Agenda*, Trenton: Africa World Press.

Oyejide, T. A. 2006a. "African Imperative in the World Trade Order: Results and Lessons" *AERC Research News* No. 9, Nairobi: AERC.

Oyejide, T. A. 2006b. "Development Interface between the WTO, EPA and Regional Negotiations for African Countries," report prepared for UNCTAD, Geneva.

Oyejide, T. A. and D. Njinkeu. 2002a. "African Preparation for Trade Negotiations in the Context of the ACP-EU Cotonou Partnership Agreement," *Special Paper* No. 37, Nairobi: AERC.

Oyejide, T. A. and D. Njinkeu. 2002b. "African Pre-conditions and Positive Agenda for a New Round of Multilateral Trade Negotiations," *Special Paper* No. 40, Nairobi: AERC.

Oyejide, T. A. et al. 2004. "Market Access, Competitiveness, and African Export Supply Response Capacity," paper prepared for the Africa Bureau, New York: UNDP.

Thomas, Harmon. 2006. Ed. "Trade Reforms and Food Security – Country Case Studies and Synthesis," Rome: FAO.

WTO. 2006. *Recommendations of the Task Force on Aid for Trade*, Aid for Trade Task Force, WT/AFT/1, 27 July.

Wuyts, M. 2004. "An Evaluation of the AERC Research Programme: 1997–2003," *Special Paper* No. 42, Nairobi: AERC.

16 The Role of International Research Institutions and Networks in Supporting Low-Income Countries in Trade Policymaking and Negotiations

ANN WESTON

1 Introduction

A remarkable development in the last decade has been the emergence in the trade policy community of many different sources of research focusing on the interface between trade and poverty. Alongside the more traditional and well-established international institutions such as the UN Conference on Trade and Development (UNCTAD) and the World Bank, there is now a wide range of organizations producing trade-related research to support low-income countries in their development of national trade policies and in their participation in international trade negotiations. These include intergovernmental and governmental organizations, universities, think-tanks, non-governmental organizations (NGOs), and others in the private sector.

Underlying this trend is a widespread recognition that if trade policy is to be effective, national governments must work with civil society and the private sector in their countries to monitor and analyze trade developments, formulate and implement trade policies, and participate effectively in international trade negotiations (OECD, 2001). Many countries have now created multi-stakeholder committees as well as inter-ministerial groups to consider trade policy interests and options. The question is whether they have the analytical tools, type of institutions, and access to data to produce the trade policy research needed for these consultative and decision-making bodies.

This chapter reviews the emergence of this now extensive array of research programs, assesses how successfully they interact with governments in low-income countries, and considers their role in the Aid for Trade initiative. Section 2 maps the range of institutions and networks contributing to the pool of trade research available to low-income countries. With the constantly evolving trade environment, it is difficult for this type of mapping exercise to be exhaustive; instead, the aim here is to cover the larger institutions and networks. Section 3 examines the relevance of contributions from research organizations. Specifically, it looks at whether their contributions respond to developing countries' needs (that is, issues around *effectiveness*); whether they have had an impact on trade policies and practices (*management and efficiency*); and whether they have contributed to building longer-term capacity nationally and regionally (*sustainability*). Section 4 presents some ideas about how trade research can both benefit from and contribute to Aid for Trade.

2 Mapping international trade research institutions and networks

Due in large part to the efforts of international development agencies in highlighting the relationship of trade to development and poverty reduction since the 1990s, there has been a proliferation of organizations undertaking research on trade. This has occurred in a climate of uncertainty about the appropriate trade strategies for low-income countries to follow in the wake of trade liberalization's failure to generate anticipated benefits. At the same time, these countries have been engaged in trade negotiations on multiple fronts. In response, several organizations involved in international development stepped up their research efforts around trade policy options and the consequences of growth on poverty reduction in low-income countries.

The increase in research and analysis of trade and development has paralleled the expansion in support for trade-related capacity building (TRCB), as monitored by a database managed by the World Trade Organization (WTO) and the Organization for Economic Cooperation and Development (OECD). According to the WTO/OECD Database, funding support in 2004 exceeded US$3 billion, up from US$2 billion in 2001.[1] However, since the database does not distinguish amounts devoted to research, it is difficult to say by precisely how much support for this area has increased. In the area of trade policy and regulations, research projects are included in the various issue-specific categories such as accession, trade and competition, and so forth, as well as in the category of trade education/training, which includes funding for academic programs. Similarly, categories such as "trade promotion strategy and implementation" and "market analysis and development" include several projects involving trade-related research. For instance, one "market analysis and development" project funded by the Canadian International Development Agency (CIDA) involved support to the Global Forum on Agricultural Research, while a study on ethical trade in African horticulture funded by the UK Department for International Development (DFID) fell in the "trade promotion, design and implementation" category.

Another problem is that many projects involve research that includes a range of components. For instance, one European Commission project on trade opportunities and policy in Uganda included a trade research fund, training for a trade negotiations team, and setting up technical trade advice centers, among other activities. Nonetheless, the WTO/OECD Database does provide some useful information about the types of research projects being undertaken.

2.1 Intergovernmental Organizations

Among intergovernmental organizations, several have undertaken research on trade and development issues particularly addressing the interests of low-income countries. These include many organizations traditionally associated with trade and development such as UNCTAD, the World Bank, the International Trade Centre (ITC), the Food and Agriculture Organization (FAO), regional development banks and commissions such as the Inter-American Development Bank (IDB) and the

[1] See WTO/OECD (2007), a compendium of all trade-related assistance programs.

UN Economic Commission for Latin America and the Caribbean (ECLAC), and plurilateral organizations such as the Commonwealth Secretariat.

Within the UN family, **UNCTAD** has played a lead role, with research and analysis being one of its three pillars (the others are technical cooperation and intergovernmental consensus building). As UNCTAD Secretary-General Supachai Panitchpakdi has said, "Without research and analysis, we cannot deliver policy advice or provide useful technical cooperation" (Khor, 2006). UNCTAD has shifted its focus from commodity trade issues and South-South commerce in the 1970s–80s to include issues such as non-tariff barriers, trade in services, and trade and environment in the 1990s. More recently, its areas of work have included accession, investment, country experiences with adjusting to liberalization, export performance and the new regionalism, as well as the agricultural and industrial market access issues on the WTO negotiating agenda. UNCTAD also maintains a number of industrial and agricultural trade databases available for others to use in their research.

While UNCTAD has its own research and analytical capacity, some of its studies are carried out by researchers based in other organizations in the North and the South. These researchers may be brought together in intergovernmental expert groups or in looser networks, especially for those that have a global orientation accounting roughly for over half of its projects, according to UNCTAD's July 2006 Review of Technical Cooperation Activities (UNCTAD, 2006a).

In the case of the **World Bank**, research on trade policies and specifically the lessons to be drawn from "inward oriented" approaches were the focus of work in the 1980s, together with market access and other issues on the Uruguay Round agenda. After a decline in the 1990s, trade-related activities expanded considerably from 2001, particularly after the creation of the new trade department in 2002 (World Bank, 2006). The Bank more recently moved to address issues around regional economic integration, those on the Doha Development Agenda (DDA), and broader concerns such as the links between trade and development, firm-level analysis of trade impacts on productivity, and behind-the-border issues such as agricultural standards. This research is usually led by Bank analysts with the ad hoc involvement of outsiders from North and South. The results are intended to feed into Bank programming, policy-based loans, and policy discussions with developing countries. Results are further meant to improve developing country officials' understanding of the subjects of trade negotiations and to highlight the development costs and benefits of the international trade architecture and national trading practices (such as Northern agricultural subsidies). In order to ensure that this large volume of research is widely used and contributes to policy reform, the Bank has adopted a more explicit advocacy role in recent years. Finally, it supports research by other trade analysts by making available its databases and simulation tools, producing handbooks, and providing training and other support through the World Bank Institute of networks such as the **African Economic Research Consortium (AERC)** (see Chapter 15 in this volume).

The **WTO** has built up its own research on the links between trade, poverty, and development, while at the same time giving support to researchers from developing countries through various initiatives. One example is a recent volume of forty-five case studies on managing the challenges of WTO participation for developing countries, undertaken with funding from the Australian aid agency, **AusAid** (WTO, 2005). It has organized various on-line fora on trade issues and annual dialogues on trade with academics, NGOs, and others. An innovation in recent years has been the delivery of three-month WTO training courses for developing country officials in collaboration with academics in regionally-based universities. The preparation and exchanges involved have helped to reinforce a network – even if this is still fairly loosely knit – of trade experts in each region.[2]

More recently, several other institutions have joined the search for alternative trade strategies to complement their own institutional efforts to reduce poverty. The **UN Development Programme (UNDP)**, to strengthen its human development approach, entered into the debate in the 1990s, culminating in the report "Making Global Trade Work for People" in 2003. This has been followed up by a series of research-based reports in different regional bureaus. UNDP's Asia-Pacific Bureau, for instance, has produced several discussion and policy papers as part of its Asia-Pacific Trade and Investment Initiative, and most recently published a report on trade and human development in the Asia-Pacific region (UNDP, 2006). The **UN Economic Commission for Africa** has an African Trade Policy Centre within its Trade, Finance and Economic Development Division, which carries out studies and helps to organize meetings to discuss their findings and policy implications.

The **World Health Organization (WHO)** began its work on trade-health linkages in 2001, prompted by concern about policy space around health. In the context of the WTO, the WHO is concerned about what effects rules such as trade-related intellectual property rights (TRIPS), sanitary and phytosanitary standards and technical barriers to trade (SPS/TBT), and the General Agreement on Trade in Services (GATS) may have for traditional health objectives such as food safety and security, and access to medicines and health services. After an initial report jointly undertaken with the WTO Secretariat (WTO/WHO, 2002) it began to fund various studies and meetings and to encourage the collection of relevant data. For instance, in 2003–04, it funded research on the GATS and trade in health services and evolving national trade commitments, and how these affected equity, access and the quality of country health systems. More recently, it has focused on coherence between national health systems and issues such as TRIPS and SPS as well as the GATS. The aim is to provide health policy-makers with the empirical evidence and tools to evaluate various trade policy options and to take part in the preparation and process of trade negotiations (Blouin et al., 2005). To date, the work has involved a loose and interdisciplinary network of trade and health researchers. It may be consolidated, however, as the WHO expands its trade-related work, following a resolution in May 2006 by the World Health Assembly calling for the WHO to support members' efforts to improve collaboration between health and trade ministries (ICTSD, 2006).

The **International Labour Organization (ILO)** has become involved in research work on trade, particularly following the report of its World Commission on the Social Dimensions of Globalization in 2004, and the release of its "Decent Work for All" agenda. For instance, it has played an active role in monitoring and analyzing the consequences of the end of the Multi-Fibre Arrangement (MFA) for working conditions in the textile and clothing sectors, and has used this work to inform its

[2] PhD students whose research thesis is on trade can also apply for a three-month residency at the WTO Secretariat in Geneva. Additionally, the UN University's Institute of Advanced Studies in Japan has a joint program with the WTO to train university lecturers on trade matters.

efforts in countries such as Bangladesh, Cambodia and Morocco to promote decent work in the face of increasing global competition (ILO, 2005).

Finally, the **OECD** has produced several studies and related policy briefs on trade and development issues, including a range of studies on trade facilitation, and has organized various regional meetings with trade experts and stakeholders to discuss these and other trade subjects.

2.2 Donors and academic and research institutes

In parallel with their support of multilateral trade research, donors have stepped up their own bilateral projects on trade issues involving research, as well as policy dialogues, training, and infrastructure, along with direct support to the private sector to improve competitiveness and address supply-side constraints. Data weaknesses make it difficult to list key funders and how these have changed in recent years. But several donors have research activities listed in the WTO/OECD Database.

In the case of **DFID's TRCB**, there is a strong policy-oriented research component in many of its trade projects and programs. According to the World Bank, "DFID has been one of the most active development partners, producing extensive analytical work related to the Doha Development Round" (World Bank, 2006). DFID's Regional Trade Facilitation Programme (2004–2007) in Southern Africa includes a series of studies on the future of the Southern African Customs Union (SACU), cross-border informal trade, and ways to assist small-scale producers enter the export market. The program further includes practical elements such as the creation of a customs bond fund and a series of workshops on regional rules of origin. DFID's International Trade Department has funded several studies to inform its own policy advocacy work on trade and development and its relations with other donors and developing countries. One such study, for instance, addressed the likely impacts on African, Caribbean and Pacific (ACP) countries of the erosion of sugar preferences. There have also been trade-related studies funded by other units in the Policy Division, as well as by other parts of DFID, including the Central Research Unit. Examples include studies of the impact of trade liberalization on the informal economy in India, liberalization in fish trade, and ethical trade in African horticulture. One evaluation of DFID TRCB in 2002–04 found that the studies fell into four broad categories in terms of trade policy and regulations: (i) trade and poverty linkages; (ii) negotiating interests (offensive and defensive); (iii) impact assessment of alternative negotiating options; and (iv) institutional needs. In terms of trade development, DFID's studies focused on the enabling environment and more specific supply-side constraints facing developing country exporters. As with other donors, DFID had no comprehensive inventory of all of these studies, let alone a website or other single source from which copies of the final reports or key findings (in the case of otherwise confidential studies) could be obtained (de Masellis et al., 2004).

Canada's **International Development Research Centre (IDRC)** has been an important instigator and funder of trade research, and since the 1990s has focused on the development of regional trade research networks such as the **Latin American Trade Network (LATN)** and the **Southern African Trade Research Network (SATRN)**, as well as supporting research on trade by AERC and others. Typically, these networks of predominantly Southern researchers – in universities, institutes and government and intergovernmental agencies – are coordinated by Southern institutions. Through a mix of research, outreach, and training, the networks aim to strengthen the capacity of developing country governments to identify national trade priorities and proactively come forward with proposals during trade negotiations, rather than simply reacting to those forwarded by others. IDRC has also funded trade-related activities focusing on particular themes such as competition policy and health. Similarly, other donors have funded networks of researchers concentrating on particular thematic or sectoral issues such as the African Clothing and Footwear Research Network, funded by the Dutch government, and coordinated out of **Institute for Development Studies (IDS)** offices in Nairobi.

Academic and research institutes are another central source of research on trade and development issues. Organizations such as **IDS** at Sussex University, the **Overseas Development Institute (ODI)**, the **South Centre**, the **International Institute for Sustainable Development (IISD)**, and the **North-South Institute (NSI)** are key research contributors. As already noted, however, many academics have been associated with research undertaken by international organizations and donors, as well as with NGOs and for-profit organizations, as discussed later in this chapter. For instance, in a DFID project on African Trade and Poverty, ODI was contracted to provide the analytical framework for national studies on trade and poverty linkages that were then intended to guide programming in each participating country. ODI, IDS, and the South Centre have carried out several studies for DFID analyzing various aspects of the DDA, often in partnership with analysts from developing and developed countries. NSI has worked closely with the WHO and a number of developed and developing countries in two of its health and trade projects. The **UN University** has commissioned research on various aspects of trade and development through the Institute of Advanced Studies (UNU/IAS, 2007) and the **World Institute for Development Economics Research (WIDER)**.

Several universities have set up centers for trade policy research as well as training. In Canada, for instance, the **Centre for Trade Policy and Law (CTPL)**, attached to the University of Ottawa and Carleton University, has received funding from CIDA and other donors to support the development of similar centers in Eastern Europe and the former Soviet Union and in a number of developing countries. Through these initiatives, together with its annual training courses on commercial diplomacy, CTPL has been able to develop a loose network of trade experts, some of whom are involved in its research on trade and development issues. In Australia, the **Institute for International Trade**, at the University of Adelaide, undertakes a wide range of studies and capacity building courses, many of them for Asia-Pacific developing countries.[3]

There are also now a large number of research centers, without any particular university affiliation, that are working on trade issues. In South Africa, for instance, these include **Trade and Industrial Policy Strategies (TIPS)** and the **Trade Law Centre for Southern Africa (TRALAC)**. In Switzerland, the **IDEAS Centre**, created

[3] See Institute for International Trade (2007). A recent project being supported by the WTO and AusAid is a study on the connections between trade and poverty reduction – the sort of trade policies needed to bring benefits to the poorest communities in the Asia-Pacific region.

by former WTO Director-General Arthur Dunkel, brings together a network of former officials and trade negotiators, many now consultants, to provide developing countries with trade policy advice.

IISD in Canada has been closely engaged in research around the contribution of trade to sustainable development. For example, IISD created the Trade Knowledge Network (TKN) in 1997 in collaboration with the **International Centre for Trade and Sustainable Development (ICTSD).** TKN has brought together researchers from North and South, with particular focus on eight countries (Argentina, China, El Salvador, Pakistan, South Africa, Vietnam, Bangladesh and Chile). Through research and dialogue, it aims to build capacity on trade and sustainable development in research institutions, governments and NGOs. For instance, TKN helps countries explore what sectors might be at risk by the greening of foreign markets, and which might benefit by undertaking environmental improvements.

Moving outside the more traditional academic/analytical centers, there are several organizations that promote trade-related information with a strong critical and analytical component – with research being an important focus. These would include for example **ICTSD**, the **European Centre for Development Policy Management (ECDPM), International Lawyers and Economists against Poverty (ILEAP)**, and, based in the South, **Third World Network (TWN), the Southern and Eastern African Trade, Information and Negotiations Institute (SEATINI)**, and **EcoNews Africa**. ICTSD and TWN have been major sources of regular information on trade negotiations, particularly those going on in Geneva (through BRIDGES Weekly Trade News Digest and South-North Development Monitor or SUNS, respectively). This has been important for researchers as well as for officials. Drawing on their excellent access to information and their own strong analytical capacities and networks with researchers, these organizations have also undertaken research projects and encouraged the research of others in various ways. For example, ICTSD has introduced small research grants and organized dialogues on particular issues such as biotechnology and trade and sustainability (Meléndez-Ortiz and Sánchez, 2005). TWN has published several reports on globalization and impacts on the poor, including a report on trade, industrialization and the non-agricultural market access (NAMA) negotiations by Yilmaz Akyuz and a series of papers on the impact of liberalization on poor rural producers. TWN-Africa has sponsored research on gender and trade, a subject that is the focus of an international network, the **International Gender and Trade Network (IGTN)**, based in the United States. SEATINI, based in Zimbabwe, is a regional non-governmental organization founded in 1996. It produces analytical work on the WTO and EU/ACP Economic Partnership Agreement (EPA) negotiations, regional trade agreements, and national trade issues from an alternative perspective. EcoNews Africa, based in Kenya, has published a number of policy briefs on the WTO negotiations, the EPAs, and other trade issues.

ECDPM in the Netherlands has a program focused on the development dimensions of the EPAs that addresses the trade rules that might be involved, complementary measures and processes, and funding required for their implementation. It has emphasized research, dialogue, communication of the results, and capacity building. Its various studies ("practical and strategic research") seek to build on – and synthesize – the large amount of primary research on EPAs by others and to draw out specific proposals for development support. Its extensive outreach program includes policy briefs and discussion papers drawing on this work and together with ICTSD it publishes Trade Negotiations Insights, a newsletter focused on bringing different perspectives to the EPA negotiations. It has created a network of trade expertise on EPAs in order to help governments find advisors as needed.

Among the newer networks, **ILEAP**, based in Canada, has a somewhat similar mandate, namely to provide practical, timely, independent and inter-disciplinary advice on trade negotiations for low-income countries in Africa and the Caribbean. It has created an international network of experienced lawyers and economists, and related institutions with both official and academic experience, to work with developing country governments and help them prepare for and participate in trade negotiations. Some of this work has involved publishing studies (for instance on a range of aspects relating to Aid for Trade, financial services, and agricultural and non-agricultural market access proposals) prepared by experts or advisory groups, as well as running workshops and training courses. It also integrates junior professionals in the preparation of background material as a way of building their policy-relevant expertise. It works closely with governments, regional secretariats, and international organizations.

2.3 Non-governmental organizations (NGOs)

One of the most striking changes in the global trade policy landscape over the last decade is the emergence of a wide range of national and international NGOs based in developed and developing countries engaged in international trade policy research.[4] This evolution partly responds to the increasing recognition that trade is no longer an issue for technocrats alone but one in which citizens' groups should be informed and involved, particularly given the expanded scope of trade policies. NGOs have undertaken trade research to inform their interventions in the increasingly participatory discussions around trade. In many cases, their analysis has drawn on their connections with the grassroots – with small farmers, farm workers, microentrepreneurs, garment workers, workers in the informal sector, consumer groups and others whose lives are affected by trade in one way or another. Many NGOs try to bring the voices of the poor and marginalized to the policy table – helping them to tell their "stories" whether directly or indirectly. NGOs have also engaged academic researchers as staff and/or as partners to undertake serious research and develop evidence-based policy recommendations, which they are able to use with increasing effect as the basis for dialogue and advocacy with government and international organizations.

For instance, **Maquila Solidarity Network (MSN)** based in Toronto, Canada, has produced an extensive body of work on codes of conduct that has been used by workers' organizations, activists and corporations to discuss ways of improving conditions for garment workers in the increasingly competitive global garment industry. NGOs now recognize that research is an integral part of the change process

[4] A recent issue of ITC's International Trade Forum lists twenty-three NGOs involved in trade development internationally – from those engaged in trade policy and negotiations, to others working on economic development for poor communities, financing and training of businesses to be involved in international trade. See UNCTAD/WTO (2005) p. 22.

that they are actively promoting – that research along with outreach and training is needed to achieve changing attitudes and beliefs about the links between trade rules and practices, on the one hand, and low commodity prices, declining terms of trade, poor working conditions, and poverty, on the other.

In the NGO community, the **Oxfam** family emerged as a leading source of research on international trade issues with the publication in 2002 of "Rigged Rules and Double Standards". That report helped to establish Oxfam as a well-respected source of creative ideas for increasing the benefits of globalization for the poor. It has produced many other reports covering a wide range of issues from cotton subsides affecting poor farmers in West Africa and the distribution of benefits along the coffee supply chain, to tariffs and the NAMA negotiations and Vietnam's accession to the WTO. The World Bank's Independent Evaluation Group (IEG) notes that Oxfam has been extremely active in drawing attention to ways of making the multilateral trading system fairer, and that on some subjects, such as cotton, their research and advocacy work preceded that of the Bank (World Bank, 2006). Certainly, Oxfam has been able to command the attention of the media and policymakers when it launches its research reports. The organization is often consulted by national governments and international organizations about its research and views on trade issues.

Within the international development NGO community, it seems that Oxfam's Make Trade Fair campaign – which was heavily research-based – helped to make trade a development issue, one that many NGOs had previously overlooked, if not rejected. There is some evidence that Oxfam's work helped to shift the discourse and attitudes about issues affecting developing countries in trade. For instance, its research on cotton subsidies contributed to West African governments becoming more vocal in their criticism of Northern agricultural policies. Further, several coffee retailers and roasters have been persuaded that fair trade coffee can be profitable and as a result have expanded their fair trade coffee business. Many of Oxfam's reports are written by staff members, with inputs (such as brief case studies) from their field offices. The organization has also increased the engagement of academics based in developing and developed countries, including partnerships with Southern research institutes and international organizations such as the South Centre. In Bangladesh, for instance, Oxfam has supported research by Unnayan Onneshan on rice trade, and collaborated with the Centre for Policy Dialogue on working conditions in the garment sector. In India in 2004, Oxfam created the Centre for Trade and Development (CTD), an independent policy research and advocacy organization. CTD was set up to undertake research on South Asian trade issues for Oxfam South Asia and other parts of the Oxfam family, and more generally to fill a perceived gap in India between those Indian organizations doing "high research" and no advocacy, and those doing advocacy using the research of others. This think-tank, together with India's **Consumer Unity and Trust Society (CUTS)**, are examples of the many new actors at the national level, which it is not possible here to map exhaustively at the global level.

Some NGOs, such as **ActionAid International**, based in South Africa, have used trade research as the basis for popular briefs used in their campaigning for trade justice, for instance on the implications of trade liberalization for developing country industries and appropriate principles for industrial tariffs.

2.4 Private sector

Finally, it is important to acknowledge the work at the **private sector** level of the trade and development research community, operating on a for-profit basis. These range from big international law firms such as Sidley Austin and consulting firms such as Ernst and Young and IBM Consulting, to much smaller firms based in the North or South of one or two consultants specializing in trade and development issues (such as Oxford Policy Management in the UK, which has prepared several policy studies for DFID). Some of these firms are involved in the creation and management of networks of analysts that are able to service developing country needs for technical advice in trade negotiations, dispute resolution, or national policy development. One of the difficulties in assessing their role in low-income countries is that even if their work may be funded by governments (donors/recipients), typically it is not in the public domain.

To sum up, there has been a surge in the amount of research on trade and development issues in recent years. The differentiation between intergovernmental, academic, NGO and private sector networks has become blurred – with analysts from one sector often being involved in the research, training, information sharing, dialogue and advocacy activities of another. Instead, what has emerged are networks of individual experts, information networks, and knowledge networks, following a typology put forward by Creech and Willard (2001). The key differentiating factors are the extent to which networks involve individuals or institutions, the nature of their collaboration, the scope and depth of their focus, and their engagement with practitioners and broader communities. How these contribute to resolving the trade challenges facing low-income countries – their strengths and their weaknesses, and particularly their role in Aid for Trade – is discussed in the next two sections.

3 Connecting to trade research needs in low-income countries

The proliferation of organizations and networks involved in research on trade and development suggests that there is considerable demand for this type of work, even if some of it may have been supply-driven. Here we consider whether the research and research networks have been relevant to low-income countries, whether they have been effective and well-managed, and whether they are sustainable.

On the issue of *relevance*, it is clear that there has been a significant increase in demand from Southern governments and groups outside government for research and analysis that provides them with a better sense of what the consequences of alternative trade policies might be, at an aggregate and a disaggregated level (macro-micro, sectoral, gender-differentiated), and what measures are needed to complement or even compensate for these changes. Likewise, governments have recognized the importance of understanding and anticipating the consequences of the changing global division of labor, the restructuring in global supply chains, and what government policies might improve national producers' positions within these. Diversity of research sources, multidisciplinary approaches, and qualitative as well as quantitative analysis are all needed. While some of this is being met by the range of organizations and networks now active in trade research, a recent survey of

TRCB in nine countries (CUTS, 2006) found there was still an unmet need for more research. Several interviewees wanted research on the likely consequences of different proposals on the regional and international trade negotiating agenda, what strategies they might propose themselves, and how they could then help their own producers and other groups respond to the changing trade environment nationally and internationally. Officials from outside the trade ministries in many countries felt this need even more strongly – suggesting that much of the trade research to date has been fairly narrowly defined, and even where it was of broader relevance it may not have been distributed as widely as needed.

In many international organizations, the demand for research has been internally generated, to help them better achieve their mandates. Organizations such as UNCTAD and the World Bank that are involved in delivering trade or broader economic policy advice, or trade support, have needed to better understand the country- and sector-specific contexts within which they were working, as well as the implications of their policy proposals. Others, such as the WHO, FAO, and UNDP, have found it critical to know the ways in which trade rules might affect the sectors (health, agriculture) or groups (farmers, women, small entrepreneurs) with which they are operating. They further want to know how best to anticipate – and take advantage or limit – these effects, and to ensure that national counterparts effectively participate in national debates about trade policies and adjustment mechanisms. Similarly, in the case of development NGOs, research and analysis have been used to strengthen their own campaigning to influence policy.

According to a review of the World Bank's trade work by the IEG, this has not been effectively linked to programming needs. It found that the research had been driven by researchers and less by demand from country economists. The latter called for more work on the transitional adjustment costs of trade reforms, empirical analyses, comparative research and global value chains. Unfortunately, the report noted, "no systematic method of gauging demand exists" (p. 60) – a comment that can be applied more generally. The IEG was also critical of the Bank's trade department for overlooking some issues and approaches that are priorities for developing country officials (World Bank, 2006). For instance, its survey found that many countries were keen to have analysis and tools to help them manage external shocks and adjustment arising from trade liberalization. Also, they wanted more training to be able to do their own analysis of the implications.

Another suggestion made during our review of WTO TRTA was for better networking of researchers and trade officials. As Creech and Willard note in their description of an effective Trade Knowledge Network, bringing these groups together at both regional and national levels can help to inform both the issues being researched – to enhance their relevance – and the use of the research findings, and thus their likely impact (2001). Certainly, there was a sense that if Southern researchers are able to share ideas for research with governments and other stakeholders, this would help to increase its usefulness. Also, such research was needed to provide relevant case-study material for trade-related training – something that has been found lacking in most such training to date.

Despite the large volume of TRCB, and specifically the amounts now invested in trade research, analysis and networking, there has been less attention until recently to its *effectiveness*, in terms of its direct impacts on policy and its longer-term contribution to improving the benefits of international trade for low-income countries.

From 2004–2006 a number of evaluations of TRCB were undertaken. Many of these evaluations found that much of the trade research is considered high quality, widely cited, and useful for improving understanding. However, they also found only weak evidence of the impact of TRCB.[5] Some have pointed to the importance of complementary measures – such as supply-side measures. Others focus on political action and the need for training in how to ensure that research is used with effect – it is important for national groups to understand the political context of policy advocacy.

Nonetheless, there are some examples to suggest that research – particularly when it is designed in response to particular needs, and has results that are clearly articulated and shared with trade policy communities broadly defined – can make a difference. For instance, it seems that the considerably greater participation by many African countries in the DDA, as measured by the number of proposals they have advanced, results from their national delegations being able to draw on various studies defining areas of possible offensive and defensive interests, and setting out the possible consequences of different ideas on the negotiating table. This is further supplemented by training programs and available resources to participate in the negotiations. More specifically, the capacity of some of the poorest West African countries to put Northern cotton subsidies on the international trade agenda in 2003 followed some timely research by Oxfam and other groups, along with coordinated political action.

Besides research, low-income countries need help in synthesizing and digesting the various studies now available – which may explain the emergence of trade knowledge networks and the proliferation of bodies (such as ICTSD, ILEAP, ECDPM and others) to promote and operationalize the findings of others. Reports need to be available in both technical and non-technical formats. In some cases, it may be important for officials to participate in "learning-by-doing" exercises. Donors can facilitate this process, and especially the transition from research to programming, for example by providing support for developing country officials to participate in international meetings, where they may apply lessons learned from research studies to the negotiating process, or for addressing behind-the-border constraints.

Turning to the issue of *management and efficiency*, there is a risk of duplication of effort and failure to make the most of existing research, given the lack of a database of what has been undertaken, let alone any coordinating mechanism in most countries and regions. While avoiding duplication may be difficult given the broad scope of the work and the many different groups now involved, a step in this direction could be through the replication of networks such as LATN and SATRN at the regional level. Another, more ambitious, suggestion from the recent Eminent Persons' Panel that examined UNCTAD's role and impact is for UNCTAD to serve as a focal point for a global network of trade and development think tanks. While the Panel believed that this would contribute to the relevance and reach of UNCTAD's research and policy analysis, perhaps more importantly adopting its suggestions might help to maximize the development impact of the entire network's research.

In terms of dissemination, there is a lot more research on trade policy now, at both a national and sectoral level, but it is often not publicly available or is

[5] See, for example, World Bank (2006) p. 84.

hard to find (especially work commissioned by donors). In some cases this may be appropriate, for instance when national negotiating positions are involved. More generally, however, it would be very useful for more research to be placed on portals such as ELDIS,[6] so that it can be widely accessed.

The creation of research networks, and especially Southern-based regional networks, may be one way to address the question of *sustainability*. As in the case of TRTA generally, much of the assistance has been short-term rather than directed at building longer-term capacity. Many research studies have been undertaken on an ad hoc basis, led by Northern-based trade researchers. They have been linked to particular projects (in the case of donors/IGOs) or campaigns (in the case of NGOs). They may have led to the creation of short-term and/or informal networks, rather than more formal or long-lasting ones. Even where Southern researchers have been involved, it has often been as part of one-off projects. The development of Southern networks that can tap into various funding sources over a longer period, to accomplish a program of research, is essential to build up a trade research community that can produce the analysis needed by governments and other stakeholders. Several of the international organizations already mentioned – both intergovernmental and non-governmental – have begun to move in this direction, providing Southern researchers with the tools (databases, software), financial and technical support, and opportunities to undertake this type of research. But more funding, especially longer-term, is needed to support these efforts.

4 Moving beyond trade research to Aid for Trade

There are several ways in which trade research networks can connect to Aid for Trade. Three in particular stand out:

1. Using Aid for Trade for Southern trade research networks

First, Aid for Trade may be used to support the evolution of trade research. This includes its scope (expanding the issues being addressed, the disciplines, the level of disaggregation, and so forth), the networks involved in its design, and implementation and dissemination of its findings. While trade research capacities have increased in some countries, they are still scarce in many, both in governments and outside in universities, parliament, civil society and the private sector. Certainly, Aid for Trade could fund more research that is Southern-based – whether through existing channels or through the creation of new demand-driven funds to be drawn down as needed by low-income country governments and stakeholder partners.

2. Putting research into action

Second, as previously mentioned, officials and other groups with interests in trade in low-income countries could benefit from having funds to translate research findings into action. This could involve funds for organizing national multi-stakeholder meetings to develop national policy positions, for meetings with potential coalition partners, or participation in negotiating meetings.

[6] ELDIS is one of a "family of knowledge services" provided by the Institute of Development Studies, Sussex. See http://www.eldis.org/trade/index.htm.

3. *Defining Aid for Trade*

Finally, research can help to inform various ways in which Aid for Trade might evolve, as other chapters in this volume show. There have been several studies on behind-the-border issues and others such as trade facilitation, which identify how additional funding might support efforts to expand developing country trade. Trade policy research has identified areas for complementary programming under Aid for Trade. For instance, studies have underlined the need for complementary action to address supply-side constraints (as in the case of the Bank's research on cotton in Zambia or of Oxfam's research on coffee cooperatives producing for fair trade markets). Others have addressed the issue of post-trade agreement impacts and compensatory policies.

REFERENCES

Blouin, Chantal, N. Drager, and D. Smith. 2005. Eds. "International Trade in Health Services and the GATS: current issues and debates," Geneva: WHO.

Creech, Heather and Terri Willard. 2001. "Strategic Intentions: Managing knowledge networks for sustainable development," Winnipeg: IISD.

CUTS, FLACSO, and NSI. 2006. "Strategic Review of WTO-provided TRTA Activities," http://www.cuts-citee.org/PDF/WTO-FinalReport.pdf.

de Masellis, Luigi, Chantal Blouin, and Ann Weston. 2004. "Evaluation of DFID Support to Trade Related Capacity Building – Descriptive and Statistical Overview of DFID's TRCB," Working Paper No. 1, Ottawa: NSI.

ICTSD. 2006. "Services negotiations waiting for movement on Ag, NAMA," *Bridges*, 10(19), Geneva: ICTSD.

ILO. 2005. "Promoting fair globalization in textiles and clothing in a post-MFA environment," report for discussion at the Tripartite Meeting on "Promoting Fair Globalization in Textiles and Clothing in a Post-MFA Environment," Geneva: ILO.

Institute for International Trade. 2007. "Homepage," http://www.iit.adelaide.edu.au/.

Khor, Martin. 2006. "Supachai reveals expert panel's proposals on UNCTAD," South-North Development Monitor (SUNS) # 6045, Penang: TWN.

Meléndez-Ortiz, Ricardo and Vicente Sánchez. 2005. Eds. "Trading in Genes – development perspectives on biotechnology, trade and sustainability," London: Earthscan Publications Ltd.

OECD. 2001. "The DAC Guidelines – Strengthening Trade Capacity for Development," Paris: OECD.

Oxfam. 2002. "Rigged Rules and Double Standards: trade, globalization, and the fight against poverty," Oxford: Oxfam International.

UNCTAD. 2006a. "Review of the Technical Cooperation Activities," TD/B/WP/188, New York and Geneva: United Nations.

UNCTAD. 2006b. "Report of the Panel of Eminent Persons, Enhancing the Development Role and Impact of UNCTAD," New York and Geneva: United Nations.

UNCTAD/WTO. 2005. "International Trade Forum: Why Services Matter, No. 2," Geneva: ITC.

UNDP. 2003. "Making Global Trade Work for People," London: Earthscan Publications Ltd.

UNDP. 2006. "Asia-Pacific Human Development Report 2006 – Trade on Human Terms: Transforming Trade for Human Development in Asia and the Pacific," Colombo: Palgrave Macmillan and UNDP.

UNU/IAS. 2007. "WTO and Sustainable Development," http://www.ias.unu.edu/research/tradesd.cfm.

World Bank. 2006. "Assessing World Bank Support for Trade, 1987–2004," Independent Evaluation Group, Washington, D.C.: World Bank.

WTO. 2005. "Managing the Challenge of WTO Participation: 45 Case Studies," Cambridge: Cambridge University Press.

WTO/OECD. 2007. "Doha Development Agenda Trade Capacity Building Database," http://tcbdb.wto.org.

WTO/WHO. 2002. "WTO Agreements & Public Health: A joint study by the WHO and the WTO Secretariat," Geneva: WTO and WHO.

17 Civil Society Perspectives in the Aid for Trade Debate

ALDO CALIARI

1 Introduction

Issues around Aid for Trade have been a subject of analysis and positioning among civil society organizations (CSOs)[1] for a number of years. CSOs maintain an important role vis-à-vis governments in discussions around international economic policy, namely the ability to articulate a global vision and take into account systemic realities and factors. This is a perspective that no country on its own can bring, as governments represent the politically expressed interests of a localized community of citizens. Any attempt by a government to analyze an issue in the global context will always be conditioned by the limits of what is possible within the boundaries of its own interests. These interests also tend to be borne out at the intergovernmental level. In addition to offering viewpoints that go beyond national boundaries and interests, civil society can make important contributions by fostering open and informed debate, improving accountability and transparency, and providing checks and balances on what would otherwise be a purely government-driven discussion.

The policy discussion on Aid for Trade is no exception to this role for civil society. CSOs are likely to play a part in the implementation and delivery of Aid for Trade. But, rather than staying confined to such a role, they are also helping to shape the agenda. This chapter assesses the role and perspectives of civil society in Aid for Trade for low-income countries, and looks at how their advocacy and other work on trade and financial policy can help bring a broader and more critical perspective to the issue-area.

At first sight, the introduction of Aid for Trade seems to present an opening to make the links between trade and finance visible. However, as this chapter attempts to show, the context in which this issue is emerging calls for a cautious approach. The concept of aid to help low-income countries better take advantage of trading opportunities, within the context of their own development priorities, is a welcome one from which many of these countries stand to benefit. The first concern for many international non-governmental organizations (NGOs) providing policy advice on Aid for Trade is to ensure that this concept does not take the place of development,

[1] Civil society is by nature diverse, and there are a large number of groups active in the area of trade and finance, operating from a variety of perspectives. An indicative list of such groups could include actors such as Jubilee, Eurodad, International Centre for Trade and Sustainable Development (ICTSD), Oxfam, Christian Aid, and so forth. On aid, trade, and finance issues, the terms civil society organizations (CSOs) and non-governmental organizations (NGOs) are often used interchangeably.

but is seen in a holistic perspective that links trade and finance on the grounds of supporting development.

Section 2 of this chapter provides some brief background on the role of CSOs in undertaking advocacy on trade and finance policies, and traces the evolution of their work in addressing trade-finance linkages. Section 3 locates the Aid for Trade discussion in the broader context of developing countries' needs in the multilateral trading system. Section 4 goes into some specific conditions that civil society has identified as requirements in order for Aid for Trade to be effective in yielding development results in low-income countries. Section 5 provides reflections on the specific features that a delivery mechanism for Aid for Trade should have. Section 6 provides some concluding remarks.

2 Trade and finance linkages and civil society

International civil society groups have become more involved in influencing policy-making processes around international aid, finance, and trade in the last two decades. For instance, lobbying and actions by NGOs from around the world played a major role in hastening the demise of the Organization for Economic Cooperation and Development's (OECD's) proposed Multilateral Agreement on Investment in 1998. Concerted NGO action was also critical in highlighting the concerns of developing countries and helping to boost aid committed at the UN Monterrey Summit of 2002 and at the 2005 G8 Summit in Gleneagles. At Gleneagles, due in no small part to the work of civil society groups such as Jubilee, G8 governments adopted language calling for "100 percent debt cancellation" for a number of highly indebted poor countries. The adoption of language that not more than a decade earlier was considered laughable and utopian is perhaps the most striking example of the impact that consistent campaigning from civil society can have on the international agenda.[2]

With regard to trade issues, one can look at the experiences of the World Trade Organization's (WTO's) failed Seattle and Cancun Ministerial Conferences, where NGOs arguably played a strong part in the events' respective collapses. Coordinated civil society campaigns against the inclusion of the four "Singapore issues" (investment, competition, transparency in government procurement, and trade facilitation) in the Doha agenda also had a hand in the eventual abandonment of the first three of these issues from the WTO negotiations after Cancun. NGOs continue to play an important role in trade policy, due in part to their ability to help amplify the growing voice of developing countries in the multilateral trading system, and to provide these countries with background research and analysis to facilitate their engagement with the trading system.

In the last few years, CSOs have begun to reflect on the results and effectiveness of their work. A few examples of results that are under debate are the following:

- After long campaigning, debt reduction materialized through the Heavily Indebted Poor Countries (HIPC) Initiative. Several beneficiary countries, however, saw the gains in debt relief erased a few years later due to the fact that the initiative overlooked their export structures.

[2] However misleading the language was in the light of the actual proposals being advanced in its name.

- While CSOs campaign to achieve increases in aid, 51 cents of every aid dollar are "lost" through commodity price losses as a result of agricultural subsidies and declining terms of trade.
- First through the discussions on a "Development Box," and now through the discussions on Special Products, civil society has been struggling to open policy space for tariff protection for subsistence agriculture. Yet, in developing countries the existing space for tariff protection tends to be underutilized due to restrictions on tariffs imposed by international financial institutions (IFIs). Likewise with regard to the prospects for subsidizing input services and maintaining marketing boards.
- While three of the four "Singapore issues" have been dropped from the multilateral trade negotiations' agenda for the time being, similar requirements are being pursued by developed countries through bilateral and regional negotiations, and through the influence of conditions set and technical advice provided by the IFIs.

These are just the most obvious examples of dynamics that are in no way new, but seem to have been neglected due to a general trend to develop work programs oriented to influence a specific international organization or its policies. There is nothing intrinsically wrong with this practice and, in fact, it would seem that the more focused a program is on the agenda of a particular institution, the more likely it will be to enter the policy-making agenda of the organization. However, CSOs are now becoming aware that, in the longer term, shifts and linkages between trade and financial policy instruments can defeat the ultimate goal of the best-designed advocacy program.

This state of affairs is prompting CSOs to balance their concentration on specific global institutions with the establishment of effective mechanisms to exercise what some have called "cross-institutional" monitoring. Cross-institutional monitoring refers to the ability of organizations to draw upon a holistic picture of how trade, debt, and aid link to each other, even as they prepare highly specialized advocacy programs oriented toward a particular institution. With respect to trade policy, a growing number of CSOs believe in the need to redefine trade and finance linkages through a vision that promotes people-centered development, human rights, environmental protection, and gender equality.[3]

3 Aid for Trade in a development context

The Doha Round was launched in 2001 in the context of the realization by developing countries that the Uruguay Round (1986–94) had not brought them the benefits

[3] For instance, a first meeting convened by Center of Concern and other groups in 2002 with the goal of exploring the issues of linking trade and finance brought together more than seventy civil society organizations. Since then, advocacy activities around the link between trade and finance have been present in almost all meetings of the Bretton Woods institutions (the World Bank and the IMF), the WTO, and the UN Financing for Development process. Starting in 2005, a series of Regional Meetings on Trade-Finance Linkages has helped galvanize action fronts at the regional level to address trade and finance in an integrated way. Currently, the Center of Concern's 2002 initiative has turned into an International Working Group on Trade-Finance Linkages that brings together over 300 organizations and networks worldwide. For an archive of these documents and the activities of the International Working Group on Trade-Finance Linkages, see Center of Concern (2007).

that had been expected or promised.[4] While East Asian countries – which were already integrated in the global trading system – had experienced rapid growth since the 1970s and 1980s, exports from most developing countries were still concentrated on products derived essentially from the exploitation of natural resources and the use of unskilled labor. Even figures showing a rise in exports of high-value products were misleading in that they hid exporting countries' participation mostly in the low-skill assembly stage of transnational chains of production, making the capture of benefit from these products elusive (UNCTAD, 2002a). By the time of the Third WTO Ministerial in Seattle in 1999, developing countries had compiled a long list of concerns emerging from the Uruguay Round that they wanted addressed – these came to be known as "Implementation Issues" (Das, 2005).

Not being at ease with the implementation of the existing commitments, developing countries were therefore wary of another round of further trade liberalization. That is why they were able to accept a new round of negotiations only under the promise that it would focus on redressing the negative impacts of the previous ones, thus giving the round its moniker of the Doha "Development" Agenda (DDA).

The reference to development, nonetheless, came to be more prominent in the title than in the actual content of the subsequent negotiations. The negotiations tended to reflect a focus by developed countries on the continued promotion of liberalization (of markets of interest to their large corporations) and little focus on the demands of developing countries, especially those that called for a review of Uruguay Round commitments. The attempt to bring up development concerns tended to be frustrated by the lack of receptivity of a system not built around the notion of development, but rather around promoting the progressive liberalization of trade transactions among its members.

One example of the low-income countries' attempts to raise matters that had been neglected in the Uruguay Round is illustrative and helpful in situating the subject matter of this chapter in its proper context. This was the attempt to articulate the linkages between trade and finance in ways that supported their development goals. This demand was embodied in the WTO Doha Ministerial Declaration's call to establish a Working Group on Trade, Debt, and Finance. The Working Group's mandate was to carry out:

> an examination . . . of the relationship between trade, debt and finance, and of any possible recommendations on steps that might be taken within the mandate and competence of the WTO to enhance the capacity of the multilateral trading system to contribute to a durable solution to the problem of external indebtedness of developing and least-developed countries, and to strengthen the coherence of international trade and financial policies, with a view to safeguarding the multilateral trading system from the effects of financial and monetary instability. (WTO, 2001a)

Ideally, and since the linkages cut across all areas of negotiation, the outcomes of the group could have permeated the rest of the Doha Work Programme (Tortora, 2001) and been brought to bear on each of the items under negotiation in the round. However, being no more than a Working Group, with no negotiating power,

[4] For a review of problems associated with the outcome of the Uruguay Round, see Finger and Nogues (2001); Das (1998); and Chapter 3 by Finger in this volume.

it became quickly marginalized, with its agenda being of hardly any relevance to the ongoing negotiations.

In the lead-up to the WTO Ministerial Conference at Hong Kong in December 2005, developing countries pushed to elevate the Working Group to the status of a Committee of the WTO, but faced the opposition of developed countries, which wanted to shut down the Working Group altogether. A compromise result was the status quo, which has been reflected in the Hong Kong Declaration (WTO, 2005). In other words, it was agreed that trade and finance linkages would continue to be addressed through a Working Group, thereby depriving the issue of its potential to have an impact on negotiating results.

The fate of the Working Group illustrates how various development aspects are being treated in the context of the Doha negotiations. Were the development content to have been taken seriously, it would have led to a critical re-evaluation of the existing system that would have been open to rolling back some of the existing rules, while creating or reinforcing others. However, rolling back trade liberalization, reinforcing rules on special and differential treatment (SDT), and finding solutions to many of the implementation issues would run counter to the logic of an organization predicated on the principle of progressively opening trade. Thus, a tension arose between what the development content of the round would require and the imperative to lower trade barriers (and, by many, to measure "success" or "ambition" in terms of how much those barriers have fallen).

In the preparations for the WTO Ministerial at Hong Kong, the response to this disconnect developed in the form of a so-called "development package." Two of the package's main components were proposals for duty-free, quota-free market access into developed countries for the exports of Least Developed Countries (LDCs), and Aid for Trade. Various developed countries made announcements during the Ministerial about increases in Aid for Trade (see the Introductory chapter in this volume), but of these increases it is unclear how much is to be provided bilaterally or through other means. It is also unclear how much these new figures represent additional resources or funding shifted from other areas.

At first blush, the introduction of Aid for Trade seems to present an opening to make the links between trade and finance more concrete. However, given the context explained above, there is a need to be cautious. The first concern for international NGOs providing policy advice on the Aid for Trade package is to ensure that Aid for Trade does not preclude progress on other development issues, but rather is implemented in the context of a holistic perspective that links trade and finance in supporting development. This approach includes the following two key elements:

1. The avoidance of trade-offs between Aid for Trade and ongoing negotiations

It is important not to tie Aid for Trade to the current round of negotiations or, for that matter, to any other set of negotiations. The idea of aid to help low-income countries better take advantage of trading opportunities, within the context of their own development priorities, is a welcome one from which low-income countries can benefit. The idea of aid for compensating countries for particular concessions that are still under negotiation is not, as it may drive cash-strapped developing countries towards making concessions that are harmful or not in their best interests in the long term. Thus, the less that aid discussions are linked to compensation for specific losses related to low-income country concessions in particular scenarios under discussion in the Doha Round, the less the risk that such a trade-off – implicit or explicit – will emerge.

2. Beware the asymmetry between trade rules and financial commitments

The asymmetry between trade rules and financial commitments should be kept in mind. Low-income countries have learned the hard way that trade rules, once accepted, are next to impossible to turn around. The lack of progress on the long list of Implementation Issues that has been referred to above is one example. Even where rules were adopted with the condition of mandatory reviews that would look at their adequacy and usefulness after a certain time, attempts by developing countries to roll back harmful rules have proved frustrating. The General Agreement on Trade in Services (GATS), for instance, provides for an assessment of trade in services in overall terms and on a sectoral basis to be carried out before any new round of negotiations.[5] This assessment should look at the goal set in Article IV of the agreement, which calls for facilitating the "increasing participation of developing country Members in world trade."[6] Numerous proposals by developing countries on the implementation of this provision "do not appear to have made any effective impact on the approach of the developed countries," (Das, 2005)[7] and thorough assessments have yet to be made, despite the advanced stage of GATS talks. A similar example can be found in the Agreement on Trade-related Investment Measures (TRIMS), which stipulates in Article 9 that the operation of the agreement must be reviewed. Attempts by developing countries to have the rules reviewed based on the harm they bring to their economies have so far remained deadlocked (Raja, 2005; WTO, 2005). Regarding the Trade-related Intellectual Property Rights (TRIPS) Agreement, it was only after a painful and protracted process, aided by an international campaign by CSOs to show the effects of TRIPS on preventable diseases, that developing countries managed to extract some flexibility through the TRIPS Declaration on Public Health (WTO, 2001b). On top of this, developing countries are routinely discouraged from making use of provisions that were built into the WTO agreements to give them flexibility in implementation for development purposes.

On the other hand, pledges by industrial countries on financial support (and specifically on Overseas Development Assistance – ODA) are typically unenforceable, hard to monitor, and risk being a repackaging of existing programs. The target of 0.7 percent of industrialized countries' Gross National Product (GNP) for ODA provides a notable example. This commitment, dating back to 1970, has been met by only a few countries, and hardly survived, in modified form, the 2002 Monterrey Summit on Financing for Development.[8] Leaders at the G8 Summit in Gleneagles in 2005 promised to ramp up ODA by around US$50 billion per year for all developing countries, and by at least US$25 billion per year for Africa, all by 2010. Some

5 GATS Art. XIX.3
6 GATS Art. IV
7 In a similar sense, see Manduna (2004).
8 Monterrey Summit Outcome Document (2002), para. 43. ("In that context, we urge developed countries that have not done so to make concrete efforts towards the target of 0.7 percent of gross national product (GNP) as ODA to developing countries.")

G8 countries have already announced, though, that they will miss their targets (Williamson, 2006; Pilling, 2006), and the OECD's Development Assistance Committee (DAC) (made up of the major donor countries) has said there is a strong likelihood that they will be missed (White, 2006).

In terms of monitoring, several NGOs have questioned the accounting practices used by OECD countries to inflate aid levels.[9] If accounting practices are a problem when monitoring general aid levels, they become more so when referring to aid for particular aims (such as, in this case, trade). What is to be counted as Aid for Trade? For example, is infrastructure for updating hospital standards that can also be used for exporting health services a trade-related expense? What about funding for building a road that will be used for domestic purposes as well as for facilitating trade? And education that improves the skills of the population and makes for a more investment-competitive workforce? There is a risk that aid already committed for several purposes, or that was to be provided anyway, might easily be repackaged as Aid for Trade. Achieving more specificity on the scope of Aid for Trade could help to resolve this.

Finally, there is the issue of trade-offs between general ODA and Aid for Trade. Given the aid commitments made by the G8 in 2005, and the likelihood of them being missed, it is hard to see how any new ODA monies can still be committed that have not been committed already. And, if this is the case, is it possible to ascertain that Aid for Trade will not come at the expense of other equally deserving aid goals, such as programs for HIV/AIDS vaccines, education, and democracy-building?

4 Making Aid for Trade effective

From the perspective of CSOs, as important as the question of how Aid for Trade will be provided is the question of under which conditions any delivered aid is going to yield development results in low-income countries. In fact, the call not to take Aid for Trade as a panacea for a very flawed international trading system has become, with varying degrees of intensity, a motto in civil society pronouncements addressing Aid for Trade.[10] An important task for which CSOs are uniquely suited is that of bringing attention to these conditions in trade negotiation processes, so they are not assumed away or simply neglected in those processes. The following section identifies five such conditions that must be met if Aid for Trade is to become an effective tool for development.

4.1 Acknowledge the political impact of IFIs in trade negotiations

The policies and practices of IFIs and donors exert an enormous influence on the design of policies and negotiations by developing countries, a situation that runs to

[9] The practices in question consist of counting debt relief or forgiveness of ECA-related debt (incurred in commercial terms, thus arguably subject to the market logic of investments gone bad) as ODA. See Minder (2006), and Daneshkhu (2006).

[10] See, for instance, Khor (2005); Bello (2005); Oxfam (2005); International Gender and Trade Network-Asia (2006); Smaller (2006); Action Aid International and Public Citizen (2006); and Bretton Woods Project (2006). Moreover, that a large number of civil society organizations have kept references to Aid for Trade to a minimum (if not simply remained silent), is in itself telling of where CSOs see the priorities for action towards a pro-development trading system.

the detriment of poorer countries in the international trade system. For instance, decision-making procedures in the WTO provide for a consensus-based system that is supposed to protect a certain amount of voice for developing countries.[11] However, the system for reaching decisions in the World Bank and the International Monetary Fund (IMF) ensures that developed countries enjoy 61 percent of the vote, effectively commanding over 70 percent at the Board level.[12]

While policy interventions by IFIs and donors are not necessarily wrong-headed, they can be risky insofar as IFIs and the donors that lead them tend to have their own trade and investment interests, often not in accordance with those of recipient countries. The limitations on the capacity of developing countries to negotiate and implement strategic trade policy can be significant. For instance, it is typical to hear that developed countries want negotiations to start from "applied," rather than from "bound" tariffs, a request that puts those countries that have gone farther in liberalizing unilaterally at a disadvantage. Industrial countries tend to be reluctant to consider those tariffs bound unilaterally by developing countries as concessions. Countries that have liberalized unilaterally show also more proclivity to agree to bind at their current applied levels, thus creating an advantage for their trade partners. Sometimes they would do so due to the perception that, with their liberalization a done deal, binding levels will offer at least the chance of getting a concession in exchange. At the same time, chances are that trade partners will not value too much as a concession the binding of a level of deregulation already in place, since this means that the access to that market de facto already exists.

The mechanisms by which IFIs influence the trade and investment policies of borrowing countries and their positions in trade negotiations can be grouped into four broad categories. While policy-based conditionality is the best known of these categories, it is not the only one. Other, perhaps more subtle but equally powerful, types of mechanisms include: (a) trade-related technical assistance (TRTA); (b) research and training activities of the IFIs; and (c) "ex ante" mechanisms.

4.1.1 *Trade-related technical assistance*

TRTA is gaining new prominence within IFIs and bilateral development agencies, with the World Bank positioning itself as one of the main providers. Indeed, TRTA is a major category of Aid for Trade. Illustrative of the role played by the World Bank is the Integrated Framework (IF), an inter-agency initiative for TRTA for LDCs. In its revised version, the IF aims at "mainstreaming" trade in countries' Poverty Reduction Strategy Papers (PRSPs) (see the section on the IF in the introductory chapter of this volume).

The dominant and unchecked role of the Bank in technical assistance schemes such as the IF is cause for some concern. For example, "Being supported in [building efficient negotiation capacity] by a donor country who is also sitting at the table of negotiations (for instance in the WTO) is at best a conflict of interest."[13] This

[11] For a detailed account of how, in spite of this, biases against developing countries are embedded in rules and practices of the WTO, see Kwa (2003).

[12] For a detailed explanation of the issues surrounding the voting system within the international financial institutions, see CIDSE (2005).

[13] Solignac-Lecomte (2002); also saying that, "The support granted by donors to enhance the negotiating capacity of the recipient country in various fora may alter the negotiator's goals and incentives."

statement is equally true of the Bank, which, as explained previously, is governed by the same donors.

The goal of "mainstreaming trade" into countries' poverty reduction strategies must be monitored carefully with respect to its ultimate objectives. While generally desirable if it means an opportunity to link trade policy and poverty reduction, it could also be used in an inverse way to ensure that trade liberalization per se is included as part of poverty reduction strategies. For instance, after reviewing 17 PRSPs, a study by the development group Christian Aid concluded that,

> . . . constraints to improved trade that existed outside the relevant country's borders were only considered in six of the PRSPs studied – mostly in respect of market access restrictions. Ongoing discussions in the WTO were scarcely referred to and their consistency with national poverty reduction goals was not revisited. [. . .] the current asymmetrical power relationship between donors and poor countries . . . would mean that if trade-poverty analysis was incorporated into PRSPs it would probably be neither independent nor country-specific [but] simply to justify and legitimize existing trade rules on the grounds of poverty reduction. (Ladd, 2003)

Thus we need to be wary that mainstreaming trade is undertaken not only for the right reasons, but also is implemented by using a process that appreciates the diverse views held on the merits of trade liberalization.

4.1.2 *Research and training activities*

The World Bank provides most of the data currently used by policy-makers in developing countries, as well as the analytical tools to conceptualize trade and investment policy reforms and their impacts on growth, development, poverty, and inequality (World Bank, 1999).[14] Donor country officials also often rely on the Bank for statistical projections, judgments, and assessments that inform the decisions they make and negotiations they conduct affecting their partner countries. As one commentator put it, "when these judgments are emitted by an institution with a clear and unapologetic ideological stance on issues where there is great contestation and controversy voiced by other actors, as is the case of the links between international trade, poverty reduction and growth, this centrality and exclusiveness clearly carries inherent risks" (Brock and McGee, 2004).

Three problems emerge with regards to the research and training tools developed by the World Bank. First, such tools are presented as objective, bypassing an honest disclosure of the assumptions they are built upon, their biases, and limitations. Second, in carving out a role for itself as a knowledge provider, the Bank has tended to crowd out alternative and independent sources of development information that might present healthy competition. The IFIs' ability to lend as well as play a signaling role for other donors represents a built-in incentive for borrowers to buy into IFI research and analysis and forego alternative sources that may be dismissed by Bank and IMF staff. Finally, the research and analysis agenda itself, far from being apolitical, is heavily influenced by the governance structure of the institutions, leadership, and management selection criteria as well as promotion

[14] A World Bank survey has revealed that 84 percent of policy-makers in developing countries rely on World Bank data for their decisions.

incentives. All this tends to ensure that the agenda and mindset of the major shareholders sets the direction of analytical and research work.

In the particular case of the IMF, recent proposals are being discussed that would give it a formal role in providing countries with "analyses of adjustment impacts" of trade reform (IMF/World Bank, 2005). Given the IMF's checkered history of failures in forecasting growth, debt sustainability, and financial crises, it is hard to see what certifies it as the institution to be entrusted with a function that could influence important trade policy decisions by developing countries. Instead, mechanisms that build the capacity of institutions in the recipient country to provide these services, as well as mechanisms that incorporate checks and balances (such as trilateral commissions or research boards) would be a preferable option.

4.1.3 *"Ex ante" mechanisms*

"Ex ante" mechanisms cover an array of instruments that implicitly or explicitly require countries to adopt certain policies before they receive any loan or grant disbursement (as opposed to policy conditionality, which, typically, provides a disbursement upon a country's promise to fulfill certain requirements or implement certain policies in the future). The most important of these mechanisms are the Country Policy and Institutional Assessments (CPIAs), carried out yearly by the World Bank with the purpose of rating the policy and institutional environment in borrowing countries. CPIAs determine the amount and key conditions of lending to International Development Association (IDA)-eligible countries[15] in order to decide either increases or decreases (and in some cases total cut-offs) of funding to such countries. They also determine priorities for reform in Country Assistance Strategies that can overturn the ones set in the "country-owned" PRSPs.

In order to carry out a country performance assessment, Bank staff are asked to fill out questionnaires measuring the policies of the country under evaluation against a set of pre-established criteria. These criteria embody a one-size-fits-all model of policies that are presumed to be "good," usually drawing upon the Bank's own analytical work. As opposed to what happens with conditionality, wherein, in spite of the unequal power relations between lender and borrower, a borrowing government has to sign off on the conditionality attached to the loan it receives, under the CPIA system there is no need for the borrower to agree to the criteria upon which its policies and institutions are measured. Many of these criteria are directly or indirectly concerned with trade and investment policy. For example, under the criterion on "Trade policy and foreign exchange regime," a country with average tariffs below 10 percent, low dispersion, insignificant quantitative restrictions, and minimal or no foreign exchange restrictions on long-term capital inflows receives the highest rating. Under the criterion on "Efficiency of revenue mobilization," a country with "taxes on foreign trade"' would receive a low rating (IMF/World Bank, 2005).

[15] There are sixty-six low-income countries that fall under the IDA classification, as identified by World Bank lending criteria. See web.worldbank.org. (As of 2007, there were 82 IDA-eligible countries).

To date, there is no mechanism to hold IFIs and donors accountable when they advise policies that turn out to be wrong-headed. For instance, a recent evaluation of the World Bank activities on trade found that:

> ...Bank trade advice and support during the 1980s and 1990s was too narrow in focus. Specifically, it underestimated the complexity and sequencing of complementary policies; the role of the external environment (taking that environment as largely given); the interaction among trade, growth, and distributional outcomes; and the country-specific context (such as initial conditions and institutions) in which these policies interacted. Consequently, Bank advice was too optimistic about the benefits of trade liberalization for growth in the short run. (World Bank IEG, 2006)

In addition, there are no mechanisms to offer redress to borrowing or recipient countries for the limitations that IFIs and donors impose on their trade or investment policies and negotiating positions. Calls by CSOs to implement such mechanisms ("Civil Society" 2003; "Letter" 2003) have gone unheeded.

One way this issue has come, to a limited extent, into the purview of the WTO negotiations has been through the discussions on "credit for autonomous liberalization" in the context of services. However, the results are far from satisfactory.[16] Likewise, Caribbean countries have tried to make credit for autonomous liberalization an element to take into account in formulas for liberalization in industrial goods (Hormeku, 2005), though it appears unlikely this will be accepted by some WTO members.

Aid for Trade will hardly be more than a mitigating measure in an environment in which countries are structurally disabled to manage and negotiate trade and investment policies to their advantage. Moreover, if not implemented well, there is a danger that Aid for Trade might well compound these problems. This, for instance, would be the case if, Aid for Trade funding is given through grants and loans that include costly economic policy conditions.[17]

4.2 Capital accumulation, rather than attraction, should be the goal for trade and investment policies

Trade negotiations tend to be driven by the assumption that the financial consequences of trade and investment liberalization will be higher income through increasing exports and the attraction of foreign investment. This premise, however, should be assessed carefully before drawing firm conclusions.

It is not within the scope of this section to review the extensive literature that questions the alleged relationship between trade and investment liberalization and growth. Suffice to mention here that there is no automatic relationship between countries' average levels of tariffs and non-tariff barriers and their subsequent

[16] See an assessment before the Cancun Ministerial in Caliari (2003). See also Manduna (2004) pp. 46–47. ("Therefore the resulting process [for credit negotiations] does carry a danger that stronger countries might use their bargaining power to grant or refuse credits in order to negotiate or get other benefits.")

[17] This possibility is certainly allowed by the current language of the Hong Kong Declaration and, as we explain later in the text, the Aid for Trade Task Force has been rather shy in addressing conditionality issues.

economic growth (Malhotra, 2004). Similarly, the evidence does not support the assertion that increased foreign direct investment (FDI) necessarily leads to higher growth.[18]

The purpose of this section, rather, is to call attention to the existence of particular aspects of trade and investment liberalization policies that could likely hamper the possibility of any capital gains staying in the country and contributing to the strengthening of a national capital base. Absent a policy framework to achieve this, Aid for Trade can hardly be effective. In the best case, it will be filling financial holes; in the worst case, it will simply filter out of the target economy. Examples of these aspects are.

4.2.1 *Lower value-added in production, as a result of de-industrialization and concentration in the export of a few primary commodities*

Trade policies that support poverty reduction must not simply expand the volume of exports, but also ensure that exports are of goods with higher value-added in the national economy. The liberalization of trade and investment often facilitates a process whereby international chains of production locate certain parts of the production process in developing countries. This might increase the volume of exports, but if the elements of the production process that have been so located are low-skilled and low-technology, the gains in value produced in the country might be small, or even canceled out by the costs the liberalization process might have on national industries.

Similarly, if the increases in production are oriented to start or intensify the production of commodities whose values are plunging, as has been the case in several low-income countries, net capital effects might be neutral or negative. For this reason, consultation with local producers, industries, and civil society groups in identifying priorities for Aid for Trade delivery are crucial.

4.2.2 *Lower income from taxation*

It is important to bear in mind that for low-income countries, trade-related taxes are an important source of revenue that typically diminishes when they liberalize (IMF, 2003a; Wise and Gallagher, 2006). The negative fiscal impacts caused by trade liberalization have gained renewed attention in recent years, and developing countries have complained that the pressure to liberalize puts them in the dilemma of either defaulting on trade commitments or building unsustainable fiscal deficits (that need to be filled out by unsustainable borrowing). A team of researchers has found that "tariff losses for developing countries could outweigh the benefits [of liberalization] by a factor of four" (Wise and Gallagher, 2006).[19] This is all the more troubling when seen in the perspective that much Aid for Trade is expected to be

[18] According to UNCTAD (2003b), the impact of FDI on economic growth is difficult to trace, and this is perhaps the main reason for the lack of consensus on the role of FDI in economic development. Also see Milberg (1999) for a review of some relevant studies in this regard.

[19] Also quoting UNCTAD research that shows that tariff losses under NAMA alone could amount to US$63.4 billion in FDI.

delivered in the form of loans rather than grants, serving to sink recipient countries even further into debt.

Defenders of trade liberalization tend to argue that fiscal losses should not be an obstacle for liberalization, as they tend to be small and can be made up by resorting to other taxes (IMF, 2003a). This is problematic, as the capacity of low-income countries to recover revenue losses is limited. The switch to other taxes, such as VAT schemes, requires higher administrative capacity that many countries do not have, and can have negative consequences for income distribution ("Economic Commission" 2004). Indeed, recent IMF research has found some recognition of the practical problems of recovering revenue losses from trade, noting that middle income countries have recovered only about 35–55 cents per dollar of trade tax revenue lost, while low-income countries have recovered essentially none (Baunsgaard and Keen, 2004). However, rather than prompting the IMF to revisit its thinking about trade liberalization, this problem has instead led to the Fund simply recommending greater caution in designing tax reform to recoup lost revenue.

The liberalization of investment can also bring about negative fiscal consequences. One commonly understood way this happens is through the phenomenon of tax competition. The costs of strategies that rely upon lower taxation in order to attract FDI might well outweigh any benefits expected from such investment flows. The costs are associated with the loss of revenue for the host government, coupled with the difficulty of effectively administering such schemes in developing countries. Neither should the impact of practices such as transfer pricing be underestimated. Transfer pricing is associated with the increasing internationalization of the transfer across borders between foreign affiliates and parent corporations of goods, services, know-how, and intellectual property. While transfer pricing frameworks should promote reasonable tax revenues for all countries involved, this is hardly the most common case. Transfer pricing thus has direct effects on host and home countries' tax revenues. Chief among the policy measures that can reduce the damage caused by transfer pricing are certain performance requirements typically banned by the process of investment liberalization.[20]

4.2.3 *Lower level of national capital formation as a result of investment liberalization*

The incorporation of managerial, know-how, technology, training, and backward and forward linkages that foreign companies can bring to the economy of a developing country are usually mentioned as one of the benefits of foreign investment. However, in the presence of growing international consolidation and competition, the ability of host countries to incorporate these benefits into a national capital base depends on their ability to utilize policy tools, such as requirements on foreign companies regarding technology transfer, employment, know-how, and so forth. According to Chang (2003), "there is a growing consensus that accepting a "package" of finance, technology, managerial skills, and other capabilities offered by transnational corporations (TNCs) may not be as good for long-term industrial

[20] See, for example, Tang 2003 for an explanation of how certain performance requirements can prevent the negative fiscal impacts of transfer pricing by foreign corporations.

development as encouraging national firms to construct their own packages using their own managerial skills – with some necessary outsourcing."[21]

Some studies point toward the emergence of a virtuous export-investment and profit-investment nexus at the root of cases of successful economic take-off (UNCTAD, 2004; WTO, 2004). The emphasis of trade and investment policies should change from attracting capital and increasing exports to increasing dynamic capital accumulation through establishing an export- and profit-investment nexus.

4.2.4 *Increased expenditures generated by trade liberalization reforms*

The demands of a growing regulatory and institutional burden as part of commitments in trade agreements has been mentioned as a source of expenditures that add to the already-beleaguered budgets of liberalizing low-income countries. One widely quoted review of the impact of new rules in developing countries puts the costs for compliance with only three areas – customs valuation, TRIPS and sanitary/phytosanitary measures – at US$150 million per country (Finger and Schuler, 2000).

Not only is this not inclusive of all rules, but it also does not include costs for upgrading production systems to bring them up to the requirements of more intense competition. Nor does it include the costs of infrastructure required to enhance competitiveness, which are also likely to generate liabilities for the public sector. If it is to truly address the supply-side problems associated with a lack of productive capacity in low-income countries, Aid for Trade will need to look beyond the narrow perspective of simply covering the costs of compliance with new rules. This is addressed in greater detail in the following section.

4.3 The role of financial compensation for trade-related losses

It has become commonplace, even by staunch supporters of trade liberalization who would strongly argue its long-term benefits, to recognize the short-term losses arising from lowering tariffs and the merits of compensation for these losses (Zedillo et al., 2005; Bhagwati, 2005). However, there are several concerns with this approach.

First, it relies on the assumption that trade liberalization is necessarily good in the long term, a contention that is still in dispute (Malhotra, 2004). Those who take a more skeptical view about the benefits of trade liberalization per se, therefore, would argue that no amount of financial compensation can replace a trade policy that is managed in conformity with the requirements of a national development strategy. The preservation of flexibility to do this is a prerogative that can hardly be exchanged by compensation promises.

Second, while the WTO Aid for Trade Task Force recommended including trade-related adjustment as a category, certain risks may accompany aid delivered under this category. Support for adjustment purposes might mean that the most important Aid for Trade tasks (financing for infrastructure, regional integration, or private

[21] See, along similar lines, UNCTAD (2003a). The study states that its findings "raise serious questions about the strategies adopted in a number of developing countries for activating a dynamic process of capital accumulation and growth through a combination of increased FDI and reduced public investment and policy intervention."

sector development) may be neglected for the sake of a situation that international financial institutions were, in the first place, created to deal with.

To the extent that trade liberalization might bring setbacks to development outcomes, there is a case to be made for international public intervention to compensate for trade losses. The need for a strong and functional financial system that can provide a proper cushion for the trade-related losses of countries that choose to introduce trade liberalization as part of their development strategy is undeniable. This is especially so when variations in trade performance are prompted by reasons beyond that which domestic policy would have reasonably foreseen (such as the case of exogenous shocks). This is by no means a new phenomenon. In fact, the creation of the IMF as a mechanism to address short-term balance of payments problems was partly inspired by this need.[22] Several mechanisms at the regional and bilateral levels are also meant as a response to losses that are attributable to trade dynamics.[23]

Existing mechanisms, however, have often proved to be dysfunctional and insufficient in terms of accessibility, price, and conditions imposed on recipient countries. It stands as a witness to this growing dysfunctionality of the financial system that some countries are now seeking to make these compensatory functions part of the Aid for Trade initiative. But it should not be forgotten that developing countries that join the IMF have the right to such compensation without needing to demonstrate any particular trade-related problem or outcome. By including compensation under an Aid for Trade umbrella, developing countries might narrow the extent of this legitimate claim they have on the international financial system. This is even assuming the non-guaranteed scenario of Aid for Trade not being tied to particular outcomes in ongoing trade negotiations.

Third, compensation for losses tends to be calculated using figures for existing and utilized market access (IMF, 2003b). It is mistaken to argue that just because a country receives some compensation for lost market access that this takes care of the issues involved in searching for a new market niche, a position in a chain of production, or improving its competitiveness. It is, at best, a remedial patch that can help temporarily without addressing the root problem. For instance, Jamaica is one of the losers in the recent reform of the EU sugar quota regime. If one were to think of using Aid for Trade as a compensation for lost sugar export revenue, losses would be calculated in terms of what effectively Jamaica was exporting to the EU under its previously existing quota. If, however, one thinks of Aid for Trade as a way to ensure that Jamaica develops a market advantage on another product that can replace sugar, or help produce sugar at a price that can compete with the economies of scale of larger sugar-producing countries such as Guyana or Brazil, the needed amounts would necessarily be much higher. As it is highly unlikely that Jamaica can actually out-compete Brazil in sugar production, the idea of improving

[22] The purposes of the IMF, as outlined in Article 1 (1944), include: "To facilitate the expansion and balanced growth of international trade, and to contribute thereby to the promotion and maintenance of high levels of employment and real income and to the development of the productive resources of all members as primary objectives of economic policies . . . To give confidence to members . . . providing them with opportunity to correct maladjustments in their balance of payments without resorting to measures destructive of national or international prosperity."

[23] For example, the IMF's Compensatory Financing Facility, at the global level, and the European FLEX mechanism, established under the Cotonou Agreement in 2000 which replaced the previous European STABEX and SYSMIN programs.

competitiveness in sugar production should probably be ruled out, and space left for the consideration of shifting production. This is a highly capital-consuming project for which any compensation for lost exports will, most likely, fall far short.

Thus, it is perfectly possible to separate the legitimate calls for compensation for balance of payments from the claim for assistance in better utilizing the opportunities that might be opened by trade and investment liberalization. Countries should not, riding on the apparent momentum around Aid for Trade, give up on their long-term claims for functional international financial institutions, independent from any particular trade liberalization outcomes.

4.4 Financial and exchange rate stability and trade performance

The trade performance of low-income countries is disproportionately affected by exchange rate and financial instability.

As for exchange rates, the logic of international trade negotiations rests on the assumption of an international monetary system that provides exchange rate stability ("Civil Society" 2003). Concessions should be exchanged and market access opportunities valuated based on these assumptions.[24] It has been found, however, that the volatility of exchange rates significantly affects the competitiveness of trading countries and offsets gains in domestic productivity.[25] The distortions generated in allocation render the traditional calculations of trade negotiations meaningless.[26] The interaction between exchange rate regimes and trade performance has acquired greater relevance lately due to the rising current account deficit of the United States. [27] In fact, it is generally the case that the distortions originate in misalignments and uncoordinated movements among the exchange rates of large hard-currency issuers (WTO, 2002a).[28] Due to the relative size of the economies, the resulting volatility tends to have a disproportionately higher impact on developing than on industrialized economies.

[24] Keynes quoted in UNCTAD (2004): "It is extraordinarily difficult to frame any proposals about tariffs if countries are free to alter the value of their currencies without agreement at short notice. Tariffs and currency depreciations are in many cases alternatives. Without currency agreements you have no firm ground on which to discuss tariffs." See also Raghavan (1997): "What the WTO and others are trying to achieve is what Keynes and others saw was not possible, namely trade liberalization... in a non-functioning monetary and financial system."

[25] UNCTAD (2002). However, the IMF carried out a study in 1984 and another one, more recently, in 2004, on the influence of exchange rate volatility on trade flows. In the last study it finds that "the general presumption that trade is adversely affected by an increase in the exchange rate fluctuations depends on a number of specific assumptions and does not necessarily hold in all cases, especially in general equilibrium models where other variables change along with exchange rates." See IMF (2003c): pp. 10–11.

[26] UNCTAD (2004): p. 2. "If exchange rate movements follow a random walk, i.e., if changes in the international value of money are in no way related to the fundamentals of countries with open markets for goods and capital, traditional trade theories quickly lose their grasp on reality and trade liberalization loses much of its alleged justification."

[27] Several reports by global economic institutions have warned about the potentially disastrous consequences that a sudden and disorderly adjustment of the U.S. exchange rate could have on the economies of developing countries. See for example World Bank (2005), ch. 3.

[28] See also Goldstein (1999): p. 125. "But the impact of the global economy on emerging countries is driven significantly by swings among the currencies of the three major economic powers. In recent years, these swings have been enormous, volatile, and frequently unrelated to underlying economic fundamentals."

As for financial stability, the repeated financial crises that have wrecked developing country economies have shown that financial booms and busts tend to generate sharp swings in international trade flows. At the same time, the fluctuations in costs and availability of external financing that are associated with financial crises deeply determine financing arrangements for trade by making importing and exporting more costly, even after large devaluations (UNCTAD, 2003a).

The general conditions of the international financial system such as exchange rate fluctuations seem far removed from the practicalities of Aid for Trade design. However, given the relevance of these conditions to the trade performance of low-income countries, the shortsightedness and likely futility of implementing an Aid for Trade package that ignores these conditions becomes obvious. After all, it is generally expected that Aid for Trade plays the function of unleashing or catalyzing processes of private investment conducive to production for exports. Absent the right signals and incentives, especially for domestic investment, Aid for Trade would be largely fighting an uphill battle, with ultimately dubious effectiveness.

4.5 Engage the financial implications of foreign investment

The need to overcome balance of payments disequilibria has been a strong force driving low-income countries' push to attract foreign investment.[29] At the outset, it is worth noting that balance of payments disequilibria have accompanied episodes of premature trade liberalization, being attributed to a consequential rapid increase in imports, while exports failed to improve.

Many civil society voices have criticized the impact of FDI on social, environmental, and human rights objectives, and have highlighted the potential threats from FDI to labor and other public interest regulations. Concerns about the social and environmental costs of FDI are often perceived as elements to be traded off against financial advantages brought by the foreign investment. There is a general belief that increased capital inflows will help overcome the balance of payments problems of developing countries. This belief is based on the perception that FDI is a net positive source of foreign exchange, and that FDI has an export-boosting effect, by increasing the efficiency and volume of production for exports that in turn generates foreign exchange. However, a growing body of evidence around the financial impacts of FDI is now putting into question whether these impacts are ultimately positive or negative.

One analyst finds that only FDI that creates new capacity in the export sector and where all output substitutes for imports, rather than for existing import-substituting production, non-tradable goods, or savings, has clearly positive balance of payments effects (Woodward, 2001). In another assessment, "...the 'disintegration of production' may result in FDI having a more negative effect on host developing countries' balance of payments. While the increasing vertical disintegration of production has meant more imports and exports for each unit of domestic production, profit and royalty outflows have only risen...In the longer run, as

[29] According to UNCTAD (2006), by 2004 the number of international investment agreements had expanded to 2,392, from less than 1,000 in the period before 1990. In 2002, 236 of 248 regulatory changes in seventy countries in the direction of facilitating FDI took place (UNCTAD, 2003a). International financial institutions have also, through their programs and activities, favored the attraction of foreign investment.

the investment begins to pay off, profit repatriation will only increase" (Milberg, 1999).[30]

Thus, there is a need to examine the costs (in balance of payments terms) of foreign investment and adopt, in trade and investment reform efforts, remedies and clauses with the aim of compensating for the negative financial effects of foreign investment on the balance of payments.

The importance of considering the implications and type of FDI as a prerequisite to making Aid for Trade effective has two aspects. First, Aid for Trade might be conditioned on, or encourage the implementation of, policies that bring FDI with net negative financial impacts. Second, preventing financially-negative FDI may free up resources that can constitute a more reliable and efficiently delivered source of funds that the government – or the domestic private sector – can direct to the same goals of Aid for Trade.

5 Delivering Aid for Trade

The preceding sections have focused on how CSOs have considered Aid for Trade in the context of a holistic framework linking trade and finance, and looked at certain conditions required in order to make it effective. CSOs have also provided reflections on the question of the Aid for Trade delivery mechanism.

5.1 Scope and monitoring

Looking at what has been suggested by international institutions, donors, and recipients regarding what Aid for Trade should finance, two categories in particular stand out as priorities from a civil society perspective:

A. *Aid to overcome supply-side constraints*. Specifically, aid directed to improve recipients' capacity to produce and export competitively, and to improve access to existing and new markets. Trade-related infrastructure needed to address supply-side constraints should be included here.
B. *Aid to improve in-country policy analysis capacity*. This would be directed towards enabling recipients to meaningfully negotiate better terms in trade-related agreements, loans, and grants.

Category A is reflected in the report by the WTO Aid for Trade Task Force under "Trade-related infrastructure" and "Building productive capacity" (WTO, 2006). Aid directed to enhance the supply-side capacity of the recipient seems to be the best way to ensure existing market access is well used. While the creation of a special fund for this purpose – as has been proposed by some analysts (Stiglitz and Charlton, 2006) – would be a promising step forward, this appears unlikely, as WTO members have opted to work with existing delivery mechanisms.

With respect to category B, by in-country policy analysis capacity, we refer to the capacity of local officials and private research institutions in the recipient country

[30] See also on this issue Woodward (2001): 145. "Clearly, it is possible for a country to attract enough new direct investment to receive an inward net transfer of resources. In principle, it is even possible to maintain inward net resource transfers for a prolonged period... However, there may be a high cost attached to attracting inward net transfers: in general, any individual inward investment will ultimately require an outward net transfer much larger than the initial capital inflow."

aimed at ensuring the funded agenda and work programs are decided on the basis of the priorities of the recipient country. As such, funding for this area is a much-needed investment in low-income countries, which suffer from dependency not only on outside capital, but also on outside knowledge, to shape their agenda.

It is unclear to what extent the category "Trade policy and regulations," also mentioned within the scope of Aid for Trade by the Task Force, is intended to provide this type of assistance. Based on its definition, it might not exclude aid simply oriented to having local officials comply with or take for granted existing trade rules and regulations, or expensive contracting of foreign expertise, rather than building long-term expertise at the national and regional levels.[31]

As discussed in this chapter in Section 4.3, Aid for Trade should avoid focusing on aid directed purely to compensate for the negative impacts of trade reforms, namely assistance under the Task Force's category of "Trade-related adjustment." Aid to compensate for trade-related losses should be provided by IFIs independently of any Aid for Trade mechanism, and what the Task Force calls "adjustment costs" should be clearly differentiated and additional.

The rationale proposed here for establishing fewer criteria is linked to concerns around the adequate monitoring of the additionality of Aid for Trade relative to other types and forms of ODA. This concern was nominally recognized in the Task Force report, which explicitly mentions the need to establish "a border between Aid for Trade and other development assistance" (WTO, 2006). But the breadth of scope and of its definition is likely to create problems for monitoring additionality.

The Task Force report goes as far as stating that "projects and programmes should be considered as Aid for Trade if these activities have been identified as trade-related development priorities in the recipient country's national development strategies" (Ibid). This neglects the possible distortionary impact that aid priorities might have, namely, leading applicant countries to depict priorities as trade-related even though they may not necessarily include trade-related ODA needs. Or, worse, the possibility that countries might add trade elements into strategies that do not call for them, just to improve the chances of getting these strategies financed. It is in order to ensure that Aid for Trade can be effectively monitored that some criteria have to be agreed upon concerning what exactly constitutes Aid for Trade.

5.2 Quantity

Whatever the quantities pledged as Aid for Trade, it is desirable that the quantity is predictable, that there are ways to monitor the quantity and its additionality and, ideally, also enforce what should become donor obligations in this regard.

This is, indeed, a high bar to set. There is no history of donors becoming bound to provide aid, much less providing it as an obligation.[32] In the context of the negotiations on the Economic Partnership Agreements, some African countries have

[31] WTO (2006) defines "Trade policy and regulations" as "training of trade officials, analysis of proposals and positions and their impact, support for national stakeholders to articulate commercial interest and identify trade-offs, dispute issues, institutional and technical support to facilitate implementation of trade agreements and to adapt to and comply with rules and standards."

[32] The limitations of the 0.7 percent target agreed to in 1970 have already been referred to at the beginning of this chapter.

tried timidly to establish some binding connection between trade liberalization commitments and aid promises (Williamson, 2006). The cold response given by the European Commission to this request speaks volumes about the feasibility of implementing this feature in the context of Aid for Trade at the multilateral level.

5.3 Quality

In terms of the quality of Aid for Trade, civil society has insisted that it be unconditional, non-debt creating, and that programs and projects should be driven by the needs of the recipients, in consultation with civil society in each country (Center of Concern, 2005).

Consistent with their critique of conditionality in financing arrangements, CSOs have called for no conditionality to be attached to Aid for Trade. Some conditions related to whether promised Aid for Trade projects have been actually been carried out are probably warranted. However, the attachment of any policy-related conditionality would be hard to justify, especially in the interest of ensuring that recipients are able to fit particular projects into a home-grown development strategy.[33] Many developing countries have clearly expressed their requirement that Aid for Trade be delivered in an unconditional way.[34] It is rather unfortunate that the Aid for Trade Task Force chose to fudge the issue of conditionality, and stuck to the rhetoric on "ownership," which leaves open the possibility of conditions on economic policy (WTO, 2006).

With many countries receiving significant debt relief in the last two decades, the requirement that Aid for Trade should be non debt-creating is a key element to ensure both that debt relief is not undermined and that other countries do not accumulate debt in order to build trade capacity. While many funded trade activities could be well-positioned to generate foreign exchange, thereby offering the opportunity for further loan repayment, a development-oriented approach would favor proceeds from trade being used in the country rather than paid out as debt service. The generation of an "export-investment nexus" – that is, a virtuous circle by which increased export earnings are reinvested in productive capacity in the country, in turn expanding and diversifying exports – has been at the heart of almost every success story of trade-led development (UNCTAD, 2004).[35] Diverting export earnings to the repayment of debt service can break this cycle, putting on hold forever the attainment of sustained development results (UNCTAD, 2002b).[36] The Aid for Trade Task Force chose to remain silent on the non-debt-creating nature of Aid for Trade, which is regrettable, given that several countries reportedly pledging Aid for Trade funding have done so on a clearly non-grant basis (Taro, 2005).[37]

33 Unfortunately, one can only be skeptical about the likelihood that donors will not judge the general policy framework of the recipient (maybe unofficially) in order to award Aid for Trade.

34 For example, WTO communications from Brazil, LDCs, African countries.

35 For specific case studies see, for example, Dabee (2002) (describing the case of Mauritius, where export earnings from the sugar boom in the 1970s were used to finance investment in manufactured exports in the export-processing zone), and Akyuz and Gore (1996) (describing how this process was at work in the East Asian industrializing economies).

36 UNCTAD actually talks of the emergence of export-debt repayment cycles.

37 For instance, Japan has pledged up to US$10 billion in Aid for Trade, but most, if not all, are expected to be delivered in the form of concessional loans.

Importantly, Aid for Trade projects must be driven by the needs of the recipients, in consultation with civil society. Donors themselves have recognized this priority, which they have acknowledged as essential for the successful implementation of projects. Still, there is a long way to walk between the conceptual consensus and the current reality, in which donor agencies tend to be guided by their own preferences and policy priorities.

5.4 The mechanism

A central question for CSOs is whether the mechanisms for delivery of Aid for Trade will best be able to ensure implementation in the scope, quantity and quality that are required to ensure that trade competitiveness is built in recipient countries. One particular aspect is whether Aid for Trade should be delivered through existing means or through a new facility (such as, for example, a global fund of the sort advocated by Nobel laureate Joseph Stiglitz) (Stiglitz and Charlton, 2005).

At the time of writing, the Aid for Trade Task Force had advocated against a stand-alone Aid for Trade facility. The World Bank and the IMF have both opposed the creation of a vertical fund on the grounds that a new fund would "distort development priorities" (IMF/World Bank, 2006).[38] They reject the idea of "new and unproven institutional arrangements to manage and deliver aid for trade," relying instead on existing donor coordination structures (Ibid). The WTO membership also has decided that Aid for Trade should be provided through existing structures.

The decision to leave Aid for Trade to several donors under a coordinated approach, rather than through the establishment of a dedicated fund, raises its own set of questions for civil society. This is because in the past it has proved more difficult to ensure uniformity with such an approach and, consequently, more difficult to monitor quantity, additionality, and quality. As different aid agencies usually have their own priorities and compete for niches in the "aid market", using existing delivery mechanisms will make it highly challenging to implement a consistent Aid for Trade approach. CSOs have developed sophisticated critiques of several existing delivery mechanisms, including those of the World Bank and of regional banks. As a result, the recommendation to rely on these mechanisms instead of opening up the possibility of developing and shaping a new one is regrettable. It has reduced the credibility of Aid for Trade approaches and tied their fate to the questionable credibility of existing institutions.

A dedicated Aid for Trade fund approach would facilitate movement towards a unified strategic direction inspired by agreed-upon goals and provided under a designated governance mechanism. Starting the discussion afresh would have provided for a new advocacy space, probably allowing for a more positive reaction from civil society.[39]

[38] This is arguably the case of any vertical fund (including several of the Trust Funds the World Bank runs itself).

[39] A pooled or dedicated fund is not, however, exempt from questions, as it raises the thorny issue of how much say donors vs. recipients and donors among themselves would have in a dedicated Aid for Trade facility. Especially in light of experience with the Integrated Framework after more than a decade, it is hard to place a lot of hope on pooled funding to guarantee the availability of aid in sufficient quantity and on a predictable basis. However, if the political will to provide Aid for Trade exists, then it should be possible to surmount this obstacle.

6 Conclusion

Civil society perspectives on policies about trade, as well as financial issues around aid and debt, have gained increasing influence in recent years. However, CSOs have tended to focus on either organizations with jurisdiction on trade or on those with jurisdiction on finance. As the Aid for Trade initiative gains momentum, many CSOs are taking a more holistic approach to monitoring the actions of both the multilateral trade regime and international financial institutions. As a result, they are starting to devise ways to ensure their efforts are more strategic in establishing and factoring the linkages between trade and finance into their work on specific global and local institutions and policies dealing either with trade or with finance.

To some extent, these efforts parallel the challenges faced by low-income countries. Trade and finance policies are inextricably interrelated in these countries' development strategies. However, they have yet to make strategic use of the linkages between trade and finance in their decision making and negotiations.

Aid for Trade should not be tied to the current Doha Round (or, for that matter, to any particular trade negotiation), and the asymmetry between trade rules (generally enforceable, concrete, and monitorable) and financial commitments (generally non-enforceable, vague, and hard to monitor) should be kept in mind.

Moreover, CSOs have referenced, in a number of statements, the need to refrain from seeing Aid for Trade as a panacea for what are systemic and persistent flaws affecting the participation of developing countries in the global trading system. Some conditions in the trading environment should be tackled alongside any Aid for Trade package if this is to become an effective tool for development. In this chapter, we have identified five such requirements:

- Provide mechanisms for redress as a response to the political impact of IFIs in limiting the capacity of developing countries to negotiate advantageous policies and terms of insertion in the international trading system.
- Allow for a policy framework conducive to capital accumulation in low-income countries.
- Avoid including demands in Aid for Trade that are not specific to trade and that should be covered under existing work and mandates of the IFIs. If the IFIs are not responding appropriately to the needs of low-income countries, they should be reformed. But a debate on Aid for Trade should not be stretched into becoming a venue to discuss such reforms. On the contrary, Aid for Trade should be clearly predicated separately and in addition to the needed reform of those institutions.
- Address the limitations that exchange rate and financial instability create for low-income countries.
- Pave the way to avoid reliance on Aid for Trade over the long term. In this regard, it is crucial to prevent the attraction of types of FDI with negative balance of payments consequences. Aid for Trade itself should not condition or encourage the blind attraction of FDI without examining its financial impacts.

Some proposed delivery mechanisms of Aid for Trade have been advanced. Their scope should be limited to as few categories as possible, in order to simplify monitoring and the additionality to other ODA funding, and to facilitate the accountability of donors. The chapter argues, in fact, for only two categories: aid to overcome supply-side constraints, and aid to improve the in-country policy analysis capacity of recipient countries. Quantities, whatever levels are agreed to, should be predictable, additional to existing promises, and be enforceable donor promises. In terms of quality, Aid for Trade should not be tied to any condition that is not, in a narrow way, related to the specific implementation of the project for which it is provided, and should be non-debt-creating. Finally, programs and projects should be driven by the needs of the recipients, in consultation with CSOs in each country.

REFERENCES

Action Aid International/Public Citizen. 2006. "The WTO's Empty Hong Kong 'Development Package': How the World Trade Organization's 97% Duty-Free Proposal Could Leave Poor Countries Worse Off," Washington, D.C.: Public Citizen's Global Trade Watch.

Akyuz, Yilmaz and Charles Gore. 1996. "The investment-profit nexus in East Asian Industrialization," *World Development*, 24(3): 461–470.

Baunsgaard, Thomas and Michael Keen. 2004. "Tax Revenue and (or?) Trade Liberalization," Draft, Washington, D.C.: IMF.

Bello, Walden. 2005. "The Development Package: Deceptive and Dangerous," statement at Press Conference on behalf of Focus on the Global South, Hong Kong, December.

Bhagwati, Jagdish. 2005. "Strong blend puts trade talks back together," *Financial Times*, 19 December.

Bounds, Andrew. 2006. "Brussels rejects moves to link trade with aid," *Financial Times*, 28 November.

Bretton Woods Project. 2006. "Aid for Trade: Distraction from a Bad Deal," http://www.brettonwoodsproject.org/art.shtml?x=507701.

Brock, K. and R. McGee. 2004. "Mapping trade policy: understanding the challenges of civil society participation," IDS Working Paper 225, UK: Institute of Development Studies.

Caliari, Aldo. 2003. "Some Selected Issues in the Coherence Agenda of the WTO and the Bretton Woods Institutions," Washington, D.C.: Center of Concern.

Center of Concern. 2005. "NGO Principles on 'Aid for Trade'," prepared by Aldo Caliari and Pam Sparr, Washington, D.C.: Center of Concern.

Center of Concern. 2007. "Homepage," http://www.coc.org.

Chang, Ha-Joon. 2003. "Globalization, Economic Development and the Role of the State," Zed Books Ltd. (London and New York) and TWN (Penang).

CIDSE. 2005. "Long Due Reform? The International Monetary Fund, the World Bank and Global Economic Governance Sixty Years Later," CIDSE Position Paper, Brussels: CIDSE.

"Civil Society Statement on Policy Coherence (Signed by 40 Networks and NGOs)," ECOSOC Special High-Level meeting with the Bretton Woods Institutions and the World Trade Organization, 14 April 2003.

Dabee, Beealasingh. 2002. "The Role of Non-Traditional Exports in Mauritius," in G.K. Helleiner (ed.), *Non-Traditional Export Promotion in Africa – Experience and Issues*, The United Nations University WIDER, Studies in Development Economics and Policy Series, Helsinki: Palgrave Macmillan.

Daneshkhu, Scheherazade. 2006. "Debt relief 'accounts for bulk of the increase in aid'," *Financial Times*, 4 April.

Das, Bhagirath Lal. 1998. "The World Trade Organization: A Guide to the Framework for International Trade." London and New York: Zed Books Ltd.

Das, Bhagirath Lal. 2005. "The Current Negotiations in the WTO – Options, Opportunities and Risks for Developing Countries," Zed Books Ltd. (London and New York) and TWN (Penang).

Economic Commission for Africa. 2004. "Economic Report on Africa 2004: Unlocking Africa's Trade Potential," Addis Ababa: Economic Commission for Africa.

Finger, J. Michael and Julio Nogués. 2002. "The Unbalanced Uruguay Round Outcome: The New Areas in Future WTO Negotiations," International Trade 0502010, EconWPA.
Finger, J. Michael and Philip Schuler. 2000. "Implementation of Uruguay Round Commitments: The Development Challenge," *The World Economy*, 244(4): 511–525.
Goldstein, Morris. 1999. "Safeguarding Prosperity in a Global Financial System – The Future of the International Financial Architecture," report of an Independent Task Force Sponsored by the Council on Foreign Relations, Washington, D.C.: Institute for International Economics.
Group of Eight. 2005. "Chair's Summary," Gleneagles Summit, Gleneagles, UK, 6–8 July.
Hormeku, Tetteh. 2005. "Trade: Caribbean countries propose new formula at NAMA meeting," South-North Development Monitor (SUNS) #5836, Penang: TWN.
IMF Articles of Agreement. 1944. Adopted at the UN Monetary and Financial Conference, Bretton Woods, New Hampshire, 22 July.
IMF. 2003a. "Liberalizing Trade and Safeguarding Public Revenue," communication to the WTO from the International Monetary Fund, WT/TF/COH/16, 14 February.
IMF. 2003b. "Financing of Losses from Preference Erosion," communication to the WTO from the International Monetary Fund, WT/TF/COH/14, 14 February.
IMF. 2003c. "Exchange Rate Volatility and Trade Flows – Some New Evidence," prepared by Peter Clark, Natalia Tamirisa and Shang-Jin Wei, with Azim Sadikov and Li Zeng, http://www.imf.org/external/np/res/exrate/2004/eng/051904.pdf.
IMF/World Bank. 2006. "Trade Progress Report – The Doha Development Agenda and Aid for Trade: Hong Kong and Beyond," submitted to the Development Committee of the IMF and the World Bank, Washington, D.C.
IMF/World Bank. 2005. "Doha Development Agenda and Aid for Trade," prepared by the staffs of the IMF and World Bank, Washington, D.C.
International Gender and Trade Network – Asia. 2006. "Trade-Finance Linkages and Gender: Implications to Asian Women," IGTN-Asia Economic Literacy Packet, Quezon City: IGTN-Asia.
Khor, Martin. 2005. "Aid for LDCs: Only a Face Saving Device Without Substance?," *LDC Trade and Development Perspective*, 1(1).
Kwa, Aileen. 2003. "Power and Politics in the WTO," Bangkok: Focus on the Global South.
Ladd, Paul. 2003. "Too hot to handle? The absence of trade policy in the PRSPs," Christian Aid, http://www.christian-aid.org.uk/indepth/0304toohot/toohot.pdf.
"Letter to the WTO Working Group on Debt, Trade and Finance Signed by 30 NGOs and Networks," Center of Concern, http://www.coc.org/index.fpl/1264/article/1923.html.
Malhotra, Kamal. 2004. "Trade, Growth, Poverty Reduction and Human Development: Some Linkages and Policy Implications," paper prepared for the XVIII G-24 Technical Group Meeting, Geneva.
Manduna, Calvin. 2004. "The WTO Services Negotiations: An Analysis of the GATS and Issues of Interest for Least Developed Countries," Working Paper 23, Trade-Related Development and Equity Series, Geneva: South Centre.
Milberg, William. 1999. "Foreign Direct Investment and Development: Balancing Costs and Benefits," *International Monetary and Financial Issues for the 1990s*, 6: 99–116.
Minder, Raphael. 2006. "EU nations accused of overstating aid figures," *Financial Times*, 3 April.
Oxfam. 2005. "Scaling up aid for trade: how to support poor countries to trade their way out of poverty," Oxfam Briefing Note, Oxford: Oxfam International.
Palley, Tom. 2003. "International Trade, Macroeconomics, and Exchange Rates: Re-examining the Foundations of Trade Policy" (On file with the author). April.
Pilling, David. 2006. "Call for aid cuts puts Koizumi pledge in peril," *Financial Times*, 24 May.
Raghavan, Chakravarthi. 1997. "A New World Order in a World of Disorder?," in Jo Marie Griesgraber and Bernard Gunter (eds.), *World Trade: Toward Fair and Free Trade in the 21st Century (Rethinking Bretton Woods)*, London: Pluto Press.
Raja, Kanaga. 2005. "Differences remain on SDT, implementation issues in TRIMs," in South-North Development Monitor (SUNS), Penang: TWN.

Smaller, Carin. 2006. "Can Aid Fix Trade? Assessing the WTO's Aid for Trade Agenda," Minneapolis: Institute for Agriculture and Trade Policy.

Solignac-Lecomte, H.B. 2002. "Building capacity to trade: what are the priorities?," paper prepared for an International CTA seminar on "Meeting the Challenge of Effective ACP Participation in Agricultural Trade Negotiations: The Role of ICM," Paris: OECD Development Centre.

Tang, Xiaobing. 2003. "Experience of Implementation of the WTO Agreement on Trade-Related Investment Measures – Difficulties and Challenges faced by Developing Countries".

Taro, Aso. 2005. Ministerial Conference, Sixth Session, Hong Kong, 13–18 December 2005, *Statement by H. E. Mr. Taro Aso, Minister of Foreign Affairs of Japan*, 14 December.

Stiglitz, Joseph E. and Andrew Charlton. 2006. "Aid for Trade: A Report for the Commonwealth Secretariat," London: Commonwealth Secretariat.

Tortora, Manuel. 2001. "The 'Doha Issues' in WTO and FTAA: Priorities on the LAC Trade Agenda," Sistema Económico Latinoamericano (SELA), Capitulo 63.

UNCTAD. 2002a. Trade and Development Report 2002 – Developing Countries in World Trade," New York and Geneva: United Nations.

UNCTAD. 2002b. "The Least Developed Countries Report 2002 – Escaping the Poverty Trap," New York and Geneva: United Nations.

UNCTAD. 2003a. "World Investment Report 2003 – FDI Policies for Development: National and International Perspectives," New York and Geneva: United Nations.

UNCTAD. 2003b. "Trade and Development Report 2003 – Capital Accumulation, Growth and Structural Change," New York and Geneva: United Nations.

UNCTAD. 2004. "The Least Developed Countries Report 2004 – Linking International Trade with Poverty Reduction," prepared by the UNCTAD secretariat, New York and Geneva: United Nations.

UNCTAD. 2006. "International Investment Agreements: Trends and Emerging Issues," UNCTAD Series on International Investment Policies for Development, New York and Geneva: United Nations.

White, David. 2006. "Africa grows but development goals are unmet," *Financial Times*, 15 May.

Williamson, Hugh. 2006. "Germany doubts ability to achieve aid target," *Financial Times*, 20 January.

Wise, T. and Kevin Gallagher. 2006. "Doha Round and Developing Countries: Will the Doha deal do more harm than good?," RIS Policy Brief No. 22, New Delhi: RIS.

Woodward, David. 2001. "The Next Crisis? Direct and Equity Investment in Developing Countries," London and New York: Zed Books in association with Eurodad (Brussels).

World Bank. 1999. "The influence of World Bank research on policy in the developing world," World Bank Research Program, Washington, D.C.: World Bank.

World Bank. 2003. "Country Policy and Institutional Assessments: An External Panel Review Panel Recommendations and Management Follow-up," Washington, D.C.: World Bank.

World Bank. 2005. "Global Development Finance 2005: Mobilizing Finance and Managing Vulnerability," Washington, D.C.: World Bank.

World Bank Independent Evaluation Group. 2006. "Assessing World Bank Support for Trade, 1987–2004," Washington, D.C.: World Bank.

WTO. 2001a. Ministerial Conference, Fourth Session, Doha, 9–14 November 2001, *Ministerial Declaration*, WT/MIN(01)/DEC/1, 20 November.

WTO. 2001b. *Declaration on the TRIPS agreement and public health*, WT/MIN(01)/DEC/2, 20 November.

WTO. 2002a. *Communication from UNCTAD*, Working Group on Trade, Debt and Finance, WT/WGTDF/W/5/Rev.1, 31 July.

WTO. 2002b. *Communication from Brazil and India*, The Mandated Review of the TRIMs Agreement. Paragraph 12(b) of the Doha Ministerial Declaration Implementation-related issues and concerns (tiret 40), G/C/W/428G/TRIMS/W/25, 8 October.

WTO. 2004. *Communication from UNCTAD*, Working Group on Trade, Debt and Finance, WT/WGTDF/W/27, 24 November.

WTO. 2005. Ministerial Conference, Sixth Session, Hong Kong, 13–18 December 2005, Doha Work Programme, *Ministerial Declaration*, WT/MIN(05)/DEC, 18 December.

WTO. 2006. *Recommendations of the Task Force on Aid for Trade*, Aid for Trade Task Force, WT/AFT/1, 27 July.

Zedillo, Ernesto et al. 2005. "Strengthening the Global Trade Architecture for Economic Development: An Agenda for Action," GTA Policy Brief, http://www.ycsg.yale.edu/focus/gta/GTA_policy_brief.doc.

PART THREE

Way Forward

18 Aid for Trade and Private Sector Development

HAVELOCK R. BREWSTER AND DOMINIQUE NJINKEU

1 Introduction

At the 1996 World Trade Organization (WTO) Ministerial Conference in Singapore, WTO members set up an Integrated Framework for Trade-Related Technical Assistance (IF) for the Least Developed Countries (LDCs). Its activities consisted mainly of diagnostic studies that identified needs in such areas as trade policy, trade facilitation, trade capacity and, policy coordination, and market access. At the Doha Ministerial meeting in November 2001, members reaffirmed their commitment to provide "well-targeted, sustainably financed technical assistance and capacity building." This was followed in July 2004 by a Framework Agreement, in which the WTO General Council stated that LDCs, as well as low-income countries, should be provided with enhanced trade-related assistance and capacity building to increase their effective participation in negotiations, facilitate their implementation of WTO rules, and enable them to adjust and diversify their economies. Thereafter, at the WTO Hong Kong Ministerial Conference in December 2005, members adopted a Declaration on Aid for Trade in which they undertook to help developing countries, particularly LDCs, build supply-side capacity and trade-related infrastructure with the aim of assisting them implement and benefit from WTO agreements, and more broadly expand their trade. The Task Force set up for this purpose delivered its recommendations to the WTO General Council in July 2006; these were endorsed a few months later in October. Following up from this process, the next steps in 2007 and beyond will be to ensure effective implementation of these recommendations.

This chapter argues that Aid for Trade needs to involve the private sector, as it is business that ultimately engages in the act of trading. As exporters and productive drivers of countries' economies, private sector firms are best prepared to identify the main impediments to trade expansion and explore related opportunities for poverty reduction. Whether such a private sector-led process materializes depends greatly on:

- The knowledge by private sector operators of trade rules and of the rights that these give as well as the obligations they impose;

The authors are grateful for research assistance provided by former ILEAP interns Monmi Goswami and Serah Kimani. Dirk Willem te Velde provided very useful comments on an earlier version of the chapter.

- Knowledge of new opportunities for trade created by liberalization commitments undertaken by countries during negotiations;
- The ability of private sector operators to proactively bring to the notice of their governments problems encountered in international transactions so that their governments can raise them in appropriate WTO forums and, if necessary, invoke WTO dispute settlement procedures;[1] and
- The ability of firms to produce goods and services competitively so as to take advantage of terms and conditions that would enable them to fully exploit market opportunities arising from liberalization.

The objective of this chapter is to consider the extent to which low-income countries, particularly LDCs and countries in the African, Caribbean, and Pacific (ACP) regions, are equipped to generate private sector-led growth. While most of these countries lack most of the ingredients needed for dynamic private sector development, there have been enough successful experiences in private sector development to point to a way forward. As such, the Aid for Trade initiative comes at an opportune time.

The chapter is in four main sections. Section 2 reviews lessons learned and shows that the experience with private sector trade capacity building (TCB), particularly in Africa and the Caribbean, has not been adequate. Section 3 discusses the contours of a private sector component in Aid for Trade. Before providing an action plan for implementing the Aid for Trade Task Force recommendations to the benefit of the private sector, which we present in Section 5, we review and draw lessons from selected TCB programs in Section 4. We emphasize in particular the need for a central role for regional development banks.

2 Lessons learned and principles for private sector capacity building

There has been some success in creating an environment conducive to private sector development in low-income countries, but much remains to be done. The cost of doing business in these countries is still high due to inadequate physical infrastructure and poor access to credit, investment capital, and banking services. In these countries, the overwhelming majority of private business units are micro, small or medium enterprises (SMEs) co-existing with a formal sector.[2] These enterprises are often too small to achieve an optimal division of labor and internal specialization in their business operations.

The challenges facing the private sector in its attempts to take advantage of new trading opportunities can be illustrated by industry-specific information from the ACP Group (see Brewster, 2006). Many programs developed under the Cotonou Agreement – an extensive aid and trade framework between the EU and the

[1] See ITC/UNCTAD/WTO (1995) pp. 51–52.

[2] In 2002, the average share of the informal sector in GDP ranged from a low of 27 percent in Northern Africa to a high of 41 percent in sub-Saharan Africa. The informal sector in Africa accounts for over 75 percent of the total non-agricultural employment on average, compared to 57 percent and 45 percent in Latin America and Asia respectively. In the towns and cities, informal employment is estimated to absorb over 60 percent of the urban labor force. It is estimated that over 90 percent of all new employment opportunities in the African region in the 1990s were generated in the informal sector.

ACP – precede the new-found interest in trade-related aid, and can be considered as precursors to present initiatives.

The Cotonou Agreement provides for dialogue between donors and recipients on the broad parameters of export development and promotion programs for specific export industries of interest to the ACP Group. Many of these include trade-related assistance provisions. Discussions in the context of these programs have taken place directly between the European Commission (EC) and the private sector interests concerned – with the latter acting as members of their governments' delegations. Although these did not come up with a target figure for aid, in side-understandings the "ballpark size" of the resource expectation was discussed. These de facto Aid for Trade framework agreements, called Declarations, were appended to the Cotonou Agreement following its entry into force in 2003. Detailed discussions ensued on the specific needs and projects to be undertaken in integrated sector-specific aid programs, and on the precise allocation of resources for their execution.

The sectors dealt with in the Declarations were among the major ACP private sector export industries, which include rice, rum, and bananas. Other sectors for which private sector Aid for Trade needs were identified include sugar, citrus, and tourism. In the **rice sector**, the identified challenges included improvement of the conditions of production and enhancement of quality through action in the following areas:

- Research;
- Harvesting and handling;
- Transport and storage;
- Enhancing the competitiveness of existing exporters of rice;
- Assisting ACP rice producers meet environmental and waste management standards and other norms in the international market, including the European Community;
- Marketing and trade promotion; and
- Programs designed to develop value-added products.

For **rum**, the following areas were identified (see Annex A for a further description of support to the ACP rum sector):

- Enhancing the competitiveness of existing exporters of rum;
- Assistance in creation of rum marques or brands by ACP region or country;
- Enabling market campaigns to be designed and implemented;
- Assisting rum producers meet environmental and waste management standards and other norms in the international market, including the Community market;
- Assisting the ACP rum industry move out of bulk commodity production into higher value branded rum products.

Final illustration is provided by the Special Framework of Assistance for the **banana** producers of Eastern Caribbean States. Identified needs include:

- Construction of inland reception facilities;
- Improvement of environmental management of banana farms;
- Training in drainage and irrigation techniques and farm management forecasting;

- Establishment of systems for land use and information systems for agricultural diversification;
- Improved road access; and
- Promotion of fair trade and organic products, and of niche markets.

2.1 Principles of private sector Aid for Trade development

To be effective, Aid for Trade must pay particular attention to the private sector. The rationale for directing Aid for Trade to the private sector derives from the fact that while the private sector is actually the locus of production and trade, it often lacks the technical and financial resources needed for investment. At the same time, the business environment and physical and institutional infrastructure necessary for it to thrive are largely outside of its control. Firms are thus caught in a vicious circle of inefficiency. Market access alone has not guaranteed export expansion. A case in point is that of many ACP countries in which, after decades of virtually free access to the European Union markets, there is little to show by way of export growth and diversification. The Independent Evaluation Group (IEG) of the World Bank concluded that while the majority of developing countries have significantly improved their environment for trade and economic growth following two decades of assistance from the World Bank for trade reform, these initiatives were less successful in generating a dynamic and sustained growth path. According to the Bank, this is primarily due to the fact that trade policy reforms were not complemented with investments, institution-building, and measures to mitigate adverse trade effects.

Efficient and competitive private sector firms do not develop solely because of their own internal capabilities. While innovative entrepreneurs, skilled managers, a dedicated and trained work force, and efficient administrative and operational procedures are important, the number, size and efficiency of enterprises in a country are affected by a host of external factors. The private sector needs an enabling environment that allows firms to operate efficiently, and specific institutions and policies to promote private sector development. Thus, however free access conditions may be, and however advanced governments' trade policy capacities may be, unless the infrastructure is in place, the business environment is propitious, and production and export capacity are sufficiently competitive to take advantage of the new trading opportunities, much Aid for Trade will be wasted. Similarly, while financial compensation for adjustment costs may be made available, if resources do not actually reach firms, much of such transfers would amount to little more than a holding operation.

It is important that activities to be supported prioritize filling gaps that currently exist in the development aid spectrum. There would be little value-added in so expanding Aid for Trade that it virtually incorporates the whole development agenda. If Aid for Trade to the private sector is to be efficiently utilized, it must be integrated into more comprehensive national development strategies or programs. Likewise, while additional financing for private sector activities will be necessary, Aid for Trade should build on and enhance existing programs and sources of development assistance. There are, for example, programs catering to a range of areas, including trade credit, venture capital, investment promotion, transport and shipping, institutional capacity building, financing for micro-, small and medium-sized enterprises, trade-related policy software (trade-related rules, regulations, and institutions), macroeconomic policy, governance, the labor market, and the business climate. All these forms of aid are of positive benefit, but they are widely dispersed in the portfolios of numerous international and bilateral aid agencies.

Moreover, the private sector should be engaged in the design, management and monitoring of any Aid for Trade initiative intended to be of benefit to it. In the framework of specific private sector/donor agency discussions, agreement should be reached based on professional diagnostic studies and needs assessments, the requirements of a results-based, realizable program of assistance, and arrangements for a semi-continuous monitoring system using mutually agreed benchmarks. Such a collective approach should have the additional benefit of improving coherence and coordination of actions among multiple donors.

The following is a summary of lessons from various efforts to strengthen the capacity of the private sector in low-income countries. Some of the pitfalls that Aid for Trade should avoid are:

1. Failure to rationalize and prioritize the kinds of activities to be supported and to mobilize the resources needed for them to be effectively executed. Often in the past, minimal resources have been spread wafer-thin over countless activities, in many cases with an unverified connection to the ultimate objective. For example, in its first eight years the Integrated Framework (IF)[3] covered some thirty LDCs, with the paltry sum of US$30 million by six major international institutions. Or, consider trade-related aid to a typical small vulnerable island economy, Dominica. According to the WTO/Organization for Economic Cooperation and Development (OECD) TCB Database (2007), total trade-related aid to the country between 2002 and 2005 amounted to US$8 million, funding about sixty interventions, practically all of which consisted of financing participation in various seminars, conferences, meetings, and workshops, many staged in Geneva.

2. A near total lack of bona fide coordination among donors. Virtually every international organization and every developed country is involved in the area of TCB. Aid has often been disbursed with little apparent concern for coherence, consistency, efficient management, or cost and development effectiveness. Donors, in particular bilateral agencies and non-specialized international organizations, appear to determine their priorities independently of each other, despite decades of efforts around coordination. As a result, there has been a heavy overlapping of trade-related assistance. With increasing attention to upstream support for the "enabling environment" for the private sector (defined by policies, laws and regulations affecting private sector development) (te Velde, 2005), it will become increasingly important that the principles of the 2005 Paris Declaration on Aid Effectiveness (including ownership, harmonization, alignment, managing for results, and mutual accountability) are put into practice.

3. Inadequate attention to monitoring and evaluation. It is not possible, even in broad terms, to say what perceptible difference the various seminars, workshops, conferences, capacity-building, WTO participation have made to negotiated outcomes.

[3] See Introductory chapter of this volume.

4. Inadequate attention to the concerns of domestic private sectors, especially small and medium-sized enterprises. Most efforts have been limited in recent years to supporting the enabling environment and improving the investment climate, including macroeconomic strategies, governance issues, and policy, legal and regulatory frameworks. Programs will need to do more to stimulate innovation and industrial and technological development.

3 Scope of a private sector Aid for Trade program

Activities suitable for Aid for Trade directed to the private sector should give prominence to those that assist the sector take advantage of trading opportunities. A prerequisite is an overall "enabling environment" that allows private firms to operate efficiently. Such an environment would constitute the presence of specific institutions and policies that promote private sector development. Importantly, the environment would look to address the supply-side constraints that bedevil businesses operating in most developing countries, making operation by these enterprises difficult, expensive, and therefore less competitive and profitable. The range of supply-side constraints falls broadly into trade-related infrastructure constraints and production and marketing-related constraints. There would also be benefit from considering a value-chain approach.

3.1 Trade-related infrastructure

Trade-related infrastructure constraints are generally considered to refer to, for example, ports, shipping, roads, electricity, and telecommunications. Trade-related infrastructure constraints need to be broken down into appropriate categories. A disaggregation helps to clarify what might or might not be appropriate for the Aid for Trade initiative to fund. Financing could come from official development assistance (ODA), 'other official flows,'[4] or development finance institutions such as the World Bank. Notably, there is a need to distinguish between infrastructure preparation, soft infrastructure, and hard infrastructure.

Infrastructure preparation includes such activities as project identification, the preparation of programs, plans, and projects for funding. This includes prefeasibility and feasibility studies, project design, and document preparation and revision to support financing requests and/or for bidding purposes. It further comprises studies related to project viability, the financing structure and rating of project proposals of public sector- sponsored projects, and, on a contingency recovery basis, of private sector projects.

Soft infrastructure is shorthand for technical assistance in setting up systems for the efficient operation of infrastructure. It would include, for example, the legal framework for maritime activity/ports; norms and standards for airport infrastructure; regulatory legislation and institutions for public utilities such as

[4] Other official flows refers to transactions by the official sector with recipient countries which do not meet the conditions for eligibility as ODA or official aid, either because they are not primarily aimed at development, or because they have a grant element of less than 25 percent. This includes various activities of regional development banks.

electricity and telecommunications, and community legal regimes for region-wide projects. Soft infrastructure would aim to create an overall hospitable business environment that keeps transaction costs low.

Hard infrastructure deals with infrastructure construction. This is the actual physical construction, rehabilitation, or upgrading of such trade-related infrastructure as mentioned above. The activities of regional development banks are of particular importance in funding in this area, thus Aid for Trade in this sense would encompass more than traditional ODA.

Recent experience of the multilateral development finance institutions is instructive as to the extent to which Aid for Trade could be relevant. Most of them are highly liquid, but massively under-spending. Total lending by the Inter-American Development Bank (IDB) declined from a peak of US$10 billion in 1998 to an average of US$6 billion in 2002–2006. Infrastructure now accounts for merely 23 percent of total lending, compared with the 65 percent devoted to the social sectors and governance. In the World Bank Group, over the past four years project lending has hardly increased, averaging about US$19 billion a year. And in the African Development Bank (AfDB), there has been a similar stagnation in project lending around the US$1 billion mark. This has rebounded somewhat in 2004/2005. Development finance institutions spent US$45 billion in 2005, of which US$21 billion went to the private sector and a third of this, US$8 billion, was allocated to infrastructure. This is the same amount as all ODA to infrastructure in 2005. However, only 16 percent went to African countries.

It can hardly be said that there is a shortage of loan capital. To the contrary, some of these institutions are now actively promoting infrastructure projects, using such innovative devices as flexible mixed private-public combinations and non-sovereign guarantees. For example, the IDB proposes to lend to Latin American and Caribbean countries no less than US$12 billion in 2007–2010 for infrastructure. According to the Infrastructure Consortium for Africa, an initiative launched by donors in 2005, donor commitments reached more than US$7.7 billion in 2006, up from about US$7 billion in 2005.

The value-added of Aid for Trade could therefore lie in its being endowed with resources that could be used for grants on a fairly massive scale. In such a case, country eligibility criteria would be drawn more sharply into question, as would the issue of private sector participation in such investments. The proposal then would be to use Aid for Trade in the trade-related infrastructure field for the first two purposes – that is, infrastructure preparation and soft infrastructure. This could be a good means of accelerating investment in infrastructure construction by the multilateral development finance institutions.

Should an Aid for Trade initiative be endowed with resources for investment in infrastructure, further thought would need to be given to how such resources can best be used in combination with the resources of multilateral and regional development banks. One possibility is to use such resources to subsidize the interest rate on loans secured from those institutions, and in special cases, such as the Highly Indebted Poor Countries (HIPCs), to make partially and/or wholly reimbursable or non-reimbursable grants, as appropriate. An issue arising in this connection is the determination of a country's relative priorities for the use of concessionary resources, say infrastructure versus education. It is not a new issue, as in the past there has been a presumption that social sector projects have been more deserving of concessionality, since they were income yielding only in the distant future. Such a presumption may now need to be reviewed, given the rationales more recently being advanced for investing in infrastructure in developing countries.

3.2 Production and marketing-related constraints

Production and marketing-related constraints refer to a variety of production and marketing problems that beset firms trying to export their products and services, ranging from lack of business information, to a paucity of exportable products, to poor technical standards. Two subcategories can be considered here: export product competitiveness development, and export promotion and market access.

Export product competitiveness development. Activities in this field are aimed at improving competitiveness, and thus expanding the volume of production of exports and exportable goods and services. Examples are: product upgrading, including the use of cost-reducing technology; support for product innovation; workforce/management training; e-commerce readiness; the application of quality, technical, health, and sanitary and phytosanitary controls and standards; labeling and packaging; rationalization of production; and the adoption and tailoring of products to specific market demands.

Export product promotion and market access. Activities in this category would include accessing business and transport information; market intelligence; information and communications technology (ICT) databanks; identifying the requirements for accessing new export goods, new markets and niche markets; trademarks, product design and quality and environmental certification of productive processes; formation of strategic alliances and partnerships with importers; development of country trademarks; customs procedures and trade facilitation; debureaucratization; and computer literacy, including the development of digital signatures and the encryption of commercial documents.

It is also worth noting that imports form an important part of many low-income country exports. Phasing out barriers to these inputs, which businesses themselves can help to identify, must also form part of a private-sector led development strategy.

3.3 A cluster-based approach

Firms have a variety of supply chain connections, and are often related to other firms through buyer-supplier relationships and a shared set of fundamental economic factors such as workers, financial capital, technology, infrastructure (such as port facilities), natural resources, institutions, legal environments, and policy regimes. Private sector capacity building is therefore best built by clusters. A cluster could be comprised of a variety of enterprises and associated supporting organizations. The competitiveness of a country or region depends on the development of its various clusters of inter-connected companies, specialized suppliers, service providers, and associated institutions in a particular field, as well as the quality of its microeconomic business environment. The development of the private sector will depend on the institutional and policy constraints to business development, new technologies or new ways of using existing technologies, and new ways for firms to develop complementary or interdependent relationships. Industries can be re-positioned such that firms enter niche markets for products or profit from higher value-added products.

The experience of USAID (2003) and others offers a sizable set of lessons for Aid for Trade:

- The most important determinant of success is the "sweat-equity" investment of the cluster participants.
- To gauge success in assisting cluster development and economic growth impact, there is a need for clearly defined, meaningful performance indicators and regular tracking of implementation.
- Leadership matters and must come from the local community; donor-funded consultants play a facilitating role and cannot be expected to substitute for local leadership. Absence of emerging leadership in a cluster is a warning sign that the cluster may fail to coalesce or progress in spite of outside assistance. The local private sector must therefore be empowered to own and drive the process of cluster development.
- Don't over-water the garden. Funneling too much money through a competitiveness initiative may weaken local initiative.
- Cluster-based competitiveness initiatives (where similar firms are brought together) are not a "quick-fix" – they take time to work, so expectations of results should be tempered accordingly. There is a need for a longer-term perspective.

4 A synopsis of private sector programs

A number of development finance institutions and banks have moved or are moving to support the private sector in developing countries. Various donors and institutions including regional development banks in developed and developing countries have designed various TCB programs to address both the trade-related infrastructure constraints and the production and marketing-related constraints. The EC has taken this route with funds administered by the European Investment Bank (EIB) (IDA, 2004). Other institutions are offering a range of instruments for private clients, including guarantees, loans without sovereign counter-guarantees, and equity instruments. The European Bank for Reconstruction and Development (EBRD),[5] the Netherlands Development Finance Company (FMO), and the Industrialization Fund for Developing Countries (IFU) also provide various forms of finance to the private sector. The other major multilateral institutions and regional banks, including the IDB, the AfDB, and the Asian Development Bank (ADB) have also been engaged in private sector development. Given that several of these are recent phenomena, it should not be difficult to introduce a monitoring scheme, such as for example a database recording flows according to the classification proposed by the Aid for Trade Task Force. The database provided by the World Bank

[5] EBRD, established in 1991, has a strategy focusing on supporting banks and other institutions that have an institutional commitment to SMEs. It also provides a full range of financing structures in infrastructure operations, including private, sovereign, sub-sovereign, and public-private partnerships.

International Finance Corporation (IFC) (2007) provides an indication of what could be done in this area.

4.1 Multilateral development agencies

The World Bank Group (WBG) programs for the private sector are a collaboration between the International Development Association (IDA), the IFC, and the Multilateral Investment Guarantee Agency (MIGA). These programs cover such areas as the investment climate, new approaches to public-private partnerships in infrastructure, and joint support work on SME support. The WBG delivers freestanding advisory services.[6] Collaboration between members of the WBG is also geared towards public-private partnerships. Examples of such collaboration include the IFC's innovative Pamir project,[7] the IDA and IFC Cote d'Ivoire Azito Power Project,[8] and the Ghana IDA and IFC power project.[9] Given that Aid for Trade may be implemented on a regional basis (Africa, Asia and the Pacific, and Latin American and the Caribbean), we focus on the coverage of regional development banks.

4.2 Latin America and the Caribbean

The Inter-American Development Bank (IDB) Group includes the Inter-American Investment Corporation (IIC) and the Multilateral Investment Fund (MIF). Its portfolio for private sector development is similar to that of the World Bank. Its TCB programs provide financing to both the private and public sectors for infrastructure projects and legal and regulatory reforms. IDB has set up the IIC to support SMEs in Latin America and the Caribbean with loans, guarantees, and equity investments. IIC began operations in 1989 with subscribed capital of US$200 million, increasing to US$700 million in 2006. It provides long-term loans and guarantees, and makes equity investment in private enterprises that have difficulty raising finance from other sources on reasonable terms. It provides Letters of Credit to financial intermediaries.

The MIF, established in 1993, finances programs for policy change, training, and improved access to credit to help member countries strengthen their private sectors. The MIF consists of a technical cooperation facility that helps identify and implement policy changes to promote the private sector, a human resources facility that helps retain displaced workers and strengthen worker productivity, and

[6] For example, in Kenya, following the successful completion of a Foreign Investment Advisory Service (FIAS) Administrative Barriers study in July 2004, the World Bank incorporated FIAS analysis and recommendations in its economic and sector work and in its private sector development policy dialogue with the government. Subsequently, the Bank/IDA and IFC jointly designed the Kenya SME Project, approved by the IDA Board in July 2004. This project includes reforms in such areas as speeding up the legal and institutional changes to ease business entry and licensing, SME tax simplification, and initiatives to promote increased SME access to finance.

[7] This project will generate and supply electricity under a 25-year concession, taking control of the state utility and expanding generation capacity through rehabilitation of existing plant, transmission, and distribution assets. In addition, the project will provide tariff subsidy mechanisms to ensure basic provision of electricity to the poorest, supported by IDA investment and a grant from the Government of Switzerland.

[8] This is a US$223million power project including a 300MW gas-fired power station and a 225 Kv transmission line. An IDA partial risk guarantee covering sovereign and political risk was considered a crucial credit enhancement to secure commercial bank financing.

[9] In this project the IDA and IFC have joined efforts to provide advice and financing to help Ghana's government reform the power sector and unblock much-needed investment by the private sector.

a small enterprise development facility that helps broaden economic participation by the poor, women, and minorities. The IDB has a private sector department that is tasked to place up to 10 percent of the bank's total loan portfolio in private projects related to infrastructure, capital markets development, and trade finance. Project limits are up to US$75million or 25 percent of total project costs, except for smaller countries, where a limit of up to 40 percent of project costs applies.

The First Credit Guarantee Initiative supports capital markets developments, while the Regional Trade Finance Facilitation Program, established in 2001, provides fast-tracked loans to support all areas related to strengthening a country's institutional capacity in trade negotiations and other issues emerging from trade agreements. To increase competitiveness in trade, the IDB, using the Lending Program for Trade, Integration and Competitiveness, allows countries to combine the bank's investment loans, policy based loans, and technical cooperation into a single package to ensure a socially inclusive transition to free trade. The program funds economic re-conversion, assistance for displaced labor, customs facilitation, promotion of exports and foreign direct investment, infrastructure, tax reforms, and enhancement of the domestic business environment. Further, the IDB in cooperation with the Organization of American States (OAS) and the Economic Commission for Latin America and the Caribbean (ECLAC) supports a developmental program in entrepreneurship, affordable housing, basic infrastructure, micro-finance, and modern communication technologies.

The IDB also has as one of its components the Medium Term Action Plan for Development Effectiveness (PRODEV), a joint program between the IDB and the World Bank. PRODEV develops results-based monitoring systems to monitor and evaluate the performance of various development programs and public institutions. The IDB, the Andean Development Corporation (CAF), and the Financial Fund for Development of the River Plate Basin (FONPLATA) provide technical support and financing to countries under the Initiative for the Integration of Regional Infrastructure in South America (IIRSA), launched in 2000 to support the development and integration of energy, transport, and telecommunication infrastructure across twelve South American countries.[10] The Puebla-Panama Plan (PPP), launched in 2001, is supported by the IDB, the Central American Bank for Economic Integration (CABEI), the World Bank, and ECLAC, with IDB acting as financial adviser. The PPP focuses on trade facilitation, infrastructure development, and tourism services in southern Mexico and Central America.[11]

4.3 Africa

The African Development Bank's private sector development strategy is anchored on the Bank Vision and Strategic Plan 2003–2007 (see AfDB, 2006). The strategy identifies avenues to more fully integrate private sector concerns in the bank's overall operations, increase direct investment and lending to support private sector operators, and augment synergies between non-secured interventions by the private

[10] IIRSA has identified physical infrastructure requirements for ten integration hubs in the region and 335 related priority projects involving an estimated investment of US$37.5 billion. From this set, governments have selected thirty-one priority projects worth US$5.8 billion for implementation through 2020.

[11] A multi-billion, multi-year program that is to run through 2020, the PPP is financed by contributions from participating countries, the private sector, and bilateral and multilateral donors.

sector window and sovereign guaranteed operations of the public sector departments. In 1991, the bank created a window dedicated to direct financing interventions in private sector enterprises without recourse to sovereign guarantees. The cumulative private sector approvals between 1991 and 2003 stood at US$1.2 billion for 66 projects in 26 countries and seven regional projects. Direct investment in infrastructure represented 10.35 percent of total approvals; manufacturing was at 7.5 percent; oil, gas and mining represented 18.8 percent; tourism at 3.3 percent; agribusiness and fisheries took 2.9 percent; and health and energy took 0.2 percent. Other programs by the bank geared towards private sector development and TCB include the New Partnership for Africa's Development (NEPAD) Unit, aimed at the promotion and development of regional infrastructure. Further, AfDB, in collaboration with the World Bank, is involved in regional cooperation. For example, the West Africa Power Pool project aims at establishing a well-functioning cooperative power pooling for West Africa as a means to increase access in ECOWAS to stable and reliable electricity at affordable costs. The World Bank also supports transit and corridor projects in major regions of sub-Saharan Africa.[12]

AfDB has a private sector department responsible for private sector lending. The efficient functioning of local financial markets is crucial for private sector development. Since 2002, the department has extended lines of credit (LOCs) for a total amount of US$700 million, enabling local banks to on-lend to their clients, thus stimulating industrialization. OPSD also provides technical assistance packages to these banks concurrently with the financing of LOCs.

To help create capacity in the private sector, AfDB has set up the African Management Service Company (AMSCO) to assist African companies – especially SMEs – to become profitable, globally competitive, and sustainable by providing experienced hands-on professional management to selected private companies with the aim of strengthening management teams while developing local management capacity.

Another program that works toward creating capacity in the private sector is a joint initiative with the United Nations Development Programme (UNDP) and IFC to assist African entrepreneurs with project preparation; it also helps sponsors with financing market research and conducting technical and feasibility studies. The African Development Fund (ADF) set up by the AfDB provides financing and technical assistance to SMEs that are unable to borrow on the non-concessional terms. The Nigeria Trust Fund (NTF) set up under the AfDB assists in the development efforts of the poorer ADB members. The NTF is required by its Agreement to use its resources to provide financing for projects of national or regional importance which further the economic and social development of the low-income companies whose economic and social conditions and prospects require financing on non-conventional terms.

On a different front, the AfDB is involved in strengthening the institutional capacity of the judiciary, anti-corruption bodies, and legislatures to reinforce legal and judicial reforms. It also provides support for public sector reforms, strengthening

[12] For example, the East Africa Trade and Transport Facilitation Project aims to improve the trade environment through the effective elimination of tariff barriers in the EAC Customs Union Area, to enhance logistics services' efficiency along key corridors by reducing non-tariff barriers and uncertainty of transit time, and to improve railway services in Kenya and Uganda.

institutions, enhancing accountability, and supporting decentralization of local governance. These efforts go a long way in creating a favorable business climate.

4.4 Asia and the Pacific

The mission of the Asian Development Bank (ADB) is to help its developing member countries (DMCs) reduce poverty and improve the quality of the lives of their citizens (ADB, 2000). Traditionally, ADB's assistance has been effected through its public sector operations by extending LOCs to state-owned and private financial intermediaries of its DMCs through the government, or with government guarantees specifically to support investment in productive private SMEs. By the year 2000, the ADB had approved 110 credit lines totaling about US$4.4 billion for use by sixty-five intermediaries in twenty-three DMCs. These have benefited over 22,000 SMEs. Several ADB-assisted development finance institutions have evolved into profitable institutions that play important roles in their countries' economic growth. This list includes the China Development Corporation, ICICI Ltd. (India), Korea Development Bank and Korea Long-Term Credit Bank, the Development Bank of Singapore, and the Industrial Finance Corporation of Thailand. The LOC operations contribute to institutional enhancement, capacity building, and human resource development in the financial sector, dialogue with DMCs on financial sector reforms, and capital market development issues.

The ADB, in creating an enabling business environment, has assisted DMCs in formulating and implementing reforms that promote private sector development by removing market distortions, strengthening domestic financial markets, and promoting good governance standards. Program loans have been used to support policy and institutional reforms in the financial sector in India, Indonesia, Sri Lanka, Thailand and Vietnam; agriculture in Bangladesh, Lao PDR, Nepal, Pakistan, Papua New Guinea, Philippines, Samoa, and Sri Lanka; industry in Bangladesh, Mongolia, Nepal, and Pakistan; trade in Indonesia; and road transport in Philippines. Further, in an effort to create an enabling environment for private investment, ADB has provided support aimed at stable macroeconomic management; investment, trade, and price control; well-functioning financial and capital markets; flexible labor markets; good infrastructure; and a legal system protecting and enforcing contractual and property rights. In the agricultural sector, ADB has been active in the commercialization of agriculture.[13]

Other efforts by ADB include collaboration with the OECD in setting up an anti-corruption action plan to support ADB member countries' efforts to build up effective and sustainable anti-corruption mechanisms through fostering dialogue, policy analysis, and capacity building.

4.5 Bilateral donors and Aid for Trade

Several bilateral donors have private sector development programs. Some of the most important include the UK's Department for International Development

[13] During the 1970s and 1980 and into the 1990s, most of the DMCs were subject to heavy public intervention in the agricultural sector, consisting of price support and input subsidies for producers, and price controls on items consumed by the poor.

(DFID), the U.S. Agency for International Development (USAID), the Swedish International Development Agency (SIDA), the Danish International Development Agency (DANIDA), and German and Japanese programs. While all programs center on enabling the business environment, most increasingly go further.

Bilateral private sector development programs share the same central concerns as those of the multilateral development banks described previously. They aim to promote economic growth and profitable production, create jobs and income, and broaden the tax base. Actions considered often include measures to foster trading conditions and improve the potential for exploiting opportunities created by globalization, such as improvements of legal, institutional and political frameworks.

In addition to bilateral cooperation, EU member states intervene via the European Commission, which has established its own agencies such as the Centre for Development of Enterprises (CDE) and the European Investment Bank (EIB). Established in 1977 as the Centre for Development of Industry (CDI), and transformed to the CDE with the Cotonou Partnership Agreement, CDI/CDE provides incentives for the development of small and medium sized industrial enterprises in ACP countries. The CDE does not provide direct financing for projects, but finances pre-and post-investment technical assistance activities to companies in the ACP, such as identification of projects and potential partners, operations prior to the implementation of a project, financial and legal structuring of projects, project start-up, and development. CDE's contribution is limited to a maximum of EUR150,000 per project, per year. In addition, the cumulative amount of all contributions to the same project/company must not exceed EUR300,000, and must be less than 20 percent of the total investment, except in the case of pilot projects. Annual budgets for CDE are currently around EUR20 million. Some of the drawbacks raised regarding the CDE are useful lessons to inform Aid for Trade in this area (see te Velde, 2005).

- The CDE has too small a resource base to make a real impact. An average of EUR250,000 per ACP country is too low for that;
- The use of regional antennae as opposed to national ones has (at least in the Caribbean) created a lack of awareness among most businesses about the services offered by the CDI and how to access them; and
- There are cumbersome, centralized, bureaucratic procedures, while the private sector needs quick and just-in-time services.

A second EC project of interest to the Aid for Trade debate is the EIB, founded in 1958. The main EIB instruments are loans and equity financing. The loans are long-term (up to 25 years), require government guarantees, will usually finance not more than 50 percent of the total project costs, and often fall between EUR1.5 million and EUR25 million. Some salient features to take into account in designing Aid for Trade are as follows:

- The effectiveness of EIB as a vehicle for providing investment finance is limited by its lack of local knowledge and local representation;
- Credit lines to financial intermediaries may be committed only gradually, and it is unclear whether credit lines for on-lending are actually used to finance new investment;

- Some firms have difficulties accessing EIB loans, either because firms are too small, or because firms cannot use favorable terms, as the EIB has often provided risk capital to government at favorable terms for on-lending on market-based terms;
- The role of credible outside investors (in tandem with the IFC and bilateral investors) provided by the EIB is a sweetener for foreign investment; and
- The EIB often relies on repeat loans to the same client including the parastatal sector, instead of identifying new projects.

In summary, and drawing from the experience of Norway in strengthening private sector development in low-income countries, the following list provides a useful illustration of the types of actions that can be undertaken to improve private sector development:[14]

1. *Reduce marginalization*: Help to improve international framework conditions and reduce the marginalization of the poorest countries, thereby reducing the risk they run of failing to benefit from the development potential of globalization.
2. *Strengthen South-South trade*: Strengthen the regional perspective and trade between developing countries, which is an underexploited potential.
3. *Make comprehensive efforts at country level*: Establish a comprehensive country-specific perspective for providing support for private sector development, with adequate emphasis on identification of bottlenecks, needs, and priorities in individual countries. Improve the consistency and synergy between efforts at different levels and through different channels.
4. *Improve framework conditions*: Continue to support macroeconomic reforms, while placing greater emphasis on supporting the development of good governance and improving institutional conditions, such as a well-functioning financial sector as well as civil society organizations and trade unions.
5. *Promote investments*: Actively promote investments in developing countries, particularly in the poorest countries. Stimulate long-term investment and involvement by international commerce and industry.
6. *Promote trade with developing countries*: Strengthen current arrangements for imports from developing countries to Norway, and increase the priority of general measures to increase the export and trade of developing countries.
7. *Support untying*: Continue active support for untying of development assistance, both in the OECD/DAC and through the gradual untying of bilateral development assistance schemes in step with other donor countries.
8. *Increase the use of local procurement*: Promote local procurement in aid-financed projects.
9. *Make active and targeted use of donor expertise*: Actively utilize donor resource base, including in commerce and industry, when this meets identified and expressed needs in developing countries. Strengthen the dialogue between bilateral development cooperation authorities and commerce and industry concerning private sector development and investment opportunities in developing countries.

[14] See Ministry of Foreign Affairs, Norway (1998).

4.6 Specialized agencies

Most specialized agencies have TCB programs in place that aim to support private sector development. For example, the UN Industrial Development Organization (UNIDO) has a program under various modules aimed at strengthening private firms.[15] The program supports the formulation and implementation of overall industrial strategies conducive to strengthening private sector development and promoting SMEs, and in providing the seedbed for developing and testing entrepreneurial talent (see UNIDO, 2007a). In order to assist SMEs overcome challenges to doing business, the program offers specific sets of services, including information services for business, SME cluster and networking development, and rural and women entrepreneurship development. UNIDO also has an Agro-Industries service module that comprises a range of technical assistance interventions and know-how, encompassing key areas such as (see UNIDO, 2007b):

1. Support and advice to official and private sector decision-making bodies in various sub-sectors (food, leather, textiles, wood, and agro-machinery) on techno-economic development options for strengthening the agro-industrial sector and fostering the equitable integration of small-scale, agro-based enterprises into market-oriented agro-produce systems.
2. Capacity building at the institutional and industry levels to enhance industrial productivity and marketing performance in the agro-industrial sector.
3. Support to traditional agro-industries to improve their productivity and efficiency, increase their integration into global value chains, and support rural livelihood diversity. This is achieved through upgrading of technical skills, process optimization, diffusion of appropriate agro-engineering systems, product innovation/diversification, and the introduction of working methodologies and guidelines. Special attention is given to marketing support, such as participation in trade fairs and missions, as a means of exposing the target beneficiaries to market requirements.

The role of business associations is also key to private sector development at a more "collective action" level. Business associations can act as cheerleaders for domestic policy reform and regulatory control. They also develop and provide access to training tools relevant to their members, and utilize the clout that comes with representing a broader swathe of business. These associations act as trade promotion vehicles, thus increasing the volume and profitability of the domestic private sector. They also act as trainers and as a source of market information for exporters. National chambers of commerce can play an important role in this regard. Linkages between businesses, government, and civil society can lead to comprehensive solutions in creating favorable business environments. For example, in tackling corruption, industry-specific initiatives among businesses and other stakeholders have been effective, as they impact local business practices beyond the capacity of any single company. Business associations face various challenges, since their members tend to be small firms with limited resources. In the case of private sector businesses trading in services, most of these enterprises do not realize that they are exporting, and they always need to be educated about what constitutes a traded

[15] See for example te Velde and Morrissey (2005).

service. Sometimes, trade promotion officers do not have the types of contacts needed by exporters to network and establish credibility in export markets. Small enterprises often lack marketing skills, and business associations always face an urgent need to help these firms undertake business development.

5 Possible ways forward for a private sector Aid for Trade program

Based on the preceding discussion, this chapter proposes the following five features for inclusion in an Aid for Trade program for the private sector:

5.1 Supportive business environment

An efficient private sector cannot emerge and prosper without an overall environment conducive to running businesses efficiently. Such a framework would be characterized by macroeconomic stability, an efficient financial system, competitive markets, regulation that ensures competition and fair trade, adequate infrastructure, political and social stability, a legal framework to ensure all operate under the rule of law, a policy framework that provides adequate support to the private sector, access to resources, and support services. Aid for Trade that will be beneficial to the private sector should therefore promote a ***comprehensive framework***, given that relevant actions encompass socio-economic and political issues that lie beyond the scope of private sector operators or government decision-makers responsible for private sector development. Such a comprehensive framework for private sector development will nurture a strong private sector that can compete effectively in world markets and enter into partnerships with international firms. The development of such an internationally competitive private sector, in turn, will require an enabling environment for enterprises and an adequate institutional capacity. Some of this is currently considered in the World Bank work on "Doing Business."

5.2 Networking

The literature stresses the role that networks play in disseminating information about innovations, lowering transaction costs, increasing the potential for the division of labor between enterprises, and fostering collective action. Networks can affect enterprise performance directly by providing information about technologies and markets. Networks may improve entrepreneurs' access to information about the world. Much of the uncertainty facing enterprises in low-income countries is due to a lack of contract discipline, leading in turn to delayed supplies, unreliable quality, and late payments or repayments by customers and debtors. Part of the problem here is one of information asymmetries that can lead to high, unavoidable transaction costs. For example, in sub-Saharan Africa, while many institutions exist, they tend not to permeate the environment within which most enterprises, SMEs in particular, operate. Instead, entrepreneurs rely on their networks to reduce information asymmetries by facilitating flows of information.

Networks can help substitute for formal market-supporting institutions by allowing information about agents to flow. Networks can be of two types (Barr, 1998). Those that enhance enterprise performance by allowing information about market opportunities to flow between their members are called "innovation networks." Those designed to reduce uncertainty by allowing information about agents to flow are "solidarity networks". In innovation networks we are likely to find larger enterprises. In solidarity networks we are more likely to find enterprises that have restricted access to and operate within an environment unregulated by formal, market-supporting institutions and that employ traditional, static technologies and sell primarily to end-users in local markets. Smaller enterprises generally display these characteristics. While solidarity networks may have a marginal effect on enterprise productivity, it is the more far-reaching, innovation networks that have a large and significant impact. The nature and relative importance of the private and spillover effects also depend on the role and consequent structure of the network. Solidarity networks tend to generate significant positive spillovers; within their bounds it is difficult for individuals to exclude others from the benefits of their own networking activity. On the other hand, the innovation networks to which large enterprises belong tend to generate high private returns. Strengthening formal market-supporting institutions and making them more accessible to small enterprises should be an important area to consider promoting in Aid for Trade.

5.3 Private sector development with specific attention to SMEs and women entrepreneurs

Within the private sector, particular attention should be paid to SMEs, as these account for the majority of domestic firms and have high potential for addressing core poverty. SMEs have specific characteristics and potentials that distinguish them from larger enterprises. SMEs are especially disadvantaged by burdensome regulations and administrative requirements. Women also face a variety of constraints to establishing and operating businesses. The case of South Africa illustrates. The entrepreneurial activity rates of men and women in South Africa are highly skewed as a result of the higher entrepreneurial opportunities available to men.[16] Women entrepreneurs in South Africa remain on the periphery of the national economy; they generally lack the necessary resources for starting and developing their own businesses; they have less human capital for the management and development of their businesses; and they are under-represented in value-adding business opportunities.

The key challenges facing SMEs and women entrepreneurs in particular include access to formal credit; higher vulnerability to adverse effects of trade reform; limited ownership of assets such as land; lack of information to exploit opportunities; higher educational and occupational barriers; and insufficient networking.

Aid for Trade could provide the opportunity for beneficiary countries to consolidate ongoing efforts toward enterprise development, particularly aspects related to SMEs and women. Aid for Trade in the private sector should encourage and assist relevant business support initiatives; provide appropriate financial assistance to SMEs and women entrepreneurs; make available to them general information and education programs, especially business skills training and facilitation of business incubation; develop and/or facilitate information and communication technologies that bridge the gap between new enterprises and established businesses; support mentoring programs and establishment of networking links and international

[16] South African Women Entrepreneurs' Network (2005).

partnerships; and stimulate changes to trade, investment, and tax policies that impede women entrepreneurship.

5.4 Access to finance

Shortage and cost of finance is the most important constraint to private sector development. Whether creating a new business or expanding an existing one, entrepreneurs need financial resources to stay competitive and they need help to introduce new technologies and grow. Despite the fact that financial institutions have a great deal of liquidity, firms in low-income countries are mostly constrained by lack of funds. SMEs in particular suffer from under-capitalization: they rely too heavily on short-term loans, which are relatively expensive and therefore increase the risk of failure. They have restricted access to collateral, hence limited access to loan finance. Indeed, according to a poll conducted with 107 SMEs in the Caribbean (E. Brewster, 2006), the main support required by SMEs of government is to facilitate access to finance. The reduction of taxation and the publication of information for small businesses follow as the next most significant measures which would help SMEs. Notable among the responses, and cited by 58 percent of respondents, is the need for governments to create a one-stop shop for SMEs. Aid for Trade could help address these constraints with particular attention to the following:

1. Establish or improve loan and mutual guarantee schemes to help entrepreneurs that have a problem with collateral;
2. Establish or improve schemes to attract small amounts of capital into small enterprises to reduce dependence on bank loans;
3. Promote capital investment into expanding and hi-tech firms by private investors and through venture capital schemes;
4. Introduce measures to facilitate the transfer and the continuation of an enterprise; and
5. Identify and spread good practice in financing start-ups.

5.5 Analytical and institutional capacity building for the private sector

The effectiveness of the private sector policy will be limited if the majority of private sector operators do not know the opportunities afforded by liberalized markets, or if they do not have the ability to draw on appropriate quantitative and qualitative data and information. Access to such data and information by the private sector is often limited, and this situation significantly reduces the contribution of the private sector to policy decisions; it also limits their ability to tap into market opportunities created by liberalization.

A crucial requirement for ensuring that the business sector can exploit market opportunities is the existence of strong and efficient trade support institutions. Such institutions should be able to provide technical and technological support to the private sector, and enable it to overcome the growing range of non-trade barriers in such areas as quality management, standardization, and safety. Aid for Trade resources could be devoted to nurturing trade-effective support institutions such as trade and investment promotion agencies, chambers of commerce, and business associations.

There is a key role to be played by the public sector. One of the lessons from the first generation of structural adjustment is the role of government in supporting the private sector. The public sector's role should not be to replace the private sector but to stimulate the provision of services through private sector providers and enable private enterprises to access the resources they need to compete in the global market. This would include stimulating the provision of business services by profit-making firms, leaving the private sector to provide directly the services, and providing enterprises with mechanisms to address their own needs. SMEs in particular lack the capacity to identify opportunities for subcontracting work from larger firms, and to identify joint venture partners from whom they could obtain financing, technology, and marketing benefits. Aid for Trade could facilitate networking between SMEs (formal and informal) and larger firms that are often better connected to international markets, hence with access to up-to date technology and know-how.

Partnerships between the private and public sectors are becoming commonplace, and these provide avenues for ensuring that government policies give priority to addressing the main impediments to local private sector development. In many countries, specific structures are being established to institutionalize this public/private partnership. Aid for Trade could strengthen this process, or help nurture it where it is lacking or grossly under-developed.

5.6 Concluding remarks

This chapter has provided some general ideas for what could constitute a private sector component of Aid for Trade. These would need to be reviewed in the context of specific countries or regions. It is useful to be mindful of some complications that are likely to occur, as the case of the rum industry illustrates (see Annex A). Grant-based resources are not traditionally used for financing capital investment for the private sector, and as such it could be hard to justify large sums of Aid for Trade coming in the form of grants directed to private sector development. More likely, Aid for Trade grant resources could be used as seed money to attract the participation of commercial banks in economic activities. Of particular interest is the mix of grant and loan resources which could ease the terms and conditions for accessing resources. This would involve greater incentives to staff of development financial institutions, including the IFC, to process applications from LDCs and other low-income countries to be the target of Aid for Trade.

There could also be competition of interests if funds destined for poverty reduction in social sectors were used instead to assist firms in profit-making activities, especially if in so doing they would be competing with firms from donor countries. One possibility would be to limit Aid for Trade resources to SMEs.

There would be a need for some elements of private-sector diplomacy, as in most cases the private sector may be called upon to play a lead role. Dunlop (2004) suggests some elements, drawn in part from the case of the Caribbean rum industries. The list of suggested actions to be championed by the private sector is as follows:

1. Public-private dialogue with government officials and trade negotiators in beneficiary and donor capitals to forge a unified public-private position and set of common negotiating objectives;

2. Be proactive and commit time and effort to the trade negotiating process to promote the industry position, including through regular visits to donor countries;
3. Development of strategic alliances in donor countries and in other low-income countries;
4. Ensure that industry players set aside any competing commercial interests for the greater good of the sector;
5. Put in place a committed and united industry leadership that is respected by trade negotiators and officials on both sides; and
6. Establish a mechanism for the constant exchange of information between industry and negotiators, including through the production of written briefs and other documentation.

For these actions to materialize, Aid for Trade capacity building should improve the knowledge level of private sector actors regarding the constraints and opportunities associated with trade negotiations. Such capacity building could be designed and implemented with local private sector associations or other trade support institutions. The success of the rum case was driven by the high level of expertise mobilized from among its membership across the Caribbean by the West Indies Rum and Spirits Producers Association (WIRSPA). A cluster-based approach at the regional level appears as the best organizing framework for this type of private sector capacity development.

ANNEX A: A SUCCESSFUL CASE OF A PRIVATE SECTOR PROGRAM: SUPPORT TO THE ACP RUM SECTOR[17]

From the 1970s to 1996, ACP exports of rum flowed to Europe under the Rum Protocol that provided a duty-free access quota to the European market for ACP rum exporters.

In November 1996, only a few months after the EU finally removed quotas on ACP rum, as part of a deal on the Information Technology Agreement at the Singapore WTO Ministerial Conference, the EU and U.S. agreed to a "Zero-for-Zero" Agreement on Distilled Spirits.

The EU General Affairs Council approved a Declaration on 24 March 1997 that recognized the likely impact of the EU-U.S. agreement on the ACP exports of rum to the EU market, and confirmed that this would be taken fully into account in any future negotiations and arrangements related to the rum sector.

The West Indies Rum and Spirits Producers Association Inc. (WIRSPA) played a crucial role in the discussions. WIRSPA is an association of national associations of rum producers in the ACP Caribbean aiming to promote and protect the interests of members concerned in the production, export, and/or marketing of rum and other locally produced sugar cane-based spirits.

WIRSPA took the lead and developed a number of strategic alliances with other industry groups in Europe; in particular, the association established a dialogue with other rum producers that had also been disadvantaged by the Zero-for-Zero

[17] Based primarily on materials from Dunlop (2004).

agreement, and signed with their representative association a series of mutually supportive ioint accords.

WIRSPA encouraged the interest of the European Parliament, particularly the Development and Budget Committees, in the ACP rum dossier. During 1999, the Parliament's Budget Committee agreed to create an EU budget line to support ACP rum producers, but with no resources attached (a so-called "budget line pm"). This nevertheless signaled to the EC and EU member states that the Parliament was politically supportive of the rum industry's case for transitional assistance to help it cope with the effects of the Zero-for Zero-Agreement.

During the post-Lomé trade negotiations, the rum case was made an issue of principle by the ACP Group. This led to identification of the main elements of the support program. As a result, the EC agreed to provide sufficient funds to finance during the preparatory period, in consultation with the ACP sector concerned, **an integrated sector-specific program for the development of ACP exporters of rum**, that could in particular include the following measures:

- Enhance the competitiveness of existing exporters of rum;
- Assist in creation of rum marques or brands by ACP region or country;
- Enable marketing campaigns to be designed and implemented;
- Assist ACP rum producers to meet environmental and waste management standards and other norms in the international market, including the Community market; and
- Assist the ACP rum industry to move out of bulk commodity production into higher-value branded rum products.

Turning what had been agreed politically into a practical program of transitional assistance that met the industry's needs was a challenge. In November 2001, the EDF Committee approved a four-year package of transitional support with a grant contribution. A year later in August 2002, the program became operational – four years and five months after market liberalization began in March 1997, or four months before market liberalization was completed on 1 January 2003.

DIAGNOS – an analysis unit at the service of the ACP Governments – was established as a support mechanism for the ACP private sector, and its role was to undertake diagnostic studies of the constraints facing priority ACP sectors; it has leaner procedures and could provide support to the ACP private sector within a defined time frame. It was recognized that normal EDF criteria and timescales do not fit well with the need for rapid delivery, in a finite period, of time-sensitive programs that involve the private sector.

In conclusion, while not completely trouble-free, this case provides a good success story and interesting lessons for Aid for Trade for the private sector. Salient features include the broad-based political support on both ACP and EU sides and the lead role of WIRSPA.

REFERENCES

"ACP-EU Partnership Agreement," ACP/CE/en1, http://ec.europa.eu/development/ICenter/Pdf/agr01_en.pdf.

ADB. 2000. "Private Sector Development Strategy," Manila: Asian Development Bank.

AfDB. 2006. "Homepage," African Development Bank, http://www.afdb.org.

Barr, Abigail M. 1998. "Enterprise Performance and the Functional Diversity of Social Capital," Working Paper WPS/98-1, Oxford: Centre for the Study of African Economies – Institute of Economics and Statistics.

Brewster, Erwin E. 2006. "Finance for Small and Medium-sized Enterprises in the Caribbean," Economic Paper 76, London: Commonwealth Secretariat.

Brewster, Havelock R. 2006. "The Competitiveness of Caribbean Countries," Georgetown: Caribbean Community Secretariat.

CDB. 2002. "Report on Regional Agriculture," Barbados: CDB.

Chauffour, Jean-Pierre (IMF representative). 2006. "Criteria for Effective Aid for Trade Delivery: the IMF Perspective," COMSEC/UNCTAD/South Centre meeting on "Aid for Trade," Geneva, 21–22 March.

CTO. 2003. "Caribbean Regional Sustainable Tourism Development Programme," Barbados: CTO.

Dunlop, A. 2004. "A strong cocktail or a weak punch? A case study of EDF assistance to the ACP private sector," ECDPM Discussion Paper No. 52, Maastricht: ECDPM.

FTAA-Consultative Group on Smaller Economies. 2003. "National Strategy to Strengthen Trade-Related Capacity," Dominica.

IDA. 2004. "Strengthening the Private Sector in IDA Countries: Status of the World Bank Group Collaboration," Washington, D.C.: IDA.

IDB. 2006. "Delivering Aid for Trade: The Inter-American Development Bank's Experience," COMSEC/UNCTAD/South Centre meeting on "Aid for Trade," Geneva, 21–22 March.

IFC. 2007. "Homepage," International Finance Corporation, http://www.ifc.org.

ILEAP. 2005. "Aid for Trade: Why and How?," presented at the WTO Hong Kong Ministerial Conference, Toronto: ILEAP.

ILEAP. 2006. "African Perspectives on Aid for Trade," paper commissioned by the African Union, Toronto: ILEAP.

ITC/UNCTAD/WTO. 1995. "Business Guide to the Uruguay Round," London: Commonwealth Secretariat.

Johnson, H. F. 2006. "Aid for Trade Architecture: The Why's, what's and How's – and who should deliver?," Commonwealth Conference on "Aid for Trade," Geneva, 21–22 March.

Ministry of Foreign Affairs, Norway. 1998. "Strategy for Norwegian Support of Private Sector in Developing Countries," http://www.regjeringen.no/nb/dep/ud/dok/rapporter_planer/rapporter/1998/Strategy-for-Norwegian-support-of-private-sector-development-in-developing-countries.html?id=420023

OAS. 2005. "The OAS Support to Trade-Related Capacity-Building in the Americas," Washington, D.C.: OAS.

Prowse, Susan. 2006. "'Aid For Trade' – Increasing Support for Trade Adjustment and Integration – a Proposal," UK: DFID.

South African Women Entrepreneurs' Network. 2005. "South African Women Entrepreneurs: A Burgeoning Force in our Economy – A Special Report 2005," Pretoria: Department of Trade and Industry – Republic of South Africa.

South Centre. 2006. "Elements for the Architecture of Aid for Trade," South Centre Analysis Series, Geneva: South Centre.

Stiglitz, Joseph E. 2006. "Aid For Trade: Complements For Development," New York: Initiative for Policy Dialogue – Columbia University.

Stiglitz, Joseph E. and Andrew Charlton. 2006. "Aid for Trade," London: Commonwealth Secretariat.

te Velde, Dirk Willem. 2005. "Aid for private sector development," in S. Page (ed.), *Trade And Aid: Partners Or Rivals In Development Policy?*, London: Cameron May Publishers.

te Velde, Dirk Willem and Oliver Morrissey. 2005. "Supporting Industrial Development: Overcoming Market Failures and Providing Public Goods," Vienna: UNIDO.

UNCTAD. 2006. "Aid for Trade: Note by the Secretariat," Geneva: UNCTAD.

UNIDO. 2007a. "Service Module 4: Private Sector Development – Overview," http://www.unido.org/doc/5069.

UNIDO. 2007b. "Service Module 5: Agro-Industries – Overview," http://www.unido.org/doc/5070.

USAID. 2003. "Promoting Competitiveness in Practice: An Assessment of Cluster-Based Approaches," prepared by the Mitchell Group Inc., Washington, D.C.

World Bank. 2006. "Aid for Trade, Economic Development and Doha Round," Washington, D.C.: World Bank.

World Bank Independent Evaluation Group. 2006. "Assessing World Bank Support for Trade, 1987–2004," Washington, D.C.: World Bank.

WTO. 2003. *Final Report of the Evaluation of the Integrated Framework*, Integrated Framework Steering Committee, WT/IFSC/6/Rev.2*, 26 November.

WTO. 2006a. *Recommendations of the Task Force on Aid for Trade*, Aid for Trade Task Force, WT/AFT/1, 27 July.

WTO/OECD. 2007. "Doha Development Agenda Trade Capacity Building Database," http://tcbdb.wto.org.

19 Regional Aid for Trade[1]

DIRK WILLEM TE VELDE

1 Introduction

Aid for Trade has emerged rapidly as an important topic for those interested in both aid and trade.[2] Aid for Trade became firmly established as a concept when the World Trade Organization's (WTO) Sixth Ministerial Conference in Hong Kong in December 2005 led to the set up of a Task Force on Aid for Trade. The Task Force reported to the WTO membership in July 2006, and the General Council endorsed its recommendations on 10 October 2006.

The Aid for Trade Task Force suggested that the scope of Aid for Trade include support for trade policy and regulations, trade development, trade-related infrastructure, building productive capacity, trade-related adjustment, and other trade-related needs. However, despite the laudable results of the Task Force, it may take some time for the precise operationalization of Aid for Trade to emerge.

The Director-General of the WTO, Pascal Lamy, followed up on the Task Force recommendations (WTO, 2006a) in the "Director-General's Report on Aid for Trade to General Council," 14–15 December 2006 (WTO, 2006b). He suggested that the operationalization of the initiative should predominantly be evident from monitoring activities, which should take place at three levels: (i) monitoring to assess global Aid for Trade flows using the OECD-DAC CRS[3] database to increase transparency on pledges and disbursements; (ii) monitoring evaluation reports by development agencies; and (iii) monitoring and evaluation of successful cases of in-country Aid for Trade. He also recommended that there be a section in WTO Trade Policy Reviews on Aid for Trade.

There are several gaps and concerns not properly addressed in post-Hong Kong Aid for Trade discussions. First, it is by no means certain that current pledges will actually lead to additional Aid for Trade, not only because it is not clear how additionality of funds is to be measured, but also because the amounts announced differ and are re-announced several times. Second, Aid for Trade is ultimately to help the private sector to trade, but there have been few inputs from the private

1 This chapter was originally a paper for ILEAP prepared for a meeting of African trade ministers in Addis Ababa, Ethiopia, on 15 January 2007. It has benefited from inputs and suggestions from Sheila Page, Lauren Phillips, and Dominique Njinkeu.

2 See ODI (2007) for references to the literature. See Page (2007) for a comprehensive account of the Aid for Trade initiative.

3 Organisation for Economic Cooperation and Development (OECD) Development Assistance Committee (DAC) Creditor Reporting System (CRS).

sector. Third, there seems to be a view that the Paris Declaration on Aid Effectiveness, a process which sets a group of donors against individual recipient countries in order to reduce transaction costs of aid delivery, would be sufficient to secure effective administration of Aid for Trade. Of course, national processes work less well for international challenges, where international delivery and coordination mechanisms seem more appropriate (see Annex A to this chapter).

Regional Aid for Trade features in post-Hong Kong Aid for Trade discussions (World Bank, 2006; WTO 2006a). For instance, the WTO Aid for Trade Task Force recommendations state: strengthen the functions in relation to regional, sub-regional and cross border issues; assign responsibility for these functions; and explore the merits of establishing a Regional Aid-for-Trade Committee (see Annex A). However, it is not apparent that these ideas are being followed up, as new delivery mechanisms suggested by the IMF/World Bank (2006) were rejected, and the Director-General's report of December 2006 failed to elaborate on the regional context.

Most attention on Aid for Trade focused initially on resources, and then on the operationalization of *national* Aid for Trade programs, with an emphasis on the monitoring aspects. Despite the fact that much trade policy-making and challenges to trade competitiveness are currently at the regional level, the current discussions implicitly assume that national aid programs are adequate for all challenges, whether they be national, regional or international. This paper argues that regional programs are required alongside national ones (and multilateral programs). Regional Aid for Trade is defined here as Aid for Trade coordinated and/or implemented at a level involving more than one country.

This chapter argues that effective delivery of Aid for Trade will need to include a strong regional element, and outlines parameters around structuring Aid for Trade at the regional level. Section 2 provides a rationale for looking at regional Aid for Trade in addition to national Aid for Trade. Section 3 provides a brief overview of regional Aid for Trade programs. Section 4 suggests possible ways forward, and Section 5 concludes.

2 Rationale for regional Aid for Trade

The two motivations for Aid for Trade are (i) in broad terms, to help developing countries build up the productive sectors to trade and benefit from trade liberalization, and (ii) in narrow terms, to provide payments to countries to meet the costs of implementing trade agreements. WTO agreements on further liberalization are associated with preference erosion, higher bills for net food-importing countries, and implementation and adjustments costs such as retraining or changing a trade tax system to a value-added tax system.

The two motivations differ in their implications for how regional Aid for Trade might be viewed. On the one hand, when Aid for Trade is viewed broadly, regional Aid for Trade is regarded as solving regional challenges not covered at other levels, of which national level programs are the most predominant. On the other hand, when regional Aid for Trade is seen as closely connected to the WTO, *regional* Aid for Trade is a "constraint" (Page, 2007) or a sub-set of *multilateral* Aid for Trade (potentially harming the efficiency of Aid for Trade). The case for regional Aid for Trade is strongest in the first approach, but not entirely absent in the latter.

The rationale for regional Aid for Trade rests on three pillars:

- *To support the provision of regional governance public goods*. Effective international economic governance promotes economic development. Some challenges are best met at the national or multilateral level, but some policy-making occurs at a regional level in parallel with national trade policy-making. There has been an increase in regional policy-making and in the number of regional trade agreements over the past decades. As these evolve to consider deeper regional integration, particularly the liberalization of sensitive service sectors or the provision of social projects (which make sense in a regional context) (te Velde, 2006b), there is a need for regional institutional development and regional governance.
- *To provide regional knowledge public goods*. A regional approach facilitates learning and sharing of information related to trade development and trade policy. This could be relevant when national Aid for Trade programs have common elements in them. For instance, a regional discussion on trade in services and appropriate regulatory frameworks and regulators might benefit all stakeholders.
- *To overcome other market and coordination failures, and to provide and coordinate activities with strong regional externalities*. Many competitiveness challenges are regional in nature; for instance, a landlocked country is dependent on appropriate infrastructure in other countries for trade in goods. Some externalities are not geographically limited to a region, but others relate to neighboring states only. National programs will not normally consider activities with strong international externalities, so that some Aid for Trade programs that are regionally optimal may not take place because the benefits cannot be fully appropriated nationally.[4]

If one takes a narrow approach (that Aid for Trade emerged as an issue at the WTO to respond to WTO-related adjustments), then earmarking Aid for Trade for specific purposes such as national programs or regional programs would be a constraint on Aid for Trade (see Page, 2007). However, as most Aid for Trade is currently programmed at the national level, the binding constraint is the limiting national focus, and therefore the earmarking of additional resources for cross-country and regional programs would alleviate some of those constraints. In addition, in certain cases, it would be better to provide regional as opposed to multilateral Aid for Trade if its aim was to benefit only a handful of neighboring states (e.g. providing physical cross-border infrastructure), as involvement of too many countries would make decision-making inefficient.

The case for regional versus multilateral Aid for Trade has parallels in the discussion on regional versus multilateral trade liberalization. Specifically, African regions are likely to see few benefits from regional tariff liberalization because it might lead to trade diversion and because intra-regional trade is low (te Velde, 2006b). As such, regional tariff liberalization does not need disproportionate attention at the regional level as opposed to the multilateral level. However, deeper integration – involving harmonization of rules and mutual recognition and finding common standards in regions – is politically easier and economically more

[4] See IMF/World Bank (2006) for a discussion of a power project benefiting Malawi, but with a need for financing in Mozambique.

meaningful as a stepping stone to multilateral trade liberalization. Trade diversion is less of a problem for regional liberalization in services. Services trade through temporary migration tends to be heavily restricted, and loosening up this one category is unlikely to lead to trade diversion away from other categories or other sources of supply; instead, temporary services providers might displace or complement host country labor rather than other foreign labor. There is also no serious loss in tariffs in the possible event of trade diversion. Hence, the problem of trade diversion is smaller when using regional trade in services preferences. Consequently, regional Aid for Trade could usefully support deeper regional trade liberalization (for example in services) rather than goods liberalization alone.

The examples in Table 19.1 show regional, national and multilateral dimensions of the Aid for Trade categories identified by the Task Force.

While the rationale is clear, there may be practical challenges for regional Aid for Trade. For instance, regional approaches may not be seen to benefit all countries the same, and some form of sharing the costs and benefits will need to be agreed. For this, all countries need to have the capacity to engage in such negotiations. Further, regions need to have the analytical capabilities and tools to facilitate negotiations and joint decision-making.

3 Overview of current regional Aid for Trade

Multilateral and regional development banks, bilateral donors, and the European Community have already provided regional Aid for Trade. This section reviews existing programs/projects from the following donors:

- Regional development banks (Asia, Latin America and Africa) and regional projects of the World Bank;
- EC European Development Fund (EDF) programs, including Regional Indicative Programmes (RIPs), those delivered at the "all African, Caribbean and Pacific Group (ACP)" level, and those linked to the EU-ACP Economic Partnership Agreement (EPA) proposals (EPA +), such as the fund for Eastern and Southern Africa; and
- Bilateral donors, such as the UK Department for International Development (DFID) and the U.S. Agency for International Development (USAID).

3.1 Regional development banks and regional World Bank projects

Provision of regional Aid for Trade by the regional development banks is already well underway, and there are already some existing instruments intended to provide Aid for Trade regionally. There is strong support from the Asian, African, and Inter-American regional development banks for Aid for Trade (ADB, 2006b). They are also committed to strengthening intra-institutional coordination on the topic, and have organized a Task Force on related technical issues. A summary of the regional development banks' submissions to the Trade Task Force are reviewed in Annex D.

The Inter-American Development Bank (IDB) is the most active of all regional banks on Aid for Trade. It highlights its strong track record of supporting infrastructure and supply-side capacity in the region, as well as its more recent track record in providing trade capacity building. In a report on its activities (Rey de

Table 19.1. Three dimensions of Aid for Trade

Task Force category	Regional projects (see Annex B for project descriptions)	Other	
		National projects	Multilateral projects
Trade policy and regulations	Coordinating national services baselines (e.g., COMESA, see Annex C on RTFP) Regional trade facilitation (e.g., SADC RTFP) Regional trade policy and analytical capacity	Studies for capital-based trade officials	Training WTO negotiators in Geneva
Trade development	Regional investment funds (e.g., as suggested by COMESA)	Support for export/ investment promotion agencies	Multilateral programs with a learning element (e.g., at ITC, UNCTAD, World Bank)
Trade-related infrastructure	Regional power or road projects (e.g., Organisation pour la Mise en Valeur du Fleuve Sénégal – (OMVS), ECOWAS) Coordination of the East African Submarine System fiber optic cable	Local roads	
Building productive capacity	ASEAN Industrial Cooperation scheme promotes joint manufacturing and industrial activities between ASEAN-based companies EADB Lake Victoria Development Project seeks to promote development and trade by sustainable management of lake Regional innovation systems	National science and technology, human resource programs	Multilateral programs with a learning / knowledge sharing element (e.g., UNIDO)
Trade-related adjustment	Eastern and Southern African adjustment fund, Sugar Action Plan.	Human resource programs to diversify into non-traditional sectors.	Trade Integration Mechanism (TIM) at the IMF dealing with preference erosion.
Other trade-related needs	Not yet defined.		

Marulanda, 2006), it states, "Aid for Trade is not new for the IDB: many of the Bank's traditional lending instruments were designed to support the very elements of what is today perceived as the broader aid-for-trade agenda, including infrastructure development (transport, energy and communications) and strengthening countries' productive capacities. The IDB also has a long track record of providing adjustment related lending, some of which has been directly related to trade" (see also Chapter 10 in this volume).

The World Bank has highlighted the difficulties of securing regional loans for trade-related issues: "Lending for regional trade-related projects is limited owing to the difficulties in securing agreement between countries and the appropriate guarantees for multi-country loans . . . More fundamentally, a key issue is that regional projects are less likely to find their way into national development plans as a result of coordination problems" (IMF/World Bank, 2006). Several regional development banks have some funding available for regional issues, but multi-country programs constitute only 2–6 percent of the portfolio of regional development banks. Only US$1 billion out of US$34.4 billion of IDA-14[5] funds are earmarked for regional projects. There is a new multi-donor trust fund in the World Bank to address regional infrastructure gaps, but the trade-related parts of World Bank lending for regional projects have recently amounted to around only 1 percent of total lending.

The WTO/OECD Trade Capacity Building Database provides data on trade-related assistance projects; the projects shown for the regional development banks include one for the African Development Bank in 2004, three for the Asian Development Bank in 2003, and twenty for the IDB over 2003–2005. While this might be an understatement of what is going on, it is indicative of the fact that total Aid for Trade through the regional development banks (with the exception of infrastructure) is still low.

3.2 European Commission

The EC is a major donor of trade-related assistance (TRA), including at the regional level. Aid for Trade is programmed in National and Regional Indicative Programmes (NIPs and RIPs) for the ACP and other regions. The ACP received EUR1325.9 million in TRA over 2001–2004, out of a total of EUR3343.8 million in EC TRA disbursed worldwide. The Commission notes: "TRA in the aggregated data for the ACP are dominated by regional and all-ACP programs in part designed to prepare for the EPAs. There are only relatively few ACP States that have a trade program, even though this number is increasing reflecting increased attention for trade and development over the past few years. In contrast to the ACP countries, the share of TRA within country programs is higher in Asia and in Latin America" (Kennes, 2005).

Regional ACP programs are prepared and justified in RIPs, and account for around 20 percent of total TRA (see Table 19.2). All-ACP programs also account for a large part of EC TRA. Annex B shows all-ACP and regional programs as part of the 9th EDF. The 10th EDF will be implemented in the period 2008–2013.

[5] IDA-14 refers to the 14th replenishment of the International Development Association's (IDA's) resources, which promised US$33 billion to the world's 81 poorest countries during the fiscal years 2006–2008.

Table 19.2. Trade content of ACP regional indicative programs, 2002–07

	Trade and regional integration (RI) %	Transport %	Other %	Total EUR (million)	Of which Trade and regional integration EUR (million)
Central Africa	25–30	15–25	25–40	55	14–17
West Africa	50	35	25	236	118
Eastern and Southern Africa and Indian Ocean	45–55	15–25	25–30	223	100–123
Southern Africa (SADC)	35–45	35–45	up to 20	101	35–45
Pacific	31		69	29	9
Caribbean	75–90		14–18	57	43–51
Total (approx)					340
Memo items:					
(a) Trade in ACP RIPs, 2002–07 annualized					68
(b) EC TRA to ACP (2001–04), annualized					331.5
Ratio (a) / (b)					20.5%

Source: RIPs, te Velde et al. (2006).

3.3 Bilateral donors

Bilateral donors also provide regional Aid for Trade directly. We cannot provide a complete overview, but have selected the work of DFID and USAID in Southern Africa as an example.

3.3.1 *DFID*

DFID's Southern Africa Regional Plan (DFID, 2006) suggests that regional approaches are necessary to create regional public goods (it includes under this: regionally integrated systems of infrastructure such as road and rail systems, ports and airfreight capacity, energy, and communications).[6] There is no sophisticated underlying needs assessment, but the plan indicates that "the state of Africa's infrastructure is so poor, with such detrimental impacts on productivity, that a recent meeting of African finance ministers identified infrastructure as the top priority for promoting growth." It then says "the need for massive infrastructure development is a key continental priority that needs integrated-level planning." Finally, it mentions that "regional institutions can promote networking and lesson sharing across the region, provide a challenge function to country-based initiatives, deliver economies of scale through regional programs and act as intermediary between country focused institutions and pan-African and global processes and policies."

[6] See Annex D for a mapping of Aid for Trade activities onto public goods.

In part based on this argumentation, the plan selects areas of engagement. There does not seem to have been a regional needs assessment akin to a Diagnostic Trade Integration Study (DTIS) at the national level. DFID's support for regional integration and trade issues in the region includes implementation of regional and national projects, many of which have been set up using regional mechanisms. Current regional programs include (see Annex C for further details):

- Regional Trade Facilitation Programme (£11.4 million);
- Program on regional standards (£4 million);
- ComMark Trust Programme stimulating high-growth commodity sectors in the Southern African Customs Union (SACU) (ComMark, 2007) (£10 mn); and
- A planned regional infrastructure for growth program (£5 million).

3.3.2 *USAID*

USAID has financed the Southern Africa Global Competitiveness Hub, which aims to:

- Enhance the competitiveness of Southern African products and services;
- Expand the role that trade can play in African poverty reduction strategies;
- Promote U.S./Southern African business linkages;
- Improve the delivery of public services supporting trade;
- Strengthen Southern African capacity for trade policy formulation and implementation; and
- Strengthen the enabling environment for Southern African business.

The Hub includes two important programs. The trade competitiveness project (USAID, 2007a) is a six-year project which seeks to improve the capacity of regional businesses and clusters to produce and market competitive goods and services. It furthermore aims to develop value-adding export relationships within the region and internationally by providing enhanced access to technical assistance.

The project on trade facilitation and capacity building (USAID, 2007b) assists the region to benefit from more effective integration with the global economy. It works with governments, the private sector, and regional institutions, and the project facilitates and supports trade capacity building initiatives that reduce the transaction costs of trade and promote competitiveness. It supports Southern African countries to maximize the potential of these opportunities, resulting in increased investment and economic growth. The project team is intended to support capacity building, trade facilitation, and dialogue activities in ten countries in Southern Africa.

3.3.3 *Conclusion*

There are various regional approaches to supporting regional integration and trade, including through regional development banks, multilateral institutions, the EC's RIPs and bilateral donors. Regional approaches address cross-border issues not fully addressed in national approaches. There does not seem to be the same coordination of Aid for Trade at the regional level as there is at the national level, and there does not seem to be the same needs assessments equivalent to the DTISs at the national level.

4 Possible ways forward

Regional approaches to Aid for Trade have a clear rationale, and this is reflected in the presence of a variety of regional initiatives. However, there are limitations to the ways donors can engage at a regional level in regional projects; for example, the World Bank and even the regional development banks need to implement these projects through national-level programs, accompanied by regional coordination. Further, the process by which regional Aid for Trade is determined seems less systematic than the process used at the national level, which at least for LDCs is informed by a DTIS. It may fall upon donors to provide a rationale and suggest relevant projects. Thus, a (developing country-owned) regional needs assessment that can link in with donors' regional approaches and instruments seems to be lacking.

4.1 Possible content of regional programs

Based on the rationale for regional Aid for Trade, three types of activities could be considered to add value to national Aid for Trade programs.

- Support that helps a region to take a *coordinating* role on trade issues, particularly for those that make sense at a regional level (such as trade in services, harmonization and/or mutual recognition), or where the regional processes reinforce and complement multilateral processes (for example, trade in services regulatory baselines need to be done once but are helpful for both regional and multilateral negotiations).
- Support that facilitates *knowledge sharing and learning* within a region, by trying to identify commonalities and share lessons from national Aid for Trade programs. This would require a regional list of country-based activities in the areas of:
  - trade policy and regulations;
  - trade development;
  - trade-related infrastructure;
  - building productive capacity;
  - trade-related adjustment; and
  - other trade-related needs.
- Support for the development of *regional approaches* to providing regional public goods and activities with externalities. This could include mechanisms such as regional investment funds or cross-border infrastructure projects.

4.2 Processes for regional Aid for Trade

Much attention has been paid to the lack of mainstreaming (Aid for) Trade in national development programs (Prowse, 2006). This relates to issues such as the lack of capacity in ministries, the different timing of trade needs assessments, and the conclusion of national development programs. If there is little trade content in national development programs, there will be little aid available to support trade, and funds instead will go to other causes. These issues will only be more pronounced at the regional level.

In fact, while national needs assessments are being done (though perhaps not always followed up), it is not clear what is being done at the regional level. Without regional needs assessments, it is difficult to assess what Aid for Trade could in practice be best coordinated or delivered at the regional level. Such a regional needs assessment should go hand-in-hand with national needs assessments in order to ascertain the value-added of each.

The WTO Director-General's report to the General Council of December 2006 suggested that adequate monitoring of Aid for Trade flows should ensure more effective Aid for Trade. He suggested that national Aid for Trade committees be set up. However, while the Task Force recommended exploring "the merits of establishing a Regional Aid-for-Trade Committee, comprising sub-regional and regional organizations and financial institutions, to oversee the implementation of the sub-regional and regional dimensions of Aid for Trade, to report on needs, responses and impacts, and to oversee monitoring and evaluation", the Director-General's report failed to elaborate on these.

We suggest that a regional Aid for Trade committee would be required to monitor regional Aid for Trade in order to facilitate:

- Monitoring of regional trade policy integration;
- Sharing of knowledge and learning across the region;
- Providing needs assessments of cross-border Aid for Trade projects (including a regional DTIS);
- Developing proposals for mechanisms to share costs and benefits of cross border projects across countries;
- Reviewing the adequacy of existing mechanisms to finance regional Aid for Trade; and
- Training and developing regional analytical capacity and regional private sector representation.

In order to ensure adequate content and value-added of regional programs, we suggest that the regional Aid for Trade committees comprise not only regional organizations and development banks (as suggested above), but also representatives of national Aid for Trade committees. For the African regions, it might make sense to also have a pan-African committee that could include some of the more effective regional groupings.

4.2.1 *Financing*

Because there is a rationale for regional Aid for Trade alongside nationally-focused programs, effective *financing* mechanisms are likely to differ substantially, and ought not to be national only. It is unwise to speak of one global Aid for Trade fund or of national Aid for Trade programs only. For example, how would regional infrastructure be implemented without regional coordination? How can knowledge on trade (development) policies be coordinated? How can a system of regional trade rules be developed and sustained? How can the profile of trade issues be raised?

These are mostly international challenges, and many of them need a regional financing approach.

The IMF and World Bank have suggested three financial options for delivering regional Aid for Trade (IMF/World Bank 2006):

- Improve existing grant instruments and mechanisms, complemented by greater monitoring of the extent to which identified needs and priorities have been addressed.
- Establish a dedicated grant funding mechanism that would mobilize resources to both address coordination problems and support regional management and regulatory bodies.
- Mobilize dedicated grant funding to support a broader agenda, going beyond grants for upstream analysis and related "software," to cover all or part of the implementation costs associated with cross-border projects.

The IMF/World Bank Development Committee suggested using existing grant elements better, rather than expanding the range of instruments. However, a proper assessment could lead to different conclusions, and it is feared that regional Aid for Trade may not reach its potential fast enough to meet pressing needs. A proper review of the available mechanisms ought to be part of regional Aid for Trade itself, and could perhaps be the first task of a regional Aid for Trade committee.

Parallel work is required on the side of the EC budget. There has been a push by the European Parliament to set up a budget line that can finance multilateral or regional Aid for Trade projects that is not determined by the existing regional EPA configurations. Such a budget line could be flexible and inter alia could be used to finance regional Aid for Trade efforts.

5 Conclusion

Discussions on Aid for Trade have emerged during the current WTO trade negotiations, but are not part of the single undertaking, and are about helping developing countries to trade or adjust to trade liberalization. Several issues are not yet addressed adequately in the current discussions, such as additionality of Aid for Trade funds, the role of the private sector, over-reliance on donor coordination at country level to safeguard effective Aid for Trade, and the lack of regional Aid for Trade. While ideas on regional Aid for Trade featured in post Hong-Kong discussions, it is not apparent that these are currently being followed up, as new mechanisms suggested by the IMF/World Bank were rejected and the WTO Director-General's report of December 2006 failed to elaborate on the regional context of Aid for Trade.

There is a clear rationale for regional Aid for Trade: to support the provision of regional governance public goods; to provide regional knowledge public goods; and to overcome other market and coordination failures and coordinate activities with strong regional externalities. Some regional Aid for Trade is already occurring. Multilateral and regional development banks, bilateral donors, and the EC have provided regional Aid for Trade. However, the process by which regional Aid for Trade is determined seems less systematic than that used at the national level.

Three types of regional activities add value to national Aid for Trade programs: (i) support that helps a region take a coordinating role on regional trade issues, particularly for integration efforts; (ii) support directed at knowledge sharing and learning within a region; and (iii) support for activities with cross-border externalities, such as regional infrastructure projects. Regional Aid for Trade committees could be set up to monitor regional Aid for Trade in order to facilitate the monitoring of regional trade policy integration, the sharing of knowledge and learning across the region, and conduct needs assessments of cross-border projects (for example a regional DTIS). They could further develop proposals for mechanisms to share the costs and benefits of cross-border projects, and review the adequacy of existing mechanisms to finance regional Aid for Trade.

In conclusion, we suggest the following key points:

- Provide regional Aid for Trade alongside national Aid for Trade programs;
- Establish regional Aid for Trade committees (taking into account WTO and EPA negotiations);
- Give these committees the responsibility to monitor regional Aid for Trade by:
  - Supervising a regional DTIS to assess the costs and benefits of cross-border projects most in need of Aid for Trade at the regional level;
  - Collecting and analyzing information on national Aid for Trade programs for the benefit of learning and knowledge sharing;
  - Supporting regional analytical capacity and private sector representation; and
  - Reviewing the adequacy of existing mechanisms to finance regional Aid for Trade;
- Make regional Aid for Trade a topic at WTO General Council annual debates on Aid for Trade; and
- Take practical steps towards the creation of appropriate regional Aid for Trade programs (see Annex E for an example).

ANNEX A: AID FOR TRADE TASK FORCE RECOMMENDATIONS ENDORSED BY THE GENERAL COUNCIL, PASSAGE RELEVANT FOR *REGIONAL AID FOR TRADE*[7]

F.5.2 Regional level

Many countries require cross-border infrastructure and regional policy cooperation to trade more effectively. The ability to identify cross-border and regional needs should be strengthened at the country, regional and multilateral level. Once needs have been identified, donors and agencies must improve their ability to respond. In particular, assistance in formulating and financing accompanying measures could help to make regional integration an effective building block for the multilateral trading system. At the forthcoming September Development Committee Meeting, strengthening support for regional, sub-regional and cross-border needs will be discussed.

[7] *Source*: WTO (2006a).

Recommendations:

- Strengthen the following functions in relation to regional, sub-regional and cross-border issues:
  - diagnosis of needs;
  - costing of projects;
  - preparation of project proposals; and
  - the coordination of donor response, including brokering and co-financing of needs that at present are difficult to finance through country-based processes, (e.g., cross-border infrastructure and policy-integration projects).
- Assign responsibility for these functions. In doing so, priority should be given to improving and strengthening existing mechanisms, including those at the multilateral and regional level, before considering a new mechanism. In exploring the most efficient solution, the conclusions from the discussions at the forthcoming Development Committee should be taken into account. Any solution should involve all relevant stakeholders and give priority to existing regional integration programs that lack funding.

Explore the merits of establishing a Regional Aid-for-Trade Committee, comprising sub-regional and regional organizations and financial institutions, to oversee the implementation of the sub-regional and regional dimensions of Aid for Trade, to report on needs, responses and impacts, and to oversee monitoring and evaluation.

ANNEX B: EC TRADE-RELATED ASSISTANCE BY REGION[8]

Trade-related assistance (TRA) for the ACP under the 9th European Development Fund (EDF – implemented from 2003 to 2007) is provided at three levels:

1. At the "all-ACP" level, facilities cover mostly short-term needs or needs in specific trade-related areas (such as sanitary and phytosanitary requirements). These facilities are accessible to all ACP countries and regional institutions upon submission of requests. Total amount: EUR150 million. This includes:
   - Facility to support EPA negotiations (EUR20 million). An additional amount of EUR4 million has been approved.
   - Facility to support ACP countries in WTO negotiations (EUR10 million). Additional funding of EUR2 million has been approved.
   - Trade.Com (EUR50 million)
   - Pesticides Initiative (EUR29 million)
   - Fisheries program (EUR42 million)
2. The bulk of the TRA support is provided under Regional Indicative Programmes, in line with the ACP EU priority attached to regional integration. The total amount is approximately EUR350 million.
   The overall envelope available to the *SADC Regional Indicative Programme* is EUR171 million. The main programs are the following:
   - SADC EPA Negotiations Support Facility (EUR7.5 million)

[8] *Source*: EC Trade and Development website, http://ec.europa.eu/trade/issues/global/development/index_en.htm.

- Support to SADC regional integration and multilateral trading system (EUR1.09 million)
- Development of Standards, Quality Assurance, Accreditation & Metrology (SQAM) infrastructure in the SADC region (EUR14.2 million)
- ESIPP Programme (EUR18.3 million) to encourage private investment in the region
- Technical Cooperation Facility (EUR1.9 million) provides some flexibility to take on board various trade activities.

The overall envelope available to the *ESA & Indian Ocean Regional Indicative Programme* is EUR302.6 million. The main programs are the following:

- Regional Integration Support Programme (RISP). (EUR30 million).
- Regional Information & Communication Technologies Support (EUR21M)
- Infrastructure projects (EUR63.3 million).
- Trade Integration Budget Support Facility (EUR50 million). Under preparation.

At the regional level, the focus in *CEMAC* of the EUR16 million PAIRAC (Programme d'Appui à l'intégration Régionale) is regional integration and trade support for related programs. This includes building a customs union, common market and supporting regional institutions (EUR1.9 million). The regional Technical Co-operation Facility has also financed export and trade related studies (EUR1.3 million) with more planned. There are related regional activities such as transport infrastructure (EUR20 million).

The focus in *West Africa* of the EUR235 million Regional Indicative Programme is regional integration and trade, with EUR118 million to support related programs, including building an ECOWAS customs union and common market and EUR82 million for transport facilitation. There is also an EUR65 million PAIRAC support for an UEMOA customs union. Other relevant regional programs include EUR15 million to support accreditation, standardization and promotion of quality under the PAIRAC private sector programs.

The overall envelope available to the *Pacific Regional Indicative Programme* is EUR29 million. The main programs are:

- Pacific Regional Economic Integration Programme (EUR9.2 million), aimed at supporting regional economic integration, EPA and WTO negotiations, mainly through technical assistance.
- DEVFISH (EUR3 million), aimed at promoting the development of domestic tuna fishery.
- PROCFISH (EUR12.5 million), aimed to contribute to long-term sustainable management of fisheries resources of the Western & Central Pacific Ocean and costal fisheries development.

3. At the national level, several ACP countries have earmarked additional funding for projects complementing those funded under the all-ACP and regional programs, mainly focusing on technical assistance and capacity building related to trade.
    - Burundi: SPS project under STABEX
    - Ethiopia: trade capacity building
    - Kenya: TRA funded out of STABEX KEPLOTRADE Programme
    - Madagascar: Funding for technical assistance
    - Mali: EUR3.7 million to support EPA negotiations

- Namibia: Trade Integration Programme (EUR3 million)
- Nigeria: EUR2 million for EPA preparation and EUR15 million for private sector support
- Papua New Guinea: Support to trade and capacity building
- Rwanda: Funding for technical assistance
- Senegal: EUR3 million to support for capacity building in trade policy and regulation
- Solomon Islands: Allocation for institutional support
- Tanzania: Project to support NAO covers a trade advisor to the Ministry of Finance
- Uganda: TRA funded out of STABEX
- Vanuatu: Funding for private sector support
- Zimbabwe: Trade capacity building for the private sector

ANNEX C: DFID'S REGIONAL SUPPORT[9]

Regional Trade Facilitation Programme (RTFP) (£11.4 million)

The RTFP is one of several programs funded by DFID in Southern Africa, all aimed at supporting different aspects of Southern African development.

1. *Contributions to the strengthening of regional trade arrangements*
   These activities are designed to contribute to the closer harmonization and effectiveness of trade facilitation measures taken by the integration organizations of the region (SADC and COMESA). The following activities are currently being implemented:
   - SADC and COMESA trade advisors
   - Customs bond guarantee
   - National consultations on rules of origin
   - Assistance to Southern African Customs Union (SACU)
   - Secretariat support for the SADC/COMESA/ESA Task Force
2. *Trade facilitation measures designed to directly benefit the poor*
   - Monitoring of Cross-Border Trade
   - One Stop Border Posts
3. *Market development of commodities and natural products produced by the poor*
   Several small-scale producers' associations have approached RTFP to provide assistance in trading their products –particularly in marketing them within the region (and especially into South Africa). Three commodities – tea, coffee and nuts (macadamia, cashew and groundnuts) – have already been identified for assistance, and a study has just been completed which identifies how assistance can be provided in the natural products sector.
   - Tea
   - Coffee
   - Capturing value for smallholder nut producers in southern Africa
   - Trade component of the Programme on Natural Products (NATPRO)

[9] *Source:* http://www.rtfp.org.

4. *Support for Trade in Services Negotiations*
   - COMESA Trade in Services Programme
   - Migration and Mode IV – a Towards a trade and development approach
5. *Support to WTO and EPA Negotiations*
   - Assistance to Zambia in its capacity as coordinator of the LDCs
   - Support for the EPA Negotiations
6. *Regional Tax Policy and Administration*
   - SADC Tax Adviser
7. *Contributions to the Harmonization of the region's standards and SPS regimes*
8. *Research on trade-related policy work in the region*

ANNEX D: VIEWS ON AID FOR TRADE BY REGIONAL DEVELOPMENT BANKS – SUBMISSIONS TO THE AID FOR TRADE TASK FORCE

Question	Inter-American development bank	Asian development bank	African development bank
What is the current scope and content of your Aid for Trade programs?	Trade is embedded in the four priority activity areas of the Bank. Regional integration is key to IDB mission and much related to trade. Trade-related Technical assistance (TRTA) and trade capacity building are undertaken and trade is incorporated into other development discussions. Dedicated loans for trade.	US$730.2 million for trade projects between 1987 and 2005. Also US$14 million TRTA.	Direct support for private sector development, help for African trade negotiators, capacity building in other forms, regional efforts, funding of trade-related research.
Are there, in your view, important outstanding trade-related needs that are not met today?	Supply-side capacity and adjustment to future liberalization continue to be neglected.	Serious infrastructure gaps in the Asia and Pacific region, including linked to trade. Have also looked at behind-the-borders barriers to trade.	Regional infrastructure constraints, behind-the-border issues, trade related institutional reforms, adjustment costs of implementation of WTO agreements.

Question	Inter-American development bank	Asian development bank	African development bank
Has trade been adequately addressed in countries' development plans and poverty reduction strategies? If not, what are the main reasons and how could this be corrected? What are the lessons learned?	Not sufficiently mainstreamed into governments' development programs. This is partially because of lack of capacity and lack of dialogue.	Not in a position to judge.	Not answered.
How, in your view, should trade related needs and priorities be identified?	Comprehensive and broad-based technical analysis. Constraints are capacity to undertake such work.	Not answered.	Should be demand-driven and country-led. WTO can facilitate and advocate.
Is the existing system of delivery mechanisms for Aid for Trade adequate? If not, where are the gaps, and what options might exist to address these gaps?	There should be more predictable, long-term grant based money available given developing countries fiscal constraints. A multi-sector approach is critical. There should also be a flexible rapid response facility.	Not in position to judge, but looking for more flexible delivery mechanisms under their own initiatives.	Should be headed up and located within the ADB as most of beneficiaries of a scheme are African. Should be grant based.
What should be the role of the private sector in identifying needs and implementing responses?	Should be one of several types of stakeholders involved in the process of identifying needs.	Private sector involvement and PPP are likely to be critical to success.	Critical, should be encouraged to participate more.
How should Aid for Trade reinforce the principles of aid effectiveness and coherence, as agreed in the Paris declaration and as embodied in individual poverty reduction strategies?	Coordination is a major challenge and needs to be enhanced to minimize duplication.	All efforts should be country-led, and donor behavior has to conform to these principles.	Must have additionality involving substantial increases in resources. Also needs to be predictable, transparent, well-coordinated and monitored.
Are there other important gaps in the delivery of Aid for Trade?	None.	Infrastructure.	Not answered.

ANNEX E: TOWARDS AN APPROPRIATE REGIONAL AID FOR TRADE PROGRAM

Based on section 4, above the following items might help to establish appropriate regional Aid for Trade programs.

Monitoring of regional trade policy integration

- How far have countries liberalized tariffs according to the RTA
- What common standards and regulatory framework are in place, and are there any commonalities across countries
- Conduct a regional Trade Policy Review

Sharing of knowledge and learning across the region

- Collect and share experiences on capacity building for trade (which Aid for Trade projects work and why)
- Collect and share experiences of service sector regulators (utilities, central banks, etc.) in dealing with liberalized trade in services regimes
- Collect and share experiences on trade facilitation reforms such as customs reforms
- Build regional knowledge and trade policy networks by promoting regionally oriented trade policy think-tanks and research institutes as well as linkages amongst country researchers
- Train and develop regional analytical capacity and regional private sector representation.

Providing needs assessments of cross-border Aid for Trade projects

- Collect and analyze data by scanning national DTIS and other national needs assessment to assess the regional content of available trade needs assessments. The guiding principles are that regional Aid for Trade projects will be complementary to national Aid for Trade projects, and
  - Provide governance public goods, or
  - Provide knowledge public goods, or
  - Deal with cross-border challenges with large cross-border externalities.
- Engage (in Africa) with AfDB and NEPAD, and relevant countries, to provide a list of cross-border infrastructure projects with expected costs and benefits
- Scope in a set of common trade challenges facing the region for further research.

Developing proposals for mechanisms to share costs and benefits of cross-border projects across countries

- Calculate costs and benefits of cross-border projects and suggest how costs and benefits can be shared
- Build up organizational, negotiating and analytical capacity to deal with cross-border projects that have varying costs and benefits across countries in a region.

Reviewing the adequacy of existing mechanisms to finance regional Aid for Trade

- Provide road maps for the financing of regional Aid for Trade projects
- Discuss solutions to constraints, such as lack of appropriate guarantees for loans for regional projects.

REFERENCES

ADB. 2006a. "Regional Cooperation and Integration Strategy," http://www.adb.org/documents/policies/RCI-strategy/final-RCI-strategy-paper.pdf.

ADB. 2006b. "Regional Development Banks and Aid for Trade: An Opportunity to Help Developing Countries Benefit from Trade Liberalization," News Brief, http://www.adb.org/Media/Articles/2006/10040-aid-for-trade-an-opportunity-to-help-developing-countries-benefit-from-trade-liberalization/.

ComMark. 2007. "Homepage," http://www.commark.org/pages/default.asp.

DFID. 2006. "Southern Africa – Regional Plan," http://www.dfid.gov.uk/pubs/files/southern-africa-regional-plan.pdf.

Duval, Y. 2006. "Strengthening trade research for policy making: The case of ARTNeT," presentation to UNCTAD Ad Hoc Expert Meeting on Building Skills in Developing Countries – "Training, Networking and ICTs," Geneva, 27–28 November.

IMF/World Bank. 2006. "Doha Development Agenda and Aid for Trade," submitted to the Development Committee of the IMF and World Bank, Washington, D.C.

Kennes, Walter. 2005. "EC Trade-Related Assistance (TRA) – some key facts and figures," draft note.

Nijnkeu, D. and B. Powo Fosso. 2006. "Intra-African Trade and Regional Integration," prepared for the ADB/AERC International Conference on Accelerating Africa's Development Five Years into the Twenty-first Century, Tunis, 22–24 November.

ODI. 2007. "Projects – Aid for Trade," International Economic Development Group, http://www.odi.org.uk/IEDG/aid4trade.html.

Page, Sheila. 2007. "The Potential Impact of the Aid for Trade Initiative," G-24 Discussion Paper Series No. 45, UNCTAD, New York and Geneva: United Nations.

Prowse, Susan. 2006. "Mega-coherence: The Integrated Framework," in S. Page (ed.), *Trade and Aid: Rivals or Partners in Development Policy*, London: Cameron May.

Rey de Marulanda, N. et al. 2006. "Aid for Trade: The Inter-American Development Bank's Experience in Latin America and the Caribbean," Integration and Regional Programmes Department, Washington D.C.: IDB.

te Velde, Dirk Willem. 2006a. "Financing International Public Goods – A Framework to Address Aid for Trade," ILEAP Negotiation Advisory Brief No. 14., Toronto: ILEAP.

te Velde, Dirk Willem. 2006b. Ed. "Regional Integration and Poverty." Hampshire: Ashgate Publishing.

te Velde, Dirk Willem, Massimiliano Cali, Adrian Hewitt and Sheila Page (2006), A critical assessment of the EU's trade-related assistance (TRA) to third countries – lessons from the past, policy options for the future, report to the European Parliament.

USAID Regional Center for Southern Africa. 2007a. "Trade Competitiveness Project (TCP)," Southern Africa Global Competitiveness Hub, http://www.satradehub.org/CXA_html/trade_comp.html

USAID Regional Center for Southern Africa. 2007b. "Trade Facilitation and Capacity Building," Southern Africa Global Competitiveness Hub, http://www.satradehub.org/CXA_html/tradeFac_overview.html

WTO. 2006a. *Recommendations of the Task Force on Aid for Trade*, Aid for Trade Task Force, WT/AFT/1, 27 July.

WTO. 2006b. *Follow-up to the Aid-for-Trade Task Force Recommendations (WT/AFT/1) – WTO Monitoring and Evaluation*, Report by the Director-General, JOB (06)/262, 12 December.

WTO. 2006c. *Communication from the African Development Bank*, Aid for Trade Task Force, WT/AFT/W/7, 28 April.

Index

Note: A *b* following a page number denotes a box on that page; a *c* following a page number denotes a chart on that page; an *f* following a page number denotes a figure on that page; an *n* following a page number denotes a note on that page; a *t* following a page number denotes a table on that page.